Travel proverbially broadens the mind. At the same time, it can be both refreshing and fascinating, because it shows us new horizons and reveals to us different ways of life. But overseas travel is often arduous, occasionally dangerous, and usually expensive. For this reason, many of us prefer to supplement our occasional real-life journeys with heavy doses of armchair travel.

The armchair traveller enjoys many advantages over his "real" counterpart. He never gets bored hanging around in airport lounges, and he is never "bumped". He does not have to worry about punctures, empty fuel tanks or breakdowns. He never gets carsick, seasick or airsick. The sun does not scorch, the rains dampen, nor the bitter winds freeze, his spirits. He has no language problems. His "journey" costs a tiny fraction of real travel - the price of a book - and no insurance is necessary. He need never leave his favourite armchair, with choice refreshments within reach.

A whole dimension of experience is available to the armchair traveller which lies entirely beyond the grasp of his "real" counterpart - that of time travel. The armchair "time-traveller" can journey in an age ignorant of mass tourism and globalisation, when there was more to travel than comparing the Macdonalds outlets in different countries; when to travel really was to enter upon an adventure of discovery, and an encounter with strange and exotic ways of life.

The seeker after variety could do no better than visit Greece. While always identifiably Hellene, each of its many communities, isolated from its neighbours by the formidable barriers of mountain and sea, once enjoyed its own distinctive ways and customs. *Travellers' Greece* brings to the reader the pick of the best of the writings of visitors to each distinctive region of this diverse and fascinating country, during more than three centuries. Valuable historical records in their own right, their narratives are frequently also vastly entertaining. They depict ways of life which have passed away for ever. The also frequently betray, in the traveller himself, depths of egocentricity and prejudice which are no longer possible to an educated man today. But whether we admire the beauties of a vanished landscape, deplore the harsh realities of lost ways of life, or smile at the smug self-absorption and ignorance unwittingly revealed by the narrator, we are always engaged and entertained.

Cover design: Aris Karey

Cover picture: *Athens in 1839* (W. von Weller)

John L. Tomkinson lives in Athens, where he divides his time between teaching History and the Theory of Knowledge, and writing.

His books include the following in the series *Greece Beyond the Guidebooks,* also published by *Anagnosis:*

> *Athens: The City*
>
> *Athens: The Suburbs*
>
> *Attica*

Travellers' Greece

Memories of an Enchanted Land

compiled by

John L. Tomkinson

Anagnosis

Anagnosis
Harilaou Trikoupi 130
145 63 Kifissia
Athens, Greece
Website: www.anagnosis.gr

ISBN 960-87186-4-3

Photoset by:
Alphabeto A.E.B.E.
Digeni Akrita 13
114 72 Athens
www.alphabet.gr
Printed and bound by:
K. Pletsas - Z. Karadri O.E.
Harilaou Trikoupi 107
Athens
www.typografio.gr

Preface

The reader of a "travel book" opens it with certain expectations: descriptive passages conveying the atmosphere of the lands visited and the societies observed, detailed historical background , lively anecdotes of incidents in course of the travellers' adventures, including vivid pen-portraits of striking characters.The writer may also, often unwittingly, provide us with an insight into his own character, outlook and prejudices, and those of his own class or nation. Always, it is the travel writer's right to digress; to reflect upon and philosophise about what he may come across on his journey, offering an insight into, or a *critique* of, a particular society, or even of human nature in general.

In *Travellers' Greece*, the publishers, *Anagnosis*, have sought to bring before a wider public a broad selection from the rich body of travel literature which has been inspired by those lands which are now part of the Greek state.

In making my selection, I have sought to cover the entire range of travel writing: descriptive, narrative and reflective. However, I have deliberately avoided passages of background material, such as might have been extracted from a history book, together with the once customary, and now tedious, demonstrations of the authors' Classical erudition. Inevitably, earlier descriptions, which tend to be rather general, have sometimes been included because they have historical value, and are of considerable interest to both the student and the general reader precisely because they provide the only picture we have of a place at the date when they were written. I have included passages of "fine writing", and also passages which, while having no literary merit whatsoever, are unquestionably informative, interesting or entertaining. I have included the views of those many who were obsessed with Hellenism, its past, its people and its destiny; and those others who found themselves, equally violently, repelled by what they saw, or more usually, by what happened to them. I have sought to cover each part of this varied country, although inevitably greater space has been given to the much-visited regions, such as Attica and those of the islands which lay on main shipping routes. The lowlands of Thrace, in particular, seem to have been avoided by travellers, who would usually opt to make the journey by sea. The authors selected span the period from the very early years of travel writing in English to the beginning of the twentieth century. Most are British, while some are from the USA.

There is a vast body of such literature, and I have but scratched the surface. The choice of what to include has necessarily, in the last resort, been a personal one, and many familiar with the field may find their most cherished passages, and even their favourite authors, omitted entirely. Others will wish that I had included more of one type of writing rather than another, or covered a particular area in greater depth. However, I *have* sought to provide something for all tastes.

John L. Tomkinson
Athens, June 2002

Editorial Notes

For the scholar, archaic font, spelling and punctuation, with all their idiosyncracies and inconsistencies, add charm to the process of reading, but it is clear that they may prove irritants to the general reader, and some compromise between a literal rendering and a thorough and consistent modernisation of the text is inevitable. I have consistently used modern spelling for all words except archaic words, or word forms which have fallen out of use, and which, consequently have no contemporary form. I have chosen to modernise the spelling and punctuation, but not the grammar or syntax. In the interests of uniformity, those variant spellings peculiarly characteristic of North American writers have also been rendered into their standard English forms.

Several further exceptions have been made to a wholesale modernisation of the spelling. Firstly, proper names, including place names, have in all cases been left in their original forms. A glossary of these, giving their modern equivalents, has been provided.

Secondly, some writers were in the habit of liberally sprinkling Greek terms throughout their English text, sometimes in Greek script, sometimes Latinised. In the interests of the general reader, these have been omitted wherever convenient, for example, if followed by an equivalent in English. Those it has been inconvenient to remove have simply been presented in Latin characters. The scholar, about his business of research, will, of course, require access to the original, but he will, in any case, have to pass beyond the pages of this compilation in order to inspect the complete original texts first hand.

Finally, there are some Greek words, referring to institutions etc. peculiar to Greece, which are used so frequently, and by most writers, because they have no exact and succinct equivalent in English. It would significantly change the effect of what was written to attempt to substitute English words for these, and they have been left in their original forms, but again, a glossary has been provided.

This set of compromises will, it is hoped, provide just enough of the flavour of the originals to convey something of their undoubted period charm, while avoiding so much archaism that it becomes tiresome to the general reader.

The extracts are organised by place, and within each area, chronologically. The dates above the extracts are, as close as it is possible to make them, the dates when the journeys described took place, and not the dates of publication, which were sometimes considerably later.

"'They are ungrateful, notoriously, abominably ungrateful' – this is the general cry. Now in the name of Nemesis, for what are they to be grateful? Where is the human being that ever conferred a benefit on Greek or Greeks? They are to be grateful to the Turks for their fetters, and to the Franks for their broken promises and lying counsels. They are to be grateful to the artist who engraves their ruins, and to the antiquary who carries them away; to the traveller whose janissary flogs them, and to the scribbler whose journal abuses them. This is the amount of their obligation to foreigners."

(Lord Byron, Note to Childe Harold''s Pilgrimage II.lxxiii)

Acknowledgements

I would like to take this opportunity to express my warmest thanks for all their help to Aris Karey, Vicky Aggeli and Linda Booker; and particularly to the ever-patient and always-helpful librarians of the British School of Archaeology in Athens and the Gennadeion.

Contents

Glossary

Place names

Only the most common variants are listed, alternative spellings should be readily identifiable.

Anapli - Nauplia
Candia - Crete
Candy - Iraklio
Cerigo - Kythera
Cervi - Elafonisos
Corcyra - Kerkyra, Corfu
Ipsara - Psara
Lepanto - Messolonghi
Longo - Kos
Morea - Peloponnese
Napoli, Napoli di Roma - Nauplion, Nauplia
Negropont, Nigroponti - Chalkis, Chalkida

Nikaria - Ikaria
Nio - Ios
Sta. Maura - Lefkada
Scio - Chios
Peterasso - Patras
Salona - Amphissa
Serigo - Kythera
Stanccow, Stanchio - Kos
Thermia - Kythnos
Vostizza- Egion
Zante - Zakynthos
Zeitoun - Lamia

General Terms

Only the most frequent terms and spelling variants are included here.

ataghan, yataghan - Turkish scimitar
bastinado - punishment by beating with canes on the soles of the bare feet, a standard Turkish punishment still administered in Turkish police stations and prisons today
cadi - Turkish judge
caloyer - monk
demarch, demark - mayor
derveni - guardhouse, often in a mountain pass
firman, firhman - an imperial document of authorisation
Frank - Westerner
fustanella, juktanillas - kilt
Ghiaour, Giaour, Djowr - infidel, non-Muslims
haratch, kharatj - poll tax
hegoumenos, igoumenos - abbot
janissary - Turkish soldier
khan - Ottoman inn
khanjee - inn-keeper, ostler
konak - the forced quartering of soldiers in private houses

metohi - monastic grange
monoxyla - small boat for use in shallow-waters
palikari, pallecari - warrior
pappas - priest
Porte - the Sultan
primate - village headman
protopappa - senior priest
pyrgo - a fortified house in the form of a tower
raki, rakhee - spirits
rayah - non-Muslim, an inferior citizen
rema - bed of a river or stream
Romaic - the name Greeks gave to themselves and their language, recognising their identification with the Byzantine, or late Roman, Empire.
serai - enclosure, palace
Skipetar - Albanian
tjiftlik - large Turkish estates
vaivide, veivode, voivode - Turkish governor

The Arch of Hadrian, Athens (Stuart & Revett, 1751)

The Ionian Islands

Under Venetian control since the fourteenth century, the Ionian Islands escaped the long centuries of Turkish occupation, although at times their fate hung in the balance. Corfu alone was besieged in 1537, 1570 and 1716. Venetian rule has left the islands with an Italianate character, which they retain to the present day. In 1797 the Republic of Saint Mark fell to the French forces under Napoleon Bonaparte, and the French took control of the islands. After only two years a combined Russian and Turkish fleet drove them out, and in 1800 the Septinsular Republic was created, under a facade of independence. Nominally the Sultan was suzerain, but in reality the islands were under Russian control. In 1807, forced to sue for peace, the Russians handed the islands back to the French, and they became, administratively, three *departements* of France. The British took them from the French one by one, and in 1815 the "Seven Islands" were once more accorded a purely nominal independence, this time under British control. This period saw considerable improvements in the life of the people, with the laying of roads and a sewage system, and the erection of some fine public buildings. But nationalist feeling was stirring in Greece, and with the establishment of the new Greek state in 1830 on the southern mainland, the islanders sought union with their fellow Greeks. The British made Greek, for the first time in modern times, the official language of the islands, and then transferred them to the Greek kingdom in 1864.

"Sappho's Leap" Lefkada (J. Cartwright, 1821)

1609-10 William Lithgow

Battle with a Turkish Man o' War

For early travellers at sea in this region, approaching vessels might mean imminent death, or a lifetime of slavery in the galleys.

... I embarked in a Greekish carmesalo, with a great number of passengers, Greeks, Slavonians, Italians, Armenians, and Jews, that were all mindful to Zante, and I also of the like intent; being in all forty eight persons. Having some winds, and a fresh gale, in twenty-four hours we discovered the isle Cephalonia the greater; and sailed close along Cephalonia minor, or the lesser Ithaca, called now Val di Compare, being in length twenty, and in circuit fifty six miles, renowned for the birth of Laertes' son, Ulysses.... On our left hand toward the main, we saw an island called St Maure, formerly Leucas, or Leucada; which is only inhabited by Jews, to whom Bajazet II gave it in possession after their expulsion from Spain: the chief city is St Maure, which not long ago was subject to Venice. This isle St Maure was anciently joined with the continent, but now rent asunder, and environed with the sea.

During the course of our passage, the captain of the vessel espied a sail coming from sea. He presently being moved therewith, sent a mariner to the top, who certified him she was a Turkish galley of Biserta, prosecuting a straight course to invade our back: which sudden affrighting news overwhelmed us almost in despair. The affrighted master having demanded of every man what was most proper to be done, some replied one way, and some another; insomuch, that the most part of the passengers gave counsel rather to surrender than fight, being confident their friends would pay their ransom, and so relieve them. But I, the wandering pilgrim, pondering in my pensive breast my solitary estate, the distance of my country and my friends, could conceive no hope of deliverance. Upon the which troublesome and fearful appearance of slavery, I absolutely arose, and spoke to the master, saying, "The half of the carmoesalo is your own, and the most part also of the loading, (all which he had told me before); wherefore my counsel is, that you prepare yourself to fight, and go encourage your passengers. Promise to your mariners double wages, make ready your two pieces of ordinance, your muskets, powder, lead, and half-pikes; for who knoweth but the Lord may deliver us from the thraldom of these infidels." My exhortation ended, he was greatly animated therewith, and gave me thanks; whereupon, assembling the passengers and mariners, he gave good comfort, and large promises to them all so that their affrighted hopes were converted to a courageous resolution; seeming rather to give the first assault, than to receive the second wrong.

To perform the method of our defence every man was busy in the work; some below in the gun-room, others cleansing the muskets, some preparing the powder and balls, some their swords, and short weapons, some dressing the half-pikes, and others making fast the doors above; for so the master resolved to make combat below, both to save us from small shot, and besides for boarding us on a sudden. The dexterous courage of all men was so forward to defend their lives and liberty, that truly, in my opinion, we seemed thrice as many as we were. All things below and above being cunningly perfected, and everyone ranked in order with his harquebuss and pike, to stand in readiness for his own defence, we recommended ourselves into the hands of the Almighty; and in the meanwhile attend their fiery salutations.

In a furious spleen, the first hola of their courtesy was the progress of a martial conflict, thundering forth a terrible noise of galley roaring pieces; and we, in a sad reply, sent out a back-sounding echo of fiery flying shots, which made an equivox to the clouds, rebounding backward in our perturbed breasts the ambiguous sounds of fear and hope. After a long and doubtful fight, both with great and small shot, (night parting us) the Turks retired till morning, and then were mindful to give us the new rencounter of a second alarm.

But as it pleased him, who never faileth his mercy to send down an irresistible tempest, about the break of day we escaped their furious designs, and were enforced to seek into the bay of Largostolo in Cephalonia; both because of the violent weather, and also for that a great hole was sprung in our ship. In this fight there were of us killed, three Italians, two Greeks, and two Jews, with eleven others deadly wounded, and I also hurt in the right arm with a small shot. But what harm was done by us amongst the infidels, we were not assured thereof, save only this, we shot away their mid mast, and the hinder part of the poop; for the Greeks are not expert gunners, neither could our harquebusadoes much annoy them, in respect they never boarded. But howsoever it was, being all disbarked on shore, we gave thanks to the Lord for our unexpected safety, and buried the dead Christians in a Greekish churchyard, and the Jews were interred by the seaside.

1825 Lytton Bulwer

The Farce of Constitutional Government

Under British rule the islanders enjoyed a semblance of self-government. The astringent pen of Lytton Bulwer reveals to what extent this was nothing more than an empty facade, covering absolute rule by the British High Commissioner.

Sir Thomas Maitland, allowing him some good qualities, was still a most abominable tyrant, and disregarded all laws when they affected himself...

The Senate consists of five members, who are selected from the Primary Council (a body of eleven) and supposed to be chosen by the islands, the four largest of which name one each, and the smallest, one alternately. The Primary Council, with the additional number of twenty-nine, forms the Legislative Assembly.

If it were not too serious a subject to excite a laugh, the election of this representative assembly would be really ludicrous. In the event of a vacancy therein, the Secretary of the Primary Council transmits to the island for which it occurs, the names of two trustworthy persons, (i.e.) worthy of the trust of the Lord High Commissioner, of whom the ... electors have their choice, verifying thus the old couplet of

> "How vast a difference we may see
> 'Twixt tweedledum and tweedledee."

The [electors] have become ashamed of this popular privilege, and never meet. In which case, the *form* of the election is in the Senate. Every act of the Senate, as well as of the Legislative Assembly, must be inspected and approved by the Lord High Commissioner, who in his capacity is doubly culpable:- first, in mocking a people with the form of a constitution; secondly, in reigning, *de facto*, as absolute as the Dey of Algiers.

But what shall we say to such an enormity as this, that, when the Ionians have been flattered with the right of petitioning our Government at home, their petitions have been stopped in their way thither, pronounced libels, and their authors prosecuted and imprisoned?

Corfu

1609 William Lithgow

"The Forts of Christendom"

Venetian government was based upon a worldly-wise distrust of human nature, especially of its own agents.

The city Corfu, from which the isle hath the name, is situate at the foot of a mountain, whereupon are builded two strong fortresses, and environed with a natural rock. The one is called Fortezza Nova and the other Fortezza Vecchia. They are well governed, and circumspectly kept, lest by the instigation of the one captain, the other should commit any treasonable effect. And for the same purpose, the governors of both castles, at their election before the senators of Venice are sworn neither privately, nor openly to have mutual conference, nor to write one to another, for the space of two years, which is the time of their government. These castles are inaccessible, and unconquerable, if that the keepers be loyal, and provided with natural and martial furniture. They are vulgarly called "The Forts of Christendom" by the Greeks; but more justly "The strength of Venice"; for if these castles were taken by the Turks, or by the Spaniard, who would as gladly have them, the trade of the Venetian merchants would be of none account; yea the very means to overthrow Venice itself...

General View of the Forts and the Harbour of Corfu (Julianus Bezier, 1807-10)

1682 George Wheler

Testing a "Miraculous" Icon

Among the more unfamiliar features of life in the Eastern Mediterranean which English visitors usually noted in their writings, to conjure up a sense of place, are the profound differences of religious feeling, and the novelty of the flora and fauna.

The first place we arrived at is a ruined city now called Cassopo; but anciently Cassiopia, famous for the temple of Jupiter Cassius; of which I have several medals... And hard by it a church called Panagia, which they name the blessed Virgin, kept only by three or four caloyers, or Greek monks. This little church is famous for a picture of Our Lady, to which they attribute miracles, and whereof I had a mind to try the skill. The way is thus:

Strangers that have a mind to know whether their friends are alive or dead go to the picture, and clap a piece of money upon it, thinking of some friend. If the person they think of be alive, the piece will stick fast; but if dead, it will drop down into a sack placed underneath; so that, dead or alive, the priest is sure of the money. I applied some farthings which I had, to try how and where they would stick; but had no other thoughts nor end, being before well-satisfied that it was but a ridiculous juggling. Some of them indeed stuck, but all to one and the same place; those that were clapped on anywhere else, falling still to the ground. The picture is painted upon the walls, and is very smooth and shining, so that I attribute the sticking to some clamminess of the varnish, which they take care shall never be wanting in some part of it.

Among the ruins of the castle I saw a vast great snake; I believe above two yards long, and big as the small of a man's leg, of a dark brown colour; thicker also at the tail than ours are; so that I take it for a different species from ours. I saw another afterward of the same kind, but not so big.

"Spying" on the Fortifications

A meticulous, note-taking traveller, George Wheler was frequently in some danger of being taken for a spy.

The next day being the eighteenth of July we came to the city now called by the name of the island. It is not a hundred years since this city was nothing but the old castle. But now it is a good large city, and well-fortified, with the walls on the south, and two castles at the east and west ends; though the side towards the harbour be not so well-fortified, as not so much needing it. It would be a town almost impregnable, were it not for a rock that standeth towards the west and commandeth the adjoining fort with a great part of the town. The other castle or fort stands upon a rock every way inaccessible, running out, like a promontory, in the sea. This is the place of residence of the Venetian Generals of the Levant by Sea and Land, and to whom from the other Providentours of Zant and Cephalonia, etc. appeals may be made, and a new hearing had of all civil causes before him, as chief judge under the Senate, as well as chief commander of all their forces. He who had this command then was Signior Priuli.

We being taken notice of here for designing places as we passed, were taken for spies; so that the order was given by the general that none should be admitted into the forts; inasmuch as we could not at that time well know their strength. But as I returned and touched here, I had so much time as to see this castle, which is well-provided with ammunition and artillery.

The Patron Saint of the Island

Every visitor to Corfu was to note the special veneration accorded by the islanders to Saint Spyridion. This is one of the earliest references in English.

To the westward side of [the castle of the Venetian Governor] is a large place which they call the Splanade; from the middle of which beginneth a large street that runneth westwards through the city. On the right hand in this street standeth the cathedral church, dedicated to Saint Spiridion, first bishop of that place [*Spyridon was never bishop of Corfu, ed.*], whose body they are persuaded they have, and there with great veneration preserve it. They attribute to him the doing of a miracle about three years since, restoring sight to a blind man, who came and prayed to him, prostrating himself before his body. And of this they keep an annual remembrance ever since, which happened when we were there.

They make a profession of the Greek religion, but are in most things Latinised, except in obedience to the see of Rome, the infallibility of the pope, and the procession of the Holy Spirit. They have not a Greek bishop allowed them, but there is a Latin one, and a protopappa Greek. This church [*of Saint Spyridon*] is well-furnished with silver lamps; and one of gold, given by a gentleman of Corfu; who by his will left 5,000 chichins (which amount to about £3,000 sterling) to buy it...

1817-18 Peter Edmund Laurent

The Moral and Spiritual State of the Garrison

A series of earnest and puritanical visitors were offended by the morals of the islanders and of the soldiers garrisoned there.

It has been remarked that soldiers, placed for any length of time in one town, lose all activity of mind, and become indifferent to surrounding objects; to the truth of the observation I feel inclined to assent. The only amusement of a soldier, garrisoned at such a place as Corfu, is sauntering on the fortifications; lounging through the streets, and abusing the natives. Vice naturally ensues, and the town becomes a seat of dissipation and, libertinism. These reasons would, perhaps, authorise government to change the garrisons of their forts oftener than now is practised; but, in military affairs, the morals of the soldier are, I fear, the last thing attended to; even those regulations which have been made on the subject are but too often neglected. When we were at Corfu the service was not performed on one Sunday because a little wet had fallen in the morning; on the following Sunday a circumstance equally frivolous was alleged as an excuse for a similar neglect...

c.1818 H. W. Williams

A Socially Acceptable Form of Concubinage

Another visitor during the same period has more detailed complaint on the same subject.

A few days after our arrival, we had a splendid ball and supper at the palace; the ladies were well-dressed and numerous, but in the French taste. They were not in general handsome, although among them were one or two that might be called beautiful. The ladies of the islands are much secluded. In Corfu, however, the French introduced a considerable change in manners and unfortunately in morals too, which here, and indeed, throughout the Seven Islands, are extremely lax.

A sort of agreement is not infrequent, by which a young woman is made over by her parents to her admirer (her own consent being first obtained) at a stipulated sum. The usual sum is 200 dollars, and a small provision for life. This species of concubinage frequently terminates in marriage, when the girl is respectable, and there happen to be children. It produces at the same time, much infidelity in the married state.

c.1828 John Fuller

"Society"

By contrast, this account of "Society" on the island suggests that Corfu may have been a rather boring place in which to live. The collector of extreme cases of unassailable smugness prejudice may particularly relish the final sentence of this extract.

The society of Corfu is extremely limited. The old nobility has been impoverished by the frequent revolutions which the islands have in the last twenty years experienced. Some have gone to seek service in foreign countries; and the hospitality of those who remain shows itself only in an occasional splendid entertainment, after which they relapse into the most private and parsimonious mode of life. Occasional "Sociétés" are held at the Government House, and are frequented by the principle inhabitants and by a few English civilians and officers of the garrison; but they are, to a stranger, exceedingly dull, the greater part of the company being seated round a large table playing at the favourite but most insipid game of "trianda mia" or one and thirty, a sort of long *vingt-et-un*. The intercourse between the English and the natives is

The city and port of Corfu (Jos. Cartwright, 1821)

extremely limited, owing perhaps in part to that feeling of contempt for all foreigners which forms a distinguishing feature in our national character, and which is particularly annoying to the vanity of the Greek.

1829 The Rev. Rufus Anderson

Carnival and the Profanation of the Sabbath

The puritan consciences of many U.S. visitors, in particular, were profoundly disturbed by what they found.

A custom fell under our observation while in Corfu, that serves to illustrate the manners of the people. It is that of promenading in masked dresses during the carnival. We arrived after carnival had properly ended, the people having relinquished the use of meat the Sunday before. But Lent had not commenced, as cheese and eggs were allowed during the following week. The maskers were now more numerous than at any time before. Nearly two hundred might be seen on the public walks in front of our lodgings, every afternoon when the weather was good, habited chiefly in the female dress, though all were not females. Few of the costumes were strikingly fantastic, we saw none that were immodest, and the law defends the maskers from insult, and prevents them from insulting others. The following Sabbath was terribly profaned. Maskers were seen on horseback and in phaetons, the dresses became more grotesque, martial music was brought in to animate the scene, and a comical, impious cavalcade was repeatedly followed round the esplanade by a laughing, shouting mob. Could anything be more painful to the feelings of a Christian, than to be assured that the leaders in this buffoonery were men who had been born and educated in one of the most enlightened and Christian countries in the world?

1836 Edward Giffard

A Grotesque Execution

A few weeks before our arrival a man had been hanged for murder, and one who was an eyewitness described it as a peculiarly disgusting sight. The executioner was dressed in a party-coloured suit of red and blue, with a mask of the same colours, with one huge Cyclopean eye in the centre, resembling nothing so much as the clown in a Christmas pantomime: thus, to our English ideas at least, mixing up horror with mummery; - but perhaps, after all, the party-coloured executioner may look as awful in the eyes of the Corcyrans, as if he were dressed in sables, and that his mask had two eyes.

1838 William Mure

Accommodation in Corfu Town

Despite being a gateway to the East, nineteenth century Corfu Town was remarkably deficient in places for visitors to stay.

The family of the Lord High Commissioner, Sir Howard Douglas, comprised several old and valued friends of my own, whom I had requested by letter to provide the best accommodation the place supplied, against the day of my arrival. Their answer, however, had not reached me before my departure from Ancona. I therefore, on disembarking, proceeded with an English fellow-passenger to secure quarters for myself, in a lodging-house which had been recommended to us as affording the best in the town.

This establishment, dignified by the title of "Taylor's Hotel", or, in more homely phraseology, "Sergeant Taylor's lodgings", (being kept by the wife or widow of a retired officer of the name and rank above mentioned,) was one of the most diminutive of the small mansions of the city. It contained several spare rooms, dark, close, and dismal, but not uncleanly, with an aspect into an equally dismal-looking street, at prices equal to what would be asked for the best apartment in a good Italian hotel. It seems a strange thing that the capital of an important British dependency, containing a population of 20,000 souls, with a large garrison, and numerous civil and military functionaries of our own nation, besides the native nobility and gentry, and forming the leading point of intercommunication between Eastern and Western Europe, should not contain so much as a tolerable inn. An attempt was made some years ago to establish one, the failure of which was ascribed chiefly to the circumstance, that visitors are in the habit of depending more for their entertainment on the hospitality of their own acquaintance, or of persons to whom they may be recommended, than on any species of public accommodation. But although the English tourist may in most instances reckon upon a bed in the quarters of a countryman, this can hardly be the case as regards the numerous travellers from other parts of Europe, who annually visit the island. The reason therefore, although perhaps the best that can be assigned, seems hardly sufficient.

My own experience, it is true, went far to justify it; for while we were making arrangements with the landlady, a young officer of the garrison, who, on return from leave of absence, had been our fellow navigator, came to announce that there was a vacant bed at the English Club House, which he politely placed at our disposal. The offer was eagerly accepted by my companion, who was more offended with the homeliness of the sergeant's apartments than myself, and to whom I ceded my claims. A few minutes afterwards I heard my name called by familiar voices at the door, and in less than a quarter of an hour was established in most luxurious quarters at the palace, leaving the poor landlady not a little disconcerted at being thus suddenly robbed of two promising guests.

"An Honest Greek Travelling Servant"

The following lengthy but fascinating pen portrait of an Albanian from Ioannina hired in Corfu as a servant to accompany the author in his projected travels on the mainland, reveals much about the state of Greece, and of travelling in what is now northern Greece, during the middle of the nineteenth century..

A portion of the morning was occupied in making such arrangements for my land journey, as were necessary to ensure the small degree of comfort that could reasonably be hoped for at the halting-places in the inhospitable regions through which it lay. The first and most important business was to hire one of that peculiar description of travelling servants who devote themselves to the attendance on tourists in the Levant, and who combine, or profess to combine, the offices of guide, cicerone, purveyor, cook, interpreter, and valet. Corfu is the chief rendezvous for this class of persons, some of whom are usually to be found on the quay, like *lacquais de place* in the seaports of western Europe, ready to prefer their claims to the traveller as he steps out of the packet. They are, as may be supposed, for the most part Greeks or Albanians, and attired in the national costume. Some, however, presented themselves equipped in the first style of European fashion, obviously for the purpose of creating a favourable impression by their smartness and civilization; although, in my own case, the effect was quite the reverse of what they intended. I had with me the address of one who had been highly recommended by a friend, and whom I was fortunate enough to find disengaged. He was, upon the whole, one of the most original characters I have happened to meet with in the course of my travels, and a good sample of a class of beings unknown among ourselves, and perhaps little common in any other country. As a further apology for digressing somewhat more widely in my description of him, than the subject may seem to deserve, I may urge the opportunity it will afford of adding a few remarks on the general plan and conduct of a tour in Greece, and on the habits of those with whom the traveller is likely to be brought into contact, which may perhaps be not altogether unprofitable to my successors in the same route, or unacceptable to the general reader.

Nicola, for so he was called, was as strange a mixture of the barbarian and the civilized man as can well be imagined. An Albanian of the purest caste, a native of the province of Joainnina, he wore the beautiful dress of his country, and his whole appearance was in the highest degree picturesque. A complete Hercules in form, with a somewhat Scythian cast of countenance, and a slight tendency to corpulence, as that hero is not uncommonly represented, he was, like him, active, and patient of fatigue. The expression of his coarse weatherbeaten image, though gloomy and even ferocious, had a certain tinge of sincerity and simplicity which prevented it from being offensive. His manner was gruff and rude, sometimes even surly and insolent, yet certainly not intentionally so; and he was obedient to orders, and submissive when seriously found fault with.

He spoke seven languages; Albanian, Greek, Italian, Spanish, French, Turkish, and I forget what other oriental dialect. Of the English he was totally ignorant; and yet for many years he had been chiefly attached to the service of British travellers; but he said he never could master its difficulties. He kept his accounts in Italian, which tongue was also our medium of communication, with the greatest order and regularity, in an excellent hand, and with an orthography that might put many a member of the native noblesse to the blush. Although I had no occasion to try him, I have little doubt that his penmanship might have been found equally available in any other of the written languages of which he was master. But, with these attainments as a linguist and a scribe, his progress in the march of intellect seemed to have been suddenly arrested, as in all further respects he was as deficient in educational knowledge, and displayed as great contempt for every thing of the sort, as the most unsophisticated shepherd of his native mountains. How or where he acquired so unusual a stock of elementary learning, I never could exactly ascertain. He was not by nature communicative; and as the few observations he hazarded were laconic and inexplicit, and he did not like to be cross-questioned, it was difficult to get much information from him on any subject on which he did not volunteer to enlarge; and even then his accounts were dry and unconnected enough. There may possibly have hung some mystery over the early part of his previous life, as is very frequently the case with men of the world of his nation and rank, more especially with those who, after having taken an active part in the turbulent vicissitudes of their native land, have adopted at a maturer age comparatively tranquil and domestic habits.

It may perhaps at first sight appear a startling, or even a calumnious imputation, to say that a large proportion of the adult population of Greece and the neighbouring countries have, during some period of their life, exercised, in one shape or other, the profession of robber; but a very little reflection on their past history and actual habits, can leave little doubt that it is a correct one. The mountain fastnesses of many of these provinces of the Turkish empire, were, even during its more flourishing periods, in the half-independent possession of the natives, ranged under patriarchal chiefs, similar in character and habits to the robber knights in the unsettled districts of Europe during the middle ages, and who gloried in the title of *klepht*, or thief. This profession they exercised somewhat in the mode of our Rob Roys, Robin Hoods, or Johnny Armstrongs, exacting blackmail from their weaker neighbours as the price of protection from their rivals, or from the common Turkish oppressor, against whom their predatory warfare was chiefly directed. From this class of robber chiefs sprung many of the heroes whose names have acquired the greatest celebrity in the war of independence, Kolokotroni, Mauromichali, Androuzzos, Gouras, and others, the survivors among whom have felt some difficulty in conforming to the habits of regular government or civilized society. But besides this more organized system of brigandage, a favourite resource of the desperate or the unfortunate of all ranks was a retreat to the mountains, and the life of a freebooter. During the war, the population of whole villages, towns, or districts, were frequently reduced to live in rocks, caves, and forests, where plunder, when opportunity occurred, became a virtue of necessity, as the only means of supporting existence; and in such cases but little distinction would be made between friend and foe. Still more demoralizing, perhaps, was the effect of the few years of civil dissension that intervened between the emancipation from the Turks and the establishment of the present government, during which these predatory campaigns were carried on between rival factions of the Greek nation itself. The necessary result of such a state of things was a general indifference to the value of human life among all classes, which was not a little fostered during the war by the universal practice of butchering the Turks in the mass, or the individual, whenever they fell into their hands; and I have heard it remarked, in well-informed quarters, that if the European traveller, as he passed along the road or the street, could instinctively detect those among the natives whose hands, apart from the adventures of regular warfare, had been deliberately stained with human blood, a large proportion of this population, who, with all their faults, appeared to me, from the little experience I had of them, friendly and kind-hearted, would become objects of disgust and abhorrence. That habits thus formed, during a long period of anarchy, should suddenly give way before the outward signs of regular government which are now displayed in the land, was hardly to be expected; and I had, during my own passage through the country, practical evidence that the mountain and the carbine still remain as formerly, the resource to which, on occasion of any social embarrassment, the lower orders are in the habit of instinctively resorting. The present corps of *gens d'armerie*, a well-disciplined and efficient body, is notoriously composed, in a great measure, of persons who were formerly professional brigands; and their services are considered, according to our own vulgar proverb of "Set a thief to catch a thief," the more valuable on that account. Under the present government it has also been the practice, especially in the northern frontiers, the chief seat of systematic outlawry, to detach the bands from their lawless mode of life, by enrolling them as light-armed infantry in the national service, and conferring military commissions on their chiefs - a short-sighted policy, which must be the greatest possible encouragement to the evil it professes to cure.

To return, however, to my own Albanian. - That his personal experience of human life was not deficient in the foregoing particular, I had, it must be admitted, no other ground of belief than the following heads of circumstantial evidence:- First, the simple fact of his being an Albanian; secondly, the nature of the service in which he had during the early part of his life been engaged; thirdly, his perfect familiarity, which in the course of our travels I had frequent opportunity of putting to the test, with the habits of the freebooter; and lastly, several incidental circumstances or remarks on his own part, in the course of our acquaintance, which seemed to indicate that his abstract views of the rights of property were not so rigid as those which the courtesy of his present mode of life enjoined. This peculiarity, however, ought by no means to count as an unfavourable item in the estimate of such a character; as being, on the one hand, quite consistent with rigid fidelity to an employer and benefactor, and tending, at the same time, for the reasons above assigned in the case of the Greek police, to promote the efficacy of his services.

His knowledge of the Spanish tongue, on which he especially piqued himself, he described as having been acquired in very early youth, during a sojourn in Spain itself, in the service of a traveller. On his return to his native land, he served in a military capacity under Ali Pasha, of whom he was a great admirer, and whose energetic character, strenuous assertion of his authority, and summary administration of justice, were subjects of warm commendation, and unfavourable contrast with what he considered the weak and languid police of his successor, or of the new Hellenic government. His cruelty, avarice, and treachery, did not seem to enter at all into the balance on the other side. After the fall of this chieftain, to whom he adhered to the last, he espoused, with other Albanian adventurers, the Greek patriotic cause, and formed part of the garrison of Mesolonghi during Lord Byron's command of the place. He afterwards married and settled at Corfu, and for the last twelve years had followed his present profession, during which time, besides every corner of Greece and its islands, he had travelled through the greater part of the Turkish empire, Asia Minor, Palestine, and Egypt.

In spite of his peregrinations and extensive knowledge of life and its vicissitudes, he was woefully deficient in every kind of general information, and either could not or would not give any connected or intelligible account of a single country he had visited, or scene he had witnessed. In fact, one of his most amusing peculiarities was a scornful indifference to things in general, beyond what he considered the immediate sphere of his own duties or avocations, in the prosecution of which he displayed an equal degree of zeal, activity, and energy. His was in fact the philosophy of the savage, or natural man, shrewd and penetrating as regards the present, around which it is concentrated, but ignorant or careless of both past and future, unless in so far as their concerns appear tangibly connected with the more engrossing, and for the most part sensual, objects of momentary interest. What seemed less easy to explain, was not so much his indifference to the objects which alone or chiefly attracted strangers to the places whither he was in the habit of conducting them, but his complete ignorance, in very many cases, of their site or existence - although perfect master of the topography of Greece in other respects. On this score I had frequently occasion to find fault with him, as he had, when hired, boasted of his familiarity with the curiosities we were to explore. His apology was, that he had never been in the habit of accompanying his previous employers in their rambles upon such occasions, but had been left in charge of the horses and baggage, while they found local ciceroni who performed this service. If so, they were more fortunate than myself, as one of the greatest inconveniences of which I had to complain, amid the ignorance of my habitual guide, was the difficulty, often the impossibility, of finding anyone in the least degree competent to act in this capacity; and as it usually happened, that the names by which the objects I was in quest of were known among the natives were different from their scientific titles, I have frequently been obliged to range for hours the whole surface of an ancient city, or other interesting locality, as a pointer-dog would hunt a field, in order to discover them for myself, to the infinite loss of time and patience, and occasionally without ultimate success. It appeared that the journeys of many of his previous employers had been directed to other than classical objects. He had been at different times in the suite of the commissioners of boundaries, and other persons travelling in a diplomatic capacity. I advised him, however, to take this, or any other opportunity that might offer, of perfecting himself in what was certainly an important branch of his profession. Although at first he seemed to treat with great contempt the notion of troubling himself about old stones and rubbish, as he called them, yet, apparently convinced of the reasonableness of my advice, he gradually began to devote a certain degree of attention to them. He even went the length of taking special notes of several localities, which were either first fully explored by myself, or previously little known or frequented; and would sometimes, in the warmth of his newborn zeal, tease me with accounts of wonders to be found here and there, which of course turned out to exist but in the delusions of his own or the popular ignorance.

He affected much contempt for the degraded state and beastly habits of his countrymen, the native Graeco-Albanian population, and yet his own were in a great measure similar; while the easy and natural manner in which he conformed to them in all their most offensive particulars, while our lot was cast in the region where they exclusively prevailed, showed that they were still in all respects as congenial to his taste as those of the semi-civilized life to which, since his marriage and settlement in Corfu, he had been accustomed. Of the habits here alluded to, the fundamental one is the aversion of the Christian population of the whole country formerly called Turkey in Europe, to ablution or change of raiment, or even to divesting themselves of the garments they habitually wear, and which are allowed to go to decay on the person of the proprietor, until necessity, or regard for the decency of the exterior man, induce him to procure a substitute. These customs are not peculiar to the lower class, but extend in a greater or less degree to the nobles and chieftains, who consider filth as one of the characteristics of martial genius or veteran service. On setting out on a campaign they put on a clean smock or fustanella, soaked in grease, which remains on their person, as a matter of military etiquette, night and day, until their return home, when their wives have a new suit ready to replace it. The consequence is, that the persons and habitations of all classes swarm with vermin, to an extent unknown probably in any other country. The Albanians are in the habit of wearing belts or bandages smeared with mercurial ointment, said to act as a partial preventive of the too rapid propagation of their personal livestock, or as an antidote to the unwholesome consequences of its supera-bundance. Not only are undressing on going to bed, and sleeping within sheets and blankets, things unheard of, but so much as bed or bedding of any kind, other than rush mats or their shaggy hair capottes and goatskin mantles, are luxuries to which, together with a table or chair, the Greek population below a certain rank are altogether strangers. A German staff-surgeon in a central military depot of the Morea employed to inspect the country recruits under the new conscription act, assured me, that the clothes of many of them were found so tightly glued to their bodies by accumulated filth and vermin, that they could not be drawn off without considerable pain to the wearer, and were frequently obliged to be cut up on his person, and detached piecemeal. It is indeed probable that, in proportion to the amount of the population, that of the filth, personal and domestic, which prevails in these countries, is greater than in any other district of Europe, or perhaps of the globe. Most other semi-barbarous nations, favoured with a fine climate are but scantily clad; whereas the Greek dress is remarkable for quantity, and the voluminous flow of its drapery. It must further be remembered, that, by the expulsion of the Turks, almost the whole aristocracy or upper class of the previous nation has been swept off the face of the land, and little more than the lower orders remain. This is a consideration of much importance, as bearing not only on these petty points of domestic manners, but on the whole social and political state of the country, and which has been far too little taken into account in the ordinary speculations on the present condition or future prospects of the so-called regenerate race. The Turks, though not in our sense of the term a cleanly people, were yet by their law under the obligation to frequent ablution; and, as being the wealthier and better class, their example may probably have exercised some little influence on their subjects. With them, therefore, a large share of whatever may formerly have existed, either of attention or encouragement to cleanliness, has become extinct; and the native peasant and artisan are now left to the enjoyment of the same unsophisticated mode of life as the cattle on their mountain sides, or as the dogs that defend the hovels which afford man and beast a common shelter from the sunbeam or the storm.

Let it not be supposed, however, that the case was quite so bad as regards my own worthy Arnaut; yet I believe a change of smock at Athens, and perhaps another at Patras, were the utmost dereliction of national manners of which he was guilty during the eight weeks he was in my service; but, as he was a man of a naturally sound and wholesome habit of body, I never found any thing seriously offensive in his personal vicinity. Not so, however, as regards his stewardship of my goods. For the conveyance of refreshments, and other necessary articles of occasional use on the road, we were provided with two or three moderate-sized goats' hair bags, which, with a little attention, might easily have admitted of such a distribution of their destined contents, as would have prevented any unpleasant collision of uncongenial bodies. Our stock of provisions consisted chiefly of salted meats, hard-boiled eggs, cheese, dried figs, etc. In addition to these, there were various other loose articles of a very different description - such as sketchbooks, itineraries, and a few pocket volumes of the classics; besides travelling caps, handkerchiefs, and other small pieces of extra clothing, which the hourly variations of temperature in a Greek spring rendered it convenient to have continually at hand, and which consequently could not be permanently embodied in the luggage, properly so called. These latter items I particularly directed to be lodged in a separate repository. But in spite of all my precautions, amid the frequent extractions and insertions which took place in the course of our day's march, often without stopping or dismounting, I almost invariably found, on emptying our treasures at the halting-place, that sausages, salt herrings, cheese, figs, sketchbook, journal, woollen comforter, Homer, Pausanias, Gell, had all been thrust into the same receptacle, and came forth presenting, both to the sight and the smell, too palpable tokens of the uncongenial contact into which they had been forced. On the first two or three occasions of the kind, I could not help being diverted by the delinquent's total unconsciousness of having been in the wrong, and the contempt which he plainly exhibited, when taxed with his fault, for my squeamish attention to such trivialities. But this feeling soon gave place to unmixed wrath at the inveterate slovenliness of his ways. Finding it, however, impossible entirely to correct them, I was obliged in the end patiently to submit; and, keeping as good a lookout as I was able on the more precious part of my stock, to leave the rest to its fate.

Among the few subjects on which he was communicative, were the glories of the late revolutionary war, and the praises of the "bravi guerrieri" who had fought out the independence of their country. On these points he was the faithful organ of all the most exaggerated popular traditions relative to combat, siege, or individual act of heroism... This pride of Hellenic patriotism, however, did not, as in many other instances even among the lowest class of Greeks, connect itself in the remotest degree with any associations of ancient national renown - matters concerning which he was as profoundly ignorant as he was indifferent; and the interest I attached to the plains of Plataea or Marathon, was to him as much a mystery as the anxiety I displayed to examine the big stone of Orchomenus, or the arched bridge of Xerokampo. It may indeed appear that, not being himself a native Greek, he had no real cause to participate in this species of classical enthusiasm...

For the Bavarians, my attendant participated in the cordial hatred, as well as contempt, which is the feeling of all classes of the Greek population towards them...

In regard to religion, although I never heard him formally profess infidel principles, yet from the habitual tenor of his allusions, Nicola was evidently a decided latitudinarian; - a rare phenomenon in these countries, where superstition - religion it can hardly be called - exercises unlimited sway over the minds of the people. All Christian persuasions, at least, seemed to him much the same, and all their observances alike matters of empty ceremonial or cunning priestcraft, and in so far objects of ridicule or disgust; and not a few of the shrewd caustic remarks with which he occasionally entertained me, were directed against sectarian zeal or superstition in all its forms, more especially as exemplified in the case of his native Greek church.

Upon the whole, as regards his qualifications for the essential duties of his office, it would probably be difficult to find a better man. The entire economy of our journey, paying bills, hiring horses, guides, etc., was left to his management; and I invariably found him perfectly honest, regular in his accounts, and zealous in all ways for the interest of his master. Of his probity and economy I had good evidence in the comparison of his books with those of other members of his profession, and still better in the surprise expressed by several Philhellene acquaintances, to whom I communicated some of the items, at the strange phenomenon of an "honest Greek travelling servant." The only point on which I had occasion to complain of extravagance, was the high fees paid for the venal hospitality of the country khans and cottages where we lodged. This, however, was but in compliance with a mischievous but inveterate custom, and indispensable to secure the tranquil enjoyment of the best of the miserable accommodation they afford.

His tact and temper in the management of the muleteers and boatmen, were admirable. The exacting spirit and disposition to cheat and squabble on the part of these people, which are so frequent a source of complaint among travellers, and so common a subject of enlargement in the pages of their journals, were inconveniences to which I was altogether a stranger. In my own experience I never knew a more tractable, good-humoured, or obliging race. For this difference of impression, I can only fairly account by the excellent discipline in which they were kept by Nicola, partly by severity where refractory, partly by a spirit of good fellowship, and mutual accommodation, where reasonable. It is true, indeed, that in most parts of the country he was known among the class of persons who profit by the visits of tourists, and whose interest it was to oblige him. He was well skilled in such elementary branches of the art of cookery as were requisite for the preparation of my frugal meals, and upon the whole cleanly in their exercise: and marvellous was the rapidity with which, on arriving at our night's quarters, he procured, killed, plucked, and boiled a fowl into rice pottage for my supper, with the very indifferent apparatus at his disposal.

c.1850 N. Parker Willis

"Mrs. Mary Flack's Greengrocery in the Gardens of Alcinous"

This US visitor seems to have been deeply affronted by the visible signs of British rule.

The entrance to Corfu is considered pretty, but the English flag flying over the port divested ancient Corcyra of its poetical associations. It looked to me a commonplace seaport, glaring in the sun. The "Gardens of Alcinous" were here, but who could imagine them with a red-coated sentry posted on every corner of the island.

The Lord High Commissioner of the Ionian Islands, Lord Nugent, came off to the ship this morning in a kind of Corfiote boat, called a scampavia, a greyhound-looking craft carrying sail enough for a schooner. She cut the water like the wing of a swallow. His lordship was playing sailor, and was dressed like the mate of one of our coasters, and his manners were as bluff. He has a fine person, however, and is said to be a very elegant man when he chooses it...

Went on shore for a walk. Greeks and English sailors mix oddly together. The streets are narrow and crowded with them in about equal proportions. John Bull retains his red face, and learns no Greek. We passed through the bazaar and bad English was the universal language.

There is but one square in the town, and round its wooden fence, enclosing a dusty area without a blade of grass, were riding the English officers, while the regimental band played in the centre… The appearance of the officers retaining all their Bond Street elegance, and mounted on English hunters, was in singular contrast with the general shabbiness of the houses and people.

I went into a shop at a corner to enquire for the residence of a gentleman to whom I had a letter. "It's werry 'ot, sir," said a little red-faced woman behind the counter as I went out, "Perhaps you'd like a glass of vater." It was odd to hear the Wapping dialect in the "Isles of Greece". She sold green groceries, and wished me to recommend her to "the hofficers." Mrs. Mary Flack's "grocery" in the Gardens of Alcinous!

A Meeting with the Lord High Commissioner

Lord Nugent, the third High Commissioner, was a firm Philhellene, remembered most for fostering various literary projects.

Called on Lord Nugent with the commodore. The governor, sailor, author, antiquary, noble-man (for he is all these, and a jockey to boot), received us in a calico morning frock, with his breast and neck bare, in a large library lumbered with half packed antiquities and strewn with straw. Books, miniatures of his family (a lovely one of Lady Nugent among them), Whig pamphlets, riding whips, spurs, minerals, hammer and nails, half-eaten cakes, plans of fortifications, printed invitations to his own balls and dinners, military reports, Turkish pistols, and lastly, his own just-printed answer to Mr. Southey's review of his book, occupied the table. He was reading his own production when we entered…

The conversation was rather monologue than dialogue; his Excellency seeming to think with Lord Bacon that "the honourablest part of talk was to give the occasion, and then to moderate and pass to something else." He started a topic, exhausted and changed it with the same facility

The Procession of Saint Spyridion (Joseph Cartwright, 1821)

and rapidity with which he sailed his scampavia. An engagement with the artillery mess prevented my acceptance of an invitation to dine with him tomorrow, a circumstance I rather regret, as he is said to be, at his own table, one of the most polished and agreeable men of his time.

The Procession of the Saint

The body of saint Spyridon was carried through the streets of Corfu today, sitting bolt upright in a sedan-chair, and acclaimed by the whole population. He is the great saint of the Greek Church, and such is his influence that the English Government thought proper, under Sir Frederick Adam's administration, to compel the officers to walk in the procession. The saint was dried at his dearth, and makes a neat black mummy, sans eyes and nose, but otherwise quite perfect. He was carried today by four men in a very splendid sedan, shaking from side to side with the motion, preceded by one of the bands of music from the English regiments. Sick children were thrown under the feet of the bearers, half dead people brought to the doors as he passed, and every species of disgusting mummery practised. The show lasted about four hours, and was on the whole attended with more marks of superstition than anything I found in Italy. I was told that the better educated Christians of the Greek Church disbelieve the saint's miracles. The whole body of the Corfiote ecclesiastics were in the procession, however.

A Memorable Night Under the Stars

I pass the first watch in the hammock-nettings tonight, enjoying inexpressibly the phenomena of this brilliant climate. The stars seem burning like lamps in the absolute clearness of the atmosphere. Meteors shoot constantly, with a slow liquid course over the sky. The air comes off from the land laden with the breath of wild thyme, and the water around the ship is another deep blue heaven, motionless with its studded constellations. The frigate seems suspended between them.

c. 1850 Henry M. Baird

A Saint's Vengeance

As it was yet early, I walked with my friend first of all to the famous shrine of St. Spyridon, the patron saint of the island. His bones, which are reputed to be possessed of miraculous properties, and which, doubtless, exhale that singular sweetness peculiar, according to the legendaries, to saintly relics, are encased in a silver sarcophagus, and deposited in a corner of the chancel. My companion told me that thousands of the labouring classes visit the church every morning before going about their daily work, in order to kiss the silver coffin, and expect by this pious act to insure good success in all their occupations.

A recent occurrence has tended to raise to a still higher pitch the awe in which the relics are held. A lawyer, as the story goes, not long since brought suit against a former client for about one hundred dollars, due as a remuneration for his services. The respondent averred that he had paid the money some months previous; but confessed that, relying on his lawyer's honesty, he had taken no receipt. This the plaintiff stoutly denied, and confirmed his denial by all oath taken on the Gospel. The judges having long since perceived that the people are more afraid of perjuring themselves when sworn on the relics of St. Spyridon than when they merely kiss the

Scriptures, resorted to this expedient in order to extort the truth. The lawyer, however, still persisted in his demand, and invoked upon himself the vengeance of St. Spyridon if a word of what he said was false. Thus he gained his suit. Not long afterward, his right hand, with which he had touched the silver sarcophagus, began to mortify; and the gangrene spread so rapidly that it could only be checked by the amputation of his arm. The superstitious immediately inferred his guilt, and attributed his misfortune to the efficiency of the relics. The incident has very sensibly augmented the veneration of the common people; and this feeling is fostered by the ecclesiastics, who profit by the increased amount of contributions to the funds of the church.

1861 Dr. Corrigan

A Trip into the Interior of the Island

At ten o'clock we started, in company with a kind friend of ours, Dr. Carroll, 9th Regiment, for the Pass of Pantaleone, about thirteen miles from the town, and one of the favourite drives for strangers. It is a beautiful drive, occupying about three hours and a half, for a great portion of the latter part of the way is up a winding road of short turns to gain the pass. It affords a magnificent view of the greater part of the island, which lies like a hollow basin under you - circled round by a ridge of hills. This immense plain is a valley of verdure, from its groves of olive and fig trees, and further rendered still more beautiful by the numerous cypress trees, like tall green pyramids scattered over the landscape, out-topping all other trees. On reaching the pass don't let your coachman stop there: let him drive down a distance of about two miles to "The Oak." This is the largest oak tree, I heard, in the island. Beside it is a spring of delicious cold and clear water running from the rock. Near the oak is a cypress, the tallest, greenest, and best proportioned I have ever seen. It would seem as if cypress and oak had each sent its best tree to contest for superiority. The oak is at once grand from its size of trunk, gnarled arms, and breadth of foliage; but the cypress, from its beautiful proportions, does not give an idea of its size until you go close to it, and then, to your astonishment, you find that, with outstretched arms, you cannot compass more than two-thirds of its trunk. All around are clumps of wild myrtle, jessamine, and tall Mediterranean heaths; and directly under the oak tree, and beside the cold spring, is a round stone table, with a granite flag for top, and a seat cut out of the soft native rock beside it.

A neighbouring farmhouse supplied us with two chairs; our wine, soda water, and grapes were laid in the running stream to cool; our sandwiches on the table, the oak gave us shade, and the journey gave us appetite, and we sat and enjoyed ourselves, wishing that we had our friends at home to share our enjoyment. We spent two hours here with the oak shade over head and the olive grove around - and an olive grove in Corfu is beautiful, for its foliage is a rich green; and the trees are allowed to throw out their naturally graceful extended branches, not pollarded as they are in other places. They make, in consequence, a rich forest of shade over head, while their bare stems do not interfere with the extended view beneath.

We were, however, not alone. Every few minutes Greek girls, carrying large jars on their heads or backs, came through the forest paths to fill their jars at the spring. Others came with flocks of goats and sheep, with the tinkling bells announcing their approach before they were in sight. The goats disdained to drink unless from the spring as it issued from the projecting groove in the rock, and waited until the Greek girl stopped the stream with her hand; then the goat, standing on its hind legs, and resting its forefeet on the projecting ledge, drank from the source. Now and then a patient donkey, with its large wooden saddle, passed, laden with every variety of article. The Greek girls wore white dresses, wide sleeves, blue skirts, and generally red belts; and on their heads a flat framework, covered with a thick white linen or calico, which depended for some way down the neck and shoulders, as a protection from the sun. Nearly all, young and old, carried the never-ceasing distaff and spindle, with which they are for ever at work while tending their goats and sheep. There appeared now other visitors on the scene-two fat, but active, merry pigs, in charge of two little Greek girls. The pigs seemed to know the spring well. Immediately on approaching it they rooted in the channel through which the water ran off until they made it muddy to their pleasure, thus evincing a taste altogether different from the goats, and then lay down in perfect content, while one Greek girl dashed her pig's face with water, and another carefully washed her charge all over. The pigs then rose, and did what I never saw pigs do before, wagged their tails with delight, and set off to join their more active companions, the goats and sheep. A beautiful little lizard, with its piercing diamond black eyes, and intelligent look and nimble movements, paid our table a visit in the midst of our repast. I have reserved for the last, and they deserve no better place, the Greek men. On our arrival a party of men and boys placed themselves on a bank just overhanging the spring, and never once took their eyes off us the whole time we were there - lying or squatting on the sod and smoking, the very impersonation of laziness: not one ever stirred to assist a Greek girl to fill her water jar, or place it on her head or back.

We left at half-past three o'clock; and, as the sun sank, the view became more beautiful in lights and shadows, and the verdure greener; and, for the first time, I had a view of the graceful and gorgeously crested hoopoe in his native haunts.

c.1897 Charles Edward Lloyd

Monument of a Grieving Mother

The queenliest and most beautiful empress in Europe, Elizabeth of Austria, loves the enchanting island and has built a winter palace which she calls Villa Achilleion, about four miles from the city of Corfu. The location is an ideal one. She has spent several million dollars in making the palace and park suited to the superb site. They say a wound in her own imperial heart, thought to be invulnerable, suggested the name "Villa Achilleion." Greek ideas dominate generally throughout the villa and grounds.

The architect was an Italian whose given name is Raphael, and he has done some work almost worthy of it. A colossal white marble statue of Achilles, with a look of torture on his face, trying in vain to pull the fatal spear from his wounded heel, is near the entrance to the park... The views of mountains, islands, and sea from every part of this temple are indescribably beautiful. The marble columns which surround it look absolutely pure and white against the background of Attic sky and ocean. The violet tints, of which Sophocles sings, are nowhere in Greece more discernible than in this charming spot.

The corridor opening on the courtyard of the palace, suggests some of the most artistic conceptions of luxurious Pompeii. The artistic masterpiece in the grounds, which can be seen from the windows of the empress' boudoir, is a monument to her son, the late Crown Prince Rudolph, who committed suicide for the sake of a woman he thought he loved. He lacked the courage of his brave mother, and could not, or would not, force his heart to be subservient to a sense of duty. The medallion on the pedestal is said to be the best likeness of the late prince in existence. Above this medallion, the Genius of Life holds the torch of life, reversed and extinct. While residing in this palace, the Empress Elizabeth spends much of her time studying the Greek language and literature. She speaks modern Greek fluently.

1926 Paul Wilsach

A Private Audience with a Saint

"That," the shop-keeper made it known, "is the procession of Saint Spiridion" [referring to a picture hanging on a wall.]

"And what is that upright case in the centre of the throng?"

"That is the saint himself."

"Do they carry the saint about town. Does one actually see him?

"Of course."

Whatever the involuntary expression that came out upon my face, the shopkeeper translated it his own way, and asked if I would like to see the saint. Now, never having seen a saint, except in plaster or stone, or in pigment proxies, I assented without thought of discretion or consequences.

He directed me to the church of Saint Spiridion, in the very next street. In the presence of the sacristan, however, I was deaf and dumb; he spoke no English and I, if possible, rather less Greek. In a square near by I found a young Israelite, messenger for the Ionian Bank, who exhibited some odds and ends of Italian and French, with which I pooled my own, and he proved an accommodating interpreter.

The sacristan was delighted to find that his visitor wished to see his saint, and at once began ringing the bell above the church. It was so entirely unexpected that I inquired why he had done it.

"To call the papas," he was interpreted, using the Greek word for priest. "No one but a priest can show the saint. If he is not in the church he always comes when I ring the bell."

I had visions of an interrupted dinner, or nap, or card-game, or call, but some mumbled regrets for trouble I might be giving were gestured aside. As the volunteer interpreter had now returned to finance, the wall, as far as communication was concerned, was up once more between the sacristan and me. He disappeared his way and I employed the interval to observe the church and the faithful.

In ten minutes, however, the bell rang out again, a little more positively. Still the priest did not come. After another interval another peal, this one quite impatient, I thought, and hunted the sacristan to beg off. But he remained in hiding. I went into the square in hope of finding my interpreter, but he had no idea of how much he was needed there. There was nothing else to do but be patient and continue to cultivate acquaintance with the church...

When finally the priest arrived, he donned a stole and lighted a candle, and took his position at the end of the silver coffer. Like all Greek priests his beard and hair had been allowed to grow untrimmed. As it was a warm day his hair was gathered and twisted into a small knot at the back of his head. The sacristan admitted another Corfiote, thus crowding four people into the little chamber; and then closed and locked the doors.

With considerable dispatch he unlocked the silver chest, which now seemed to have taken on enormous proportions, and turned the top back and dropped the entire front, disclosing brilliant scarlet linings and a crystal casket in which lay at full length the mummified remains of the saint. Only his head was visible for otherwise he was covered with vestments and his feet were encased in high red velvet slippers heavily embroidered in gold bullion. The top panel is in two sections and these the sacristan slid to the middle so as completely to expose face and slippered feet.

As priest and sacristan held a smoking guttering candle at each end of the reliquary, the priest intoned from memory a rather extended prayer and I was able to observe this strange survival of the early church. The head was complete, and the features were ascetically thin and curiously life-like, except for the dark bluish colouring. The head leaned slightly to the left and the expression on the lips suggested scarcely less than a smile. Others might affect to find a meaning in that smile in such circumstances. To me it gave at least a welcome relief from an exhibition that could have been trying. It removed one far from the actuality of living in the present to be locked in that sombre smoking chamber, an inscrutable language mumbling at one's ear, a regal blaze of crystal and precious metal and shimmering silk framing this silent smiling human reality of sixteen hundred years ago.

When the prayer was finished the priest gave me a sign I did not understand. The fourth person relieved the situation by stepping up on a stool, bending over and, with his head buried in the casket, reverently kissing the foot of the saint. As he retired the priest repeated his polite gesture, which I now understood, and, as offense might have resulted from restraint, I too stepped on to the stool, and buried my head in the casket, and placed my lips very near the sacred feet.

When I withdrew I noticed for the first time a silver salver on the crystal slides and rather doubted it had been there before. There was no mistaking the priest's fixed and expectant gaze as the sacristan made an obvious gesture toward the plate. The contribution having been deposited, the priest transferred it to his pocket, and with a delicate reticence allowed the sacristan to pantomime pathetically that that contribution would go to the saint, or perhaps to the shrine, and what might there be for the ecclesiastic and himself. When that additional transaction had been completed the door was unlocked and I was permitted to depart.

The Harbour of Corfu from Gouvia (A. G. de Saint Sauveur, 1801)

Ithaca

1823 E. J. Trelawney

A Visit by Lord Byron

Our party made an excursion to the neighbouring island of Ithaca; contrasted with the arid wastes and barren red hills of Cephalonia, the verdant valleys, sparkling streams, and high land, clothed in evergreen shrubs, were strikingly beautiful. After landing, it was proposed to Byron to visit some of the localities that antiquaries have dubbed with the titles of Homer's school, - Ulysses' stronghold, etc. He turned peevishly away , saying to me, 'Do I look like one of those emasculated fogies? Let's have a swim. I detest antiquarian twaddle. Do people think I have no lucid intervals, that I came to Greece to scribble more nonsense? I will show them I can do something better: I wish I had never written a line, to have it cast in my teeth at every turn.' Brown and Gamba went to look for some place where he might pass the night, as we could not get mules to go on until the next day. After a long swim, Byron clambered up the rocks, and, exhausted by his day's work, fell asleep under the shade of a wild fig-tree at the mouth of a cavern. Gamba, having nothing to do, hunted him out, and awakened him from a pleasant dream, for which the Poet cursed him. We fed off figs and olives, and passed our night at a goatherd's cottage.

1838 William Mure

"Murder Most Foul"

Our arrival at Ithaca took place at a moment when the minds of its population were under the influence of an excitement, unequalled perhaps, in the annals of the place, since that consequent on the destruction of the flower of the native nobility by the arrows of Ulysses, and like it, produced by the commission, within the bounds of their own little island, of a mysterious deed of blood. The interest excited by this occurrence was not confined to Ithaca itself; but had spread throughout the Septinsular Republic. The crime, indeed, was one of those to which, in point of complication and horror, it would perhaps be difficult to find a parallel in the *Newgate Calendar*, or the *Causes célèbres*, and, occurring in the bosom of a small and simple community, possessed a special claim on my attention, which induced me to note its details. As they tend also to throw a curious light on the social condition of the island, a brief statement of them may perhaps not be uninteresting to others.

Upwards of twenty years ago, a Frank by the name of Soleure had established his domicile at Vathy, with a wife and only son. He was a person of some education, and of extensive knowledge of the world. Hence, as his character had been irreproachable since his settlement in Ithaca, he had been appointed teacher in the public grammar school, and had acquired considerable influence among the more intellectual class of the inhabitants. There was some mystery attached to his early life, which, even according to his own account, had not been of the most creditable description. He gave himself out for a Frenchman, native of Avignon, yet he spoke Italian better and more fluently than French – a circumstance which might, perhaps, be explained by a residence of more than half his life in countries where the former was the prevailing dialect. He described himself as having held a captain's commission in the French imperial army in Spain, where he had been taken prisoner during the early part of the war, but had effected his escape in the disguise of a capuchin friar to Malta. To account for his not returning to his own country to resume his military duties, he pleaded a distaste for the service, and a constitutional nervousness which disqualified him for the profession of a soldier. This latter statement, although in itself perfectly true, naturally suggested to those who were disposed to cavil at his story, the further question, how a person of such a temperament should have managed to attain the rank of captain in Napoleon's army. At Malta, and subsequently at Zante, he continued to support his character of capuchin. In the latter island, however, he attached himself to a female, with whom he eloped to Patras, where he threw off his canonicals, abjured the Catholic for the Greek persuasion, and married his mistress. Afterwards he kept a school at Sta. Maura, from whence he removed to Ithaca, where he was now settled under the circumstances previously stated.

For some years past, freemasonry had been much in vogue in the Ionian islands, and more especially in Ithaca. As it comprised many British members, the society was viewed without suspicion by the government, and thus afforded opportunity to the more enlightened classes for private convivial meetings to discuss matters of public interest, without the suspicion which would attach to organized political clubs, or other secret associations. Soleure from the first took a lead in the affairs of the lodge, and for several years past had officiated as its master. During this period the society had fallen under the displeasure of the clergy, who saw in it but a medium for the dissimulation of principles calculated to open the minds of the people to the absurdity of their own system of superstition, and, by consequence, a conspiracy against their authority and influence. They therefore took every means to inflame the minds of the lower orders against it, and their exertions were crowned with complete success. To such an extent was the popular feeling carried, that the council of the lodge, during the early part of the year 1837, fearing disturbances or acts of violence against their own persons, had deliberated on the propriety of its dissolution. Some of the leading members, however, objected to this plan as a mean subserviancy to popular clamour, and an act of injustice to the people themselves, by still further countenancing and confirming their foolish prejudices; and so it fell to the ground.

Soon after, a violent sermon was preached by the bishop against masonry, and the same night the lodge was broken into, and robbed of arms and other articles used in the ceremonial of the society. Soleur, as the head of the establishment and a foreigner, was the chief object of popular odium. He was frequently mobbed in the streets; and, as he resided at some little distance from the town, he requested and obtained from the superintendent of police, a retired British officer of great respectability, a constable to guard his house by night until the excitement had subsided. A few nights afterwards, several hours before daybreak, the superintendent was roused by the servant maid of the Soleure family, who announced that the work of murder was going on in the house; she could give no further particulars, as, on hearing a tumult and screams in the family apartment from another part of the dwelling where she slept, she had fled for assistance. He immediately proceeded to the spot, where the unfortunate woman and her son were found lying quite dead and fearfully mutilated on the floor. Soleure himself was stretched on the bed in a corner of the room, also apparently lifeless from terror, but with no other bodily injury than a slight wound in the flesh of the arm. His account was, that when the assassins broke in, the family were preparing to retire to rest; that becoming aware of their purpose, he instinctively took refuge in the bed, where he had swooned from terror; and that the wound in his arm had been inflicted by a random thrust, aimed at him as he lay enveloped in the clothes. Nothing tending to afford any trace of the murderers was found, but the scabbard of a sword lying on the bed by his side.

By a coincidence which appeared almost too singular to be the effect of accident, the constable appointed to guard the house, was, upon some pretext absent from his post that night. Soleure, although he did not pretend to recognise his person, which was disguised, denounced as the murderer a man formerly a freemason, but who had been expelled the lodge, by his sanction and authority, for disreputable life. This individual had since become a sworn foe of his former brethren, and of Soleure in particular, identifying his cause with that of the priests, by whom he had been absolved from his previous crime of participation in the profane mysteries, and received into special favour and confidence. The superintendent proceeded, therefore, at once to the house of this man, who was not found within; and it was afterwards proved that he had been seen that morning at three o'clock, in company with the son of a priest distinguished for the violent part he had taken against the freemasons. The only reason he could assign for this circumstance was, that he was an early riser, and fond of exercise in the morning; and he was accordingly placed under arrest. Suspicion, however, at the same time, fell upon Soleure himself, and, as will appear in the sequel, not altogether without reason. Public feeling ran, as might be expected, strongly against him – partly from his previous unpopularity, partly from a patriotic anxiety on the part of the Ithacans to shift the odium of so horrible a crime from their own shoulders upon those of a foreigner - and he was also taken into custody.

The office of crown prosecutor for the island about this time became vacant, and, owing, to the importance and mystery of the case, a lawyer of distinguished ability was sent from Corfu to follow out the investigation. During several weeks, nothing more was elicited tending to throw light on the affair; and, according to the usual custom on such occasions, a solemn procession, partly of a judicial, partly of a religious nature, was held, in which the authorities, civil and ecclesiastic, paraded the streets of the town, headed by the bishop, summoning all those who had any information to give, to come forward, and pronouncing, unqualified excommunication on all who, after this invitation, should hold back. Upon this an individual appeared, and deposed - "That on the night of the murder, while passing, along the quay near the shipping, he saw a man come down as if from the direction of Soleure's house, and throw something into the water, and that he resembled Soleure in stature and general appearance." A search was immediately instituted at the place pointed out, and a sword found smeared with blood, which on trial exactly fitted the scabbard discovered in the apartment where the murder was committed. The appearance of the weapon, however, was such as to render this evidence very suspicious; for, although it must have been already seventeen days under water, its general surface was comparatively bright and free from rust or corrosion, while the traces of blood exhibited a freshness which it was scarcely possible they could have preserved during so long a period of immersion. On the witness being questioned as to what he himself was doing in the streets at that late hour, he answered that he was on his return from a visit to sick friend. An epidemic fever, it is true, was prevalent at the period, and the friend in question was then afflicted by it. On enquiry, however, it turned out that no such visitor had been admitted that night. The explanation given was, that on arriving at the door of the house, and finding it closed and the family retired to rest, he had not cared to disturb them. Another suspicious circumstance was, that the spot from whence he stated the sword to have been thrown, was not in the direct road from his own house to that of his friend. Soon after, a person who kept a small shop in the town came forward and stated, that, some time before the murder, Soleure had come to his house, and showing him a sword he held in his hand, had asked him its value, adding, "that it was a good weapon, and before this time had killed both a mother and son!" - that he weighed the sword and entered the weight in his books, and that the weight of the one found in the water corresponded with his entry. On inspecting the books, however, the style of the entry showed it to have been made subsequent to the date under which it was inserted. His explanation was that he had neglected to make it at the time, and that, when it afterwards occurred to him to do so, he had, for the sake of regularity, assigned it a place under the proper date. Why he should have thought it necessary to record the weight at all, did not appear, as he had not purchased the sword. The servant girl was next brought forward with a statement tending to implicate Soleure; namely, that during the tumult in the room, while the crime was committing, she heard the young man call out – "What! wilt thou murder me?" The distinction between *thou* and *you*, which with us is but one of usage, is, it need hardly be observed, of considerable importance in most other European tongues, in regard to the sense of the expression; the former mode of address being customary only between relations or very attached friends, while the latter is that of ordinary social intercourse. This statement, however, was found to be broadly at variance with her deposition as formerly made before the superintendent of police, where she had no less distinctly and emphatically ascribed to the young man expressions of a very different nature. This was, in fact, so clear a case of perjury, that the witness was sentenced to three years imprisonment, which she was undergoing at the period of my visit to the island.

Such was the cream of the direct testimony against Soleure - lame enough, no doubt, and bearing much in its own face tending to show the existence of a conspiracy against the unfortunate old man. On the other hand, there were certainly some strong points of circumstantial evidence of an unfavourable nature. In the first place, it seemed strange that a plot on the part of his own enemies, and of those of freemasonry, should have been so bungled as to wreak its malice on the wife and son, while he himself escaped comparatively uninjured. Hence it was assumed by the party unfavourable to him, that the flight to the bed, the terror, and the swoon, were mere pretexts, and that the wound in the arm was inflicted with his own hand, the better to avert all suspicion from himself. And yet no reasonable motive was ever suggested that could have instigated him to so monstrous an act. Something, indeed, was said of a feeling of jealousy having been occasionally expressed by him towards his wife; but no weight was attached by impartial persons to this circumstance. The parties were both well past the period of life when conjugal harmony is exposed to much risk of interruption from any such cause, and there was every reason to believe that whatever had passed between them on the subject was but in jest. Nor would this have accounted for the destruction of his only son, whom there was abundant proof he tenderly loved, and with whom there was no evidence of his ever having had a quarrel. Many, too, of those who knew him best, ridiculed the notion that so weak, nervous, and timid an old man, even had he been ferocious enough to form the design, should have been able to muster sufficient energy, either of mind or body, successfully to carry into effect an assault of this kind against two persons much more active and able-bodied than himself. It was moreover proved, that his right arm, from the effects of an old hurt, added to constitutional debility, had for many years been incapable of any great exertion; and it was hence argued by his counsel, that it would have been impossible for him to have thrown the sword to the distance at which it was found from the shore.

The newly appointed advocate, considered a man of great talent, but apparently altogether devoid of principle, on observing how strong the tide of popular feeling set against the prisoner, had, shortly after his arrival, thrown aside even a pretence of impartiality, and completely identified himself with his enemies; exerting himself, with a zeal almost amounting to enthusiasm, to fix the stain of guilt upon him, and remove it from others on whom suspicion might have fallen.

The ex-freemason who had been arrested at the commencement, and against whom so much circumstantial evidence existed, was released by him shortly after his arrival.

Immediately on being set at large the man started for Constantinople, but returned two or three months afterwards; when, hearing that the servant-maid had been imprisoned for perjury, he again decamped after a two days' stay in the place, and has not been heard of.

For a long time the feeling, not only of the populace, but of all classes, even of the English residents, was unfavourable to Soleure, owing to the apparent plausibility, at first sight, both of the testimony and of the circumstantial evidence against him. But upon more full investigation, a change took place; and, although opinions were still divided, the conviction of the majority of impartial persons of the upper class, including most of the English, seemed now to be, that a foul conspiracy existed to involve the unfortunate man and his family in the cruellest species of destruction. It was conjectured, to explain the apparent singularity in the selection of the two principal victims, that the plot had been to kill the wife and child before the father's eyes, and then to fasten the guilt of the action upon himself, and bring him to the scaffold. This, however, seemed a refinement of iniquity scarcely conceivable and hence others preferred the supposition, that the plan had been to murder the whole family, but that its authors had been prevented, by some sudden alarm, from the complete execution of their purpose. The perjury of the servant girl, of the tradesman, or of other witnesses for the prosecution, did not in itself seem to be considered as necessarily implying the existence of a conspiracy; it being, as I was informed, not altogether inconsistent with the principles of modern Greek morality, where a firm conviction prevailed of the guilt of an individual, and an excessive desire for his conviction, to promote the desired object even by false testimony! This, at least, was the mode in which the more intelligent believers in the guilt of Soleure proposed to set aside the argument which the palpable falsehood of a great part of the evidence supplied of his innocence.

The Crown advocate's own fate furnished a striking episode in this tragical history. In the full ardour of his zeal against the prisoner, and while basking in the sunshine of popular favour, he suddenly became deranged, and was sent off and placed in confinement at Corfu. The circumstance was naturally turned to account by the friends of Soleure, as a Divine judgment against his persecutor; and there was reason to believe it had not been without its effect on the minds of the superstitious populace. Owing to this and other incidental causes of delay, upwards of a year had elapsed before the opening of the trial, and the process was now at one of its most interesting stages. The prisoner, if deficient in physical courage, displayed no small degree of that mental firmness which might be the result either of philosophy or of despair. He was entitled by law to claim his release, if not brought to the bar within the year. But he disdained to avail himself of this privilege, asserting that, if he were to live, he would not live under the odium of so horrible a crime; and if he were to die, it mattered but little, as he had lost all that made life dear to him, The newly appointed advocate - himself a native of the place, a personal friend of Soleure, a mason, and engaged as a witness for the defence – was incapacitated by these causes from performing his functions, which were transferred to the individual holding the same office in the neighbouring island of Cefalonia. This person, a man of honour as well as of ability, made no secret of his conviction of the innocence of the accused; and it was even said, that so strong was his sense of the futility of the charges against him, that it was not his intention to reply to the speech of the counsel for the defence.

It rained hard the whole morning - I therefore the more readily acquiesced in Captain W -'s proposal to accompany him to the court, where the proceedings promised to be interesting. In approaching the Ithacan *agora*, the mind instinctively reverted to the description of the second book of the *Odyssey*; and the contrast between the scene which now presented itself, and the image long familiar to my fancy of that where Telemachus, like this poor schoolmaster, the victim - with his family - of a cruel conspiracy of his fellow-citizens, expostulates with his oppressors, added much to the interest of a first view of the humble council-hall, and the assembly that filled it. It was a small two-storied edifice of the most homely architecture, with a wooden staircase outside, according to the prevailing fashion of the islands, and of the whole of continental Greece, in the few cases where access to an upper floor is required. The tribunal offered much the appearance of the room set apart for the meetings of justice courts in a second-rate English market town. The judges, three in number, sat at one extremity, on a platform considerably raised above the level of the floor; the crown advocate in the corner below, to their right, near whom Captain W - and myself were accommodated with chairs; on the other side, the clerk of the court. The prisoner, who was also allowed a seat at the bar, was a thin infirm-looking old man, with a haggard, careworn countenance, in which a naturally mild and placid expression was nearly effaced by one of deep and poignant grief: behind him, the remainder of the floor was filled with spectators, who, though very attentive, displayed little of that intense interest in the proceedings which their rancorous prejudice against him might have led one to expect. The pleadings were in Italian, in which language the whole business of the court was conducted, unless in the case of witnesses of the lower and less educated class, who were examined in their native Greek. The form of process differed in no great degree from that of our own tribunals. When we entered, the counsel for the defence, a young Cefalonian lawyer, was speaking to the evidence of the discovery of the sword, which he impugned with some ability. The sword itself was produced, and handed round the court for inspection. After he had concluded, testimony was brought forward to the character of the prisoner. The most important and interesting was that of the crown advocate of the island, a remarkably pleasing, good-looking young man, an intimate friend of my host, and who dined that afternoon at his table. He recapitulated with much eloquence and feeling a number of proofs, which he himself had witnessed, of the fond affection borne by the unfortunate old father to his murdered son, who it seems had been a youth of remarkable promise; of the pride he had taken in him; how often he had boasted of the excellent education he had given him; and with what delight he looked forward to the honour that would crown his own gray hairs, from the distinction he was destined to attain in whatever civil or literary career it might be his lot to pursue. The countenance of the old man, who had hitherto listened in mute apathy to what was going on, here became slightly convulsed, and torrents of tears rolled down his cheeks; but he remained silent, and in other respects motionless. It certainly was a most affecting scene, and ought to have gone far to convince of his innocence even those among his bitterest enemies whose hearts were not as hard as the rocks of their native island. It would, indeed, be difficult to conceive a more horrid destiny than that of the poor sufferer, assuming him to be guiltless: after having witnessed the murder of a wife and only son, the joy and hope of an otherwise forlorn and comfortless old age, to be impeached and exhibited in public as their assassin; to lie in prison in a foreign land during a year, under so odious an imputation; and to have, from day to day, all the revolting details of their massacre forced upon his recollection, by enemies unremitting in the exercise of every art of ingenuity or treachery to fasten the stigma of it on himself.

During a pause in the proceedings, the judges retired to a small side apartment, where coffee was handed round, of which we also partook. Their appearance and conversation gave a favourable impression of their character; and as there was no real ground to suspect their impartiality, it was the more amusing to observe how necessarily it seemed to be assumed, even by the more intelligent of the prisoners' friends, that their decision might be influenced by motives such as with us no one would ever imagine could interfere with the rectitude of a verdict. One, it was said, was a Catholic, and would bear ill-will to Soleure because he was a renegado from that persuasion; another was a native of Ithaca, and connected by blood with some of the parties most hostile to him: a third had a great dislike to freemasonry, and so forth...

The only species of external influence which there seemed to be any plausible ground for apprehending, was the fear of popular outrage in case of acquittal; and the general belief was, that the verdict would be of that ambiguous and unfair description, which in England is unknown, but in Scotland is admitted under the name of "not proven;" and which, without too rudely clashing with the prejudices of the community, would at the same time evade the sin of punishing an innocent man. Soleure, however, had declared he would be satisfied with nothing less than a full acquittal, and in the case of any decision of the nature above mentioned, would appeal to the Supreme Court of Corfu for a new trial. On my return, I heard that the verdict had been in his favour, but whether by the full or half species of acquittal, I could not ascertain. The real perpetrators of the mysterious crime remained still undiscovered.

Vathy, Ithaca (E. Dodwell, circa 1800)

Paxoi

Early 1870s Mrs. Annie Brassey

Waterspouts

The serene blue waters of the Ionian Sea can be stormy and dangerous at certain times of the year, but rarely as spectacularly as when Mrs. Brassey encountered it.

At 3 am. we left Paxos behind. About 9.30 am. we were all called in a great hurry to see a waterspout. The sea was rushing up violently like an immense fountain jet, while from the cloud above, which was intensely black, an inverted cone came down to meet the sea. Another water-spout, farther off, looked like a long black trough, pouring down from the heavens above into the cone-shaped fountain in the sea beneath. While we were all gazing at these over the starboard side, another small waterspout rushed by under our stern, so close that the man steering, using the sailor's proverbial expression, said "you could have pitched a biscuit into it," and before he could even call us to look, it was miles away, so swiftly was it flying.

It was a fortunate chance it missed us, for these waterspouts are very dangerous, the force with which the water falls often driving ships' decks in, and sometimes causing them to founder. Men-of-war frequently fire into and break them to prevent such an accident.

Paxoi (Edward Lear)

Lefkada

1682 George Wheler

The Curious Geography of Lefkada

[W]e were obliged to touch at a port of it called Chimeno, which is the best in the island, having good depth and anchorage. From thence the fancy took us to go see the fortress, and to that end took a boat, called *monoxylo*, to carry us thither. We rowed four or five hours in the narrow channel that separates it from the continent before we arrived at it. Strabo saith that it was anciently joined to the land, and that this strait was dug to separate it; which is likely enough. For in the straitest part it doth not much exceed fifty paces over, and almost everywhere three or four feet of water. It is in this narrow part of the strait that the ancient city of Leucada had its situation, upon an eminence a mile from the sea, of which some remains are yet to be seen; having for its port the whole channel, especially those parts where there was water enough... The fortress is good, and hath some round bastions, situated upon a very low ground. But that which renders it considerable is that it neither can be approached to by land nor sea, unless in those *monoxylos*, or little barques, which draw not above a foot of water. It is separated by a ditch of thirty or forty feet wide, from two little islands, which are as the suburbs to the fortress, and are inhabited by Turks and Greeks. Their houses are very low, and built of wood; but to make amends, they themselves go very well-clothed, and are great pirates in those seas.

The Basha of the Morea came thither this year to burn their little galleys ... We left our little boat ashore, and went to Saint Mauro on an aqueduct a mile long, which serveth as a bridge for those that would go thither on foot, though it be not above a yard broad, and without any hold; which would make the stoutest man tremble in passing it, especially if he meet any other person thereon. For it is as much as two can do to pass by one another.

There is above five or six thousand inhabitants in the citadel and suburbs. But we had very hard cheer there, without the fish we carried with us; for we found nothing there but bad wine, bad bread and worse cheese.

There are about thirty villages on the island, inhabited by

Santa Maura

(Fullart, 1850)

poor Greeks that manure the land and catch fish; being under the jurisdiction of a bishop whose revenues apparently are but mean. The isle is fruitful enough in corn, oranges, lemons, almonds, and pasture for their cattle, and is about thirty or forty miles in compass.

1802-09 Colonel William Leake

The Chief Town

The modern capital of Leucas, named Amaxikhi, resembles Mesolonghi, as well by its situation on the lagoon as in the form of the houses, which are very unlike those of Corfu, being built chiefly of wood on a substruction of stone or brick, with galleries supported by wooden pillars. The greater part of them are of one story only, which, as well as the wooden construction, is said to have been adopted in consequence of the frequency of earthquakes. Some of the larger houses are fitted up with tapestry in the Venetian taste. The town is composed of a single street, from which branch some narrow lanes of small wooden tenements. At the northern termination of the street, near the head of the aqueduct, is a small square called the Piazza di San Marco; from the other end branch two roads which are practicable for carriages for two or three miles, and then become mere horse-paths. Amaxikhi may perhaps have taken its name from being the only place in the island where amaxia, or wheel carriages, are or can be used. The women are generally handsome, as at Mesolonghi, and in some other situations in Greece which have every appearance of being unhealthy; but many of the men have a sickly complexion...

Sept. 12. - Cross the lagoon in company with Count Orio to the fortress, in a small flat-bottomed boat which is punted, and sails back without any danger under the lee of the aqueduct, though there is a strong south-wester without. The aqueduct is so narrow, that when the wind is very strong it sometimes happens that careless or drunken men fall, or are blown over into the water and smothered in the mud. The Russians in garrison, who have just received a year's arrear of pay and clothing, are commanded by a rough Russian colonel, who has learnt few words of Italian at Naples and in these islands, and says that he should prefer the most miserable village in Russia to his present solitary and disagreeable station. Formerly the fortress was the seat of government, and there were houses in it for the *proveditori ordinario* and *straordinario*. The profile is low, and the wall is very weak, especially towards the lagoon. But it is well placed for protecting the strait just where it is easily forded from the opposite heights in Xeromero, called Lamia, on the extremity of which is a Tekieh of Dervises. The shallow channel extends two or three miles to the north of the fort, separated only from the open sea by a continuation of the Plaka, which terminates at the southern side of the entrance of port Dhemata, or St. Nicolas. This harbour, being the only one between Viskardho and Prevyza, is of some importance, though the depth of water is sufficient for ships only at the entrance; it communicates eastward by a narrow channel with the Lake of Vulkaria. The fortress of Santa Maura is the only place where I have seen date trees growing on the western coast of Greece; they are now bearing fruit, but it never ripens here.

The Collection of Salt

Lefkadha produces corn enough for its own consumption, and some oil for exportation. A great quantity of salt, and wine sufficient not only for home consumption, but for exportation in considerable quantities to Corfu, Prevyza, and other places. Besides the salt-works of Kaligoni, there are some smaller near the town. The salt-chambers are separated from one another by other chambers in which no salt is made; the stagnant water in these and in the ditches causes malaria. The salt is piled up in large pyramids, and covered with a roof of tiles. At Corfu it is formed into little hillocks. The manufacture there is not so good as it is here, nor the salt so much esteemed.

1817-18 Peter Edmund Laurent

Sick and in Quarantine

In the afternoon of the second day from our departure, we landed at the town of Santa Maura. It was not till the surgeon of the British garrison stationed on the island had reconnoitred us that we were allowed to disembark. My companions, whose humanity claims my lasting gratitude, carried me in their arms to land. We were there placed in a room to perform fourteen days quarantine. Several papers which hung on the walls were removed, and two Greek guards were placed at the door to see that the laws of quarantine should not be infringed. Each of these sentinels held a long bar of iron, at the end of which was a separation, in which any written communication we had to make was placed, in order, ere it was delivered, to be properly fumigated. We were daily visited by the British officers of the garrison, anxious to give us proofs of the simple and genuine hospitality peculiar to their nation. The surgeon of the regiment attended me assiduously, and, thanks to his kind attention, my fever was, if not entirely cured, at least for a time repelled.

So disgracefully are the most rigid laws of the quarantine infringed by the sentinels ... that we not infrequently found our servant playing at cards with them: from us, however, those conscientious gentlemen would never receive the smallest paper until it had been properly discoloured with smoke, and sometimes partially burnt.

The Quarantine Station, Lefkda (J. Cartwright, 1821)

Cefalonia

1809-10 Dr. Henry Holland

The Evil Potato

The priests in the island, though very numerous, are inferior in respectability to both the former classes. They are generally taken from a lower rank in society, and their education is of a very limited kind; a circumstance not peculiar to this island, but common to the other isles, and to the continent of Greece. In Cephalonia, two papas or priests were for some time very active in opposing the schemes of improvement which have lately, been carried on there. It is a curious instance of their tendency to resist innovation, that when Major Du Bosset wished to introduce the culture of the potato, many of these men laboured to convince the peasants that this was the very apple with which the serpent seduced Adam and Eve in Paradise.

Unfortunately, the potato experienced a more serious obstacle in two successive bad seasons, and in the necessity which was found for renewing the sets from England at the expiration of this period.

Kefalonia (Cartwright, 1821)

1825 Lytton Bulwer

A Reserved Memorial of Lord Byron

I paid a visit to the house which Lord Byron occupied in this island previously to his entering Etolia. There is nothing to distinguish it from a common cottage, except the classic air which we still suppose it breathes.

Just by, is a small but beautiful villa, belonging to a poor little doctor, whom we found almost dying of the fever. In common with all whom we have seen, he appeared enchanted by the manners of his late neighbour; who was, in fact, a far more popular character than would be conjectured from the mere perusal of his writings.

1898 Samuel J. Barrows

A Visit to the Monastery of Saint Gerasimos

The monastery of Saint Gerasimo is really a nunnery with an abbess and a few priests and acolytes who conduct the religious services in the chapel. The country people respect and love the abbess, or Mother Superior, as do the inmates of the convent, where she has been for over thirty years. She lives in the main building which stands between the men's court and the women's. The latter was the more interesting, with its row of little whitewashed houses, each having a bit of garden under the windows, shaded by vines and fig-trees. In each tiny house live two sisters, whose busy fingers decorate their living-rooms with embroidery, patchwork and knitted tidies. Some of the younger girls were drawing water at the well as we crossed the courtyard. Several others ran out to peep at us, holding back with shy curiosity. One sister had been to France, and she was pushed forward as interpreter. The rest kept behind her, clinging to one another's skirts; but they soon lost their fear and followed us into the chapel.

The monastery is distinguished for two things, - the remains of Hagios Gerasimo, and the underground cell in which he lived. Neither of them was particularly attractive, but the little sisters would have been disappointed if we had not begged the privilege of seeing what is left of their patron saint. To the chapel we went, then, where the priests and the little boys who drone the responses were already gathered. Anastasios the priest asked us to write our Christian names on a bit of paper. Then we took our places in the stalls, with the other worshippers, and service was conducted for our especial benefit. On a great shelf built into the wall lay what had once been Gerasimo, a poor brown mummy, laden with rings and votive jewels. Before his shrine the priest stood chanting a prayer. Now and again we could catch our own names – "Guilielmos," "Triantaphylle," "Mavilla" - as he presented each one to the saint. Then, when the introductions were over, we were allowed to step within the sacred enclosure, and bow before his saintship. The fervour of the worshippers made the service solemn, and even we Americans were touched.

The very small hole in the floor, through which we had to wriggle down into the saint's cell, shows that Gerasimo must have been an abstemious man. How could a man dig a hole for himself in the rocks underground, and live in that foul dampness, when he might have enjoyed God's sunshine? But men thought differently four hundred years ago, and Gerasimo was considered wise and holy and possibly clean.

Beyond the pain where the convent stands rises Mt. Aenus. The view from its summit is the finest to be had in the Ionian islands. We planned to climb it in time to see the sunrise. "Please have the mules ready and wake us at three," we said, as we went to our rooms.

At three the convent bells and the clatter of hoofs beneath our windows woke us. It was raining hard. No sunrise, no mountain! We mournfully gathered in the refectory to decide what we should do.

"In the first place," said our practical escort, "let's have some tea." So we sat around in the dim candlelight and held an informal "afternoon tea" at three am on Sunday. Glimmering through the rain we could see the lights of the chapel, where the monks and the sisters were already at mass. [*At that hour it was probably not mass but part of the monastic office (ed.).*] We splashed across the court and slipped in behind the pillars. The service was antiphonal. On one side stood a young priest who was reading the liturgy at a rate which would have made the most rapid phonograph green with envy. What a cataract of words! And all the time his eyes were scarcely on the book; one of them at least was busy scanning the newcomers. It is not a common event to have such a party at early morning prayers. On the other side stood an old priest at a second reading-desk with a large illuminated prayer-book which now and then caught the drippings of the candle he held in his hand. Very prominent was the sharp nasal tone of the principal boy as he sang out, - Kyrie eleison.

The old priest invited Mavilla and myself to look over with him and follow the Greek text. We each held a naked candle, while the priest kept track of the place with one of his fingers. He had been a sailor in his early days and had seen a little of the world. His literal devotion to the service did not prevent him from keeping up a broken conversation with us, which he interjected between the responses.

"You come from America?"

"Yes."

"Kyrie eleison, Kyrie eleison – What part?"

"From Boston."

"Ah! Kyrie eleison, Kyrie eleison – I was there once. It was many years ago."

Then another volley of Greek addressed to Heaven, and suspended at the proper pause to make sure that his communications with earth were not cut off. The expression "Lord have mercy" (Kyrie eleison) when he learned that we were from Boston seemed to us strangely inappropriate. He was greatly pleased to establish this relationship, and more than the ordinary amount of melted candle dripped upon the sacred page. The service was thoroughly mechanical, and I did not see why a phonograph run by water power would not have been as devotional. But it was a free and novel lesson in the modern Greek pronunciation.

" I moved away," says Mavilla, and let the priest talk with my father. The stone floor was cold, and I was sleepy. Two or three nuns were nodding in their stalls; another, crouched on the floor, was rocking back and forth, throwing up her hands and moaning. The little choir boys yawned, and pulled each other by the sleeves when it was time for their responses. The splash of the rain mingled with the monotonous drone of the priest; the incense made me dull, and the candles flickered weirdly before my sleepy eyes.

"When will the service be over?" I whispered to Mr. Woodley.

"In three hours," he replied cheerfully. "It lasts every morning from two to seven."

Mavilla gave one look at the picturesque two by the reading-desk – "the dark, grey-bearded priest and the pale clergyman, paler than ever in the dim candlelight" -and quietly stole back to bed. It was not long before the paternal clergyman followed.

For their hospitality the monks made no charge, but accepted with thanks the contribution we offered.

Zakynthos

1599 Thomas Dallam

Venturing onto a Strange Shore

This charmingly naive account of a first landing in a strange land,,conveys the sense of adventure occasioned in an untravelled man by arriving in this part of the world.

Whilst we lay, thus for six days upon the sea before the town, I took great notice of a little mountain, the which, as I thought, did lie close to the sea, and seemed to be a very pleasant place to take a view of the whole island and the sea before it. It showed to be very green and plain ground on the top of it, and a white thing like a rock in the middle thereof. I took such pleasure in beholding this hill that I made a kind of vow or promise to myself that as soon as I set foot on shore I would neither eat nor drink until I had been on the top thereof; and in the meantime did labour with two of my companions, and persuaded them to bear me company. One of their names was Myghell Watson, my joiner; the other's name Edward Hale, a Scotchman. The day being come that we should go a shore, I challenged my associates with their promise, and got their good wills to go with me before we went into the town. This hill is called by the Greeks Scopo (i.e., outlook). It is from the town more than a mile, but I gave our sailors something to carry us in the coke boat, as we thought to the foot of the hill; but when we were set a shore we found it to be almost two miles unto it. When we came to the foot of it, by great fortune we happened on the right way, the which was very narrow and crooked. It was early in the morning, and we were told, two or three days before, that no man must carry any weapon with him when he went ashore, and therefore we went only with cudgels in our hands. So, ascending the hill about half a mile, and looking up, we saw upon a storey of the hill above us a man going with a great staff on his shoulder, having a clubbed end, and on his head a cape which seemed to us to have five horns standing outright, and a great heard of goats and sheep followed him.

My friend Myghell Watson, when he saw this, he seemed to be very fearful and would have persuaded us to go no further, telling us that surely those that did inhabit there were savage men, and might easily wrong us, we having no swords or daggers, neither any more company; but I told him that if they were divers, I would, with God's help, be as good as my word. So, with much ado, we got him to go to that storey where we saw the man with his club; and then we saw that that man was a herdsman. Yet, for all this, Myghell Watson swore that he would go no further, come of it what would. Edward Hale said something faintly that he would not leave me, but see the end. So we two travelled forward, and when we came something near the top, we saw two horses grazing; with pack saddles on their backs, and one man coming down the hill towards us, having nothing in his hands. Quoth I to my fellow: "Ned, we shall see by this man what people they be that inhabit here." When this man came unto us he lay his hand upon his breast, and bowed his head and body with smiling countenance, making us a sign to go up still. Yet then Ned Hall began to dissuade me from going any further ; but I told him it would not stand with my oath to go back until I had been as far as I could go. Coming to the top there was a pretty fair green, and on one side of it a white house built of lime, and some square, the which had been the house of an anchorite, who, as I heard after wards, died but a little before our coming thither, and that she had lived five hundred years. Right before us, on the farther side of the green, I saw a house of some twenty paces long, and walled about one yard high, and then open to the eaves; which was about a yard more. And I see a man on the inside reach out a copper kettle to one that stood without the wall. Than said I to Ned Hale: "I will go to yonder house and get some drink, for I have great need. The weather was very hot, and I was fasting. But Ned Hale told me that I had no reason to drink at their hands, neither to go any nearer them. Yet I went boldly to the side of the house, where I saw another man drink, and made a sign to him within that I would drink. Then he took up the same kettle which had water in it, and offer it me to drink. And when I did put out my hand to take it, he would not give it me, but set it further off, and than came near the wall again, and lift up a carpet which lay on the ground, and there was six bottles full of very good wine, and a fair silver cup, and he filled that silver bowl full of a reddish wine, which they do call Rebola, and he gave it me to drink. And when I had it in my hand I called to my friend Ned Hale, who stood afar off, for he was afraid to come near. Here, Ned, quoth I, a carouse to all our friends in Inglande. I pray you, quoth he, take heed what you do. Will you take what drink they give you? Yea, truly, quoth I; for it is better than I have as yet deserved of. When I had give God thanks for it, I drank it of, and it was the best that ever I drank. Then he filled me the same bowl with white Rebola, the which was more pleasant than the other. When I had much commended the wine, and told Ned Hale that he was a fool to refuse such a cup of wine, then he came near the house, and desired to have some water; so he had the kettle to drink in. When this was all done, I was so well pleased with this entertainment, that I knew not how to thank this man.

I had no money about me but one half dollar of Spanish money, and that money is best accepted of in that country. I offered to give that piece of silver to this man, but he would not by any means take it. Then I remembered that I had two several knives in my pocket. I took one of them and gave it him, and the blade gilded and graven. When he had taken it out of the sheath and looked upon it, he called with a loud voice: "Sisto! Sisto!" Then another man came running, unto whom he showed but only the haft of it, and then they began to wrestle for the knife; but he that I gave it unto kept it and leaped over the wall to the side where I was, and bowing himself unto me, he took me by the hand, and led me about by the end of that house, and so into a little cloister, through the which we passed into a chapel, where we found a priest at mass, and wax candles burning. He put me into a pew where I sat and saw the behaviour of the people, for there were about twenty men, but not a woman amongst them; for the women were in a lower chapel by themselves, yet might they hear and see. Ned Hale came after, but having lost sight of me, at his coming into the chapel he kneeled down near unto the women, but saw them not; but they saw him, and wondered at his behaviour; for, after I had kneeled down, I stood up in my pew to look for him, and then I saw two women put out their heads and laughed at him - as indeed they might, for he behaved himself very foolishly. Neither he nor I had ever seen part of a mass before, neither were we thing the wiser for that. This chapel was very curiously painted and garnished round about, as before that time I had never seen the like.

Service being ended, we departed out of the chapel; but presently one came after us, who did seem very kindly to entreat me to go back again, and he led us through the chapel into the cloister, where we found standing eight very fair women, and richly apparelled, some in red satin, some white, and some in watchell damask, their heads very finely attired, chains of pearl and jewels in their ears, seven of them very young women, the eighth was ancient, and all in black. I thought they had been nuns, but presently after I knew they were not. Then were we brought into that house where before I had drunk. Cloth being laid, we were requested to sit down, and served with good bread and very good wine and eggs, the shells of them coloured like a damask rose, and these made like an alla compana root, for they keep it in the earth, because nothing will there take salt. My fellow, Ned Hale, would neither eat nor drink anything but water, yet I did eat one egg, bread and cheese, and I drank two bowls of wine. Whilst we sat there, the gentlewomen came in, and three of them came very near us, and looked earnestly upon us. I offered one of them the cup to drink, but she would not. Then I offered to give him that tended upon us my half dollar, but he would not take any money. These women standing all together before us, I thought they had been dwellers there, because no money would be taken. I presented my other knife, of 2*s.* price, unto the old gentlewoman, the which she was unwilling to take, but at last she took it, and then they all flocked together, and, as it seemed to me, they wondered much at it. When they had all well looked upon it, they came altogether towards me and bowed their bodies, to show their thankfulness.

So Ned Hale and I took our leaves and went away very merrily; but when we came to the place where we left our faint-hearted friend Myghell Watson, who all this while had lain in a bush, when we had told him the wonders that we had seen, and of our kind entertainment, he would not believe us, for he was ashamed, and desired to make haste to the town that he might get some victuals; but we made the less haste for that, and went to see another monastery.

1609-10 William Lithgow

Addiction to Currants

The puritan conscience of this Scot was gravely offended by the new, and obviously morally degenerate fashion, common among the English of course, for adding currants to their food.

Here in Zante a Greek surgeon undertook the curing of my arm, and performed condition within time.

And on the top of a Hill, above the town, standeth a large, and strong fortress (not unlike the Castle of Milaine) wherein the Providitore dwelleth, who govemeth the island. This city is subject yearly to fearful earthquakes, especially in the months of October and November, which oftentimes subvert their houses, and themselves, bringing deadly destruction on all. This lie produceth good store of *rasini di Corintho*, commonly called currants, olives, pomegranates, citrones, oranges, lemons, grenadiers, and melons...

The islanders are Greeks, a kind of subtle people and great dissemblers; but the seigniory thereof belongeth to Venice. And if it were not for that great provision of corn which is daily transported from the firm land of Peloponnesus to them, the inhabitants in a short time would famish.

I was credibly informed here by the better sort, that this little isle maketh yearly (besides oil and wine) only of currants, one hundred and sixty thousand zechins, paying yearly over and above for custom, twenty-two thousand piasters, every zechin of gold being nine shillings English, and every piaster, being white money, six shillings, a rent or sum of money which these silly islanders could never afford, (they being not above sixty years ago, but a base beggarly people, and an obscure place), if it were not for some liquorish lips here in England of late, who forsooth can hardly digest bread, pasties, broth, and (*verbi gratia*) bag-puddings, without these currants. And as these rascal Greeks becoming proud of late with this lavish expense, condemn justly this sensual prodigality. I have heard them often demand the English, in filthy derision, what they did with such liquorish stuff, and if they carried them home to feed their swine and hogs withal. A question indeed worthy of such a female traffic; the inference of which I suspend: there is no other nation but this, thus addicted to that miserable isle."

1610 Sir George Sandys

A Lawless Land

The inhabitants of this land are generally Grecians... in habit they resemble the Italians, but transcend them in their revenges, and infinitely less civil. They will threaten to kill a merchant that will not buy their commodities: and make more conscience to break a fast than commit a murder. One of them ... being here pursued a poor sailor (an Englishman) for offering but to carry a little bag of currants aboard uncustomed, and killed him running up a pair of stairs for succour. He is weary of life that hath a difference with any of them, and will walk abroad after daylight. But cowardice is joined with their cruelty, who dare do nothing, but suddenly upon advantages, and are ever privately armed.

[They are] encouraged to villainies by the remissness of their laws, for no one will lay hands upon an offender until fourteen days after that he be brought to the Scale, an eminent place where one doth stand and publicly cite the offender, who in the meantime hath the leisure to make his own peace, or else absent himself. If he then appear not, they banish him, and prepare a reward, according to the greatness of the offence, to him that shall either kill or take him alive. And if it be done by one that is banished, his own banishment (the least reward) is released.

The labourers go into the fields with swords and partigans, as if in an enemy's country, bringing home their wines and oils in hog's skins, the insides turned outward.

Methods of Guarding the Integrity of Marriages

It is a custom amongst them to invite certain men into their marriages, whom they call compeers. Every one of these do bestow a ring, which the priest doth put upon the bride and her groom's fingers, interchangeably shifting them, and so he doth the garlands of their heads. Of these they are never jealous, an abuse in that kind reputed as detestable a crime as if committed by a natural brother, so that they choose those for their compeers that have been formerly suspected too familiar.

The bridegroom, entering the church, sticks his dagger in the door, held available against enchantment. For here it is a common practice to bewitch them. Made thereby impotent with their wives until the charm be burnt or otherwise consumed, inasmuch that oftentimes (as they say) the matters of the betrothed, by way of prevention, do bewitch themselves, and again unloose them as soon as the marriage is consummated; a practice whereof former times have been guilty...

The nuptial sheets ... are publicly shown, and preserved by their presents as a testimony of their uncorrupted virginities.

Foreign Residents

The Jews here have a synagogue, of whom there are not many, one, having married an English woman and converted her to his religion. They wear a blue ribband about their hats for distinction.

The foreign merchants resident here are for the most part English; who by their frequent deaths do disprove the air to be so salubrious as is reported; who have their purchased internments in gardens, neither suffered by the Greeks nor Latins to be buried in their churches.

1682 George Wheler

A Shake-Up

The town is well-built of freestone; but the buildings not very high by reason of the frequent earthquakes that happen there; which in the spring are, some years, once or twice a week, and so shake all the houses, that the stone walls of some are full of great cracks. I happened when I was there, at my return from Athens, during my quarantine in the pest-house. That day it happened the sun looked a yellowish colour, which was looked upon as ominous. I was sitting leaning upon a table; when on a sudden the earth was so prodigiously shaken that I thought the place (which was but one storey high) would have immediately fallen on my head, it gave such a crack, and the chairs, stools and table so clashed together that they rattled again. The unusualness of the thing made so deep an impression on my fancy that I hardly believed the earth stood still, so long as I stayed on the island after it. But the inhabitants are so used to them that they make little or nothing of them.

Rival Churches

They profess the Greek religion, but are very much Latinized in doctrine, although they extremely hate the Roman Catholic Church. They are not allowed a bishop, but a *protopappa*; and submit themselves to the bishop of Cephalonia. There is a Latin bishop; whom they are hardly constrained to use civilly. A new one arrived while I was there, and he made his public entry; the Greek priests were commanded to attend him to the cathedral church in the fort. He was likewise attended by the several orders of friars that have convents there; who sing his entry after the Latin way; but were derided by the Greeks that followed them.

Reprehensible Absence of the Church of England

Towards the point that lieth opposite to Cephalonia is a little Greek church called Saint Veneranda, about which the English used to bury their dead; but since upon some dispute with the *pappa*, they have lately altered their place of burial, it being made a mile or two off the town, at a little church in the plain behind the castle. At the first are several monuments of our English merchants, who have left their bodies there; but few marks of their religion are to be observed, whether of the living or the dead, in this, and in several other of our factories abroad; to the great dishonour of the reformed religion; there being none to administer comfort to their souls, by preaching the word or administering the sacraments to them, when they are in health, or in the greatest extremities of sickness and death. For they have neither church, chapel, nor priest. So that they seem to the people of the place to live without religion, and to die without hope, as they really are buried without decency. This is a very great scandal to those without; and therefore a very great fault to those within our church. You shall nowhere see a factory of the Roman religion, but they will have one or more priests, when, perhaps, they are not well able to maintain themselves. But ours, on the contrary, are rich and wealthy, and able to maintain many; but will keep none… Because it gives occasion of reflection upon our church, and the excellent religion we profess, to its ignorant and malicious enemies abroad, it would, in my opinion, be a matter highly becoming the pious zeal of our reverend fathers, to whom God hath committed the care of his Church, to consider some proper expedients, if any may be found, to prevent such scandals, and supply the defects of this nature in foreign countries with whom we have any, although but small, commerce.

An Alternative Attitude Towards Currants

This is now the chief island from whence the currants come, whereof we make so many pleasant dishes here in England... They grow not upon bushes like our red or white currants, as is vulgarly thought, but upon vines, like other grapes, only their leaf is something bigger. They are also without stones; and in these parts are only red, or rather, black... In August, when they are ripe, they are laid thin on the ground until they are dry; then they are gathered together, cleaned, brought into town, and put into warehouses they call seraglios, into which they are poured through a hole above, until the room be filled up to the top. By their own weight they cake so together that they are forced to dig them out with piked irons, and this they call stirring. When they barrel them up to send into these parts, a man getteth into the vat with bare legs and feet; and as they are brought out and poured in, he keeps stamping and treading of them down, to make them lie close together. They are worth here about twelve dollars the thousand more or less, and pay as much to the state of Venice for custom. The island beareth enough of them yearly to charge five or six vessels: Cephalonia three or four, Nathatigo, Mesalongia and Patras one; of which some few are brought down from the Gulf of Lepanto.

The Fortress and port of Zakynthos (Baron von Stackelberg & Deroy, 1834)

59

To maintain this trade, the English have a little factory here, consisting of a consul and five or six merchants. The Dutch have a consul and one or two merchants; and the French have a consul and merchant in the same person. The English have the chief trade here; and good reason they should; for I believe they eat five or six times as much of their fruit as both France and Holland do. The Zantiotes have not long known what we do with them; but have been persuaded that we use them only to dye cloth with; and are yet strangers to the luxury of Christmas pies, plumpotage, cake and puddings, etc.

An Unimpressive Devil

We had to pass about, from this port, a long promontory, stretched-out towards the Morea, and thence to return to the port on the other side of it. In that bay are two other little rocks or islands, one of which is called Marathronesa, or the Fennel Island, from the abundance of that plant which groweth there…

In it there is only a little church, with a caloyer or two, who look to a woman they pretend is possessed with a devil. But, as my companion saith, it is a foolish one. For it told us that he was of Jodua, though it could not speak one word of Italian; nor could it tell us of what country we were, or whether married or bachelors; nor indeed make any pertinent answer, but speak in rhyme, but to little purpose.

1740s Richard Pococke

Island of Rubbish

This is not the only island about which the following folk-tale was told.

The state of this island is very miserable, for it is divided into two great parties under Count Metaxas, and the family of Anno, who judge in all affairs of their clients by force of arms, it being a great aim of each party to destroy the other. Another powerful family is the Conphani, his ancestor was a fugitive from Naples, and with whichsoever side he joins, that party is sure to be the stronger; there are besides these other families of condition, which take part on one side or other, and they are all descended from fugitives, so that the whole island is full of very bad people; and the Venetian governors find their account in these divisions.

A story they have invented will give some idea of the character of these people, as well as some others, they say that the Creator, when he had made the earth, threw all the rubbish here; and that there being notorious rogues he sent one to this island, another to St. Maura, and the third to Maina."

1809-10 Henry Holland

Taking Risks with Public Morality

There are few public amusements of any kind in Zante. At the time I was there, the question was agitated, whether an opera might not be safely admitted into the city; and I heard various opinions on this subject among the principal inhabitants. The prevailing sentiment appeared adverse to it; and even many of those who did not object on the score of religion or morals, yet spoke of the evil of changing the ancient habits of the people; and especially of the female part of the community. The English garrison of the island occasionally gave balls and other entertainments which, however, are only very partially frequented by the natives.

1811-12 C. R. Cockerel

A Special Zantiote Method of Murder

Although a murderous lot, the Zantiotes had, in the mind of C. R. Cockerel, a much more grevious fault.

The Zantiotes, as they have been more under Western influence - for Zante belonged to Venice for about three centuries - are detestable. They are much less ignorant than the rest of the Greeks, but their half-knowledge only makes them the more hateful. Until the island was taken in hand by the English, murder was of constant occurrence, and so long as a small sum of money was paid to the proveditor no notice was taken of it. For accomplishing it without bloodshed they had a special method of their own. It was to fill a long narrow bag with sand, with which, with a blow on the back scientifically delivered, there could be given, without fuss or noise, a shock certain sooner or later to prove fatal. Socially they have all the faults of the West as well as those of the East without the virtues of either. But their crowning defect in my eyes is that they have not the picturesque costumes or appearance of the mainland Greeks.

1814 The Rev. Thomas Smart Hughes

The Pitch Wells

The pitch wells of Zakynthos, known since ancient times and mentioned in Herodotus, were a natural curiosity which became an essential port of call to all passing travellers.

Next morning we made an excursion to the celebrated pitch wells under some low hills near Port Cheri; exactly similar, in situation and appearance, to what they were when visited and described by the father of Grecian history. [Herodotus, *Histories* I, iv, 195.] The inhabitants also collect the pitch in small quantities, as they may require it, according to the ancient method; for we observed some of them dipping myrtle branches attached to long poles into the ebullient sources.

Every peasant we met was armed with a musket, and many of these fellows had ferocious countenances: our guide pointed out a deserted house into which five of them had entered not more than a month before, in open day, and murdered every member of the family, even to an infant sleeping in the cradle; an act of retaliation, because the master of it had given information against them in some of their malpractices.

The Presence of Royalty

Royalty inspired a tone all-too familiar to us in today's "society pages".

We dined this day with General Airey, the ex-governor, whose house was sweetly situated amidst olive groves and sloping hills, about five miles from the city. At his table we met some of the best society which the island afforded; and amongst them a royal pair, wandering at this time almost without a home, although now raised by the eventful occurrences of our times to the splendours of a throne. These illustrious personages were the Archduke Francis [first cousin to the Emperor of Austria, and reigning Duke of Modena] and his lovely bride, whom he was carrying away from her paternal court of Sardinia. He appeared an affable, well-informed man, but the character and manners of the princess were peculiarly interesting. Young, beautiful, and accomplished, she inspired by her presence life and soul into society, without ever losing sight of her dignity or that decorum which females of high rank in the south of Europe are too frequently accused of violating. They had resided in this island about two months, being furnished with an excellent house and every other accommodation by the hospitality of Mr. Foresti.

1825 Lytton Bulwer

Violent Visitors

Not all the violence on the island was to be put down to the credit of the Zantiotes.

Cephalonia, Santa Maura, and Ithaca are infested by daring robbers, who find no difficulty in crossing the narrow channel which separates those islands from Epirus, and returning to the continent the same night-too frequently after having committed some horrid act of barbarity or revenge.

Shortly before our arrival at Zante, Sir Frederick Stovin apprehended three ruffians who had passed over from the Morea, and attacked the house of a Zantiot nobleman. Not being able to discover some treasure, which they imagined he had concealed, these wretches thrust pins into the flesh below his nails; and put him to every sufferance which they thought likely to extort a confession of where they were deposited.

1898 Samuel J. Barrows

The Restless Earth

This author is propelled into some interesting reflections by the inconstancy of the earth.

It was four days after the great shock which left town and village sadly shattered that I had my first experience with an active earthquake. It was a sort of shuddering reminiscence of what had gone before, a premonition, too, of what was to follow, not the kind of dessert you want for your dinner. It was not what it did that frightened one, so much as what it seemed capable of doing. Emotionally at least you had considered this "terrestrial ball" as solid and inert. You are suddenly amazed to find it alive. It is arching its gigantic back; it is trembling with anger or pain. More fearful than the thought that its motion is voluntary is the terribly swift suspicion that it may be involuntary; that the great creature cannot help it; that it is the victim of internal distress. If you were not so frightened, you might even be sympathetic; you are immensely relieved when the shaking stops; but you have no surety that it will not come again.

In this pale incertitude none of us left the table. We might have done so had it not been for the stolid indifference of the hotel keeper. He was the only person or thing in the vicinity that in the midst of the general agitation seemed to be absolutely unmoved. He felt perfectly sure, he said, that his hotel would stand. Did he hold a mortgage on the land?

The next morning at six o'clock occurred the most powerful shock after the first ruinous one. We were sleeping, my companion and myself, in two iron bedsteads, each of which had a frame above, terminating in a gilded crown for the support of a mosquito netting. The affirmation of Shakespeare, "Uneasy lies the head that wears a crown," seemed to have in it an element of prediction. The King of Greece, however, had taken off his crown, or the jaunty little yachting-cap that serves the same purpose, and gone to a safe place on his yacht. Our gilded crowns were a part of the bedstead. I do not know how the king felt, but as for myself, the sensation I had at six o'clock that morning was unlike anything I had ever experienced. For a moment it seemed as if the bottom had dropped out of everything. We waited expectantly for the tremendous crash with which the building would collapse and bury us in its ruins. What a mighty ague! It was not a wave, not an undulation, but a wrenching, shivering, shattering, Titanic power. It is only three or four seconds in duration, but each second is a brief eternity .What can you do ? If you are able to rush into the street, you may be killed by your neighbour's walls; if you stay in your house, you may be buried under your own. On the whole, the safest thing is to do nothing. Your fate will be decided for you.

One needs to experience an earthquake to know what terror might reside in the old time in the designation of Poseidon as the earth-shaker. Had the sea god waked up to wreak his vengeance on Christian shrines?

The time for you to make your preparation, when you live in an earthquake country, is when you build your house. And if you build as in the sight of the gods, you can put up a house that will endure on this tremulous island the repeated shocks of seven hundred years. So the Venetians built here, and so the English who followed them. This is one reason why there is little appearance of earthquake ruin as you sail into the harbour of Zante today .The great buildings, the lofty towers, were made to last. Not so the houses built by the Greeks living in the outskirts of the town and in the villages on the island. They have been built with stones and earth, without the grip of lime, and when the day of reckoning comes they go down.

Just how the earth-shaker troubled Zante in ancient times, I do not know; but in the present century several visitations have been recorded. Severe shocks were felt in 1873 and 1886, but the last great convulsion before that of 1893 was in 1840, on Saint Luke's Day. It did a great deal of damage, but there was only one shock. The earthquake of 1893, however, was signalled by slight premonitions, and by several succeeding shocks of great power. The strongest, which did immense damage and endangered the lives of thousands of people, occurred at half-past five on the morning of January 3rd. It was followed by one at two o'clock the next day, and by a third at six o'clock the day following. February 2. Between these were a great number of minor shocks, which served to continue and heighten the alarm and to heap up another instalment of ruins in the outskirts of the city.

Excitement and terror were widespread. The nomarch, or governor of the island, lost his head completely, and was found on the shore hunting for a boat in which to escape with his family from the island. Five hundred people immediately sailed for Patras, and as many more left the next day. Those who owned anything in the shape of a wagon or carriage, pulled it out in the square or on the quay and slept in it. Others hired carriages for the same purpose. No one went to bed. The country people stayed out of doors. On the third day the terror was increased by a tremendous storm of thunder and lightning, and a general panic ensued.

The condition of a large number of people was certainly unfortunate. They were suddenly rendered homeless. Some had nothing but the clothes on their backs. The climate of Zante is usually mild, even in winter; but that week the cold was more severe than for many years. The rain poured into the roofless cellars in which many families had taken refuge. From the Greek naval station, about three hours by water, one hundred tents were sent to the island, where several thousand were needed. Half of these tents were taken possession of by the soldiers, who had left their barracks. The Athenian papers loudly rebuked this form of military cowardice, and the nomarch and the commandant were dismissed.

The poorest part of the town is on the south side, in what is known as Neachori. The havoc of the earthquake here was great, so far as property is concerned. Few houses were totally demolished. In nearly every case one or two walls were left standing, and in almost all cases the front. This fact is significant. The system of house building in Zante in the last thirty years has been disgracefully careless. No lime is used in the construction of the walls except on the facades, which are the only parts that stand. A wall of earth and stones may bear the slight exposure of such a mild climate as that of Zante, but it is no protection against a wrenching, jostling earthquake. That more people were not maimed or killed is due to the fact that the inhabitants well know where the weak part of the house is, and so have their sleeping-rooms in the front, and the kitchen and dining-room in the back. The most destructive shock was at half-past five in the morning, before they had risen. There were thus few people on the streets to be hit by falling stones.

Earthquakes undoubtedly have their freaks; but they do have some respect for good architecture. In the larger buildings, for the most part, the damage was confined to falling ceilings, tiles and copings. Yet some of the churches fared badly, the Roman Catholic having an immense hole in the side wall through which the morning sun shone on the damaged picture of the Virgin.

The City of Zakynthos from the Square (Antoine-Laurent Castellan)

The Peloponnese

Although the Peloponnese, then known as the Morea, was conquered by 1473, the inhabitants were never reconciled to Turkish rule. The mountain fastnesses and the peninsula of Mani were usually left to themselves. Admiral Morosini took the peninsula for Venice during 1685-7, and it was ceded to Venice by the Treaty of Carlowitz of 1699. This settlement did not last, however, and in 1715 Ali Pasha reconquered it. In 1770 an insurrection against the Turks was incited by the Russian nobleman Orloff, but the Russians soon abandoned their Greek allies to their fate. In 1821 the Greek independence struggle was launched in the Peloponnese by bishop Germanos of Patras. Many leaders in this area, including the brigand Kolokotronis and the Bey of the Mani, Petros Mavromichales, supported the struggle, which was initially successful. Then in 1825, Ibrahim Pasha landed with a large Egyptian army, with the intent to depopulate the entire region, resettling it with Egyptian Muslims. But after the defeat of Navarino and the landing of a French force, Ibrahim withdrew. The Peloponnese became part of the new kingdom of Greece, although resistance to the imposition of the Bavarian monarchy upon the country by the Great Powers led to a brief revolt in the Mani during 1831.

Patras as seen from the Mainland (Contemporary engraving, 1836)

Achaias

1609 William Lithgow

Summary Justice

Peterasso is a large and spacious city, full of merchandise, and greatly beautified with all kind of commercers. Their chief commodities, are raw silks, cloth of gold and silver, silken-growgranes, rich-damas, velvets of all kinds, with satins and taffeties, and especially a girnell for grain. The Venetians, Ragusans, and Marseillians have great handling with them. Here I remember there was an English factor lying, whom the Subbassa or Governor of the town, a Turk, caused privately afterward upon malice to be poisoned, even when I was wintering at Constantinople, for whose death the worthy and generous ambassador, Sir Thomas Glover, my patron and protector, was so highly incensed, that he went hither himself to Peterasso, with two jannizaries, and a warrant sent with him from the emperor, who in the midst of the marketplace of Peterasso, caused one of these two janizaries, strike off the head from the shoulders of that sanzack; and put to death divers others also that had been accessory to the poisoning of the English consul; and the ambassador returning again to Constantinople, was held in singular reputation even with the Turks, for prosecuting so powerfully the course of justice, and would not shrink for no respect, I being domestic with him the self same time.

*Patras
(1860)*

1770s George Wheler

The Realities of a Shepherd's Life

Venturing into the mountainous interior, Wheler finds the reality of the life of a Greek shepherd somewhat different from what he had been led to expect by his study of literature.

One day, to take the air, I went to the mountains, with our Greek, and a guide, to get provisions; and having passed by some flocks, not above two miles from us; not finding the shepherds with them, we began to ascend the foot of the mountain; and being gat up upon a hill, at a good distance we saw thirty or forty, fitting in a round heap together. This made me presently to call to mind the pleasant stories I had heard of the Arcadian shepherds, from whose country we were now not far distant. I thought of nothing, but being diverted by some festival, some sport or other among them; or, at least, that there had been the nuptials of some fair shepherdess, then celebrated; at which the shepherds being weary of dancing, were now let down to entertain themselves with the noble wine of the country, a fat lamb of their flocks, or with some rustic sonnets, and old wives tales. But approaching nearer, I was soon undeceived; finding an old grey-bearded Turk sitting in the middle of the circle, like a conjurer, with his lap full of pebbles, pen, ink, and paper by him, and giving each of them their task, which was to turn five of those stones into so many dollars by the next day at that time, upon pain of being made slaves, and sent chained to the galleys if they failed. This was for their caratch, or poll-money. There were other accounts also to be made up among them, for their flocks are not their own, but the Grand Signior's, of which they have the tenth part of the profit, and fruit for their labour; paying the other duties that are imposed upon them. The number of pebbles that were then to be made dollars, was four hundred and thirteen; by a people, that I dare engage, knew nothing of the Philosopher's Stone.

Their manner of living there, is in little huts, made of long sedges which they join together with sticks, and withies, in such sort, that a covering of them keeps off the rain from the top; and as for the wind, as that changeth, so they turn their doors to the lee of it; making a fire before it. There are their winter houses, when they are forced from the tops of the mountains covered with snow, into the Valleys. For in the summer they have villages they live in upon the Mountains; and there with greater security feed their sheep, and winter in these little huts; therein crowding themselves, and wives, and children together.

Their habit is ordinarily made of white cloth, of the coarser wool of their flocks; being a large cloak, with a hood of the same joined to it, and hanging down behind, or to cover their heads with, when they have occasion. For ordinarily; on their heads they wear a kind of hat, made of wool, in which their hoods enter not; but is flat, and fits close to their heads, having a good big knob on the top, and tied under their chin with long strings, like a cardinal's cap; by which, when they please, they can let it hang on their shoulders, and put on their hood. Their undergarment is commonly a fustian shirt, made so wide, that they let it hang sometimes quite on the outside their breeches.

The women have a very odd kind of dress for their heads; being a half circle, or crescent, of tin or brass, set on end upon their heads; with a girdle about their middle of the same metal, composed of many scales of brass; which is girded about such a linen garment, as the men wear; but longer, and embroidered with red yarn about the neck, sleeves, and bottom.. Their shoes are only dried skins, laced together with leather or strings about their feet.

1818 H. W. Williams

Dangerous Easter

The celebration of the Greek Easter has been a constant source of comment by travellers, many of whom were alarmed by some of its less restrained aspects.

Fortunately we arrived at the time of a festival of the Greeks, the celebration of the Resurrection of our Saviour. This afforded us an opportunity of seeing some of their gaieties and amusements. Processions with music began at a very early hour, with a constant firing of muskets: fiddles, bagpipes, and tambourines, were to be heard in every street, and never certainly was any thing more distracting or confounding : the discordant union of the bagpipe with the fiddle sounded to our ears like the squealing of children and the squeaking of pigs; yet to this music, if so it may be called, they paraded and danced. The firing of the guns made us start at every instant, for we found that they were often loaded with ball, and there is rarely a festivity without some disaster. We heard the balls distinctly in the air, and when we paid our visit to the castle, and the great cypress tree in the plain, balls passed us within a yard or two, whizzing in our ears: one actually went through the room in which Mr. Parnell was seated, and a poor child had its knee shattered to pieces! On enquiring what would be done with the transgressors, we were told that, if they could be discovered they would be banished; but that there was little chance of finding them, where so many were engaged in the same pastime. This may afford a little insight into the nature of their police; and some idea of the value they have for human life. In short, the scene, instead of being a rational enjoyment, seemed to be one of uproar and confusion.

The streets of Patras are very narrow, and being never cleaned, are disgustingly filthy; the shops are quite contemptible; the roofs of the houses meet; which, no doubt, is intended for shade in this warm climate; but the air, corrupted by various nuisances below, can hardly find a way to escape. The Turks and Greeks sit under shelter, on the outside of the steps, and appear as if they had no concern or employment to engage their thoughts. It is well they have some baths to which the better sort of people occasionally resort. The common class are filthy beyond measure, and the cloth they wear next their skin, is seldom changed or washed!

It is generally the steam bath which is used at Patras. The steam is introduced, in almost suffocating abundance, into an apartment in which there is a reclining seat: the person who receives the bath places himself: in this seat, and a Greek in attendance proceeds to pull the joints of the fingers and toes, and places one hand under the middle of the back; with the other he presses the breast, till he makes the joints of the back to crack. The whole body is thus at once loosened, and while the skin is soft, it is rubbed violently with a bag stuffed with cotton, till the cuticle peels off, as our informer emphatically said, like macaroni! We were advised to take this bath as an excellent preparative for the fatigues which we were about to encounter, but we preferred bathing in the waters of the ocean, which is in this country an inexpressible luxury.

c. 1828 John Fuller

An Alien Land

Comment such as the following remind us how different mainland Greece under Ottoman rule must have seemed to travellers from Western Europe.

Every man will feel a little forlorn and solitary when for the first time in his life he lands on the Turkish shores, when he bids to the Christian tongues a long adieu, and finds himself among a people whom he has been used to consider s almost savage. But his curiosity at the same time cannot fail to be highly gratified by the perfect novelty of the scene around him. The points of difference between other European nations bear no proportion to those in which they resemble each other. But here, a person coming from the nearest port seems to be entering a new world, and finds a total and striking change in the face of the country, the style of the building, and the dress, manner and general appearance of the inhabitants.

An accidental circumstance too, which occurred as we arrived at Patras, served to remind us that we were no longer in a civilized country. An affray had taken place between the townspeople and the soldiers of the Boluk-bashi, or governor. Several persons had been killed; others were seen wandering about as if attempting to hide themselves in the gardens which surround the town. Straggling shots were heard in all directions, and we were not sorry to find ourselves safely lodged in the house of the English consul.

It ought to be mentioned, however, as some compensation, that we were free from all those vexatious custom-house researches which in other countries await the tired and exhausted passenger at the end of his voyage.

1829 The Rev. Rufus Anderson

Profanation of the Sabbath

Sometimes it is the attitudes of the visitor, rather than those of the visited, which require explanation.

Our stay at Patras was prolonged till Monday, April 20th. The Sabbath was Easter Sunday with the French troops, and Palm Sunday with the Greeks, and at an early hour the President, Capo d'Istrias, arrived on a tour he was then making through the Peloponnesus. From these causes we were much incommoded by the firing of guns great and small, and the running and shouting of Greeks about our house, which happened to be near the President's quarters. The tumult was increased by the lamentable fact, that the Sabbath is the principal market-day in the place, and many of the peasants had come in from the country for purposes of traffic. I therefore sought refuge upon the broken hills behind the castle: but there being no shade on those tiresome heights, I soon felt the force of that expressive figure in the Scriptures, "the shadow of a great rock in a weary land." How refreshing such a shade, in such a land, "with a water-brook near by: and how much more refreshing God's gracious presence. But deprived, at that moment, of those cheering views of divine providence, which I endeavour habitually to cherish, and oppressed by the heat, for once I gave way to melancholy feelings, as I sat upon the brow of a hill overhanging the town. It was my first Sabbath in Greece. The crowds of people beneath were exulting in the possession of their newborn liberty. They could no longer be oppressed by the Moslem - the robber and the pirate had been disarmed - and hill and valley plain and shore, were now equally safe to the inhabitant. But then I could see no traces of the SABBATH - the true palladium of liberty, the safeguard of Christianity itself, and that one thing without which we must not anticipate a general revival of pure and undefiled religion. I did not look for preaching in the churches, nor indeed for any of those services in the language of the people which make the Sabbath a delight in my own land. I expected to see shops open, trade in the marketplace, mirth in the streets, and thoughtlessness everywhere. But I was not prepared to see the principal weekly fair for all the surrounding country, held on that day; and should we find this profanation extending through the provinces, (as we did in some others,) I thought how formidable an obstacle it would be to the prevalence of truth and righteousness. At last I took refuge in the power and grace of our Lord Jesus Christ, who, when he sent Paul into Greece, encouraged him to take his stand in the most corrupt of Grecian cities, with the assurance that he had much people there to be transformed in the spirit of their minds and tenor of their lives, and made meet for heaven, by the Gospel. And in some instances how great the change. "Be not deceived," says the apostles to those Grecians, "neither fornicators, nor idolaters, nor adulterers, nor effeminate, nor abusers of themselves with mankind, nor thieves, nor covetous, nor drunkards, nor revilers, nor extortioners, shall inherit the kingdom of God. *And such were some of you*: but ye are washed, but ye are sanctified, but ye are justified in the name of the Lord Jesus, and by the Spirit of our God."

1838 William Mure

"Badlands"

Lawlessness increased rather than decreased following the establishment of the Greek state.

The third evening we slept at a khan close to the ancient port (now a marsh) of Panormo... A band of eleven robbers, who, the day before, had stopped all passengers, pillaged and bound them to trees, had left the khan the same morning. They had destroyed whatever they could not consume or carry away; so we had but indifferent fare. One man they had broiled on the hot embers to extort from him a discovery of some supposed treasure. The peasants were in a state of the greatest alarm, and of the deepest indignation. "Such a thing had never happened," they said, "during the anarchy of the revolution." The supplies of the soldiery have always been exacted as of right, "but to touch the belt of a Greek, to undo a female zone [*sash,* ed.], were crimes unheard of; and now that we have a regular Government, that we pay every tax, and obey every order; now that our arms are taken from us, must we endure what was unknown even in our troubled days!"

c. 1850 Henry M. Baird

Shopping in Kalavryta

Calavryta is quite an ordinary town, though better built than most of the interior places. The plain, some three or four miles long by three quarters of a mile wide, is fertile and well watered. Somewhere upon it stood the ancient city of Cynretha. On arriving, we found that our baggage had gone on toward the monastery of Megaspelion; but our horses were considerably jaded and we were tired, and hungry enough to enjoy a lunch during the three quarters of an hour we stayed at Calavryta. What time remained was profitably employed in making purchases of various articles, such as the more respectable shops were possessed of, and in replenishing J.'s tobacco-pouch, which had not been proof against the heavy drafts made upon it while we were travelling in the back districts of Arcadia. The streets, or rather lanes, are rarely more than a dozen feet wide; and the small shops, entirely destitute of windows, are thrown quite open to the street. A wide counter occupies almost the whole breadth of the front, upon which the greater part of the commodities are exposed for sale. Cobblers and tinsmiths alike sit cross-legged upon them, with their tools and wares by their sides. Thus situated, they keep a sharp lookout on everyone that passes, and can gossip as much as they please with their neighbours.

Our presence among them aroused the curiosity of the talkative townsmen, Perhaps our laying in a store of straw hats, and of the Indian weed, augmented it. At any rate, a knot of idlers soon gathered about us while we were lounging around the khan waiting for our horses, They seemed determined to find out all they could about our destination, and we had as firmly made up our minds not to gratify them. A young fellow from the Ionian Isles accosted H. in Italian, and soon contrived to inquire whether "their excellencies were bound to Patras"; to which H. replied that, though not impossible, it was yet doubtful whether we would go to that place. The questioner then mentioned a number of other towns to which he might suppose us en route; but, as the answers were somewhat enigmatical, he gained very little light in his search for information. Somewhat nettled at his poor success in eliciting that wherewith to satisfy his companions' curiosity, "we heard him suggesting to them in Greek, as they made a retreat, that most likely we were travelling without passports; but, whether our appearance did not justify them setting us down as *klefts* or smugglers, or they did not care to make the inquiry, that was the last we heard of the matter.

The Cavern-Monastery of Megaspilion

The great monastery of Megaspilion was one of the great sights of this region, and frequently visited.. This account allows us to understand how many of the monasteries managed to survive and prosper under Turkish rule.

From Calavryta we had before us a two hours' ride to Megaspelion, along the pleasant banks of the small river Buraicus, winding through a narrow valley toward the Corinthian Gulf. The monastery is by far the greatest, richest, and most famous in Greece proper. Imagine a vast cavern upward of one hundred feet in height, and much wider, as the niche in which this curious establishment is situated, and this on the steep side of a mountain at a considerable distance above the ravine. The approach is along the hillside by a path winding gradually toward it, and which might easily be defended against a host of invaders. The steep land-slopes are cultivated in front of it in a succession of terraces, each presenting the appearance of a garden. As we drew near the building, there could be nothing more singular than its appearance. A single wall, one hundred and eighty feet long, and seventy or eighty high, closes up the lower part of the cave's aperture, It is no less than twelve feet thick, and offers little hope to the assailant of his being able to force his way within. Above, it is pierced with windows, and surmounted by seven or eight wooden houses of curious and diverse aspect, built more or less lofty, according to the irregularities of the mouth, and leaning against the almost perpendicular rock that towers three or four hundred feet aloft. The light materials of which they are constructed contrast singularly with the massive proportions of the wall that supports them, and from which they project considerably in different places with staircases and covered galleries sustained by props.

We rode around to the solitary portal situated at the southern end of the great wall; and here dismounting, we were welcomed by a number of monks, who were seated on a circular seat at the door, enjoying the shade and the evening breeze. Oriental custom required us to sit down and converse with them before entering the monastery, to which they welcomed us with much apparent cordiality. It devolved on me, as spokesman, to give the chief dignitaries some explanation of the nature of our tour, and to answer whatever interrogatories their curiosity might prompt them to make. As usual, these related principally to the affairs of the capital, but more especially to any new phase which the question of the possession of the Holy Sepulchre at Jerusalem had assumed since the last advices. As it was between two and three weeks since we had left Athens, we could give them little information that was new. H. had visited Megaspelion when cruising in the Mediterranean in his own yacht, a couple of years since; but such is the number of strangers who from time to time come here to pass a night, that, naturally enough, the monks did not remember him. Profiting by a pause in the conversation, we excused ourselves on the ground of our day's travel, and betook ourselves to the room prepared for our reception, in one of those singular overhanging houses that crown the monastery wall. It seemed to be the best guest-chamber in the edifice. We were assured that we were but following in the footsteps of royalty. King Otho and Queen Amelia being uniformly entertained in this room whenever they come hither.

In the morning we were conducted through the building. The church, of course, was the part that the monks took most delight in exhibiting. Croziers and crosses, curiously carved, with other articles of solid silver, were proudly and admiringly displayed. But it was the holy "ikon," or picture of the Virgin, made, as we were informed, by the hands of St. Luke himself, and discovered during the Middle Ages by a princess of imperial blood, for which they expected the greatest veneration. The monks bowed profoundly and crossed themselves frequently before it, and reverently kissed the glass with which it is protected from the too rude salutations of the vulgar. This ugly portrait is, in fact, a bas-relief of poor execution, on a blackish wood, and does little credit to the skill of its reputed author. If authentic, it would seem to prove that St. Luke, besides being a wretched dauber, was a very inferior sculptor. Fortunately for the artistic reputation of the saint, there are tokens of its being a product of medieval times, as evident as are to be found in any portrait ascribed to the same source in the Italian churches. The brazen gates of the church, made at Jannina in Epirus, some seventy or eighty years ago, are of elaborate workmanship.

From the church we were conducted through intricate corridors and dark stairways, to the kitchens, the baking-rooms, the refectory, and the wine-cellars - each department being on a scale commensurate with the size of the monastery and the number of its inmates. There were a number of large casks of wine in the cellar, the two largest, *Stamato* and *Angelica* being enormous. Their exact capacity I can not tell; but the weight of the wine they could contain is estimated respectively at 40,000 and 60,000 pounds. The wine kept here is all produced by the vineyards belonging to Megaspelion, and intended for home consumption. Not less than 160,000 or 170,000 pounds of wine are drunk at the monastery in the course of the year. Most of the revenues of the establishment are derived from the sale of the Corinthian currant, about 400,000 pounds of which are yearly sold by its agents. This year the crop has so signally failed, that the holy friars are in great trouble respecting their resources.

The library is contained in a small, dark room, and is kept perpetually under lock and key. There seemed to be about a thousand fifteen hundred books and bound manuscripts; but in former times much larger and more valuable collections existed here. On two different occasions the library fell a prey to the conflagrations which reduced the monastery to ashes, notwithstanding the tutelar care of the sacred image of the "Panagia" in the chapel. The remaining manuscripts are principally transcripts of the Greek liturgical works and of the Gospels, and many of them are beautifully illuminated, after the manner of the Middle Ages. We could not examine the works critically in the short time at our disposal; but this had undoubtedly been done by others before us. It is a remarkable fact, that this small library is probably the largest collection of books to be found in any monastic institution in Greece; while the number contained in the monasteries of Mount Athos, in Turkey, though much larger, is not supposed to be very considerable. The incessant wars to which this fair but most unfortunate country has for ages been subject, the spoliations of western travellers, and the ignorance and carelessness of the inhabitants, all combined, are scarcely sufficient to account for such a total dearth of medieval literature.

We strolled through the gardens and along the hillside for a fine view of the monastery, to commit to paper, while the "hieromonachus," who had been our chief guide, pointed out to us the elements of its strength, and narrated the most striking incidents of its history. In 1770, during the revolt in which the Peloponnesians madly involved themselves by giving faith to the lying promises of Russian emissaries, the wary monks stood aloof, and, indeed, lent their aid to the Turkish captives, multitudes of whom they fed, lodged, and sent in safety to their own homes across the Corinthian Gulf. This kindness proved the salvation of Megaspelion, and was amply rewarded by the protection extended to the truly philanthropic monks.

Such a course was no longer practicable when the flames of the Revolution of 1821 burst out, and the conflict was a struggle, not for mere political supremacy, but for national and individual existence. The question now to be decided, was whether a single Greek should be permitted to breathe; for a deep scheme had been laid by the Sultan and his advisers to annihilate every vestige of the Hellenic race, and replace it by a barbarous horde of Albanians and Turks, that should render more implicit obedience to the Porte's commands. It was, consequently, one of the objects of the Turkish generals to reduce this fortress, commanding so important a passage between the Gulf and the interior. But the monk pointed out with pride the spot where the intruders were met and repulsed by the "Pallecaria," or braves, collected by the monastery. On a former occasion, we were informed, the enemy had climbed to the top of the cliff overhanging the cave, whence they hurled down huge fragments of rock, with the intention of overwhelming the building; but the projecting ledges themselves protected it from injury. With superstitious reverence our guide directed attention to one large boulder on the verge of the impending rock, which seems to be just about to fall. The invader had, with much toil, conveyed it to its present situation; but the Virgin, the patron of the monastery, interposed her power, and miraculously secured it fast just as it was about, to descend.

There are altogether some two hundred monks at present in the building, besides fifty more attending to the cultivation or their farms in different parts of the Morea. Their life is an easy one, and their accommodations are much superior to those of the common people, by the sweat of whose brows they live.

1858 William George Clark

A Journey along the Shore of the Gulf

After three days' stay at Patras, we set off at eleven o'clock in the morning of May the 10th. The scirocco still blew with unabated strength, producing languor and uneasiness in man and beast, This effect is due, I think, not to its heat, but to the fact that, being exceedingly dry, it holds the dust, as it were, in solution, In other words, it is fined with minute and impalpable particles, which get into the throat, eyes, and nose, and stop up the pores of the skin, We had not, however, ridden many miles when it suddenly ceased, and the angry foam of the waters of the gulf gave place to a glassy smoothness, After passing the sand-hills near Patras, we came opposite to the low, marshy spit of land which joins the Castle of the Morea to the shore; and then rode for several hours along a path sometimes dipping down to the shore, but generally keeping along the steep side of hills thickly covered with shrubs, and more sparsely with pines and other forest trees, The sea and the bleak hills on the other side were in sight on our left nearly all the way, About five o'clock we came to a more open country, where the steep hills recede and leave a ledge of fertile land between them and the sea, We saw here and there a village in the midst of vineyards and cornfields, and shortly after the large houses of Vostizza appeared in sight. We arrived about seven, and found the whole population at church. On this day and the next there were to be special services to pray for the cure of the grape disease, which had now prevailed for five years. We waited for some time before the door of the house to which we had been recommended, till the crowd poured out of church and came down the street, and among them the portly person of our intended host. He was one of the principal merchants in the place, and we had a letter to him from our kind friend the vice-consul, who was connected with him in business. He seemed at first more surprised than pleased at seeing the group collected round his door; but as soon as he had read the letter, he welcomed us with exceeding cordiality. The house was the largest and the best furnished which we had yet seen in Greece. All the family were in their dresses of ceremony - I think it was the eve of the feast of St. Alexius - the men in white kilts, the ladies in jackets of tight-fitting velvet and wearing red fez caps with long blue silk tassels embroidered with gold. Our host could only speak his own language; but there was a brother-in-law who had studied medicine in Paris, by whose aid we carried on a brisk conversation over the chibouques and coffee.

The failure of the currant-crop was the chief theme. For several years past the grape disease had reappeared as regularly as the fruit set, and neither prayers nor remedies had been found, effectual. This year a new remedy was to be tried-powdered sulphur blown on to the grapes with a kind of bellows. Some of the priests opposed the use of human means, but the fathers of Megaspelion had more worldly wisdom. They had made a bargain with our host whereby he was to furnish the sulphur and apply it to their grapes on condition of sharing half the produce. The experiment proved afterwards perfectly successful, and must have added largely to the treasures of the Kyrios Soteri Panaghiatopoulos.

Vostizza, which beyond all question occupies the site of the ancient Aegium, stands in a beautiful position at the corner of a tableland stretching from the mountains to the gulf. The torrents on either hand have thrust out tongues of alluvial plain into the gulf, and so made something of a sheltered port for the town of Vostizza. On the seaward side is a steep cliff, and between the foot of the cliff and the shore a narrow strip of level ground. Here is a fountain of abundant and excellent water gushing out from sixteen pipes, and close by a magnificent plane-tree, the pride of Vostizza, which, though past its prime, is still the largest in Greece. It measures forty-five feet in girth at a height of three feet above the ground. I have only seen two others which could compare with it - one in the seraglio at Constantinople, the hollow trunk of which is used as a baker's shop, and another between Therapia and Buyukdere. About the trunk of the Vostizza tree - as it was a holiday - a goodly number of men and boys were assembled. It is the *lesche* of the town; and a pleasanter spot for the purpose could not well be imagined. It was early morning in early May, and the place was full of pleasant sights and sounds, such as Theocritus loved - a fountain prattling at our feet; waves rippling on the beach hard by; and overhead the breeze shaking the leaves and tassels of the plane-tree together, and making the very shadows dance merrily to the music...

Before we left Vostizza we went to the house of M. Demetrios Petmazas to see two statues which had been found close by. They are both about the size of life. The one is a draped female figure with the left hand wrapped up all but the thumb and forefinger. The other, which, as a work of art, appeared to us much superior, represents, probably, Antinous holding a palm-branch.

Turning Inland

We then took leave of our host, and set off about nine am for Megaspelion. As we rode through the vineyards which cover the slopes on the south-east side of the town, where the vines grow luxuriantly among the debris of the old city-broken bricks and potsherds - we witnessed a curious ceremony. A priest was carrying the skull of St. Alexius, their most precious relic, accompanied by other priests or acolytes bearing crosses, and a large crowd of people in holiday costume, from vineyard to vineyard, stopping at each and chanting. The object of their intercession was the removal of the disease...

By-and-bye we halted under the shade of a huge perpendicular cliff of conglomerate, overlaid in places, from top to bottom, with a thick layer of stalactite, formed by the water trickling down its face. The glen up which we had come was thickly grown with myrtles and arbutus: From this point we had higher and more open ground to cross. At noon we reached a khan called, Makaron, a little to the south of the ruins which are supposed to mark the site of Bura. The trees afforded scanty shade, but it was a breezy place, and a spring flowing into a pond close by supplied good water and plenty of cresses, now, as of old, called Kardama. From thence the road continues to ascend for forty minutes through a wood-scattered planes and oaks to the top of a ridge, from which there is a grand view of Mount Khelmos, with its snows and precipices, to the south-east.

Turning to the north is a prospect which combines all the elements of picturesque beauty in a way which I had never seen paralleled. Immediately in front are broken masses of mountain, with cliffs grey below and red above, belts of dark pine on the ledges, and tracts of bright green sward on the upper slopes; beyond, looking down the ravine that parts the hills, a strip of plain by the shore, then the blue gulf, and over all the snowy heights of Parnassus and Aetolia. Beauty of form is the unfailing characteristic of Greek scenery; monotony of tint its customary defect. In this prospect the colours are vivid and various in a degree that would be remarkable anywhere. From this point there is a long descent, and nothing worthy of note, except on the hillside a fountain, which is said to be cold in summer and warm in winter. Herodotus mentions a spring in the desert with a similar property. The obvious explanation that the water is of uniform temperature and seems therefore cold in the hot season, and vice versa, though our guide scornfully rejected it, is beyond doubt the true explanation. A phenomenon exactly similar is presented by the temperature of a good cellar, and in the case of the spring the natural reservoir is probably so far below the surface that it is not affected by change in the external air.

"The Fallacies of Hope,"

We had been promised a superb night's lodging in a new khan, so new that there had not been time for it to get dirty, much less dilapidated; but oh! "the fallacies of hope," if I may use the phrase after J. M. W. Turner. The landlord was gone to a wedding, and had taken the key in his pocket. In this perplexity, after a vain effort to break open the door, we betook ourselves to a cluster of shepherds' summer huts, the kalyvia of Miria by name, and induced a family to vacate one of them and make it over to us for the night. It was of an oval shape, made of a rude wickerwork, with a steep roof supported on two poles, and entered by a door about four feet high. It was of course not proof against any weather. Fortunately the night, which had threatened storm, was windy, but not wet; and under the shelter, such as it was, of the kalyvion, we enjoyed as sound sleep as any of the shepherds or their flocks.

Korinthia

1804-06 Colonel William Leake

The Administration of Corinth

Korintho is the chief town of a kaza which is sixty miles in length, extending westward from Fonia (Pheneus) inclusive, as far as Fanari and Potamia which are situated between Epidaurus and Troezen: to the south-eastward it confines on the districts of Argos and Nauplia. There are eighty villages, besides many small tjiftliks. Wheler says that the Kadi boasted of a jurisdiction extending over 800 villages; either therefore the kaza was still larger in his time than it is now, or it is much depopulated. The latter I believe to be the case, though it is certain that the district, particularly in the vicinity of the town, has benefited much from the hereditary power of the family of Nuri Bey, which has been established at Corinth during nearly a century; for here, as in every other part of Turkey, where a powerful family has been long settled, their interest in the prosperity of the district counteracts in some degree the usual blind and eager avarice of the Turkish character, and produces an effect favourable to the security of the subject: and this is greater and more permanent in proportion to the moderation of the governor, as by avoiding the character of accumulating treasure, he is so much the less exposed to the jealousy and rapacity of the Porte.

Acrocorinth

The description of Corinth by Wheler and Spon shows that very little change has occurred here in the last 150 years; and as Nuri Bey defies the firmahn of the Porte, by which I obtained admittance into the Palamidhi and the other fortresses, asserting that his requires a particular and separate firmahn, I must be satisfied with verifying the accounts of Wheler and Spon, as well as an exterior view will permit. They were an hour in riding on horseback, by a narrow rugged path, to the first gate.

Here they were obliged to alight, and to enter on foot. The first inclosure was well covered with houses, of which a part was in ruins, but many still inhabited; for those in the town consisted at that time chiefly of occasional residences for pleasure or business: the families of both Turks and Christians keeping the best part of their moveable property in the Castle, to which they were in the habit of retiring for security, whenever the corsairs, to whose robberies the coasts of Greece were then much exposed, excited any alarm below. The fortress contained a great number of cisterns, hewn in the rock, for collecting rain water, and two natural sources, the higher of which, towards the southern side of the hill, was very plentiful: it is the ancient Peirene. There were three or four mosques in the Castle, and five or six small churches, but most of the latter were ruined. The cathedral of the metropolitan bishop, dedicated to St. Nicolas, was "a very mean place for such an ecclesiastical dignity"; but it contained two old manuscripts of the Scripture, divided according to the usual readings of the Greek Church, and two liturgies of St. Basil, written upon long scrolls of parchment, rolled upon cylinders of wood.

From the first, or outer castle, the two travellers entered the inner through a gate strongly built, with towers on each side of it. The inclosure into which it conducted comprehended all the remainder of the summit of the Acro-Corinthus; Wheler reckoned it at two miles in circumference. The wall which surrounded it was strengthened, on two of the highest points, by towers, or bastions. On the eastern pinnacle of the mountain stood a small mosque, from whence they enjoyed the same magnificent prospect which Strabo has described. It may be seen almost as well by mounting a broad slope between two crests of rock which project above the surface of the northern side of the Acro-Corinthus. This slope leads up, like a great natural road, to the very wall of that, which Wheler has described as the second inclosure of the fortress, and which, though inner in one sense, is exterior in another, since it encompasses the greater part of the summit of the hill, and has no second protection, except on the side of the western inclosure. The view comprehends perhaps a greater number of celebrated objects than any other in Greece, though in extent it is not to be compared to some others which I have seen. Hymettus bounds the horizon to the eastward, and the Parthenon is distinctly seen at a direct distance of not much less than fifty English miles. Beyond the Isthmus and bay of Lechaeum ... are seen all the great summits of Locris, Phocis, Boeotia, and Attica; and the two gulfs from the hill of Koryfi ... on the Corinthiac, to Sunium at the entrance of the Saronic. To the westward the view is impeded by a

Acrocorinth (Baron von Stackelberg, 1831)

great hill, which may be called the eye-sore, of the Acro-Corinthus, especially with regard to modern war. Its summit is a truncated peak, which may be reached on horseback, by turning to the right of the road which leads to the Acro-Corinthus... This height is particularly formidable to the western or lower inclosure of the modern fortress, which slopes towards the hill, and is completely exposed to its fire, at a distance of about 1000 yards...

As pirates of late years have not been so formidable in these seas as they were in the time of Wheler, a larger proportion of the inhabitants of Corinth now reside in the lower town, and a smaller in the Castle, and there are fewer Turks; but the amount of population seems to be nearly the same. He reckons 1500, half of whom were Turks. There are now about 200 Greek, and 100 Turkish houses... The modern town, like the ancient, is situated on the intermediate level which lies between the foot of the Acro-Corinthus and the range of cliffs. It occupies a large space of ground, being divided into several separate portions, with intervals of vineyard and corn-land, and many of the houses are surrounded with gardens of orange, fig, almond, and other fruit trees, mixed with cypresses. The most remarkable object is the palace of Nuri Bey, standing in a large inclosure, near the middle of the cliff above mentioned. It is difficult to account for the extreme unhealthiness of Corinth in the summer and autumn, as the situation seems such as to expose it to the most complete ventilation. The dews are said to be particularly heavy.

c. 1822 William Rae Wilson

A Terrible Punishment

Firearms had been discharged from time to time, under the cloud of night, into the houses of different consuls [in Corinth], and the authors of such outrages or wantonness could not for some time be discovered. After much investigation, the act was ultimately brought home to a Turk hitherto considered as respectable, when he was so frightfully bastinadoed on the soles of his feet that the nails of them dropped off during the operation, and they were actually beaten to a jelly. In opposition, however, to all expectation that this culprit would [*not* ed.] survive the rigour of the discipline, he recovered of his dreadful wounds, in consequence of the usual , and as it may appear to us, extraordinary, mode of cure adopted; namely the application of salt mixed up with onions and vinegar. And after some time he was able to walk about as usual.

1828 Henry A. V. Post

A Poor Meal

During the War of Independence much of the population of Greece was forced to become refugees. Many starved. Yet Western travellers rode majestically through all this, demanding of their hosts wherever they went the standard of food and accommodation they evidently considered their birthright.

We dined in a large cave on the side of the mountain, occupied by a number of the more respectable families, who had brought with them in their flight some portion of their effects, and were living in a state of comparative comfort. As we entered the mouth of the cavern, we involuntarily paused for a moment to gaze at the singular spectacle which presented itself within. The gloomy darkness of the apartment was faintly illumined by the glare of a small fire which was burning in the centre, and over which a number of stout and masculine figures were brooding in mournful silence. Several groups of females were sitting in the back ground, amid heaps of undressed cotton, some engaged in preparing it for the distaff, and others busily plying the spindle. The rocky walls and ceiling were black with smoke, and were hung around with Albanian muskets, and a variety of kitchen utensils. A few branches of trees and coarse blankets, which served for bed and bedding, were strewed upon the ground, and completed the simple furniture of the place. All the inmates arose to welcome our unlooked for arrival, and several of the females soon began to prepare for our refreshment such a rude repast as their scanty means afforded. A few eggs, some boiled herbs, and a small piece of half-starved meat, were set before us. Our table was a rough plank, and our chairs, the clay floor of the cavern. As soon as we were seated, a good looking damsel came round with a copper basin and ewer, and poured water upon our hands, according to the ancient and cleanly custom, which is still pre-served in the more retired parts of the country. We partook of our coarse and simple meal, sincerely grateful to the Providence which had fed us in the midst of famine, and to our kind hearted hosts, who had given us of their poverty all that they had. As we retraced our way down the mountain, and beheld for the last time the wretched objects that lay starving and shivering around us, we felt rejoiced that we had been the instruments of contributing, in however small a degree, to alleviate their calamities; but it was with the sad and chilling reflection, that hundreds of them must perish ere long, unless that Almighty Power, which once found food in the wilder-ness for the Jewish multitude, should send them other and more effectual relief, than what had already reached them.

From Loutraki we proceeded to Corinth; but the day being far spent on our arrival, we merely cast a passing glance upon the ruined city, and began to climb the toilsome ascent to the Acropolis. It was late in the evening when we reached the outer entrance of the castle, but the gates were standing wide open, and no other sentinel appeared besides three or four sleepy fellows who were lounging upon some benches in the porch, and who scarcely raised their eyes to notice us as we entered. We passed the other gates in the same manner, I and after a long, and cold, and fatiguing march, arrived at length at Jarvis' quarters. I had promised myself some indemnification for the toils of the day, in the comfortable accommodations which I should find under the roof of one of the commanders of the fortress; but never were expectations more cruelly disappointed. Instead of a decent habitation somewhat befitting the rank and title of an *antistratigos*, I found a small and ill-constructed hut, built of stones laid loosely upon each other without mortar, roughly thatched with the branches of trees, and full of yawning crevices for the admission of wind and rain. The interior of the building was in admirable keeping with its rough exterior, and as dirty and filthy as dirt and filth could make it. The only furniture consisted of half a dozen barrels placed on end for a bedstead, and furnished with a bed of myrtle branches, - a sort of couch of the same materials, - a few necessary utensils for cooking and eating, and a square stone of portable dimensions, intended to be used, as might be required, for a stool or a pillow. Such was the establishment of a general in the Greek army, and an officer high in command in the castle of Corinth!

The Acro-Corinthus itself is one of the most commanding objects in this enchanting region. It is a lofty and rocky hill, rising abruptly and precipitously in the form of a truncated cone, and standing aloof from the neighbouring group of mountains. Its summit is enclosed by walls and battlements, forming a circuit of several miles, and containing a considerable town, with a number of mosques and small churches, at present, however, in a ruined and dilapidated state. The walls are principally of modern construction, though they contain some vestiges of the most remote antiquity. In some places, particularly on the northern side, they exhibit to the eye, in regular gradation, the workmanship of successive ages: first, the rough Cyclopean, then the later Grecian, then the Roman, and lastly the Turkish and Venetian.

In that part of the castle called the Dragonera battery is a fountain, supposed to be the ancient Peirene, where Pegasus was drinking when mounted by Bellerophon; if indeed the fountain Peirene was upon the Acro-Corinthus, and not, as some contend, upon Parnassus or Helicon. On the north-eastern face of the rock is a cavern, which popular tradition has connected with the residence of St. Paul at Corinth. It is called the cave of St. Paul, and is believed to have been the apostle's favourite retreat for devotional meditation.

The only point from which this majestic fortress is at all vulnerable, is a hill a short distance to the southwest, from which it was stormed by Mahomet II, when he took it from the Venetians in 1459. This important point is now defended by a battery of five large cannon, called the Pentescouphia, or Five-Caps. By properly securing this place, the Acro-Corinthus may be considered as impregnable; yet it has several times changed hands since the commencement of the revolution. It was surrendered to the Greeks in 1822, but fell again into the power of the Turks the same year, in a manner too singular to pass over unnoticed. When the immense army of Osmali Pasha poured down upon the isthmus, the fortress was left, through the weakness and, improvidence of the government, in the hands of an inefficient garrison, commanded by a Hydriote priest, named Achilleus. As soon as they saw the Turkish hordes filing out of the Geranian passes, they abandoned their stronghold, and fled before the approaching torrent, after putting to death the Turkish commander of the castle, who had been their prisoner since its capitulation.

Hopeless of reducing the proud fortress, which towers above the Isthmus, the Turks were marching by, contented with having sent a reconnoitring party to observe it. This party, on approaching close to the walls, observed someone descending the hill, waving a white cloth. It was a Turkish woman, whom the Greeks had left, and she informed her countrymen that the fortress was deserted. Suspecting some snare, the Soldiers carried her before the Pasha, and she persisting in the same story, a party was sent to examine; they found it as she said; and in a few minutes the banner of the crescent was hung over the Acro-Corinthus.

The manner in which the citadel came into the possession of its present occupants; is still more remarkable, It had, some time before, been retaken from the Turks, but had become a subject of contention among the Grecian chiefs, In the month of July, 1827, the garrison, who had lost their commander at the battle of Athens, offered the place for sale to the highest bidder, refusing to admit the authorized agents of government. It was purchased by Tzavellas, a Suliote chief, associated with other Kapitanoi, at the price of one hundred and thirty thousand piastres.

1833-8 J. L. Stephens

Talk of the Town

The following gives some idea of the character of Turkish government, and why the Greeks were so keen to be rid of it.

The chief subject of conversation among the politicians of St. George, is an act of justice lately performed by the Pasha upon the Boluk-Bashi who commanded the police guard of Tripolitza, and who had been recently employed by the Pasha against the thieves. Instead of performing his duty he plundered the villages, cut off the heads of some of the peasants, presented them to the Vezir as the heads of robbers, and received a reward for them. The pasha having discovered his crimes, issued an order for his head, and gave the commission to the

Dehli-Bashi who commands the Pasha's bodyguard. The Boluk-Bashi being a true Albanian, brave and artful, the Dehli thought it safest to employ treachery, which indeed is the ordinary mode of operating in such cases among the Turks. He invited the Albanian to dinner, and while the latter was smoking his pipe and the servants were preparing the table, he drew out, in order that every thing should be done in form, first, the buyurdi, or written order, secondly, a pistol to shoot his guest, and thirdly, a hanjar to cut off his head, with which he proceeded forthwith to the Serai and laid it at the Pasha's feet. It is admitted that the affair was well and technically done.

Corinthian Hospitality

Standing on the Isthmus, Corinth was a natural conduit and focus for travellers. But with only one khan for miles around, it was also a place where the weary traveller might be shamelessly exploited.

As travellers having regard to supper and lodging, we should have been glad to see some vestige or its ancient luxury; but times are changed: the ruined city stands where stood Corinth of old, but it has fallen once more; the sailor no longer hugs the well-known coasts, but launches fearlessly into the trackless Ocean, and Corinth can never again be what she has been. Our servant had talked so much of the hotel at Corinth, that perhaps the idea of bed and lodging was rather too prominent in our reveries as we approached the fallen city. He rode on before to announce our coming, and working our way up the hill through narrow streets, stared at by all the men, followed by a large representation from the juvenile portion of the modern Corinthians, and barked at by the dogs, we turned into a large enclosure, something like a barnyard, on which opened a ruined balcony forming the entrance to the hotel. Demetrius was standing before it with our host, as unpromising a looking scoundrel as ever took a traveller in. He had been a notorious captain of brigands; and when his lawless band was broken up, and half of its number hanged, he could not overcome his disposition to prey upon travellers, but got a couple of mattresses and bedsteads, and set up a hotel at Corinth. Demetrius had made a bargain for us at a price that made him hang his head when he told it, and we were so indignant at the extortion that we first refused to dismount. Our host stood aloof, being used to such scenes, and perfectly sure that, after storming a little, we should be glad to take the only beds between Padras and Athens. In the end, however, we got the better both of him and Demetrias, for as he had fixed separate prices for dinner, beds and breakfast, we went to a little Greek coffee-house, and raised half Corinth to get us something to eat, and paid him only for our lodging.

Passport Control

But I had no time for deep meditation, having a long [*return, ed.*] journey to Corinth before me. Fortunately, my young Greek had no tire in him; he started me off on a gallop, whipping and pelting my horse with stones, and would have hurried me on, over rough and smooth, till either he, or I, or the horse, broke down, if I had not jumped off and walked. As soon as I dismounted, he mounted, and then he moved so leisurely that I had to hurry him on in turn. In this way we approached the range of mountain separating the plain of Argos from the Isthmus of Corinth. Entering the pass, we rode along a mountain torrent, of which the channel-bed was then dry, and ascended to the summit of the first range. Looking back, the scene was magnificent. On my right and left were the ruined heights of Argos and Mycenae; before me, the towering Acropolis of Napoli di Romania; at my feet, the rich plain of Argos, extending to the shore of the sea; and beyond, the island-studded Aegean. I turned away with a feeling of regret that, in all probability, I should never see it more.

I moved on, and in a narrow pass, not wide enough to turn my horse if I had been disposed to take to my heels, three men rose up from behind a rock, armed to the teeth with long guns, pistols, yataghans, and sheepskin cloaks - the dress of the klept, or mountain robber - and altogether presenting a most diabolically cutthroat appearance. If they had asked me for my purse, I should have considered it all regular, and given up the remnant of my stock of borrowed money without a murmur; but I was relieved from immediate apprehension by the cry of *passe porta*. King Otho has begun the benefits of civilised government in Greece by introducing passports, and mountain warriors were stationed in the different passes to examine strangers.

They acted, however, as if they were more used to demanding purses than passports, for they sprang into the road, and rattled the butts of their guns on the rock with a violence that was somewhat startling. Unluckily, my passport had been made out with those of my companions, and was in their possession, and when we parted neither thought of it; and this demand to me, who had nothing to lose, was worse than that of my purse. A few words of explanation might have relieved me from all difficulty, but my friends could not understand a word I said. I was vexed at the idea of being sent back, and thought I would try the effect of a little impudence; so, crying out "Americanos," I attempted to pass on; but they answered me "Nix," and turned my horse's head towards Argos. The scene, which a few moments before had seemed so beautiful, was now perfectly detestable. Finding that bravado had not the desired effect, I lowered my tone and tried a bribe; this was touching the right chord; half a dollar removed all suspicions from the minds of these trusty guardians of the pass; and, released from their attentions, I hurried on.

The whole road across the mountain is one of the wildest in Greece. It is cut up by numerous ravines, sufficiently deep and dangerous, which at every step threaten destruction to the incautious traveller. During the late revolution the soil of Greece had been drenched with blood; and my whole journey had been through cities and over battlefields memorable for scenes of slaughter unparalleled in the annals of modern war. In the narrowest pass of the mountains, my guide made gestures indicating that it had been the scene of a desperate battle. When the Turks, having penetrated to the plain of Argos, were compelled to fall back again upon Corinth, a small band of Greeks, under Niketas and Demetrius Ypsilanti, waylaid them in this pass. Concealing themselves behind the rocks, and waiting till the pass was filled, all at once they opened a tremendous fire upon the solid column below, and the pass was instantly filled with slain. Six thousand were cut down in a few hours. The terrified survivors recoiled for a moment; but as if impelled by an invisible power, rushed on to meet their fate. The Mussulman rode into the passes with his sabre in his sheath and his hands before his eyes, the victim of destiny. The Greeks again poured upon them a shower of lead, and several thousand more were cut down before the Moslem army accomplished the passage of this terrible defile.

The Impositions of a Foreign Army in "Independent" Greece

Following the War of Independence, the Great Powers inflicted upon the Greeks, clearly perceived as unable to govern themselves, an unasked for king. He was a youth of seventeen, chosen because he was a candidate towards whom none of the Powers had any particular objections. However, since he was a youth of only seventeen years of age, in addition to their foreign king, there descended upon Greece three Bavarian regents, appointed to rule without reference to any parliamentary representation, a host of Bavarian officials to set up a centralised administration, and a Bavarian army, which, as the following passage clearly shows, behaved as any nineteenth century imperial army of occupation. It was not to be expected that this situation would be accepted with gratitude by the newly "liberated" Greeks.

It was nearly dark when we rose to the summit of the last range of mountains, and saw, under the rich lustre of the setting sun, the Acropolis of Corinth, with its walls and turrets, towering to the sky, the plain forming the Isthmus of Corinth; the dark, quiet waters of the Gulf of Lepanto; and the gloomy mountains of Cithreron and Helicon, and Parnassus covered with snow. It was after dark when we passed the region of the Nemean Grove, celebrated as the haunt of the lion and the scene of the first of the twelve labours of Hercules. We were yet three hours from Corinth; and if the old lion had still been prowling in the grove, we could not have made more haste to escape its gloomy solitude. Reaching the plain, we heard behind us the clattering of horses' hoofs, at first sounding in the stillness of evening as if a regiment of cavalry or a troop of banditti was at our heels, but it proved to be only a single traveller, belated like ourselves, and hurrying on to Corinth. I could see through the darkness the shining butts of his pistols and hilt of his yataghan, and took his dimensions with more anxiety, perhaps, than exactitude. He recognised my Frank dress, and accosted me in bad Italian, which he had picked up at Padras (being just the Italian in which I could meet him on equal ground), and told me that he had met a party of Franks on the road to Padras, whom, from his description, I recognised as my friends.

It was nearly midnight when we rattled up to the gate of the old locanda. The yard was thronged with horses and baggage, and Greek and Bavarian soldiers. On the balcony stood my old brigand host, completely crestfallen, and literally turned out of doors in his own house; a

The Khan at Corinth (Baron von Stackelberg & C. F. Gille, 1831)

detachment of Bavarian soldiers had arrived that afternoon from Padras, and taken entire possession, giving him and his wife the freedom of the outside. He did not recognise me, and taking me for an Englishman, began "Sono Inglesi Signor" (he had lived at Corfu under the British dominion); and telling me the whole particulars of his unceremonious ouster, claimed, through me, the arm of the British government to resent the injury to a British subject. His wife was walking about in no very gentle mood, but, in truth, very much the contrary. I did not speak to her, and she did not trust herself to speak to me; but, addressing myself to the husband, introduced the subject of my own immediate wants, a supper, and night's lodging. The landlord told me, however, that the Bavarians had eaten every thing in the house, and he had not a room, bed, blanket, or coverlet, to give me; that I might lie down in the hall or the piazza, but there was no other place.

I was outrageous at the hard treatment he had received from the Bavarians. It was too bad to turn an honest innkeeper out of his house, and deny him the pleasure of accommodating a traveller who had toiled hard all day, with the perfect assurance of finding a bed at night. I saw, however, that there was no help for it; and noticing an opening at one end of the hall, went into a sort of storeroom filled with all kinds of rubbish, particularly old barrels. An unhinged door was leaning against the wall, and this I laid across two of the barrels, pulled off my coat and waist-coat, and on this extemporaneous couch went to sleep.

I was roused from my first nap by a terrible fall against my door. I sprang up; the moon was shining through the broken casement, and, seizing a billet of wood, I waited another attack. In the meantime, I heard the noise of a violent scuffling on the floor of the hall, and, high above all, the voices of husband and wife, his evidently coming from the floor in a deprecating tone, and hers in a high towering passion, and enforced with severe blows of a stick. As soon as I was fairly awake, I saw through the thing at once. It was only a little matrimonial *téte-a-téte*. The unamiable humour in which I had left them against the Bavarians had ripened into a private quarrel between themselves, and she had got him down, and was pummelling him with a broom-stick or something of that kind. It seemed natural and right enough, and was, moreover, no business of mine; and remembering that whoever interferes between man and wife is sure to have both against him, I kept quiet. Others, however, were not so considerate, and the occupants of the different rooms tumbled into the hall in every variety of fancy night-gear, among whom was one whose only clothing was a military coat and cap, with a sword in his hand. When the hubbub was at its highest, I looked out, and found, as I expected, the husband and wife standing side by side, she still brandishing the stick, and both apparently outrageous at everything and every body around them. I congratulated myself upon my superior knowledge of human nature, and went back to my bed on the door.

In the morning I was greatly surprised to find, that instead of whipping her husband, she had been taking his part. Two German soldiers, already half intoxicated, had come into the hall, and insisted upon having more wine; the host refused, and when they moved towards my sleeping place, where the wine was kept, he interposed, and all came down together with the noise which had woke me. His wife came to his aid, and the blows which, in my simplicity, I had supposed to be falling upon him, were bestowed on the two Bavarians. She told me the story herself; and when she complained to the officers, they bad capped the climax of her passion by telling her that her husband deserved more than he got. She was still in a perfect fury; and as she looked at them in the yard arranging for their departure, she added, in broken English, with deep, and, as I thought, ominous passion, "'Twas better to be under the Turks."

I learned all this while I was making my toilet on the piazza, that is, while she was pouring water on my hands for me to wash; and just as I had finished, my eye fell upon my muleteer assisting the soldiers in loading their horses. At first I did not notice the subdued expression of his usually bright face, nor that he was loading my horse with some of their camp equipage; but all at once it struck me that they were pressing him into their service. I was already roused by what the woman had told me, and, resolving that they should not serve me as they did the Greeks, I sprang off the piazza, cleared my way through the crowd, and going up to my horse, already staggering under a burden poised on his back, but not yet fastened, put my hand under one side, and tumbled it over with a crash on the other. The soldiers cried out furiously; and while they were sputtering German at me, I sprang into the saddle. I was in admirable pugilistic condition, with nothing on but pantaloons, boots, and shirt, and just in a humour to get a whipping, if nothing worse; but I detested the manner in which the Bavarians lorded it in Greece; and riding up to a group of officers who were staring at me, told them that I had just tumbled their luggage off my horse, and they must bear in mind that they could not deal with strangers quite so arbitrarily as they did with the Greeks. The commandant was disposed to be indignant and very magnificent; but some of the others making suggestions to him, he said he understood I had only hired my horse as far as Corinth, but if I had taken him for Athens, be would not interfere; and, apologising on the ground of the necessities of government, ordered him to be released. I apologised back again, returned the horse to my guide, whose eyes sparkled with pleasure, and went in for my hat and coat.

The Bazaar at Corinth (Baron von Stackelberg & C. F. Gill, 1831)

85

Labour Troubles

I dressed myself, and, telling him to be ready when I had finished my breakfast, went out expecting to start forthwith; but, to my surprise, my host told me that the lad refused to go any farther without an increase of pay; and, sure enough, there he stood, making no preparation for moving. The cavalcade of soldiers had gone, and taken with them every horse in Corinth, and the young rascal intended to take advantage of my necessity. I told him that I had hired him to Athens for such a price, and that I had saved him from impressment, and consequent loss of wages, by the soldiers, which he admitted. I added, that he was a young rascal, which he neither admitted nor denied, but answered with a roguish laugh. The extra price was no object, compared with the vexation of a day's detention; but a traveller is apt to think that all the world is conspiring to impose upon him, and, at times, to be very resolute in resisting. I was peculiarly so then, and, after a few words, set off to complain to the head of the police. Without any ado, he trotted along with me, and we proceeded together, followed by a troop of idlers, I in something of a passion, he perfectly cool, good-natured, and considerate, merely keeping out of the way of my stick. Hurrying along near the columns of the old temple, I stumbled, and he sprang forward to assist me, his face expressing great interest, and a fear that I had hurt myself; and when I walked towards a house which I had mistaken for the bureau of the police department, he ran after me to direct me right. All this mollified me considerably; and before we reached the door, the affair began to strike me as rather ludicrous.

I stated my case, however, to the *eparchos*, a Greek in Frank dress, who spoke French with great facility, and treated me with the greatest consideration. He was so full of professions that I felt quite sure of a decision in my favour; but, assuming my story to be true, and without asking the lad for his excuse, he shrugged his shoulders, and said it would take time to examine the matter, and, if I was in a hurry, I had better submit. To be sure, he said, the fellow was a great rogue, and he gave his countrymen in general a character that would not tell well in print; but added, in their justification, that they were imposed upon and oppressed by every body, and therefore considered that they had a right to take their advantage whenever an opportunity offered. The young man sat down on the floor, and looked at me with the most frank, honest, and open expression, as if perfectly unconscious that he was doing any thing wrong. I could not but acknowledge that some excuse for him was to be drawn from the nature of the school in which he had been brought up; and, after a little parley, agreed to pay him the additional price, if, at the end of the journey, I was satisfied with his conduct. This was enough; his face brightened, he sprang up and took my hand, and we left the house the best friends in the world. He seemed to be hurt as well as surprised at my finding fault with him, for to him all seemed perfectly natural; and, to seal the reconciliation, he hurried on ahead, and had the horse ready when I reached the locanda. I took I leave of my host with a better feeling than before, and I set out a second time on the road to Athens.

1839 Lord Carnarvon

Among the Albanian Shepherds

On the following morning we left the khan, and traversed a district as wild in character as that which we had left, reaching at length a little cluster of tents inhabited by shepherds. Some of these were of straw, others of goatskins, dark in colour, and reminding me of those which in former years I had often seen among the wandering Arabs in the north of Africa. We paused and greeted the shepherd patriarch. An Albanian by birth, a wanderer by profession, he stood before us equally proud of his country and independent life, a fine, erect, though weather-beaten man. In one tent sat his mother. She scarcely stooped under the burden of four-score years, and continued to rock her little grandson with untiring activity, as in his rudely-constructed cradle he slumbered, apparently born to the same untainted health and vigour that were so conspicuous in his race. Next to his mother sat his wife, carding wool. Bags, which were striped with bright colours, were lying on the ground; a little box, curiously inwrought with different-coloured pieces of wood-containing probably the family treasures - was lying oddly enough across her legs; the soles of her feet were exhibited to view, begrimed with dirt; her complexion was of the deepest olive tint, and her turbaned headdress, her flashing eye, and the long black hair, which streamed down on either side of her countenance, invested her and the whole scene with a singularly picturesque effect. In the neighbouring tent a young man was spinning, clad in the white Albanian shepherd dress, with its distinctive kilt - a dress, simple as the life which the wearers of it lead, and graceful in its simplicity. He listened to us with great interest when we spoke to him of Albania.

"Have you, too, heard of Yanina?" he said; and when we named the lake, we had evidently touched upon a chord to which every feeling of his heart responded. "That lake," he said, those shores, which I can never more behold."

"And why?"

"Because, with others of my countrymen, I took up arms against the Turks; and now we wander over Greece and ever shall wander, till death comes on us one by one."

I asked him whether they made any acknowledgment for the ground which their flocks were then occupying.

"Why should we?" he replied; "we did not beat the Turks to pay the Greeks;" but admitted immediately afterwards that when they remained for any length of time on the same ground, some slight tribute was due to the owners of the soil. It also appeared on inquiry that they paid a few lepta a head on their flock as a tax to the government. I asked him how the children fared in this wild and unsettled life. "All do not die," he said; "but all attempt to save their lives is sure to kill." He smiled at the care taken of children in the towns, and seemed to think that any effort to avert the consequences of cold and fatigue, or even to alleviate illness, in the helpless years of infancy was unnatural, unworthy of a shepherd race, and useless in its results. In this opinion the old grandmother seemed to coincide. "My children," she observed with pride, "flourish like the tall green trees. I have thirty children and grandchildren, ay, and many more - shepherds all, wanderers everyone of them; from Wallachia to the Maina my race is known; father, grandfather, brothers, all the same; never had I kinsman that was not a shepherd."

That her children should have lived when others died, and that not one should have degenerated from the credit of his ancestors, or addicted himself to the mean pursuits of settled life, was manifestly the brightest and proudest consolation of her old age.

"Do you ever expect to see again those children who have separated from your camp?"

"At my age it is scarcely likely."

"Does not this consideration grieve you?"

"It is the condition of our nature."

"Do you ever hear from them?"

"I have heard of them from shepherds who have fallen in with their tents, but have never heard directly from them."

"Does not this annoy you?"

"It is not the habit of our tribes to communicate when parted from each other."

The habits of these wandering races are singular. While living in the same encampment they form a single family, and are bound together by many powerful ties; but having once separated, they become wedded to their new associates, old attachments are superseded by new obligations, and the desire of revisiting the kinsmen of their youth seldom long survives the original separation. These shepherds are sometimes richer than those who have a greater reputation for wealth. Their habits are simple, their wants few and easily gratified, they make the cheese that they eat, and the capote that they wear; but they do not invariably consume their own mutton, if my scandal-loving Greeks spoke true; for as regards this, Elias observed, one tribe steals from another whenever the occasion serves.

c.1857 William George Clarke

A Journey to the Site of ancient Sicyon

We left Khaliani at a quarter-past six am. The path lay along a wide, bare valley, traversed at intervals by the torrents which descend from the eastern flank of Cyllene. The mountain was visible nearly all the way on the left, not cone-shaped, as it appeared from Khaliani, but terminating in a jagged ridge. We passed another amphibious lake, like that of Stymphalus, but much smaller. By-and-bye we fen in with a group of peasants of both sexes and all ages, headed by a priest marching in slow procession, and stopping at each man's field to chant a *Kyrie eleison* and invoke a blessing upon their crops. The whole way is a gradual ascent; and about ten o'clock we reached the summit of a ridge of hills running east and west and commanding a splendid prospect of both the gulfs and the isthmus between. The thin and arid soil produces nothing but a few scattered stunted oaks and a scanty undergrowth of familiar shrubs. The descent on the northern side is more rapid, down a path cut deep between chalky banks and glowing like a furnace in the midday sun. Here and there I observed traces of an old road. The monotony of the journey was relieved by an occasional assault upon a snake surprised as he lay basking in the heat. One of them was about a yard long with a disproportionately large head, spotted black and grey, and, according to the testimony of his destroyer, *poly kako*, that is, "very venomous."

At half-past twelve we came to a ruined bridge, probably ancient, at the bottom of a ravine, and then ascended the right bank by a steep path. Along the crest of the hill might be traced fragments of a Hellenic wall - the western wall of Sicyon.

A finer site for a city could not well be imagined. The mountains hereabouts fall down towards the sea not in a continuous slope, but in a succession of abrupt descents and level terraces - a series of landslips, as it were, so that green smooth pastures alternate with white steep scaurs. These are severed at intervals by deep rents and gorges, down which the mountain torrents make their way to the sea, spreading the spoils of the hills over the flat plain two miles in breadth, which lies between the lowest cliffs and the shore. Between two such gorges, on a smooth expanse of tableland overlooking the plain, stood the ancient Sicyon. On every side are abrupt cliffs, and even at the southern extremity there is a lucky transverse rent separating this from the next plateau. The ancient walls may be seen at intervals along the edge of the cliffs on all sides. The entire circuit of the city cannot have been much less than four miles. In shape it approximated to a triangle, with the apex towards the hills and the base fronting the sea.

The Argolid

1609 William Lithgow

An Uncomfortable Bed Prompts Some Melancholy Meditations

Considering the many misfortunes Lithgow endured during his enforced exile from his native Scotland, it is hardly surprising that at times he gave way to melancholy.

Here in Argos I had the ground to be a pillow, and the world-wide-fields to be a chamber, the whirling windy-skies, to be a roof to my winter-blasted lodging, and the humid vapours of cold Nocturna, to accompany the unwished-for-bed of my repose. What shall I say then, the solid, and sad man, is not troubled with the floods and ebbs of Fortune, the ill employed power of greatness, nor the fluctuary motions of the humorous multitude; or at least, if he be sensible of his own, or their irregularities, or confusions, yet his thoughts are not written in his face, his countenance is not significant, nor his miseries further seen than in his own private suffering; whereas the face and disposition of the feeble one, ever resembleth his last thoughts, and upon every touch, or taste of that which is displeasant and follows not the streams of his appetite, his countenance deformeth itself, and like the moon, is in as many changes as his fortune, but the noble resolution must follow ...

In all this country of Greece I could find nothing to answer the famous relations, given by ancient authors of the excellency of that land but the name only; the barbarousness of Turks and Time having defaced all the monuments of antiquity. No show of honour no habitation of men in an honest fashion, nor possessors of the country in a principality; but rather prisoners shut up in prisons or addicted slaves to cruel and tyrannical masters. So deformed is the state of that once worthy realm and so miserable is the burthen of that afflicted people: which, and the appearance of that permanency grieved my heart to behold the sinister working of blind Fortune, which always plungeth the most renowned champions, and their memory in the profoundest pit of all extremities and oblivion.

1804-06 Colonel William Leake

A City in Decay

Leake found Nauplia in a state of abject decay when he visited it. Not many years after his visit it was to become the temporary capital of a liberated country.

Before the year 1790, the Pasha of the Morea resided at Anapli, which brought the agas to Anapli and the Greek primates to Argos, and made the former town the Turkish, and the latter the Greek capital of the Peninsula; many Greeks were attracted also to Argos, as I have already said, by the privileges which the place then enjoyed. Much of the commerce of the Morea then centred at Anapli, and there were several French mercantile houses. The moving of the seat of government to Tripolitza in 1790, was followed in 1791 by a plague, which lasted for three years with little intermission; it prevailed in almost every part of the Morea, but was particularly fatal in Anapli. Since that time the town has not prospered; it is now only inhabited by the agas who possess lands in the Argolid, by the soldiers of the garrison amounting to about 200, commanded by a Janissary aga, who resides in the fort of Palamidhi, and by some Greek shop-keepers and artisans. The governor is a mirmiran, or pasha of two tails, whose authority does not extend beyond the walls of the fortress; but there is also resident here a voivoda for the vilayeti, a kadi, or judge; and a gumruktji, or collector of the customs, which last office is generally united with that of voivoda. The houses are, many of them, in ruins, and falling into the streets; the French consulate, a large house like the Okkals at Alexandria, is turned into a khan. The port is filled up with mud and rubbish, and capable only of admitting small polaccas, and to complete this picture of the effects of Turkish domination, the air is rendered unhealthy on one side by the putrid mud caused by the increasing shallowness of the bay, and on the other by the uncultivated marshy lands along the head of the gulf. In the midst of these miseries, however the fortifications and storehouses of the Venetians still exhibit a substantial grandeur never seen in a town entirely Turkish, and testify the former importance of the place.

Rivalry between the Woman of Nauplion and Argos

It is pretended at Anapli that the women are generally handsome, and those of Argos the contrary, and it is ascribed to the water, which, at Argos, is drawn entirely from wells, and at Anapli from a fine source in one of the rocky heights near Tiryns, which is conveyed to the town by an aqueduct. This tale is derived, perhaps, from the [*myth*] relating to the Nauplian spring called Canathus, by washing in which Juno was said to have renewed her virginity every year. I inquired in vain, however, for any natural source of water in Anapli; and could only find an artificial fountain, now dry in consequence of neglect, near the Latin church by the Custom-house: but this source having been supplied from the aqueduct which I have mentioned, could not have been the Canathus which Pausanias describes as a natural spring.

The Palamidi Fortress

It seems nothing less than amazing that Colonel Leake could wander so widely over Greece taking meticulous notes, and taking especial interest in fortifications, without arousing more suspicion than he did.

Notwithstanding a buyurdi of the Pasha of the Morea, which I bring with me, as well as a general firmahn of the Porte, I find some difficulty in obtaining permission to see the fortress of Palamidhi. Before the Pasha had read the order, an the kadi had summoned the ayans to take it into consideration, all the forenoon had passed. But at length an order is issued, and in the afternoon I ride up, by a circuitous route, to the southern extremity of the castle, and entering by the gate on that side, find the Janissary aga and his staff waiting for me at the gate; he accompanies me round the fortress. It is of a remarkable construction: the interior part consists of three cavaliers, or high redoubts, entirely detached from one another, and surrounded by an outer and lower enclosure. There are many brass-guns mounted on the ramparts, some of which carry stone-balls of a foot and a half in diameter. The outer wall is low on the side towards the sea, and the rock, though very precipitous on that side, is not inaccessible to a surprise: the profile of these outer works is low also towards the heights on the south, and they have no ditch; but there is an advanced work adjoining the rocks at the southern extremity, the salient angle of which is as high as that of the principal cavalier. Under the sea-face, at the foot of the precipice, there is a road leading along the shore.

1817-18 Peter Edmund Laurent

Roma at Argos

As we entered Argos, we were not a little surprised to find, at the gates of the town, an encampment of gipsies: their huts were made of skins; tribes of their children wandered on all sides in a state of complete nudity. They gain their livelihood by smithing and by fortune-telling, a service which several of them offered to perform for us: we were told that the language spoken among themselves by these vagabond hordes, although not Turkish, was different both from the Albanian and the Greek.

c.1820 Thomas Smart Hughes

Around Ancient Nemea

In about two hours we deviated from the direct road in the direction of Nemea, leaving Antonietti and the tchocodar to make the best of their way to Corinth. We very soon observed a large cave at the end of a long mountain on our right hand, which is supposed to have been the retreat of the Nemean lion whose destruction afforded one of the twelve labours to the Grecian Hercules: winding round this hill (the ancient Tretus) we entered upon the spacious plain, that scene of animated contests and tumultuous passions, now solitary as the desert and silent as the grave. Three lofty Doric columns, remains of the great temple of Jupiter, cast as it were a melancholy charm over its solitude, seeming as if they were spared but to impress upon man the awful moral lesson, "that all his pomp is vanity". Turning through a chasm amongst the hills behind this temple, we passed a fountain of delicious water, probably that mentioned by Pausanias under the name of Adrastea: soon afterwards we discovered the ancient road by which the chariots passed to Nemea, the rock being in many places indented to the depth of more than a foot by the constant attrition of the wheels: there is nothing to detain the traveller upon the site of Cleonae, for that ancient city – *ingenti turritae mole Cleonae* - has been long swept away by the besom of destruction.

Early 1820s Francis Hervé

Misery in Epidauros

At length, about dusk, and in a shower of rain, we arrived at the once far-famed Epidaurus. Oh! how I could have wished for an English inn, with all the delicious comforts that appertain to that dear refuge of the wanderer, that ever welcomed traveller's home! But I was in Greece, and above all, in that misery-stricken Epidaurus.

I entered with my companions a sort of hovel. We were cold and wet, and saw little chance of redress to our grievances. A fire on the floor there certainly was, but almost invisible, from the number of grim ill-looking figures which were around it, some squatted on the ground, others bending over them, in order to inhale a sniff of smoke and heat. Chairs or tables there were none, but some boxes, forming part of my companions' baggage, were arranged as seats, of one of which I availed myself, and was quietly contemplating the savage looking group around me, when I found the rain was amusing itself by pattering on my bare head, entering very unceremoniously from a hole in the roof just above me.

This splendid hotel had no other flooring than the unsophisticated earth; windows it had none, nor chimney, but its absence was not felt, as in the many apertures between the tiles, the smoke had free egress. The principal piece of furniture, nay, the only one which I remember, was such as I observed in almost all the Greek cottages, viz., a sort of table, reaching from one end of the house to the other, resembling most a tailor's shop-board, or a counter; on this the family sits, or rather squats; there they also do every species of work, and on it they spread their bedding; in fact, it answers the purpose to them of table, chair, and bedstead, and on this they hauled my mattress; and being bed time, I, like the other inmates of the dismal den in which we were stowed, sought the blessed state of forgetfulness.

But alas! it was not so easy to forget the disgusting torments with which I was surrounded, for I had not lain down five minutes before three great rats came romping, and tumbling within a few inches of my nose: I was regularly horrified; the Lady of General G. having previously entertained me on the passage with anecdotes respecting the biting of rats in the East, she, and all her sisters, having been dreadfully bitten by them at Constantinople. But at last, after many very disagreeable cogitations, "tired nature's sweet restorer," came to my relief. The next morning I caused the circumstance, through the means of an interpreter, to be mentioned to my host, not wishing another night to be exposed to the mercy of such bedfellows. In answer, he very coolly replied, "Then the gentleman did not want for company."

Another misfortune befel me when I mounted the great shop-board to go to bed, I had left my boots on the ground; consequently, in descending the next morning was bootless, and it being very dark, I did not perceive where I stepped, and set my foot in a hole in the floor, which the entrance of the rain from the aperture above had converted into a pool of black mud, giving me in appearance a half boot, but so cold, wet, and filthy that as I drew off my nasty beplastered stocking, I could not help execrating the Greeks, their dirty ways, and their beastly hovels.

Yet I was much better off than a friend of mine, who arrived at Epidaurus at another period, and was not so fortunate as to be conducted, as I was, to the best inn in the place, but was ushered into one considerably inferior, where they had not even the aforesaid shop-board; consequently, his mattress was laid on the floor, which was as usual the unspoiled earth; but, having observed that there was a great pig, which appeared to have the run of the house, he began to entertain sundry suspicions that the pig would be walking upon him in the night, whilst he might be asleep, and communicated his apprehensions to his landlord and landlady, who assured him that the pig never went into that corner where his mattress was laid. My friend, however, could not understand why that spot should be more respected than the rest by this ambulating swine, and retired to his pillow, very sceptical on the subject, his doubts, and fears for a long time keeping him awake. At length fatigue and drowsiness operating upon him, he sank into the arms of Morpheus. How long he had remained in that delicious state of unconsciousness is hard to say, when he was disturbed by a tremendous pressure on his cheek; and naturally turning his head, the pig's foot (for it was the pig's self that pressed) slipped into his mouth, being well charged with an accumulation of mud and filth, collected in its nocturnal promenades. My unfortunate friend sprung on his feet spitting and spluttering, endeavouring to clear his mouth of its unwelcome contents; at the same time with stentorian voice vociferating an anathema against the accursed hut and its inmates, he rushed into the air and sought a brook that "babbled by," and there performed an ablution which had become highly necessary. As he regained some degree of composure he stalked about the deserted village, contemplating the moon, content to find so clean a looking object whereon to fix his gaze, where so much dirt surrounded him; and, after wearing away the time till sunrise, presuming that his host, and family would have risen, and consequently be on the *qui vive* to prevent his new acquaintance, the pig, from again treating him with such indecorous familiarity, he once more entered his loathsome quarters; and having received an assurance from his landlord, that his slumbers should not again be intruded upon, he at length took to his bed, hoping to obtain one refreshing nap, to recruit his spirits for the continuation of his journey. But ah, delusive hopes! in lying down he felt a hard lump under him which instantly broke with a queer sort of squash, emitting a liquid, which, as the Americans would say, pretty considerably wetted him; and starting up, and examining the cause, from the state of the tail of his shirt a piteous tale was elicited, from which it appeared, that during his absence a hen had found his bed a very warm comfortable place, and had crept into it, and there laid an egg, and he lying thereupon had crushed it, and by that means had befouled his linen!

To return to my own case: I soon recovered my calm, after my more trifling mishaps, and at the first opportunity emerged from my rat-hole; but, as I pique myself much upon my impartiality, and am determined not to suffer dislikes or prejudices to influence my opinion to the disparagement of any one, so that when they merit praises I may even eulogise my enemies, from that same Christian spirit, I feel myself bound to declare, that however those rats to whom I have alluded were obnoxious to me, yet I must say they were the finest of the description of any that I ever beheld. I am certain that some of them would have measured at least eighteen inches from the point of the nose to the tip of the tail, and were equally stout in proportion, and I have no doubt but that amongst their own coterie they were considered complete models of their race!

c. 1825 A Companion of H.M. Queen Caroline of Brunswick

Plague-Ridden Nauplia

The population of Nauplia consisted of about two thousand persons, at the time of our arrival. The plague frequently rages during several successive years, and carries off thousands of its inhabitants. When free from this scourge, it is a very unhealthy place, the people being attacked annually with a malaria fever. The few merchants who reside here have generally country-houses, and leave the town in the summer months. The only remedy is the red Peruvian bark; but it must be administered in very -powerful doses. A traveller of Greece should consider this medicine as absolutely necessary to his existence, and never journey unprovided.

Early Nineteenth Century Argos

We employed the first day of our arrival at Argos, in examining the town and its ruins. Argos is a large straggling place, full of cottages, with few good houses. The roofs here are not flat, as in almost all parts of the east, but slope like those of northern nations. The same style of building may be observed in Athens, and in other parts of Greece. The present population consists of six thousand, including females and children. There is a school kept by a Greek priest. Being desirous to know what the children were taught, we visited the master, who seemed pleased by our inquiries, as if he had bestowed pains upon his scholars. He said they were instructed in writing, arithmetic, astronomy, physic, and rhetoric.

The houses in Argos are built with a degree of regularity, and fitted up with some comforts uncommon in this part of the world, although in other respects they are wretched hovels, They are all ranged in right lines, or in parallel lines; and each house, consisting of a single story, has an oven; so that here even the Albanians do not bake their unleavened cakes upon the hearth, as it is usual elsewhere in their cottages.

An Ancient Fraud Revealed

The antiquities of Argos, once so numerous, may be now comprised within a very short list. After visiting the remains of a theatre, we found, at the foot of the hill of the Acropolis, one of the most curious remains yet discovered among the vestiges of pagan priestcraft: it was nothing less than one of the oracular shrines of Argos, alluded to by ancient historians, laid open to inspection, like the toy which a child has broken to see the contrivance by which its music is produced. A more interesting sight for modern curiosity can hardly be conceived to exist among the ruins of any Grecian city.

In its original state it had been a temple; the farther part from the entrance, where the altar was, being an excavation of the rock, and the front and roof constructed with baked tiles. The altar yet remains, and part of the superstructure: but the most remarkable part of the whole is a secret subterraneous passage, terminating behind the altar; its entrance being at a considerable distance towards the right of a person facing the altar; and so cunningly contrived as to have a small aperture, easily concealed, and level with the surface of the rock. This was barely large enough to admit the entrance of a single person; who having descended into the narrow passage, might creep along until he arrived immediately behind the centre of the altar; where, being hid by some colossal statue or other screen, the sound of his voice would produce a most imposing effect among the humble votaries prostrate beneath, who were listening in silence upon the floor of the sanctuary. We amused ourselves for a few minutes, by endeavouring to mimic the sort of solemn farce acted upon these occasions; and as we delivered a mock oracle, from the cavernous throne of the altar, a reverberation, caused by the sides of the rock, afforded a tolerable specimen of the oracles, as they were formerly delivered to the credulous votaries of this now forgotten shrine.

There were not fewer than twenty-five of these juggling places in Peloponnesus, and as many in the single province of Boeotia: and surely it will never again become a question among learned men, whether the answers in them were given by the inspiration of evil spirits, or whether they proceeded from the imposture of priests.

c.1830 Alphonse de Lamartine

An Unimpressive Capital City

We enter a vast bay, that of Argos; we glide along with the wind aft, and with the velocity of a flight of swallows; the rocks, mountains, and islands of the two shores, fly like dark clouds from before us. Night falls; we already perceive the head of the bay, though it is six leagues in extent; the masts of three squadrons anchored before Nauplia are sketched out like a winter forest on the background of the sky and the plain of Argos. The darkness becomes soon complete; fires are lighted on the mountain slopes, and in the woods, where the Greek shepherds are tending their flocks; the ships are firing the evening gun. We see all the gunports or these sixty vessels at anchor gleaming successively, like the streets of a great town lighted by its reflectors; we enter this labyrinth of ships, and we are about to anchor in the middle of the night close to a little fort which protects the roadstead of Nauplia, in front of the town, and under the guns of the castle of Palamides.

I rise with the sun to have at length the pleasure of viewing close to me the Gulf of Argos, Arsoa, Nauplia, the present capital of Greece. What a complete deception! Nauplia is a miserable village, built on the side of a long and narrow gulf, on a margin of earth that has fallen down from the lofty mountains that cover the whole of this coast; the houses have no foreign character; they are built in the style of the most ordinary dwellings in tile villages of France and Savoy. Most part of them are in ruins, and the fragments of walls overturned by cannon in the last war, are still lying in the middle of the streets. Two or three new houses, painted in rough colours, appear on the quay, and a few coffee-houses and shops of wood project on piles into the sea; these coffee-houses and balconies on the water are crowded with some hundreds of Greeks, in their gaudiest but dirtiest costume; - they are seated or stretched out on planks or on the sand, forming a thousand picturesque groups. All their physiognomies are beautiful, but sad and ferocious; the weight of indolence oppresses their every attitude. The laziness of the Neapolitans is mild, serene, and gay – it is the nonchalance of happiness; the laziness of the Greeks is heavy, morose, and gloomy - it is a vice which is its own punishment. We turn our eyes from Nauplia; I admire the beautiful fortress of Palamides, which ranges over the whole mountain by which the town is commanded; the battlemented walls resemble the indentations of a natural rock.

We have passed two days at Nauplia. The state of Julia's health again distresses me. I remain a few days more, to wait till she is completely recovered. We are on shore, in the chamber of a wretched inn, opposite a barrack of Greek troops. The soldiers are all day stretched out under the shade of the fragments of ruined walls; their costumes are rich and picturesque; their features bear the impress of misery and despair, and of all those fierce passions which civil war kindles and foments in those savage souls. The most complete anarchy reigns at this moment over all the Morea. Each day, one faction triumphs over the other, and we hear the musketry of the *klephtes*, of the Colocotroni faction, who are fighting on the other side of the gulf against the troops of the government. We are informed, by every courier that descends from the mountains, of the burning of a town, the pillage of a valley, or the massacre of a population, by one of the parties that are ravaging their native country. One cannot go beyond the gates of Nauplia without being exposed to musket shots. Prince Karadja had the goodness to propose to me all escort of his palikars to go and visit the tomb of Agamemnon ; and general Corbet, who commands the French forces, politely offered to add to them a detachment of his soldiers. I refused, because I did not wish, for the gratification of a vain curiosity, to expose the lives of several men, for which I should eternally reproach myself.

At the Birth of a New Nation

I was this morning present at a meeting of the Greek Parliament. The hall is a hovel of wood; the walls and roof are formed of planks of fir badly joined. The deputies are seated on raised benches around a floor of sand; they speak from their places.

We sat down, to see them arrive, on a heap of stones at the door of the hall. They came in succession on horseback, each accompanied by an escort more or less numerous, according to the importance of the chief. Each deputy dismounted, and his palikars, superbly armed, went and grouped themselves at some distance in the little plain which surrounds the hall. This plain presented the image of an encampment, or of a caravan.

The attitude of the deputies was haughty and martial; they spoke without confusion or interruption, in a tone of emotion, though, at the same time, firm, measured, and harmonious.

They were no longer those ferocious figures that are so repulsive to the view in the streets of Nauplia; they were the chiefs of a heroic nation, who still held in their hands the musket or the sabre with which they had just been combating for its deliverance, and who were deliberating together on the means of securing the triumph of their liberties.

One cannot imagine any thing more simple, and, at the same time, more imposing, than the spectacle of this armed nation thus deliberating amidst the ruins of their country, under a planked roof raised in the open field, whilst the soldiers were polishing their arms at the very door of this senate, and the horses neighing impatiently to resume their path on the mountains! There were to be seen among those chiefs some heads admirable for beauty, intelligence, and heroism: these were the mountaineers. The Greek merchants of the islands were easily recognised by their more effeminate features, and by the wily expression of their physiognomies. The commerce and indolence of their towns have removed all nobility and rigour from their countenances, and stamped in their stead the impress of that vulgar skill and cunning which characterises them.

c.1850 N. Parker Willis

An Evening Walk on the Plain

Only some twenty years after Independence, it is clear not only that the fortunes of Nauplia had improved tremendously, but also that the intervening period, peace and independence had already permitted the development of a degree of elegance, at least, in the urban population of the new kingdom.

We walked beyond the walls of the city this evening, on the plain of Argos. The whole population were out in their sun costumes, and no theatrical ballet was ever more showy than the scene. They are a very affectionate people, and walk usually hand in hand, or sit upon the rocks at the roadside with their arms over each others' shoulders; and their picturesque attitudes and lofty gait, combined with the flowing beauty of their dress, gave them all the appearance of heroes on stage. I saw literally no handsome women, but the men were magnificent, almost without exception.

Among others, a young man passed is with whose personal beauty the whole party were struck. As he went by he laid his hand on his breast and bowed to the ladies, raising his red cap, with its flowing blue tassel, at the same time with perfect grace. It was a young man to whom I had been introduced the day previous, a brother of Mavromichalis, the assassin of Capo d'Istrias. He is about seventeen, tall and straight as an arrow, and has the eye of a falcon. His family is one of the best in Greece; and his brother, who was a fellow of superb beauty, is said to have died in the true heroic style, believing that he had rid the country of a tyrant.

The view of Napoli and the Palamidi from the plain, with its background of the Spartan mountains, and the blue line of the Argolic Gulf between, is very fine. The home of the Nemean lion, the lofty hill rising above Argos, was enveloped in a black cloud, as the sun set on our walk. The short twilight of Greece thickened upon us, and the white, swaying juktanillas of the Greeks striding past, had the effect of spirits gliding by in the dark.

The king, with his guard of lancers on a hard trot, passed us near the gate, followed close by the Misses Armansperg, mounted on fine white Hungarian horses. His Majesty rides beautifully, and the effect of the short, high-born flags on the tips of the lances, and the tall Polish caps with their cords and tassels, is highly picturesque.

The Lion Gate, Mycenae (Baron von Stackelberg, 1834)

1850s Julia Ward Howe

A Brigand Chief's Head

Despite the development of more civilised mode of life, for a long time the traditional violent ways survived outside the cities.

The evening of our sojourn in Argos saw an excitement much like that which blocked the street at Nauplia. The occasion was the same - the bringing home of a brigand's head; but this the very head and fount of all the brigands, Kitzos himself, upon whose head had been set a price of several thousand drachmas. Our veteran with difficulty obtained a view of the same, and reported accordingly. The robber chief of Edmond About's "Hadji Stauros" had been shot while sighting at his gun. He had fallen with one eye shut and one open, and in this form of feature his dissevered head remained. The soldier who was its fortunate captor carried it concealed in a bag, with its long elf-locks lying loose about it. He showed it with some unwillingness, fearing to have the prize wrested from him. It was, however; taken on board of our steamer, and carried to Athens, there to be identified and buried.

All this imported to us that Mycenae, which we desired to visit, had for some time been considered unsafe on account of the presence of this very Kitzos and his band. But at this moment the band were closely besieged in the mountains. They wanted their head, and so did Kitzos. We, in consequence, were fully able to visit the treasure of Atreus and the ruins of Mycenae without fear or risk from those acephalous enemies.

Arcadia

1599 Thomas Dallam

A Meteor in the Night

About noon we came to a river that we must pass through; and determining there to wait, for we had victuals ready dressed for three days, we pitched and placed ourselves under the alder trees, to keep us from the sun; for though it was Christmas Eve, yet we thought it to be as hot weather as we have it in Inglande at Whitsuntide, and swallows came flying about us. Our dinner ended, we crossed the river, and entered into a forest-like country, where we saw neither town nor village, but somtime a shepherd's hut.

At night we found three little poor cottages. In this wild country, where we rested the most part of the night; and while four of us slept, the other four did watch, for we took the place to be dangerous to sleep in. I was one of the four that did watch in the fore part of the night. Betwixt eleven and twelve of the clock we saw a ball of fire, as big as a great football, rising out of the east, and did rise of a great height, and did give a great light; then, falling towards the west, the light and fire both was less and less. Mr. Conisbe was very sorry that he had not seen that fire ball.

1609 William Lithgow

The Poets Mitigate the Traveller's Hunger

In this desert way, I beheld many singular monuments, and ruinous castles, whose names I knew not, because I had an ignorant guide. But this I remember, amongst these rocks my belly was pinched, and wearied was my body, with the climbing of fastidious mountains, which bred no small grief to my breast. Yet notwithstanding of my distress, the rememberance of these sweet seasoned songs of Arcadian shepherds which pregnant poets have so well penned, did recreate my fatigued corpse with many sugared suppositions.

1804-06 Colonel William Leake

A Truly Arcadian Scene

Here Leake gives us a sense of what the plain around ancient Megalopolis must have been like before it was dwarfed by the great power station.

Though the appearance of this noble basin might be rendered more agreeable by a certain degree of culture, desolation has not deprived it of its natural beauties, as seems to have happened in the other great Arcadian valley of Tripolitza, which, having lost its three cities, its cultivation, and its forest Pelagus, (the latter a fine contrast, probably, to the rocky steeps on either side,) is now an uninteresting monotonous level. The valley of Megalopolis, on the contrary, abounds in delightful scenery. The sides of the majestic mountains Karyatiko and

Tetrazi, and the hills at the southern end of the plain beyond Londari, are covered with oaks, chestnuts, and other trees. The eastern range in its higher regions is more naked than the others, but the lower hills are clothed both with underwood and large trees, among which are forests of oaks, extending in some places into the plain, particularly a little to the southward of Megalopolis. The valley itself, varied with hillocks, undulated ground, and detached copses, refreshed with numerous rivulets, shaded by planes, and watered by a larger stream winding through the middle, may almost rival the plain of Sparta in picturesque beauty; to which it is inferior only in the grandeur of the mountains, and their magnificent contrasts with the other features of the Spartan valley. In the present sylvan and uncultivated state of the country around the site of Megalopolis, we have a scene more resembling an ideal Arcadia, than could have been presented when there was a large city in the centre of the valley: and thus we have another example of a resemblance between the Greece of the earliest ages of its history and that of the present day. The country is now clothed in all the beautiful verdure and flowery luxuriance of a Grecian spring.

A Thief Cleanses the Country of Thieves

Turkish rule would ensure that Arcadia was no paradise on earth.

One hundred and twenty heads of thieves taken by the Pasha have been sent to Constantinople. The thieves were dispersed, and taken in detail. The Pasha hopes, by this achievement, to keep himself in place for another year. A boluk-bashi with a large body of Albanians whom he sent against the robbers, deserted, and retired to Bardhunia, where he was well received by Amus Aga. The Pasha has now sent against him 100 men, who are to be joined by 400 at Mistra... Not long ago the Pasha summoned all the Turkish voivodas and Greek hodja-bashis in the Morea, for the purpose of consulting them on the best mode of proceeding against the robbers. The voivoda of Gastuni, an Albanian, and brother of the voivoda of Mesolonghi, whom I met at Patra, neglected the summons for some time; but at length, after repeated orders, he came, and when the Pasha taxed him with his neglect, answered without showing any signs of humility. Upon this the Pasha seized a small hatchet, (an instrument often worn by the Turks more for ornament than use,) threw the voivoda on the carpet, and beat him unmercifully with the hatchet, then turned him out of the room without kauk or slippers, kept him many days in prison, and finished by obliging him to pay a sum of money. He has driven away Sotiraki and the interpreter, two men who for several years have committed with impunity all kinds of oppression on their countrymen. From Sotiraki, who has retired to Livadhla, the Pasha extorted ten purses before he allowed him to go, and as much more from Asimaki of Kalavryta, by pretending that he had received a firmahn for their heads. Papadhopulo has thus gained a triumph over his enemies; the Tripolitziotes ascribe his influence with the Pasha to his eloquence. He has absolute power in Aios Petros and Tzakonfa, where the Turkish voivoda is such an acknowledged cypher that he commonly resides at Tripolitza.

"Low Intrigues" and "Wasted Talents"

The mode in which Sotiriki procured a beautiful antique intaglio which I have purchased here, I learn today from a Corfiote practitioner of physic, who was the original purchaser of it from a peasant of Langidha. The peasant was carrying it about the streets for sale, suspended by a string, when the [physician] accidentally met him, and bought it for two piastres. He showed it to the brother of Sotiraki, who is an archdeacon, and who perceiving the stone to be valuable, informed his brother of it. The latter, as ignorant as the peasant who found it, but whose avarice was excited by the prospect of selling the gem again for a high price, communicated his wishes to the kady, a poor Turk, who may at any time be displaced by the influence of the hodja-bashis and other chief Greeks. They soon agreed that a certain baker should swear it was his property, and stolen from him by his servant, who, if necessary, was to confess the fact before the kady. The affair did not proceed, however, to such a length. The kady having sent for the Corfiote [physician], attempted at first to alarm him by representing that he had bought stolen goods; and at length obtained it from him as a present, the physician being, as he confessed to me, ignorant of its real value. Suspecting Sotiraki to be at the bottom of the affair, he had at first offered him the stone as a present, in order to ingratiate himself with such a leading character; but Sotiraki preferred obtaining it through the kady to being under any obligation to the Corfiote. Such are the low intrigues that occupy the time and talents of this naturally gifted people.

The Bird-Carriers

An idea prevails here, which I have heard repeated in several parts of the Morea, that the swallows come in the spring from Africa on the backs of the cranes. A person of good credit has assured me, that he has seen a crane light upon a ship at sea with swallows on its back. The storks arrive in the Morea at the same time as the cranes, but are not swallow carriers, whether from want of charity, or want of strength, I cannot learn.

A Criminal Impaled

March 31st - 10.55 I leave Tripolitza by the Anapli gate. Here I find by the road side, where stands the permanent gallows, a high stake with the body of a man impaled upon it. He suffered three or four days ago, for having shot his wife in a fit of jealousy. He lived twenty hours after being impaled. It is believed that after a certain time a draught of water has the effect of putting the culprit out of his misery, and the coup-de-grace is said to be generally given in this manner.

An Ancient School

In the afternoon I visit the school of Dhimitzana, the most renowned in the Morea, and which probably existed before the Turkish conquest. I find the master, in his library, which contains some valuable editions of the classics ... and numerous theological works, but no manuscripts. At present the school has few disciples, and those who learn ancient Greek read little more than the Fathers of the Greek Church, and Lucian, which is generally the first book put into their hands by the master. I have remarked this practice at other places; it had its rise, perhaps, in the early ages of Christianity, for the sake of the ridicule which the author throws on the pagan deities. The school of Dhimitzana, though still considered the best in the Morea, has much declined of late. With the increasing misery and depopulation of the peninsula, the pursuit of letters has diminished in proportion. The study of Hellenic, though so easy to those who have more than half learned it with their mother tongue, is discouraged because it leads to nothing. Meantime smaller schools have been established at Mistra, Argos, Vitina, and Kalavryta, in which is taught that mere smattering of the ancient language which is thought sufficient for boys intended for the Church. The poor [teacher] complains piteously of these changes from bad to worse, the effect of which is, that his means of existence fall off, and that he is at a loss to find any person who really esteems his occupation, or with whom he can entertain a conversation on the subjects which interest him. He seems a sensible, pleasant character, with a tolerable knowledge of the ancient authors, and a good memory; but, as usual among the modern Greeks, he is quite devoid of sound criticism, and scarcely attempts to form a judgement for himself of the authors whom he reads...

The [teacher] accompanies me to the bishop, an ignorant monk from Cyprus, who lives in the eastern part of the town, on a ridge branching towards Zygovisti. He then conducts me to the other parts of the town, and we make the circuit of it as far as a rocky summit overhanging the river, which forms a semicircle around the precipitous peninsula. All round the crest of the ridge occupied by the town are the remains of a Hellenic wall, some parts of which are intermixed with the yards and walls and foundations of the private houses. In some places there are several courses of the masonry remaining, which is partly of the third order, but contains also some fine massy pieces of the polygonal kind... There are some Hellenic foundations among the vineyards on the slope of the mountain, showing this slope to have been a part of the ancient city. On the other hand, the portion of the modern town lying on the ridge to the eastward, seems to have been excluded from the ancient enclosure. The walls traceable round the modern town are probably those of the Acropolis only.

The River Styx

The ancient Styx was thought of as the River of the Dead.

I can find no person at Solos, not even the [teacher], who is scholar enough to be sensible that he is living on the banks of the Styx; but, what is very curious, though ignorant in this respect, they preserve the old notion, that the water is unwholesome, and relate nearly the same story concerning it as Pausanias, saying that no vessel will hold the water; which, indeed, they may very safely affirm, as well as all the other fables repeated by the ancients, if it is inaccessible, as they assert, They seem also, equally with the ancients, to have neglected the consideration, that, if the Styx is a pernicious water, the stream below Solos ought to partake of the same quality, which has not been pretended either by ancients or moderns, The cascade is called Black Water, and sometimes Dragon Water. In summer, when the stream is scanty and the wind high, they describe the cascade as blown about like a torrent from a mill.

The superstitious respect in which the present inhabitants hold the Styx is probably the effect of tradition, supported by the causes which had originally produced the same influence on their still more superstitious ancestors, - such as the wildness of the surrounding scenery, the singularity of the waterfall, (which, though it might not obtain much fame in the Alps, is higher than any other in Greece, and its inaccessible position. In a rude state of society, such situations are often the fabled residence of the personified objects of worship, whose supposed presence, added to the terrors of the scene, would render an oath there taken more solemn, and its obligation more binding. We learn from Herodotus ... that five centuries before our era, the Arcadians, who were a people preserving their origin and manners more than any other in Greece, were accustomed to swear by Styx, and to meet at Nonacris for that purpose. The practice seems at that time to have been falling into disuse, for this is the only instance of it occurring in history; but the ancient Arcadian custom had probably given a celebrity to the place throughout Greece, and had often induced persons to repair thither from other parts of the country to give solemnity to their adjurations; whence it was natural that, in process of time, the poets should feign, that to swear by the Styx was an oath inviolable by the gods themselves. It was very natural also, under these circumstances, that when the Greeks adopted the fables of Egyptian origin, concerning the infernal kingdom, they should have applied the name of Styx to its imaginary river...

1818-19 Peter Edmund Laurent

Surprised at Cleanliness

At four o'clock in the morning we reached Kravata, the second khan on the road from Tripolitza. Here, after much trouble and noise with the khanjee (who at first took us for robbers, and was going to fire on us) we at length got under a small roof, heated in the same manner as the stable at Kriavrio. Fatigue rendered us much less nice in the choice of a sleeping place. Our blankets and capottes were spread on the floor. We stretched our weary limbs before the fire, and enjoyed a few hours of most delightful repose.

Early in the morning our abode was filled with peasants, who squatted themselves, down on the ground near the fire, and examined us with a savage attention. They were not a little surprised to see us wash and perform the operations of a morning toilet. I heard several times the word Turzicos, "Turks" pronounced with some emphasis by the bystanders, as though cleanliness could not reckon among the practices of a Christian. The English traveller is nowhere in Greece regarded as a Christian, by either Turk or Greek, I mean by the uneducated of either nation; this prejudice I should suppose, from their not being seen to make the sign of the cross, a gesture which alone, in these countries, distinguishes the Christian from the infidel, and is much used by the peasants, who cannot be prevailed on to pass even a ruined chapel without crossing themselves several times.

The Mosque at Tripolotza (Contemporary engraving)

The Bitter Vedict of a Traveller

Of the abilities of the ancient Megalopolitans, the present Scinaniotes offer by no means a favourable specimen: in the whole village not one person could be found who knew the roads for four miles round, and it was with the utmost difficulty we could in the evening procure a guide on to Maytomati, the site of ancient Messene. The whole mental faculties of the present inhabitants are apparently bent towards cheating and plundering their neighbours, but more particularly any unfortunate tourist who may fall into their hands. Not a field of maize, or a plot of vineyard is seen unprovided with a raised scaffold, on which, sheltered by a roof of green boughs, and armed with a long Venetian musket, an individual is stationed, to preserve the crop from the purloinings of the peasants. A pocket compass, which bad been of the greatest use to us during our stay fell a victim to this pilfering propensity. The vanity of our servant George had likewise to regret the loss of his copper ink stand, which he was wont to wear proudly displayed in his girdle. The inkstands used in, the east consist of a long metal case, of a square or octogonal shape, at the end of which is placed a small box of the same material, in which the ink is kept. Pens, seal, sealing-wax, and penknife, are contained in this case, which is worn like a poniard in the belt, and distinguishes those who have learnt to write from the more ignorant.

1825 James Emerson

An Army of Caterpillars

Near Andritzenna, and in the middle of the War of Independence, Emerson found time to make obesrvations of curiosities of natural history

The naturalist may, perhaps, be interested by being informed that our route was crossed in this place by a singular procession: it consisted of upwards of a hundred large black caterpillars, which were performing their migration from one spot to another. They were led by three ranks two deep; the remainder followed in line, each taking hold of the rear of his predecessor, and performing their movements at the same moment; the rear was again closed by three lines, two deep; and the whole moved on slowly, but with extreme precision across our path.

1828 Henry A. V. Post

An Eagles' Eyrie

The final paragraph of this passage contains one of those remarkable examples of the double standards which Western visitors were accustomed to apply to judge their own conduct and that of the local people.

We stopped at this place to pay our respects to the pappas of the village, a venerable old man whom we had formerly met at Hydra. We found him crouching over a handful of coals, in a wretched hut which had more the appearance of a smokehouse than of a human dwelling, and was entirely destitute of the simplest and most ordinary comforts of life: and yet this might be called an enviable abode, compared with the still more wretched kennels which most of the villagers inhabited. The reverend patriarch received us with the most affectionate kindness, and urged us to take shelter for the night beneath his humble roof; but we knew he was too poor to entertain us, and after some slight refreshment, we continued on our journey. Descending the steep mountain on which Kastri stands, we came in about half an hour to some scattered remains which mark the site of an ancient town. Vestiges of its citadel are visible on a huge insulated rock, rising abruptly from the side of the mountain, and overlooking a tremendous chasm. Another half hour brought us to a *metochi*, or farm belonging to the monastery of St. John the Baptist, where we took up our quarters for the night. The monastery is a large and singular building, hanging at an elevation of several hundred feet upon the side of the opposite mountain, which rises far above it in a precipice of rugged rocks. Excepting the famous establishment of Megaspelia, and perhaps one or two others, it is the richest and most extensive institution of the kind in the Morea. Nothing can exceed the romantic beauty of its situation, when viewed from the metochi. Perched upon a giddy crag where an eagle would scarcely venture to build its nest, and surrounded above, below, and on all sides by perpendicular cliffs, it seems inaccessible to the footsteps of man, and entirely cut off from all communication with the world below it. The road which leads to it is a steep and winding path cut with great labour in the face of the rock, scarcely wider than a goat track, and only visible upon a near approach. It was the fear of Turkish oppression and exaction, that so frequently induced the monks of Greece thus to sacrifice convenience to security, and to build their sanctuaries in these wild and inaccessible situations.

In the summer of 1826 the Turks attacked the monastery of St. John, and made the most desperate exertions to capture or destroy it. Jarvis was lying there at the time with a small number of Greek soldiers, and about six hundred women and children, who had fled before the enemy's approach, and to whom the caloyers had generously afforded the protection of their walls. Many of the inhabitants of the neighbouring country had also deposited there for safe keeping all their moveable treasure. Finding the place unassailable by the ordinary modes of attack, the besiegers resorted to the experiment of rolling down large stones from the top of the precipice above it; but as the building was partly sheltered by overhanging rocks, and the stones in rolling acquired a horizontal impetus, they all fell beyond it. They killed, however, a large number of mules, sheep, and other animals, that were in the court and outside of the walls. After many fruitless attempts to find some vulnerable point, the Turks perceived that there was no hope of reducing the place but by the tedious process of a blockade, and soon relinquished the undertaking. Had they persevered in the siege a few days longer, the monks could not have held out, for owing to the great accession to their number, their supply of water was nearly exhausted. They had resolved, however, if reduced to such an extremity, to blow themselves up rather than fall into the hands of their merciless enemies.

With the exception of a single room, in which a native professor of the healing art had established his mortar and pestle, the whole of the spacious buildings of the *metochi* lay before us, "where to choose our place of rest;" for the monks abandoned them at the time of the invasion, leaving nothing but the naked walls, and had not reoccupied them since that period, in consequence of the unsettled state of the country, and more particularly on account of the depredations to which they were exposed from their own lawless soldiery.

A party of Kolokotrones' troops were lying at a small hamlet close by, and devouring every thing upon which they could lay their hands; and such was the scarcity of provisions which they had occasioned, that we were unable to purchase for any money a single loaf of bread. After we had rested ourselves for a few moments, and kindled a small fire from the few remaining fragments of doors and window-shutters, (for nearly every thing combustible about the building had already been applied to a similar purpose,) our men sallied forth to forage in various directions. They soon returned, some with a supply of fuel, which they had lopped from the first trees that fell in their way, - others with a quantity of delicious honey, which they had stolen from a neighbouring hive, - and last of all came the provident Stamates, with a lamp and several other useful articles, which he had procured from the premises of the absent physician, by unceremoniously picking his lock! The stolen honey, together with a few mouthfuls of bread which we had fortunately brought with us from Arakoba, served us as an apology for a supper.

After we had finished our repast, an incident occurred, which, however trivial in itself, is worth recording … as an additional illustration of the disregard of the Greeks for the rights of property. We were all endeavouring to contrive some mode of carrying along with us for the following day's journey, several fine combs of honey which we had left untouched; but an insuperable difficulty seemed to present itself in the want of a suitable vessel to put it in. The ready-witted Stamates retired forthwith, without saying a word, and returned in a few moments with a handsome stone jar, which looked as if it had been made for the very purpose. I asked him where he had got it. "In the doctor's apartment," he innocently replied. I expressed my surprise that he should think of carrying off a thing which did not belong to him, observing that the mere act of breaking into the man's premises in the manner he had done, would be sufficient, in a civilized country, to doom him to years of imprisonment; and begged him as he valued my friendship, to return the jar immediately to its proper place.

1829 The Rev. Rufus Anderson

"Heaps of Cursing"

We soon discovered a little Albanian village, however, of twelve houses, called Psari, without priest or school, from which, through the kindness of an old widow woman, we were supplied with bread made of Indian corn, and with yogurt, milk, and water. Other similar villages exist in the neighbourhood. Beyond these villages cultivation ceases, and we had to trace our way through deep ravines and among cliffs of slate, continually ascending, until Langadia unexpectedly appeared across a valley upon a mountainous declivity. Here our curiosity was attracted by a heap of stones on the way side, which, on inquiry, we found to be a *heap of cursing*. Some family in Langadia, or perhaps the village itself, had provoked the general execration, and to express it every traveller throws a stone upon the heap with a curse. Such piles of stones are said not to be uncommon in this part of the world....

1839 Lord Carnarvon

A Lamenting Bird

After leaving Tegea, and passing by a little lake, we continued our way through a wild and stony valley; we crossed the plain where Ibrahim Pacha was defeated by Colocotroni's son; we rode through the "Monk's Pass," a singularly striking ravine lying between shattered crags and surmounted by a tower, which picturesque and ruined, "pleads haughtily for glories gone." As we advanced the country improved; wild pears were seen in abundance, the oak made its appearance, at first low in character, but soon increasing in size and occupying a greater extent of ground, till at length as the surrounding hills became covered with wood – a new and grateful sight - we entered a real forest. Here our Greeks were startled by a bird which flew across the road, and which they called "kira." That bird they said had once been a woman, who deprived of all her kindred by some great calamity, retired to a solitary mountain to bewail her loss, and continued on the summit forty days, repeating in the sad monotony of grief the lamentation of the country, "Ah me! ah me!" till at the expiration of that period she was changed by pitying Providence into a bird. So strangely live on in modern tradition the fables of heathen Greece, mingled though they may be with the incongruous accompaniments of Christian legend.

The Holy Oaks

The country was now growing singularly beautiful; the ravines were sometimes clothed with woods and the oaks stood prominently forth on the hill sides, and in the valleys. Fern grew everywhere around us, and the magnificence of the oaks reminded me of those beauteous glades in the parks of England, where the trees have been the growth of centuries, and where the property has gone on from father to son in long descent. In one part we observed a knot of oaks so peculiarly fine that we deviated from our path to inspect them more closely. A ruined church was buried under the shade of this gigantic group. Perceiving, or imagining that I perceived, a variety in the foliage of one of these trees, I asked a Greek to pick me a branch. He recoiled from the proposition and answered: "Not for the world and all its gold. I should never again have a quiet night, and the heaviest calamities would fall on any person who plucked a leaf from the holy trees; except, indeed, on the feast of the Virgin, when we may safely pick even boughs." A peasant standing by confirmed this popular belief, and added that some Mahomedan travellers on this road had picked a bough, and on returning to their homes had mysteriously perished that very evening.

A Lament for Lost Captivity

Leaving this beautiful spot, we rode on to Megalopolis. As we went, we met an old shepherd with his family. A flock of sheep, three white horses, a jackass laden with little barrels and multitudinous scraps, a pan for boiling milk, a tent, a child, and some fine attendant dogs pacing by his side, completed the picture. He entered into conversation with me, and bewailed the times. "Ah, poor Turks," he said, "where are ye now? then we were happy, then we were Rayahs, now all is tyranny; then we only paid one lepton per head, now we pay a dreary forty-five." I suspect that he exaggerated the past immunity and the present exaction; yet this lamentation over the vanished dominion of the Mussulman was a curious evidence of the insufficiency of revolution to satisfy the minds that have most desired it

Platomancy

We wound our way through scenery, of which it is difficult to exaggerate the beauty, till we reached the point at which it was necessary to diverge from the main road in the direction of the Temple of Bassae. Sending on our luggage to Andrizzena, where we proposed to stay, we struck into the hills. But we had miscalculated the time. The sun declined, and threw its last warning light over rock, and tree, and bush, just as we passed a singularly beautiful spot, where a shepherd had pitched his tent.

The sheep all round were grazing, the bells tinkling, and no sound disturbed the absolute peace of the whole scene, save the tremendous baying of the watch dogs, who saluted us as we approached their master's property. It was now clear that we were belated, and that our only course was to stop here, and to spend the night in the shepherd's tent. We halted and sent our guide to arrest the baggage mules on their way to Andrizzena, and to bring them back: but the man, half-foolish, half unwilling, demurred, from the suspicion that he might lose his recompense. "If you are not paid, may I lose my youth!" cried Elias, - this being one of their most binding adjurations.

Whereupon our guide went, and we, in spite of the dogs who stood round us baying, took possession of the tent, and waited the arrival of its owner. In a few minutes he appeared. A young Arcadian shepherd, with very handsome features, and great natural grace of manner, he wore the fustanella and red gaiters, a long shaggy coat of wool, which, however, did not conceal the embroidered edges of a white vest, and a figured cotton handkerchief bound round a tasselled fez. In his belt he carried a knife, in his hand a long shepherd's crook. Altogether he was a very picturesque being. He told me afterwards that his wife, while sitting in the noonday heat under the shelter of a great Arcadian oak, had worked for him the handkerchief which he wore, tracing the pattern on it in accordance with the light and shadow that fell upon the piece.

As soon as we had announced our intentions, he received us with the utmost hospitality, saying that it was their practice always to welcome a stranger. He then climbed up into a fine tree and lopped a large stick, which he fashioned into a smooth stake. Having done this, he went into his flock, selected a young lamb and killed it; but a minute or two afterwards, when I hoped that all life was extinct, the poor creature struggled convulsively. Our friend, however, at once approached, and conversed with it tenderly, advising and begging it to die quietly, much in the same way that a father would beg his child to submit to the extraction of a tooth, or some such necessary operation. And now, all preliminaries being accomplished, two large stones were placed just within the doorway of the tent, a fire was lit, the stake was converted into a skewer, and the lamb being fastened on it, and turned round by two men, was in due course of time roasted whole. The fire, fed by large logs of wood, blazed and flickered almost in the centre of the tent, and we all sat round, soldiers, shepherds, muleteers, and partook in common of the food provided. This is the true spirit of Greek society. They never grudge a superior in birth or position, the highest place at the board, but no one must be excluded. The Greek chief, amongst his retainers, had the best place, and all the honours belonging to it allotted to him; but though acknowledged to be the first, he was still one of them, and the exclusion of no one was ever dreamt of.

After supper, we sat on in the blaze of the fire, and wild stories were told. For a moment, indeed, the good humour of the party was disturbed by our guide, who was a surly fellow, and refused to take any part in the preparations for supper. He was now joked and bantered by one of the muleteers, but unable to bear the turn which the conversation had taken, he rose with ill-concealed temper and departed. As he left us, another muleteer wished him good night; but he only answered, "Long life to the master," meaning, by implication, no long life to you."

And now that our lamb was devoured, a curious scene took place. On baring the shoulder blade of the flesh, the bone assumes a semi-transparent appearance, though veined with many fibrous marks; and by means of this a curious species of divination is still practised in Greece. It is the common belief that one skilled in such lore can read in these natural lines the clear presage of coming events. The young Arcadian was supposed to read them well, and it was curious to see the eager interest of the party, as he studied the shoulder-blade. To me, indeed, he announced that I was on the eve of a long journey - a prophecy of pretty certain accomplishment - and that I had before me something both to please and to render that journey melancholy. He would apparently have said more but that Elias checked him. But the forecast of their own fortunes seemed full of anxiety to them. The young Arcadian showed to a brother shepherd certain fibrous marks, and he in turn, with a serious and foreboding countenance, examined them and shook his head. At last he announced that a separation from their flocks - to them a heavy calamity - was impending. Whether this was to be the result of a marriage, which might fulfil the prophecy, though without involving sorrow, was for awhile a question, but no - the signs were distinctly ominous, and some enemy or catastrophe was at hand. They consulted together; it appeared that only the week before another shoulder-blade had given a similar warning; a gloom fell upon them; conversation flagged; even the fire began to burn low; and wrapping myself in my capote, so as best to screen myself from the keen night air which blew through the open sides of our tent, I lay down to sleep...

Bad Luck

At Andrizzena we rested awhile to allow our horses to be shod. They had been shod at Calamata, but so badly that nearly all the shoes had fallen off, and one of the horses was almost permanently disabled. Trade of every kind is extremely rude out of Athens, and even amongst the best of the Greeks there is a strange improvidence on many of these matters. Elias, who is a shrewd fellow, and good on a journey, instead of attributing the inconvenience to his own omission to carry a few nails with him, could only trace the disaster to our departure on a Tuesday and to the magpie of that fatal day; and so he continued his journey inveighing against expeditions undertaken on a Tuesday, and cursing, not the magpie itself, but the father and mother and even the grandfather and grandmother of the ill-omened bird that had flown across his path.

1852 Edmund About

A Night with a Poor Peasant Family

One evening, at the end of May, after a long ride in mountains of Arcadia, our guides made us stop at the village of Cacoletri. The first house we came to invited us to it with an irresistible charm. It was not that it was better or more curious than the others; it rose, like its neighbours, from amidst a little thicket of northern and southern trees, chilly olive-trees, hardy pear-trees, fig and walnut-trees; in front of it, as of the others, was an humble loom, where the young girls of the house pass the day in weaving cotton. All these cottages are built on the same plan... True, it is the simplest plan of all, that which nature seems to have taught all men - four walls and a roof, a low door, where we rarely missed knocking our heads, and two narrow windows closed by shutters; chimney, none; chimney, none at all, the smoke escapes as it can; the roof consequently is of a beautiful black colour and as it is never swept, the soot hangs down in stalactites. The furniture is unvaried - a few large earthen jars: these are the granary; they keep there their oil and grain, when they have any; a few hollowed trunks of trees, a few baskets of osier or reeds plastered with cow dung - these are the cupboards; a few coarse felt carpets for beds, sometimes a skin hung up against the wall; this is the cellar. In the houses of the more rich, a wooden chest may be met with; it is there that they shut up the things which they deem precious, which, however, are far from being so, Money is so scarce in these country districts, that a girl's dower is paid in clothes; the inhabitants, as in the world's early days, make a direct barter of fruits for milk, and of milk for cotton. I have seen our Agoyats pay for purchases with nails. If this chest, which shuts up the treasures of the house, were opened, one would doubtless find in it the same riches as those possessed by the shepherd of La Fontaine...

The most interesting portion of the furniture is the cradle. It is so humble, this cradle of the poor man, it takes up so little room, it lies so close to the ground that one passes by it without notice, and you see it without guessing that within a little man is growing up. A few days before marriage the bridegroom goes into the neighbouring forest, chooses a tree, and sets fire to it at its foot - it falls; then the young man cuts off a piece of the trunk, or of some great branch; he takes off the bark, splits it in two, leaves one half, and in the other hollows out a little space. It is in that hollow that all his children will sleep, one after another, and that their mother will rock them by an imperceptible motion of the foot, singing the while some song…

On the threshold of this poor house we had caught sight some splendid costumes, and a family of statues. There was in the foreground a young woman, tall and well made, and with a majestic appearance almost royal. Her blue eyes looked upon us with tranquil curiosity, like the vagueness of those large eyes of the statues, which for twenty centuries contemplate the tumultuous life of men. Her face of a fine oval, had the graceful paleness of marble.. Two long tresses, falling unartificially down her cheeks, lengthened her face still more, and made it somewhat dreamy. Her waist, unconstrained by stays, showed supple grace and fresh vigour. Her hands and naked feet had such delicate joints that any duchess might have envied them; her whole being was such a flower of beauty that she would have embellished the richest dress, without receiving from it any additional beauty. Her dress, wonderfully suited to her, showed a tasteful consciousness of what most adorned her. As many costumes as there are women may be met with in these country districts - nothing varies more capriciously than the dress of these peasant women; they choose at will the pattern which most becomes the beauty of each - each one is an artist whose costume is a masterpiece.

The young woman had thrown over her head a large red and yellow handkerchief, the point of which fell down between her shoulders. The long cotton shift, which hung to her feet, was ornamented with a small red and black pattern, embroidered round the neck and sleeves like the design on a Tuscan vase. A short garment, with narrow stripes covered her breast without confining it, and fastened below the bosom; a black sash, thickly folded, was loosely wound round her waist; an apron and thick coat of white woollen, sparingly embroidered with gaudy colours, completed her dress and adornment. Her hair, hands, and neck, were loaded with coins, rings, necklaces, and pieces of glass of all kinds; and she wore below the bosom two large embossed plates of silver, like small shields, - humble luxury, ornaments of bad silver, transmitted from mother to daughter, and which have a value only from the recollections attached to them, and the strange grace which they add to beauty. This woman, thus clothed, astonished the eyes by her singular splendour.

Her husband might be about five years older than herself, that is, about twenty-three or twenty-four. He was very tall, without seeming lanky, and slender without being thin. His features, purely chiselled, had something childlike, notwithtanding the presence of a growing moustache; and his long black hair, falling over his shoulders, especially gave him the shy physiognomy of a peasant of Brittany. He wore a jacket and fustanella; sandals, or rather moccasins without heels; woollen gaiters, which stand pretty well instead of stockings; a cotton scarf, embroidered by his wife, was wound like a turban round his head; his belt, tightly wound round, was armed with a dagger with a horn hilt - an inoffensive weapon, and whose innocence I would warrant.

The father and mother of the young woman lived in the house, which belonged to them. They gave their son-in-law lodging, that is to say, a corner in the cot, and he worked for them. The father was an old man - still green, gay enough, and very active. The whole house seemed to obey him cheerfully, but he showed a certain deference to his son-in-law. He asked his advice before taking us into his house. The young man answered, "What do you fear? - they are Christians like ourselves, and will do us no harm."

The old woman was like almost all the women of the country - fat to a degree neighbouring on corpulency. She seemed full of respect for her husband and for her son-in-law. Woman in the East persists in thinking herself inferior to man. She has almost everywhere a harsh and complaining voice, which at first astonishes one. This poor sex, oppressed for so many centuries, only speaks in lamentation.

All the family, even the little children, who ran away at our approach, were of remarkable beauty, in spite of their poverty and dirt. The use of a comb is unknown in these parts, and their fine hair is as uncultivated as a virgin forest. These long and delicate hands never see soap, except when they wash the linen at the spring, and those pretty rosy nails will be everlastingly in mourning. The water of the neighbouring torrent is too cold for taking a bath in it.

The supper of these poor beautiful statues pierced our hearts. They sat on the ground, and ate with their hands some herbs plain boiled, and some wretched maize bread. A little boy of twelve or thirteen sat apart without eating; his father took from the dish a handful of herbs and gave it to the mother, who passed it on to the child, who refused to take it. He felt the first shivering of fever. The mother returned the mouthful to her husband, who ate it. After the meal, which lasted a quarter of an hour, each one threw himself down, in his clothes, on an old mat or on some tattered piece of coarse stuff. The two old people set themselves next the fire, then the children. The beautiful young woman wrapped herself in an old coverlet, and lay down on the bare ground; her husband rolled himself in a thick capote, and placed himself between the family and us. The most comfortable part of the house had been left to us, and we were on some boarding a little space above the ground.

I was next the young couple, and before going to sleep, I reflected that this hard earth had been their nuptial bed, and would be their death bed, and that the happiness and misery of ten or fifteen people were shut up, pell-mell, within these four walls.

In the morning, everybody awoke before four o'clock; they rubbed their eyes, this was their whole toilet. When we were up, there remained in a corner a sort of shapeless bundle. "There," said Garnier, "there is something asleep under that." This thing was three little girls; the eldest of them, about thirteen or fourteen years old, had beautiful fair hair and black eyes, a complexion like milk, an antique profile, and a soft and serious face. The smallest, a child of hardly six, had one of those faces from a "Keepsake," such as ... the English engraving can alone reproduce.

A Visit to a Poor Mountain Village

Despite the changes in the life of the city people, in the fastnesses of Arcadia and elsewhere, the ancient way of life continued throughout the nineteenth, and into the twentieth, centuries.

Mendicity is allowed throughout the kingdom of Greece. Beggars wander through Athens in all directions: some address themselves to those that go by in the streets or on the highroad, others go from house to house. If they find the outer door open they enter into the court, and cry out in doleful tones. If no one answer them, they make their way into the passages; if they meet with neither master nor servants, they go into the first room they find, and if the room is empty they sometimes help themselves to alms.

By the side of the ditch which traverses the new town, a number of blind people are to be seen sitting on the ground in all seasons. From as far as they can hear anybody coming, they call out at the top of their voice, "Have pity on us, Effendi! – Give us alms, Effendi!" The soldiers, the workmen, the servants rarely pass them by without giving them a centime. In Greece, as every-where else, the poor are more generous than the rich... The town-beggars are the happiest of the land, in comparison with the peasants in certain villages.

We had just visited the temple of Apollo Epicurius, in the most barren mountains of Arcadia, when Lefteri conducted us to the Albanian village of Pavlitza. It is a village perishing of hunger; there meat is only eaten at Easter; bread is never eaten. The inhabitants do not even possess that horrible maize bread, which the first day is a thick dough, and the next day falls into crumbs, which chokes you when fresh, and sticks in your throat when it is stale; they live only upon herbs and milk.

When our arrival was known, all the people were in a state of excitement. "Here are the Franks," that is to say, here is a little money. Men and women hastened to our halting-place; the women carried their children of one year old in a kind of portable cradle, consisting only of a piece of felt folded double, with two sticks at the edges. With this equipment, and with their children on their backs, they came to group themselves before our house. The house which we chose to lodge in became at once the centre of the village, and the public meeting-ground was always in front of us.

Some came there from simple curiosity; these were by far the minority - almost all had some-thing to sell to us. The men brought coins, some wretched graven stones, and even pebbles from the river; the women had for sale their dresses; they offered us one an apron, another a scarf, another a shirt, another - I would call it a pocket-handkerchief if I could forget that they have no pockets, and that they do not use handkerchiefs. They brought those squares of red silk with wide fringes, which they hold in their hands like handkerchiefs on their wedding-day, or on very solemn occasions.

At first they did not dare to address us; they confided their interests to a man who came and treated with us. But by degrees they became bolder; they came close to us, and they profited by their nearer approach. One said, "I have got no bread." Another, "It is to get a living." Another said, "I am a widow." Widowhood, which is not without some consolations for a rich woman, is for people who live by their labour, the sum of all miseries. A young girl exclaimed, blushingly, "This is to buy me a husband!" It may be easily guessed that we did not know what answer to give to such good arguments, and that we bargained only just enough to prove that we were not Englishmen.

All the garments they had for sale they had made themselves; those shirts, and cotton scarfs embroidered with silk, are, every thread, the work of their hands. They carded the cotton, they spun it with their long distaffs; they wove it on that loom standing as a fixture before their doors. The embroidery is of their invention; they extemporize without a model, without design, without master, those charming arabesques, continually varied with an ever happy fancy. All these women are artists without being aware of it; and besides, they have that enduring patience, the mother of beautiful works. The time they spend at their work would frighten the most persevering of our beautiful embroideresses of the Faubourg St. Germain. Some of these shirts embroidered at the neck, at the sleeves, at the hem, embroidered all over, has cost as much as three years of patience. The work has been begun whilst rocking the first-born of the family in that humble wooden cradle, which I have described to you; it has been finished by the side of the couch of a sick husband.

Another scarf has been embroidered by an old mother who has not had time to complete it; the daughter has added the fringe, and has piously continued the same design. It is curious to observe also, how much they attach themselves to these labours which have occupied so large a part of their lifetime! When they bring themselves to sell them, we may be sure that their minds are divided between grief at parting from what they love, and the necessity of obtaining a little money. They give them up, they withdraw them back again; they look at the money, then at their work, and again at the money; the money consideration always ends by carrying the day, and they go away in despair at seeing themselves so rich.

An old woman had brought us a large and beautiful scarf, of a magnificent design, of brilliant, I would almost say of noisy colours. The tints of the silk were certainly a little effaced, but in spite of the slight damage caused by time, it was a splendid piece of work, and no doubt resembled the fine tissue which the Penelopes of former times used to weave during long years, for the burial of the father of their husbands. As soon as we saw this masterpiece, each of us wanted to have it; but Curzon had spoken first; his rights were respected, and I bought it in his name. There was a long negotiation, in which I came to the end of my Greek and of my patience. The whole village interested itself visibly in the affair. At length the scarf was handed over to us; at what price? I dare not mention it; money in these villages is worth ten times as much as in Europe. The poor old woman withdrew with slow footsteps, looking at the money in her hand; then she turned back mechanically, came back, stood before us, and not knowing what to say, exclaimed, "Ah, it is a fine scarf, it is six piques long !" And she fled crying. This senseless grief pained our hearts. These tears suggested some humble romance, slowly developed in this mountain nook; perhaps a long drama of domestic misfortune, or maybe some love-story, fresh and smiling as the spring, and of which we were going to carry away in our baggage the last relic, and the only remembrance. But what could we do? we wanted some costumes; we were not rich, and each time we bought something we were tempted to leave the thing and give the money.

But it was when we had completed our purchases, that our real difficulties began. We wished to buy nothing more, and everybody wished to sell us something. In my capacity of interpreter, I was besieged. A woman said to me: "I too, I am poor, I am ill! why do you buy nothing from me?" another exclaimed; "You have bought from young girls; I have four children, and you will not buy anything of me; you are not just!" It was of no use to answer them that we wanted nothing more, that our journey would yet be a long one, that our horses were overloaded; they would listen to nothing.

At the same time other women brought us their children, saying, that "they are crying for a penny;" when one had given to one, all the others must have something; all had such good argument: no bread! and this terrible *no bread* is not in this place a rhetorical figure for the use of beggars. Our supply of bread was almost at an end: at no price could we have got any in the village. There are only two men there who have any wine; we bought some: it was vinegar. And this wine is considered excellent: how many of these poor people have never drunk any of it! A woman came to ask us for some sugar for some remedy or other. Sugar is like money: they get some when foreigners bring some; and about three foreigners pass by in a year. I had some conversation with this poor woman: "Have you a doctor in the neighbourhood?"

"No, Effendi."

"What do you, then, when you are ill?"

"We wait till the illness goes off."

"But when you are very ill?"

"We die."

What a night we passed! All the family, consisting of six persons, slept in a heap near us. The child cried till morning, and the mother hushed it so noisily, that the remedy was worse than the evil. A young girl talked in her sleep; the wind whistled in the roof, the cold made us shiver under our coverings, and to complete all, we were devoured by all manner of creatures. Not being able to sleep, I betook myself to reflecting. This wretched village occupies the site of a flourishing town. Pavlitza was formerly called Phigalia! Without being rich, like Athens or Corinth, Phigalia enjoyed an honourable ease: it was Phigalia that taught the neighbouring town the cultivation of corn; this town was therefore, in Arcadia, what Eleusis was in Attica, the storehouse of bread. The ancestors of these starved peasants possessed temples, statues, a gymnasium: it was they, that after a pestilential sickness summoned to their mountains the architect of the Parthenon, to raise to Apollo Epicurius the fine temple of Bassae. The walls of their town, which still exist, are among the finest monuments of the military architecture of the Greeks.

What affected me in this decay was neither the reduced population, nor the walls without soldiers, nor the ruin of a little state. That a village which had attained the rank of a town, should fall back again to the condition of a village; that a people should lose the power of oppressing its neighbours, what is all this but a text for declamation on the instability of human affairs: I do not see that mankind has suffered any misfortune thereby.

But I made the reflection, that among so many cities which have fallen from the height of their power or of their glory, there is perhaps not one that has not been compensated by some solid advantages for the loss of some external benefits, not one in which the inhabitants have not now got greater wellbeing and more enlightenment than they had two thousand years ago. The progress of sciences, the development of industry, the advantages conferred by the discovery of a new world, the four or five great inventions which day by day render more easy material and intellectual life, have carried into the smallest hamlets of Europe benefits more certain and real, than the dominion of a plain, or the empire over two mountains. But has Phigalia obtained from fate the same compensations, and have the accumulated benefits of twenty centuries given her the small change for her unpretending grandeur? I have much difficulty in believing it, and if it were allowable to doubt the law of progress, it would be in those inaccessible mountain gorges, where ignorance and misery seem everlastingly established. It is not for these poor people that printing has been invented; they will never know how to read. It is not for them that America has been discovered: the potato, which feeds our most wretched villages, is a treasure unknown in Arcadia. They have not even heard that within a few years men have learned to move like the wind, and to send their words like lightning. And what signify to them these discoveries, by which they will never profit? So long as the word shall exist, people will travel a league per hour in their mountain paths. I even asked myself once, what they can have gained by the deliverance of Greece? The Turks could take nothing from them: they had nothing. Perhaps they have gained by no longer getting the bastinado; but did the Turks ever go so high and so far for the pleasure of bastinadoing them?

Being unable to sleep, I considered within myself by what means this wretched country might be ameliorated. No doubt the present Government does not do all that is possible; but it is the impossible which ought to be done to cure an inveterate misery resulting from the distance from the towns, the height of the mountains, the exhaustion of the soil - in short, from geographical and geological causes. We have, even in France, departments given up to ignorance and poverty, which receive from the State more than they give to it, and which profit by the fertility of other provinces.

I meditated so much on this subject, that morning came. At four o'clock, I could have believed myself to have been in the open air: the holes in the roof, lit up by the pale light seemed like so many stars. We left our beds without any regret.

There will always be something inexplicable in the obstinate love of mountaineers for a soil which refuses to maintain them. The inhabitants of the mountains of Greece refuse to emigrate, or if they do make up their minds to it, they soon return to their rocks.

1850s Henry M. Baird

The Travellers Discussed

We were to have gone on directly to Dragoi, or Tragoge; but ascending into the plain of the Pamisus, J's horse had the misfortune to wrench off one of his shoes and cut his foot badly. Nicholas knew nothing of horse-shoeing, and, indeed, prided himself on his ignorance. Our only recourse was to deviate considerably from our track to the right, and hunt up the blacksmith of Meligala. This took some time; for it was St. George's Day, and the smith was reluctant to perform any work. Meanwhile, we sat in a neighbouring khan, and soon beheld a crowd of gaping countrymen collected about the doors, to whom our coming furnished a rare staple of conversation. As they supposed us, like the generality of travellers, entirely ignorant of their dialect, their comments were quite free. In short, our whole equipment underwent a rigid review, and of each article of dress they expressed their approval or dislike. What most excited the interest of the spectators was a gutta-percha riding-whip, which H. carried and twisted into all possible shapes, to the no small wonder of the peasants, who expected to see it break at every moment. They were a little disconcerted on discovering, as we were about to leave, that we could understand what they said.

1870-80s John Pentland Mahaffy

An Austere Good Friday

We experienced in this place [Andritzena] some of the rudeness of Greek travel. As the party was too large to be accommodated in a private house, we sought the shelter of a *xenodocheion*, as it is still called - an inn with no chairs, no beds, one tiny table, and about two spoons and forks. We were in fact lodged within four bare walls, with a balcony outside the room, and slept upon rugs laid on the floor. The people were very civil and honest ... and were, moreover, considerably inconvenienced by our arrival during the Passion Week of the Greek Church, when there is hardly anything eaten. There was no meat, of course, in the town. But this was not all. No form of milk, cheese, or curds, is allowed during this fast. The people live on black bread, olives, and hard-boiled eggs. They are wholly given up to their processions and services; they are ready to think of nothing else. Thus we came not only to a place scantily supplied, but at the scantiest moment of the year. This is a fact of great importance to travellers in Greece, and one not mentioned, I think, in the guidebooks. Without making careful provision beforehand by telegraph, no one should venture into the highlands of Greece during this very Holy Week ...

[A]fter having suffered some hardships from this unforeseen cause in remote parts of Italy, we travelled into the same difficulty in Greece. But I must say that a Greek fast is a very different thing from the mild and human fasting of the Roman Catholic Church. We should have been well-nigh starved, had I not appealed, as was my wont, to the physician ... of the town, a very amiable and cultivated man... The gentleman to whom I appealed in this case did all he could to save us from starvation. He procured for us excellent fresh curds. He obtained us the promise of meat from the mountains. He came to visit us, and tell us what we required to know of the neighbourhood. Thus we were able to spend the earlier portion of the night in comparative comfort. But, as might have been expected, when the hour for sleep had arrived, our real difficulties began. I was protected by a bottle of spirits of camphor, with which my rugs and person were sufficiently scented to make me an object of aversion to my assailants. But the rest of the party were not so fortunate. It was, in fact, rather an agreeable diversion, when we were roused, or rather, perhaps, distracted, shortly after midnight, by piercing yells from a number of children, who seemed to be slowly approaching our street.

On looking out a very curious scene presented itself. All the little children were coming in slow procession, each with a candle in its hand, and shouting *Kyrie eleison* at the top of its voice. After the children came the women and the older men (I fancy many of the younger men were absent), also with candles, and in the midst a sort of small bier, with an image of the dead Christ laid out upon it, decked with tinsel and flowers, and surrounded with lights. Along with it came priests in their robes, singing in gruff bass some sort of litany. The whole procession adjourned to the church of the town, where the women went to a separate gallery, the men gathered in the body of the building, and a guard of soldiers with fixed bayonets stood around the bier of their Christ. Though the congregation seemed very devout, and many of them in tears at the sufferings of their Saviour, they nevertheless all turned round to look at the strangers who chanced to witness their devotions. To those who come from without, and from a different cult, and see the service of a strange nation in a strange tongue, the mesquin externals are the first striking point, and we wonder how deep devotion and true piety can exist along with what is apparently mean and even grotesque. And yet it is in these poor and shabby services, it is with this neglect or insouciance of detail, that purer faith and better morals are found than in the gorgeous pageants and stately ceremonies of metropolitan cathedrals.

The Temple of Apollo at Bassae

This passage is a fine example of the romantic Victorian attachment to the idea that ruins may be beautiful in their own right, and not merely in virtue of the qualities of the original edifice.

We rose in the morning eager to start on our three hours' ride to Bassae, where Ictinus had built his famous but inaccessible temple to Apollo the Helper... The morning, as is not unusual in these Alps, was lowering and gloomy, and as we and our patient mules climbed up a steep ascent out of the town, the rain began to fall in great threatening drops. But we would not be daunted. The way led among gaunt and naked mountain sides, and often up the bed of winter torrents. The lateness of the spring, for the snow was now hardly gone, added to the gloom; the summer shrubs and the summer grass were not yet green, and the country retained most of its wintry bleakness. Now and then there met us in the solitude a shepherd coming from the mountains, covered in his white woollen cowl, and with a lamb of the same soft dull colour upon his shoulders...

As we wound our way through the mountains, we came to glens of richer colour and friendlier aspect. The sound of merry boys and baying dogs reached up to us from below as we skirted far up along the steep sides, still seeking a higher and higher level. Here the primrose and violet took the place of the scarlet and the purple anemone, and cheered us with the sight of northern flowers, and with the fairest produce of a northern spring.

At last we attained a weird country, in which the ground was bare, save where some sheltered and sunny spot showed bunches of very tall violets, hanging over in tufts, rare purple anemones, and here and there a great full iris; yet these patches were so exceptional as to make a strong contrast with the brown soil. But the main features were single oak-trees with pollarded tops and gnarled branches, which stood about all over these lofty slopes, and gave them a melancholy and dilapidated aspect. They showed no mark of spring, no shoot or budding leaf, but the russet-brown rags of last year's clothing hung here and there upon the branches. These wintry signs, the gloomy mist, and the insisting rain gave us the feeling of chill October. And yet the weird oaks, with their branches tortured as it were by storm and frost - these crippled limbs, which looked as if the pains of age and disease had laid hold of the sad tenants of this alpine desert - were coloured with their own peculiar loveliness. All the stems were clothed with delicate silver-gray lichen, save where great patches of velvety, pale green moss spread a warm mantle about them. This beautiful contrast of gray and yellow-green may be seen upon many of our own oak-trees in the winter, and makes these the most richly coloured of all the leafless stems in our frosty landscape. But here there were added among the branches huge tufts of mistletoe, brighter and yellower than the moss, yet of the same grassy hue, though of different texture. And there were trees so clothed with this foreign splendour that they looked like some quaint species of great evergreen. It seemed as if the summer's foliage must have really impaired the character and the beauty of this curious forest.

At last we crossed a long flat summit, and began to descend, when we presently came upon the temple from the north, facing us on a lower part of the lofty ridge. As we approached, the mist began to clear away, and the sun shone out upon the scene, while the clouds rolled back towards the east, and gradually disclosed to us the splendid prospect which the sanctuary commands. All the southern Peloponnese lay before us. We could see the western sea, and the gulf of Koron to the south; but the long ridge of Taygetus and the mountains of Malea hid from us the eastern seas. The rich slopes of Messene, and the rugged highlands of northern Laconia and of Arcadia, filled up the nearer view. There soil remained here and there a cloud which made a blot in the picture, and marred the completeness of the landscape.

Nothing can be stranger than the remains of a beautiful temple in this alpine solitude. Greek life is a sort of protest for cities and plains and human culture, against picturesque Alps and romantic scenery. Yet here we have a building of the purest age and type set up far from the cities and haunts of men, and in the midst of such a scene as might be chosen by the most romantic and sentimental modern. It was dedicated to Apollo the Helper, for his deliverance of the country from the same plague which devastated Athens at the opening of the Peloponnesian War, and was built by the greatest architect of the day, Ictinus, the builder of the Parthenon. It was reputed in Pausanias's day the most beautiful temple in Peloponnesus, next to that of Athene Alea at Tegea. Even its roof was of marble tiles...

The ruin, as we saw it, was very striking, and unlike any other we had visited in Greece. It is built of the limestone which crops up all over the mountain plateau on which it stands; and, as the sun shone upon it after recent rain, was of a delicate bluish-gray colour, so like the surface of the ground in tone that it almost seemed to have grown out of the rock, as its natural product. The pillars are indeed by no means monoliths, but set together of short drums, of which the inner row are but the rounded ends of long blocks which reach back to the cella wall, But as the grain of the stone runs across the pillars they have become curiously wrinkled with age, so that the artificial joinings are lost among the wavy transverse lines, which make us imagine the pillars sunk with years and fatigue, and weary of standing in this wild and gloomy solitude.

There is a great oak-tree, such as I have already described, close beside the temple, and the colouring of its stem forms a curious contrast to the no less beautiful shading of the timeworn pillars. Their ground being a pale bluish-gray, the lichens which invade the stone have varied the fluted surface with silver, with bright orange, and still more with a delicate rose madder. Even under a midday sun these rich colours were very wonderful, but what must they be at sunset?

There is something touching in the unconscious effort of Nature to fill up the breaks and heal the rents which time and desolation have made in human work. If a gap occurs in the serried ranks of city buildings by sudden accident or natural decay, the site is forthwith concealed with hideous boarding; upon which, presently, staring portraits of latest clown or merriest mountebank mock as it were the ruin within, and advertise their idle mirth - an uglier fringe around the ugly stains of fire or the heaps of formless masonry. How different is the hand of Nature! Whether in the northern abbey or in the southern fane, no sooner are the monuments of human patience and human pride abandoned and forgotten, than Nature takes them into her gentle care, covers them with ivy, with lichen, and with moss, plants her shrubs about them, and sows them with countless flowers. And thus, when a later age repents the ingratitude of its forerunners, and turns with new piety to atone for generations of forgetfulness, Nature's mantle has concealed from harm much that had else been destroyed, and covered the remainder with such beauty, that we can hardly conceive these triumphs of human art more lovely in their old perfection than in their modern solitude and decay.

The Temple of Apollo at Bassai (Baron von Stackelberg, 1831)

Laconia

1680s Bernard Randolph

A Decisive Way with Religious Claims

The Greeks have free exercise of their religion. The priests are very ignorant, scarce any understanding the old Greek, nor are they so superstitious in their worship to pictures as those who live under the Venetians. They have several monasteries. There was another Maddona in Misithra which did many miracles; and every year great numbers of Greeks flocked from all parts to pay their devotions to it. The Bassha of the Morea having notice, went to see the ceremony, telling the priests he was desirous to see some miracle; they telling him it had done many, he ordered one of his men to bring another picture out of any house, which being brought, he asked the priests what difference there was betwixt those two pictures. They answered that the picture which was in the church was the most sacred thing. But the Bassha caused a fire to be made, and both pictures to be put into it, saying he would worship that which escaped the fire; but both were burnt, and the Bassha, laughing at their superstition, went his way.

1801 Edward Dodwell

An Enemy of History

Among the other difficulties which confront him, the historian has to contend with the deliberate alteration or destruction of evidence of the past. In Greece, the Abbé de Fourmont was the most notorious offender.

After I had taken copies of some of these inscriptions, I observed Manusaki turning them over and concealing them under stones and bushes. When I inquired his motive for such unusual caution, he informed me that he did it in order to preserve them, because many years ago a French milord who visited Sparta, after having copied a great number of inscriptions, had the letters chiselled out and defaced. He actually pointed out to me some fine slabs of marble from which the inscriptions had evidently been thus barbarously erased.

The fact is generally known at Misithra, and it was mentioned to me by several persons as a received tradition. This must doubtless have been one of the mean, selfish and unjustifiable operations of the Abbé Fourmont... It is conjectured by many, and perhaps not without reason, that his principal object in obliterating the inscriptions was, that he might acquire the power of blending forgery and truth without detection, and that his fear of competition was subordinate to that of being convicted of palaeographical imposture.

On his return to France he produced a vast mass of inscriptions, many of which are authentic, and have since been copied in Greece, and published by various travellers. But the most curious part of his collection, and that in which his authenticity is particularly questionable, are his inscriptions of Sparta and Amyklai, in which perfect confidence ought not to be reposed without great caution. Since the time of Alaric, Greece never had so formidable an enemy...

1806   François-René de Chateaubriand

. The Site of ancient Sparta

The view enjoyed, as you walk along the Eurotas, is very different from that commanded by the hill of the citadel. The river pursues a winding course, concealing itself, as I have observed, among reeds and rose-laurels, as large as trees; on the left side, the hills of Mount Menelaion: of a bare and reddish appearance, form a contrast with the freshness and verdure of the channel of the Eurotas. On the right, the Taygetus spreads his magnificent curtain; the whole space comprehended between this curtain and the river, is occupied by small hills, and the ruins of Sparta. These hills and these ruins have not the same desolate aspect as when you are close to them; they seem, on the contrary, to be tinged with purple, violet, and a light gold colour. It is not verdant meads and foliage of a cold and uniform green, but the effects of light, that produce admirable landscapes. On this account the rocks and the heaths of the bay of Naples will ever be superior in beauty to the most fertile vales of France and England.

Thus, after ages of oblivion, this river, whose banks were trodden by the Lacedaemonians whom Plutarch has celebrated, this river, I say, perhaps rejoiced, amid this neglect, at the sound of the footsteps of an obscure stranger upon its shores. It was on the 18th of August, 1806, at nine in the morning, that I took this lonely walk along the Eurotas, which will never be erased from my memory. If I hate the manners of the Spartans, I am not blind to the greatness of a free people, neither was it without emotion that I trampled on their noble dust. One single fact is sufficient to proclaim the glory of this nation. When Nero visited Greece, he durst not enter Lacedaemon. What a magnificent panegyric on that city!...

Night drew on apace, when I reluctantly quitted these renowned ruins, the shade of Lycurgus, the recollection of Thermopylae, and all the fictions of fable and history .The sun sank behind the Taygetus, so that I had beheld him commence and finish his course on the ruins of Lacedaemon. It was three thousand five hundred and forty-three years, since he first rose and set over this infant city .I departed with a mind absorbed by the objects which I had just seen, and indulging in endless reflections. Such days enable a man to endure many misfortunes with patience, and above all, render him indifferent to many spectacles.

1804-06 Colonel William Leake

A Brigand Raid

It is said that Captain Nicetas and the only remaining body of the Kleftes, amounting to forty, (a favourite number, and meaning little more than the English word "several"), came the other day to the village of Petrina, and received bread from one of the inhabitants, who, in course, was obliged to join them, or at least to fly, as his head, by the Pasha's order, was by this action forfeited. The thieves went afterwards into the mountain on the west of Londari, where they were attacked by their pursuers, and two or three persons were killed in the action. They have since retired to Mani, and are followed by a body of the Pasha's men, and about 400 armed Greeks from the vilayeti of Londari...

The head of Nicetas is brought in today, and exhibited at the tree at the Serai, with another head, and an arm. They belonged to some robbers who were lately killed at the mills behind Kalamata, when others, to the number of twenty, escaped to Mani; a servant of Nicetas was brought in alive.

Fear of the Turks

At the sight of the high black cap of the voivoda's Dehli who accompanies me, the inhabitants of Priniko fled and hid themselves, and some time elapsed before I could procure admittance into one of the cottages. The helot who owned it, when forced at length to make his appearance, bestowed the most ridiculous flattery on the ragged Turkish soldier. When told that the new voivoda was arrived at Anapli, on his way from Constantinople, and was daily expected at Mistra, "A thousand and a thousand times welcome," he exclaimed, with a profusion of benedictions which the Turk received with a grave face, though perfectly understanding the value of these compliments to his master, and that the Greek knew as well as himself that the arrival of a new governor could make no other difference to the poor helots than the imposition of some extraordinary gratuity, and consequently that he meant nothing but curses in his heart. At dinner the Turkish soldier did ample justice to the helot's fare, who not then knowing that I should remunerate him for the damage, must have considered the effect of the Dehli's teeth as all clear loss to him. He pretended nevertheless to lament that the Dehli ate very little, and after many pressing invitations, when at length he saw the Turk fairly a-ground, ended with the reflection … "Great men never eat much." One of the cottagers told me of two or three miracles that had happened to him last year. On one occasion a wine barrel that had been long lying empty he found full of good wine. It has always been part of the Greek character to believe in [miracles]: when the traveller tells them that such wonders never occur in his own country, they reply that it is a proof of their being the especial favourites of heaven, though they admit that at present they are suffering severe punishment for their sins. The boluk bashi, who superintends the affairs of the mukatasi of Tzasi, and the two other villages, said to me, " This land of Elos is good and rich, but we are obliged to squeeze the peasants too much, otherwise it would produce a great deal more." Thus it often happens, that Turks possessing local power are well inclined to exercise it with moderation for their own sakes, but the vicious system beginning from the head, and passing through all the gradations of the Turkish government, irresistibly impels them to a contrary course.

The Recent Origins of "Greek National Dress"

The Albanian dress is daily becoming more customary, both in the Morea and in the rest of Greece: in the latter, from the great increase of the Albanian power; in the Morea, probably in consequence of the prosperity of Ydhra, which is an Albanian colony, and of the settlements of Albanian peasantry that have been made in some parts of the Morea, particularly Argolis, as well as in the neighbouring provinces of Attica and Boeotia. The dress is lighter and more manageable than the Turkish or Greek. It is common for the Turks of Greece to dress their children as Albanians, though it would not comport with their own dignity and prejudices to adopt it themselves. Hassan's son is dressed *à l'Albanoise*; - himself as a galionji, or Turkish seaman.

Inscribed Marbles in a Peasant's House

As we approach the Finikioika kalyvia, the inhabitants fly and hide themselves. I soon get permission, however, into the best cottage in the village, in which the first object that meets my eye is an inscribed marble. The house is constructed, in the usual manner, of mud, with a coating of plaster; the roof is thatched, which is not a very common mode of covering the cottages in

Greece. There is a raised earthen semicircle at one end for the fire, without any chimney; towards the other, a low partition, formed of the same materialas the walls, separates the part of the building destined for the family from that which is occupied by the oxen and asses used on the farm, one door serving for both apartments. The usual articles of furniture of a Greek cottage are ranged, or hung around, namely, a loom, barrel-shaped wicker baskets, plastered with mud, for holding corn, a sieve, spindles, some copper cooking-vessels, and two lyres. The floor is the bare earth covered, like the walls, with a coat of dried mud. An oven attached to the outside of the building, and in the garden some beans, artichokes, and a vine trailed over the roof, indicate a superior degree of affluence or industry.

The inscribed marble is inserted in the wall on one side of the door, and turns out to be an interesting monument. It was erected in honour of Caius Julius Eurycles, who, in the time of Strabo, was governor of Laconia, and was so powerful that the island of Cythera was his private property. His name is inscribed on the Lacedaemonian coinage in brass, struck under his government. Strabo adds, that Eurycles abused the friendship of the Roman emperor so much as to excite an insurrection, which, however, soon ceased in consequence of his death. Pausanias tells us, that he built a magnificent bath at Corinth. On the·present marble, unfortunately, the name of the dedicating city is not mentioned.

The master of the cottage, when he returns home in the evening from his labour in the fields, tells me that he found the stone at Blitra, as they call some ruins near Kavo-Xyli, and that a Turk, who is now dead, advised him to convey it to his house: "But how do I know," he adds, that it may not bring some mischief upon my house, having belonged perhaps to some church?" The Turk's reason for being unwilling to have any thing to do with the marble was because it had been a work of the infidels. The mischief contemplated by the Greek was my arrival with men and horses, which he thought would bring expense upon him, if nothing worse. While I was at dinner five oxen entered, and took up their abode for the night behind the low partition.

April 2.- This morning at 7.15, sending away the baggage by the direct road to Turali, in the plain of Elos, I ride towards Kavo-Xyli, to see the ruins from which the marble was brought…

1824 The Rev. Charles Swan

The Burning of Mistra

The following is a reminder that while Western travellers were ranging about Greece during the 1820s, a terrible war was going on.

On reaching Bruliah, a point of our descent toward Mistra, the whole range of Taygetus, now called Pendedactylon (Five-fingers) whose summits we had perceived for some time, opened upon us with surprising magnificence ...From this place we observed Mistra; but we saw with regret that the town was smoking in a variety of places. The way conducted us through many beautiful valleys, ornamented as well as the higher regions with olive-trees ...As we drew near to Mistra, fire broke from the houses, but not a soul was visible. A few Greeks, attracted by the hope of collecting what had not yet perished, appeared afterwards. We entered the town and beheld the flames all around us; household utensils broken and scattered in every direction. Nothing in short could equal the desolation, or the interest which it excited. In one place a cat remained the only inhabitant; in another, a dog barked at us as we passed, resolved to have the usual gratification of its spleen, though it sounded over the ruined hearth, and the broken shrine of domestic happiness.

'Tis sweet to hear the watch-dog's honest bark
Bay deep-mouth'd welcome as we draw near home -

But what a different feeling must have arisen in the mind of the owner of one of these burnt dwellings, when he returned to witness the wreck of his comforts, and the destruction of his property! The Greeks before mentioned conducted us to a house yet untouched, although surrounded by flames. Here we slept; expecting indeed to have been aroused in the night; but the escape was so easy, that we had no apprehension of the consequence. Ibrahim left Mistra in the state I have described, only this morning. He has gone forward burning and destroying: we shall follow, and be eyewitnesses of the destructions he has caused.

1839 Lord Carnarvon

Robbed in the Bishop's Mansion

The bishop and the five brothers to whom I have alluded were adherents of the English party: consequently their opponents espoused the Russian interest... There were some who seemed to envy the bishop the honour of entertaining us; but the good old prelate observed that he could not resign us to others. This feeling indeed is so prevalent that in two or three towns a little contest has occasionally occurred between the rival authorities which it has required some little management to allay, without giving offence to either side.

I retired to rest that night rather early, but feverish, and in pain. I found myself unable to sleep; with wakefulness came thought, that enemy to rest; and so, to banish all superfluous activity from the mind, I lit my lamp, and taking up Leake's *Morea*, I, singularly enough with reference to the event of the night, read his account of the lawless state of that strange country the Maina, on the frontier of which we are even now pausing. Sleep at length began to assert her influence, and extinguishing the light I lay down; but my slumbers were unrefreshing, and disturbed by wild and unconnected dreams. I was at length roused by a heavy noise overhead, listened to it for a moment, and then, out-wearied, I was overpowered by that sleep which had been So slow in visiting me at first. When I again became conscious, I distinctly recollect that I felt a pressure resting upon me, which was, however, instantly removed, and which I attributed to some vagrant cat. Immediately afterwards, as I was again subsiding to sleep, I heard, or thought I heard, a step, and the sound of whisperings. I was now so completely roused that I rose in my bed. I imagined, even then, that I could distinguish a rustling sound in the corner near me, and was possessed by that indescribable feeling or almost instinct which sometimes takes the place of the physical organs of vision, and assures us even in darkness of the presence of some unwonted object. I was on the point of applying to my phosphorus box, to determine the mystery; but feeling indisposed to any exertion, I listened attentively for a minute or two, and hearing no further sound of a suspicious character, I once more lay down on my pillow, and resigning myself to the influence which was fast steeping my senses in forgetfulness, I slept again till I was thoroughly roused by a loud noise at the end of the room, by the sound of steps overhead, and of some heavy weight dragged along the floor. I now began to suspect that the room above me was occupied by persons preparing to start upon some early expedition, and I gradually became convinced that the whispering apparently so near me had really proceeded from a neighbouring apartment for cracks and crevices are common in the walls of Greek houses; and it is not unusual to see from one story household operations carried on in another. But I was now so completely awakened that I lit my lamp, looked at my watch, ascertained that it was scarcely two o'clock, wrote in my journal for a short time, and then again composed myself to rest.

I slept heavily enough after a night of such frequent disturbance, and the first object that presented itself to my sight was my servant George, standing near me in the morning, with an amusing expression of astonishment and dismay on his truly English face. He had instantly perceived that my trunk, which was placed in a line with my bed, and only a few steps from it, had been forced open and a good deal of money taken. The events of the night were then explained; the light step in the room was not that of a cat, but of a robber; the whisperings came not from above; but from the room itself, and the pressure which I had felt was that of a hand endeavouring, in the darkness, to find the right, or rather - the wrong, path for its intrusive owner. There were still some circumstances to which I could assign no satisfactory explanation; the noises which I could no longer doubt as having arisen from operations near me, and the noises which obviously came from above had been so strangely blended as to have seemed almost simultaneous. A minute investigation of the room dispelled the uncertainty, and revealed the general plan of proceeding.

In a recess near the door, and almost concealed from view, was a staircase, for the construction of which it seemed at first difficult to assign an adequate reason, but which on closer examination led, as I found, to a trap-door in the ceiling, through which I ascended into an uninhabited room. There was in this untenanted apartment a window overlooking an open gallery, which again communicated with the courts and gardens on the ground floor. The shutter of this window had been removed, and the window itself was broken. On reflection, I thought it my duty to mention the circumstance to the bishop, though I felt that its occurrence in his house would annoy him greatly. The bishop was grieved by the intelligence. The *Procureur du Roi*, who lodged at the palace, was instantly summoned, and vigorous inquiries were instituted. The general course of the investigation satisfied the police that the entry had been made by the window, and they also came to the disagreeable conclusion that persons outside had been associated with and directed by others inside the palace. They examined the apartment of a young Greek, upon whom suspicion rested, but the examination led to no result. Ultimately my depositions were required, and these I made with caution and reserve, lest I should implicate or cast suspicion upon any innocent person. The police next insisted on examining the muleteers, of whose guiltlessness, however, I felt assured. Poor Elias walked up and down the gallery wringing his hands, and declaring that he was a ruined man; sorrow and shame would rest upon his head; would to Heaven that he had never left the walls of Athens! Would to Heaven, above all, that he had never encountered that fatal magpie! That bird had blasted his sight at the time. Bad as the whole tribe was, no previous magpie had been half so fraught with baneful influences. It had a look of most malignant meaning. He knew also, by the peculiarly wicked character of its flight, that disaster of the gravest kind was at hand. The good old bishop was agitated, in a different manner, though scarcely in a less degree. That a stranger should have been plundered when resting under his roof, was a positive calamity; it would be an undying source of shame and sorrow to his kindred, and of exultation to his enemies; no time could efface the stain that would attach to his house. He should, however, pronounce a solemn and public anathema on the robbers and on all who were party to or in any way cognizant of the act, and this awful sentence of eternal condemnation would, he said, in all human probability lead to the detection of the offenders and the restitution of the money. I was afterwards informed that in cases of robbery, when this appalling interdict had been laid by the Church upon the unknown criminals, the stolen goods were not infrequently restored by the awestruck depredators with a confession of their guilt, and with the humblest supplications that at any price or sacrifice the Church's wrath might in mercy to their stricken souls be removed. But the power of the Church over the minds of men is slowly but certainly declining in Greece.

I was really embarrassed and affected by the quiet affliction of the old bishop, and I almost regretted that I had communicated the circumstance to him. He wished me a very mournful farewell after giving me an embrace in regular Greek form. I had little notion when he said that such a circumstance would be used as a handle against him by his enemies, that any human being could seriously impute to him a share of blame in the transaction; yet so strong is party rancour, that on our arrival at Mistra a few hours later, a resident of the town when questioning us of the event, the fame of which was already widely spread through the country, said, "Ah! The bishop is a Mainote."

1850s Henry M. Baird

A Rustic Dwelling

Janni, or Merdzianni, our Arab cook, following out the instructions he had received, had, as we found, established himself with our effects in the best cottage he could procure in the village of Georgitzi, and was busily engaged in preparations for our evening meal. Let me describe the house and its inmates. They will give a fair idea of the average dwellings and the lower class of the population of Greece.

The whole building, about thirty feet long and twelve or fifteen wide, was formed of rough stone, except the roof, constructed of boards, upon which the tiles reposed. A single room composed the interior. On the right of the door there had been built a square platform of boards, raised three or four feet above the clay floor, and attainable by means of a small rickety ladder. Upon this our beds had been spread out; and here we ate off the portable table that accompanied us everywhere. Meanwhile the culinary operations might be watched at the other end of the room, where a fire had been kindled on the large stone hearth. The smoke found its way out, partly through the interstices of the tiles, partly through the paneless windows and the door. Around the cook were grouped a goodly number of Greeks, men and women, eating and drinking, and making a very babel of the place as they waxed joyous over their wine. From time to time, a crowd of children, and grown people too, might be observed peering through the door, or even intruding into our small apartment, in order to have a look at the "Frank milords." Ever and anon Nicholas, by dint of threat or entreaty, would clear them from the door; but they speedily resumed their posts of observation, with such perfect nonchalance and good humour, that we were fain to permit the gratification of their curiosity.

Around the room, as usual, were to be seen some of the products of the neighbourhood. Often there will be a heap of cotton, whose picking provides ample employment for the women during the winter months. In autumn one corner is filled with golden ears of Indian corn. Over our heads were hanging from the rafters a number of wide and shallow wicker baskets, in which the silkworms were feeding. Already a chrysalis or two might be seen suspended by its delicate constructor from the lower sides of the tiles of the roof, through the intervals of which, when night fell, the moonbeams gleamed in upon us.

On the whole, I must say, the cottages of the Greek peasantry are remarkably wanting in the air of comfort which a few slight improvements might readily impart. No neat garden, with its wallflowers garnishing the border, and the woodbine or honeysuckle climbing over a rustic porch, is to be seen, as in England, before the door of the most humble labourer. Few domestic animals are kept, except fierce watchdogs for protection, who greet the traveller in packs as often as he has occasion to enter a village. Even to the rearing of the honeybee, for which the country is admirably adapted, the people of Peloponnesus pay comparatively little attention; and a neat row of hives is rarely met with in that district. The few that you will find are made of osier baskets, merely plastered over with mud or clay and dried in the sun; and perhaps they answer the purpose well enough. This is one of not a few instances in which contrivances of a manufacture as simple as that of Homeric times are still commonly employed. Small, too, are the substantial comforts with which the labouring man's home is provided. Of furniture there is little except the mere utensils indispensable for cooking; and as the diet of the poor is simple and light, their number is restricted within a narrow compass. The articles we esteem as almost necessary to existence are wanting. Such a thing as a bedstead can not, I presume, be met with in a peasant's house from one end of Greece to the other, The poor consider themselves very fortunate if they can purchase some matting on which to lie. The greater part, so far as I know, are obliged to content themselves with the great shaggy coats, or *capotas*, in which they wrap themselves, and suffer little from the dampness of the bare ground. At the same time, the want of cleanliness pervading the houses makes them an object of disgust to every person who has not become accustomed to the sight.

1870-80s John Pentland Mahaffy

A Memorable Experience

We lodged at a very bad and dear inn, and our host's candid excuse for his exorbitant prices was the fact that he very seldom had strangers to rob, and so must plunder those that came without stint. His formula was perhaps a little more decent, but he hardly sought to disguise the plain truth. When we sought our beds, we found that a very noisy party had established themselves below to celebrate the Feast of the Liberation, with supper, speeches, and midnight revelry. So, as usual, there was little possibility of sleep. Moreover, I knew that we had a very long day's journey before us to Kalamata, so I rose before the sun and before my companions, to make preparations and to rouse the muleteers.

On opening my window, I felt that I had attained one of the strange moments of life which can never he forgotten. The air was preternaturally clear and cold, and the sky beginning to glow faintly with the coming day. Straight before me, so close that it almost seemed within reach of voice, the giant Taygetus, which rises straight from the plain, stood up into the sky, its black and purple gradually brightening into crimson, and the cold blue-white of its snow warming into rose. There was a great feeling of peace and silence, and yet a vast diffusion of sound. From the whole plain, with all its homesteads and villages, myriads of rocks were proclaiming the advent of the dawn. I had never thought there were so many cocks in all the world. The ever-succeeding voices of these countless thousands kept up one continual wave of sound, suth as I suppose could not be equalled anywhere else; and yet for all that, as I have said, there was a feeling of silence, a sense that no other living thing was abroad, an absolute stillness in the air, a deep sleep over the rest of nature.

How long I stood there, and forgot my hurry, I know not, but starting up at last as the sun struck the mountain, I went down, and found below stairs another curious contrast. All over the coffee-room (if I may so dignify it) were the disordered remains of a disorderly revel, ashes and stains and fragments in disgusting confusion; and among them a solitary figure was mumbling prayers in the gloom to the image of a saint with a faint lamp burning before it. In the midst of the wrecks of dissipation was the earnestness of devotion, prayer in the place of ribaldry; perhaps, too, dead formalism in the place of coarse but real enjoyment.

We left for Mistra before six in the morning, so escaping some of the parting inspection which the whole town was ready to bestow upon us. The way led us past many orchards, where oranges and lemons were growing in the richest profusion on great trees, as large as the cherry-trees in the Alps. The branches were bending with their load, and there was fruit tumbled into the grass, and studding the ground in careless plenty with its ruddy and pale gold. In these orchards, with their deep green masses of foliage, the nightingales sing all day, and we heard them out-carolling the homelier sounds of awakening husbandry. During all the many rides I have taken through Greece, no valley ever struck me with the sense of peace and wealth so much as that of Sparta.

1888 Thomas D. Seymour

Spartan Conditions in Sparta

Conditions for travellers in Sparta did not improve quickly.

The best hotel in Sparta had but one washbowl for its guests, and that was only as large as a good sized soup plate. The street is the ordinary slop jar. Towels are scanty and thin. The traveller needs Persian powder to protect him from vermin. He is served by unkempt boys...

The Acropolis of Sparta (Baron von Stackelberg & Dupressier)

The Mani

1670s Dr. John Covel

A Brush with the Maniotes

For three or four days the wind was full in our eye; we tacked and tumbled backwards and forwards between Cerigo and the W. end of Candia, then we got between C. Matapan and Cervi, and having been thus beaten up and down, and made no progress, and little hopes being left of a fair wind, by consent we came all to anchor on the S.W. side of Cervi; in nineteen fathom water, about five o'clock, Nov, 14, afternoon. That evening I went with the Captain in his pinnace sounding the several depths in the bay, and then went on board our Admiral, where all the captains resolved to go on shore next morning for what provisions we could find, especially of wood (whereof there is plenty), and fresh water if we could find any.

Next morning our Capt, and I and two of our gentlemen passengers went on shore in the yawl betimes, before any of the other commanders appeared. We landed at a spot where it was plain ground and an open place, and therefore free from ambuscades. Immediately came down an old Greek from the top of the mountain in a poor patched habit, in a thick coarse jacket, a woollen shirt, with no stockings nor shoes, but only some pieces of a raw hide of an ox or bull were laced on to the soles of his feet with the hair side inwards, which I suppose never go off till time and rottenness separate them. With these his feet are so pliable that he can easily go up or down a rock which our shoes will not suffer us to do, at least with that dexterity... He had a skull cap on, bordered with a lambskin, which he pulled off, and came boldly to us. We had a native Greek in our boat's crew, and he was our interpreter, for I spoke as good school Greek to him as I could in our pronunciation, but my language seemed as perfect gibberish to him as his did to me. We asked for flesh: sheep, bullocks, goats, and the like. He told us they were all driven off the island the day before, for they took us for Africans and enemies, seeing us lying so long upon their coast. We asked for water. He told us there was none but what was preserved from the rain in hollow basins in the rocks, which he directed us to; and I afterwards tasted of it, and found it good. There are no people who continually live there, but they come from the continent to till the ground, which lies on the edges of the mountain round by the sea, and had good corn then growing on it; they likewise bring sheep and other cattle sometimes from the main land to feed here. We asked him if he could procure any cattle or other necessaries to be brought over for our money. He said he would go and inform his friends, and see what he could do; he doubted not but we might have something; in the meantime he showed us where we might try for water. He answered all along with such a show of innocent simplicity as we were much pleased with him; and I gave him a Tunbridge knife which I had in my pocket, and everyone likewise gave him something, which he received with a wonderful submissive reverence, and promising us a very grateful return of our kindness, away he went, running directly up the mountain.

By this time all the other commanders (except Capt. Wild) and a great many of their men were come on shore. Most of them brought firearms with them, and in all we might then make about a hundred firelocks. All the Captains strictly commanded their men not to stir far from the shore; and our Captain, to make us more wary, told us that in the year (as I remember) 1664 our general ships passing by here for Turkey came to an anchor, and many went on shore on the mainland there, whereof three worthy merchants and six or seven others were snapped by the natives, who lay in wait for them, and it cost them 1,600 dollars for their redemption. These who live upon the rocks and mountains by the sea are a sort of lawless people, and the Turks themselves cannot govern them or reduce them into any good order. These miscreant wretches lie constantly watching upon the rocks and mountains, not so much to secure themselves from the injuries of pirates as themselves to thieve and rob whom they can catch, and all the Christian passengers which they can seize on the shore they sell to the Turks to serve in their galleys or otherwise as slaves; and I have been assured that if they can conveniently spirit away Turks themselves they will serve even them in like manner, and sell them for slaves to any Christian who will be their chapman! There was a fawning cunning varlet came to those gentlemen then, and pretended to procure them all manner of provisions which they could desire, but betrayed them then, as this vile wretch did us now. I could not but call to mind old Sinon in Virgil, for our cheat seemed to pretend to the very same motto: Poor, but very honest. Believe me, Greeks are Greeks still; for falseness and treachery they still deserve Iphigenia's character of them in Euripides: Trust them and hang them, or rather hang them first for sureness.

We kept in little bodies near the shore, where there were small thickets of juniper and myrtles with their berries then ripe, and we had excellent sport in killing fieldfares and thrushes, and such other birds, which were there at feed in great abundance, Some went towards the sandhills, where was store of game in little plashes made by the sea-water, which was cast in there by winds and storms. After we had sported our selves a while with shooting in these thickets and plashes; two or three of our Commanders invited me to a collation, and as we were set in the shade under some pieces of rocks, we saw several of our men (notwithstanding all the captains' commands, and our Captain's history) struggling up the mountain, One was habited something like our Captain, and, at a distance, appeared indeed to be him; whereupon some gentlemen coming by us would by all means have tempted my curiosity to have followed them, but our Captain's lecture at our coming on shore had stirred up such wary apprehensions and jealous reflections in my mind, as I could not possibly be persuaded that it was he; and the captains there with me were in a very great rage to see such inconsiderate people running into that danger. No sooner had these gentlemen left us but we heard three or four guns go off upon the mountain; and, looking up, we saw some of the stragglers posting down in wonderful haste; and presently appeared several men brandishing their cutlasses or scimitars, and making them glitter against the sun. We immediately rose, and went to the body of our company to hear what was the matter. It happened that five or six gentlemen had got some seamen with them, and away they had ventured up the mountain. The gentlemen (I know not whether it was by good fortune or policy) were hindermost, and just as their vanguard was got on the brow of the other side the mountain, up rose about a dozen rogues, who had lain skulking there in the thickets, and ran upon them. They being scattered abroad, and not near one another by forty or fifty yards or more, at this surprise fired upon the rogues without doing any execution (perhaps most of them were charged only with small shot). So soon as their fire was over, the rogues came more boldly on, though armed only with half, pikes and cutlasses. Our seamen, who had not in the least considered to make good their retreat, threw down their arms, and betook themselves to their heels. But our gentlemen had the start of them, and so, God be thanked, these all escaped, though very narrowly, all coming down without their arms, most without their hats, some with but a piece of a shoe, their feet and legs being battered and torn, and their bodies bruised with rushing through the shrubs and jumping down precipices, for they came right forward, thinking the shortest way was best.

Four of the poor seamen were taken ... and Francis, whom they first had slightly wounded in the face, then they seized him and tied his hands behind him, and left him with three rogues to guard him, These drove him before them, and because he often lingered and offered to stop, they pricked him forward in the back, and wounded him in several places with their half pikes. The poor man was a very stout fellow and a good wrestler, and feeling the thing which bound his hands something loose, slipped his right hand out, and, with great courage and presence of mind, turned upon the rogues, who were useless, and thought they had him safe. With this advantage, he ran the first quite over, and struck up the heels of the second; the third (who was a little behind the other) made a blow at him with his scimitar, which he saved from his head with his left arm, and laid hold of the weapon with his right hand. The rogue, drawing it a little back, cut the poor fellow's hand badly. Yet this saved him from a second stroke, for he being something under the rogue, he struck him up hand and foot, and before the other two could come at him, away he came. The great concern which he had for his dear life and dearer liberty added something more then natural vigour to his legs, and as much lightness to his heels. At last he got to us, and told us all that had passed.

There were, in another place, two of our seamen (one the native Greek) who made a very soldier-like retreat. As they straggled from us, they kept together, and, out of a thicket, up start five or six Maniotes, and made towards them. They, standing together, presented their muskets (resolving not to fire but to good purpose, and therefore not till they were very near). Down the rogues dropped again. The seamen retreated; they again followed. The seamen presented again, and they again squatted down. Our Greek at last spoke to them, and told them to keep off in their own language; at which they stopped, and so these two retired leisurely and safely to us.

After some debate what we ought to do, we all in a body were marching up the mountain to rescue our men; but Captain Wild, being all this while on board, and observing all which had happened, thought we were not strong enough; and, therefore, firing a great shot over us, called us back; and sometime after came all his soldiers on shore well armed; and then Mr. Day (his Lieutenant), a brave stout man, marshalled us all, and put us in order and away he led us up the mountain. But when we arrived, we saw we were come too late; for all the rogues had crossed the water in their boats, and were just landing on the Main, and with our glasses we could discover our poor captives amongst them, bound. The Lieutenant was earnest for bringing our boats about and going to them, for they appeared in all much short of a hundred men. Our captains, though all brave men, were utterly against that, for being, by their charter-party, bound to ply their voyage, they could not tell how they could answer such an adventure, for we knew not what event our landing on the main land in a hostile manner might produce, so some of them came back presently; but the Lieutenant and the rest rambled all over the island, where they saw not one man left, nor found so much as one house. Here and there were coves, in which they found some tattered cloths, and a few poor utensils; as likewise a sack of meal, and good store of onions and suchlike very mean booty. I hardly believe that this Maniotes do ever bring any cattle hither (though our honest Sinon told us they did), or, at least, they feed them on the other side the mountain, and not in view, for fear of African or other pirates, who would sweep them off. They only come here to till the ground and reap the corn, and now and then to make such ambuscades as these; and very slender provisions will serve them upon these occasions. Some of our men, as they marched, found some hats, swords, pistols, and such like (it seems useless) baggage, which our first Myrmidons had discreetly scattered in their retreat. At last all came down, and we went on board, much lamenting our sad misfortunes, and all concluded that if we had proceeded on at our first march, and not stayed for Captain Wild's soldiers, we had certainly rescued our men, and perhaps sufficiently chastised those Sons of Belial.

After some little conference with all the captains, we jointly agreed to contribute to their ransom, and everyone setting down their good will, we had that night subscribed about 1,500 dollars, the poorest seaman giving one. Next morning the admiral sent out his boat, and we went in ours with white flags of truce round the island, but not one man appeared to treat with us, or to take the least notice of us. Wherefore the money was collected and deposited in the Consul's hands at Smyrna, and, about two years after, the poor slaves were found in the galleys and redeemed, though they proved most ungrateful wretches, for I heard that when they got into England they offered to sue their captains for their wages, which they pretended was due to them for all that time.

1680s Bernard Randolph

The Fate of Ships Putting in on the Coast of the Mani

This passage reveals the sophistication of the Maniotes' methods of extracting ransom..

If any ship come to anchor on their coast, many arm themselves and go to the place, over against where the ship doth ride; some of them will be in priests' habits, walking by the sea side, with their wallets, in which they will have some wine and bread. Their companions lie hid behind the bushes at some convenient post. When any strangers come ashore, who do not understand their language, the feigned priests make signs to them, showing them their bread and wine, which they offer to them for money, by which the strangers being enticed from the seaside (and it may be to sit down and taste their wine) the hidden Maniotes come and make their prey. The priests will seem to be sorry, and endeavour to make the strangers believe they were altogether ignorant of any such design. So a white flag is put out, and a treaty held with the ship for their ransom. The priests endeavour to moderate the price, showing a great deal of respect to their companions, who are clothed in Turkish habits. Many ships have been thus served. Such business happening to some English ships, who (having the winds contrary) came to anchor near the island Cervi, (in one of which, Sir Paul Rycaut was a passenger going for Constantinople) several young men were taken, and they paid dear for visiting the Maniotes, and though the Earl of Winchelsea, then ambassador from his majesty at Constantinople, made complaint of it, no redress could be had.

1685 George Wheler

Lamenting a Missed Opportunity for Theft

The Magnoti, who are the inhabitants of that Country, are famous pirates by sea, and pestilent robbers by land. They have always bravely defended themselves against the Turks, and maintained their liberty, till lately...

They are naturally such thieves that when any vessel cometh into their harbour, they will go by night, and cut the cables of their ships, when they can find nothing else to lay hold of; which sometimes endangers the vessels running ashore, when not discovered in time. Some mariners of this place that were on board of us, gave us this account of their country, with many diverting stories of the same nature, which they glory in.

One of the officers of our ship, who had been at the town, related a story, that well expresseth their thieving nature. Some strangers, being at one of the villages of the Magnoti, caused their baggage to be brought into an old woman's house, whilst they baited themselves, and their horses. But soon after their hostess fell bitterly a weeping. The strangers surprised at it, began to enquire the reason. Then one of them answering for her, said, That perhaps it was because the sight of other countrymen put her in mind of the miserable estate of the Magnoti were reduced unto. But she made them this short reply, and told them it was false; her weeping was because her son was not at home to rob them of their baggage.

1738 Lord Sandwich

A Western Champion of the Maniotes

All this part of the country is at present inhabited by the descendants of the ancient Lacedaemonians, who still present their love of liberty to so great a degree as never to have debased themselves under the yoke of the Turkish empire; but flying to the mountains, which are almost inaccessible, live in open defiance of that great power, which has found means to enslave all the rest of Greece. They are a people very little given to cultivating their lands, employing their women in that sort of work, and following themselves their own diversions, the chief of which is shooting; and that indeed is a manner which maintains them; and besides what serves for their sustenance, they have a very considerable commerce for pickled quails, which they send up in great quantities to Constantinople. They never stir out unarmed, and constantly wear an iron helmet on their heads; this serves them both as a defence against an enemy and the violent heat of the sun, which, reflecting from the barren rocks, would be otherwise unsupportable. Their poverty makes them guilty of a vice, which probably, were they in a more flourishing condition, they would abhor. They are extremely given to thieving, though they seldom murder but upon an absolute necessity; abstracting this, they are a very tolerable people, and which the more refined part of the world is destitute.

1746 Lord Charlemont

Profitable Tax-Paying

The external, or more northern and inland Maina, which borders upon the Turkish settlements, has also in effect retained its freedom. The people of this district, after having for a long space bravely defended themselves against the Turks, slaughtered a multitude of their invaders, and defeated them in every conflict, wearied with continual war, and desirous of an intercourse of trade with their neighbours, were at length induced to treat with the Turks, and to promise the payment of a certain annual tribute, extremely trifling according to the original stipulation, and which is now become just what they think proper. But the principal and most remarkable article of this treaty is that it is thereby stipulated that no Turk shall ever dwell among them, that the tribute shall not be imposed or allotted by Turkish authority, nor collected by Turkish officers, but that they themselves shall levy the tax according to their own pleasure, and marching out of their country in armed bodies shall deposit the tribute in the hands of the neighbouring Agas. This ceremony they annually perform, and many of the Turks have assured me that it would be much better for them if the Maniotes paid no tribute at all, for these formidable paymasters, in their route through the country, and in their way home, rob and steal to such an amount that they do much more than repay themselves, making no sort of scruple to carry home with them, unpaid for, whatever cattle they can meet with, and whatever else may chance to fall in their way.

1795 John Morritt

The State of the Mani

The government of the Maina at the time I visited it, resembled in many respects the ancient establishment of the Highland clans in Scotland. It was divided into smaller or larger districts, over each of which a chief, or Capitano, presided, whose usual residence was a fortified tower, the resort of his family and clan in times of peace, and their refuge in war. The district they governed belonged to their retainers, who each contributed a portion (I think, a tenth) of the produce of his land to the maintenance of the family under whom he held. Each chief, besides this, had his own domain, which was cultivated by his servants and slaves, and which was never very considerable. They were perfectly independent of each other; the judges of their people at home, and their leaders when they took the field. The most powerful Capitano of the district usually assumed the title of Bey of the Maina, and in that name transacted their business with the Turks, negotiated their treaties, or directed their arms against the common enemy. In the country itself his power rested merely on the voluntary obedience of the other chiefs, and his jurisdiction extended in fact only over his own immediate dependants. The Turkish court, to preserve at least a shadow of power over this refractory community, generally confirmed by a firman the appointment of the Bey, whose own power or influence enabled him to support the title. The population of the Maina is so great in proportion to its fertility, that they are obliged to import many of the common necessaries of life. For these they must occasionally trade with the Turkish provinces, and exchange their own oil and silk and domestic manufactures for the more essential articles of wheat and maize, and provisions. To obtain these, they had recourse sometimes to smuggling, and sometimes to a regular payment of the Charatch, and acknowledgment of the supremacy of the Porte. This they again threw off, when a favourable year, or any extraordinary sources of supply rendered their submission unnecessary; and by such rebellion had more than once drawn upon them the vengeance of their powerful neighbour. The contest had been repeatedly renewed, and as often the Turks had been repulsed or had fallen victims to the determined resistance of the Mainiots, and the inaccessible nature of their country.

The coast, indented with small creeks, containing the row-boats used universally in piratical excursions, is every where surrounded by rocks and exposed to winds which render it unsafe for transports and ships of burden. On the arrival of an enemy, their villages and towers along the shore were deserted, and the people retired to the mountains, the steep ridges of Taygetus, that rise from the shore, where other villages and securer valleys afforded them a temporary shelter from the storm of invasion. Should a body of troops be landed, and wreak their vengeance on the deserted habitations, the first rising gale cuts them off from all hopes of assistance from their fleet. A hardy people, well acquainted with every path of their native mountains, armed to a man with excellent rifles, dispersing easily by day, and assembling as easily every night, would distress them every hour they stayed, and harrass them at every step, if they advanced. The very women, well acquainted with the use of arms, have more than once poured ruin from the walls of some strong-built tower, or well situated village, on the assailants, from whom they had nothing to expect but slaughter or captivity, if conquered. The country admits not of the conveyance of artillery, and their towers, ill calculated as they may seem for the improved warfare of more polished nations, offered a powerful means of resistance against the efforts of the Turks, and had more than once materially delayed their progress.

Should the Turks attack them by land, their frontier to the north is still more impenetrable. The loftiest and most inaccessible rocks, and the highest summits of Taygetus occupy the whole line, leaving only two roads that are shut in by the mountain on one side, and the sea on the other. The passes of the interior part or the country are known only to the natives, and to penetrate along the coast, while the Mainiots are in possession of the mountains, would require courage and discipline very superior to such as are generally displayed by the Turkish soldiery. In the war conducted by Lambro, with Russian money, the Mainiots were found so troublesome to the Turks, that a combined attack was made upon their country by the fleet under the Capoudan Pasha, which landed troops upon their coast, and the forces of the Morea, which marched at the same time from Misitra. The number of these two armies, probably exaggerated, was rated by the Mainiots at 20,000 men. The result of the attack by sea was pointed out to me near Cardamyle; a heap of whitening bones in a dell near the town, the remains of the Turks, who, after suffering the severest privations, were not so fortunate as the rest in finding a refuge in their fleet. The attack by land was equally disastrous. After a fruitless attempt to advance, and burning a few inconsiderable villages, their army was obliged to retire, harassed by the fury of the people, while another party of the Mainiots burst into the plain of the Eurotas, drove off whatever they could plunder, and in the flames of Misitra, a considerable Turkish town, expiated the trifling mischief they had sustained at home. .

Such are the stories at least which I heard repeated by their chiefs, and which the common people no less delighted to tell. Though easily united, when threatened by the Turk, yet frequent feuds, and party warfare, too often arose between their chiefs at home; these feuds, however, preserved alive the martial spirit of the people, and they were, perhaps, on this account more successful in their resistance than they would have been if their government was more settled, and they had enjoyed a more uninterrupted peace. By sea their warfare was still more inextinguishable. They infested with their row-boats every corner of the Cyclades and Morea, and made a lawful prize of any vessel that was too weak for resistance; or entered by night into the villages and dwellings near the shore, carrying off whatever they could find. Boats of this sort, called here *trattas*, abounded in every creek; they are long and narrow like canoes; ten, twenty, and even thirty men, each armed with a rifle and pistols, row them with great celerity, and small masts with Latine sails are also used when the winds are favourable. Every chief had one or more of these, and all exercised piracy as freely, and with the same sentiments, as appear to have prevailed among the heroes of the Odyssey and early inhabitants of Greece...

The Hospitality of a Maniote Chieftain

We remained great part of the day at Cardamyla in compliance with the wishes of our host and of his neighbours, and partook of the amusements on the green. After dining with him and his family, he attended us in his boat, the inland road being scarcely passable from the stony rugged hills that it surmounts. We viewed the situation of Leuctra, a small hamlet on the shore still retaining its ancient name, but found there few and inconsiderable traces of antiquity. About two miles and a half from hence we came to the little creek of Platsa, shut in by the rock of Pephnos, near which was a tower; the residence of the Capitano Christeia, a chief to whom we were recommended.

We had sent our letters to this chief by a messenger from Cardamyla, in consequence of which he met us at the port on our landing, attended by a large train of followers. We took leave of our friends of Cardamyla; who paid us a compliment at parting, not unusual in this country, by firing all their rifles over our heads. As this was not very carefully or regularly performed, and the pieces were always loaded with ball, the ceremony was not altogether agreeable…

We walked from the shore with our host to his castle; Capitano Christeia, the owner of it, was one of the most powerful and at the same time the most active and turbulent chieftain in this district. He had paid the price of the renown he had acquired, for he bore the marks of three bullets in the breast; the scars of two more upon his face, besides slighter wounds in his legs and arms: in fact his life was a constant scene of piracy by sea and feuds at home. He was about forty-five years of age, and showed us with much satisfaction the spoil he had amassed in his expeditions. He was friendly and hospitable to us, and lively and intelligent in his conversation. He had recently captured at sea a small French merchant ship, and related with just indignation the following trait of the captain who commanded it. After seizing on the men, money, and merchandize, which the vessel contained, he told the captain he would land him on the shore of the Morea, and offered him at his request any favour he might ask, out of the prize. The captain, regardless of the freedom of his men, or the property consigned to him, solicited only an enamelled snuff-box, with a lady's hair on the outside, and a very indecent design within the lid. Christeia, who, though a pirate, was enraged at his unmanly and heartless levity, retracted his offer, and left the captain with only a shirt and a pair of trousers in the boat, to shift, for himself. He set the crew on shore, and brought his prize to Platsa, where he showed us the snuff-box with great satisfaction. He had also been engaged the year before we were there in hostilities with a neighbouring chief, and had taken the field with a company of eighty men, and thirty women, of whom his sister had the command. A peace had been since made after several skirmishes, but not until some of his Amazons had fallen, and his sister had been wounded as well as himself. In the tower to which we were shown, we lived in a neat and comfortable room, but the walls were thick and strong, the windows barricaded with iron bars, and barrels of gunpowder were arranged along the shelves below the ceiling. The men who attended in the castle had an air of military service, and the whole place bore in its appearance the character of the master.

1804-06 Colonel William Leake

The Fighting Priests of Mani

An affair, which happened two months since at Vathy, shows the state of society in Mani. The son of a priest had by accident killed a boy, a relation of another priest. The latter papas declared war against the former, which is done in Mani in a formal manner, by crying out in the streets. The first papas went to his church to say mass with pistols in his girdle; such being a common custom in Mani; but, as is usual in such cases, he laid them behind the altar, on assuming the robe in which the priest performs divine service. The other papas entered the church with some of his party, and the instant the office was concluded, walked up to his enemy, who was still in his robes, and fired a pistol at him, which flashed in the pan: the latter, then running behind the altar, seized his arms, shot his enemy and one of his adherents, and drove all the rest out of the church. The affair was then settled by the interposition of the bey himself, in whose village it had happened. A composition in money, for the balance of blood, is the only efficient mode of making peace in these cases. When one of a family is slain, the person who takes upon him to revenge the injury often vows not to change his clothes or shave or eat meat till his revenge is satisfied.

Next to the captains, the priests are the chief men in the Maniate wars, both in council and field; and in the quarrels which so frequently occur between separate villages or families, they are generally the promoters and leaders of the strife. To pull down the adversary's house is generally the object and end of the war. The sufferer is then conquered, and seldom ventures to prosecute hostilities.

A Maniate cannot fire without resting his musket, on account of its length, but he is an excellent marksman in his own manner. The Albanians are the same, and for this reason they cannot easily be disciplined without a change in their arms. Like the Albanians, the Maniates seldom venture to face their enemy in the field, but fire from behind houses, rocks, and trees. This must, in fact, be the case wherever no discipline exists, as no individual can depend upon the conduct of his neighbour; in short, their preference of a musket which has a long range, and their mode of fighting, are the reciprocating effect and cause of their state of society. The Maniates seem to be more addicted to assassination than the Albanians, though in Albania almost any mode of getting rid of an enemy is thought justifiable. The Maniates, however, show great courage and obstinacy in their own way; and these qualities are held in the highest estimation among them. Even the women emulate the men in this respect. It is not long since a woman of Mount Taygetum stood a siege in her pyrgo, against a body of Turks; she fired upon them from the windows, and kept them employed on one side, while, at the back, she sent away in safety a female servant with two children. Though her ammunition was in reality all spent...

Maniote Vendettas

Chronic violence, in the Mani, was directed as much against each other as against outsiders.

At 1.20 I arrive at Skutari, and lodge in the pyrgo of Katzano, for whom the Bey has supplied me with a recommendatory letter. He is a man of a plain modest manner, civil, and perfectly ready to answer any questions about his country, a readiness indeed which I have observed among all the Maniates with whom I have conversed. A greater share of candour and veracity is a natural consequence of their independence, rendering falsehood and dissimulation less necessary than they are to the other Greeks, who have no other arms of defence against their oppressors. The pyrgo, garrisoned at present by fifteen soldiers, whom Katzano keeps in pay, is constructed in the usual Maniate fashion. The lower story is occupied by the garrison, the upper consists of two rooms, or rather of one long room, divided by a slight wooden partition; at one end is the fireplace and the kitchen furniture, at the other a mattress for a sofa. Mattresses and blankets are piled up in one corner of the room; all the rest of the family furniture is hung about the walls, or stowed away in wooden boxes, ranged around; the floor consists of loose boards, and, never undergoing ablution, harbours myriads of fleas in winter, and bugs in summer. Katzano has twenty-five persons in his family, of whom nine are his children; he married at the age of nineteen, his wife was fourteen; they have had fifteen children.

The hills around Skutari are cultivated in little terraces covered with wheat and barley, the latter of which is now in ear. The town is full of the ruins of Pyrghi, which have been destroyed in the Maniate wars; one belonging to the Cavaliere was ruined by the artillery of Hussein, the Capitan Pasha. In the course of conversation, Katzano informs me that formerly all the Gligoraki family lived at Skutari, but that John and Antony, alias Zanim and Andon, the heads of the two houses falling out, and all the branches taking part with one side or the other, a dispersion ensued, and Katzano, with his brother Tzingurio, are now the only two of the name in Skutari. Here, as in Khimara, which enjoys nearly the same degree of independence as Mani, the most ordinary state of hostility between two families, is that of non-intercourse and mutual observation, without any overt act. While the two branches of the Gligorakis were living here in that state, Katzano being then young, he, with his brother and another were sitting on the outside of a house, when thirteen of the opposite party passed by. Katzano and his friends saluted them; the others returned the salute in an offensive manner, or such at least as Katzano and his friends, who had been drinking, thought proper to interpret as such, and who, without another word, rose and fired upon their opponents. The fire was returned, and both the brothers were dangerously wounded. Andon then sallied out of his house with a band of followers, seized eleven of the enemy, and shut them up in a pyrgo, until his nephew's wounds were healed, intending to have had blood for blood if they had died.

Many of the Maniate women value themselves on their skill with the musket. Katzano's wife said to me, (as I was inquiring on this subject,) pointing to a place about 150 yards distant, "set up your hat there, and see if I cannot put a musket ball through it." I had too much regard for my only hat to trust her, for she has had two wounds in battle, and affects to consider her husband as no braver than he should be. Lambro, a son-in-law of Lambro, the bey's nephew, arrives at Skutari in the evening, with a train of friends, to request the interference of Katzano on the following occasion. Lambro lives at the Katjaunianika, the place which I passed through near the Castle of Passava. A Kakavuliote, whose brother had been killed by Lambro, thwarted in all his attempts to revenge himself like a man of honour, that is to say, by murdering Lambro, and perhaps rather fearful even of success, on account of Lambro's connection with the government, resolved at least to have the satisfaction of making depredations on his property. This day, in sight of Lambro and his friends, who even fired at the Kakavuliote without effect, he stole a mare belonging to Lambro, and rode off with her. The object of the embassy was to request Katzano's interference to have the mare restored, and to prevent hostilities, and there seems every reason to believe it will be effected. This shows the good effect of the influence and authority which the Captain Pasha has lately obtained over Mani, as enabling the inferiors in command to check the lawless system of retaliation which in their present uneducated state is the consequence of the independence of this people; and it leads me to believe, that the best thing that could happen to the Greeks would be for the Turks in every part of the country to have a similar authority, in such a manner that the Greeks, governing themselves in that sort of municipal form natural to this country, should at the same time be under a control sufficient to save them from the pernicious effects of the spirit of party, to which their character, arising from the same natural causes, irresistibly impels them. If the pashas and other officers in command could maintain discipline among their troops when out of their sight, such a system might be possible in the islands, and perhaps even throughout the Morea; but I fear that Turkish anarchy, bigotry, greediness of gain, and cruelty, render it impracticable.

Maniote Piety

I am informed by Katzano, that beyond the hill which terminates in Cape Stavri, (so the promontory is called, which bounds the bay of Skutari on the south, as Kremidhara does on the north,) there are some ruins called Skopa or Skopopoli, about two hours distant from hence; they are in the district of Vatas, and near the sea, and consist of arched brick fabrics, like those of Hypsus, but not so well preserved. They are probably the remains of Teuthrone. My host adds, with a grave face, and his assertion is confirmed by all around, that the sound of persons tossing over heaps of gold is sometimes to be heard there.

No people are more rigorous in the observances of the Greek Church than the Maniates. A Kakavuliote, who would make a merit of hiding himself behind the wall of a ruined chapel, for the purpose of avenging the loss of a relative upon some member of the offending family, would think it a crime to pass the same ruin, be it ever so small a relict of the original building, without crossing himself seven, or at least three, times.

A Priest With a Past

Having descended from Alika into the bed of a torrent, we enter, at 4.20, the fences of Kyparisso, once a considerable village, but now reduced to one pyrgo, a chapel, and a house for the priest. My companion of the Gligoraki family says, that his ancestors, as well as those of the Mavromikhali, came originally from hence. The old priest, whose only costume is a jacket with a pair of wide trousers of coarse blanketing of Maniate manufacture, receives me with an air of cheerfulness and hospitality; from a consciousness, perhaps, that he has nothing to give us, and that he is more likely to be entertained at our expense, than we at his. His house, which adjoins the church, offers, indeed, little hope of supply to the traveller. He points, however, without hesitation, to the only fowl he possesses, as he desires us to "take off its head", imitating the action of a pasha ordering an execution. He makes no difficulty in telling me his history; he is a Cretan, his monastic name Macarius. After having passed several years as a kaloiero at Mount Sinai, which he says is infinitely worse than Kakavulla, he was sent into Egypt to collect charity for the convent. The temptation was too great; instead of returning with the money into the desert, he came to hide himself in Mani, and has now, for thirty years, been officiating as the priest of Kyparisso. He hopes to obtain pardon, he says, by his daily prayers, for the crime he has committed, and shows me a sepulchre which he has built for himself behind the church.

Salad, and an Accusation of Murder, at a Monastery

At 11.54, leaving the Kyparsso road to the left, we proceed along the summit of the Isthmus, and then, winding round the side of the mountain which overhangs Porto Kaio, arrive, at 12.27, at the monastery called the Virgin of Porto Kaio, which furnishes by far the most agreeable lodging I have met with in Mani. On the eastern side a spring issues from the side of the hill, and falls over several terraces of garden ground on the side of the mountain, which are grown with olives, caroubs, and cypresses, mixed with a few orange-trees. The garden furnishes me with a salad for dinner, and the stores of the convent some of the choicest Maniate honey - my companions, meantime, regaling upon bean-soup and salted olives. During their repast an old man incessantly accuses Gika Mavromikhali of having killed his brother, or, at least, of being of the family of the murderer. Gika admits the latter, but urges in defence that the deed was done in an honourable way, in the course of a war between the two houses. Only sixteen days ago, Gika tells me, he destroyed a pyrgo of one of his enemies in his own village of Tzimova.

A Healthy Poverty

The misery of these Kakavuliotes is extreme. To the inquiries of my servants for the commonest articles of provisions, the answer constantly is, "where are we to find oil, or vinegar, or wine, or bread?" as if such things were luxuries in which they never indulged. The scarcity at present is undoubtedly very pressing in consequence of the insufficient harvest of last year; and to these occasional dearths, perhaps, may be chiefly ascribed the habitual penury and avarice of the people. But my Tzimova companions say, that even when the Kakavuliotes had numerous pirate boats and trattas in the Archipelago, and brought home a great deal of plunder, they still continued to live in the same miserable manner. The chief instrument of household furniture is the handmill, in which the kalambokki is ground. This is the employment of the women at night, who generally accompany the work with a song in lamentation of some

137

deceased relation who has been killed perhaps by a hostile house; and it is their custom to continue these songs during the whole period of mourning, and the men let their beards grow on the same occasions...

Except on the great feasts, none but the richest of the Kakavuliotes kill mutton or poultry: an old ox no longer fit for the plough, or a sheep or fowl already at the point of death, they sometimes indulge in. Cheese, garlic, and bread of maize, are the principal food; wine and oil, as their district produces none, they seldom use. A boy even of fifteen has a wrinkled, weather-worn appearance; but diseases are rare, they live to a great age, and their chief evil is a population disproportioned to the natural resources of the country. In soil and aspect, it resembles many of the islands, such as Kefalonfa, Tzerigo, Naxia, Zia, etc. where, as in Mani, all the productions, though excellent of the kind, are seldom plentiful. My companions, however, who are some of the first characters on the western coast, do not complain: on the contrary, they boast of the sweetness of their mutton, that they send corn, in good years, to Cerigo, that they occasionally supply the Morea with cattle, and that when the seasons favour them, they want nothing from abroad but wine and cheese.

The Loss of a Pistol

Proceed at 11, leaving Atza above us on the right; pass, at 11.25, through Paleokhora, and then falling again into the road by which we came, at 2.20 we arrive at Tzimova. Thus terminates my journey in the land of Evil Counsel, without accident or any loss, except that of a double-barrelled pistol, which was stolen out of my holster on the 12th, at the hut near Kavo Grosso, perhaps by one of my companions, for they made a most suspicious show of halting to search for it at the same place on our return. At Tzimova I am again received into the house, or rather cottage, of Gika Mavromikhali, who, to make room for me, sends all his females into the pyrgo. At night fifty sheep and twelve oxen are driven into the yard of the cottage. The Maniates are seldom in such a state of security as to leave their cattle abroad in the fields at night.

An Unfortunate French "Quack"

Not many years ago a Frenchman came to Tzimova, flying probably from justice; he set up for a physician, and resided here several years. He could cure those who believed in him, by giving them a pinch out of his snuff box, and at length obtained such credit among the Maniotes as to predict futurity. But he did not foresee his own fate. Some Kakavuliotes lay in wait for him, as he was returning one day from Koroni by sea, and murdered him, by which they gained only a few piastres.

The Towers of Mani

Each person of power and every head of a family of any influence has a pyrgo, which is used almost solely as a tower of defence: the ordinary habitation stands at the foot of it. The Bey' relations and a few of the kapitani maintain some soldiers in their towers, but in general these buildings are uninhabited, except in time of alarm. To overturn the pyrgo of the enemy and to slaughter as many of his relations as possible, are the objects of every war. The tower has loopholes in the different stories and battlements at top, and he that can get a rusty swivel to plant upon them is not easily subdued. Most of the ordinary dwellings are built with loopholes in the walls; nor are the villages, in which there is no inhabitant of sufficient opulence to build a pyrgo, the more peaceable on that account, but quarrel either among themselves or with their neighbours, and endeavour to overturn one another's houses just like their betters. Every pyrgo has a cistern, which has an arched covering of stone, with a little wooden door kept constantly locked. The villages, also, in general, have cisterns in or near them. The cactus is very commonly grown round the villages for the sake of the fruit, and these with a few figs, and grapes, and some of the commonest esculent vegetables, are the only horticultural productions of Mani.

c.1830 Alphonse de Lamartine

A Hermit Suspended between the Sea and Sky

The hermit of the Cape was a familiar sight to mariners rounding the stormy cape for so many years (centuries) that there must have been a succession of them.

The breeze is mild, and wafts us towards the cape [Malea]. The frigate, which has us in tow, hollows out ahead of us a level and murmuring path, along which we glide in her wake, amidst the wreaths of foam which her keel dashes up on its flight. Captain Lyons, who knows the coast, wishes to let us enjoy the view of the cape and the country, by passing not more than a hundred fathoms from the shore.

At the extremity of Cape St. Angelo, or Malia, which advances considerably into the sea, that narrow passage commences which timid mariners avoid by leaving the island of Cerigo on their left. This cape is the cape of tempests for Greek sailors. The pirates alone show head to it, because they know they will not be followed thither. The wind descends from this cape with such weight and impetuosity on the sea, that it often hurls rolling stones from the mountain upon the decks of vessels.

On the steep and inaccessible declivity of the rock, that forms the headland of the cape, sharpened by hurricanes and by the lashing of the spray, accident suspended three rocks detached from the summit, and arrested half way in their fall. There they remain, like a nest of sea-fowl bending over the foaming abyss of the waters. A quantity of reddish earth, also stopped in its fall by these three unequal rocks, gives root to five or six stunted fig-trees, which themselves hang with, their tortuous branches, and their large grey leaves, over the roaring gulf that whirls at their feet. The eye can not discern any footpath, any practicable declivity, by which this little mound of vegetation could be reached. However, a small low dwelling can be distinguished among the fig-trees - a house of a grey, sombre appearance, like the rock which serves for its base, and with which one confounds it on the first view. Over the flat roof of the house there rises a small open belfry, as over the door of convents in Italy: a bell is suspended from it. To the right are to be seen some ancient ruins of foundations of red bricks; in which there are three open arcades leading to a little terrace that stretches in front of the house. An eagle would have feared to build his eyrie in such a place, without a single bush or trunk of a tree to shelter him from the wind which roars continually, from the eternal noise of the sea breaking, and of the spray licking incessantly the polished rock, under a sky always burning. Well! a man has done what the bird itself would scarcely have dared to do; he has chosen this asylum. He lives there; we perceived him - he is a hermit. We doubled the cape so closely that we could distinguish his long white beard, his staff, his chaplet, his hood of brown felt, like that of sailors in winter. He went on his knees as we passed, with his face turned towards the sea, as if he were imploring the succour of heaven for the unknown strangers on this perilous passage. The wind, which issues furiously from the mountain-gorges of Laconia, as soon as you double the rock of the cape, began to resound in our sails, and make the two vessels roll and stagger, covering the sea with foam as far as the eye could reach. A new sea was opening before us. The hermit, in order to follow us still farther with his eyes, ascended the crest of a rock, and we distinguished him there, on his knees and motionless, as long as we were in sight of the cape.

What is this man? He must have a soul trebly steeped in woe, to have chosen this frightful abode; he must have a heart and senses eager for strong and eternal emotions, to live in this vulture's nest, alone, with the boundless horizon, the hurricane, and the roar of the sea. His only spectacle is, from time to time, a passing ship, the creaking of the masts, the tearing of the sails, the cannon of distress, the cries of sailors in their agony.

1839 Lord Carnarvon

A State of Nature

This thoughtful passage by the younger Lord Carnarvon on the "Journals" of his father provides some reflections on the strange state of society in the Mani.

It is not unusual for a speaker to observe with reference to particular states or times that there is neither law nor government when he only means to intimate that the administration of the day is powerless, and that justice is overborne by the accidents of the particular time, or that its provisions, at least, are dealt out with uncertainty. But the Maina, down to the close of the Greek Revolution, presented the remarkable spectacle of a country where law, as law, was unknown. The right of the strongest, tempered by the observance of certain chivalrous customs, growing out of their warlike habits, and respected for the sake of general convenience, was the only acknowledged law in the Maina. The great rule, "Thou shalt not kill," issued to man in the origin of his race and confirmed by the legislation of every time and country, had scarcely here an existence. It is, perhaps, hardly in excess of fact to say that murder was the organised and formulated expression of the national life. But although the murderer had no cause of apprehension from the arm of the law, he enjoyed a very qualified impunity. The vengeance of the injured family was not only wreaked upon him, but was extended through a long course of years to every kinsman of the hated race down to the last link in the long chain of successive generations. The only occupation considered worthy of a man was that of taking his brother's life, and such was the general distrust engendered by this strange state of society, that men were only safe when shut up – sometimes for many years together – within fortified towers, of which one of their principal towns was but an agglomeration.

Yet in this condition of affairs, when every man's hand was against his neighbour, and when society must have been utterly paralysed for every good and useful purpose of public and even of private life, there was, strange to say, in the Mainote microcosm an element of strength which enabled them to combine against foreign aggression, to maintain the limits of their barren but beloved country, and to secure fair terms from their Mahomedan master even in the height of his power. Uniting qualities at first sight perhaps opposed, joining an unbounded patriotism to an utter contempt for that security of person and property in which more civilised countries find at once their greatest strength and their greatest weakness, ready to pour forth their blood like water to preserve their national individuality, they presented a picture of engrossing interest to the writer of these Journals, whose early life had been coloured by unusually romantic incidents, and in whom the more tranquil course of English duties and domestic occupations had never extinguished the love of wild travel and adventure. "When a regular government," he observes, in one part of these MSS., "was first established in Greece at the close of the great struggle against the Turks, the Maina was not exempted from the operation of general laws; but their promulgation was little heeded by those hardy mountaineers, and when the central authority attempted to enforce them, it was met by a spirit of resistance before which the dogged and unelastic temper of the Bavarians quailed. The Regency, naturally solicitous to terminate a system of domestic hostilities utterly incompatible with the requirements of a settled government, but too stupid to effect their object by the only means which offered a prospect of success, incensed the pride of the chiefs by requiring them not only to abstain from those predatory wars in which they had indulged for centuries, but to throw down their battlements as a mark of subjection to the Crown, and as a guarantee for the future preservation of peace; - to this insulting proposal the chiefs gave the reply which could be anticipated from a people who had never yet tolerated any interference with their internal regulations. Animated by one simultaneous feeling, the Mainotes sprang to arms, to enforce compliance, a large force was sent into the Maina by the Government. It soon met with a severe reverse, and was obliged to capitulate under circumstances of some discredit – the majority of the soldiers owing their lives only to the contempt of their enemies, who sold them, naked and shivering, in the public market at the low price of twopence a-head, From this degrading position they, or many of them, were released by some friends of the Government, who bought them back at the cost of an additional penny a-piece, to the great dishonour of the recently-established Court, and amidst the jeers of a people who despised them too heartily to be much incensed. Yet those Bavarian soldiers, so sacrificed, were brave men placed in a ridiculous position by an incapable minister.

"Since that catastrophe the Government, led to adopt a more prudent policy by their fears rather than their judgment, abandoned all intention of subjugating the Maina by force, and whilst they endeavoured to conciliate the chiefs by appointing them to official posts, or undermined their influence by removing them from the natural sphere of their authority, they proclaimed to the people an absolute immunity from the taxation which was prescribed for other parts of Greece, but which they did not dare to impose on the Maina. By such means the Government, no doubt, gradually paved the way for the extinction of the civil feuds of the Maina, and the establishment of their authority in that remote part of the kingdom.

Still calm and tempest succeeded each other in frequent alternation, and every now and then there arrived at Athens the unwelcome intelligence that in consequence of some collision with the King's officers on the frontier, the Mainotes had burst from their mountains and were plundering the towns of the plain below. I believe there was not a name in Greece so hateful to official ears as that of the Maina; there was not a recollection so distasteful to official pride as that of the memorable sale of the King's troops."

It was not unnatural that it should be so; for the Mainotes system was not only at variance with the first principles of settled government, but, with the exception of the Corsican vendetta, which though less in degree was analogous in kind, and was suppressed by the French Government only within very recent times, it was one of the most extraordinary that ever existed in any age or country. A Mainote noble, if he did not inherit, would build himself a tower – sometimes, it might be, with the money which he had amassed by hard toil beyond the limits of his own country. When once the tower was built, his relatives flocked to him, and erected their own dwellings under the shelter of his castle. These were his kindred, and bore his name. But others also trooped in, unconnected with him by family ties, and these became his vassals, and gave him their allegiance in return for his protection. Thus the whole clan was consolidated and bound as one family to support the lord in all his feuds, without regard to the justice or injustice of the quarrel; and an insult or wrong offered to any member of that clan, entailed on the wrongdoer a common feud. Jealousy, a quarrel upon some delicate point of honour, a supposed slight offered to a woman, the carrying off a betrothed, were frequent and deadly causes of animosity. In one instance, some malicious women, anxious to promote strife, under the cover of night, seem to have knocked at the doors of certain houses, calling each other by the names of young men, so as to give the notion of an improper familiarity with the daughters of the house, and thus kindled a long-enduring feud.

But when once the feud was declared, the mode of its prosecution was as ruthless as it was characteristic of this strange people. The hostile families rarely engaged in open combat. It was a long trial of patience and skill, to determine which of the two parties should exterminate the other. Going forth singly or in pairs, they hid themselves among bushes or behind walls, and, patient of hunger, thirst, and weather, they lay in wait for days together to shoot any member of the rival clan who might pass by. Their towers, some of which were of great strength, were guarded night and day by two men, who paced the battlements, both to prevent a surprise, and to destroy any enemy who might walk within musket shot. Women and girls, indeed, they were content to spare, but boys of more than eight years old were doomed, as at that age they were considered capable of bearing arms.

To such an extent did this prevail, that men, when deeply involved in these family feuds, retired to the shelter of their castles, and for years never ventured forth, except when perhaps at night and by stealth they went out to murder an enemy, or to undermine his tower. Men have been born and married, have lived for twenty or thirty years, and in some cases have even spent their whole lives within the enclosure of those gloomy walls. "I was informed," it is said in one part of these Journals, "of one man who was born in his tower, and lived to the age of seventy without daring to quit it. When questioning a man at Cape Matapan, on some point of local interest, which could not have escaped the notice of anyone of common observation, I was surprised by his asking me in reply how he should know anything of the country, when almost all his life he had been shut up in a tower?" So again: "A fine young Mainote, of good family, once regretted to me, that he was unfit for everything but fighting. 'I am,' he said, 'not twenty-seven, and for more than twenty years of my life I was shut up in a tower; never leaving it but a very few times in the dead of night, for the purpose of stealing along the ground and shooting an enemy.' He had been speaking of the success of some friends or acquaintances in certain agricultural and commercial undertakings out of the Maina, where he had become painfully sensible of his own deficiencies.

During the continuance of these feuds, which, with the intervals of an occasional truce, often endured for generations, the women were allowed to go free and unmolested, to carry on their domestic avocations, to cultivate the ground, though at times the hostile party would come down upon the fields and carry off the harvest, and even to convey food to their husbands, who were shut up in their towers. Nor was the part which they took in these merciless quarrels always of this neutral character. They would sometimes walk in front, and their husbands would skulk behind them, until the men, unseen themselves, came within gunshot of their enemy, and levelled their deadly aim.

And yet this detestable system of war was not only accompanied by extraordinary patience and courage, worthy of a better cause, but it was redeemed by some great though rude virtues. The Mainote never attacked a woman. In the fiercest wars, no shot from tower or ambuscade seems to have been directed against her. Even when she served as a screen to her husband, the assailed party is said never to have returned the fire upon her. Nor less sacred was the virtue of hospitality. Poor themselves, and barely deriving a subsistence from their rugged soil, they would accept any privation or make any sacrifice for the humblest stranger who might claim their assistance. "Any stranger," says the writer of these *Journals*, "who places himself upon a bench in the church, which is understood to indicate that he is friendless, is immediately received by some chief, and tended with every care during his stay in the country; and anyone who should dare to inflict wrong or insult upon him while enjoying such protection, would call down upon himself the full vengeance of the clan." I have found in these MSS, the story of a stranger travelling in the Maina, and lodging at the house of a poor Mainote, who, having nothing to give him, with all the unselfishness of the poor man in the scriptural parable, and all the chivalry of the lover in Boccaccio's inimitable story of the falcon, sacrificed for his guest's supper his mule – the one thing on which he depended on for his own daily sustenance and support. It is impossible to conceive the higher exercise of a virtue, which has now little more than a conventional existence in many civilized countries.

But if their virtues were great, their vices were equally great. "Human life" – I resume my quotation – "is with them of no account, and the murder of an enemy, slain in what we consider the foulest manner, occasions not a moment's remorse. Yet they are scrupulous according to their notions of right and wrong. A breach of hospitality is a deadly sin; a violation of chastity is a lasting dishonour, and an offence for which no punishment is too great; for truth they have frequently a severe respect, and on points of religious form they are extremely punctilious. I was eating some fowl in one of their rude dwellings on a Friday. "I would not do that for all that the world could give me," said a young Mainote chief, who had been much with me, and whose hands were red with a hundred murders. "But," observed my muleteer, with the freedom so common in these countries, "you would think nothing of killing a man." "Oh, no,' replied my Mainote friend, "but eating meat on a Friday is a crime."

Signs and Portents

The legends of that wild country were coloured by the usages of this ruthless warfare. Thus there are fantastic tales in which the ghost appears to the murderer, not as in our colder latitudes to upbraid, reproach, and drive to madness by means of an accusing conscience, but to stimulate to fresh acts of vengeance. "Why should we care for the ghost of an enemy ?" said, on one occasion, a Mainote soldier, and in this expression spoke the true spirit of the Maina. Even religion was sometimes made to lend its countenance to these merciless acts; and the popular superstitions, more powerful than religion itself, came in to consecrate the practice of their daily warfare. If, in the voice of any friend, a moaning or melancholy sound were detected, it was held to be the sign of his approaching death. Yet not always necessarily so. The omen might be averted if three women were to work for him a scarf or shirt with the sign of the holy Cross upon it; but the workers must all be virgins of the name of Mary, the work must be completed in a single day, and that day one on which mass was said by a priest. Again, these superstitions admitted of fine distinctions. If, in the prosecution of his stealthy warfare, a man heard a moaning sound in front of him, it augured success; but if the sound came from behind, it was of evil presage, and he who heard it should instantly return. So, too, if two men went out together upon a common expedition, and one of them could not hear the tread of his enemy, whilst the other heard it, he was from that moment a lost man. "One night," says the writer of these *Journals*, "my Mainote friend told me how, when lying in ambush, he heard overhead a heavenly sound of cymbals. He accepted the sound as a favourable omen; immediately his enemy passed, and he laid him low. The shoes that men wore on these midnight expeditions were made of pigskin, to enable their wearers to tread lightly; for a practised ear could distinguish the step of an enemy, sometimes half a mile off. A man who was not at feud stepped boldly; but one who was at enmity with his neighbour, had a light and comparatively uncertain tread." The Bavarian officers," said my

Mainote companion, "complained of our tread when we were first drilled, it was so light and little assured; but it was the tread which necessity had taught us, and it was not easy to unlearn.'"

Vampires

But nowhere did the belief in witchcraft assume a darker and more awful character than in the superstitions once so common of the Vampire, who was supposed to rise from his grave at night to suck the blood of the living, and, when satiated with his unholy banquet, to return to his tomb with the earliest dawn of day. Greece and, I believe, Hungary may claim the honour of retaining this superstition when other nations of Europe had abandoned it. The Greek clergy even appealed to the fresh and undecomposed features of the supposed vampire in proof of the mystic and effective powers of excommunication which they claimed to exercise; and Tournefort, who travelled through the Archipelago about the beginning of the last century, describes the solemn act of unburying, impaling, and burning the body of one of these supposed monsters in the island of Mycone. I extract from the MSS. before me the following story of a Mainote vampire.

"Passing by a dreary and half-deserted village, I was shown a house to which another wild legend attached, and which was said to have been once inhabited by a shoemaker's widow. Her husband, however, though dead, had not entirely departed; for, being a vampire, he used a vampire's privilege, and bursting the bondage of the tomb, returned every night except on the Saturday to his old abode, and sometimes even worked at his old trade. At length the woman became pregnant. The villagers taxed her with infidelity to her husband's memory, and she in her own defence maintained that she was on the point of giving birth to no unlawful issue.

At this horrifying disclosure the villagers sallied forth to attack the vampire in his tomb, undertaking the enterprise on a Saturday morning, on which day alone the vampire's devil-imparted strength forsakes him, and the grave has power to hold his body. They found him working in his grave, making shoes. "How did you know that I was a vampire?" exclaimed the still living tenant of the tomb. A villager, in answer, pointed to a youth whose cheek a month before had been bright with health, but on which the ghastly paleness of disease and coming death had fixed its mark.

The vampire immediately spat at him. The moisture from those accursed lips burnt the man's capote as though it had been fire, but it could not hurt the man himself, because it was the blessed Saturday. Maddened by the failure of his attempt, the vampire imprudently cried, "Though I am nerveless now, yet you shall taste my vengeance to the full on every night save this alone." On hearing this alarming threat the neighbours fell upon him, tore him to pieces, and cut out his heart, dividing it into portions, and distributing the several parts among the villagers, commanding each one to eat his allotted fragment - and this," my narrator observed, "is the only real specific against Vampires; and since that event," he added, "no vampire had ever molested the village again, though for two months before persons had been perishing daily under their fatal influence." The Vampire was supposed to suck the blood of his victim, and during the still hours of night to dry up the springs of life. Every case of gradual decline was attributed to the unseen but malignant agency of this terrific creature of the imagination; the man worn out by real physical disease was startled from his unrefreshing sleep, fancying that he heard the heavy flap of the monster's wing, and, convinced in the growing weakness of his sinking frame, that he could count the precious drops of blood of which he had that night been drained."

The Devil's Pass

Once more we entered the wild rock scenery of the previous day, and traversed the Devil's Pass, where the muleteers maintained that belated travellers are attacked by demons. I asked what sort of demons. "Nobody knew," the muleteer replied, because no one passed after dark. "No one for his soul's salvation would venture to go through that haunted pass after sunset, and few would dare to go alone in daylight. Wild and accursed moanings might be heard – the voice of fiends who simulated the sounds of birds or wild beasts." One of our soldiers who, unlike the majority of our party, had been beyond the limits of the Maina, pretended to be incredulous, at which the muleteer was very angry, saying, "Did not Demetrius, who was dead, appear, and throw a child into a pail in the court of the great tower and drown him; and did not some one else hear the mill grinding the corn at night though no mortal hand was near to move it?" As I was always ready to hear a legend, I looked grave, as if duly weighing the arguments on either side; upon which the soldier, seeing that I did not scoff at all notion of supernatural agency, as he supposed a Frank must do, dismissed the semblance of incredulity which he affected, and no longer insensible to the marvellous tales which he had pretended to despise, himself told strange and characteristic stories of the manner in which ghosts had come to their friends to urge them to take vengeance in Mainote fashion upon some member of a rival family.

In such conversation the time was beguiled, till the picturesque towers of Kita and the green fields of cactus, which is said, when in bloom and seen from a distance, to have excited the admiration of Ibrahim Pacha, announced the end of our day's march.

The Passing of a Way of Life - and Death

...Kita, "the city of towers," was the most striking to a traveller. Its inhabitants were divided into the factions of an upper and a lower town, sometimes at feud with each other, sometimes at feud amongst themselves. For 30 years previously to 1839, the best blood of Kita had been drained in a deadly and embittered strife which arose out of an imaginary insult to a young girl whose scarf was held too long by her partner in the dance of some village festival. For thirty years the two factions exterminated each other; murder was not disguised, it was the avowed profession of every clansman and the recognised mode of warfare; death was atoned for by death even to the third and fourth generation, and men continually and systematically shot down men with whom they had never exchanged a word, only because they were hereditary enemies. Happily, there were intervals to this ruthless system, in which a breathing space was allowed. Sometimes, through the intervention of a third party, a truce was agreed to: the rival factions then exchanged knives, and the mediators immediately became the enemies of those who might violate the armistice. Occasionally, on the natural expiry of the truce, an attempt was made to appease the feud, but rarely with success. It was generally closed by the extirpation of one family, or their flight by night.

When the writer of these *Journals* passed through Kita a considerable change had already taken place, and these feuds were in abeyance, if not absolutely suppressed. But the recollection of them was still fresh, and was illustrated by a characteristic incident.

"The evening was closing in as we entered Kita, but the leader of our escort did not come out to meet us. Elias said that he was probably afraid of passing at so late an hour through a part of the town inhabited by families with whom he had once been at enmity. Whilst we paused in the street, and our mules were being unladen, Elias observed that no lights were burnt in Kita, "because, if I were an enemy," he said, "I should know where to direct my shot," and suiting the action to the word, he carelessly pointed his gun towards a window. Immediately the heavy shutter was closed with a loud noise."

The spirit of civil war is hardly yet laid in the country. Here in Kita on Sunday the service is not performed in church before daybreak as in many other places, from an apprehension of venturing beyond the house while it is still dark; and but a short distance out of the town we observed a tower, on the battlements of which we saw two individuals, standing as we had seen them stand some days previously when passing by the same spot on our way southwards to Matapan. They were the son and brother of a chief whose betrothed had about a year before been carried off by the owner of a neighbouring tower, and who had revenged the insult by shooting the offender. But this vengeance was purchased dearly. The usual retaliation followed. The chief himself escaped to Zante; but his ill-fated family, in pursuance of the usages of the country, were devoted, and neither son nor brother dared leave the tower. My informants ended by saying, that the outraged family would still find a mode of satisfying their vengeance...

Such were the inhabitants of this wild country, and there is perhaps little cause for wonder if in the fantastic superstitions of the Maina many of the qualities that they possessed were popularly attributed to some supernatural influence of their own rugged land, and that even those who desired to put the most favourable construction upon the Mainote habits, and to extenuate their evil disposition, sometimes declared that it was to be referred to the badness of the soil, and not to the natural temperament of its people. A Smyrniote merchant, it is said, who had two Mainote servants that, contrary to all expectation, served him well, resolved to test the truth of the tradition; and having sent for some Maina soil, placed it under their beds, and from a place of concealment listened to their conversation. Nor had he long to wait, for they soon arranged to murder their master and to plunder his property, and he then knew that the cause of Mainote wickedness was the badness of the Maina soil. But the Mainotes themselves had all the passionate love for their own country that belongs to free mountaineers. They dreaded to leave the Maina, fancying that the water of the plains was fatal to them; and the story is told of a Mainote, who, though prospering in a foreign country, sent for a little earth from his beloved Maina, and was so affected by the smell that he at once returned to his native hills. All, or nearly all, this state of feeling and things has passed away. It was rapidly passing in 1839, though the old system could not be said to have absolutely expired, and the recollections of it were fresh in men's minds and mouths. Thus, at Tzimova, I find the following entry: "My host showed me my room in the tower. On pointing to a small window he said, 'There are shutters; but you are safe; they will not shoot you.' I could not help observing that but for the bloodhead I should like to have seen one of the many fights which had taken place here a short time since. "Oh," he said, "a word would in a moment bring it back again," meaning that the feeling and spirit were the same as in former years.

So too at the little town of Vathia, a boy of twelve or thirteen years old had struck a playmate; the father had retaliated; a feud had actually been revived, and as the writer of these *Journals* passed through the place the elders were holding a conference to determine whether they should resort to the ancient practice of an exterminating war, or bend to the new system and carry the matter for settlement before the regular tribunal. "If," said one of the counsellors, who deprecated such a degenerate change of procedure, much in the spirit of an English or Scotch borderer, "if they carry up the question to such places as these new law courts, instead of settling it in the old way of their fathers, there will be no end to such matters."

It was the transitional character of the time that gave additional interest to the country and the state of society; but though the former possessors of power had either been deprived of their jurisdiction, or, like Petro Bey Mavromichale, had been induced to exchange their position of vast local influence for a place or an official title in Athens, many traces of that influence remained and were to be seen in these more distant parts of the Morea. Many even, in their disgust at the new civilization which had promised so much and done so little, which had destroyed political and feudal power, and which had given no compensation in the form of material prosperity for what it had taken away, were tempted to regret the days of Turkish rule, when a rude autonomy prevailed. The Governor of Karytena still wore his Turkish dress of honour Petro Bey's brother, the head and representative of that powerful family, showed with pride the Turkish sword that he had once worn and the scarlet robes that the Sultan had given him, and complained that they were now put aside, and that "everything had become Frank." "The time was," he said, " when he and his family had raised the Maina against the Turks; but they had done wrong. They were then at least independent; and alluding with bitterness to the days when he had marched to Kita and silenced those terrific feuds, he said that though a colonel in the King's service, he could not now go to Athens without obtaining official leave."

No Children - Only Daughters

Daybreak was ushered in by a discharge of firearms – a short time since an ominous sound in Kita - but on inquiry I learnt that it was in honour of a marriage. The man was already married, but having had no children by his wife, he was permitted, with her consent - and, it is affirmed, under the sanction of a priest - to be united to another woman of the place. It is said here that if he should have a son by this second union, that son would in the Maina be considered to be legitimate, and the first wife could be repudiated. On my asking some further questions, it appeared that his first marriage had indeed given him three daughters; but my informant repeated his statement that there were no children - so completely are girls counted as nothing in this country. One of my muleteers clinched the argument by the additional question of how could a man wish to have anything to do with a woman who brought him no sons?

Maniate
(Baron von Stackelberg
& G. Mochetti, 1825)

147

Kythera

1609 William Lithgow

The Sins of the Brothers

Although he had been forced to leave his native town in Scotland on account of an affair involving a woman, the puritan conscience of this Protestant, and his atavistic anti-Catholic prejudices, were aroused to indignation by a monastic scandal on the island of Kythera. Subsequently, while in the course of attempting to return to Scotland, he was to fall into the hands of the Holy Inquisition. This incident may have be responsible for the tone of bitterness which may be detected here.

In the time of my abode, at the village of Capsalo (being a haven for small barks, and situate below the castle) the captain of that same fortress killed a seminary priest, whom he had found in the night with his whore in a brothel-house: for the which sacrilegious murder, the governor of the isle deposed the captain, and banished him, causing a boat to be prepared to send him to Creta.

O! If all the Priests which do commit incest, adultery, and fornication (yea, and worse, *Il peccato carnale contra natura*) were thus handled and severely rewarded; what a sea of sodomitical irreligious blood would overflow the half of Europe, to stain the spotted colour of that Roman Beast. Truly, and yet more, these lascivious friars are the very epicures, or off-scourings of the earth; for how oft have I heard them say one to another "Be cheerful, be cheerful, dear brother, he that eateth well, drinketh well, he that drinketh well, sleepeth well, he that sleepeth well, sinneth not, and he that sinneth not, goeth straight through Purgatory to Paradise." This is all the care of their living, making their tongues to utter what their hearts do thus profanely think...:

> Injustly, no! Monks be called fathers, Why ?
> Their bastards swarm, as thick, as stars in sky.

1817-18 Peter Edmund Laurent

An Unenviable Post

Taken under British control during the Napoleonic Wars, an English garrison was installed on the island. Laurent evidently considered Kythera a singularly uninviting place on which to be marooned for any length of time.

Having doubled Cape Matepan, we passed sufficiently near the island of Cerigo (Cythera) to see the English sentinel, who was mounting guard at the fort. The garrison consists of seven men; and I should think that the ignominy of punishment is the only circumstance which renders the life of the New South Wales convict less comfortable than theirs.

Messenia

1804-06 Colonel William Leake

Kalamata at the Beginning of the Nineteenth Century

Kalamata, including its kalyvia, contains 400 families, of which only six are Turkish. The government is in the hands of the chief Greeks, and the voivoda is readily removed upon any complaint of theirs. The mukata of the Kazasi is generally bestowed upon some favourite at Constantinople for twelve or eighteen months, who undersells it to some other Turk for four or six months. The resident voivoda is the agent of the latter person, and a mere collector of the revenue. The kadi is, in like manner, the deputy of a principal at Constantinople, who has purchased the kadilik. An Albanian Boluk-bashi and forty men are maintained by the town, to keep the country free from robbers; like every other part of the police, they are under the direction of the archons. The town is situated at about a mile from the sea, on the left bank of a torrent, which emerges from a rocky gorge in Mount Taygetum, at the distance of a mile to the north-eastward of a hill rising from the back of the town. This height is crowned with a ruined castle of the middle ages, and is naturally strengthened by a perpendicular cliff towards the torrent, which in winter often fills a bed 100 yards wide, but is now divided into three channels. There is a small kalyvia, or suburb, on the right bank of the river, the mills and gardens of which are supplied by an artificial diversion from the river.

Holy Week

April 18 - This being the morning of Holy Thursday, by the Greek calendar, a young sub-deacon, two hours before day, knocks at all the doors, calling out, "Christians, come to church." Today, oil is permitted, but tomorrow, Good Friday, it is forbidden even to set a table for dinner. In the evening ... a service begins, which lasts till eleven; twelve masses are said [? Ed.], and as many portions of the Gospels read, descriptive of the different sufferings of Christ, previous to the Crucifixion, which they suppose to have taken place at midnight. Just as the service was beginning, there was a slight earthquake - certainly the most appropriate of all accompaniments.

April 19. - Mahmud Aga makes his entrance into the town; he is a friend of the Pasha, and comes hither on a visit of observation, connected with some efforts about to be made by the Pasha for the suppression of the robbers: he was lately in the household of Bekir Effendi, of Tripolitza, brother of Nuri Bey, of Corinth. I saw an old woman this evening searching for a strayed mule among the olive-trees, and making the sign of the cross down to the ground, every two or three steps, by way of assisting her in the search, but which, of course, retarded her not a little.

April 20. - The ceremony of the Entombment a occurs this morning, at two hours before day; the people come out of their houses in the dark, and scramble to light their candles at the priest's candle. There is then a procession, consisting chiefly of women, through the streets to the church. Kalamata is the only town in the Morea, inhabited by Turks, where the Greeks can perform this ceremony; which generally takes place within the walls of the church or monastery. In the retired villages of the mountains, of course, it may be done openly.

Easter Sunday, by the Greeks called Lambri. It is a general custom, when two acquaintances meet for the first time today for one to say, "Christ hath risen!" to which the other replies, "truly He hath risen!" The morning is occupied in visiting and drinking coffee. At about 11 dinner takes place, after which it is not unusual to sing the words of salutation just mentioned, or something equally applicable to the day.

The Rearing of Silk-worms

Almost every house in Kalamata is provided with a chamber for rearing silk-worms. The eggs are sold from two to five piastres the measure of eight drams, the price varying according to the crop of the preceding year: this year the price was five piastres. The eggs are wrapped in a cloth, and the worms hatched at the end of April or beginning of May; young mulberry leaves are then placed upon them; the worms mount upon the leaves, and are placed in round shallow baskets. In this state ... small leaves are given to it once a day, or once in two days: the leaves increasing in size as the worm increases. At the end of fifteen days it sleeps two days, sheds its skin and then becomes a *protokuli*; in which state it eats twelve days, having fresh leaves in the morning of each day. After sleeping again two days, and changing its skin, the worm ... [is given] fresh leaves twice a day, and is removed out of the basket into the *kalamoti*: this is nothing more than a frame of reeds tied together, and is usually ten, twelve, or fourteen feet long, and five or six broad. The *kalamotes* are placed one above the other at intervals of eight or ten inches, forming as many stories as the height of the room will permit. In Asia Minor the worms are commonly kept in huts built for the purpose in the mulberry grounds; here they are in the private houses. The *dhefteraki* eats for ten days, sleeps two, sheds his skin again, and then becomes a tritaki: he has now fresh leaves morning, noon, and evening, and, after eating for eight days, sleeps three, and once more sheds his skin. In the last and largest state the worms are called great; they have leaves three times a day, cease eating at the end of eight days, and then begin to climb upwards. The branches upon which they are to spin are then placed upon the *kalamotes*, and the worms form the [cocoon]; sometimes two, three, or four spin together, and make a large [cocoon]: at the end of fifteen days the [cocoons] are placed in the sun, which is now at the solstice, and the chrysalis is killed by the heat; soon afterwards the moths, eat their way out of those [cocoons] that have been reserved to furnish eggs.

The growth of the animal, the quantity he eats, and consequently the frequency of the change of leaves, depend on the weather; he advances more rapidly if it is hot, and less so if it is cold and rainy. The worms are so delicate that thunder, or even the report of a pistol, will sometimes kill them. The baskets and *kalamotes* are cleaned by merely throwing in fresh leaves, which, as soon as the worms have mounted upon them, are removed to a fresh basket, or *kalamoti*. This operation is repeated after every change of skin. The moths live three days.

The Jannissaries of Korone

May 2. - A fatal dispute has just occurred between two Turks; one a janissary of the Septinsular Consul, the other a distributor of corn from the Bey's magazine. The Consul wished to transport some corn privately to Mani, where the distress has become still greater than when I was there, but where, according to the Messenians, money can generally be found when the occasion requires it. The janissary applied to the distributor, as if for himself: the distributor would not give the proportion he desired, on which the janissary abused the keeper of the magazine and beat his Greek servant. The affair was made up for the moment, but the relatives on both sides having interfered, a challenge ensued, and the two parties met yesterday evening at the castle-gate, when they came to blows with yataghans. The guardian of the Bey's corn, finding the adverse knives likely to prevail, drew a pistol from his girdle and shot the janissary, and before the affray ceased, the janissary's father also was mortally wounded, as well as one of the opposite party. The brother of the janissary immediately mounted his horse and rode to Petalidhi, with the intention of murdering the distributor's brother, but one of Mustafa Bey's nephews anticipated him by sending advice to the man at Petalidhi, who by that means escaped. On the return of the slain janissary's brother from Petalidhi this morning, he was forbidden to land, and sent by the Bey to conceal himself in Mani.

The Greeks give melancholy accounts of the atrocities of these janissaries of Koroni, who are gradually reducing to desolation the beautiful region of olives, vineyards, and gardens, which surround the town. Before the year 1770, there were four French mercantile houses here, who exported grain, oil, and silk, from this and the surrounding districts.

1818-19 Peter Laurent

A Comfortable Night in a Khan

This is an unusual passage, since Laurent seems to have been almost alone in enjoying good luck with his khans. Other travellers paint a very different picture.

The Makryplaia road is very bad, and, indeed, infinitely worse than those who are accustomed to be whirled over the English causeways can imagine: the scenery is most beautiful and romantic. On the left rolls a torrent, on the opposite border of which, high among the forests, is seen the village of Londari: as the road advances the precipice gradually increases in depth, till at length the eye seeks. In vain to reach its bottom: the sound of the rushing waters is heard at an awful distance as the traveller advances, trembling and giddy. On both sides forests of lofty oak veil the mountain-side; but so sadly does Turkish supineness neglect these treasures, that the finest trunks are seen decaying on the ground:, and repeatedly impeding the way...

After scrambling some hours over this road, we arrived at the *derveni*, or guardhouse, one of which is erected in all the passes of the Turkish empire. Here the strait begins to open, and one sees, in the distance, the territory of Messenia, bounded by the Gulf of Coronea: numerous mountains surround the vale, above which, rising high and conspicuous, is Ithome, now called Vourkano: behind stand the ruins of the once celebrated capital of Messenia. Thither we should now, have impatiently, hastened, had not night warned us that we had already proceeded sufficiently far; we, therefore, stopped at an adjacent, khan, and passed a very comfortable night.

The Grecian khans are for the most part built in the shape of a quadrangle, in the middle of which is a well: the entrance is by an arched; gateway: stables occupy the ground floor all around, above which is built a projecting platform, of wood, to which lead two or three stair-cases, erected on the outside. The different rooms of the first story open upon the platform: these rooms are used for the accommodation of travellers and the warehousing of merchandise: they are unfurnished; for every traveller carries with him his rug and necessary utensils.

The keeper of the khan is called *khangee* - a word which all the newcomers vociferate as they enter the yard, answering to the English *ostler*. The khangee is always provided with uncooked provisions, which he sells to the traveller at a moderate price; were he to be caught overreaching, his ears would soon be nailed as an ornament to the gateway.

In the Morea khans are by far the most eligible lodgings, whether quiet, cleanliness or comfort be considered: the charges can beat no comparison; one piaster abundantly satisfies the khan keeper for lodging, and fuel, if wanted; whereas in the dirtiest of huts, for a corner in the only room it contains, hardly any sum will be found sufficient to satisfy the rapacious owner. Add also, that in no other places can provisions be procured more cheaply, and with less difficulty; for elsewhere, if indeed they are not absolutely refused, the peasant never fails to ask an incredibly exorbitant price.

The sun had not yet risen in this sequestered spot when we quitted our resting-place to pursue our journey onwards to enjoy the beauties of the morning at the first dawn of light...

From the khan the road winds in a deep descent and, after crossing a river, enters a valley, the approach to which is most strikingly beautiful: it is surrounded by lofty mountains, forming, as it were, the walls of an immense ancient theatre, having the sea for a proscenium...

In the valley are built numerous villages. These, being surrounded with lofty impenetrable barriers of prickly Indian fig-trees, bear an appearance quite novel and extraordinary: those trees thrive extremely well, and their fruit forms a principal article of food for the inhabitants. The modern Messenians find these fences very useful, as they can be penetrated neither by man nor beast, defending them much more effectually from depredation than the herds of barking mastiffs which infest the other villages.

c. 1857 W. G. Clarke

An ancient Site, a Monastery, and a Lunatic

This version of the treatment of lunatics differs markedly from another account, below.

We left Navarino at six o'clock, and taking the road by which we had come two days before, reached the forest at half-past eight, and halted for breakfast at ten. We chose a shady oak close to a guardhouse, which is the headquarters of a detachment of *nomophylakes* - the rural police, or mounted *gens-d'armes* of Greece. Two of these functionaries accompanied us to show the way; for the route now diverged from our former track, and was as new to our dragoman as to ourselves. The way was indeed exceedingly difficult to find, and puzzled even the *gens-d'armes* more than once. After getting out of the wood, we had to cross a succession of low ridges, divided by streams running between steep banks covered with thick bushes. Nothing like a path was to be seen. Here and there were patches of cultivation, but we did not come to any village till five in the afternoon. The multitude of Judas-trees all in flower, and the rich red of the broken earth banks, contrasted with the various green tints of herbage and foliage, gave to the landscape a fantastic patchwork look such as would not be credited in a picture. Our course was further hindered by the repeated tumbles of a wretched overladen baggage horse, and it was growing dark while we were still scrambling over a rocky hillside without having any resting-place in prospect. Suddenly we came upon a huge ruined wall, and we found ourselves on the site of Messene. We had, indeed, passed over it without being aware, and were now "at the gate of Laconia." A steep path to the right led down to the convent of Vourkamo, where we were to pass the night. There was a considerable preliminary difficulty in finding the door – then a parley through the keyhole. *"Tines eisthe?"* "Who are you?" said a voice from within. – *"Angloi,"* said we. – "*Lordoi*," added Alexander, for thus the dragoman designates all foreign tourists; and we were forthwith admitted.

A wild-looking monk, with long black hair and beard and gown, candle in hand, conducted us to the room set apart for guests – a large bare room upstairs with a divan, or, in Yorkshire phrase, a settle, covered with carpet at each end. Here we were visited by the abbot and all the brethren, and treated with sweetmeats, coffee, and liqueur. Our arrival gave evident pleasure. It was a break in the monotony of life at Vourkamo. We asked and answered many questions. In the monastery, we were told, there are fifteen regular monks or "caloyers," and counting the lay brethren and dependent peasants – *georgoi* and *poimenes* - sixty persons in all attached to the establishment. The building, as we found next morning, is in a beautiful situation, on the steep slope of Aio Vasili, the ancient Euan, overlooking the rich, well-watered plain of Messenia, with the sea to the right and serried ranks of mountains in front and on the left. Like all convents in Greece, the building, as an achievement of architecture, does not satisfy the expectations raised by the ruins and traditions of the monasteries of Western Europe. Outside all is strong and solid, inside all is mean and rickety, as if it had been built with a double purpose of resisting the violence and not tempting the cupidity of brigands or other constituted authorities. Outside, one doubts whether it is most like a barn or a jail, inside our comparativeness halts between a khan and a college. There is a quadrangle with a church on one side, and on the other three an upper and lower range of cells, with a wooden balcony all along. The convent is almost enclosed with an orchard and a grove of maples and cypresses. One of the hangers-on of the place is a poor idiot who was always "mopping and mowing" in the court, and whenever he caught sight of a stranger ran up to him with a sudden outbreak of gabble and grimace. These unfortunate people are treated with peculiar tenderness in Greece - at least so far as my observation went; and that not from pity or personal fear, but from a kind of superstitious reverence. This same reverence was strongly felt by the ancient Greeks, notwithstanding their habit of pelting mad people with stones.

Further experience would probably have shown that in modern Greece, too, the treatment of lunatics is not universally tender. A madman is always a stranger – no length of habit can make him familiar; we may pity him, and even tolerate his presence, but we cannot sympathise with, or love him. He is always regarded with awe, fear, pity and distrust; and among educated folk treated with uniform care, prompted by a mixture of these feelings. The ruder a people are, the more distinct are their impulses, the more fickle their conduct; hence, by children and rustics the unhappy madman is alternately worshipped and pelted. I think within the walls of the Panaghia at Vourkamo, among the grave fathers, poor Andreopoulos is safe from the latter fate. Before taking leave we had again to partake of preserves and liqueur with the Hegoumenos (or abbot). In return for the shelter and hospitality of the convent, every stranger who can afford it is expected to make a donation, as at the St. Bernard. One of the brethren asks you to come and see the church, and particularly directs your attention to a picture of the Panaghia which you cannot look at without seeing the poor-box below.

The Albanians of the Peloponnese

It was past five when we left these ruins. We followed for some miles a very rough path, if path it could be called, on the left bank of the Neda, looking with Barba Jan's eyes for a convenient place to pass the river. At last we managed to cross, and plodded on some miles more. It was now growing dark. Barba Jan had forgotten or never known the road. Luckily we met another peasant, Anastas he called himself. Him we engaged as guide; but as it grew pitch dark he lost his way too. We all floundered along, over hedges and ditches, or what seemed to be such. At last we came to the edge of a ravine, a stream roaring, as streams do roar at night, far below. Somehow we scrambled down through the wood, plashed through the water, scrambled up through another wood, and so on till about ten o'clock we arrived at Paulitza. The village had been for hours asleep, excepting the household with whom we had to pass the night. Our men had made a fire outside, and were sitting round it, wondering with pleasurable anxiety whether we had been murdered by brigands or had only broken our necks. After all, the only article broken was an umbrella.

The house where we lodged consisted of a single room. At one end, round the fire, sat the whole family, old and young, enjoying an Easter feast, probably on the strength of what they were to receive for our night's lodging. As soon as the lamb was roasted, the goodman of the house tore it to pieces and put them into a dish, from which, after it had been sent to us to taste, they all helped themselves. After which they disposed themselves to sleep round the dying embers on the hearthstone. At the other end of the room our beds were laid among a mass of household stuff. Our hosts, like most of the people in this part of the country, were Albanians, knowing only a few words of Romaic. There are about 200,000 of this people among the inhabitants of the Greek kingdom, that is to say, nearly a fifth of the whole population. They first came into the Morea in the fourteenth century; some as mercenary soldiers, who received grants of land after being disbanded; others as invited or unopposed settlers on waste ground.

In the year 14 15, the Emperor Manuel II, in a funeral oration which he delivered at Mistra in honour of his brother Theodore, who had governed the Morea as despot or viceroy, made especial mention of the pains which he had taken to introduce Albanian colonists. These colonists were for the most part shepherds and herdsmen, and occupied the pastures on the high ground on condition of paying a rent to the government and to the Sclavo-Greek proprietors in the towns and valleys. Even to this day the Albanian language is spoken almost universally in all the mountainous districts of the Morea, with the exception of the three southern peninsulas. In order to get rid of the obligation of paying rent, they took an opportunity in 1452, when the empire of Constantinople was struggling in the agonies of dissolution, to rebel in order to become lords, not tenants, of the soil; but the attempt was quelled by the interference of the Turks. They have received frequent accessions from the same causes in more recent times; but as there is a constant tendency in the less civilized races to be absorbed in and assimilated with their neighbours, so, doubtless, there are many people of Albanian blood who now rank with the Greeks, because they speak their language and have adopted their habits. They are, I was told, offended at being called Albanians or Skipetar, as they used to call themselves, and desire to be termed Hellenes. This desire on their part, and the systematic education which is now introduced in modern Greece, will in a very short time obliterate all the distinctions between them. Generally speaking, the Albanians are lighter in hair and complexion and more athletic in form than the Greeks or Sclavonians about them, but there are striking individual exceptions to the rule; as I have said, they used to call themselves Skipetar, the learned call them Albanians, their rural neighbours call them Vlachi - a misnomer, but a natural one, since before the Albanians were known in Greece the Wallachians had occupied a great part of the country north of the Corinthian gulf. In the same way the Welsh give the name of Sassenach to the Flemings settled about Tenby and Milford Haven. The mistake is perpetuated in the names of some villages inhabited by Albanians, as, for example, in Vlakho-Raphti in Arcadia, Vlakho-Khori in Laconia, etc.

1857-58 Bayard Taylor

A Disturbed Night at Kalamata

The journey to Kalamata occupied six hours, through scenery as rich and magnificent as that of Italian Switzerland. The eye ranged from orange orchards and groves of cypress on the rocky terraces near the sea, to forests of fir on the higher hills, bristling with robber towers, while, far above, the sharp white peaks flashed and glittered in the blue. While descending to the plain at the head of the Gulf, where we left the Mainote territory, I met Ariadne, carrying a load of wood on her back. Even in this position, bent under her burden, she exhibited a more perfect beauty, a more antique grace, than any woman you will see in Broadway in the course of a week. If such be the Greek race now, in its common forms, what must have been those refined Athenian women whom Phidias saw? Since I beheld Ariadne, ancient art has become a reality.

Early in the afternoon we reached Kalamata, a large, straggling, busy town, with a dismantled acropolis, and took up our quarters in the "Grand Hotel of Messenia." The filthy rooms of this establishment were not a pleasant change from the airy towers of Maina. All the afternoon, as I sat at the window, the boys tormented an idiot in the street below, and all night there was such a succession of discordant noises through the house, that we got but little sleep.

1870-80s John Pentland Mahaffy

Crossing the Laganda Pass

From this point we entered at once into the great Langada Pass, the most splendid defile in Greece - the only way from Sparta into Messene for a distance of thirty miles north and south. It is indeed possible to scale the mountain at a few other points, but only by regular alpine climbing, whereas this is a regular highway; and along it strings of mules, not without trouble, make their passage daily, when the snow does not lie, from Sparta and from Kalamata.

Nothing can exceed the picturesqueness and beauty of this pass, and nothing was stranger than the contrast between its two steeps. That which faced south was covered with green and with spring flowers-pale anemones, irises, orchids, violets, and, where a stream trickled down, with primroses, - a marsh plant in this country. All these were growing among great boulders and cliffs, whereas on the opposite side the whole face was bleak and barren, the rocks being striated with rich yellow and red veins. I suppose in hot summer these aspects are reversed. High above us, as it were, looking down from the summits, were great forests of fir-trees - a gloomy setting to a grandiose and savage landscape. The day was, as usual, calm and perfectly fine, with a few white clouds relieving the deep blue of the sky. As we were threading our way among the rocks of the river-course we were alarmed by large stones tumbling from above, and threatening to crush us. Our guides raised all the echoes with their shouts, to warn any unconscious disturber of this solitude that there were human beings beneath, but on closer survey we found that our possible assassins were only goats clambering along the precipice in search of food, and disturbing loose boulders as they went.

Farther on we met other herds of these quaint creatures, generally tended by a pair of solitary children, who seemed to belong to no human kin, but, like birds or flowers, to be the natural denizens of these wilds. They seemed not to talk or play; we never heard them sing, but passed them sitting in curious vague listlessness, with no wonder, no curiosity, in their deep solemn eyes. There, all the day long, they heard no sound but the falling water, the tinkling of their flocks, and the great whisper of the forest pines when the breeze touched them on its way down the pass. They took little heed of us as we passed, and seemed to have sunk from active beings into mere passive mirrors of the external nature around them. The men with us, on the other hand, were constantly singing and talking. They were all in a strange country which they had never seen; a serious man with a gun slung round his shoulder was our guide from Trypi, and so at last we reached the top of the pass, about 4000 feet high, marked by a little chapel to St. Elias, and once by a stone pillar stating the boundary between Sparta and Messene. It was then up this pass, and among these forests, that the young Spartans had steeled themselves by hunting the wolf and the bear in peace, and by raids and surprises in days of war.

The descent was longer and more varied; sometimes through well cultivated olive yards, mulberries, and thriving villages, sometimes along giant slopes, where a high wind would have made our progress very difficult. Gradually the views opened and extended, and in the evening we could see down to the coast of Messene, and the sea far away. But we did not reach Kalamata till long after nightfall and rested gladly in a less uncomfortable inn than we had yet found in the journey.

Kalamata (Baron von Stackelberg, 1831)

Elis

1804-06 Colonel William Leake

A "Culture of Deceit"

[I] enter Gastuni at 3.55, where I again lodge in the house of Dr. S. S complains to me, that in the Morea it is becoming daily more rare among the rich Greeks to give their children any education, and this want of encouragement to schoolmasters makes it difficult to find any good ones. The proesti, he observes, are the ruin of the nation in this, as in every thing else. In the Morea, where so many Greeks have authority, they naturally become, under the Ottoman system, a sort of Christian Turks, with the usual ill qualities of slaves who have obtained power. The chief proofs among them of a good birth and genteel education, are dissimulation and the art of lying with a good grace; which they seem often to exercise rather with a view of showing their ability in this way, than with any settled design. When I have taxed a Greek with falsehood on some occasion, the answer has been – "Why you know I must say something." The other day, at St. Luke's, I complained to the Igumenos of the false account of the distance which his brother abbot at Dobo had given me: "That was nothing;" he replied, "he knew very well your Excellency was determined to go to that village, and therefore told you the distance was shorter than the reality, not to alarm you." In other words, he wished to get rid of me, which was natural enough, as he had found, by experience, that such casual guests were both troublesome and costly, and had never before seen any travellers who are in the habit of defraying their expenses. Though it is impossible not to be disgusted with these things, one can hardly blame the Greeks for them; for what other arms have they against their oppressors? Under such a cruel tyranny, deceitfulness unavoidably becomes a national characteristic: a Greek will often answer the simplest question by a falsehood, for the mere purpose of gaining time to reflect on the most advantageous mode of answering it, or to unriddle the inquirer's motive for asking. They will afterwards, perhaps, speak the truth if, as it appears to them, there will be nothing lost in so doing…

Agriculture in Gastuni

Colonel Leake was an assiduous and systematic observer, and the following is an extremely detailed account of the agriculture of the region around Gastoun. With its many references to contemporary agricultural practices, it provides a detailed portrait of a way of life now lost.

The chief produce of the arable land of Gastuni is flax, wheat, and two kinds of Holcus, both called Kalambokki; namely, maize and the dhurra of Egypt, called, from the smallness of the grain, Small Kalambokki. For flax the land is once ploughed in the spring, and two or three times in the ensuing autumn with a pair of oxen, when the seed is thrown in and covered with the plough. The plant does not require and hardly admits of weeding, as it grows very thick. When ripe it is pulled up by the roots, and laid in bundles in the sun. It is then thrashed to separate the seed; the bundles are laid in the river for five days, then dried in the sun, and pressed in a wooden machine. Contrary to its ancient reputation, the flax of Gastuni is not very fine, which my informant ascribes to its being exposed to the cold and running water of the river, instead of being soaked in ponds; it is chiefly used in the neighbouring islands by the peasants, who weave it into cloths for their own use.

The wheat grown in the plain is the hard red wheat called Ghirinia. In the hills the white kind of Rusia is used. Land being plentiful, there is no regular succession of crops, and a fallow of two years is common. New land, or fallow is ploughed in the spring, and if there is rain, it is sown at the third ploughing with cotton, kalambokki, and sometimes with aniseed. Wheat, on secondary land, is sown in October, on the richest in November, December, and sometimes as late as the middle of January, if an excess of rain prevent its being done before. The proportion of seed is usually half a vatzeli, or measure of thirteen okes to a strema, or square of nineteen fathoms the side. A fall of rain in March, and another in April are reckoned sufficient; if there is more, thistles, tares, centauries, and golden thistles, gain head, and choke the corn. The other plagues are a black winged insect called vromusa, from its bad smell, and rain in May, which injures the blossom.

Harvest begins about June 10th, in the plain, in the hills it does not finish generally till July 20th, or beginning of August, new style. The grain is trodden out on the threshing floor by horses, when the Muktitasi takes his tithe. Good land produces ten, and sometimes thirteen to one. The corn of Gastuni weighs about twenty-six okes, the kilo of Constantinople. The kalambokkia of both kinds may be either dry, or irrigated by art; the first mode produces the better grain, the latter the more plentiful crop. Both require the best land. After three or four ploughings in the spring, the seed is ploughed in about the end of April, in the proportion of one vatzeli to sixteen stremata. The land is then levelled with an instrument called the svarna. This svarna is a piece of wood six feet long and one foot thick, which is fixed to the plough after the share is taken off, and is driven about the field while the labourer stands upon it; it breaks the clods, and levels the ground. A very dry summer is injurious to the dry, and a very rainy August to both kinds of kalambokki. The harvest begins in the middle of September. The return of maize is thirty or forty to one. The stalk makes excellent fodder for cattle. The small kalambokki is used chiefly for feeding fowls; and the quantity raised is not very great.

For cotton the best land is chosen, and that which can be easily irrigated. The seed is soaked in water two or three days, and then mixed and rubbed together with earth, that the grains may not cohere, but may be well scattered in sowing. The seed time is the same as that of kalambokki, namely, the end of April, or beginning of May, the proportion of seed, half a vatzeli to a strema: the seed is ploughed in, and the land levelled with the svarna; the harvest is in the beginning of September...

A flock of sheep consists of 500, two-thirds of which are ewes: it is attended by three men and a boy, and four or five dogs. Nothing is paid for pasture except one asper and a half a head to the Spahi of the village to which the pasture belongs. The tax to government is now one asper and a half a head per annum; besides a para a head on the fleece. Neither sheep nor goats are ever fed: the pasture is changed three or four times in the summer. The profits of a flock are derived from the lambs, the wethers, the milk, the fleece, and the skin. Four rams are sufficient for one hundred ewes. In warm situations near the sea, they are put together about July 20th, that the lambs may be dropped about December 20th. In colder places the rams are not admitted till August 6th, that the ewes may lamb about January 6th. In two months the lambs are weaned, but for another month they are allowed to suck a little after the ewes are milked. A lamb that has been fed entirely upon milk for three months, will sell at Easter, when the great consumption of lambs takes place, for four, five or six piastres. In March the ewes are separated, and for the three following months are milked twice a-day, then once a day for a month, and in July once in two or three days. A good ewe gives at every milking a pound of milk, of which are made butter, cheese, misithra, and yaourt. For butter the milk is left twenty-four hours to become sour, when it is beaten in a narrow cask with a stick until the butter swims at the top; the buttermilk is then mixed with an equal quantity of milk, and forms the tyrogalo, or milk for making cheese. Salted rennet is thrown into it when warmed. As soon as it is coagulated, it is beaten up until it resembles milk again, after which the cheese is allowed to separate, is then put into a form of cloth, or wood, or rushes, and squeezed dry by the hand. The remaining liquid is called nerogalo, milk water.

To make misithra. The nerogalo after the cheese has been extracted is placed upon the fire; about a tenth of milk is added to it, and after a short boiling the misithra is collected on the surface. Goat's milk makes the best misithra, even though the butter has been extracted from it.

Yaourt, which seems to be a Tartar invention introduced into Greece by the Turks, is made from the best milk of sheep or goats. To make the ... coagulum - take some leaven of bread, that is to say, flour and water turned sour, and squeeze a lemon upon it, dissolve it in boiling milk, and keep it twenty-four hours. To make the yaourt - boil some new milk till it foams, stirring it frequently, leave it till it is cool enough for the finger to bear the heat; then throw in the pityá, of which a Turkish coffee-cup full is sufficient to make several quarts of yaourt. Then cover it that it may not cool too fast, and in three hours it is fit for use. On all future occasions a cup of the old yaourt is the best pitya for the new.

The sheep-shearing takes place from April 20th to May 10th; no washing or preparation of any kind is thought necessary; it is performed with scissors. The ewes give about three, the males four pounds of wool, which now sells for about ten paras the pound. About three-fourths of the wool produced in the district is exported, the remainder is wrought at home into coarse cloaks, or into carpeting, or the furniture of beds and sofas. An ewe's or wether's skin, unshorn, is worth thirty or thirty-five paras; a ram's, forty or forty-five paras; a lamb's, ten. The curriers purchase them, make some into leather at Gastuni, and send the rest to the islands.

The flocks suffer occasionally from wolves and jackals, The principal disease of the sheep is called the evloghia or plague; it carries off great numbers, but seldom occurs oftener than once in five or six years, and is not peculiar to any season, They have a practice of inoculating for this distemper, by taking a small quantity of matter from an ulcer of the diseased sheep, and rubbing the ear of the still healthy sheep with it; it is confessed, however, that little benefit is derived from this process. If the evloghia carries off half the ... uninoculated, perhaps sixty per cent, of the inoculated may live, Another disorder is called kholianitza, which is supposed to proceed from unwholesome food, The vidheia is ascribed to feeding in marshy places in August and September, when it is imagined that an insects from the plant finds its way to the sheep's liver.

From the middle of June till the autumn the sheep feed only in the night, and require water once a day, There are supposed to be about 800,000 sheep and goats in the Vilayeti of Gastuni, besides which, 150,000 come from the mountainous parts of the neighbouring districts in the winter. These pay two aspers a head to the Spahi, instead of one and a half. The proportion of goats to sheep is about a fourth.

The uncultivated land serves for the pasture of cattle as well as sheep... The herds of Gastuni supply Zakytho and the other islands with beef in considerable quantities. In the Morea, beef is little used; and they would rather give fifteen paras an oke for goat's flesh, or eighteen for mutton, than ten for beef. But there is a constant demand in the Morea for cattle for the plough, both oxen and buffalos. A good pair of oxen costs one hundred and fifty to one hundred and eighty piastres; a bull about thirty-five; a cow sixteen to twenty. When natural fodder is scarce, oxen are fed with wheaten straw, with the rovi, or with vetches and tares, which are sown for the purpose and plucked up by the roots; but poverty and oppression prevent the proprietor of oxen from cultivating this useful provision for his cattle, and in summer they are almost starved. Like the sheep, the ox is occasionally subject to a peculiar epidemical disorder. On these occasions there are some quacks of cow leeches who administer a herb, which they pretend to bring from Filiatra, but, as may be supposed, without much effect. Ox-hides are exported to Zakytho; but there is a great internal consumption of them here also, as the shoes, both of the cultivators and shepherds, are made of ox hide.

Corinth is reckoned to possess the best race of cattle, and bulls have sometimes been brought from thence to Gastuni, to improve the breed; but the cattle of Elis are still inferior to those of the Corinthia.

1813 The Rev. Thomas Smart Hughes:

Muslim Greeks

We left Zante in a small boat and arrived at Pyrgo the following morning, where we parted from Mr. Gropius, and made our way to Miracca near the site of the once famous Olympia, of which there are no remains worth notice. I am of opinion, that the Alpheus has overflowed and buried many of its edifices.

We sojourned in the tower of a Turkish Aga, mounting a high staircase to enter it, and then crossing a drawbridge: the best room, at the top, must be ascended by ladders, all light being excluded for the better defence against, attacks. In such a tower a Turk named Ali Farmarki, about four years since, defended himself with a hundred men against the whole force of the Pasha during a siege of two months; at the end of which he capitulated to march out with all the honours of war. The peasants of the Morea celebrate his feats in many characteristic songs.

At Miracca not a word of Turkish is spoken except the common oaths; the greatest part of the inhabitants being apostates from the Christian faith: its situation is exceedingly romantic; the houses, which are made of brushwood and clay in the form of beehives, standing on the summit of a small hill.

1818-19 Peter Edmund Laurent

A Journey into the Mountains

Descending from the monastery of Vourkano, and crossing once more the Mavrozume, we took the road to Pavlitza, the spot we intended next to visit.. Near it are found the remains of the ancient city of Phigalia, and the temple of Apollo Epicurius, whence the Phigalian frieze in British Museum was taken...

The road lies through a lovely wood of oak, between the trees of which is seen, peeping in a romantic manner, an ancient fort, of Venetian structure. It is not, however, always permitted to the traveller to indulge his feelings in the admiration of one of the sweetest views of nature I ever beheld, for the fort is generally infested with robbers, who plunder every traveller as he passes, and bid defiance to the efforts of the Turks to dislodge them.

.After enjoying for some hours the beauties of this enchanting scene, we arrived at a khan, much to the joy of poor George and the other servants, who were nearly dead with fright, and would not stay one moment on the road.

The khan is built, as usual, near a derveni, and by the side of a rivulet. Seated under a large plane tree, which shadowed its banks, were five or six Turks. They had lighted a fire, and were roasting some ears of Turkey wheat, a very usual refreshment among them; these they shared generously with us, and we, of course, in return offered some of our coffee: thus a close intimacy was established between us very shortly. One of their train actually wished to become our shakshish, or janissary for the rest of our journey. We had no idea, he coolly told us, how he could bastinado the Greek peasants, and make them show ... the stones. His offer was refused, and the party, having mounted on their fine accoutred steeds, galloped off, pipe in hand, towards Arcadia, a new seaport town, near the site of Cyparissia, in ancient Messenia, mostly inhabited by Turks, and about three days' journey from Patrass...

We wished to take a guide, but were precluded from so doing by their exorbitant demand of twelve piasters; this charge, as the distance was only three hours, we deemed by far too high. We therefore proceeded alone, keeping on the right towards, the village of Vlachi, situate at the bottom of the mountain, across which lies the road to Pavlitza. The peasants were busied in harvesting the Velani acorns; the men, climbing the trees, beat down with a pole, the fruit, which was gathered up by the women. The village of Vlachi is inhabited by Albanians; it is situated at the foot of the range of Mount Lycaeus...

The ascent of this mountain, seldom undertaken by men or horses, occupied us nearly two hours. The greatest part of the time was taken up in removing the fallen trees, which obstructed the path, and often made us doubt the possibility of proceeding by this way to the top. At last, however, we succeeded, when a fine and extensive view repaid us for the fatigue and labour of climbing so high. Before us lay the whole plain of Messenia; at its bottom the Aegean waters, purple as the cornflower, and Mount Ithome; to the right a beautiful woodland of hill and vale: beyond was seen the unrippled surface of the Ionian Sea...

Having enjoyed this prospect a considerable time, and hailed with lively emotions the first view, on our return, of the Ionian Sea, we again endeavoured to continue our journey towards Pavlitza, but we were not able to discover the track, a task of no small difficulty among these mountains, known, as it were, only to the herds of cattle which graze on their tops. Luckily, however, we found a company of shepherds sitting round a fountain, one of whom we at length persuaded to show us the road.

These men were, both in dress and physiognomy, the most barbarous you can possibly imagine; they seemed but one step above the sheep which they tended, and indeed, in countenance were not unlike them, the most stupid and uncouth beings with whom a straying traveller could meet. The general food of these peasants consists in the wild fruits, of which their forests produce a great abundance...

The pincipal wild fruits are the acorns, which they eat roasted, the arbutes, and Siliqua Edilis, the sweet pulpy pods of which are eaten by the poor thoughout Greece...

The language of these people is one of the broadest of the dialects heard in Greece. Our Athenian servant, when conversing with them, was almost lost in the confusion of the rustic sounds which were poured forth from their lips: But, however, without their assistance it would have been impossible to find the way, as there absolutely is not a vestige of a path.

The spot in which we were, and the country through which our road lay, are doubtless the most beautifully romantic which the fancy of the painter could trace, or that of the poet describe; to the scorching atmosphere of the valley had succeeded the cool air of spring; shielded from the rays of the sun by the impenetrable foliage of the velani oak, we continued our way, treading on the greenest turf, in a silence interrupted only by the tinkling of the sheep browsing on the sides of the mountains, accompanied by their shepherds; at each turn new beauties offered themselves to feast the eye. At one time ridges covered with verdure were seen extending to the sea; at another a deep glen, affording the wildest scenery, or a torrent, impetuously rushing through steep crags, covered with woods of cedar and pine - all equally beautiful, arrested our attention, and worked up our minds to a state of awe and admiration. The poets in vain have endeavoured to describe this land; at every step one sees new and beautiful scenes, which nature has hidden in these solitudes, as though she were loth to unfold all her beauties to the eye of man.

We descended by a terrific zig-zag path, overgrown with bushes, and slippery by the thick moss which covered the rock. The horses of the Morea descend these dangerous passes with astonishing safety; the traveller dismounts; the bridle is tied up, and the muleteer, pulling with all his force the tail of the animal, hinders him from tumbling headlong down the rocks.

On the opposite side of a deep glen, watered by the Neda, is the supposed site of ancient Phigaliao. Represent to yourself a river, darting from a narrow pass between the rocks, rapidly flowing at an immense depth below a bridge overhung with myrtle, bay, and arbutes, and soon after lost by the eye between two perpendicular and approaching cliffs, the trees of which seem to unite their branches, and form one lofty mass of forest; then a steep road, leading to a fountain, overhung with weeping willows and wild olives, rushing from the rock, under an immense natural arch, and afterwards dashing with a loud noise its foaming waters to feed the river.

Over this, built among hanging masses of stone, which the first blast threatens to hurl down the abyss, some miserable cottages, commanded by a mountain crowned with ancient walls:, the extent of which seem to indicate the habitation of the giant warriors of old; such is the situation of the little village of Pavlitza: here we passed the night. We were treated wretchedly; we, however, had an opportunity of convincing ourselves of the dread which these people have of the power of their commanders, the Turks. On our first arrival nothing could be obtained, neither bread, eggs, nor any provision whatever; so that we had no prospect than that of going to bed supperless - a circumstance by no means agreeable to persons who had been twelve hours travelling. We had in one of our portmanteaus and old *firman* the Sultan's permission for a ship to descend the Hellespont; it was given to us by the Captain of the *Gertrude* just after we had quitted the Dardenelles. This, after having made one last effort to obtain by gentle means what was necessary, we shewed to the astounded peasants. The effect was instantaneous. Hardly had the immense folds of parchment discovered long dark lines of the Sultan's mandate than we were surrounded with people offering to us all sorts of provisions, apologies, etc. We contented ourselves with a few eggs, wine for our muleteers, and a bottle of excellent honey.

A Narrow Escape

We intended to sleep at Concurra, a small village, three or four miles distant from Olympia. ... It was by God's mercy that we escaped assassination in this miserable hamlet; the circumstances I shall briefly, detail; they offer a lesson of prudence to those whose curiosity leads them to visit spots subject to no government, and inhabited by the vicious and the lawless.

We arrived very late, and proceeded to some cabins situate at the foot of the hill. We found it impossible to obtain a lodging; we therefore took one of the peasants as a guide, and ascended to the upper part of the village. The house of the cogia-bashi or governor, a fellow as miserable and ragged as his subject clowns, was pointed out to us by our guide, who quitted us precipitately, leaving us to gain admittance. Lodging was here peremptorily refused by the master of the house, who carried his inhospitality so far as to deny us even a light to kindle a fire under a neighbouring shed; and we were left standing ... shivering with cold, and wearied with fatigue. Giorgio, our servant, was taken for a janissary and as such called *Aga mou*, the mode of address, used ,by the Romaics to the Turks. Proud of the mistake, our Athenian resolved to augment the similitude by thrashing the landlord. The effect was directly contrary to his expectations. At the sound of the cogia-bashee's voice the, whole clan assembled, armed with bludgeons, sabres, and guns. The servant and myself were the only persons who had dismounted; the horses, the baggage, and my companions were, with the rapidity of lightning, hurried down the hill by our cowardly muleteers, leaving us to defend ourselves as well as we could. Giorgio cocked the gun which he wore slung on his shoulder. We prepared to resist, and, if possible, to make good our retreat, although pursued by the peasants; who shook the air with the cries of "Horned, horned!" (a term of reproach often used by the modern Greeks,) "down with the sabre."

Stones were poured upon us by the women, and a few musket shots were fired. The report of the guns luckily alarmed some Turkish soldiers who were garrisoned at the foot of the hill, in the villa of the Vaivode of Pyrgo, a neighbouring town. They came to our assistance, and enabled us to escape to the Turkish house, where we received most hospitable treatment, and passed a quiet night.

1852 Edmund About

On Seeing Some Nomads Returning to the Mountains in Spring

One morning, when we were asleep after our breakfast, a few leagues from Pyrgos, we were suddenly awakened by a confused noise of voices and footsteps. On opening my eyes, I saw, passing on the road, a long caravan of men, women, and children, of horses and donkeys loaded with baggage. Wretched baggage! there were tents, coarse furniture, clothes, and a few babies thrown in confusion amongst some hens. I remembered the first canto of Hermann and Dorothea, and that sad and touching picture of an emigration. But our Arcadian emigrants were not flying from their village; they were returning to it. One of them, a handsome old man, told me their story. They inhabit a mountain, which every winter covers with snow. At the first cold, they fold up their tents, and descend to Pyrgos. The winter is not very long; during about three months, the strongest go out as workmen or as servants; the weaker ones, and the little ones, live by the labour of the others. And all, on the return of spring, again take the road to the mountain and to freedom. Their faces were contented; they gaily endured the burden of fatigue and heat. Yet their joy was not noisy. It is in the East especially that "happiness is a serious thing."

I watched them going by in a line, meditating on the lot of these human swallows, whom a pious instinct brings back again to their nest each spring. The old man, to whom I spoke, must have taken the road to Pyrgos more than eighty times in his life; and it has never entered into his thoughts to abandon his wretched hamlet for a milder climate and a more fertile soil. I then recollected a melancholy and simple song, which is perhaps the work of a shepherd of this village. "I make a project once, and I make a project twice, and I make the project three and five times, to leave the country, and go to a foreign land. And to all the mountains which I crossed, I said to them all: 'My dear mountains, do not cover yourselves with snow; fields, do not grow white with hoar frost; little fountains of fresh water, do not freeze, whilst I go and come, until I return.' But the foreign land has estranged me - the foreign land where one is alone. And I have chosen foreign sisters, and foreigners rule over me; and I have taken a foreign sister to wash my garments. She washes them once, she washes them twice, she washes them three and five times; and at the end of five times, she throws them into the street, "Stranger, pick up your linen; gather up your garments; and return to your place, and return to your house. Go away and see your brothers, stranger; go away and see your relations!

1898 Samuel J. Barrows

Dreaming Beside the Alphaeos

As we rode down from Mazi, approaching Olympia from the southeast, the hill of Cronion and the Alpheius winding below came in sight. I tried to imagine myself in the seventy-seventh Olympiad (472 BC.), riding with Themistocles as a barbarian spectator to the Olympian games. For centuries before that date the flower of the Greek nation had crossed these mountains, over the same trails, and seen Cronion and the two rivers and peaceful Zante in the calm sea. It is one of the insensible charms of travel in Greece that you may frequently surrender yourself to illusions which for a while there is nothing to disturb. The imagination dilates in a congenial atmosphere, and what you see is some soft refraction of reality, or the diffused glow of a sunset of poetry and tradition not yet faded into night.

Then the illusion is dispelled, but you are surprised again to find how much reality is left. A jolt of your horse brings you back suddenly to the nineteenth century. Your dream is gone. You expect to see the hills and the islands dissolve too, but they stay there, and you feel and know that you are indissolubly united to ages that are past by this very reality , by the constancy and truth of a beautiful picture. Sky, mountain, rivers, sea, island and plain were theirs, and they are yours.

We reached the Alpheius. It is still a live river. W e were ferried across with our mounts in two or three relays in a large flat boat, and with the enthusiasm of youthful cavaliers galloped up to the *xenodocheion.*

1880-90s John Pentland Mahaffy

A Journey over the Mountains

Travellers going from Olympia northward either go round by carriage through Elis to Patras - a drive of two days - or by Kalavryta to Megaspilion, and thence to Vostitza, thus avoiding the great Alps of Olonos ... and Chelmos; which are among the highest and most picturesque in Greece. After my last visit to Olympia (1884) I was so tantalised by the perpetual view of the snowy crest of Olonos, that I determined to attempt a new route, not known to any of the guidebooks, and cross over the mountain, as directly as I could from Olympia to Patras. It was easy for me to carry out this plan, being accompanied by a young Greek antiquarian... and by Dr. Purgold from Olympia, who had travelled through most of Greece, but was as anxious as I was to try this new route.

We started on a beautiful spring morning, up the valley of the Kladeos, with all the trees bursting into leaf and blossom, and the birds singing their hymns of delight. The way was wooded, and led up through narrow and steep, but not difficult glens, until, on a far higher level, we came in three or four hours to the village of Lala, once an important Turkish fort. Here was a higher plain, from which we began to see the plan of that vast complex of mountains which form the boundaries of the old Elis, Achaia, and Arcadia, and which have so often been the scenes of difficult campaigns. From Lala, where we breakfasted, we crossed a sudden deep valley, and found ourselves, on regaining the higher level, in a vast oak forest, unlike anything I had yet seen in Greece. The trees had been undisturbed for centuries, and the forest was even avoided in summer by the natives, on account of the poisonous snakes which hid in the deep layers of dead leaves. In that high country the oaks were just turning pink with their new buds, and not a green leaf was to be seen, so we could trust to the winter sleep of the snakes, while we turned aside again and again from our path, to the great perplexity of the muleteers, to dig up wood anemones of all colours, pale blue, pink, deep crimson, scarlet, snowy-white, which showed brilliantly on the brown oak-leaf carpet.

We spent at least two hours in riding through this forest, and then we rose higher and higher, passing along the upper edge of deep glens, with rushing streams far beneath us. The most beautiful point was one from which we looked down a vast straight glen of some fifteen miles, almost as deep as a canon, with the silvery Erymanthus river pursuing its furious course so directly as to be clearly visible all the way. But though ascending the river from this point, where its course comes suddenly round a corner, the upper country was no longer wooded but bleak, like most of the Alpine Arcadia, a country of dire winters and which we began to see the plan of that vast' complex of mountains which form the boundaries of the old Elis, Achaia, and Arcadia, and which have so often been the scenes of difficult campaigns. From Lala, where we breakfasted, we crossed a sudden deep valley, and found ourselves, on regaining the higher level, in a vast oak forest, unlike anything I had yet seen in Greece. The trees had been undisturbed for centuries, and the forest was even avoided in summer by the natives, on account of the many poisonous snakes which hid in the deep layers of dead leaves. In that high country the oaks were just turning pink with their new buds, and not a green leaf was to be seen, so we could trust to the winter sleep of the snakes, while we turned aside again and again from our path, to the great perplexity of the muleteers, to dig up wood anemones of all colours, pale blue, pink, deep crimson, scarlet, snowy-white, which showed brilliantly on the brown oak-leaf carpet.

We spent at least two hours in riding through this forest, and then we rose higher and higher, passing along the upper edge of deep glens, with rushing streams far beneath us. The most beautiful point was one from which we looked down a vast straight glen of some fifteen miles, almost as deep as a canyon, with the silvery Erymanthus river pursuing its furious course so directly as to be clearly visible all the way. But though ascending the river from this point, where its course comes suddenly round a corner, the upper country was no longer wooded but bleak, like most of the Alpine Arcadia, a country of dire winters and great hardship to the population, who till an unwilling soil on the steep slopes of giant precipices.

We were much tempted to turn up another tortuous glen to the hidden nest of Divri, where the Greeks found refuge from Turkish persecution in the great war - a place so concealed, and so difficult of access, that an armed force has never penetrated there. But the uncertainties of our route were too many to admit of these episodes, so we hurried on to reach the Khan of Tripotamo by the evening...

Nor were the bugs perhaps the worst. Being wakened by a crunching noise in the night, I perceived that a party of cats had come in to finish our supper for us, and when startled by a flying boot, they made our beds and bodies the stepping stones for a leap to the rafters, and out through a large hole in the roof. By and by I was aroused by the splashing of cold water in my face, and found that a heavy shower had come on, and was pouring through the cats' passage.

So I put up my umbrella in bed till the shower was over - the only time I felt rain during the whole of that voyage... We did not see more than two showers, and were moreover so fortunate as to have perfectly calm days whenever we were crossing high passes, though in general the breeze was so strong as to be almost stormy in the valleys.

Next morning we followed the river up to the neighbouring site of Psophis, so picturesquely described by Polybius in his account of Philip V and his campaigns in Elis and Triphylia. This town, regarded as the frontier-town of Elis, Arcadia, and Achaia, would well repay an enterprising excavator. The description of Polybius can be verified without difficulty, and ruins are still visible.

We found out from a solitary traveller that our way turned to the north, up one of the affluents of the Erymanthus, and so we ascended in company with this worthy man to a village (Lechouri) under the highest precipices of Olonos. He was full of the curiosity of a Greek peasant - Who were we, where did we come from, were we married, had we children, how many, what was our income, was it from land, was it paid by the State, could we be dismissed by the Government, were we going to write about Greece, what would we say, etc. etc.? Such was the conversation to which we submitted for the sake of his guidance. But at last it seemed as if our way was actually at an end, and we had come into an impassable cul-de-sac. Perpendicular walls of rock surrounded us on all sides except where we had entered by constantly fording the stream, or skirting along its edge. Was it possible that the curiosity of our fellow-traveller had betrayed him into leading us up this valley to the village whither he himself was bound? We sought anxiously for the answer, when he showed us a narrow strip of dark pine-trees coming down from above, in form like a little torrent, and so reaching with a narrow thread of green to the head of the valley. This was our pass, the pine-trees with their roots and stems made a zigzag path up the almost perpendicular wall possible, and so we wended our way up with infinite turnings, walking or rather climbing for safety's sake, and to rest the labouring mules. Often as I had before attempted steer ascents with horses in Greece, I never saw anything so astonishing as this.

When we had reached the top we found ourselves in a narrow saddle, with snowy heights close to us on both sides, the highest ridge of Olonos facing us a few miles away, and a great pine forest reaching down on the northern side, whither our descent was to lead us. About us were still great patches of snow, and in them were blowing the crocus and the cyclamen, with deep blue scilla. Far away to the south reached, in a great panorama, the mountains of Arcadia, and even beyond them the highest tops of Messene and Laconia were plainly visible. The air was clear, the day perfectly fine and calm. To the north the chain of Erymanthus still hid from us the far distance. For a long time, while our muleteers slept and the mules and ponies rested, we sat wondering at the great view.

The barometer indicated that we were at a height of about 5500 feet. The freshness and purity of the atmosphere was such that no thought of hunger or fatigue could mar our perfect enjoyment. In the evening, descending through gloomy pines and dazzling snow, we reached the village of Hagios Vlasos, where the song of countless nightingales beguiled the hours of the night, for here too sleep was not easily obtained.

The journey from this point to Patras, which we accomplished in twelve hours, is not so interesting, and the traveller who tries it now had better telegraph for a carriage.

Epirus

Despite the seizure of strong points on the coast of Epirus by the Venetians during the fifteenth and sixteenth centuries, most of this region remained nominally part of the Ottoman Empire until the early twentieth century. However, in 1788 the Albanian, Ali Pasha from Tepelini, was made Pasha of Trikkala. He seized Ioannina and made himself a virtually independent sovereign, extending his control over much of what is now Northern Greece, until his death in 1822. Although a bloodthirsty tyrant in the Turkish tradition, he was for some time courted and assisted by the British as an ally in the region against Napoleon, and received many British visitors. At the Congress of Berlin in 1878 the Great Powers assigned the area of Arta to Greece, and the Turks conceded most of this in 1881. It was only during the Secoond Balkan War, in 1913, that triumphant Greek forces were able to liberate Ioannina and the rest of Epirus.

The Bridge of Arta (Contemporary print)

167

Arta

c. 1692 D.Urquhart

The Ruins of Arta

The river of Arta, opening from the hills, is met by a prolonged sandstone ridge, running north and south. The river bends back, and encircles its northern extremity, skirts it on the western side, then runs southward to the Gulf. On the low point of this ridge, to the north, stands the castle, a long and narrow structure, with lofty towers, of all forms and dimensions, over them; and over the wall the ivy rambles, fills up the embrasures, and even clusters round the muzzles of the few harmless guns. Storks, the only visible occupants, stand sentry on the towers, or solemnly pace the battlements, undisturbed by the flocks of crows, with gray crops and bright green plumage, that croak and flutter around them. This structure is rendered quite Eastern and allegorical, by a ruined tower, that rises above the others, bearing aloft a date-tree, which waves "the banner of the clime," beside a tall dark cypress, the dismal telegraph of the times. Behind the castle, but still on the low ground, are spread the ruins rather than the town, remarkable for the number of the arcades, arches and built columns, still standing amongst them. The ancient circumference of the walls embrace four times the extent of the present town: they are of old Hellenic construction, but, on the eastern side, the structure is perfectly unique. The stones are joined with the greatest precision, the surface hewn perfectly smooth, the layers exactly parallel, but the stones not always rectangular. The first layer is of five feet, and the stones are some of them six, seven, and nine feet in length, and four in width: we found one eight feet by ten and a half, and four in thickness.

The church of Parygoritza is a large square building of brick and mortar, with well-turned arches and good masonry. It contains marble and granite columns, taken from Nicopolis. Its external appearance is strange and curious, and, as we approached Arta, it looked like a palace. At Barletta, and in other parts of Apulia, there are similar churches, which are erroneously termed Gothic, or Lombard. The Albanians had been bivouacking in the church, and defacing the little that remained.

1809-10 Dr. Henry Holland

Nomadic Shepherds

We left Cinque Pozzi at eight o' clock, after several parties of Turks and Albanians had already quitted the Khan. The route from hence to Ioannina, a journey of six or seven hours, was extremely interesting. Descending for some way from the khan, we continued our progress a few miles along a narrow plain, still on a high level, but cultivated throughout the greater part of its extent. Several small hamlets appeared in the landscape, though not sufficiently numerous or extensive to give it the appearance of a well-peopled country. When advanced eight or nine miles in our journey, and crossing another ridge of high and broken land, we were highly interested in a spectacle, which, by a fortunate incident, occurred to our notice. We met on the road a community of migrating shepherds, a wandering people of the mountains of Albania, who in the summer feed their flocks in these hilly regions, and in the winter spread them over the plains in the vicinity of the Gulf of Arta, and along other parts of the coast. The many large flocks of sheep we had met the day before belonged to these people, and were preceding them to the plains. The cavalcade we now passed through was nearly two miles in length, with few interruptions. The number of horses with the emigrants might exceed a thousand; they were chiefly employed in carrying the moveable habitations, and the various goods of the community, which were packed with remarkable neatness and uniformity. The infants and smaller children were variously attached to the luggage, while the men, women, and elder children travelled for the most part on foot; a healthy and masculine race of people, but strongly marked by the wild and uncouth exterior connected with their manner of life. The greater part of the men were clad in coarse, white woollen garments; the females in the same material, but more variously coloured, and generally with some ornamented lacing about the breast. Their petticoats scarcely reached below the knee, showing nearly the whole length of the stockings, which were made of woollen threads of different colours: red, orange, white, and yellow. Almost all the young women and children wore upon the head a sort of chaplet, composed of piastres, paras, and other silver coins, strung together, and often suspended in successive rows, so as to form something like a cap. The same coins were attached to other parts of the garments; and occasionally with some degree of taste. Two priests of the Greek church were with the emigrants, and closed the long line of their procession.

These migratory tribes of shepherds are chiefly from the mountainous districts, which in their continuity form the great chain of Pindus, traversing the country very far from north to south, with many collateral branches. The people whom we now met were reported to us to be of two different tribes, one of which had already been travelling for eight or ten days. They generally come down from the mountains about the latter end of October, and return thither from the plains in April, after disposing of a certain proportion of their sheep and horses. In travelling, they pass the night on the plains or open lands; arrived at the place of their destination, they construct their little huts or tents of the materials they carry with them, assisted by the stones, straw, or earth which they find on the spot. Such is the simple life of the migrating shepherds of Albania!

1848 Edward Lear

An Unusual Theory on the Hatching of Tortoise Eggs

During this morning's ride I have seen upwards of twenty large vultures; but now, the ornithological denizens of this wide tract of marshy ground are storks, which are walking about in great numbers, and their nests are built on the roofs of the houses, clustered here and there in the more cultivated part of the district. Snakes and tortoises also were frequent during the morning, concerning which last animals Andrea volunteers some scientific intelligence, assuring me that in Greece it is a well-known fact that they hatch their eggs by the heat of their eyes, by looking fixedly at them, until the small tortoises are matured, and break the shell.

Thesprotia

1802-09 Colonel William Leake

The Town of Paramythia

Paramythia occupies the entire side of a hill which rises to half the height of Mount Kurila, and is separated only by a small space from its cliffs. Like the generality of Albanian towns, it covers a large space of ground, and is divided into clusters of houses, occupied by ... family alliances, which often make war upon one another when in want of an external quarrel. Before the reduction of the place by the Vezir , there were 600 inhabited houses, but many families having fled with Isliam Pronio, Aly's chief opponent, there are now not more than 400 Musulman and 40 Greek. The houses are built of the roughly hewn calcareous stone of the mountain, and where they stand close together, the usual Albanian filth prevails, but nothing can be more beautiful than the general appearance of the town. On the summit, which is surrounded with cliffs, stands a ruined castle; below, on the declivity of the hill, the picturesque houses are dispersed among gardens, watered by plentiful streams descending in every direction, and the spaces between the clusters of houses are grown with superb plane trees, or occupied by mosques and fountains, shaded by cypresses and planes. These beautiful features are admirably contrasted with the cliffs and fir-clad summits of the great mountain which rises above the castle. As in other Albanian towns, all the ordinary articles of Albanian or Turkish dress and furniture are manufactured here, chiefly by Musulmans. The Greeks are for the most part only retail shop-keepers.

The castle, which is surrounded by precipices, except towards the town and the south-west, formerly contained, as usual in Turkey, a great number of private houses; but these having been ruined in the war which preceded the capture of the place by Aly, it now serves only to lodge an Albanian garrison. The Vezir's governor occupies the house of Pronio, who was head of the family alliance, formerly the most powerful in Paramythia; this house, together with five or six others, which belonged to relatives of the same chieftain, is situated below the castle, on a slope terminating in another fortified rocky summit named Galata, which lies three quarters of a mile below the castle, and midway between it and the extremity of the town in the valley. The Vezir has made many repairs and additions to the fortress of Galata.

The Tribute of the Shepherds

This day I was present at a presentation to the Vezir of some of the chiefs of his shepherds who were admitted to the *proskynyma*, and kissed the hem of his robe. They come to pay their annual dues. Their first visit was to the ... Secretary, who desired all but the chief person to withdraw. "We are all equal," they replied. They are Albanians, and are here named Karagunidhes, or black-cloaks, as a distinction from the Vlakhiotes, though elsewhere, and often even in common parlance at Ioannina, it is very customary to call them all Karagunidhes, which is the more natural, as the black or white cloak is no longer a distinction, and they all come from the same great ridge of Pindus.

When the flocks are their own, they pay to the farmer of the Sultan's dues for every sheep, male or female, more than half a year old, 41/4 piastres, a small portion of which consists of a ... capitation on the animals, the rest is for ... pasture. These dues belong to the royal revenue, and are farmed by the Vezir throughout the countries which he governs. But he is moreover the greatest proprietor of sheep in northern Greece, and owns flocks in every part of Epirus and Thessaly. His shepherds are accountable for an increase of twenty per cent every year upon the number of animals, besides a certain quantity of cheese. They pay all expenses, and reckon upon an average profit to themselves of a piastre a year from each ewe, from which is to be deducted a small loss upon the males.

1849 Robert Curzon

A Narrow Escape

Towards the afternoon, when we were, by computation, about twenty-five miles from Paramathia, as we were proceeding at a trot along a narrow ledge above a stream, the baggage horse, or mule I think he was, whose halter was tied to the crupper of my horse, suddenly missed his footing, and fell over the precipice. He caught upon the edge with his forefeet, the halter supported, his head, and my horse immediately stopping, leant with all his might against the wall of rock which rose above us, squeezing my left leg between it and the saddle. The noise of the wind and rain, and the dashing of the torrent underneath, prevented my servants hearing my shouts for assistance. I was the last of the party; and I had the pleasure of seeing all my company trotting on, rising in the stirrups, and bumping along the road before me, unconscious of anything having occurred to check their progress towards the journey's end. It was so bad a day that no one thought of anything but getting on. Every man for himself was the order of the day. I could not dismount, because my left leg was squeezed so tightly against the rock, that I every moment expected the bone to snap. My horse's feet wore projected towards the edge of the precipice, and in this way he supported the fallen mule, who endeavoured to retain his hold with his chin and his forelegs. There we were – the mule's eyeballs almost starting out of his head, and all his muscles quivering with the exertion. At last something cracked: the staple in the back of my saddle gave way; off flew the crupper, and I thought at first my horse's tail was gone with it. The baggage-mule made one desperate scrambling effort, but it was of no use, and down he went, over and over-among the crashing bushes far beneath, until at length he fell with a loud splash into the waters of the stream.

Some of the people hearing the noise made by the falling mule, turned round and came back to see what was the matter; and, horse and men, we all craned our necks over the edge to see what had become of our companion. There he was in the river, with nothing but his head above the water. With some difficulty we made our way down to the edge of the torrent. The mule kept looking at us very quietly all the while till we got close to him, when the muleteer proceeded to assist him by banging him on the head with a great branch of a tree, upon which he took to struggling and scrambling, and at last, to the surprise of all, came out apparently unhurt, at least with no bones broken. The men looked him over, walked him about, gave him a kick or two by way of asking him how he was, and then placing his load upon him again, we pursued our journey.

Before dark we arrived at Paramathia, and went straight to the house where we had been so hospitably received before. We crawled up like so many drowned rats into the upper room, where we were met by the whole troop of ladies, giggling, screaming, and talking, as if they had never stopped since we left them a week before. When the baggage came to be undone, alas! what a wreck was there! The coffee and the sugar and the shirts had formed an amalgam; mud, shoes, and cambric handkerchiefs all came out together; not a thing was dry. The only consolation was that the beautiful illuminated manuscripts of Meteora had not participated in this dirty deluge.

I was wet to the skin, and my boots were full of water. In this dilemma I asked if our hosts could not lend me something to put on until some of my clothes could be dried. The ladies were full of pity and compassion; but unfortunately all the men were from home, not having returned from their daily occupations in the bazaar, and their clothes could not be got at. At last the good humoured young bride, seeing that wherever I stood there was always, in a couple of minutes' time, a puddle upon the floor, entered into an animated conversation with the other ladies, and before long they brought me a shirt, and an immense garment it was, like an English surplice, embroidered in gay colours down the seams. The fair bride contributed the white capote, which I remembered on my former visit, and a girdle. I soon donned this extempore costume. My wet clothes were taken to a great fire, which was lit for the purpose in another room, and I proceeded to dry my hair with a long narrow towel, its ends heavy with gold embroidery, which one of the ladies warmed for me, and twisted round my head in the way usual in the Turkish bath - a method of drying the head well known in most eastern towns, and which saves a great deal of trouble and exertion in rubbing and brushing according to the European method.

The Port of Ioannina and the Palace of Ali Pasha (C. R. Cockerell, 1811)

Ioannina

1802-09 Colonel William Leake

Petitions to the Traveller

Among the numerous instances of resemblance between ancient and modern customs observable throughout Eastern Europe and Western Asia, there is none more remarkable, or that better serves perhaps to mitigate the miseries of despotism, than the system of clienteia, which pervades all ranks, and which was common even among the republicans of Greece and Rome. It is a part or consequence of this system, that the request of one person to another in favour of a third, when made under particular relation of consanguinity or supposed friendship between the two former, cannot easily be refused. Even the most despotic chiefs are in great measure bound by this custom, and it is often considered a matter of certainty that the pardon of an offender may be obtained from the Vezir Aly, if some particular person of known influence can be induced to petition in favour of him. To the traveller this is attended with great inconvenience, as all sorts of requests are made to him, founded upon this maxim, sometimes the most trifling and ridiculous, at others such as he would gladly be the means of promoting, were not compliance in any case imprudent, as it would produce an endless repetition of such demands, and many inconveniences. This morning a woman of Vissiani intreats my interest with the Vezir to procure the freedom of her son, who is in prison at Ioannina, and a man who has been married three or four years to a woman without having children, wishes by the Vezir's interference with the Church to obtain a divorce and marry again, his wife being, as he asserts, wicked and perverse, and resisting all his arguments to persuade her to a separation. Another request to me for an antidote to the magic arts of an enemy, by which a husband has become *empodismenos*, is addressed to the medical knowledge, which every Frank is supposed to possess.

The Town of Ioannina

Of these houses the greater part exhibit a picture of misery not to be exceeded in any part of Turkey, many families living all the year in this severe climate in apartments defended only on three sides from the open air. Beyond this unclean quarter, the northern side of the citadel is occupied by a range of official buildings, among which is the fatal prison so much the object of horror throughout the greater part of Northern Greece, and which contains at present two hundred and fifty persons, some of whom have been two or three years immured here. An irregular esplanade between these buildings and the palace is terminated at the north-eastern angle of the citadel by the principal mosque, surrounded with cypresses, a cemetery, and a small range of buildings for the use of the imams, with a portico in front of them. This mosque, which is said to have been built, as well as that of the harem at the south-eastern angle, on the site of a Greek church, is a conspicuous object in the beautiful scenery of Ioannina, and commands one of the finest panoramas in Greece, rich as this country is in the sublime and picturesque. A drawbridge leads out of the gate of the citadel over a small esplanade, which is the ordinary place of execution, into the bazaar. This is an extensive quarter in the centre of the lowest part of the town, and consists of several narrow, intricate, dirty, ill-paved streets, occupied entirely by shops. From either end of it along the margin of the lake, branches a street occupied by the poorer classes of Greeks, and which, though not in its appearance of misery to be compared to that of the Jews, is the abode of more real poverty. All the better houses of the town are towards the slope of the hill of St. George.

Ioannina contains about 1000 Musulman houses, 2000 Greek, and 200 Jewish. The Musulman families are not more numerous than the houses, but of Greeks there are supposed to be near 3000 families, and of Jews not less than four to each house upon an average. The Christians have six or seven churches served by fifty *papadhes*, or secular priests, who attend also to the private religious observances of the Greek families. The bishop and the priests attached to the metropolitan church, are, as usual, of the monastic order. There are sixteen mosques, including the two in the citadel, where the Jews have two synagogues. Since Ioannina has been the residence and capital of Aly Pasha, its permanent population has been gradually in part exchanged for that of a more transitory kind. The town is now constantly full of the natives of other parts of Greece and Albania, attracted here by the affairs or the expenditure arising from its being the seat of government of a large portion of Greece and Albania. Many families from distant parts of the country are forced to reside here as a security for the fidelity of their relatives who may be in the Viziers employment either here or in other parts of his dominions. The house-hold establishment and troops of the Vezier and his sons, together with the Albanian soldiery, who are constantly here in their passage from one part of the country to another, increase the moveable population, but probably have not much augmented the whole amount beyond that which Iannina contained fifty years ago, as many of the old families, both Greek and Turkish, have removed elsewhere to avoid the perils and extortion of the present government, and particularly the inconvenience of lodging Albanians, from which the Turkish houses are not exempt.

A Turkish Mansion

Some of the Greek and Turkish houses in the higher parts of the town are among the best that are to be found in the provincial towns of European Turkey, though their external appearance gives little indication of it, in consequence of the custom which prevails here, as in other parts of Turkey, of avoiding the appearance of opulence, of having few windows towards the street, and or guarding them with iron bars of the rudest workmanship.

The house which I occupy ... was built by a Turkish bey, upon whose demise without heirs, or at least without any whose claims the Vezir thought proper to admit. It was seized upon by his Highness. It is situated at the angle of two streets, covers a square of about 100 feet the side, and consists, as usual, of two stories, of which the upper only is inhabited by the family.

The house is divided into three parts, of which the inner was the harem. In the middle the master received and entertained visitors, and the outer served for persons in waiting and their horses, or for strangers, who were not admitted any further into the house. In each division is a court open to the sky. A wide gate, very near the angle of the two streets, sufficient for the admission of wheel-carriages, but used only for horses, there being not even a cart like those of Thessaly in the district of Ioannina, leads into the outer court, at the end of which are two small chambers on a level with the court; these served to lodge strangers and persons who came to the Bey from the country on business. A second wide gate leads into the middle court, and opposite to it is a flight of steps, which is open laterally to the court, but is protected by a roof and ascends into the principal gallery. These steps are the only stairs in the house, except a sort of ladder, from the third court into the gallery of the harem. The middle court is paved with stone; the two others covered only with coarse gravel. According to Turkish custom, persons of superior or equal rank to the Bey rode up to the steps across the middle court, after which their horses were led back to the outer; but inferiors entered the middle court on foot. The gallery, which is about fifty feet by twelve, and forms an agreeable apartment in summer, opens at the end, to the right, into the chamber of reception, and leads, at the same extremity, by a passage at right angles to the great gallery, into two smaller ones looking down upon the third court and leading into the apartments of the harem. The pavement of the middle court extends under the chamber of reception; this in summer is the only place of refuge from the heat, which, when no clouds intervene, completely penetrates, by the hour of two in the afternoon, all the upper apartments, which have nothing above a slight ceiling but a roof of concave tiles; so that towards the evening every part of the house is intolerably hot, and more than half the night is required to restore it to the temperature of the atmosphere. Such a flimsy construction is of course equally incapable of keeping out the cold in winter, against which there is no complete protection in such dwellings but a clothing of fur. A shed at the end of the middle court, opposite to the chamber of reception, is one of the stables: the other is below the gallery of the smaller apartments of the harem; both are open towards the respective courts, and here the horses stand on the bare stone pavement without any litter, and are watered only in the evening, after which their barley is given. Instead of the chopped straw, which is the common food of horses in Turkey during the day, hay is here substituted, and the quantity of barley at night is smaller.

No windows in the house look to the street, except those of the two rooms on a level with the outer court, together with a single window in one corner of the principal apartment of the harem, which is closely latticed, but projects from the wall so as to afford a view of the street in either direction. A dim light, however, is derived from the street in the two principal apartments by means of small fixed panes of stained glass not far below the ceiling. These, with the painted ceilings and wainscots, some parts of which are very gaudy, are the only decorations in the house. All these windows look into the courts, and are closed with wooden shutters within which are bars of iron. In general, the better houses of Ioannina have an inner window-frame behind the bars, containing small panes of a very bad kind of glass brought from the Adriatic; this addition, which is seldom seen in Asiatic Turkey or the warmer climates of Greece, is here rendered necessary by the long winter and the rudeness of the climate in every season.

Greek Mansions

The best Greek houses differ not much in plan from the Turkish just described; but they are rather more comfortable, partly because the Greeks, especially the travelled merchants, have acquired some of the feelings of civilized Europe in this respect, and partly from the difference which is produced in the distribution and economy of the family, from the women not being so much concealed. There is seldom more than one court, and a small one perhaps at the back of the house; but the court is more spacious, with a wider and more ostentatious flight of steps leading to a larger wooden gallery into which all the principal apartments open. The gallery is supported by an arcade of stone continued perhaps along the side of the yard, in which is the gate leading into the street. A small garden sometimes occupies one side of the court, and at the end of the capacious gallery there is generally a raised kiosk. The gallery and kiosk are the usual residence of the family in summer; and here some of the men generally pass the night in that season. As usual both in Greek and Turkish houses, the sofa is the only furniture in sight, the bedding which is spread upon the sofa at night being deposited in closets on the sides of the chambers, and the small table with the round metal tray, which forms the only apparatus for meals, being put aside also when not in immediate use. In these respects Greek customs are nearly the same at Ioannina as in other parts of Turkey, though in some houses a table and chairs of European form are to be found, and Venetian or German mirrors are commonly suspended on the walls. In one or more of the rooms hangs a picture of the Virgin, with a lamp perpetually burning before it; and generally that of the saint whose name is borne by the master of the house, or who, for some reason, is a favourite. Some of these pictures are covered (except the face) with silver, like those in the churches. All the houses of Ioannina are constructed in the lower story of small stones rudely squared and very ill cemented: the upper apartments are in general of wood. Every large house is furnished with a well, affording, at no great depth, an abundant supply of excellent water, which is very cold even in the midst of summer. But Ioannina is otherwise well situated to afford the luxury of cool liquors - Mitzikeli and Olytzika supplying snow in the early part of the season, and the mountain of Syrako to the latest period.

The domestic manners of the Greeks of Ioannina have in general been very little affected by the long residence of many of the merchants in foreign countries, and, as in other parts of Turkey, seem not to have undergone any great alteration since the time of Homer. That they are almost identical with those of the Turks, except in those points in which their respective religions have drawn a line, or given rise to a difference, may be attributed to the tincture of Oriental customs, which is traceable in the language and manners of the Greeks of every age, arising from their position on the borders of the eastern world. But though the resemblance may thus partly be traced to a common origin, the greater part of the Turkish customs have probably been adopted by the Turks in the progress of their conquest or Asiatic and European Greece, during which they gradually exchanged the rude and simple habitudes of Tartary for the refinement and luxuries of the Byzantine empire.

"She Walks Like a Goose"

The Greek women of Ioannina are as uneducated as the Turkish, and are held in that degree of subserviency which is their common lot throughout Greece, and which seems indeed to have been their ordinary condition among the ancients.

Little respect is paid to age, especially when the parents, as often happens, are in part maintained by their children, and live in the same house. Girls are never married without a portion; to provide for which, and to make a suitable alliance for their daughters is the most anxious care of the parents, and is generally done without consulting the girl, or even allowing her to see her future lord and master. Brothers often supply their sisters, with portions; and it is even common among the young Greeks to refrain from taking a wife themselves until their sisters are married.

Young women seldom or never go out of the house before marriage, except to church, which is generally in the night. When they begin to visit, it is considered that themselves and parents have given up all hope of matrimony; but they are the more unwilling to come to this determination, as parents, aided by the custom of seclusion, sometimes succeed in concealing the age of their daughters. From such manners naturally arise ignorance, inelegance, and an early decay of beauty. The walk of the women is particularly uncouth, not so much caused by their confinement or their dress as by a persuasion prevailing among all but the peasantry, who walk as nature has taught them, that a rolling, waddling gait, is a proof of refinement; so that it is a compliment to tell a lady that she walks like a goose.

Education

One of the chief distinctions of Ioannina is its two colleges for education, and the libraries belonging to them. There is a collection of books also at the metropolitan church, but the Fathers and the Byzantine history are almost the only works which the *kalogheri* have to boast of. At the head of the old school, the origin of which is beyond tradition, is Cosma Balano, a very respectable old man, whose father was master before him. In this establishment, which lately has derived its chief support from the Zosimadhes, grammar and the usual Hellenic authors are taught, as in many of the schools of Greece. In the other, one hundred scholars are instructed in Greek, history, geography, and philosophy. The latter college was founded by Pikrozoi, a native merchant, who bequeathed 800 purses, the interest of which, together with other donations, affords a salary of 2000 piastres to the *archididaskalos* Athanasius Psalidha, besides supporting two assistants, and giving a small yearly donation to each scholar. The same Pikrozoi built a church and hospital at Ioannina. The total of the ... annual interest of the funds of the two schools, is now 60 purses. Besides these are several small grammar schools, kept by individuals generally of the secular priesthood, whose acquirements do not extend beyond the Hellenic of the Greek Testament. In the midst of summer it is not uncommon to see one of these teachers seated under a tree in the suburbs of the town surrounded by thirty or forty scholars. They receive generally a piastre a week from the poorest of their scholars.

It is said that one of the most efficient instruments in persuading the Greeks to establish schools as the best mode of improving the nation, was a monk of Apokuro named Kosma, who during eight years travelled over the country as a preacher, and made this subject a principal theme of his discourses. He was in other respects also a reformer, as he succeeded in persuading the women of Zagori to lay aside a great shapeless headdress, similar to those of some of the Aegean islands, for a simple kerchief. He fell a martyr to his zeal, having been put to death in 1780 by Kurt Pasha.

It is probably rather a consequence of the Vezir's indifference to the distant consequences of his measures, and with a view to some supposed immediate advantage, than with any better feeling, that he has always encouraged education among the Greeks. He frequently recommends it to the attention of the bishops, the generality of whom thinking only of accumulation and acting exactly like Turks in office, are too much disposed to neglect it. To the old schoolmaster, Balano, he often holds the same language, exhorting him to instruct the youth committed to his care with diligence, to give them a good example, and never to entertain any doubts of receiving his countenance and protection. His oppression is light upon monasteries compared with that which he exercises upon villages and individuals, and he has lately in particular favoured the monastery of St. Naoum, between Korytza and Akhrida. Not that he is ever at any personal expense on these occasions: for example, when a rock not long ago, fell upon the convent of St. Pandeleimona, in the island of the lake of Ioannina, he ordered the expense of the repairs to be defrayed by an assessment upon some of the chief Greeks of Ioannina; and Kyr. D. A. the most eminent merchant here, having recently given him some cause of discontent, became the principal sufferer by the fall of the rock.

The Greek spoken at Ioannina is of a more polished kind than is usually heard in any part of Greece proper; its phrases are more Hellenic, and its construction more grammatical. This is a natural consequence of the schools long established here, and of the residence of many merchants, and others who have travelled or dwelt in civilized Europe. The observation applies however to the Greeks alone. Among the Turks and Musulman Albanians every tenth word of the Greek which they speak is Turkish, and this among the native Mahometans is often all the

Turkish they know. In Epirus, as in every other part of Greece, some words remain in use among the vulgar, which though not employed elsewhere, nor even entering into the more polished language of the better classes on the spot, are of pure Hellenic derivation; they may not be found perhaps in any extant ancient author, but have been preserved in the same manner as in every country ancient forms are sometimes employed by rustics which have long been obsolete in cities... The long residence of the Sclavonic race in this part of Greece has however left its traces in the dialect, but still more perhaps in the names of places, and in the termination and mode of pronouncing those which are of Greek derivation. Many Italian words have also been introduced into the vernacular tongue from the neighbouring islands, and by means of the commerce of Ioannina with Italy.

Some Notable Buildings

The appearance of Ioannina has been greatly improved, since I was here in the year 1805, by the large serai, which the Vezir has erected upon the hill of Litharitza, according to the intention which he then communicated to me. In its form and decorations it is preferable to any other of his Highness's buildings, and though not so spacious as the Sultan's palaces on the Bosphorus, deserves still greater admiration in respect of the surrounding scenery. Standing upon the summit of a fortress which now encloses the hill of Litharitza, it forms by its light Chinese architecture a striking contrast with the solid plainness of the basis on which it rests. The parapets of the fortress are armed with cannon, and the lower part of it consists of casemated apartments, so that it may stand a siege after all the upper structure is destroyed.

Another building with which Aly has adorned Ioannina, though not adding like Litharitza new embellishment to the beautiful scenery, because it is concealed by trees, is a large kiosk situated in the midst of a rude park or garden in the northern suburb on the slope of the hill of St. George, where he has built also a small palace, and keeps some deer, a lion, and other wild animals. The Kiosk is a circle having a diameter of about 250 feet, the central half of which is paved with marble, and consists in the middle: as usual in Turkish kiosks, of a basin of water. In the centre is a rude model of a fortress mounted with cannon, which when the fountain is at work spout forth water, and are answered by a similar discharge from besieging cannon round the edge of the basin. If instead of this silly bauble in the childish taste of the Turks, there had been some more simple and elegant fountain, the building would have been as perfect a work of its kind as can be conceived. As it is, I doubt whether the Sultan himself possesses any kiosk more elegant, or more agreeable in the heat of summer. The space around the central pavement is divided into eight parts. One of these is an entrance hall, opposite to which, in a corresponding recess, is a narrow staircase and an exit to the garden. The stairs lead up to a chamber having a window which looks down into the kiosk, but is covered with a lattice painted with a landscape in such a manner as effectually to conceal the existence of the window from those in the kiosk. It is of course intended for any of his women whom he may favour by bringing them here, and who may from thence see and hear what is passing below. Of the other six recesses, the two opposite ones of which the axis is at right angles to the two first mentioned, are vacant spaces paved with marble. The others are four apartments splendidly furnished with sofas on three sides, and on the fourth open towards the fountain.

On the western side of the fortress of Litharitza, on an eminence almost equally high, stands the serai of Mukhtatr Pasha, and to the southward of it, in a lower situation, that of Vely Pasha, They are both on the edge of the great burying ground, on the southern side of the city, and not far from the shore of the lake. These houses of the two sons of Aly resemble those of Turks of high rank in other parts of the empire, except that the furniture and decorations of Vely's are a little more European than those generally seen in Turkish palaces. Mukhtar's, on the contrary; is correctly in the Turkish taste. The walls display in several places, both within and without, large paintings in their hideous style, representing actions alluding to Mukhtar's several qualities of governor, landholder, and hunter; - such as the decapitation of a Greek, the operations of agriculture, and the sports of the field. Besides the serais of the Kastro, and Litharitza, and the garden of the northwestern suburb, Aly has a large house near the northern extremity of the lake on its eastern shore at the village of Perama, where, standing on a rocky insulated height at the foot of Mount Mitzikeli, it commands a fine view of the city, with the mountains towards Arta in the distance. It is particularly agreeable in the spring, as it looks down, in an opposite direction, upon that beautiful meadow which extends from Perama as far as the lake of Lapsista, and which then, free from inundation, begins to be clothed with herbage, and a profusion of gay or odoriferous herbs...

The Lake and Island

The Nisi, or Island of Ioannina, is half a mile long and one-third as much in breadth. It contains a house for the Vezir, five small monasteries, and a village of 100 houses, inhabited by fishermen, who pay 15,000 piastres a year to the Vezir for the monopoly of the fishery, besides which they are subject to the kharatj, and to a fixed contribution of firewood for the use of the Semi. The village is situated amidst gardens and plane-trees; and the neatness of the cottages is such as would be sought for in vain among the lower classes of Ioannina, or the villages of its district, or indeed in any part of the surrounding country, except among the Vlakhiotes of Mount Pindus. The women spin cotton, and soak and bleach the cotton cloths, which are made in the city. There are only two or three monks in the island, the monasteries being now used for the lodging of prisoners collected from every part of the Vezir's dominions. As the confinement in the island, compared with that in the castle, is health and liberty, it is inflicted only for offences of a lighter kind, or upon those who are detained as hostages for absent relatives. The largest monastery is now occupied by the women and children of the Suliotes, who fled to the Seven Islands when Suli was taken... These poor creatures are allowed only a ration of koromana, and for the rest are dependent upon charity.

The commonest fish in the lake are carp and eels; but there are also pike, perch, and tench, and a small fry ... supposed to be a species of perch, which are particularly caught in the Trokhoto, in fine nets of silk made for the purpose. Water serpents are numerous, and may very commonly be seen in calm warm weather swimming on the surface. Their haunts are along the margin and at the foot of Mount Mitzikeli, where I have often witnessed them suddenly darting upon the frogs, which equally abound there: though the frog died instantly, I could never perceive that the serpent swallowed it.

All the shallow parts of the lake, particularly northward of the citadel and around the edges, abound in tall reeds and rushes, intermixed with the nymphaea both with the yellow and white blossom... Among the rushes the most common is the papyrion, from whence *ta papyria* is the term in common use to express the parts of the lake overgrown with reeds and rushes. The papyri has a single round stem without leaves, often ten feet high, of a bright green, soft, and tapering to the top, where it ends in a small tuft. It is full of a honeycombed pith, and is used to make a very useful kind of mat which forms the ordinary carpeting of the houses of Ioannina, and is exported to Corfu and other places. The reeds of the lake are chiefly used for roofing the inferior class of houses, and for making the huts and sheds of the shepherds. The papyria shelter a few cormorants and cranes, and all immense number of wild ducks of several varieties. Some of these furnish food to the birds of prey of the kite and vulture kind, which build on Mount Mitzikeli, and are often seen soaring above its sides; but the great body of the ducks are decimated by the sportsmen of Ioannina, who are continually following them in monoxyla. Passages are cut through the papyria for this purpose, and the pursuit furnishes sport occasionally to the Vezir, and still oftener to Mukhtar Pasha, the keenest sportsman of the family, and who allows the public to take their pleasure on the lower part of the lake, provided the northern, which has the best cover, is reserved for himself. When the Vezir goes forth on a shooting excursion, the lake presents a most animated scene; every boat and monoxylo being employed in surrounding the papyria, and in raising the game for him, while every gun in Ioannina is employed in bringing down the birds.

Climate

The climate of Ioannina renders it more subject to the diseases of northern than of southern Europe. In consequence of the post meridian showers the heat is seldom very oppressive until the middle of July, and the air is sensibly cooler in the beginning of September. That long continuance of heat, therefore, which is so pernicious to northern constitutions in many parts of Greece, and the South of Europe, rendering the body unable to resist the effects of the marshy exhalations, or of the first chilly breezes of autumn, is much abridged at Ioannina, and seldom felt for more than six or seven weeks. Even in that interval it does not often happen that the thermometer of Fahrenheit is above 85° in the shade, though sometimes for several days it rises about 2 pm. to 95°, and even 100°.

But though the climate of Ioannina, notwithstanding its marshes, is not generally unhealthy, the lower part of the town forms an exception: here the action of the sun upon the stagnant borders of the lake, and the effluvia of putrid matter which quickly accumulates in the streets when the rains have ceased, being aided by poverty, wretched lodgings, and unwholesome diet, dysentery prevails, as well as autumnal fevers, which if not immediately fatal, are often the commencement of obstinate intermittents, and other disorders.

A peculiarity of Ioannina, or at least of the upper part of the town, is the absence of gnats, at least of that kind which is so tormenting in other southern countries, and an abundance of which is considered by Italians as a sure sign of malaria. During two summers which I have passed here, I have never discovered any, though particularly sensible to their tormenting attacks, and have even found a mosquito curtain unnecessary. But if there is something adverse to the propagation of the venomous gnat in the air of this place, it is not so with other winged insects, of which such clouds rise from the borders of the lake in the summer evenings, that unless when the rain was falling, scarcely an evening has passed in which my candles have not been repeatedly extinguished by the immense numbers of them attracted by the flame, particularly a small kind of gnat. Among the nuisances of vermin, are brown rats of the largest kind, and it is almost needless to add, bugs, since not a house in Turkey, except in some of the mountain villages, is, in summer at least, exempt from these pests, or from fleas.

So strongly does a first view of the low situation of the greater part of the town on the borders of an apparently stagnant lake, surrounded by marshes, give the impression of unhealthiness, that it was with great difficulty I could persuade the celebrated Roman artist Lusieri, who arrived here in the latter end of June, to prolong his stay beyond a day of two, so much was he alarmed at those which his Italian opinions led him to consider as infallible symptoms of malaria. But the picturesque beauties of the place had such a powerful attraction for him that he was induced to hazard a longer visit, until his fears having been calmed by my own experience, and that of the Ioannites in general, he prolonged his stay for six weeks. The longer he remained the more he was impressed with the feeling, that in the great sources of his art, the sublime and beautiful, and in their exquisite mixture and contrast, Ioannina exceeds every place he had seen in Italy or Greece.

A Cave-Monastery

This afternoon having recrossed the bridge at the foot of the mountain of Kalarytes, I leave to the right the ordinary road to Ioannina, which crosses the ridge of St. George, and follow that which leads to Pramanda and Arta along the eastern side of the same ridge. At the end of an hour from the bridge, we arrive at Kiepina, a monastery formed like that of Megaspilio in the Morea, by means of a wall built in front of a cavern, but on a diminutive scale compared with that building, and containing only a small church with two apartments, inhabited by two monks and a young laic. The cavern is very curious, as being the entrance of a horizontal passage into the body of the mountain, of which the monks affirm, that neither they nor any other person have ever yet reached the extremity. I followed the passage for twenty minutes by the watch, without any considerable ascent or descent, over a level ground of hard clay, and without meeting any impediment, except occasionally that of stooping under some projections of the roof, or of climbing over some hollows where a single plank would save the trouble. Not having been able to procure a sufficiency of candle, I was obliged to return; the air was cold and loaded with vapour; which increased as I advanced. Near the entrance of the cavern, the sides are a bare calcareous rock; in the farther parts are some large stalagmatic columns. The monastery is situated exactly in the gorge which gives passage to the united stream, formed by the three branches of Matzuki, Kakardhista, and Kalarytes, or Syrako, and not far above the junction of this river with the Arta, or Arachthus. It commands a magnificent view of mountain scenery. Below the monastery, on the side of the hill towards the river, are some gardens watered by springs, which there issue from the mountain.

Protecting Sheep with Dog Bones

Some shepherds who are feeding their flocks around Kiepina confirm the existence of an absurd custom in these mountains, which I had of tell heard mentioned by the Kalarytiotes. With the view of making their sheep healthy and strong, and the flesh coarse and ill-flavoured, the first for the sake of enabling the sheep to resist the weather, and the latter to render it less tempting to the wolves, they are in the habit of taking a piece of the fibula of a dog, two inches long, and of inserting it into the fleshy part of the thigh of the lamb when it has nearly attained its growth, after which the opening is sewed up, So persuaded are they of the efficacy of this custom, that the shepherd at Kiepina expressed his belief, that lambs born of a ram or ewe so treated have a similar bone, Such a practice could only obtain, where the greater part of the lambs were destined only to be shorn, to breed, and to make cheese. The bone, doubtless, is soon carried away by suppuration. As education extends in Greece, this absurd custom, which is already ridiculous among the higher class, will gradually cease, as well as the use of charms and some other superstitious practices which still prevail among the common people, especially among the women.

Vampires

It would be difficult now to meet with an example of the most barbarous of all those superstitions, that of the *vrukolaka*. The name being Illyric, seems to acquit the Greeks of the invention, which was probably introduced into the country by the barbarians of Sclavonic race... The Devil is supposed to enter the vrukolaka, who, rising from his grave, torments first his nearest relations, and then others, causing their death or loss of health. The remedy is to dig up the body, and if after it has been exorcised by the priest, the demon still persists in annoying the living, to cut the body into small pieces, or if that be not sufficient, to burn it. The metropolitan bishop of Larissa lately informed me, that when metropolitan of Grevena, he once received advice of a papas having disinterred two bodies, and thrown them into the Haliacmon, on pretence of their being *vrukolakas*. Upon being summoned before the bishop, the priest confessed the fact, and asserted in justification, that a report prevailed of a large animal having been seen to issue, accompanied with flames, out of the grave in which the two bodies had been buried. The bishop began by obliging the priest to pay him 250 piastres: (his holiness did not add that he made over the money to the poor). He then sent for scissors to cut off the priest's beard, but was satisfied with frightening him. By then publishing throughout the diocese, that any similar offence would be punished with double the fine and certain loss of station, the bishop effectually quieted all the vampires of his episcopal province.

1809-10 Dr. Henry Holland

Along the Vale of Acheron

The landscape here is singularly fine; and the sudden change in the character of the scenery of very extraordinary kind. The river of Suli rises by different streams in the country to the west of Cinque Pozzi; passes the village of Sestron or Sestroni, which gives name to a part of its course, and in the valley just alluded to, flows underneath a high ridge of mountain, called Valdunesi. From the place where I reached its banks, to the castle of Suli and the plains of Paramithia, the scenery along its course is altogether more singular than any other I have seen in Greece; striking as this country is in all its natural features.

Crossing the river by a deep ford, where it makes this sudden turn to the north, I ascended the mountain on the eastern side of the pass, or chasm, which it now enters, and which is so much contracted by opposing cliffs, to the height of some hundred feet above the stream, that no access is possible, except along the higher ledges of its mountain boundary. The ascent was one of extreme difficulty, and some danger. Skirting under the summit of the mountain, upon narrow and broken ledges of rock, I came to a spot where the interior of: this profound chasm opened suddenly before me, vast and almost perpendicular precipices conducting the eye downwards to the dark line, which the river forms in flowing beneath. The view from this place I have never seen surpassed in grandeur; if grandeur indeed be a word which expresses the peculiarity of the scenery; not only its magnitude, but also the boldness and abruptness of all its forms; and a sort of sombre depth and obscurity in its features, to which it would not be easy to find a parallel. In one view you may trace the progress of the river for six or seven miles, between mountains some of which are upwards of 3000 feet in height; their precipitous sides beginning to rise even from the edge of the water; their projecting cliffs and ledges covered with small oaks and brushwood; and higher up, where they recede further from the perpendicular line, retaining the same sombre character from the dark thickets and rows of pines which appear at intervals among the rocks.

Over the Pindus to Thessaly

We recommenced our journey at an early hour on the 17th, and accomplished in the course of this day a journey of ten hours, or from 30 to 34 miles, by a route the most interesting we had yet travelled in this country. The first and principal point in the journey was the passage of Pindus. We had been strongly advised to take with us from Metzovo, some peasants acquainted with the route to assist our progress over the mountains, and our tartar had engaged three or four people for this purpose. They did not, however, arrive at the appointed time, and the weather had fortunately now become so clear and serene, that we ventured upon the journey without this, assistance; accompanied as the day before, by several men on horseback, who were travelling from Albania into Thessaly. That part of the ridge of Pindus which we had now to cross, is directly opposite to the face of the hill on which Metzovo stands, and intervenes between the sources of the river of Arta, and of the Salympria or Peneus. The comparative facility of ascent, afforded, by the valleys of the torrents which form these rivers, has led to the choice of this place of passage; where the elevation of the chain also is less than in those parts of it further to the south. Opposite Metzovo, a mountain stream forms a deep hollow to the very base of the summit ridge, and along; this steep and rugged channel, the road, or rather, track, is continued for two or three miles. While pursuing slowly this part of the route, we met a large train of Albanian soldiers, who, though the day was still little advanced, had already crossed the ridge of Pindus, from a khan on the eastern side. Where we quitted this channel, it seemed as if the further progress of the ascent were utterly impracticable and we looked upwards with astonishment at an impending promontory of rock, which at this time was nearly 1,000 feet above us, but which the Tartar explained to be one point in our route to the summit of the mountain. Our ascent thither was rendered possible only by long detours, to avoid the numerous precipices which appeared on each side of our tract; yet notwithstanding this circuitous direction of the road, the declivity was such, that we had much difficulty in urging our horses to continue their progress forwards. In winter, this part of the passage of the mountain is often wholly impracticable; and even when there is only a small quantity of snow on the ridge, the ascent becomes so dangerous, that guides are necessary to the security of the traveller. A violent wind is almost equally dreaded in traversing these lofty regions: sweeping through the deep hollows and recesses of the mountain, it forms whirlwinds so strong and impetuous, that the passage even if possible, becomes extremely dangerous. We were fortunate in avoiding both these difficulties. The day was perfectly calm, and the snow, lying only in the clefts of the mountain, in no degree impeded our progress. Even at the summit of the ridge a little after 9 o'clock, the thermometer did not fall below 34 degrees; and we suffered no inconvenience in remaining some time on this elevated point, to gaze on the extraordinary scene, around us.

A ridge, it may indeed be called, to which a laborious ascent of two hours from Metzovo had conducted us. The summit where we crossed it is scarcely a yard in width, and the same wedge-like form of this vast mountain chain appears to be continued far towards the north. At this point, even the general calmness of the day did not exempt us from a strong wind, which, when increased in degree, renders the passage extremely difficult. The inspiration of Apollo and the Muses, the deities of Pindus, must be powerful indeed, which could produce a stanza in this spot on a winter's day; yet the view hence might well suggest the subject of a thousand. The plains of the ancient Thessaly lie expanded in the landscape before you. The Peneus of Tempe, a river well known to poetic lore, issues in mountain streams from the rocks below your feet. Its beautiful valleys, luxuriant in the foliage of woods; picturesque, or even sublime, in the hills which form the boundary, may be traced league after league, into the distant landscape. Beyond this, a succession of mountains and plains conduct the eye, in the remote distance is the ever memorable Olympus; now, as in ancient times, covered with snows which even the summer sun of these climates does not entirely remove. Other heights appeared to the south of this great mountain, which, from their situation, we supposed to be Ossa and Pelion; (and with respect to the former at least, the conjecture was founded in fact. With some earnestness we sought to discover the coast of the Archipelago, and the outline of the sea; but if they are actually to be seen from this remote point, the state of the sky, which in the horizon was covered with fleecy clouds, prevented us from obtaining this part of the view. The chain of Pindus itself was not the least remarkable object in the landscape; having a strength and majesty of outline, which cannot easily be surpassed in mountain scenery; its narrow ridges to the north of the spot where we stood covered with woods of pine, even to their summits; to the south, rising into much greater heights, which were deeply covered with snow; these heights forming the great mountains which intervene between the sources of the Achelous and the river of Arta.

1810 John Hobhouse

Social Equality

Many English travellers remarked upon the way in which a "great man" in the East would dine with his social inferiors without any outward sign of condescension. They persisted in regarding this, rather than their own absurd social pretensions, as requring explanation.

The Greeks are all traders in some degree. This circumstance, together with the Turkish oppression, and the want of hereditary dignities, occasions a kind of equality amongst them, and does away with all those distinctions which are so rigorously observed in England. I was one day a little astonished at the house of Signor Nicolo at Ioannina, to see a tailor who had just been measuring one of us, seat himself in the room with ourselves and the rest of the company, and, by the invitation of our host, take a dish of coffee, to which he was helped by the Signor's brother with the usual ceremonies. There is nothing that implies familiarity, and, at least, temporary equality, so much as eating together: but according to the customs of both Greeks and Turks, in many points exactly similar, and which may be called oriental, the very lowest person is often indulged in this liberty by his superiors. A great man travelling does not have a table spread for him alone, but some of his attendants always partake with him round the same tray. One of the young Pashas at Ioannina insisted upon our servant George sitting down at the foot of the sofa opposite to him, and taking coffee and sweetmeats at the same time with himself and his guest. It must, however, be recollected that as almost all in Turkey receive the same sort of education, and consequently imbibe somewhat the same manners, there is in that country none of that awkwardness and confusion in society, which arise amongst us when a person of inferior quality is admitted by sufferance into better company than he has been accustomed to keep. Neither our dragoman nor our tailor would have been distinguished by a stranger from the company about them by any want of ease, or other deficiency in their manners. There is an air of great kindness, and even of ceremonious attention, in their treatment of servants and dependants; and when a rich, or, in other words, a great man, meets an inferior in the street, he not only returns his salute, but goes through the whole round of complimentary inquiries which are always usual upon a casual encounter, and prefatory to any other conversation. Two Greeks will ask one another how they are, with the same inquiries after their wives, daughters, sons, family, and affairs, twenty times over, before they begin to converse, and often when they intend to separate instantly...

1813 The Rev. Thomas Smart Hughes

The Stoning of a Girl

On the day when I departed for the north of Albania, a Turkish girl, of extraordinary beauty, was stoned to death. As my two friends and myself were proceeding to the palace, we heard a person proclaiming something in the Turkish language; and on inquiring of our interpreter, we found it was an order for "every true believer in the faith of Mahomet" to go and throw a stone at this poor girl. Her crime was that of intriguing with a Christian, a Neapolitan in the vizir's service, for which the laws of Turkey subjected her to this horrible punishment.

The interviews between herself and her lover had been facilitated by a Jew; but this worthy descendant of Iscariot was the first person to betray them: he supped at the Neapolitan's table on the fatal evening, and had scarcely retired from it half an hour before his information caused them to be arrested by the Turkish guard. The following morning, Geliscm (this was the unfortunate girl's name) was condemned to die. Soon after sentence was passed, her face was uncovered and exposed to the public gaze, which is the greatest indignity that can be offered to a Turkish female. She was then conducted, amidst the groans and curses of the Mahometans, to a plain at a short distance from the town; and had no sooner reached the fatal spot, than she was partly stripped, and her long black tresses loosened about her neck and shoulders. One would suppose that her appearance at this moment might have disarmed even Turks of their vengeance: but no! She was obliged to descend into a hole dug for the purpose, when these barbarians began to pelt her with stones, uttering at the same time a volley of groans and curses. She was tortured thus for nearly a quarter of an hour, the pebbles being inconsiderable in size and striking her mostly about the neck and shoulders: at length an Albanian soldier, who had more humanity than the rest, took up a large stone, and, throwing it upon her head, put an end to her misery. She was then left buried under the mass.

The Neapolitan's fate can be considered as little less severe. After having been permitted to remain at Ioannina long enough to witness the barbarities exercised upon his mistress, he was cruelly beaten and then sent to be imprisoned in the city of Argyro-Castro, where the plague was violently raging, and where two-thirds of the inhabitants had already fallen victims to its fury. The people indeed demanded his blood, and Ali spread a report that he had been executed; but being his principal engineer, he could not spare him for sacrifice.

What rendered the fate of these unfortunate lovers more melancholy was, that the girl, who was but nineteen years old, was in a state of pregnancy, and the man wished to marry her; but this could not be permitted, according to the laws of the country, I was informed, however, that he might have saved her life as well as his own by renouncing his religion. The girl too had means of escaping the punishment of death; but she afforded a singular instance of female heroism as well as of that extraordinary attachment which the Turks bear to their religion. When she arrived at the fatal hole dug in the ground, she was desired by the priest to leap into it, *"if a true believer in Mahomet: - if not, to leap over it."* She took the former resolution, though the consequence of not doing so would have been the preservation of her life: she would indeed have been degraded, scourged, and spit upon by the Turks; but her life would have been spared.

Of course, we had no wish to be spectators of this horrid scene; nor should we have been permitted to see it, so enraged were the Mahometans against the Christians, or, as they are pleased to term them, "the Infidels." Indeed it was said at the time (and considering the source from whence I received the information, I have reason to believe it true) that a dervish went to the vizir next day, and represented to him the necessity of sacrificing thirty Christian heads, in order to save the girl's soul; but Ali had him turned immediately out of the room. Had this measure been adopted, my head might possibly have counted as one.

We walked through the streets this day as usual; but were afterwards told that we had acted imprudently in doing so. There are certainly many parts of Turkey where we might have been exposed to the fury of the Mahometans: but considering the authority of Ali Pasha, as well as his extreme care not only to protect but even to please the English, I believe we incurred very little danger.

Second-Hand Brides

The same evening, after changing our dress, we witnessed a very extraordinary marriage procession from the window of another of Nicolo's relatives: it was the deportation of one of Ali's own concubines from his harem to the house of an officer to whom he had given her in marriage. One would have thought it impossible that a victim who had just escaped from the bars of such a prison, in which sensuality reigned without love, luxury without taste, and slavery without remission, could have complied so far with custom as to walk, in the first ecstasies of liberty, with a motion not much quicker than the minute hand of a town-clock. She was attended by no persons of her own sex, but her train-bearer and supporters were Albanian soldiers, friends of her future spouse. From the great number of torches carried in procession, we were enabled to get a perfect view of her face, which was by no means handsome. Her figure was lusty, but this among the Turks is considered more beautiful than the proportions of the Medicean Venus. She was superbly attired, but we were informed that the pearls and brilliants which adorned her head and neck were only lent for the occasion, and would be returned next day to the seraglio. The dress she wore, and two other suits, which, together with the furniture of the bridal bed, were carried after her by the Albanian guards, was all the dowry she received from her former master.

It was not by any means an unusual thing with Ali thus to dispose of the females of his harem; he gave them to his Turkish, Greek and Albanian retainers; but most willingly to Franks who entered into his service, as means of detaining them in his dominions. At Tepeleni we saw two Italian gardeners who had been thus generously provided with consorts: but, as I have before observed, he was free from many Turkish prejudices, and very ready to dispense with any forms, civil or religious, for the promotion of his own interest. Perhaps some of my readers may not give him much credit for liberality in this case, when they are informed that he possessed about six hundred female victims, guarded by eunuchs, and immured within the impenetrable recesses of his harem; though it may be supposed that most of these were retained merely to augment his dignity, and to wait upon his favourites. Before age had chilled his blood his sensuality was unbounded: wherever his satellites heard of a beautiful child, of either sex, they dragged it from the paternal roof, and massacred the family or burned the village if any resistance was offered. One of his most beautiful females was torn from the hymeneal altar whilst she was pledging her vows to a fine young man, son of the primate of Vonizza, who, unable to bear the loss, or to avenge it, blew out his own brains with his pistol. Such disgusting scenes are reported to have been acted within his harem, and especially that of his son Mouchtir, as are little fit for description in these pages: even the Turks themselves were accustomed to speak of them with astonishment and abhorrence. His favourite was a young Greek slave, named Vasilikeé, born at Paramithia and brought up in the serai from a child: she was said to have been extremely beautiful, and bore an excellent character for charity; whilst her kind disposition was frequently shown in mitigating the severities of her lordly lover towards his subjects. Wherever he went this favourite constantly attended him; she retained his affections longer than any other woman; and in 1816 he married her with great pomp and ceremony, permitting her to retain her own religious rites and doctrines.

A Degenerate Court

Ali's infamous excesses brought him to a dreadful state of suffering, in which he often sought relief by application to the best Frank physicians, as well as by those arts of quackery with which his own subjects contrived to cheat him. In 1806 he was at his particular request supplied by Sir A. Ball with a skilful surgeon from Malta; and that gentleman, in a very interesting narrative, thus alludes to a communication which the Vizir made to him on the subject of his disordered constitution. "It would ill become my professional character, were I to particularize what passed during this and subsequent visits, to harrow up my best feelings, and to kindle in my breast mingled emotions of horror, indignation, and surprise! Of surprise, that one bearing on his proud front the stamp and image of his maker, and intellectually gifted in no ordinary degree, should have degraded himself beneath the level of the vilest reptiles whose gross instinctive propensities engage physiological inquiry, and have afforded all example of the passions which reason ought to have controlled, unblushingly directed to objects repugnant in their nature! I speak not of the garden scene - of the modern Antinous, environed by his ever-watchful guardians - neither is it my wish, lovely Vasilikeé to dwell on thy cruel lot, doomed like Tantalus to the most mortifying endurances. Though still of tender age thou wert for six tedious years the degraded but not the subdued victim of this satyr in human shape! But if, as well as the more prominent and energetic traits, those of the privacy of exalted characters belong to posterity, either as a lesson or a guide, then ought it to be recorded - that in the gratification of his depraved appetites, Ali Pasha, of all known modern sensualists the most sensual, exceeded whatever the most *impure imagination can conceive*, whether it may have drawn its sullied stores from scenes of high-varnished debauchery, or from the obscurely tinted perspective of the low haunts of infamy and vice.

This gentleman also declares, and I am not inclined to doubt his veracity, that he afterwards met Ali's agent, Signore Colvo, in Malta, who earnestly applied to him for a tasteless and colourless poison of which his master had need, and in search of which he had sent him to Sicily: doubtless he had heard of the rediscovery made in that island of the celebrated *aqua tofana* which had the properties above alluded to. Colvo, however, failed to procure it, and loath to return home without executing his commission, made his shameless application to a British officer, and received the answer which one would expect on such an occasion.

1820s David Urquhart

The Meeting of Two Ottoman Nobles

At the gorge, a troop of Arslan Bey's horse was drawn up. They made their obeisance in the most lowly guise as the Bey approached, and, when he had passed, joined the throng behind him. The ground was broken, and there was now a general rush from behind forward; the men on foot had been gradually expelled from the centre by the weight of the horses, and we entered the meadow in a dense mass at full gallop. The press, the confusion, the dust, were such that we could distinguish neither where we were going, nor the ground we were passing over; and I am sure that, if a hundred muskets had been discharged at us, a general scamper and rout must have taken place, and we should have upset each other, attacked our friends, or have fled from them. It is a very singular thing to see warfare conducted between enemies wearing the same costume, speaking the same language, and without any distinctive signs, marks, or watchwords. Here soldiers are instruments, but not machines; the most powerful assemblages of troops may be melted away in a moment, and gatherings may as suddenly assemble, fit to change the face of provinces and of empires, through agency of a moral character, which is most painful for a stranger to trace with accuracy, but which is still one of the most interesting features, and one of the deepest enquiries, presented by the East.

Between European and the Eastern commander there is this most remarkable difference, that the intercourse of the first with his men ceases with the duty of the field; he is known to them only through the discipline he enforces and the services he commands, and makes no appeals to their affections in social life. The Eastern commander, on the contrary, is the Patriarch of his followers ; - he is the arbitrator of their differences - the chief of their community - knows each, and the affairs of each - and such is the equalizing effect of those manners which appear to us to place so immeasurable a distance between man and man, that the humblest soldier may, under certain circumstances, be admitted to break bread with his general. The characters which there ensure fidelity and raise to power, are ability indicated by success ; and the disposition to repay loyalty by protection, indicated by generosity. And if I were to place in order the qualifications which lead to greatness, I should say: justice first, then generosity; and only after these, military skill and personal valour.

In the middle of the little plain, and close to a clear fresh stream, stood a splendid weeping willow: this was the spot chosen for meeting, and here Veli Bey dismounted; he was soon seated on his carpet, and a circle of Beys and men formed around him. It appeared to us extraordinary that Arslan Bey was not already here, and the more so, as the higher ground all around was occupied by his men. Many suspicions crossed our minds, and my companions and myself retired up the side of the hill to make our observations, and to escape the effects of the first discharges, which we had now no doubt would, at some preconcerted signal, be poured on the crowd in the plain. There, thought I, are those men with the eye-ball of destruction glaring upon them, sitting with the same infatuation that year after year lures to their fate the chiefs and the rebels of Turkey! There scarcely is an example of a revolt that has not been subdued, or of a struggle between rival chieftains which has not been concluded by an act of treachery, in which the party deceived has been led into the noose with a facility which appears to us both childish and incomprehensible. The reason of this I at that time was just beginning to see. These movements, not being connected with general principles, can be annihilated only in the person of their conductors ; and that apparent confidence by which so unaccountably those appear to be betrayed, is the result of the daring and decision upon which alone their authority depends.

In the midst of these reflections a cloud of dust arose at the opposite extremity of the meadow, and shouts of "He comes! He comes!" arose on all sides. An alley of two hundred paces was opened from the willow tree, lined on both sides by the troops of Veli Bey. At the extremity were planted in the ground the two standards of our chief – the one pure white, the other white and green, bearing a double-bladed sword and blood red-hand, and some masonic diagrams. A troop of about two hundred horse dashed up in most gallant style, and with a greater air of regularity than I had ever witnessed before. When they reached the standards they pulled sharp up, trotted on to the willow-tree, filling up the whole breadth of the alley, and then wheeling right and left, ranged themselves behind the lines of Veli Bey's foot soldiers. At this moment Arslan Bey himself reached the standards - he there dismounted; at the same moment Veli Bey stood up under the willow-tree. This was a signal for a general discharge of the whole muskets of both parties; and when the smoke cleared away we saw the two chiefs embracing each other in the centre of the alley, to which, with equal steps, they had advanced from either extremity. Each then embraced the principal adherents of his antagonist ; - this was the signal for the respective troops to follow their example; and all around nothing was to be seen but figures bending down and rising up with such a motion as a field of battle presents when men are struggling hand to hand, and closing in the embrace of hate. This was a strange meeting of the rival hordes of a *Firmanli* and his commissioned executioner; and whoever looked upon the fervour and simplicity of that meeting "where they fell and wept on each other's necks." - might have deemed it that of Lot and Abraham with their households. In embracing, they bend down as they meet each other, kiss the mouth, then press cheek to cheek, while they either formally extend their arms, or more or less closely press each other. But the lowness to which they stoop, whether or not the kiss on the lips is given, or one or both cheeks are pressed, or the embrace is formal or close, constitute an endless series of shades and distinctions, indicating degrees of acquaintance, friendship, affection, relationship, station, relative rank, authority and command.

Broken and abrupt ground rising on either side, over which fell in little cascades the water that turned several mills; well-wooded hills beyond, in which fir predominated, and above these, the lofty and precipitous cliffs of the Pindus, displayed to the best advantage the troops bristling along each summit, or crowded in the valley. Beneath the willow was assembled the principal group; - five thousand men were scattered in parties, above, below, and around us; - congratulations, embracings, elaborate compliments and loud laughter, activity, bustle, and ever-varying and pleasing confusion; - variety and power of expression, beauty and diversity of costume, richness of accoutrement, strangeness of arms, brilliancy and contrast of colours – fatigued the curiosity they could not cloy. ..

The public conference lasted about a quarter of an hour; a general movement then informed us that the chieftains were about to retire to a khan near at hand for private discussion. We pressed forward to obtain a closer view of Arslan Bey. The two walked on, half embraced, when Veli Bey, perceiving us, stopped, and patting Arslan Bey on the breast, cried out – "Here is the Turk! You see we have caught the klepht you were so anxious to fight with." Taking this for an Albanian mode of presentation, we bowed low, whilst the young "Lion", drawing himself to his height, scanned us from head to foot; but strange as our figures were, his thoughts were evidently not with his eyes. They moved on and entered the khan; the doors were closed upon them, and a negro attendant of each chief defended them against the throngs of palicars that pressed like swarms of bees around their queens.

The scene of agitation sank gradually into one of repose. The palicars, in social groups, nestled themselves in the bushes; nothing was to be seen but groups of grazing horses. After an hour's scramble, exhausted by the midday heat, we turned towards the khan. From every bush, as we passed, we heard the words repeated, "Will you write this?" Meaning - Will you print it? The constant, and not friendly stare of the Albanians of the other party almost determined us on retiring to the first encampment, when Abas Bey again came to our assistance, and proposed our entering the chamber, as the conference was drawing to a close, and we could not interrupt it, not understanding the Skipt. The passage was consequently cleared, and we had the satisfaction of being present at a conference on which such immense results depended.

The two chiefs were seated on a mat under a small window, which gave the only light to the room, which fell , with full power and with deep shadows on the group: a white cloak, hung up on the opposite side, increased the effect, by throwing back a pale glare over their countenances. The remainder of the dungeon-like apartment was dark. In a remote corner, from time to time groaned a sick man, who had been removed out of hearing from a pallet on which we were seated. A bowl of raki, a bottle of Samian wine, and a plate of salt-fish, stood between the Beys. We sat for three hours, during which their conference was still prolonged, sometimes gravely animated, sometimes in scarcely audible whispers, whilst they leaned forward and seemed to look into each other's soul. Several times drops of large perspiration started from Arslan Bey's brow, and once Veli Bey impressed a kiss on his forehead.

Our anticipations had been excited by the praises we had constantly heard lavished on Arslan Bey; nor were we disappointed. His person was good, though below the middle size; his features fine, with a mild expression, but a fierce eye; a dark handkerchief bound the small red cap over his high and beautifully formed forehead; his dress was plain and soldierlike, and youth gave additional interest to the ideal character which we always suppose, and to the natural powers of mind and body that must always be combined in a, leader who struggles with constituted authority. They told us he was only twenty-two, but I should say he was twenty-five... He held the destinies of Albania in his hands; his will or caprice was actually the ruling power, and a word from him might let fall the thunderstorm now lowering over it. Yet, what ultimate benefit could he expect from the disaster? If he exerted his influence to arrest the catastrophe, he thereby deprived himself of power; and what assurance of recompense, what guarantee of pardon, could he obtain? These arguments we imagined we could trace in the imposing tones and manner of Veli Bey, and in the deep abstraction of his antagonist, who, although he had his rival in his hands, suffered him to assume so decided a superiority. Veli Bey's cares were not less anxious, nor his breast more quiet, whatever the serenity that sate on his brow; but all that I then knew of his inward thought, and of his actual circumstances, I have already detailed.

We remained silent and motionless, catching at every word, tone, or gesture, to which we could attach a meaning, and marking the expression with which were uttered the words, "Sadrazem", "Cogana," "Lufe," "Padeshah," etc., Veli Bey had, from time to time been handing us over *rakki* and giving vent to his satisfaction in rallying Arslan Bey, and asking us how we liked the Klepht; but he could not induce the fixed features of the young rebel to relax into a smile. At length, Veli Bey called for dinner, and some of the principal officers, who thronged the passage without, in the most anxious expectation, burst into the apartment. We ourselves were perfectly ignorant of the result, nor could we exclude the idea that the conference might terminate in blood; and each unexpected movement in the chiefs instantly riveted our attention. When the Beys entered the room, Veli Bey exclaimed, "Brothers, it is peace!" Those of his party again embraced Arslan Bey, but more fervently than before; they then attempted to tear from his forehead the kerchief that bound it; he struggled for a moment, but they tore it from him, and stamped upon it. Veli Bey seemed delighted, laughed, and pointed out to us the new Tactico (Nizzam). During dinner the conversation was principally in Albanian, in which Arslan Bey, with remarkable versatility of powers and character, took the lead; peals of laughter followed every word he uttered. When we had eaten, washed, and drank a cup of coffee, the room was again cleared. The chief adherents of Arslan Bey were then called back by name, and collected by Veli Bey in a circle around him: he addressed them in a long discourse. Often as I have had to lament the ignorance of language, never did I deplore that ignorance as on this occasion. The continuity, the oratorical sweep of his periods, the variety of intonation, action, and expression - the scorn, reproach, and, finally, pity, of which the men before him were evidently themselves the objects, exhibited powers no less extraordinary than ,judgment, and not less courage than rhetoric ; and we learned that day a lesson, with respect to the characters of the Eastern mind, that neither, probably, will soon forget. When he had completely mastered his hearers, his manner changed entirely, and their reconciliation was sealed in a formal manner. One was placed opposite to Veli Bey, two others on either side; they rose together, leaned forward, and each stretching out his arms, the four stood locked in one embrace. Veli Bey kissed each separately, repeating, "We have peace."

The conference, after eight hours of painful anxiety, being thus happily concluded, Veli Bey and Arslan Bey left the khan as they had entered, half embracing each other. The men started up, thronging around them; the Tambourgi's alarum sounded, and we again ascended the hill, to see the separating squadrons reiterating adieus, galloping round their leaders, whirling their spears and muskets, and running races up the hills or through the valley.

We returned to the encampment, and had our tent pitched in it. Veli Bey took up his quarters with us. He had previously few thoughts or words to spare; but now, in the exultation of success, he opened to us his own prospects, and his hopes for Albania, and spent the greater part of each day in giving us the history of the Grand Vizir, of the Greek war, of his feud with Selictar Poda, and of every thing he thought might be interesting or instructive. The organisation of Albania was the subject he dwelt on with the greatest satisfaction; and his own appointment to the command of twelve thousand men, which was the immediate recompense held out for his reducing this insurrection. He seemed to take delight in speaking to us, in the midst of his men, of the plans that had been formed for organising Albania, as if to sound their feelings, and to gain support from the approbation of Europeans. On the other hand, the men said to us, "Tell our Bey to leave us our fustanels, and we will become any thing he pleases." With equal earnestness, Veli Bey entered into the commercial interests and prospects of his country, the ameliorations that might be introduced; above all, the necessity of establishing friendly feelings between his own people and Europe, through which foreign capital would pour in, and, by facilitating the means of conveyance, greatly increase the wealth of the country and the value of land. He anxiously inquired into every improvement and discovery in agriculture or machinery, with the view of turning his triumph, as he said, to the advantage of their children; so that, when an old man, he might bring his grandsons to see the valley in the Pindus, where the projects were conceived.

Brigands at the Pass

Mezzovo, one of the most important, perhaps the most important, pass of all Roumeli, situated amidst such natural defences, having so large a population of armed Greeks, with little landed possessions, had been hitherto singularly respected and peculiarly favoured. It was now in a state of the utmost panic and alarm; every door not occupied by troops was barricaded, and apprehension was deeply imprinted on every countenance. The sheep, cattle, and horses, were dispersed and hidden among the rocks. The town was occupied by the troops of a Turkish Binbashi, by those of Gench Aga, and by those belonging to the municipality. On the road to Milies, to the north, were the troops of Arslan Bey; to the west, those of Veli Bey; to the east, those of the Greek captains, Gogo and Liacatus, were engaged in a separate war, contending for the Capitanato of Radovich.

No answer arriving from Arslan Bey, we determined on setting forward immediately, without waiting for the detachment. Ten men and a captain, the most savage-like travelling companions it had as yet been my lot to fall in with, were given us as an escort. Before we had been half an hour on the road, the captain began to treat us with the utmost insolence; and receiving a rebuke unaccustomed from a Giaour, he stopped with his men; but after appearing to remain some time in consultation, they followed us. We pushed on to overtake some Greeks belonging to Gogo. We had scarcely reached them, when they quitted the road and took to the hills; their appearance and manners were. However, not much more inviting than that of the party we had hoped to leave. We were now winding lip the steep ridge of the highest chain of the Pindus, the most dangerous part of the road. The place was full of broken rocks, from behind which sure aim could be taken; and we were surrounded by banditti that knew no chief and were fighting among themselves, who wanted neither opportunity, inclination, nor a sense of impunity.

It being impossible either to halt or to return, we trusted to Kismet and went on. Presently we perceived a captain with some mounted men following us. Taking them to be of a higher caste, we slackened our pace till they came up, and, after the customary salutations, we proceeded together. In scrambling up the rock, his horse passed that of our interpreter, who seemed by no means disposed to allow himself to be thus shoved out of the narrow path: the captain turned round upon him, calling him *pezeveng* and *kereta*, and was answered in the same style. One man was close to the captain. I returned to support the servant; and in a moment we four stood, each with a cocked pistol in one hand, and a knife or a dagger in the other. The captain's men, a little higher up; and our men, who were now close to us below, on the first movement unslung their guns, dropped down behind the stones, and lay with their pieces levelled on the group in the centre; which stood up to their full height, watching each other's eyes. Seeing the pause, the chief of our guard rushed forward and interposed; the weapons were gradually lowered, then put up, and we marched on as if nothing had happened, passed over the sharp ridge, and descended to the khan close to it on the other side. It was only there that we began to think how romantic a fate had been ours, had our funereal lotion been fresh poured from the urn of Peneus, and our turf decked by the Dryads of Pindus.

There was something very business-like in the sudden drop of the men behind the stones: familiar practice was marked in the first alertness and the subsequent indifference. This incident illustrated the advantage, in this world, of having foes. Our escort, from whom we were endeavouring to escape, and who entertained towards us, while we had no need of their aid, no more friendly feelings than we to them, now instantly, seeing us attacked, proposed to risk their lives in our defence, and to send their bullets through their countrymen's hearts for our sakes.

At the khan we found ourselves in a most beautiful situation; the summits were covered by lofty beech, straight as arrows, dropped, like plummet lines, on the inclined sward. This was the finest timber of its kind I ever saw; in the lower part there is nothing to be compared to it. These lofty trees shut out the view of the plains to the east, and left our confined echappees embellished but by the trees themselves, glaring lights and deep shade, cool breezes and crystal springs, amid glassy rocks of every hue, The klefts collected round the khan, chiefly deserters from Gench Aga, might have delighted the spirit of a Salvator Rosa; but we at the time paid but little attention to the picteresque of the landscape, or to the romance of the figures in the foreground. We looked at the cover they had at every point; we marked every inquisitive glance cast on our baggage, our arms, and our persons. We, too, were Tartars in our way, and might have passed for cousins of Robinson Crusoe, our clothes torn by thorns and thickets, with a pistol, a dagger, or a knife, appearing from each pocket-hole. We were deliberating whether we should advance, or barricade ourselves within the khan for the night, when a detachment of the cavalry of Gench Aga galloped up, inquiring loudly for us. Subsequently to our departure, learning the state of the road, he had sent on these, in all haste, to accompany us to Triccala.

1848 Edward Lear

A Plague of Vultures

We pursued the paved post-track to Yannina for nearly two hours and as the pace over those causeways is of the slowest, I am on the lookout for incidents of all kinds, and find sufficient amusement in watching the birds which haunt these plains; there are jays and storks, and vultures, in greater numbers than I had supposed ever congregated together. Even the unobservant Andrea was struck by discovering on a near approach, that multitude of what we thought sheep, were in fact vultures and on our asking some peasants as to the cause of their being so numerous, they said, that owing to a disease among the lambs, greater quantities of birds of prey had collected in the plains than the oldest inhabitant could recollect. A constant stream of these harpies was passing from the low grounds to the rocks above the plain and they soared so closely above our heads, that I could perfectly well distinguish their repulsive physiognomies. I counted one hundred and sixty of them at one spot, and must confess that they make a very grand appearance when soaring and wheeling with outstretched wings and necks. All the ground in this marshy part of the plain was covered with the most brilliant yellow iris in full bloom.

A Painter in Ioannina

Three days passed at Yannina, but with constant interruptions from showers. The mornings are brilliant, but clouds gather on Mitzikeli about nine or ten, and from noon to three or four, thunder and pouring rain ensues. The air is extremely cold, and whereas at Parga I could only bear the lightest clothing, I am here too glad to wear a double capote, and half the night am too cold to sleep.

Apart from the friendly hospitality of the Damaschino family, a sojourn at Yannina is great pleasure, and were it possible, I would gladly pass a summer here. It is not easy to appreciate the beauty of this scenery in a hasty visit; the outlines of the mountains around are too magnificent to be readily reducible to the rules of art, and the want of foliage on the plain and hills may perhaps at first give a barren air to the landscape. It is only on becoming conversant with the groups of trees and buildings, picturesque in themselves, and which combine exquisitely with small portions of the surrounding hills, plain, or lake, that an artist perceives the inexhaustible store of really beautiful forms with which Yannina abounds.

During these days time passed rapidly away, for there was full employment for every hour; one moment I would sit on the hill which rises west of the city, whence the great mountain of Mitzikeli on the eastern side of the lake is seen most nobly: at another, I would move with delight from point to point among the southern suburbs, from which the huge ruined fortress of Litharitza, with many a silvery mosque and dark cypress, form exquisite pictures: or watch from the walls of the ruin itself, the varied effect of cloud or sunbeam passing over the blue lake, now shadowing the promontory of the kastron or citadel, now gilding the little island at the foot of majestic Mitzikeli. Then I would linger on the northern outskirts of the town, whence its long line constitutes a small part of a landscape whose sublime horizon is varied by mountain forms of the loftiest and most beautiful character, or by wandering in the lower ground near the lake, I would enjoy the placid solemnity of the dark waters reflecting the great mosque and battlements of the citadel as in a mirror. I was never tired of walking out into the spacious plain on each side the town, where immense numbers of cattle enlivened the scene, and milk-white storks paraded leisurely in quest of food: or I would take a boat and cross to the little island, and visit the monastery, where that most wondrous man Ali Pasha met his death: or sitting by the edge of the lake near the southern side of the kastron, sketch the massive, mournful ruins of his palace of Litharitza, with the peaks of Olytzika rising beyond. For hours I could loiter on the terrace of the kastron opposite the Pasha's serai, among the ruined fortifications, or near the strange gilded tomb where lies the body of the man who for so long a time made thousands tremble! It was a treat to watch the evening deepen the colours of the beautiful northern hills, or shadows creeping up the furrowed sides of Mitzikeli.

And inside this city of manifold charms the interest was all varied and as fascinating: it united the curious dresses of the Greek peasant - the splendour of those of the Albanian: the endless attractions of the bazaars, where embroidery of all kinds, firearms, horse-gear, wooden-ware, and numberless manufactures peculiar to Albania were exhibited -the clattering storks, whose nests are built on half the chimneys of the town, and in the great plane-trees whose drooping foliage hangs over the open spaces or squares: these and other amusing or striking novelties which the pen would tire of enumerating, occupied every moment, and caused me great regret that I could not stay longer in the capital of Epirus. And when to all these artistic beauties is added the associations of Yannina with the later years of Greek history, the power and tyranny of its extraordinary ruler, its claim to representing the ancient Dodona, and its present and utterly melancholy condition, no marvel that Yannina will always hold its place in memory as one of the first in interest of the many scenes I have known in many lands.

A Journey to Suli

This is an indication of the enormous amount of baggage which the traveller of this period would take with him on such a journey as a matter of course.

On leaving the Yannina road, we held on our course westward, and crossed the plain to the village of Strivina on the banks of the river Luro, which we followed for more than an hour. The scenery of this part of Epirus is not unlike that of the Brathay near Ambleside, but the closely wooded sides of the hills are here and there enlivened by a Greek scattered hamlet, giving its own character to the scene. Higher up the stream the trees are of a larger size, and fringe the lower hills beautifully and when, at 1 pm we reached Pasheenas bridge, I thought I had never seen a more romantic bit of English-like scenery. It is delightful to rest below the fine old oaks and planes in this spot, whence as far as the eye can reach thick foliage gladdens the sight. Crossing the Charadrus, we started once more at two, and in one hour - the route always leading through glades and wild woodland - came to the little Lake Zero, which I had been strongly recommended by Mr. Saunders not to omit seeing. And, in truth, it is well worth a visit, not that it has any character peculiar to Epirus or Greece (for it is more like Nemi than any lake I am acquainted with), but on account of the surpassing beauty of its deep and quiet waters, from whose (clear surface bold red rocks rise on all sides, hung with thickest ilex, and summited by dense woods of oak which extend to the very summit of the hills above. There was barely time to make two sketches of Lago Zero, ere the sinking sun warned me onward, and another hour brought us to the vale of Lelovo, a village which is built on the western side of the hills enclosing the glen; the other, as I entered the hamlet, became gloriously bright in the last rays of sunset, all the detail of rock and tree changing from red and purple, and cold grey, until finally lighted up by the bright full moon.

A very comfortable lodging was obtained at the top of the village of Lelovo, in a house which, like all in these parts, stands alone in a courtyard, and is well arrayed with galleries and stairs. Its tenants were a Greek priest (Lelovo is a Christian community), and a very old nun; they allowed me to occupy for the night, one of their rooms, a clean and good one. The scenery through which I have passed today and yesterday has greatly delighted me; it is rare in Greece to find such rich foliage combined with distant lines of landscape, and this, indeed, is a beauty peculiar to the southern parts of Epirus; towards Yannina, and to the north of it, such clothing of vale and mountain is not frequent.

At sunrise the vale of Lelovo is full of mist, and resounding with the lowing of invisible cows, on hearing which domestic sound, I thought, of course, there would be no milk, but for a wonder, there was. How enjoyable was the walk through the meadows as we left the village on our route to Suli. The song of birds, the fresh breeze, and all those charms of early morning which to the experienced sojourners in southern lands, marks the best hours of the day! We halted but once at a shepherd's capanna, for a bowl of fresh milk, ere we began a severe ascent, which in two hours brought us to Kragna, a little village among noble old oaks, whence the views extended over the gulf of Arta with the Tzumerka and Yannina hills. But the people of Kragna were cross-grained and disobliging, and no offers would induce them to furnish us with another horse (that which carried the baggage not being a very strong one), nor would they show us the road to Zermi, on the way to Suli, except for a minute's walk beyond their village. About eight we left it, and passed from dell to dell, by very difficult paths, steep, narrow and rocky, with no little fear of losing the way in places where the track was quite obliterated by torrents. We steered well, however, and finally leaving the thick oak woods, arrived at the hill of Zermi, high up on which is the scattered village of the same name, guarded by troops of angry dogs, as is the custom in these parts.

We went to the house of the primate and found him and all his family at dinner: it was the fête of St George, today being with them the 23rd of April. With the heartiest hospitality they insisted on our sharing the feast, which was by no means a bad one, as it consisted of roast lamb, two puddings made of Indian corn, one with milk and herbs, the other with eggs and meat, besides rakhee. The room was extremely neat and clean, and the best in all respects I had seen in southern Albania but, sitting in a draught of air when heated by exercise, that premonitory feeling which indicates coming fever, obliged me to quit the society almost immediately. We waited for some time in expectation of another horse, but at half past twelve tidings came that it had escaped, and so we divided our baggage into two parts, in order to lessen the feebler steed's burden, and thus arranged set out again.

Descending the hill of Zermi we came in less than an hour to the vale of Tervitziana, through which the river of Suli flows ere, "previously making many turns and meanders as if unwilling to enter such a gloomy passage", it plunges into the gorge of Suli. We crossed the stream, and began the ascent on the right of the cliffs, by narrow and precipitous paths leading to a point of great height, from which the difficult pass of the Suliote glen commences. And while toiling up the hill, my thoughts were occupied less with the actual interest of the scenery , than with the extraordinary recollections connected with the struggles of the heroic people who so lately as forty years back were exterminated or banished by their tyrant enemy. Every turn in the pass I am about to enter has been distinguished by some stratagem or slaughter: every line in the annals of the last Suliote war is written in characters of blood.

But my reflections were interrupted by a disagreeable incident: in a rocky and crabbed part of the narrow path, the baggage horse missed footing and fell backward; fortunately, he escaped the edge of the precipice; but the labour and loss of time in rearranging the luggage was considerable; and when we had scaled the height, and I sat looking with amazement into the dark and hollow abyss of the Acheron, a second cry and crash startled me - again the unlucky horse had stumbled, and this time, though safe himself, the baggage suffered - the basket containing the canteen was smitten by a sharp rock, and all my plates and dishes, knives, forks, and pewter pans - which F. L. had bequeathed to me at Patras - went spinning down from crag to crag till they lodged in the infernal stream below. These delays were serious, as the day was wearing on, and the "Pass of Suli" was yet to be threaded. This fearful gorge cannot be better described than in the words of Colonel Leake: "A deep ravine, formed by the meeting of the two great mountains of Suli and Tzikurates - one of the darkest and deepest of the glens of Greece; on either side rise perpendicular rocks, in the midst of which are little intervals of scanty soil, bearing holly oaks, ilices, and other shrubs, and which admit occasionally a view of the higher summits of the two mountains covered with oaks, and at the summit of all with pines.

1849 Robert Curzon

Sadistic Brigands

November 6th. - I had engaged a tall, thin, dismal-looking man, well provided with pistols, knives, and daggers, as an additional servant, for he was said to know all the passes of the mountains, which I thought might be a useful accomplishment in case I had to avoid the more public roads - or paths, rather - for roads there were none. I purchased a stock of provisions, and hired five horses -three for myself and my men, one for the muleteer, and the other for the baggage, which was well strapped on, that the beast might gallop with it, as it was not very heavy. They were pretty good horses - rough and hardy. Mine looked very hard at me out of the corner of his eye when I got upon his back in the cold grey dawn, as if to find out what sort of a person I was. By means of a stout kourbatch – a sort of whip of rhinoceros hide which they use in Egypt - I immediately gave him all the information he desired; and off we galloped round the back part of the town, and unquestioned by any one, we soon found ourselves trotting along the plain by the south end of the lake of Yanina. Here the waters from the lake disappeared in an extraordinary manner in a great cavern, or pit full of rocks and stones, through which the water runs away into some subterranean channel - a dark and mysterious river, which the dismal-looking man, my new attendant, said came out into the light again somewhere in the Gulf of Arta. Before long we got upon the remains of a fine paved road, like a Roman way, which had been made by Ali Pasha. It was, however, out of repair, having in places been swept away by the torrents, and was an impediment rather than an assistance to travellers. This road led up to the hills; and, having dismounted from my horse, I began scrambling and puffing up the steep side of the mountain, stopping every now and then to regain my breath and to admire the, beautiful view of the calm lake and picturesque town of Yanina.

As I was walking in advance of my company, I saw a man above me leading a loaded mule. He was coming down the mountain, carefully picking his way among the stones, and in a loud voice exhorting the mule to be steady and keep its feet, although the mule was much the more sure-footed of the two. As they passed me I was struck by the odd appearance of the mule's burden: it consisted of a bundle of large stones on one side, which served as a counterpoise to a packing-case on the other, covered with a cloth, out of which peeped the head of a man, with his long black hair hanging abut a face as pale as marble. The box in which he travelled not being more than four feet and a half long, I supposed he must be a dwarf; and was laughing at his peculiar mode of conveyance. The muleteer, observing from my dress that I was a Frank, stopped his mule when he came up to me, and asked me if I was a physician, begging me to give my assistance to the man in the box, if I knew anything of surgery, for he had both his legs cut off by some robbers on the way from Salonica, and he was now taking him to Yanina, in hope of finding some doctor there to heal his wounds. My laughter was now turned into pity for the poor man, for I knew there was no help for him at Yanina. I could do nothing for him; and the only hope was, as his strength had borne him up so far on his journey, that when he got rest at Yanina the wounds might heal of themselves. After expressing my commiseration for him, and my hopes of his recovery, we parted company; and as I stood looking at the mule, staggering and slipping among the loose stones and rocks in the steep desert, it quite made me wince to think of the pain the unfortunate traveller must be enduring, with the raw stumps of his two legs rubbing and bumping against the end of his short box.

I was sorry I did not ask why the robbers had cut off his legs, because, if it was their usual system, it was certainly more than I bargained for. I had pretty nearly made up my mind to be robbed, but had no intention whatever to lose my legs: so I sat down upon a rock, and began calculating probabilities, until my party came up, and I mounted my horse, who gave me another look with his cunning eye.

Paying for Shade and the Power of the Turkish Language

We continued on Ali Pasha's broken road until we reached the summit of the mountain, where we made a short halt, that our horses might regain their wind; and then began our descent, stumbling, and sliding, and scrambling down until we arrived at the bottom, where there was a miserable khan. In this royal hotel, which was a mere shed, there was nothing to be found except mine host, who had it all to himself. At last he made us some coffee; and while our horses were feeding on our own corn, we sat under the shade of a walnut tree by the roadside. Our host, having nothing which could be eaten or drunk except the coffee, did not know how in the world he could manage to get up a satisfactory bill. I saw this very plainly in his puzzled and thoughtful looks; but at last a bright thought struck him, and he charged a good round sum for the shade of a walnut tree. Now although I admired his ingenuity, I demurred at the charge, particularly as the walnut tree did not belong to him. It was a wild tree, which everybody threw stones at as he passed by, to bring down the nuts…

Little did the unoffending walnut tree think that its shade would be brought forward as a cause of war; for then arose a fierce contest between Greek oaths and Albanian maledictions, to which Arabic and English lent their aid. Though there were no stones thrown, ten times as many were hard words hurled backwards and forwards as there were walnuts on the tree, showing a facility of expression and a redundance of epithets which would have given a lesson to the most practised ladies of Billingsgate.

When the horses were ready the khangee came up to me in a towering passion, swearing that I should pay for sitting under the tree. "Englishman," said he, "get up and pay me what I demand, or you shall not leave this place, by all that is holy." "Kiupek oglou," said I, without moving from the ground, "Oh, son of a dog! go and get my horse, you chattering magpie!" These few words in the language of the conqueror had a marvellous effect on the khangee. "What does his worship say?" he inquired of the dismal-faced man. "Why, he says you had better go and get his excellency's worship's most respectable horse, if you have any regard for your life: so go! be off! vanish! Don't stay there staring at the illustrious traveller. 'Tis lucky for you he doesn't order us to cut you up into kebabs; go and get the horse; and perhaps you'll be paid for your coffee, bad as it was. His excellency is the pasha's, his highness's, most particular intimate friend; and if his highness knew what you had been saying, why, where would you be, O man?" The khangee, who had intended to have had it all his own way, was taken terribly aback at the sound of the Turkish tongue: he speedily put on my horse's bridle, gave his nosebag to the muleteer, tightened up his girths, helped the servants, and was suddenly converted into a humble submissive drudge. The way in which anything Turkish is respected among the conquered races in Syria or in Egypt can scarcely be imagined by those who have not witnessed it.

Leaving the khangee to count his paras and piastres, with which, after all, he was evidently well satisfied, we rode on down the valley by the side of a brawling stream, which we crossed no less than thirty nine times during our day's journey. Our road lay through a magnificent series of picturesque and savage gorges, between high rocks. Sometimes we rode along the bed of the stream, and sometimes upon a ledge so far above it that it looked like a silver ribbon in the sun. Every now and then we came to a cataract or rapid, where the stream boiled and foamed among the rocks, tossing up its spray, and drowning our voices in its noise. In the course of almost eight hours of continual scrambling up and down all sorts of rocks, we found ourselves at another wretched shelter dignified with the name of khan. Here, after a tolerable supper, we all rolled ourselves up in the different corners of a sort of loft, with our arms under our heads, and slept soundly until the morning.

Ioannina (C. R. Cockerell, 1830)

Macedonia

Macedonia remained under Turkish rule until the Balkan Wars which immediately preceded the outbreak of the First World War. These were preceded by a struggle between various armed groups of Greeks, Serbs and Bulgarians to ensure that after liberation it would be annexed by their respective countries. The Greek army under Crown Prince Constantine settled the issue by defeating the Turks and liberating the region in 1912. On 26th October, the feast of the city's patron, Saint Demetrius, the Greek army under the command of King George I marched into Thessaloniki.

Triumphal Arch, Thessaloniki (Fauvel, 1831)

1795 John Bacon Sawry Morritt

A Hypocritical Tirade

It helps to put Morritt's indignation into an appropriate context if we bear in mind that it was his custom to cheat the local people remorselessly to get his hands on "marbles". In other passages in this collection he even boasts about it.

The few miserable villages we passed though are entirely inhabited by Greeks or Jews. The Greeks here have the power in their hands, and exercise it in so rascally a manner that we enquired after Turks as easily as we should elsewhere after Englishmen... Everything you have to buy or order in these villages is a signal for the whole body to unite in cheating you.

1801 The Rev. Edward Daniel Clarke

Clothed Dogs

On Saturday, December the twenty-sixth, we left Katarina; journeying towards the east, over a wretched sandy common, covered with brakes, in the plains near Katarina, the Arnaut shepherds are seen armed with large pistols and poniards. Their dogs make a singular appearance, wearing body-clothes; the only instance we had ever seen of the same kind. The animals under their care, beside sheep, were hogs, buffaloes, and oxen.

Preveza

Nothing ever exceeded, in dirt and wretchedness the condition of this town; or ever equalled the horrid filth of the khan here. The trees were knee deep in every species of ordure. It was therefore by no means desirable to move from the gate of the khan, except with a view to escape from the place; and this we were anxious to do, as quickly as horses could be procured...

1802-09 Colonel William Leake

The Mining Villages of Chalcidike

This passage illustrates a rare large-scale industrial enterprise with a long history.

Nizvoro contains three or four hundred houses, divided into two nearly equal Makhaladhes, situated half a mile apart, the one inhabited by Greeks, at the head of whom is the bishop of Erissos, one of the suffragans of the metropolitan of Thessalonica, and styled also bishop of Aghion Oros; the other by Turks, and the residence of Rustem Aga, who, as Madem Agasi, has the direction of the neighbouring silver mines, together with the government of twelve eleftherokhoria ["free villages"] in the Chalcidic peninsula, which from this union of the Mukata are named the Sidherokapsika, or Mademokhoria.

Not long since Rustem was nearly expelled from his post by the united complaints of all the villages under his government, but having, by the powerful support of Ibrahim Bey of Serres, his patron, overcome all difficulties, as well at Saloniki as at Constantinople, he revenged himself upon the Greek Proestos of Nizvoro, who was instigator of the combination against him, by putting him into a well, and keeping him there till he had gradually extorted all his property, when he cut off his head. My Janissary, who relates this anecdote, considers it, as a proof of Rustem being a[n] ... upright man.

Rustem pays the Porte 120 purses and 200 okes of silver for the mukata of the villages and mines, but as he never makes more than 100 okes from the mines, he is obliged to supply the difference in money. This he is enabled to do by the Greeks of the Sidherokapsika, who are well content to make good the deficiency for the sake of the advantages they derive from belonging to the government of the mines. The owner of the house in which I lodge pays 300 piastres a year in ["gifts"] of all kinds.

Belon, who visited the mines of Sidherokapsa in the middle of the sixteenth century, asserts that he found five or six hundred furnaces in different parts of the mountain, that besides silver, gold was extracted here from pyrites, that 6000 workmen were then employed and that the mines sometimes returned to the Turkish government a monthly profit of 30,000 ducats of gold. The name Sidherokapsa, although implying a smelting of iron, is generally applied to places where any appearances of metallurgy remain; it is not probable that there ever existed any iron works in this place. The villages attached to the government of the Mines are chiefly situated in the highlands of the Chalcidic peninsula on either side of the central ridge, and in a part of the country to the south-west of Nizvoro, towards the isthmus of Sithonia...

The mines now wrought are about half an hour from Nizvoro, between two hills, in a deep ravine, where a stream of water serves for the operations of washing, as well as to turn a wheel for working the bellows for the furnace. The whole is conducted in the rudest and most slovenly manner. The richest ore is pounded with stones upon a board by hand, then washed and burnt with charcoal; the inferior ore is broken into larger pieces, and burnt twice without washing. The lead, when extracted from the furnace, is carried to Kastro, where the silver is separated, in the proportion of two or three drams to an oke of 400 drams. When the present shafts are exhausted, the mines will probably be abandoned. From the mines I return, by a circuitous path, to a point not far above Nizvoro, and set off from thence on the road to Stavros at 4.30 (Turkish time).

The heaps of wrought ore, some of which I passed yesterday, but which are seen in much greater quantity on the side of the mountain below the present works, show how very extensively these mines have once been wrought. The lofty mountains which lie at the back of Nizvoro are covered with forests, consisting on the southern side chiefly of elms, on the summit of chestnuts, and to the north of oaks. Some of the elms are very fine trees. All the forenoon we travel amidst the clouds, which, as the wind is to the south-east, hang low upon the hills, and at 6.30 descend upon the southern corner of the plain of Lybjadha, around which all the sides of the hills are covered with great heaps of scoriae, similar to those near the Maden of Nizvoro, but much larger and more numerous.

The plain, which is a dead level in the form of an equilateral triangle, surrounded by woody mountains, is covered with fields of Kalambokki, and intersected with torrents shaded by large plane trees. The scoriae are seen in the greatest quantities in the bed of one of these torrents, below the corner where we descended; but a peasant who has the care of a magazine for the maize, informs me, that towards the summit of the mountain there are heaps of the same substance larger than any near the valley, and shafts of a much greater depth and size. Some of these may be works, perhaps, of the ancient Macedonians, whence a part of the silver money was derived, the prodigious quantity of which is proved by the proportion of it still existing. I am not aware, however, that any ancient author has noticed mines in this part of the country.

A Fishery

Neokhori, as the word implies, is of recent construction. It is inhabited by forty Greek families, and is included in the district of Zikhna, a town situated between Dhrama and Serres, at the foot of the great mountain which borders the Strymonic plains to the northward. Neokhori seems chiefly to owe its existence to the profitable fishery of those Strymonian eels which were celebrated among the ancients for their size and fatness, and were considered not inferior to the eels of the lake Copais. They are caught at a dam which crosses the stream half a mile below the bridge of Neokhori, and which serves as well for this purpose as for a mill-head. Were it not for this artificial impediment, the river, although rapid, would be navigable to Neokhori and into the lake. The mill belongs to the convent of Pandokratora on Mount Athos, but the fishery, since it has become valuable, has been claimed by the Sultan, and is now farmed by Feta Bey of Zikhna, whose deputy I find at the mill, counting the fish as they are caught. Some thousands of eels had just been taken, many of which are of enormous size. Grey mullet and other migratory sea-fish are sometimes intercepted here in the same manner, but always in a small proportion to the eels. Possibly the Strymonic lake is too distant from the sea for the mullet. The freshness of the water can hardly be an objection, as many of the lagoons of Greece and Asia Minor most productive of mullet are of mixed water; and some, as that of Buthrotum, are quite fresh. The Bey as Mukatesi levies on the spot 20 paras for each zevgari, or pair, of large eels; and the people of Neokhori sell them either fresh or salted at 30, 40, or 50 paras a pair, according to the distance to which they are sent. The fishery is said to produce annually about 40,000 brace of large eels, besides the smaller and other fish.

A Suspicious Official

The late ruins have rendered the moment favourable for fishing, which is an unfortunate accident for me, having brought hither Feta Bey's agent to superintend the fishing, from his usual residence at a village an hour distant, of which he is voivoda. He refuses a present of a pair of pistols, gives orders to prevent my visiting the summit of the hill, and issues a proclamation forbidding the people to sell me any antiquities, but is afterwards so far pacified, though still refusing any present, as to retract the latter part of the order, and to send a messenger to the Bey, who is now at Ziliakhova, a village to the eastward of Zikhna, for permission that I may view the place. My firmahn he cannot read.

Nov. 9. - The answer of the Bey of Zikhna is unfavourable: the only reason of which appears to be the persuasion among these barbarians that the site of Amphipolis contains hidden treasures. I am obliged, therefore, to leave this interesting site with a transient view of it, and it is not without difficulty that I succeed in copying an inscription in the wall of a fountain in the village; for inscriptions are supposed by Turks to inform us where to dig for treasures: I fortunately observed it yesterday evening, and had transcribed it as soon as there was light enough, this morning, just when some of the Myrmidons of the Aga, who had probably formed some suspicion of my intention, arrived with the design of preventing me. It is a document of great interest, as being written in the Ionic dialect, and as containing the exact words of some of the laws of Athens as cited by the Athenian orators, both which peculiarities, are referrable to the fact of Amphipolis having been an Attic colony. The letters are small, but beautifully engraved, and have the form which is supposed to indicate a date earlier than that of Alexander. The record is that of a decree of perpetual banishment from Amphipolis and its territory, enacted by the people against two of their citizens, Philo and Stratocles, and their children. If they were ever taken they were to suffer death as enemies. Their property was confiscated, and a tenth of it was to be applied to the sacred service of Apollo and of Strymon. Their names were to be inscribed by the Prostatae upon a pillar of stone; and if any person should revoke the decree, or by any art or contrivance give countenance to the banished men, that man's property also was to be forfeited to the people, and he was to be banished from Amphipolis for ever.

A "Moderate" Governor

A large portion of that part which is in the district of Serres, is the private property of Ismail Bey and his family, one of the richest and most powerful subjects of the Sultan, if he can be called a subject who is absolute here, and obeys only such of the orders of the Porte as he thinks fit, always, however, with a great show of submission. Besides his landed property he is engaged in commerce, and derives great profits from his farm of the imperial revenues. He has been rapidly increasing in power during the last ten years, and his authority now extends northward to the borders of Sofia and Felibe, to the westward to Istib inclusive, and to the eastward as far as Gumurdjina inclusive. His troops are now fighting with Emin Aga of Haskiuy beyond Gumurdjina, whom he will probably soon reduce. To the southward and westward the summits of the mountains which border the plain, separate his dominions from the district of Saloniki. His forces do not amount to more than 2000 in constant pay, who are chiefly Albanians, but upon occasion he might easily raise 10,000. When he builds a new palace, or repairs a road, or builds a bridge, the villages furnish the materials and labour, so that his household and troops are his principal expenses.

Deficient in the extraordinary talents of Aly Pasha, he is said to be free from his cruelty, perfidy, and insatiable rapacity. Though he never conceals his contempt of Christians, and treats them with the usual harshness of the most haughty Mussulman, he is spoken of by the Christians themselves as a just, attentive governor, and whose extortions are comparatively moderate. Hence his territory presents a more prosperous appearance than any part of Aly Pasha's. The culture of cotton being very advantageous to him, he is anxious to encourage its exportation, in which he is himself engaged, and hence the Greek merchants of Serres, who carry on an extensive trade with Vienna, enjoy sufficient protection, though personally they are often ignominiously treated by him.

As to the rayahs in general, it is sufficient to mention one of the labours and exactions imposed upon them, to show their condition even under a governor who has the reputation of being indulgent. Every village is bound to deliver the Bey's tithe of the cotton in a state fit for immediate exportation, that is to say, cleared of the seeds and husks, instead of supplying it as it comes from the field; and even to make good the loss of weight caused by the abstraction of the seeds, by the addition of an equal weight of cleared cotton. The Turks justify this oppression, by alleging that it is customary in all cotton districts; the only kind of answer they ever deign to give, when they are the strongest.

The Bey has four sons, of whom the eldest, Yussuf, carries on all the active business of the government, while his father enjoys a rather indolent retirement at the Adda tjiftlik. The Greek community is governed with very little interference from the Bey, by the Greek metropolitan bishop, and the archons, of whom the chief is a Greek merchant, Matako Dhimitri, whose brother is established at Saloniki. Another merchant, named Sponty, who acts as consul for several nations, is of a French family long settled in Candia, and here I again meet a Dr. P. of Ioannina, who after having served for some time as surgeon in the French army of Italy under Bonaparte, narrowly escaped being put to death by Aly at Prevyza on his return: he attended Vely Pasha in the siege of Suli, and was eyewitness to the heroism of the woman Khaïdho, and eight Suliotes, who came disguised into the middle of the Albanian camp in the night, and when discovered the next morning, retreated with such bravery and conduct as to kill or wound twenty Albanians in the retreat, without receiving a hurt.

Tobacco Farming

From the baths of Pella to Yenidje is a ride of fifty minutes. Two miles to the right of the last tumulus of Pella is the village of Alatjaushluk, standing on the slope of the mountain. Iannitza, or Ghianitza, more commonly known to the inhabitants, being chiefly Turks, by the corrupted Turkish form of Yenidje, appears to have declined considerably of late years, as the number of houses is now by no means proportioned to the eight minarets which the town still exhibits. There are however several good Turkish dwellings, and in the middle of the town that of Abdurrahman Bey, an Osmanli of an ancient family, and possessor of a large proportion of the neighbouring lands, which produce grain, cotton, and tobacco. The last of these, which occupies most of the land in the immediate vicinity of Yenidje, is renowned in every part of Turkey for its aromatic tutun, which, together with coffee, supplies the Turks with a stimulant at least as agreeable as the meagre ill-made wines of modern Greece. The leaves have been lately gathered, strung together, and hung up to dry, which operations are chiefly performed by the women: every wall in the town is now festooned with tobacco leaves, but particularly the open galleries which surround all the houses, and into which the inner chambers open. As the apartments in general have hearths only, without chimneys, the smoke of the wood which is burnt upon them circulates amidst the tobacco leaves, and gives the tobacco a peculiar flavour, which Italians object to, but Turks admire. The herb of Yenidje is of the species called garden tobacco, and has a small yellowish leaf.

Naoussa at the Beginning of the Nineteenth Century

Although now in the power of Aly Pasha, it is still governed by its own magistrates, whose authority, the place being an imperial appanage, and the inhabitants well armed, has been generally respected by all the neighbouring Pashas and other men in authority, including the robbers, though Niausta has occasionally been at war with them all. By an effect of the republican system of the place, I am detained two hours in an empty house, while the powers are consulting as to the konak in which I am to be lodged; at length I am conducted to the house of Thomas, who is married to the widow of Lusa Papafilippo, a name of some note in Macedonia, and formerly proestos of Niausta.

The decline of the place, and its subjection to Aly, which will be followed by the usual consequences of his insatiable extortion, is to be attributed to that spirit of dissension which seldom fails to ruin the Greeks when they have the power of indulging in it. Not many years ago Niausta was one of the most commercial places in Northern Greece, and like Verria, Siatista, and Kastoria, had merchants who traded to Christendom as well as Turkey, but not one of whom now remains here.

Papafilippo, who is spoken of in terms of high respect by his own adherents as a benefactor of his native town, was poisoned with several others, about twenty years ago, by the adverse party, at the head of which was one Zafiriaki, son of Theodosius, who afterwards became proestos, and enjoyed all the authority until last year, when the party of Papafilippo, by applying to Aly

Pasha, gave him the long-desired excuse for introducing his myrmidons into the town. But he met with a stout resistance from Zafiraki and his brother Konstantino Musa assisted by a party of Albanians, under two Albanian brothers Vrakho and Litjo. Those whom the Pasha first sent having been fired upon from an inclosure of mud bricks, which is the only artificial defence of the place, he found it necessary to increase their numbers to 2000, who quickly destroyed every thing on the outside of the town, but not having cannon, could not ruin the fortifications, slight as they are. They proceeded therefore ... building towers on a level with the walls, from which they could fire into the town. Their loss was very great, according to the people of Niausta, of whom about fifty were slain. At length the besieged, after having lived for some time upon wild herbs, branches of trees, and bread made of the refuse of their rice mills, were obliged to surrender, but not until the four chiefs above mentioned had fought their way one night through the besiegers with fifty palikaria, and had arrived safe at Saloniki, where I saw them, and where they still remain. All the persons found in Zafiraki's house have been carried to Ioannina, where they are now in prison, and the house is occupied by the Albanian commandant, and by a Stambuli Bostanji residing here as agent of the Sultana, who enjoys the revenue of the town and its district. In one year Aly has exacted 500 purses from the people, and no longer apprehending any resistance, has reduced his Albanian guard to twenty, which, united with those stationed at Verria and Vodhena, are sufficient both to maintain his interests and to protect the passes against the robbers, to whom he has been indebted for his justification with the Porte for introducing his troops here. These kleftes during the last summer blockaded Verria as well as Niausta, and advancing to the walls of the latter, carried away children, cattle, and sheep. At length Aly sent his trusty Tepeleniote Mutjobon ... who has dispersed or taken them all, except a few men under a Musulman Albanian named Sulu Proshova, who not long before was at the head of 700 men, for the most part Christians. He still haunts these mountains which as far as Bitolia, Prillapo, and Velesa, furnish so many impenetrable retreats, that it is almost impossible to eradicate the thieves from them. Not long since, Sulu took a boy of Niausta going to Verria, who was to have been ransomed by the village for sixteen purses, when, two days before the money was to be paid, the boy escaped, and arrived here a day or two ago.

The principal church, dedicated to St. George, has a monastery attached to it, and is surrounded by a quadrangle of cells or small apartments for the monks, which they generally let to strangers. The people of Niausta were formerly noted for working in gold and silver, and still carry on the manufacture in a smaller degree. The productions of the territory are wheat, barley and maize in the plain; rice in the immediate neighbourhood of the marshes adjacent to the lake of Iannitza; on the heights vines, supplying one of the best wines in Macedonia, in sufficient quantity for a large exportation, and in the valley mulberry plantations, which yield about 300 okes of silk per annum. The town is well supplied with fish, particularly with large pike from the lake of Iannitza, and with trout from their own river, the principal source of which is at a short distance above the town. Many persons suppose it to be the discharge of a katavothra in the lake of Akridha, but can give no better reason for this opinion, than that the lake is the only one in Macedonia which produces trout. The sheep which feed on the mountains behind the town, furnish a fine wool, and mutton of the best quality.

Verria

Verria ... stands on the eastern slope of the Olympene range of mountains, about five miles from the left bank of the Vistritza or Injekara, just where that river, after having made its way in an immense rocky ravine through the range, enters the great maritime plain. The territory produces corn and maize in the lower plain, and at the foot of the mountain hemp and flax, which are supplied with the necessary irrigation from the rivulet on the northern side of the town. This stream, which has its origin in the mountains to the westward, emerges from a rocky gorge in them, falls in cascades over some heights which rise abruptly above the town, and after turning several mills, rushes down the mountain between steep rocky banks to the bridge, over which we crossed it, and from thence into the plain.

The town contains about 2000 families, of which 1200 are Greek. The houses are lofty, and for Turkey well built. Water flows through every street, supplied either from springs or from the rivulet; which advantage, together with the lofty and salubrious situation, the surrounding gardens, many fine plane-trees interspersed among the houses, the vicinity of the mountains, and a commanding view over the great level to the eastward, renders Verria one of the most agreeable towns in Rumili. The manufacturing part of the population spin the hemp and flax grown at the foot of the mountain, and make shirts and towels, particularly the makrama, or large towel used in the public baths, and of which there is a great consumption in all Turkish towns, four of them being required for each bather, besides two more for sheets to the bed on which he reposes after the bath. Many of the water-mills around the town are for fulling coarse woollens and carpets, which are made in the surrounding villages or by the Jews of Saloniki.

The Sign of a Wineshop

In this part of Macedonia it is customary for the keepers of wine-houses to suspend an evergreen bush before them, being the same as the old English custom, from whence the proverb, "Good wine needs no bush." In the southern parts of Greece, it is generally a long stick with shreds of painted paper on a string.

Fleet of Foot

I have frequently had occasion to notice the extraordinary celerity of some of the ... foot-messengers in Greece. A celebrated one of Verria may compete with any of them. He carried letters on foot to Saloniki in seven hours, remained there one hour, and returned to Verria at the end of the fifteenth hour. After having performed this feat more than once, he was commonly known to the day of his death by the name of Anemos [Wind].

Into the Mountains

Dec. 4. - The weather, which has been fine, with a northerly wind, ever since the day of my arrival at Saloniki, as well as on the road from thence, is said to have been the reverse at Verria for several days, and last night the rain fell heavily. At 6.30, Turkish time, I set out for Kozani, accompanied by one of Aly Pasha's tatars, a guard of six Albanians supplied by Metjobon, and Musa Pasha's tatar, who has accompanied me from Saloniki. We begin immediately to ascend the hills at the back of the town, and soon enter a narrow vale watered by the stream which descends to the town. At the upper end of this valley, at 8.4, stands the derveni, a straw hut for lodging the Albanian guard, from whence we begin to ascend Mount Bermium, in defiance of the assertion of Herodotus, that it is impassable, and although the historian has every possible advantage in the season, and weather, that of last night having covered the mountain with snow to a great depth.

Very soon after entering a forest of large chestnut trees, we arrive, at 9.40, at Kastania, a small village, of which all the houses, except two or three, are now deserted, in consequence of the demands for provisions, which were alternately made upon them by the robbers and their

Albanian opponents. Aly Pasha endeavours to encourage their return, and declares his intention of building here a large village, with kules on the mountain for his soldiers, and thus to secure to himself this important pass between Lower and Upper Macedonia. The mountain abounds with wolves, wild boars; fallow deer, and roes. The swine are killed for the sake of their skins, which are in request for making shoes. A peasant informs me that not long since he shot one of these animals in the woods, which weighed 90 okes. The flesh of the roe is esteemed by these people, but not that of the deer.

Dec. 5. - We leave Kastania at 3,5, Turkish time. The snow continued to fall during the night, but the weather has now become bright and calm, with a hard frost. As we advance the woods are of birch, in the highest parts of beech, and amidst them numerous traces of the wild animals are observable. On the summit, which is not more than three miles in a straight line from the Vistritza, we leave the highest point of the mountain now called Dhoxa, or more commonly Xerolivadho, from a village of that name which once stood near it, six or eight miles on our right, and descend to Khadova, a village of about 50 Turkish families, from whence there is a further descent of about three miles to the Vistritza, which is seen from our road....

1830 David Urquhart

A Living Mummy

In passing through this village [Gomati], I was struck with the sight of a stiff and shrivelled corpse, clothed and seated in a chair laid slanting against a wall, so that the feet were in the air, and the head was bent down upon the breast. While I stood looking at it, I was startled by a jerking motion in the right arm and then seeing two black and vivid eyes straining to catch my attention. This was a human and a living thing, which had existed in this shrivelled and motion-less state for twenty-eight years; flesh seemed to have disappeared from his bones; the skin had shrunk, and was almost black. I have seen mummies that appeared in a better state of preservation. The joints were all fixed, with the exception of the right shoulder and the jaws. His freedom of the shoulders amounts, however, only to three inches of a seesaw movement of the forearm, and he keeps working it backwards and forwards, as he says, for exercise; his hands are closed; all his joints doubled up; the pelvis is as a pivot; and the only change of attitude is resting his back against the wall, or his feet on the floor; in bed, he lies upon one side only. He says, he first began to have his joints contracted twenty-eight years ago; he had successions of boils upon them, and one after the other they became immovable. During the last two or three years, he has experienced little change for the worse, and he hopes he will preserve what he calls the use of his right hand, to the grave. He is forty-five years old, and was a priest. When he saw me start on perceiving the living eye in what I took to be a corpse, he laughed heartily; his tongue and teeth, he said, were better than those of walking men; and his large clear eyes had a brilliancy not very common in health. I told him he might very soon make his fortune in London; he replied, he was very well pleased with his own village, and did not want to lose in travelling any of the time he had yet to live.

Captured by Brigands

The reader must make his own judgement about the following narrative; but certainly, the picture it paints of the steadfast courage of its author, and the dominance he wielded over a band of brigands by the sheer force of his personality, puts a considerable a strain upon the credulity of the reader.

We had not proceeded more than an hour, when we stopped to drink at a fountain, before engaging in the passes which are termed the Gates. Here the guards I had got at Ozeros left me, saying they had orders to turn back, as we were now almost in sight of the Koulia, a post that guards the entrance of the isthmus; and they had shown such symptoms of cowardice, that I was glad to be rid of them. As we sat on our horses drinking at the fountains, we laughed heartily at the haste of their retreat; my Greek servant Hadji, who wore my arms, and looked more like a Cavash than a Rayah, pointed at them with disdain, and asked contemptuously if such men were worthy of liberty. Inspired by the words, he began to sing a Greek song, which arrested the triggers of levelled guns that marked and singled us out at the very moment, and we continued our journey without a suspicion of the fate we had so narrowly escaped. We had left the fountain about fifteen minutes, and I was fifty paces ahead, winding round the side of a steep and wooded hill, in a narrow path, which jutted over a deep dell on the left, and had a bank and depending trees overhanging it on the right, when I was arrested by a loud shriek, followed by sounds that boded no good. I saw through the trees the crowding of men, white fustanells and arms! Whether or not escape was practicable, it did not enter into my mind to enquire; resistance was out of the question; but, in the confidence which extensive practice among these men had given me, I felt only incensed at the outrage, and reckoned on instant submission. I therefore turned and galloped towards them. I was certainly led into another train of reflection, when I saw a couple turn at me, holding their muskets levelled. I held up my hands, unarmed, (I was unarmed, except a pair of horse pistols in my holsters,) but they made a rush on both sides, vociferating imprecations, and distorting their faces into the most hideous and exasperating grimaces; at the moment I saw only two besides, so I thought resistance not impracticable; but the priming of the horse pistols was six months old; both successively missed fire, and I was struck senseless to the ground. The next thing I recollect was a blow on the back, as I was raised on my knees, which is generally preparatory to the act of decollation. How I escaped this, I had not sufficiently recovered my senses to know; but an object which may appear comparatively trifling aroused me; this was a ball of strong twine, which one of them was hastily measuring out. Recovering, at this sight., my senses and my limbs, and finding myself loose, I leaped up, and stood prepared with a stout stick to do what might he practicable, to prevent myself from being bound. My companions in misfortune were on their knees, calling out "Amaun! Amaun!" and with stream-ing eyes held up their joined hands to be bound. The bandits had no wish to be pushed to extremities in the vicinity of the guard-house, and with the guards that had left me at no very great distance; so they listen well to me, and left me alone. The others were quickly bound in silence; one of the party, the only very ferocious one of the set, turned to me with the cord. I offered him my breast to strike. His yatagan was in an instant bare; when a youth, of slender and even elegant air and appearance, and who had been looking at me, pushed him back. The others then approached, and told me to go quietly, and that I should not he bound. I told them (this seemed to me the only way to produce an effect) that I was perfectly resolved not to move a step, unless not only relieved from all insult, but treated with respect: "nor will I stir from this spot," I continued, "unless that man," pointing to one who seemed the chief, "whose countenance I will trust, gives me his word that the wretch who has insulted me shall not be allowed to approach me while I remain unarmed."

Not only was the promise given, but my mule was brought to me; and I even insisted that my harmless pistols should be replaced in the holsters. We now plunged into the depths of the wood. I had, therefore, immediately again to dismount; but the point was gained, and, after about an hour's most fatiguing run, arrived at an elevated spot, whence we could command a view of the sea on either side, as well as of every access to the isthmus.

It was now most essential for me to improve rapidly the position I had established among them, and on my way I had anxiously considered how that was to be done. What I had more particularly to fear was, that having seized an Englishman, they would dread pursuit by the English cruisers that were in those seas, while the Turks would cut off their retreat by land; they might, therefore, seek to retard pursuit and prevent detection by despatching me there, and effacing every trace of the party. My plan, therefore, was first to conciliate their respect to myself; and, secondly, to convince them that I sympathised with them in their wrongs, and that Europeans were inclined to use their best endeavours to relieve them from oppression. But amongst them was that savage Albanian, who was evidently intent on my destruction, and who had twice so nearly effected it, and with whom these considerations would be of no avail. I therefore determined upon keeping no terms with him; which, indeed, offered me two advantages, that of keeping up the character I had assumed, and the chance of effecting a division amongst them. On arriving at the spot where we were to halt, I directed that my servant should be unbound, that he might unlade the baggage and spread my carpet. After a moment's hesitation, without any remark, this was done. I took the opportunity of reproaching him for his dastardly conduct. I might, I said, have overlooked his not using his arms in my absence and against Greeks, but that his imploring for his life made him so despicable in my eyes, that from that hour I should no longer consider him my servant. He was, at the moment, filling my pipe. I snatched it from him, and turning to the young man who had before saved me, I told him that he should fill it, for I was sure he never would disgrace the arms he wore, or the master he served. It was caught with alacrity, and more than one jackomaki (flint and steel) was pulled out to strike a light. Emboldened by this first success, which was most critical, I found immediately a number of little wants, which, one after another, employed them all in serving me; while poor Hadji, who in his terror, first for *klephti* and next in his amazement at me, had stood rooted to the spot where I took the pipe from him, kept whispering instructions and directions to the palikars, as to how I ought to be served; so that had he been up to his part, he could not have played it more dexterously.

The klephts were only six; they had been ten at the fountain, where they first intended attacking us, upon seeing us part company from the four guards. The captain and three men had followed these, to despatch them, if their companions within their hearing, had to make use of their firearms. We were four - a guide, a muleteer, (both unarmed,) my servant, and I.

When I was comfortably arranged on my carpet, with coffee and pipe, I seized the moment, before the Palikars sat down, to tell them to be seated. The Albanian, all this time looking on with no less surprise than dissatisfaction, at length came forward and said, "This is all nonsense, we are robbers, and you are our prey; your coffee is ours. Your money is ours, and your blood is ours ... every one is in debt to the robber. I am sultan here; I am king of England here; and you pretend to treat us as if you were a Pasha." I vouchsafed him neither regard nor answer; but, turning to the Greeks, I exclaimed with great warmth, for I am sure I felt it, "What is there in that Hellenic blood, that so distinguishes its race from the barbarians that defile its soil?" A movement was made to repress the violence of the Skipetar. He called them fools, and was called in return a brute by my young friend; a schism was established. The only one I could, however, yet reckon on my side, was the youngest and least influential; but even this was an acquisition in such circumstances. The others were inclined, I thought, in my favour; but the Albanian kept constantly handling his weapons, and looking at me, as if he wanted neither the consent nor the assistance of his comrades. The absent party, and the captain, if I could hold out till their return, would of course turn the scale. They now left me with two, while the others went to consult; and these two were again relieved by others. Hadji was called and recalled, and examined and cross-examined. The point they seemed most anxious to ascertain was my being an Englishman; had I turned out a German, a Frenchman, or a Russian, my fate would have been instantly sealed. The baggage was visited, all the better parts of the habiliments of my attendants were gradually abstracted; and I was requested, but respectfully, to deliver up what I had in my pockets, excusing themselves by saying nothing less would satisfy the Albanian. During this time I was not unemployed finding out the history of each, and the cause of his being driven to the woods; and I found each most anxious by himself to impress upon me the belief that wrong had reduced them to so wretched an alternative; and that now, but fore the others, he would be glad to see me released. This gave me an opportunity of sympathising with each. I took an opportunity, during these hours of mortal suspense, to interrogate the lad who had proved my friend. He was a native, he said, of free Greece, and had corne to Atheto because betrothed there to a maid, who had attracted the eye of the Aga of Cassandra. He had related to me the persecution that had driven him to the woods, when I supplied the name of his Aglae. I had now my story to tell him, and in five minutes we were sworn brothers. Vasili now set about the work of my liberation in earnest, and declared that he was ready to risk his life, if necessary, to save mine.

He soon returned from the party which was seated in consultation at a little distance, to tell me that the prevailing opinion was, that I should be released, on paying 50, 000 piastres. "But where, Vasili," said I, "am I to find 50,000 piastres?"

"Oh!" he replied, "they well know a paper with your seal is as good as gold," "And will they release me on giving them such a paper?" "That will depend on the captain."

The subject was then discussed in my presence; and it was settled, under the condition of the captain's approval, that I should send Hadji for 10,000 piastres to Salonica, and should remain with them until his return with the money; and that my head should answer for his discretion,

At length the captain was descried, and Vasili ran to meet and if possible, to gain him. His reception was now my grand stroke; and I whispered to Hadji, instructing him as to minute details. What I had heard of their chief led me to admit favourable expectations; and I prepared myself for my fresh task with the utmost solicitude, As the newcomers broke through the thick boughs into the opened space we occupied, they were evidently struck with our relative positions; for by this time none of them ventured to sit down. As the captain approached, I rose not, stirred not, looked not even towards him; till, having come close up, he saluted me by making the temenaz, which I returned with a slight motion, and then indicated the corner of my carpet. He seated himself exactly on the designated spot, In a couple of seconds I turned my eyes gravely upon him, and, to remind him fully of the yoke to which he had been broken, repeated in Turkish the ordinary salutation, which he returned in the humblest manner. Coffee had been prepared; I now called for it, and Hadji took care that a proper interval should intervene between the presenting of my cup and his. The few minutes that thus elapsed appeared most irksome to the captain, who looked like a sober and homely farmer; the newcomers spoke not, but turned wondering eyes on me, and inquiring looks at the others, who seemed rather ashamed of themselves; while to me these moments were of more intense anxiety than any former period. I now held so rnany strings in my hands, it was no longer a matter of irnpulse, but of calculation, and that too of the minutest points; while the slightest indication of plan or design would have destroyed all. My heart throbbed, so that it shook me. When the coffee-cups were taken away, (and in Turkey, coffee is always despatched before business is commenced,) and after two or three long and deep whiffs - changing my manner entirely, I turned abruptly round, and, with warmth, addressed him to this effect:

"I have long known the Greeks - I have long admired their character, and pitied their misfortunes; I have wandered over every mountain, from Makronows to Trickeri - from Zitza now to Agion Oros; I have eaten Calamboki witll the black Rayah, Mgithra with the Vlach, and roasted kids with the klepht; I have been ever received as a friend, and parted as a brother. I would, but for this day, have carried these impressions with me to Europe; but you have taught me to do the Turks justice! I have gone to seek out and visit the armatoles of Olympus, and the klephts of Thessaly, thinking that amongst these men I should see the true descendants of the Hellenes. Had I feared you, I could now have been accompanied by guards that would have set you at defiance; but, on the contrary, had I known where you were, I should have come to visit you alone; expecting more hospitality at your hands than I do from these monasteries. But it seems you make war, not on your oppressors and the Turks, but upon mankind and Christians. And how are you so mad as to lay your hands on me, the well-wisher of your race - an Englishman; for whom vengeance will be sought, both by his countrymen and the Turks; and one who has shared the hospitality of all the Capitani around you? However," I added, "I can in part excuse your men; they knew me not, - my capture originated in a mistake, which I see you both regret and are ashamed of; and I must say, the subsequent conduct of most of them has gone far to efface the impressions of their first violence.

The captain's reply fully justified this appeal to their nationality; for he commenced by attempting a justification. "The boys will tell you, that though I am not a young man, I am no old robber. Not very long ago I had houses, lands, and children. Why should I have been a robber ? For what I am now, those who drove me to it must bear the blame; and if these allow me some authority over them, it is not for my Tufenk's sake, out by memory of some kindness I once showed to this band. Look at those men, some of them barefoot, with clothes of strings rather than cloth, with empty tobacco-bags, and empty stomachs; what makes them lead such a life, and what restraint can you place on men who live so? What care they for life; and why should they? Does the injury they do to others bring any good to them? And what serves the feasting of a night, and the plunder of a day, when they can carry nothing with them against a week's cold, rain, or hunger? Speak not, then, to such men of your English shire, nor of Turkish gibbets; but tell them that one is come from Europe, but tell them that one is come from Europe, who will tell again how their name is disgraced; how they are driven like oxen in the fields, or hunted like bears in the mountain. Speak to them but words of consolation and kindness, and they will lay their heads on the ground, and put your foot on them....

The discourse which followed it, would be too long to relate. They afterward retired a little way back into the wood to consult, not even leaving a guard over me. I felt relieved until the length and loudness of the discussion again awakened my apprehensions. However, they were of short duration; for presently Vasili came running, and kissed my hand, telling me that all was arranged; he was followed by the rest, who clamorously surrounded me, telling me they have determined on making me their captain. I, without the slightest indication of satisfaction or surprise, - without a betraying word of thanks, - asked whether they allowed me a voice in the matter, and whether they thought the picture they had drawn of their life was so very attractive? This was quite an unexpected difficulty to come from one whose life was in their hands; but as in their new frame of mind they had lost sight of the connection, I took care to lead them as far away from it as possible. They now set about persuading me that the whole country was distracted by the Turks and by the robbers; that the present oppression was like the knife reaching the joint; that the Turks had no strength, and the whole country would turn *klephti* if they could be respectable; and that the *klephti* would unite among themselves, and protect the people if they had a chief; that during the last insurrection, if they had a chief on whom they could have depended, and to whom they could have looked, the Turks would have as easily conquered the moon as reconquered their country; that now, if it was known that an English Bey Zadeh was their leader, they could collect 500 men in three days, carry some fort, which would the signal for the rising of the whole country. "Where," said they, "is the man to oppose us...?"

Dread, doubt and confusion, at that time throughout the Ottoman Empire, pervaded men's minds and opinions. This incident but served to confirm the conclusions at which I had already arrived. I felt that a soldier of daring, and a man of en energy , might have changed the face of the East, if philosopher enough to ascend to the sources of the distinct currents of opinion from the East and the West then meeting and struggling in this arena. I was convinced also that the name of Englishman alone might instantaneously have given importance to such a gathering, and led to rally round it sections, interests, and races, which scarcely any other watchword could call together. These views I frankly entered into with these men. I pointed out to them what qualities and qualifications were requisite in the chief of so desperate an undertaking: where there was no middle position between destruction and success; where success would almost be miraculous. That if such a man could be found to lead such a movement, it might perhaps succeed; that such men were found only once in ten centuries; but that, whether it succeeded or failed, there would be a curse on the projectors. They gradually became thoughtful, mournful, and subdued: and thus this strange vision flitted by.

The Albanian was my warmest partisan; we talked over "Alvanitia," Veli Bey, and Arslan Bey, with whom I found he had been at Milies; and we thus were old friends. He now had a great deal to tell his companions about me, and summed all up by saying that I ought to have been an Albanian.

After the Grand Divan was over, they proposed sending to a flock of the monks to fetch a sheep; but though it was near sunset, I preferred making for the nearest monastery, seven or eight miles off. Our "plunder" was brought out: whatever was mine was punctually restored; and amongst these were silver and gold articles. I made them a present, after finding that nothing was missing, of my money and a telescope: my baggage-horse was laden, my mule brought to me - one held the bridle, another the stirrup; and they accompanied me down to the road. They then pressed round me to shake hands; and, as this was an exceptional case, I did shake hands with them. The captain said, "We trust implicitly in you: we have exacted no promise from you, that you would not cause search to be made for us. When you speak of us, we know it will be to plead our cause; when you think of us, we know it will not be with anger." I assured them of the gratification I should feel, not only in preventing search being made for them, but in contributing to their pardon and restoration to their homes. Our parting was more like the severing of affectionate friends than of robbers from their prey; and I had left them some fifty paces, when the Albanian shouted after me, "If you have any friends coming this way, just give them a ... note, and we will take care that no one hurts them."

When we found ourselves again alone, our very mules seemed to step out, to put as much space as possible between us and the *klephts*. Our first impression was that of wonder at the reality of our escape; the next was the recollection of the wanton cruelties from which even the monks were not exempt; one poor wretch had at this place, a few days before, been ransomed by the monastery, and was sent back - without nose, lips or ears!

We hurried on, without exchanging a word, until we were long out of both ear and musket-shot. At length we made a halt, when Hadji dismounted; and running up to me, showed me, with the most extravagant demonstrations of joy, a small black thing, exclaiming, "This has saved us, and I have saved it !" A bit of holy wood, (wood of the cross,) within an envelope of wax-cloth, to save it from the wet, was the object thus displayed. Hadji told me that, from the moment of his capture, all his fears had not been in the least about himself, but about the holy wood: before he was stripped, he had confided it privately to Vasili; and nothing now could exceed his joy at its being restored to him, which restoration had been our deliverance. Here he devoutly kissed it. I entreated to be allowed to look at it, to which he at length consented. I unfolded the wax-cloth, - three several coverings of paper and silk; I then got to some cotton in the middle: "There it is," said he, "in the cotton; but it is not a very large bit." "No, Hadji," I said, "it cannot be very large; for I call neither feel nor see it." The holy wood had vanished!

1848 Edward Lear

A Journey Seen through the Eyes of an Artist

By 7 am the four post-horses and the Soorudji are ready. In these parts of Turkey, blessed with a post-road, you have no choice as to your mode of travelling, nor can you stop where you will, so easily as you may with horses hired from private owners. Yiannitsa being the next post from Salonica (reckoned ten hours), thither must I go. The Soorudji or post-boy, always rides first, leading the baggage-horse, and is almost always fair food for the pencil, for he wears a drab jacket with strange sky-blue embroideries, a short kilt, and other arrangements highly artistical.

The morning was sultry and uninviting. We left the ill-paved, gloomy Salonica by the Vardhari gate, which at that early hour was crowded with groups of the utmost picturesqueness, bringing goods to market in carts drawn by white-eyed buffali: immense hears of melons appeared to be the principal article of trade; but their sale being prohibited within the walls of the city, on account of the cholera, the remaining inhabitants came outside to buy them, taking them in *nascostamente* [secretly].

The broad, sandy road, enlivened for a time by these peasants, soon grew tiresome, as it stretched over a plain, whose extent and beauty were altogether hidden by the thick haze which clung close to the horizon. Hardly were the bright white walls of Salonica long distinguishable; and as for the mountains and Olympus, they were all as if they were not, - a colourless, desert "pianura" - such seemed my day's task to overcome. Nevertheless, though the picture was a failure as a whole, its details kept me awake and pleased, varieties of zoology attracting observation on all sides. Countless kestrels hovering in the air or rocking on tall thistles; hoopoes, rollers, myriads of jackdaws, great broad-winged falcons soaring above, and beautiful grey-headed ones sitting composedly close to the roadside as we passed - so striking in these regions is the effect of the general system of kindness towards animals prevalent throughout Turkey - the small black-and-white vulture was there too, and now and then a graceful milk-white egret, slowly stalking in searchful meditation.

The usual pace of the Menzil [the Turkish postal agents] is a very quick trot, and the great distance accomplished by Tatars [couriers] in their journeys is well authenticated; but not being up to hard work, I rode slowly: besides, the short shovel stirrups and peaked saddle are troubles you by no means get used to in a first lesson. At half past eleven we reached the Vardas, a broad river (the apple of discord between Greek and Turk, as a boundary question), and here crossed by a long structure of wood, bristling with props and prongs: near its left bank stands a khan - destined to be our midday resting-place.

A sort of raised wooden dais, or platform, extends before the roadside Turkish khan: here mats are spread, and day wayfarers repose, the roof, prolonged on poles, serving as shelter from sun or rain. Three Albanian guards - each a picture - were smoking on one side, and while Giorgio was preparing my dinner of cold fowl and an omelette on the other I sketch the bridge and watch the infinite novelty of the moving parts of the scene which make this wild, simple picture alive with interest, for the bridge and a few willows are foreground and middle distance: remote view there is none. Herds of slow, bare-hided buffali, each with a white spot on the forehead and with eyes of bright white - surrounded by juvenile buffalini, only less awkward than themselves; flocks of milk-white sheep, drinking in the river; here and there a passing Mohammedan on horseback, one of whom, I observed, carried a hooded falcon, with bells on his turban; how I wished all these things could be portrayed satisfactorily, and how I looked forward to increasing beauty of costume and scenery when among the wilder parts of the country .

1 pm. Again in travelling trim and crossing the rickety bridge; we trotted, or galloped for three hours across a continuous, wide, undulating bare plain, only enlivened by zoological appearances as before, all the distant landscape being hidden still. Near the road many great tumuli were observable on either side during the day, and a large portion of the plain near the Vardar was white with salt, a kind of saline mist appearing to fall for more than an hour. At the eighth hour we had approached so near the mountains that their forms came out clearly through the hazy atmosphere and one needle-like white column, the minaret of the chief mosque of Yiannitsa was visible, the town itself being nearly reached at the ninth hour, an event which, with a stumbling horse and fatigued limbs, I gladly hailed.

An Extremely Polite Turk

While taking a parting cup of coffee with the postmaster I unluckily set my foot on a handsome pipe-bowl (pipe-bowls are always snares to near-sighted people moving over Turkish floors, as they are scattered in places quite remote from the smokers, who live at the farther end of prodigiously long pipe-sticks) - crash; but nobody moved; only on apologising through Giorgio, the polite Mohammedan said: "The breaking such a pipe-bowl would indeed, under ordinary circumstances, be disagreeable; but in a friend every action has its charm!" - a speech which recalled the injunction of the Italian to his son on leaving home, "Whenever anybody treads upon your foot in company, and says, "Scusotemi," only reply: "I beg pardon. On the contrary, you have done me a pleasure*!*"

A Dervish's Tomb

By five I was out on the road to Yiannitsa, at a dervish's tomb, not far from the town, a spot which I had remarked yesterday as promising, if weather permitted, a good view eastward. All the plain below is bright yellow as the sun rises gloriously, and Olympus is for once in perfect splendour, with all its snowy peaks; but the daily perplexity of mist and cloud rapidly soars upward and hardly leaves time for a sketch ere all is once more shrouded away.

The dervish's or saint's tomb is such as you remark frequently on the outskirts of Mohammedan towns in the midst of wide cemeteries of humble sepulchres - a quadrangular structure three or four feet high, with pillars at the corners supporting a dome of varying height; beneath its centre is usually the carved emblem of the saint's rank, his turban, or high-crowned hat. As these tombs are often shaded by trees, their effect is very pleasing, the more so that the cemeteries are mostly frequented by the contemplative faithful. Often, in their vicinity, especially if the position of the tombs commands a fine view or is near a running stream, you may notice one of those raised platforms with a cage-like palisade and supporting a roof in the shade of which the Mohammedan delights to squat and smoke. There is one close by me now in which a solitary elder sits, in the enjoyment of tobacco and serenity, and looking in his blue and yellow robes very like an encaged macaw.

Thessaloniki

1609-10 William Lithgow

Thessaloniki at the Beginning of the Seventeenth Century

From thence ... I arrived at a town in Macedonia, called Salonica, but of old Thessalonica, where I stayed five days, and was much made of by the inhabitants, being Jews. Salonica is situate by the sea side, between the two Rivers Chabris and Ehedora: It is a pleasant, large and magnificke city, full of all sorts of merchandise; and it is nothing inferior in all things (except nobility) unto Naples in Italy. It was sometimes for a while under the Seigniory of Venice, till Amurath the son of Mahomet, took it from this republic. And is the principal place of Thessaly which is a Province of Macedon, together with Achaia, and Myrmedon, which are the other two Provinces of the same. This City of Salonica is now converted in an university for the Jews; and they are absolute Signiors thereof.

1745 Richard Pococke

Drinking Turks

"The Turks drink much, and to that may be imputed their being very bad people in this place; the janizaries in particular are exceedingly insolent."

1788 "An Italian Gentleman"

The Peoples of the City

The Jewish population of Thessaloniki was so prominent that the city was sometimes referred to as "The Mother of Israel."

This town is ... surrounded by a pretty strong wall. The houses are of wood, painted red, and edged toward the roof with black. On the corners of them there is frequently a verse of the Koran, or some scraps of poetry written in gilt letters. They are decorated with terraces, and the courts are often ornamented with Cyprus trees, which the Turks, who are of a melancholy turn, greatly delight in. The principle parts of the streets, on account of the heat of the sun, are covered with wood, which does not tend to make them more wholesome, as it prevents a proper circulation of air. Others swarm with sparrows, doves, crow, ravens, and storks, and also with dogs and cats. No one dare molest these animals; for the Turks, though they do not, like the Egyptians, exalt them into devils, would like them consider the person who injures them a murderer, and treat him accordingly. The shops are fastened with small bolts, for, thanks to the influence of religion, there are here no thieves. The surrounding country is well-cultivated, and abounds with partridges, hares, pheasants, hedgehogs, and a great number of tortoises.

The inhabitants of the place are computed at 80,000. The Jews, who amount to 23,000; the Greeks and Franks to 20,000; and the remainder are Turks. The Greeks and Latins have their respective churches in which they pray as much as they please without fear of molestation. The streets in which the Jews live may be known by their stench. The Jewesses are in general dirty; some of them may be seen, especially on Saturdays, who are handsome, clean and well-dressed. As we were going out of the Jewish quarter, the children came in crowds to ask us for paras, to which they were encouraged by their mothers, with a view probably of inspiring them with an early taste for the property of others. The Jews, however, do not meet here with the best of treatment. If a Turk has occasion for the service of a Jew, he seldom fails to honour him with the epithet of pimp or cuckold, or with some other title equally respectable. The Jews, it is true, are not much affected by contempt, and even bad treatment, provided they are well paid. They are the principle vendors of provisions, and in this business acquit themselves with much ability. They exercise the functions also of boatmen, porters, usurers, brokers, etc.

The country is governed in regard to criminal matters by a mullah, a name which denotes a cadi or judge of superior rank. The police is under the inspection of a pasha, a title given only to viziers and governors... These offices are bought, or obtained, by interest. The government, properly speaking, is in the hands if the janissaries, who act like petty despots. Some of them, when in a state of intoxication, have, to gratify their sanguinary disposition, or in order to try their powder, shot a Greek or a Jew. Others of them commit the like enormities through treachery, and in cold blood.

1802-09 Colonel William Leake

Some Notable Buildings

Salonica, as the Italians and English name this city, is by the Turks called Selanik, Saloniki by the Greeks, and by all the educated among them Thessaloniki. Being situated in great part upon the declivity of a hill rising from the extremity of that noble basin at the head of the Thermaic gulf, which is included within the Capes Vardar and Karaburnu, and being surrounded by lofty whitened walls, of which the whole extent, as well as that of the city itself, is displayed to view from the sea, it presents a most imposing appearance in approaching on that side. The form of the city approaches to a half circle, of which the diameter is described by a lofty wall, flanked with towers, extending a mile in length along the sea shore, and defended by three great towers, one at each extremity, the third overlooking the skala or landing place, where stands a small suburb, between the tower and the sea shore. Since the invention of gunpowder, batteries on a level with the water have been added to the maritime defences in the most important points, and a fortress, or fortified inclosure, has been constructed at the western angle of the city.

The eastern and western walls follow the edges of the height, where it falls on either side towards a small valley watered by a rivulet, and terminate above in the walls of the citadel, which has a double inclosure towards the town flanked with square towers. The heads of the valleys on the east and west are separated only by a ridge connecting the citadel with the falls of Mount Khortiatzi, which command it at a short range. The citadel, like that of Constantinople, is called ... the Seven Towers; for doubtless at both places the name is older than the Turkish conquest. Saloniki bears the usual characteristics of a Turkish town; no attention is paid to cleanliness or convenience in the streets, the exterior of the houses is designed to conceal all indications of wealth, nor can any correct opinion be formed of the population from the central part of the town, or a visit to the bazaar, where crowds are collected during the greater part of the day, while the rest of the city is a solitude. The houses in the lower part of the town are shut out from all external view by the narrow streets and the high town walls, but in rising higher, a noble prospect opens of the grand outlines of Olympus, Ossa, and Pelium, seen above the promontory of Karliburn, together with a part of the Chalcidic peninsula to the southward, and to the westward the immense level which extends for 50 miles to Verria and Vodhena.

The principal mosques were formerly Greek churches, and two of them were Pagan temples, which had been converted into churches, The most remarkable is that which is still known to the Greeks ... vulgarly [as] Eski Metropoli, an appellation employed also by the Turks, Hence it seems to have been, in the time of the Byzantine Empire, the cathedral church of the metropolitan bishop. It is a rotunda built of Roman bricks, with two doors, one to the south, the other to the west. The thickness of the walls below is 18 feet, their height about 50 feet, the diameter within, 80 feet: above these walls was a superstructure of slighter dimensions, the greater part of which, as well as the dome which crowns it, may perhaps have been added when the building was converted to the service of Christianity. It is lighted by windows in the middle height of the building, which in all is about 80 feet. Possibly these windows also are a Christian repair, the ancient temple having perhaps been lighted from the dome. The inside of the dome is adorned with the representation of buildings and saints, in mosaic, interspersed with inscriptions which, as usual in Greek churches, explained the subjects, but are now too much injured to be decipherable, though the Turks have not destroyed any of these ornaments, nor even a figure of the Almighty which occupied a niche opposite to the door where once stood the Pagan idol. In one place they have supplied a fallen mosaic with a painting in imitation of it.

Eski Djuma, or Old Friday, is the name of another mosque, the masonry and form of a great part of which shows that it was once a building of the same age as the Eski Mitropoli, or perhaps still older, but such have been the repairs and alterations which it has undergone in its conversion first into a church and then a mosque, that the ancient plan cannot easily he traced. It is supposed by the learned to have been a temple of Venus. Ai Sofia is a mosque, so called by the Turks, and which like the celebrated temple at Constantinople, was formerly a church dedicated to the Divine Wisdom. The Greeks assert it to have been built by the architect of St. Sophia, of Constantinople: its form at least is similar, being that of a Greek cross with an octastyle portico before the door, and a dome in the centre, which is lined with mosaic, representing various objects much defaced; among these I can distinguish saints and palm trees. The Turks, contrary to their usual custom of destroying, or at least of hiding with a coat of plaster, the figures in the Greek churches which they have converted into mosques, have allowed all the figures of St. Sophia to remain, with the exception of a piece in the centre, which they have replaced by an Arabic inscription, having been justly shocked, perhaps, by a huge human face, looking down, as I have frequently seen in Greek churches, and which is generally inscribed with the word *Pantokrator*.

St. Demetrius is a long church with a triple aisle, supported by a double order of columns of several kinds of variegated marble, and very much resembling an old Latin church, such as are seen in Italy, Sicily and the Holy Land. It may possibly have been built by the Latins when in possession of Thessalonica in the 13th century. Within this temple a sepulchral marble is inserted in the wall, which very much resembles many similar monuments in Christendom, being in that common form which represents the end of a sorus crowned with a pediment. It is ornamented with flowers well executed, within which is an inscription in twenty-two Greek Iambic verses, in honour of one Luke Spanduni, who is described as a scion of Byzantium and the Hellenes, and who died in the year 6989, or AD. 1481, whence it would seem that the Turks did not deprive the Greeks of their church of St. Demetrius immediately after the conquest...

Among the ecclesiastical antiquities, in which Saloniki exceeds any place in Greece, as the churches just mentioned show, are two of the most ancient pulpits in existence; they are single blocks of variegated marble, with small steps cut in them, One of these *bemata*, as they are still called by the Greeks, is in the mosque of Eski Mitropoli: the other is lying in the yard of a church of St. Minas, which is still appropriated to the Greek worship.

Among the remains of pagan times, may be mentioned some small portions of the walls, which there is every reason to believe, follow the line and foundations of the inclosure of Cassander, and which being in their general structure much higher and more solid than such as the Ottomans build, seem to consist for the most part of successive repairs of the Macedonian work, before the Turkish conquest. Therme we can hardly suppose to have been so large as Thessalonica, and as it could not have left the citadel unoccupied, probably did not extend as far as the sea. That the main street, and two principal gates, and consequently the whole inclosure, of the Roman Thessalonica, corresponded with those of the modern town, we have an infallible proof, in two ancient arches which still cross that street; one already mentioned near the Vardar gate, the other not far from the corresponding gate at the eastern end of the same street. The latter, which had two smaller lateral arches annexed to it, now destroyed, consists of two piers 14 feet square, faced with stone, which were covered on all sides with a double range of figures in low relief, representing the sieges, battles, and triumphs of a Roman Emperor. A great part of the piers are concealed by shops of the bazaar, which cover all the lower parts of the figures on one side, and the whole of them on the other. Entering a bakehouse in the latter situation, I found the sculpture still more defaced than in other parts, but in none is it in good preservation, and the whole appears to have been of a very declining period of art. The arch which rests upon the piers is still more deprived of its facing, and is now a mere mass of Roman tile and mortar...

To the westward of this arch, near the main street, are the ruins of a portico with a double order of architecture, consisting of four Corinthian columns, not of the best design or execution, and the shafts of which are now half buried in the ground. On their architrave stands an upper order, consisting of four plain pilasters, on the opposite faces of which are Caryatides, eight in all: the figures are of the human size, or near it, and each of them represents a different subject. On one of the pilasters the two opposite figures are Leda and Ganymede ; the former embraces the swan, whose head reposes upon her breast: Ganymede is held by the eagle, whose wings are spread over his back, and whose talons; rest on his hips, while the head of the eagle reaches over the left shoulder of the youth, looking in his face. This is a very good piece of sculpture, and not much injured by time. The other figures seem inferior in merit as they are in preservation; nor can the subjects be easily understood. The next to Ganymede, on the same side, is a man with a Phrygian bonnet, at whose feet is a bull's head; the third and fourth are females in light drapery, the latter with wings. On the opposite side, or that of the Leda, the figures are so much ruined that I cannot distinguish the subjects. This monument is in the house of a Jew, and is known in the Spanish dialect of the Jews by the name of Incantada, "the Enchanted," on the supposition that the figures are human beings petrified by the effect of magic. Its central position, and the nature of the construction, support the idea that it was connected with the ancient agora. The space which lies between the sea and that part of the main street where the Incantada and arch of Constantine are situated, is said to have been occupied by the hippodrome, noted for having been the scene of a promiscuous massacre of the assembled people of Thessalonica by order of Thcodosius.

In many parts of the town, particularly at the fountains, sepulchral stones and inscribed sori are to be found. Wherever figures occur upon the latter, their heads have, as usual, been destroyed by the Turks, nor is it easy to find an inscription that is perfect...

The Peoples of the City

The population of Saloniki is reckoned at 80,000, but probably does not exceed 65,000, of whom 35,000 are Turks, 15,000 Greeks, and 13,000 Jews, the remainder Franks and Gypsies...

The Yuruks cultivate their own lands chiefly in the mountainous districts. The Janissaries are the garrisons of the fortified places, among whom are generally enrolled the greater part of the heads of families engaged in trade or manufactures, or who have landed property in the neighbouring plain. A thousand pounds sterling a year in land is considered a large estate. Hadji Mustafa, the Bash Tjaus of the Janissaries, has seven tjiftllks worth 20,000 piastres a year (or 1200*l*.), though he lives at the rate of not more than eight or ten thousand. Under a government which makes everyone feel danger in displaying his wealth, and renders property and life insecure even to its most favoured subjects, the extremes of parsimony and extravagance are naturally to be found. Turks as well as Jews often carry the former to excess, and the latter is by no means uncommon among the young Osmanlis. An under-employée in the Mekheme is pointed out to me, who in a few years dissipated 2000 purses and seven tjiftliks. These Turkish landed proprietors, however, are the persons of the greatest stability in Turkey; and the Frank merchants who bargain for their corn, cotton, and tobacco, can, without much risk, make advances upon their crops.

The Jews of Saloniki are descended from the largest of those colonies, which settled in Greece at the time of their expulsion from Spain at the end of the fifteenth century; but a considerable portion of them have become Musulmans since that time, though without being altogether acknowledged by the Osmanlis, and forming a separate class under the denomination of Mamins. Inheriting the Jewish spirit of parsimony and industry, they are generally rich, and among them are some of the wealthiest Turks at Salonlki. Hassan Adjik, one of the ministry at Constantinople, and his brother, who is Gumrukji, or collector of the customs at Saloniki, are Mamins. They are naturally objects of extreme dislike to the idle, poor, and profligate Janissaries of the lower class. They go to mosque regularly, and conform to the Mahometan religion in externals, but are reproached by the other Turks with having secret meetings and ceremonies, with other peculiarities of which the best attested is their knowledge of the Spanish language. They are said to be divided into three tribes, two of whom will not intermarry with the third, nor will the latter give their daughters in marriage to the Osmanlis.

The ... Greek community, is presided over by the metropolitan bishop, who with the archons arranges all civil disputes in which Turks are not concerned, unless when the Christians think fit to resort to the Mekheme... There are some opulent Greek merchants at Saloniki, most of whom are indebted for the undisturbed possession and increase of their wealth to the protection which they have enjoyed as dragomans or barataires of the European missions. Now that these protections are about to be abolished, their situation will be much more precarious.

There are three sorts of kharadtj paid by the rayahs; the first, called edina, is of 3 piastres, to which boys under fourteen are subject, but which is generally exacted from all under eleven; the second, the efsat, of six piastres, is paid by artisans, servants, and all the poor, even beggars; the third, alia, taken from all the classes above the last, amounts at Salonica to twelve piastres a head. Mr. N-, the principal Greek merchant, who is procurator for Mount Athos, informs me that he pays only 3000 kharatjes for the whole population of the peninsula, though there are 4000 monks alone, besides laics.

It is almost the only place where the kharatj is underrated. Those who farm it having generally the means of making good their claims for an increase in the rayah population, it most frequently happens that individuals pay more than the regulated sum, and scarcely ever the reverse. Some-times they are called upon for the double or triple. The Turks are probably aware that Mount Athos is rated below its numbers, but being the abode of persons devoted to religion, it is entitled to favour by the Turkish usages, for custom is a powerful argument among them, though seldom employed, as in the instance just mentioned, for the benefit of any but themselves. A Pasha of Saloniki having received orders to join the Grand Vezir's army, was waited upon by a merchant acting as English consul, to whom he was indebted about 30*l*. My friend, said he, where am I to find a para? I have not money to pay the bread have been eating here; the Porte indeed has sent me 500 purses, but it will not discharge one fourth of my debts. At least, says the consul, you will give me an acknowledgment in writing. ... It is not the custom; was the only reply. It is the custom to admit Christians to see the mosques of Saloniki, which have been once churches, probably because the imam gets a fee by it...

Economy

The ordinary price of silk is 50 piastres the oke; and almost every family raises silkworms. Ordinary cotton and woollen stuffs for the clothing of the common people are also woven in the private houses as well as in the surrounding villages. A considerable quantity of cotton towels are made here, sometimes with a border of gold threads, for the ... washing of the upper classes before and after meals, which in every part of Greece is practised as in the time of Homer. Silken gauze for shirts and mosquito curtains, are another fabric of the city, but the chief manufacture is the tanning and dyeing of leather, which is entirely in the hands of the Janissaries. The commerce of Saloniki has very much declined during the war, and even since Beaujour described it in 1797. Tobacco sent from hence in imperial ships is now the only considerable export. No English ship has loaded here for 12 years. The beys have their magazines full of corn, which by a firmahn of the Porte, issued last year and renewed this year, they are forbidden from sending to Christendom. Meantime the Porte demands a certain proportion from all the most productive corn countries of the empire, Macedonia among the rest, at a low price, on the pretence of fitting out fleets and armies. The consequence has been, that last year, when the price of corn at Athens was very high, it was sold by the government at Constantinople to foreigners, at a much lower price than they might have received for it in Greece, including the expense of sending it there. Three or four hundred thousand Stambul kila of wheat might be procured here in a month, and cattle in any number that could be required. The Beys of Saloniki suffer more than the more distant landlords, because the smuggling of corn can be more easily carried on from any other part of the coast, In general the orders of the Porte against the exportation of corn are converted into a source of profit to the local governor; but in a fortified place, under the eyes of a Pashai, and in time of war, more attention to the imperial orders is necessary.

Some Observations on Turks

In reading descriptions of China one is struck by the similarity of the customs of that country with those of Turkey, arising from the same Tartar origin. Their dress and architecture, their custom of interchanging presents, their habit of smoking, and the amusements at their festivals, are almost, identical. Public employments are generally venal, in spite of the Sovereign. The quantity of escort when a man goes out, is the measure of his grandeur. It is unpolite to speak of any but agreeable subjects at visits, and even to use certain words conveying hateful ideas. The

Emperor gives only two audiences to ambassadors, one at coming, the other at departing. When a great man passes through the streets, his approach is indicated by a small drum. A drum marks the watches of the night. Provincial governors are changed very frequently...

The Turks have a certain manly politeness, which is the most powerful of all modes of deceit, and which seldom fails in giving strangers an erroneous impression of their real character, It covers a rooted aversion to all European nations, as well as to the individuals who have the misfortune to have any dealings with these plausible barbarians. Though in the most splendid era of their history their feelings may have been those of contempt, founded upon ignorance, fanaticism and the pride of conquest, it has been changed by their weakness and their dread of the Christians of Europe, into a mixture of fear and hatred. Thus there are two things which the European who has any political dealings with the Turk, should never lose sight of: 1, that he hates us: 2, that he fears us. By the latter only can we counteract the effects of the former, added as it is, to the most profound dissimulation, a keen sense of self-interest, and an obstinate perseverance in defending it. The Turks have so long experienced the advantages of conduct founded on this basis, and that of the mutual jealousy of the several European powers, that we may rely upon their adhering to it, as long as they have a foot of land on the continent of Europe. To say that the Turks have more honour and honesty than their Christian subjects, is a poor commendation: they have not the same necessity for the practice of fraud and falsehood. What other arms against their tyrants, are left to the unfortunate rayahs!

1848 Edward Lear

Thessaloniki in a Time of Cholera

This passage demonstrates the disruption of normal life in a city of considerable size, together with the general panic, occasioned by an outbreak of pone of the epidemic diseases which, during tyhis period, spread from city to city along the shores of the Mediterranean.

At sunrise the highest peaks of Athos were still visible above the long, low line of Cape Drepano, and at noon we were making way up the Gulf of Salonica, Ossa and Olympus on our left-lines of noble mountain grandeur, but becoming rapidly indistinct as a thick sirocco-like vapour gradually shrouded over all the features of the western shore of the gulf.

N'importe - the Vale of Tempe, so long a dim expectation, is now a near reality; and Olympus is indubitably at hand, though invisible for the present. There were wearily long flat points of land to pass (all, however, full of interest as parts of the once flourishing Chalcidice) ere Salonica was visible, a triangle enclosed in a border of white walls on the hill at the head of the gulf; and it was nearly 6 pm. before we reached the harbour and anchored.

Instantly the wildest confusion seized all the passive human freight. The polychromatic harem arose and moved like a bed of tulips in a breeze; the packed Wallachians and Bosniacs and Jews started crampfully from the deck and disentangled themselves into numerous boats; the Consular Esiliati departed; and lastly, I and my dragoman prepared to go, and were soon at shore, though it was not so easy to be upon it. Salonica is inhabited by a very great proportion of Jews; nearly all the porters in the city are of that nation, and now that the cholera had rendered employment scarce there were literally crowds of black-turbaned Hebrews at the water's edge, speculating on the possible share of each in the conveyance of luggage from the steamer. The enthusiastic Israelites rushed into the water and, seizing my arms and legs, tore me out of the boat and up a narrow board with the most unsatisfactory zeal; immediately after which they fell upon my enraged dragoman in the same mode, and finally throwing themselves on my luggage each portion of it was claimed by ten or twelve frenzied agitators who pulled this way and that way till I who stood apart, resigned to whatever might happen confidently awaited the total destruction of my *roba*. From yells and pullings to and fro, the scene changed in a few minutes to a real fight, and the whole community fell to the most furious hair-pulling, turban-clenching, and robe-tearing, till the luggage was forgotten and all the party was involved in one terrific combat. How this exhibition would have ended I cannot tell, for in the heat of the conflict my man came running with a half-score of Government Kawasi, or police; and the way in which they fell to belabouring the enraged Hebrews was a thing never to be forgotten. These took a deal of severe beating from sticks and whips before they gave way, and eventually some six or eight were selected to carry the packages of the Ingliz, which I followed into the city, not unvexed at being the indirect cause of so much strife.

In Salonica there is a Locanda - a kind of hotel - the last dim shadow of European "accommodation" between Stamboul and Cattaro [Kotor]: it is kept by the politest of Tuscans, and the hostess is the most corpulent and blackest of negresses. Thither we went; but I observed, with pain, that the state of the city was far more melancholy than I had had reason to suppose: all the bazaars (long lines of shops) were closed and tenantless: the gloom and deserted air of the streets was most sad, and I needed not to be told that the cholera, or whatever were the complaint so generally raging, had broken out with fresh virulence since the last accounts received at Constantinople, and nearly three-fourths of the living population had fled from their houses into the adjacent country. And no sooner was I settled in a room at the inn than, sending Giorgio to the British Consulate, I awaited his return and report with some anxiety.

Presently in came Giorgio with the dreariest of faces, and the bearer of what to me were, in truth, seriously vexatious news. The cholera, contrary to the intelligence received in Stamboul, which represented the disease as on the decline, had indeed broken out afresh and was spreading or - what is the same thing as to results, if a panic be once rife - was supposed to be spreading on all sides. The surrounding villages had taken alarm and had drawn a strict *cordon sanitaire* between themselves and the enemy; and, worse than all, the monks of Mount Athos had utterly prohibited all communication between their peninsula and the infected city; so that any attempt on my part to join C.M.C. would be useless, no person being allowed to proceed beyond a few miles outside the eastern gate of Salonica. No one could tell how long this state of things would last; for, although the epidemic was perhaps actually decreasing in violence, yet the fear of contagion was by no means so. Multitudes of the inhabitants of the suburbs and adjacent villages had fled to the plains, and to pass them would be an impossibility. On the south-western road to Greece or Epirus, the difficulty was the same: even at Katerina, or Platamona, the peasants would allow no one to land...

Whatever the past of Salonica, its present seems gloomy enough. The woe, the dolefulness of this city! - its narrow, ill-paved streets (evil awaits the man who tries to walk with nailed boots on the rounded, slippery stones of a Turkish pavement!); the very few people I met in them carefully avoiding contact; the closed houses; the ominous silence; the sultry, oppressive heat of the day; all contributed to impress the mind with a feeling of heavy melancholy. A few Jews in dark dresses and turbans; Jewesses, their hair tied up in long, caterpillar-like green silk bags, three feet in length; Greek porters, aged blacks, of whom - freed slaves from Stamboul - there are many in Salonica; these were the only human beings I encountered in threading a labyrinth of lanes in the lower town, ascending towards the upper part of this formerly extensive city. Once, a bier with a corpse on it, borne by some six or eight of the most wretched creatures, crossed my path; and when I arrived at the beautiful ruin called the Incantada two women, I was told, had just expired within the courtyard, and, said the ghastly-looking Greek on the threshold, "you may come in and examine what you please, and welcome; but once in you are in quarantine, and may not go out," an invitation I declined as politely as I could and passed onward. From the convent at the summit of the town, just within its white walls, the view should be most glorious, as one ought to see the whole of the gulf and all the range of Olympus; but, alas I beyond the silvery minarets relieving the monotonous surface of roofs below and the delicately indented shore and the blue gulf, all else was blotted out, as it were, by a curtain of hot purple haze, telling tales to my fancy of miasma and cholera, fever and death.

Willing to exercise the mind as much as possible in a place so full of melancholy influences, I examined, in order, every ruin and record of old Thessalonica - the mosques in the lower town, and in the courtyard of one of these the pulpit said to be St. Paul's, the Roman arch, with its *bassi rilievi*, and the Hippodrome; and, although there was no one of these I particularly regretted that I could not draw, yet I saw an infinity of picturesque bits, cypresses and minarets and latticed houses; and doubtless, under more cheering circumstances, a week in Salonica might be well spent. But the fear of fever deterred me from great exertion, and sent me home long ere noon. Sad, gloomy, and confused memories of Salonica are all I shall carry away with me. In the afternoon, Mr. C. Blunt, our Consul, came to me, and strongly recommended my own decision as the best, his account of Athos and the west coast being confirmatory of that I had previously heard. The evening was passed with his agreeable family, long resident here.

Ancient ruins, Thessaloniki (Fauvel,1831)

223

Mount Athos

1802-09 Colonel William Leake

The Holy Mountain at the Beginning of the Nineteenth Century

At Karyes resides the Turkish governor of the Holy Mountain: a bostanji of Constantinople, who is supported, together with a guard of Albanians, at the expense of the holy community; but without having any authority except for the general police of the mountain, and for its protection against thieves and pirates. Towards the centre of the town the houses are more closely built, and there is a sort of bazaar containing shops of grocery, with those of a few artisans, among whom blacksmiths and locksmiths are the most numerous. On Saturdays there is a ... market, to which the manufactures of the mountain are brought for sale. Karyes is the residence also of the Archons or Epistatae. These are Caloyers deputed from the twenty monasteries to superintend the civil affairs of the mountain, to take cognisance of any matters in which the whole community is interested, to assign to each monastery its portion of the payments to the Turks, and to enforce the collection of it. The revenue and internal government of each convent is its own concern. The Epistatae are four in number, and are changed every year; each monastery sending one deputy in its turn, but in such manner that one of the four is always from one of the five great monasteries, Lavra, Vatopedhi, Iviron, Khilandari, and Dhionysiu. Besides these principal officers the community have an agent at Saloniki and another at Constantinople. Ecclesiastically the Oros depends immediately on the patriarch of Constantinople. The archons are competent to punish small offences, and to determine such differences between the monasteries as are not sufficiently important to be decided at Constantinople, where, however, the monks are too apt to carry their causes and to spend money in litigation for the benefit only of the Turks. In the time of the Greek Empire the mountain was under the direction of a great ecclesiastic ... whence the name Protáto still attached to the church at Karyes where he resided. This church is supposed to be the most ancient on the peninsula, and to have been built by Constantine the Great. It is celebrated on the mountain for a miraculous picture which once called out to the officiating priest to read his liturgy quicker, in order that he might administer the communion to a dying monk. Near Karyes to the southward is Kutlumusi, situated in one of the most cultivable parts of the peninsula, amidst gardens, vineyards, olive plantations, and cornfields. It was founded by the Emperor Alexius Comnenus, but partook of the fate of all the early buildings in being destroyed by plunderers. It was afterwards renewed and enlarged by several successive Waiwodes of Wallachia. Kutlumusi boasts of possessing the other foot of St. Anne among its relics. Like the other monasteries it has a port, which is below Karyes, not far to the north-west of the Arsanas of Iviron.

After dining at Karyes, I proceed in two hours to Iviron, situated near the northern shore of the peninsula, in a small bend of the coast, midway between the other two principal monasteries of this shore, Lavra and Vatopedhi. The road descends the hills obliquely by a rugged path through vineyards, and amidst a great diversity of hilly ground covered with wood. Iviron, or the monastery of the Georgians, was so called as having been founded by four pious and wealthy men of that nation, of whom three were brothers, and the fourth was Tornicius, a general officer of the Emperor Romanus, who, having been recalled from his retreat by the widow of Romanus, to defend the frontiers of the empire against the Persians, received from the empress, on his successful return to Constantinople, the means of building the present church, which is the largest on the peninsula next to that of Lavra. It stands in the midst of an irregular quadrangle, comprehending also a church of the Panaghia surnamed Portatissa. This church is renowned for a picture which was thrown into the sea in the reign of the iconoclast Theophilus, and some years afterwards made its appearance again on the neighbouring shore. Besides several valuable Metokhia in the adjacent parts of Macedonia, it has a large dependent monastery at Moscow, and another in Wallachia, and it has always been the favourite and most protected monastery of the Russians. No convent on the Oros is so rich in relics. There are 300 monks belonging to the house, but a third of them are either absent on eleemosynary missions, or dwelling on the metokhia and kellia of the monastery. The library, which is kept in tolerable order by an old Didascalus, consists chiefly, as he observes, of the fathers, or books appertaining to the church service; but it contains also several Greek and Latin classics, a recent gift of a Mavromati of Arta, who was bishop of that see, and whose nephew I met there last year. None of the Latin books have been touched, because nobody can read them: indeed, the whole library is nearly useless, such is the extreme ignorance of the monks. The house has the reputation of being the best ordered on the mountain. Like all the monasteries, or at least the larger, Iviron has an hospital for the sick, presses for wine and oil, and among the monks some tailors and shoe-makers, who make all the clothes of the inmates. It is often the residence of retired Greeks. The Patriarch of Constantinople, who was deposed eight years ago, and who has lived here ever since, has just been recalled to the capital, on the change of the Turkish ministry to resume the patriarchal throne.

Oct. 25.- In the afternoon I proceed to the convent of Filotheu, in the way to Lavra: the road follows the slope of the mountain through a thick forest of chestnuts, oaks, and elms, mixed with a great variety of shrubs, particularly the arbutus, now covered with ripe fruit. The oaks are small, but many of the chestnuts are fine trees: a small portion of the fruit is consumed on the mountain, or exported in the boats which come to load firewood; the remainder perishes on the ground, or is washed into the sea by the torrents. The monasteries levy a small contribution upon the woodcutters.

In a green valley near the sea, between Iviron and Filotheu, stand the ruined monidhi, or subordinate monastery of Mylopotamo, and a tower belonging to Lavra. Filotheu, though one of the smaller establishments of the peninsula, is among the most ancient; it was founded by one Philotheus, in company with two other Greek saints named Arsenius and Dionysius, the last of whom was founder of the great monastery of St. Dionysius on Mount Olympus...

Oct. 27. - The stormy weather still continues. At a kelli above Iviron I find some monks employed in building a boat on the side of the mountain, a mile from the sea, and learn from them that boats are sometimes built in much higher situations, as they find it easier to convey the boat to the sea side than the timber for building it.

Oct. 28. - From Iviron to Vatopedhi in three hours : first crossing a projection of the mountain, on which to the right stands the monastery of Stavronikita, and then descending to Pandokratora, which is midway to Vatopedhi. Stavroniklta was founded by a Patriarch of Constantinople named Jeremiah. It is agreeably situated just above the shore, in the midst of gardens and orange groves, and contains a celebrated picture of St. Nicolas of Myra, to whom the church is dedicated. This picture is called the Stridhas, because it has an oyster upon it, which is sup-posed to prove the tale related of it, namely, that it was thrown into the sea in the time of the iconoclast contest, and long afterwards found its way again to the shore. Pandokratora was built in the 13th century by two brothers, one of whom was Alexius, the general of Michael Palaeologus, who recovered Constantinople from the Franks. On a summit to the left is St. Elias, a large *askitiri*, occupied entirely by Russians.

From Pandokratora we cross another ridge, passing constantly through woods to Vatopedhi. This monastery, which, with its lofty walls flanked by towers mounted with cannon, looks more like a fortress than a religious house, is beautifully situated on a commanding height, separated from the shore of a little bay by slopes covered with plantations of olives and oranges. The bay is the termination of a small valley, surrounded by steep woody heights, and watered by a torrent. These heights are separated by the vale of Karyes from the hills which lie between the latter and Xeropotami, so that the longitudinal ridge of the peninsula here becomes double. Vatopedhi is larger than any of the monasteries except Lavra, and is the most ancient of all, its first foundation having been by Constantine the Great... No monastery has larger possessions of olive plantations, vineyards, and foreign metokhia, the best of which are in Moldavia, and none is better provided with all sorts of internal conveniences. The treasury nevertheless is now poor, in consequence of a cause which the monastery has lately gained against Zografu, concerning the property of a metokhi, and in which they prevailed, not so much by the evidence of their ancient charters, as by the expenditure of 200 purses at Constantinople; the Grand Vezir, before whom the cause was heard, took occasion at the conclusion to give the parties a good lecture on their folly. The ordinary annual expenses of the house are 200 purses, including all the imposts which they pay to the Turks. Three hundred monks are attached to the establishment, but more than half of them are absent in the Metokhia or in eleemosynary missions; besides these, are a great number of cosmics, both in the house and the kellia. The affairs of the monastery are directed by twelve [abbots], among whom the chief dignities are the ... sacristan, the ... inspector ... and the ... secretary. One of the oldest residents, but who has no direction of affairs, is the Bishop of Moskopoli, whose fears of Aly Pasha drove him from that place twelve or fifteen years ago.

On a hill adjoining the monastery is the school of Vatopedhi, now empty, but which for a short time, under the learned Eugenius Bulgari, of Corfu, attained such reputation, that he had more scholars than the building could well lodge, although it contains 170 cells for students. But notwithstanding the advantages which the healthy situation, beautiful scenery, and seclusion, seem to promise in Mount Athos, as a place of education, the friends of learning among the Greeks have been compelled to apply their exertions elsewhere. The ignorant are generally persecutors of knowledge: the school was viewed with jealous eyes by all the vulgar herd of caloyers, and there were other objections to the Holy Peninsula which, combined with the former, proved at last the ruin of the school.

The monks at the head of the monasteries of Mount Athos are generally those who have brought some money to the treasury; sometimes those who have travelled to collect charity, and who, by retaining a part of the produce, acquire thereby the means of influencing the Patriarch, who has always some weight in the election of the Igumeni, though nominally they are annually elective, wherever the monks are [idiorhythmic], as they are at Vatopedhi, and in the greater part of the monasteries of the Oros. When so denominated, they contribute something to the treasury on entering the society, receive a cell and a ration of bread and wine, but provide every thing else themselves. The *coenobitics*, on the other hand, are headed by a single [abbot], appointed by the Patriarch. They dress and live uniformly, receive raiment as well as food from the house, and are in every thing more despotically governed. Seven only of the twenty monasteries of the Oros are *coenobitic*, namely, Karakalo and Simenu, on the northern coast, and on the southern, Dhionysiu, Simopetra, Russiko, Xenofu, and Konstamonitu. The monks are of three degrees of rank: in a state of preparation, bearing the sign of the cross, and of the highest rank. When the *kellia*, or detached houses, are in small clusters, the monks and laics who inhabit them are under an elder of the parent monastery , but many of these cells are solitary cottages occupied by hermits. There are more than 300 scattered kellia on the mountain. The *kelleiotai* are either cultivators of vineyards, gardens, or cornfields, of which latter however there are very few, or they tend the bees and cattle of the peninsula. Some of the inmates of all the monasteries are employed in spinning wool and making articles of clothing, generally those confined to the house by incapacity for out door employment, but the manufactures are chiefly carried on in the retreats called *askites or skites* , from whence the bazaar at Karyes is supplied with articles of monastic dress, caps and bonnets of almost every kind used in Greece, beads, crosses, wooden spoons, and other ordinary implements used in the monasteries. Some of the ... ascetics, particularly at St. Anna, are bookbinders, painters, and framers of church pictures, and there are some calligraphers, the last remains of a profession which was very extensive before the invention of printing, and was probably a great resource to the monks of Athos. The *asksites* is under the direction of a monk of the monastery on which it depends... The principal *askites* besides those dependent on Lavra, are the new skiti of St. Paul, that of Xenofu, St. Elias of Pandokratora, St. Demetrius of Vatopedhi, Prodhromo, or the skiti of Kutlumusi, the *skiti* of A. Triadha near Simopetra, and a monidhi of St. Basil on the shore not far from Karyes.

The Oros supplies its inhabitants with timber, firewood, oil, olives, figs, walnuts, potherbs, grapes, and wine, but for bread corn they are entirely dependent upon their *metokhia* beyond the isthmus: of which the Oros [mountain] possesses no less than fifty-five in the adjacent parts of Macedonia, or in the island of Thaso. Fish is the only animal food permitted on the peninsula, except to strangers of distinction, who are always expected to contribute something to the treasury. The ordinary food therefore of the Aghiorites, even when there is no fast, is vegetables, salt-fish, olives, and cheese. Fresh fish they make little use of: their timid and indolent habits, the deep and tempestuous sea that surrounds them, and the want of boats, combining to deprive them of the best nourishment their rules allow. The mountain is forbidden ground to all animals of the female sex. Neither cow, nor ewe, nor sow, nor hen, nor she-cat, is to be seen; but of course the wild animals and birds defy them; rats and mice multiply and devour them, and they are obliged to confess their obligations to the queen bee, without whose assistance they would be deprived of one of their staple productions. All the buildings swarm with wild pigeons in search of food, fortunately for the carnivorous traveller, who without this resource, and that afforded by a few cocks which are kept either for his sake or for a retired prelate in case of illness, would find it difficult to make a dinner. The vulgar believe, or affect to believe, contrary to the evidence of their senses, that nothing feminine can live upon the peninsula; and I have heard the sailors of the Aegean relate stories of women who have been punished with immediate death for having had the audacity to land upon it.

The pastures of the mountains are chiefly peopled with mules and young bulls, which, as well as some oxen, rams, and goats, are bred at the metokhia beyond the isthmus, and brought here to grow and fatten. A sheep or goat is killed occasionally at Karyes for the use of the Aga and his household, but even he cannot have any female in his house.

The amount of the contributions to the Porte and to the Pasha of Saloniki is about 150 purses... Most of the monasteries, if not all, have a debt, for which they pay a high interest, and like some larger communities find this part of their yearly obligations more burthensome than their direct taxes and current expenses.

The inhabitants of Mount Athos are assembled of course from all parts of Turkey, and consist chiefly of men in the decline of life, who retire hither from motives of piety, or more commonly for the sake of securing the remainder of their days from the dangers of Turkish despotism. Any man who brings money with him is welcome; if old, he is not received without it, but the young and laborious are admitted free of expense, and after serving for some years as cosmics they become caloyers. As these persons merely seek their living, they are generally of the lowest classes. Not a few of every period of life are fugitives from the effects of their own crimes, or from Turkish vengeance, whether just or unjust. Hence it seldom happens at present, though it was probably otherwise during the Byzantine empire, that more than a few of the monks in each monastery know any thing beyond the liturgy, the remainder being at the utmost just able to read the church service. Several were pointed out to me, who having formerly become Musulmans and then repented, have fled to this place as the only one where they can return to the church and save themselves from the punishment which awaits the Turkish apostate. Not long since a young Jew of Salonlki came to the Oros to embrace Christianity and the monastic life; but as soon as he had been well-clothed, returned to Saloniki, and there received new favours from the Jews for renouncing Christianity. One of the monks of Vatopedhi, who had been instrumental to his first conversion, informs me that he found this Jew soon after at Adrianople practising as a physician. A young Turk of Constantinople, who, being the son of a Janissary of the Patriarch, had been brought up in the constant view of the ceremonies of the church, and had thus become thoroughly acquainted with them, finding himself totally destitute on his father's death, came to Vatopedhi and served for three years as… one of the priests who take their turns to say the daily mass, and who have frequent opportunities of sharing in the gifts of pilgrims or others. After having conformed himself during that period to all the forms of confession as well as to the usual mortifications, such as an occasional retirement to a hermitage to live on bread and water, he became tired at length of such a life, and desirous of spending some of the piastres which he had collected. Presenting himself therefore one day to the Igumenos, he asked his commands for Constantinople, stating that he had now finished his affairs at the Oros, and that his name was once more Ismail. These tricks are the more ridiculous at Vatopedhi, as this monastery is noted for the strictness of its discipline. It is probably a consequence of their diet that cutaneous disorders and ruptures are very common among the monks in general. The ordinary punishment for breaking the rules of fasting, or other venial offences, is that of… repentances, which are generally reckoned by the hundred. The … great repentance, is to make the sign of the cross followed by a prostration of the body to the ground. The … little *metania*, is a cross and bend without prostration. The price of a … vigil and mass for the benefit of the purchaser's soul, is 25 piastres, of the *parrisia* , 50 piastres: by means of the latter sum the donor is mentioned in a particular prayer on certain feast days as long as the monastery endures.

Among the present inmates of Vatopedhi is an old Chiote, who has been long in the Russian service in various parts of Europe, and now enjoys a pension as a retired captain: he had intended to pass the remainder of his days on the Oros, but disgusted with the companions whom he finds here, is about to return to Teresopol, where he has a daughter married to a Russian colonel. He was at Kherson when Catherine, anxious for the prosperity of her newly-founded city of Kherson, sent thither the Corfiotes Eugenius Bulgari, and Theotoki, with the princess Gkika, all persons well qualified to improve their countrymen, many of whom had been induced to settle there by the advantages which the empress held out. The governor, however, was a Russian, and as such, hated the Greeks. To a new colony, at such a distance from the capital, this was fatal. The poorer settlers perished in great numbers in the winter of 1780; and in 1784 the plague was introduced into Kherson, by which the Chiote captain lost five grown children in four days.

1834-7 Robert Curzon

A Genuine Hermit

We steered for a tall square tower which stood on a projecting marble rock above the calm blue sea at the S.E. corner of the peninsula; and rounding a small cape we turned into a beautiful little port or harbour, the entrance of which was commanded by this tower and by one or two other buildings constructed for defence at the foot of it, all in the Byzantine style of architecture. The quaint half-Eastern, half-Norman architecture of the little fortress, my outlandish vessel. The brilliant colours of the sailors' dresses, the rich vegetation and great tufts of flowers which grew in crevices of the white marble, formed altogether one of the most picturesque scenes it was ever my good fortune to behold, and which I always remember with pleasure. We saw no one, but about a mile off there was the great monastery of St. Laura standing above us among the trees on the side of the mountain, and this delightful little bay was, as the sailors told us, the ... landing-place for pilgrims who were going to the monastery.

We paid off the vessel, and my things were landed on the beach. It was not an operation of much labour, for my effects consisted principally of an enormous pair of saddlebags, made of a sort of carpet, and which are called *khourges*; and are carried by the camels in Arabia; but there was at present mighty little in them: nevertheless, light as they were, their appearance would have excited a feeling of consternation in the mind of the most phlegmatic mule. After a brisk chatter on the part of the whole crew, who, with abundance of gesticulations, all talked at once, they got on board, and towing the vessel out by means of an exceeding small boat, set sail, and left me and my man with the saddlebags high and dry upon the shore. We were somewhat taken by surprise at this sudden departure of our marine, so we sat upon two stones for a while to think about it. "Well," said I, "we are at Mount Athos; so suppose you walk up to the monastery, and get some mules or monks, or something or other to carry up the saddlebags. Tell them the celebrated Milordos Inglesis, the friend of the Universal Patriarch, is arrived, and that he kindly intends to visit their monastery; and that he is a great ally of the Sultan's, and of all the captains of all the men of war that come down the Archipelago: and, added I, "'make haste now, and let us be up at the monastery lest our friends in the brig there should take it into their heads to come back and cut our throats."

Away he went, and I and the saddlebags remained below. For some time I solaced myself by throwing stones into the water, and then I walked up the path to look about me, and found a red mulberry-tree with fine ripe mulberries on it, of which I ate a prodigious number in order to pass away the time. As I was studying the Byzantine tower, I thought I saw something peeping out of a loophole near the top of it, and, on looking more attentively I saw it was the head of an old man with a long grey beard, who was gazing curiously at me. I shouted out at the top of my voice, *Kalemera sas, ariste, kalemera sas* (good day to you, sir); *ora kali sas* (good morning to you). He answered in return, *Kalos orizete?* (how do you do?). So I went up to the tower, passed over a plank that served as a draw-bridge across a chasm, and at the door of a wall which surrounded the lower buildings stood a little old monk, the same who had been peeping out of the loophole above. He took me into his castle, where he seemed to be living all alone in a Byzantine lean-to at the foot of the tower, the window of his room looking over the port beneath. This room had numerous pegs in the walls, on which were hung dried herbs and simples. One or two great jars stood in the corner, and these and a small divan formed all his household furniture. We began to talk in Romaic, but I was not very strong in that language, and presently stuck fast. He showed me over the tower, which contained several groined vaulted rooms one above another, all empty.

From the top there was a glorious view of the islands and the sea. Thought I to myself, this is a real, genuine, unsophisticated live hermit; he is not stuffed like the hermit at Vauxhall, nor made up of beard and blankets like those on the stage; he is a genuine specimen of an almost extinct race. What would not Walter Scott have given for him? The aspect of my host and his Byzantine tower savoured so completely of the days of the twelfth century, that I seemed to have entered another world, and should hardly have been surprised if a crusader in chain-armour had entered the room and knelt down before the hermit's feet. The poor old hermit observing me looking about at all his goods and chattels, got up on his divan, and from a shelf reached down a large rosy apple, which he presented to me; and it was evidently the best thing he had, and I was touched when he gave it to me. I took a great bite; it was very sour indeed: but what was to be done? I could not bear to vex the old man, so I went on eating a great deal of it, although it brought the tears into my eyes.

We now heard a holloing and shouting, which portended the arrival of the mules, and, bidding adieu to the old hermit of the tower, I mounted a mule; the others were lightly loaded with my effects, and we scrambled up a steep rocky path through a thicket of odoriferous evergreen shrubs, our progress being assisted by the screams and bangs inflicted by several acolytes, a sort of lay-brethren, who came down with the animals from the convent.

A Ruined Library

On my inquiring for the library, I was told it had been destroyed during the revolution. It had formerly been preserved in the great square tower or keep, which is a grand feature in all the monasteries. I went to look at the place, and leaning through a ruined arch I looked down into the lower story of the tower, and there I saw the melancholy remains of a once famous library. This was a dismal spectacle for a devout lover of old books – a sort of biblical knight errant, as I then considered myself; who had entered on the perilous adventure of Mount Athos to rescue from the thraldom of ignorant monks those fair vellum volumes, with their bright illuminations and velvet dresses and jewelled clasps, which for so many centuries had lain imprisoned in their dark monastic dungeons. It was indeed a heart-rending sight. By the dim light which streamed through the opening of an iron door in the wall of the ruined tower, I saw above a hundred ancient manuscripts lying among the rubbish which had fallen from the upper floor, which was ruinous, and had in great part given way. Some of these manuscripts seemed quite entire - fine large folios; but the monks said they were unapproachable, for that floor also on which they lay was unsafe, the beams below being rotten from the wet and rain which came in through the roof. Here was a trap ready set and baited for a bibliographical antiquary. I peeped at the manuscripts, looked particularly at one or two that were lying in the middle of the floor, and could hardly resist the temptation. I advanced cautiously along the boards, keeping close to the wall, whilst every now and then a dull cracking noise warned me of my danger, but I tried each board by stamping upon it with my foot before I ventured my weight upon it. At last, when I dared go no further, I made them bring me a long stick, with which I fished up two or three fine manuscripts, and poked them along towards the door. When I had safely landed them, I examined them more at my ease, but I found that the rain had washed the outer leaves quite clean; the pages were stuck tight together into a solid mass, and when I attempted to open them, they broke short off in square bits like a biscuit. Neglect and damp and exposure had destroyed them completely. One fine volume, a large folio in double columns, of most venerable antiquity, particularly grieved me. I do not know how many more manuscripts there might be under the piles of rubbish. Perhaps some of them might still be legible, but without assistance and time I could not clean out the ruins that had fallen from above; and I was unable to save even a scrap from this general tomb of a whole race of books. I came out of the great tower, and sitting down on a pile of ruins, with a bearded assembly of grave caloyeri round me, I vented my sorrow and indignation in a long oration, which however produced a very slight effect upon my auditory; but whether from their not understanding Italian, or my want of eloquence, is a matter of doubt. My man was the only person who seemed to commiserate my misfortune, and he looked so genuinely vexed and sorry that I liked him the better ever afterwards. At length I dismissed the assembly: they toddled away to their siesta, and I, mounted anew upon a stout well-fed mule, bade adieu to the hospitable *agoumenos*, and was soon occupied in picking my way among the rocks and trees towards the next monastery.

A Wealthy Monastery

This is the largest and richest of all the monasteries of Mount Athos. It is situated on the side of a hill where a valley opens to the sea, and commands a little harbour where three small Greek vessels were lying at anchor. The buildings are of great extent, with several towers and domes rising above the walls: I should say it was not smaller than the upper ward of Windsor Castle. The original building was erected by the Emperor Constantine the Great. That worthy prince being, it appears, much afflicted by the leprosy, ordered a number of little children to be killed, a bath of juvenile blood being considered an excellent remedy. But while they were selecting them, he was told in a vision that if he would become a Christian his leprosy should depart from him: he did so, and was immediately restored to health, and all the children lived long and happily. This story is related by Moses Chorensis, whose veracity I would not venture to doubt...

This church contains a great many ancient pictures of small size, most of them having the background overlaid with plates of silver-gilt: two of these are said to be portraits of the Empress Theodora. Two other pictures of larger size and richly set with jewels are interesting as having been brought from the church of St. Sophia at Constantinople, when that city fell a prey to the Turkish arms. Over the doors of the church and of the great refectory there are mosaics representing, if I remember rightly, saints and holy persons. One of the chapels, a separate building with a dome which had been newly repaired, is dedicated to the "Preservation of the Girdle of the Blessed Virgin," a relic which must be a source of considerable revenue to the monastery, for they have divided it into two parts, and one half is sent into Greece and the other half into Asia Minor whenever the plague is raging in those countries, and all those who are afflicted with that terrible disease arc sure to be cured if they touch it, which they are allowed to do "for a consideration." On my inquiring how the monastery became possessed of so inestimable a medicine, I was gravely informed that, after the assumption of the Blessed Virgin, St. Thomas went up to heaven to pay her a visit, and there she presented him with her girdle. My informant appeared to have the most unshakeable conviction as to the truth of this history, and expressed great surprise that I had never heard it before.

The library, although containing nearly four thousand printed books, has none of any high antiquity or on any subject but divinity. There are also about a thousand manuscripts, of which three or four hundred are on vellum; amongst these there are three copies of the works of St. Chrysostom: they also have his head in the church - that golden mouth out of which proceeded the voice which shook the empire with the thunder of his denunciations. The most curious manuscripts are six rolls of parchment, each ten inches wide and about ten feet long, containing prayers for festivals on the anniversaries of the foundation of certain churches. There were at this time above three hundred monks resident in the monastery; many of these held offices and places of dignity under the *agoumenos*, whose establishment resembled the court of a petty sovereign prince. Altogether this convent well illustrates what some of the great monastic establishments in England must have been before the Reformation. It covers at least four acres of ground, and contains so many separate buildings within its massive walls that it resembles a fortified town. Everything told of wealth and indolence. When I arrived the lord abbot was asleep; he was too great a man to be aroused ; he had eaten a full meal in his own apartment, and "He could not be disturbed. His secretary, a thin pale monk, was deputed to show me the wonders of the place, and as we proceeded through the different chapels and enormous magazines of corn, wine, and oil, the officers of the different departments bent down to kiss his hand, for he was high in the favour of my lord the abbot, and was evidently a man not to be slighted by the inferior authorities if they wished to get on and prosper. The cellarer was a sly old fellow with a thin grey beard, and looked as if he could tell a good story of an evening over a flagon of good wine. Except at some of the places in Germany I have never seen such gigantic tuns as those in the cellars at Vatopede. The oil is kept in marble vessels of the size and shape of sarcophagi, and there is a curious picture in the entrance room of the oil-store, which represents the miraculous increase in their stock of oil during a year of scarcity, when, through the intercession of a pious monk who then had charge of that department, the marble basins, which were almost empty, overflowed, and a river of fine fresh oil poured in torrents through the door. The frame of this picture is set with jewels, and it appears to be very ancient. The refectory is an immense room; it stands in front of the church and has twenty-four marble tables and seats, and is in the same cruciform shape as that at St. Laura. It has frequently accommodated five hundred guests, the servants and tenants of the abbey, who come on stated days to pay their rents and receive the benediction of the *agoumenos*. Sixty or seventy fat mules are kept for the use of the community, and a very considerable number of Albanian servants and muleteers are lodged in outbuildings before that great gate. These, unlike their brethren of Epirus, are a quiet, stupid race, and whatever may be their notions of another world, they evidently think that in this there is no man living equal in importance to the great agoumeños of Vatopede, and no earthly place to compare with the great monastery over which he rules.

A Successful Haul

Xenophou, which stands upon the sea shore. Here they were building a church in the centre of the great court, which, when it is finished, will be the largest on Mount Athos. Three Greek bishops were living here in exile. I did not learn what the holy prelates had done, but their misdeeds had been found out by the Patriarch, and he had sent them here to rusticate. This monastery is of a moderate size; its founder was St. Xenophou, regarding whose history or the period at which he lived I am unable to give any information, as nobody knew anything about him on the spot, and I cannot find him in any catalogue of saints which I possess. He monastery was repaired in the year 1545 by Danzulas Bornicus and Badulus, who were brothers, and Banus (the Ban) Barbulus, all three nobles of Hungary, and was afterwards beautified by Mattheus, Waywode of Bessarabia.

The library consists of fifteen hundred printed books, nineteen MSS. on paper, eleven on vellum, and three rolls on parchment, containing liturgies for particular days. Of the MSS. on vellum there were three which merit a description. One was a fine quarto of part of the works of St. Chrysostom, of great antiquity, but not in uncial letters. Another was a quarto of the four Gospels bound in faded red velvet with silver clasps. This book they affirmed to be a royal present to the monastery; it was of the eleventh or twelfth century, and was peculiar from the text being accompanied by a voluminous commentary on the margin and several pages of calendars, prefaces, etc., at the beginning. The headings of the Gospels were written in large plain letters of gold. In the libraries of forty Greek monasteries I have only met with one other copy of the Gospels with a commentary. The third manuscript was an immense quarto Evangelistarium sixteen inches square, bound in faded green or blue velvet, and said to be in the autograph of the Emperor Alexius Comnenus. The text throughout on each page was written in the form of a cross. Two of the pages are in purple ink powdered with gold, and these, there is every reason to suppose, are in the handwriting of the imperial scribe himself; for the Byzantine sovereigns affected to write only in purple, as their deeds and a magnificent MS. in another monastic library, of which I have not given an account in these pages, can testify: the titles of this superb volume are written in gold, covering the whole page. Altogether, although not in uncial letters, it was among the finest Greek MSS that I had ever seen – perhaps next to the uncial MSS, the finest to be met with anywhere.

I asked the monks whether they were inclined to part with these three books, and offered to purchase them and the parchment rolls. There was a little consultation among them, and then they desired to be shown those which I particularly coveted. Then there was another consultation, and they asked me which I set the greatest value on. So I said the rolls, on which the three rolls were unrolled, and looked at, and examined, and peeped at by the three monks who put themselves forward in the business with more pains and curiosity than had probably been ever wasted upon them before. At first they said it was impossible, the rolls were too precious to be parted with, but if I liked to give a good price I should have the rest; upon which I took up the St. Chrysostom, the least valuable of the three, and while I examined it, saw from the corner of my eye the three monks nudging each other and making signs. So I said, "Well, now what will you take for your two books, this and the big one?"

They asked five thousand piastres; whereupon, with a look of indignant scorn, I laid down the St. Chrysostom and got up to go away; but after a good deal more talk, we retired to the divan, or drawing-room as it may be called, of the monastery, where I conversed with the three exiled bishops. In he course of time I was called out into another room to have a cup of coffee. There were my friends the three monks, the managing committee, and under the divan, imperfectly concealed, were the corners of the three splendid MSS. I knew that now all depended on my own tact whether my still famished saddlebags were to have a meal or not that day, the danger lying between offering too much or too little. If you offer too much, a Greek, a Jew, or an Armenian immediately thinks that the desired object must be invaluable, that it must have some magical properties, like the lamp of Aladdin, which will bring wealth upon its possessor if he can but find out its secret; and he will either ask you a sum absurdly large, or will refuse to sell it at any price, but will lock it up and become nervous about it, and examine it over and over again privately to see what can be the cause of the Frank's offering so much for a thing apparently so utterly useless. On the other hand, too little must not be offered, for it would be an indignity to suppose that persons of consideration would condescend to sell things of trifling value – it wounds their aristocratic feelings, they are above such meannesses. By St. Xenophou, how we did talk! For five mortal hours it went on, I pretending to go away several times, but being always called back by one or other of the learned committee. I drank coffee and sherbet and they drank arraghi; but in the end I got the great book of Alexius Comnenus for the value of twenty-two pounds, and the curious Gospels, which I had treated with the most cool disdain all along, was finally thrown into the bargain, and out I walked with a big book under each arm, bearing with perfect resignation the smiles and scoffs of the three brethren, who could scarcely contain their laughter at the way they had done the silly traveller.

Then did the saddlebags begin to assume a more comely and satisfactory form. After a stirrup cup of hot coffee, perfumed with the incense of the church, the monks bid me a joyous adieu; I responded as joyously: in short every one was charmed, except the mule, who evidently was more surprised than pleased at the increased weight which he had to carry.

A Man Who Could Not Remember Seeing a Woman

The same evening I got back to my comfortable room at Xeropotamo, and did ample justice to a good meagre dinner after the heat and fatigues of the day. A monk had arrived from one of the outlying farms who could speak a little Italian; he was deputed to do the honours of the house, and accordingly dined with me. He was a magnificent-looking man of thirty or thirty-five years of age, with large eyes and long black hair and beard. As we sat together in the evening in the ancient room, by the light of one dim brazen lamp, with deep shades thrown across his face and figure, I thought he would have made an admirable study for Titian or Sebastian del Piombo. In the course of conversation I found that he had learned Italian from another monk, having never been out of the peninsula of Mount Athos, his parents and most of the other inhabitants of the village where he was born, somewhere in Roumelia – but its name or exact position he did not know – had been massacred during some revolt or disturbance. So he had been told, but he remembered nothing about it; he had been educated in a school in this or one of the other monasteries, and his whole life had been passed upon the Holy Mountain; and this, he said, was the case with very many other monks. He did not remember his mother, and did not seem quite sure that he ever had one; he had never seen a woman, nor had he any idea what sort of things women were, or what they looked like. He asked me whether they resembled the pictures of the Panagia, the Holy Virgin, which hang in every church. Now, those who are conversant with the peculiar conventional representations of the Blessed Virgin in the pictures of the Greek church, which are all exactly alike, stiff, hard, and dry, without any appearance of life or motion, will agree with me that they do not afford a very favourable idea of the grace or beauty of the fair sex; and that there was a difference of appearance between black women, Circassians, and those of other nations, which was, however, difficult to describe to one who had never seen a lady of any race. He listened with great interest while I told him that all women were not exactly like the pictures he had seen, but I did not think it charitable to carry on the conversation further, although the poor monk seemed to have a strong inclination to know more of that interesting race of beings from whose society he had been so entirely debarred. I often thought afterwards of the singular lot of this manly and noble-looking monk; whether he is still a recluse, either in the monastery or in his mountain farm, with its little moss-grown chapel as ancient as the days of Constantine; or whether he has gone out into the world and mingled with its pleasures and its cares.

A Female Intruder on the Holy Mountain

The aga apologised for having no good room to offer me; but he sent out his men to look for a lodging; and in the meantime we went to a kiosk, that is, a place like a large birdcage, with enough roof to make a shade, and no walls to impede the free passage of the air. It was built of wood, upon a scaffold eight or ten feet from the ground, in the corner of a garden, and commanded a fine view of the sea. I one corner of this cage I sat all day long, for there was nowhere else to go to; and the aga sat opposite to me in another corner, smoking his pipe, in which solacing occupation to his great surprise I did not partake. We had cups of coffee and sherbet every now and then, and about every half-hour the aga uttered a few words of compliment or welcome, informing me occasionally that there were many dervishes in the place, "very many dervishes," for so he denominated the monks. Dinner came towards evening. There was meat, dolmas, demir tatlessi, olives, salad, roast meat, and pilau, that filled up some time; and shortly afterwards I retired to the house of the monastery of Russico, a little distance from my kiosk; and there I slept on a carpet, on the boards; and at sunrise was ready to continue my journey, as were also the mules. The aga gave me some breakfast, at which repast a cat made its appearance, with whom the day before I had made acquaintance; but now it came, not alone, but accompanied by two kittens. "Ah!" said I to the aga, "how is this? Why, as I live, this is a she cat! a cat feminine! What business has it on Mount Athos? And with kittens too! a wicked cat!"

"Hush!" said the Aga with a solemn grin;" "do not say anything about it. Yes, it must be a she-cat; I allow, certainly, that it must be a she-cat. I brought it with me from Stamboul. But do not speak of it, or they will take it away; and it reminds me of my home, where my wife and children are living far away from me."

I promised to make no scandal about the cat, and took my leave; and as I rode off I saw him looking at me out of his cage with the cat sitting by his side. I was sorry I could not take aga and cat and all with me to Stamboul, the poor gentleman looked so solitary and melancholy.

c.1878 Mrs Annie Brassey

Sacrilege on Sacred Soil

Mount Athos was visible, rising grandly from the sea, 6,000 feet above Cape Santo. On the summit there is the strictest monastery in the world. Not a female animal of any kind is allowed within miles, so that the monks have to do without milk, or fresh eggs even, and travellers are not allowed to carry even dead hens on their saddles for provision. A few years ago two English ladies landed here from a yacht. As most of the men here wear petticoats, and the women trousers, and the monks have not a chance of much experience in such matters, they did not discover the sacrilege that had been committed for some time; and then you may imagine their horror and disgust, and the penances they had to perform...

Khan near Kavalla

(1814)

Thrace

An area of mixed ethnic groups, Thrace fell to the Turks in the 1450s when they besieged and captured Constantinople, and remained firmly under Turkish rule until the early years of the twentieth century. Parts of the area had a majority of Muslim inhabitants, and a considerable Muslim community of Greek citizens flourishes there to this day. During the Balkan Wars of 1911-13 Western Thrace, and for a short time much of Eastern Thrace, was occupied by the Bulgarians, a plan favoured by the Russians during the late nineteenth century, but never effected. By the treaty of Sèvres at the end of the First World War, Greece was awarded most of the region by the representatives of the Allied Powers meeting in Paris, but after the disastrous Graeco-Turkish War of 1922, Eastern Thrace was returned to Turkey in the Treaty of Lausanne.

Turks Dancing Dall' Acqua & Lazaretti, 1816)

The Rev. Edward Daniel Clarke

The Rigours of Ramadan

At sunset we arrived at Yeniga: here we found the inhabitants discharging their tophaikes and pistols to celebrate the beginning of the Ramadan; which made it dangerous to appear in the streets. During this fast, they abstain from every indulgence that can be considered as the smallest gratification of sense - even from smoking or drinking water - the whole time that the sun is above the horizon: the consequence is, that the moment sun-set is proclaimed by the (muezzin) crier of a mosque, from a minaret, the Moslems abandon themselves to the most profligate excesses; - and woe be to the infidel Christian, who happens to fall in their way during these moments of their frantic licentiousness. There is, however, much pretence in the rigour with which the Turkish fasts are said to be observed; as in all countries where similar privations are enjoined by religion. There are some of the Moslems, no doubt, who observe the strictest abstinence; owing to the sincerity of their devotion: but there are many other who will both eat and drink when they can do this without being observed by one of their own religion. The Dervishes are, of all others, the most likely to violate the rules prescribed by the Koran, when they have an opportunity; and we often supplied them with the means. When alone with us, they would eat pork, and drink wine, and laugh at the absurdity of considering such things as forbidden. The most amusing instance of this kind was afforded, during the Ramadan, by our Tchohodar. Having observed that the poor fellow, in his fatiguing journeys, took no refreshment when we halted for this purpose, although naturally corpulent and fond of good living, - but that he had the additional mortification of seeing us feed heartily upon such occasions, we endeavoured, by every persuasion, and by putting before him the best provisions that the country afforded, to induce him to break his fast. It was all to no purpose; he shook his head and sighed, saying, that it was contrary to his religion. and therefore impossible. At last we hit upon an expedient which enabled us to keep him in better plight for. the future. We wrapped up the legs of a baked turkey in paper, with bread and salt; and when he was on the road, at a distance from any town or village, where he could not be observed by any other Moslem, one of us, coming behind him, conveyed the packet into his hand. He no sooner saw what it contained, than, muttering his "God be praised," with great energy he fell to work, making as hearty a meal as any of us had done before: and in this manner we took care afterwards that he should be regularly supplied, leaving him to slake his thirst, as he could, from the fountains which we passed upon the road...

The following morning (Jan. 6), being that of the celebration of a Greek festival, great difficulty occurred in procuring either horses for the road, or any surudji to accompany them. The author, with the Tchohodar, waited upon the Agha, and made known his situation; at the same time exhibiting his firman and passports. The Agha boasted that the firman was to him a matter of little consideration: he knew how to do his duty towards Djours; without any such authority. The conference ended, however, in his sending an officer to enforce the attendance of post-horses at the khan. The persons who came with them betrayed a manifest reluctance: first arrived a Turkish surudji, with his own, and two other horses: afterwards, a Greek guide, with five other horses. The two first horses being ready, and the surudji impatient to start. Mr. Cripps and the author set out with this man; leaving the Tchohodar to follow with Antonio and the other guide with the baggage. Having proceeded about half an hour from Gymmergine, the Turkish surudji, in an authoritative tone, commanded them to halt, and wait until the rest of the party should arrive: and upon their persisting in continuing the journey, the miscreant drew forth his ataghan threatening to stab Mr. Cripps, and made him descend from his horse, and stand in the mud; using every menacing expression at the same time. They were armed only with one of the large Turkish poniards, which they were accustomed to use in digging up the roots of plants, when collecting specimens for their herbary; but two Englishmen, even if unarmed, ought to be a match for one Turk with all his weapons. It would have been no difficult matter, therefore, to have dispatched this fellow, and to escape with the horses; but they waited very patiently, and even endeavoured to pacify the mutineer until the Tchohodar came; who said it was necessary to endure it all; and that every one of the party would have been impaled alive if a blow were given to any of the inhabitants; that it was well nothing worse had happened, there being neither government nor religion in the country, and he wished himself well out of it. The ill-humour of the surudji proceeded solely from his long fast, for the Ramadan; but the whole district was in a state of open rebellion, and bade defiance to all authority.

Heroic Hospitality

We traversed again the long and dreary Plain of Tchouagilarkir, for two hours, when we arrived at a bridge of eight or nine arches. Half an hour from this bridge we passed a small village, and one hour afterwards another village, with an ancient bridge of eight arches over a small river. We then came to another village and a ruined bridge, distant four hours from Gymmergine. In this manner we continued riding through this dreary plain for another hour, when it began to grow dark: and as the surjdjees were so surly, that they refused to answer any of our questions, finding that we were close to a village called Tchafts-tcheyr, or Shaft-cheyr, we resolved to halt for the night. Here a new difficulty occurred, for we could not prevail upon any of the inhabitants to lodge us: but as it gave occasion to one of the most remarkable instances of hospitality perhaps ever known, it becomes a duty to relate our adventure more part.icularly.

The rascally surudjees who were with our baggage had already dismounted it, and were leaving us upon the bare earth, when an old Turk, casually passing, and hearing some altercation between these men and the Tchohodar, demanded the cause of the dispute. Being informed that the surudjees refused to proceed any farther, and that some poor djowrs were in danger of being exposed all night houseless in the mud, he ordered them to bring our baggage to his house, and bade us all follow him. This being done, we were received into an open inclosed court, while a room was prepared for us. As soon as we were conducted to this apartment, we found the floor covered with clean mats, and a blazing fire kindled. The owner of this dwelling was not rich; yet he caused a supper to be sent to us from his little harem, where it was prepared by his women. Of the sacrifice thus made to hospitality by a Moslem, we were not yet aware. We were supplied with every necessary for our comfort and repose; and the next morning, when we rose to depart, horses were waiting for us at the door. To our regret, as well surprise, when we tendered payment for our nights lodging and provisions, our benevolent host would accept of nothing, as he said,but our good wishes; and bidding us a good journey withdrew from our sight.

Soon after quitting this hospitable mansion, perceiving that a volume of plants belonging to our herbary was missing, one of us returned in search of it; and found that the family, who had so kindly entertained us, had actually carried out and broken the earthen vessels out of which we drank water; and were besides busily employed in completing the ceremony of purification, by fumigating the mats, and scouring the room which they conceived to have been defiled by the presence of Christians. The inconvenience, therefore, and the loss, which our visit to this liberal Moslem had occasioned in his family, will shew to what an extent the virtue of hospitality is sometimes carried out among the Turks.

Thessaly

Ruled in the Middle Ages by Vlachs, the Turks conquered Thessaly as early as 1389. There were periodic uprisings against Ottoman rule, most notably that under the bishop, Dionysios Skylosophos, in 1618. Only after the Albanian, Ali Pasha, was made ruler of Trikkala, and set up a semi-independent state based upon Ioannina, was it governed locally. Thessaly was excluded from the boundaries of the kingdom of Greece set up after the War of Independence. At the Congress of Berlin in 1878 the Great Powers assigned it to Greece, and the Turks conceded most of the area in 1881. However, they held on to the northern part of Thessaly, which was liberated only during the Balkan Wars of 1911-13.

The Gorge of the Peneus (Contemporary print)

1609-10 William Lithgow

Olympia and Mount Olympus

Some of the earliest travellers were rather vague in their understanding of geography. This rather dramatic mislocation" of Thessaly is probably a result of the author's further confusing Olympia, site of the ancient Olympic Games, in the Peloponnese, with Mount Olympus, home of the Greek gods, in Northern Greece.

Thessaly a long the sea side, lieth betweene Peloponnesus, and Achaia: wherein standeth the hill Olympus, on which Hercules did institute the Olympian games, which institution was of long time the Grecian epoch, from whence they reckoned their time.

1802-09 Colonel William Leake

The Climate of Thessaly

The obstinacy and violence of the Etesian winds in July and August … are well known to those who have had to struggle with them in the Aegean in that season. As a contrast for this sometimes disagreeable, though probably always salutary characteristic of the climate of Greece, nothing can be more delightful than the general tranquillity of the autumn and early winter throughout the eastern side of the Grecian continent, beginning generally about the middle of November, and sometimes lasting the greater part of the month of January, between which and April is generally the true winter in Greece. The wind, since I have been in this province, has generally been light, whether with or without rain, and during the last month there have been only two violent gales; one of these occurred yesterday, the other at Aghia, and neither of them lasted more than twelve hours. Eastern Greece, however, is subject to greater extremes of temperature than the country to the westward of Pindus, where southerly and westerly winds are so prevalent during the winter, that the cold is seldom very durable or very severe, except in the parts near the central ridge. Daniel and Gregory of Milies state in their "Geography", that the olive trees of Magnesia, where the climate is milder than in any other part of Thessaly, were killed by the frost in 1782. In 1779 the lake Boebis, which was then so full as to extend to Kastri, was frozen entirely over, so that persons passed from Kanalia to the opposite side. The flocks perished, and many a Vlakhiote shepherd returned to his mountains without a single sheep. The authors confirm the truth of their account by describing the peculiar sound caused by the cracking of the ice from one end of the lake to the other, a phenomenon remarkable to them from its rare occurrence in so southern a latitude. I have met with many similar testimonies as to the occasional severity of the winter, particularly in Upper Thessaly, where only two years ago the sheep perished in great numbers, and where the plains are covered sometimes for a fortnight with snow to the depth of eight or ten palms; this may be seen also in Epirus, in the interior plains.

Karditsa

1802-09 Colonel William Leake

The Fisheries of Lake Tavropon

He [the Mukhtar Pasha] is entitled to a third of the produce of the fishery, the Kanaliotes enjoying the sole right of fishing, which in plentiful seasons they relax in favour of some of the neighbouring villages. The only fish are carp, a small flat fish, and eels. They are caught with seines and hand-nets, but chiefly in inclosures made of reeds which grow in the lake, and are called *mandrakia*, because the fish follow the leader into them like sheep into a fold [*mandra*], the entrance, of course, being so constructed that they cannot return. When the fishing takes place, carriers attend on the shore with their "things", by which is here meant either horses or asses, and having paid for the fish, transport them forthwith to the surrounding markets. In summer fish caught in the evening are thus sold at daybreak in Larissa, Aghia, Armyro, or Fersala: in winter, Katerina, Trikkala, and even Metzovo, are supplied from hence. The agents of the Zabit, as the farmer of the Sultan's share is styled, attend at the landing places to take an account of the sums received by the Kanaliote fishermen, and receive the third at their houses in Kanalia. At present there are no carp in the lake, as they all come through the Asmaki on the overflowing of the Peneius into the Nessonis, and thence into the Boebeis; and this year, according to the local expression, "the mother has not come down." Nor was there any considerable inundation last year, so that few fish were caught in the summer, and none have been taken this winter. A deficient inundation is often followed by the farther calamity, that the fish remaining in the reduced lake are killed by the sun, as happened last summer, when the heat and drought were excessive. The wind too is sometimes fatal to them, by raising the water on the lee-side of the lake, and then suddenly abating, by which the fish are stranded or left in small pools, where the heat of the sun soon kills them. The Etesian winds in particular have this effect, as they occur in the hottest season, and when the lake is generally at the lowest.

To make amends for the want of fish this year, there has been a plentiful crop of corn from the banks of the lake, which, as the harvest was indifferent in other parts of Thessaly, and in some places failed entirely, has borne a good price; and hence the Kanaliotes have been induced this winter to sow the borders of the lake to a great extent, and with the more confidence, as after a scanty inundation, a more than usually plentiful one is required to restore the lake to its average limits, and consequently they have a good chance that their crop of corn will not be injured by the water. Sometimes, though very rarely, the lake is quite dry, as it will be next winter if there should be no inundation in the course of the year. Indeed, they say that it would now be dry but for the torrents which have poured into it from the mountain. The inundation generally takes place from the middle of February to the middle of April ... and brings with it fish full of roe, which is soon afterwards converted into young fish... When the seasons are favourable for two or three successive years, the quantity caught is immense, and the fish are sold at six or eight paras the oke, at other times from ten to twenty. The fishing times are not regulated by natural causes, but by the calendar, the principal object being to supply the market with fish during the Greek fasts, and to those who fast strictly on the days of "suspension", when ... instead of ... shell-fish, star-fish, and botargo, fish having blood is allowed, as well as eggs, milk, and cheese, and which days are therefore in reality feasts.

Trikkala

1802-09 Colonel William Leake

The Miseries of Kalambaka

Kalabaka has suffered extremely of late from the vexations of the last hodja-bashi Ianaki, who built a superb house with the produce of his plunder, and ended his days in the prison at Ioannina. But it is injured more permanently by the expense of konaks, to which it is continually subject, in consequence of its lying at the exit of the most frequented pass in Greece.

The master of the house in which I lodge, who among his other misfortunes has left an eye with the thieves, had the honour not long since of having a Bey with a party of Albanians quartered upon him for ten or twelve days: they burnt his furniture and his silk frames, and finished by borrowing a valuable mule, which he saw no more.

To increase the misery of Kalabaka, the crop of silk has been bad this year, and the spinners have been obliged to purchase it at 30 piastres the oke, instead of 20, the usual price...

The Christian Trikkalini admit that Aly Pasha has relieved them from the insolence and oppression to which they were formerly subject from the Turkish beys. Vely Pasha is following the same plan in the Morea, where the Turks were much in want of this discipline. His Highness and his sons adopt the surest method of effecting it, by obtaining all the landed property of the Turks... by every possible contrivance of fraud, injustice, and oppression. At a small expense they have thus converted the greater part of the plain of Trikkala formerly belonging to the beys of Trikkala, or to the Elefthero-khoria of the Greeks into *tjiftliks* of their own. Aly and Mukhtar transport their share of the crops to Ioannina to feed their Albanians, and that of Vely is sent to the Morea for the same purpose; while the Porte, according to its usual practice in several of the most fertile districts of the empire, is supplied with a certain quantity of grain from Thessaly at its own price. Thus, in the midst of a most productive country, the inhabitants retain no more than is barely sufficient for existence; and the price, even of the necessaries of life, is beyond their means. The wars of the Porte on one side, and those of Aly on the other, are the chief cause of this distressing oppression, which the people of Trikkala never recollect to have been so great as it is at present; and for this reason alone have hopes of seeing diminished: one of their complaints is, that the Vezir's Subashis, for the purpose of irrigating his lands, draw off the water of the river, upon which the town chiefly depends; so that in summer nothing but a little heated muddy water remains in the bed of the Peneius. Nothing can more strongly show the misery of the place than the want of this commonest of all Turkish conveniences, especially as fountains might easily be supplied by an aqueduct from numerous sources in the hills of Khassia.

Freethinking Dervishes

Nov. 27. - Trikkala has lately been adorned by the Pasha with a new Tekieh, or college of Bektashli dervises, on the site of a former one. He has not only removed several old buildings to give more space and air to this college, but has endowed it with property in khans, shops, and houses, and has added some fields on the banks of the Lethaaeus. There are now about fifteen of these Mahometan monks in the house with a Sheikh or Chief, who is married to an Ioannite woman, and as well lodged and dressed as many a Pasha. Besides his own apartments, there are very comfortable lodgings for the dervises, and every convenience for the reception of strangers.

The Bektashli are so called from a Cappadocian sheikh who wore a stone upon his navel; in memory of which his followers wear a stone which is green ... suspended to the neck, and hanging upon the naked breast. The important part which Hadji Bektash played in the establishment of the Janissaries is well known. The Bektashli particularly insist like other Mahometans on the unity of the Deity, but do not exalt Mahomet so high as other Musulman sects, and are free thinkers in the practical part of their religion, considering that every thing is given us for enjoyment, and therefore they smoke and drink and live merrily. It is their doctrine to be liberal towards all professions and religions, and to consider all men as equal in the eyes of God. Though the sheikh did not very clearly explain his philosophy to me, he often used the word *anthropos*, with some accompanying remark or significant gesture conveying a sentiment of the equality of mankind. The Vezir, although no practical encourager of liberty and equality, finds the religious doctrines of the Bektashi exactly suited to him. At the time that Christianity was out of favour in France, he was in the habit of ridiculing religion and the immortality of the soul with his French prisoners; and he lately remarked to me, speaking of Mahomet, "...and I too am a prophet at Ioannina." It was an observation of the bishop of Trikkala, that Aly takes from every body and gives only to the dervises, whom he undoubtedly finds politically useful. In fact, there is no place in Greece where in consequence of this encouragement these wandering or mendicant Musulman monks are so numerous and insolent as at Ioannina.

1834-37 Lord Curzon:

The Rocks of Meteora

The scenery of Meteora is of a very singular kind. The end of a range of rocky hills seems to have been broken off by some earthquake or washed away by the Deluge, leaving only a series of twenty or thirty tall, thin, smooth, needle-like rocks, many hundred feet in height; some like gigantic tusks, some shaped like sugar-loaves, and some like vast stalagmites. These rocks surround a beautiful grassy plain, on three sides of which there grow groups of detached trees, like those in an English park.

Some of the rocks shoot up quite clean and perpendicularly from the smooth green grass; some are in clusters; some stand alone like obelisks; nothing can be more strange and wonderful than this romantic region, which is unlike anything I have ever seen either before or since. In Switzerland, Saxony, the Tyrol, or any other mountainous region where I have been, there is nothing at all to be compared to these extraordinary peaks.

At the foot of many of the rocks which surround this beautiful grassy amphitheatre, there are numerous caves and holes, some of which appear to be natural, but most of them are artificial; for in the dark and wild ages of monastic fanaticism whole flocks of hermits roosted in these pigeon-holes. Some of these caves are so high up the rocks that one wonders how the poor old gentle-men could ever get up to them; whilst others are below the surface; and the anchorites who burrowed in them, like rabbits, frequently afforded excellent sport to parties of roving Saracens; indeed, hermit-hunting seems to have been a fashionable amusement previous to the twelfth century. In early Greek frescos, and in small, stiff pictures with gold backgrounds, we see many frightful representations of men on horseback in Roman armour, with long spears, who are torturing and slaying Christian devotees. In these pictures the monks and hermits are represented in gowns made of a kind of coarse matting, and they have long beards, and some of them are covered with hair; these I take it were the ones most to be admired, as in the Greek church sanctity is always in the inverse ratio of beauty. All Greek saints are painfully ugly, but the hermits are much uglier, dirtier, and older, than the rest; they must have been very fusty people besides, eating roots, and living in holes like rats and mice. It is difficult to understand by what process of reasoning they could have persuaded themselves that, by living in this useless, inactive way, they were leading holy lives. They wore out the rocks with their knees in prayer; the cliffs resounded with their groans; sometimes they banged their breasts with a big stone, for a change; and some wore chains and iron girdles round their emaciated forms; but they did nothing whatever to benefit their kind. Still there is something grand in the strength and constancy of their faith. They left their homes and riches and the pleasures of this world, to retire to these dens and caves of the earth, to be subjected to cold and hunger, pain and death, that they might do honour to their God, after their own fashion, and trusting that, by mortifying the body in this world, they should gain happiness for the soul in the world to come; and therefore peace be with their memory!

Getting into the Barlaam Monastery

On the top of these rocks in different directions there remain seven monasteries out of twenty-four which once crowned their airy heights. How anything except a bird was to arrive, at one which we saw in the distance on a pinnacle of rock was more than we could divine; but the mystery was soon solved. Winding our way upwards, among a labyrinth of smaller rocks and cliffs, by a romantic path which afforded us from time to time beautiful views of the green vale below us, we at length found ourselves on an elevated platform of rock, which I may compare to the flat roof of a church; while the monastery of Barlaam stood perpendicularly above us, on the top of a much higher rock, like the tower of this church. Here we fired off a gun, which was intended to answer the same purpose as knocking at the door in more civilized places; and we all strained our necks in looking up at the monastery to see whether any answer would be made to our call. Presently we were hailed by some one in the sky, whose voice came down to us like the cry of a bird; and we saw the face and grey beard of an old monk some hundred feet above us peering out of a kind of window or door. He asked us who we were, and what we wanted, and so forth; to which we replied, that we were travellers, harmless people, who wished to be admitted into the monastery to stay the night; that we had come all the way from Corfu to see the wonders of Meteora, and, as it was now getting late, we appealed to his feelings of hospitality and Christian benevolence.

"Who are those with you?" said he.

"Oh! most respectable people," we answered; "gentlemen of our acquaintance, who have come with us across the mountains from Mezzovo."

The appearance of our escort did not please the monk, and we feared that he would not admit us into the monastery; but at length he let down a thin cord, to which I attached a letter of introduction which I had brought from Corfu; and after some delay a much larger rope was seen descending, with a hook at the end to which a strong net was attached. On its reaching the rock on which we stood the net was spread open; my two servants sat down upon it; and the four corners being attached to the hook, a signal was made, and they began slowly ascending into the air, twisting round and round like a leg of mutton hanging to a bottle-jack. The rope was old and mended, and, the height from the ground to the door above was, we afterwards learned, 37 fathoms, or 222 feet. When they reached the top I saw two stout monks reach their arms out of the door and pull in the two servants by main force, as there was no contrivance like a turning-crane for bringing them nearer to the landing-place. The whole process appeared so dangerous, that I determined to go up by climbing a series of ladders which were suspended by large wooden pegs on the face of the precipice, and which reached the top of the rock in another direction, round a corner to the right. The lowest ladder was approached by a pathway leading to a rickety wooden platform which overhung a deep gorge. From this point the ladders hung perpendicularly upon the bare rock, and I climbed up three or four of them very soon; but coming to one, the lower end or which had swung away from the top or the one below, I had some difficulty in stretching across from the one to the other; and here unluckily I looked down, and found that I had turned a sort or angle in the precipice, and that I was not over the rocky platform where I had left the horses, but that the precipice went sheer down to so tremendous a depth, that my head turned when I surveyed the distant valley over which I was hanging in the air like a fly on a wall. The monks in the monastery saw me hesitate, and called out to me to take courage and hold on; and, making an effort, I overcame my dizziness, and clambered up to a small iron door, through which I crept into a court of the monastery, where I was welcomed by the monks and the two servants who had been hauled up by the rope. The rest of my party were not admitted; but they bivouacked at the foot of the rocks in a sheltered place, and were perfectly contented with the coffee and provisions which we lowered down to them.

My servants, in high glee at having been hoisted up safe and sound, were busy in arranging my baggage in the room which had been allotted to us, and in making it comfortable: one went to get ready some warm water for a bath, or at any rate for a good splash in the largest tub that could be found; the other made me a snug corner on the divan, and covered it with a piece of silk, and spread my carpet before it; he put my books in a little heap, got ready the things for tea, and hung my arms and cloak, and everything he could lay his hands on, upon the pegs projecting from the wall under the shelf which was fixed all round the room. My European clothes were soon pitched into the most ignominious corner of the divan, and I speedily arrayed myself in the long, loose robes of Egypt, so much more comfortable and easy than the tight cases in which we cramp up our limbs. In short, I forthwith made myself at home, and took a stroll among the courts and gardens of the monastery while dinner or supper, whichever it might be called, was getting ready. I soon stumbled upon the *agoumenos* (the lord abbot) of this aerial monastery, and we prowled about together, peering into rooms, visiting the church, and poking about until it began to get dark; and then I asked him to dinner in his own room; but he could eat no meat, so I ate the more myself, and he made up for it by other savoury messes, cooked partly by my servants and partly by the monks. He was an oldish man. He did not dislike sherry, though he preferred rosoglio, of which I always carried a few bottles with me in my monastic excursions. The abbot and I, and another holy father, fraternised, and slapped each other on the back, and had another glass or two, or rather cup, for coffee-cups of thin, old porcelain, called fingians, served us for wine-glasses. Then we had some tea, and they filled up their cups with sugar, and ate seamen's biscuits, and little cakes from Yanina, and rahatlokoom, and jelly of dried-grape juice, till it was time to go to bed; when the two venerable monks gave me their blessing and stumbled out of the room; and in a marvellously short space of time I was sound asleep.

A Collector At Large

The library contains about a thousand volumes, the far greater part of which are printed books, mostly Venetian editions of ecclesiastical works, but there are some fine copies of Aldine Greek classics. I did not count the number of the manuscripts; they are all books of divinity and the works of the fathers; there may be between one and two hundred of them. I found one folio Bulgarian manuscript which I could not read, and therefore was, of course, particularly anxious to purchase. As I saw it was not a copy of the Gospels, I thought it might possibly be historical, but the monks would not sell it. The only other manuscript of value was a copy of the Gospels, in quarto, containing several miniatures and illuminations of the eleventh century; but with this also they refused to part with it, so it remains for some more fortunate collector. It was of no use to the monks themselves, who cannot read either Hellenic or ancient Greek ; but they consider the books in their library as sacred relics, and preserve them with a certain feeling of awe for their antiquity and incomprehensibility. Our only chance is when some worldly minded *agoumenos* happens to be at the head of the community, who may be inclined to exchange some of the unreadable old books for such a sum or gold or silver as will suffice for the repairs of one of their buildings, the replenishing, of the cellar, or some other equally important purpose. At the time of my visit the march of intellect had not penetrated into the heights of the monastery of St. Barlaam, and the good old-fashioned *agoumenos* was not to be overcome by any special pleading; so I told him at last that I respected his prejudices, and hoped he would follow the dictates of his conscience equally well in more important matters. The worthy old gentleman therefore pitched the two much-coveted books back into the dusty corner whence he had taken them, and where to a certainty they will repose undisturbed until some other bookworm traveller visits the monastery; and the sooner he comes the better, as mice and mildew are actively at work...

A Collector Frustrated

Having seen all that was worthy of observation, I was waiting in the court near the door leading to the place where the monks were assembled to lower me down to the earth again. Just as I was ready to start there arose a discussion among them about the distribution of the money which I had paid for the two manuscripts. The agoumenos wanted to keep it all for himself, or at least for the expenses of the monastery; but the villain of a librarian swore he would have half. The agoumenos said he should not have a farthing, but as the librarian would not give way he offered him a part of the spoil; however, he did not offer him enough, and out of spite and revenge, or, as he protested, out of uprightness of principle, he told all the monks that the *agoumenos* had pocketed the money which he had received for their property, for that they all had a right to an equal share in these books, as in all the other things belonging to the community. The monks, even the most dunderheaded, were not slow in taking this view of the subject, and all broke out into a clamorous assertion of their rights, every- man of them speaking at once. The price I had given was so large that every one of them would have received several pieces of gold each. But no, they said, it was not that, but for the principle, of justice that they contended. They did not want the money, no more did the librarian, but they would not suffer their rules to be outraged or their rights to be trampled under foot. In the monasteries of St. Basil all the members of the society had equal rights - they ate in common, they prayed in common, everything was bought and sold for the benefit of the community at large. Tears fell from the eyes of some of the particularly virtuous monks; others stamped upon the ground, and showed a thoroughly rebellious spirit. As for me, I kept aloof, waiting to see what might be the result.

The *agoumenos*, who was evidently a man of superior abilities, calmly endeavoured to explain. He told the unruly brethren exactly what the sum was for which he had sold the books, and said that the money was not for his own private use, but to be laid out for the benefit of all, in the same way as the ordinary revenues of the monastery, which, he added, would soon prove quite insufficient if so large a portion of them continued to be divided among the individual members. He told them that the monastery was poor and wanted money, and that this large sum would be most useful for certain necessary expenses. But although he used many unanswerable arguments, the old brute of a librarian had completely awakened the spirit of discord, and the ignorant monks were ready to be led into rebellion by any one and for any reason or none. At last the contest waxed so warm that the sale of the two manuscripts was almost lost sight of, and every one began to quarrel with his neighbour, the entire community being split into various little angry groups, chattering, gesticulating, and wagging their long beards.

After a while the *agoumenos*, calling my interpreter, said that as the monks would not agree to let him keep the money in the usual way for the use of the monastery, he could have nothing to do with it; and to my great sorrow I was therefore obliged to receive it back, and to give up the two beautiful manuscripts, which I had already looked upon as the chief ornaments or my library in England. The monks all looked sadly downcast at this unexpected termination of their noble defence of their principles, and my only consolation was to perceive that they were quite as much vexed as I was. In fact, we felt that we had gained a loss all round, and the old librarian, after walking up and down once or twice with his hands behind his back in gloomy silence, retreated to a hole where he lived, near the library, and I saw no more of him.

My bag was brought forward, and when the books were extracted from it, I sat down on a stone in the court yard, and for the last time turned over the gilded leaves and admired the ancient and splendid illuminations of the larger manuscript, the monks standing round me as I looked at the blue cypress-trees, and green and gold peacocks, and intricate arabesques, so characteristic of the best times of Byzantine art. Many of the pages bore a great resemblance to the painted windows of the earlier Norman cathedrals of Europe. It was a superb old book. I laid it down upon the stone beside me and placed the little volume with its curious silver binding on the top of it, and it was with a sigh that I left them there with the sun shining on the curious silver ornaments.

Amongst other arguments it had been asserted by some of the monks that nothing could be sold out of the monastery without leave of the bishop of Tricala, and, as a forlorn hope, they now proposed that the *agoumenos* should go to some place in the vicinity where the bishop was said to be, and that, if he gave permission, the two books should be forwarded immediately by a trusty man to the khan of Malacash, where I was to pass the night. I consented to this plan, although I had no hope of obtaining the manuscripts, as in the present unsettled state of the country the bishop would naturally calculate on the probability of the messenger being robbed, and on the improbability of his meeting me at the khan, as it would be absolutely necessary for me to leave the place before sunrise the next day.

All this being arranged I proceeded to the chamber of the windlass, was put into the net, swung out into the air, and let down. They let me down very badly, being all talking and scolding each other; and had I not made use of my hands and feet to keep myself clear of the projecting points of the rock I should have fared badly. To increase my perils, my friends the *palicari* at the bottom, to testify their joy at my reappearance, rested their long guns across their knees and fired them off; without the slightest attention to the direction of the barrels, which were all loaded with ball-cartridge: the bullets spattered against the rock close to me, and in the midst of the smoke I called down and was caught in the arms of my affectionate thieves, who bundled me out of my net with many extraordinary screeches of welcome.

When my servants arrived and informed them of our recent disappointment, "What!" cried they, "would they not let you take the books? Stop a bit, we will soon get them for you!" And away they ran to the series of ladders which hung down another part of the precipice: they would have been up in a minute, for they scrambled like cats; but by dint of running after them and shouting, we at length got them to come back, and after some considerable expenditure of oaths and exclamations, kicking of horses, and loading of guns and saddlebags, we found ourselves slowly winding our way back towards the valley of the Peneus.

After all, what an interesting event it would have been, what a standard anecdote in bibliomaniac history, if I had let my friendly thieves have their own way, and we had stormed the monastery, broken open the secret door of the library, pitched the old librarian over the rocks, and marched off in triumph, with a gorgeous manuscript under each arm! Indeed I must say that under such aggravating circumstances it required a great exercise of forbearance not to do so, and in the good old times many a castle has been attacked and many a town besieged and pillaged for much lighter causes of offence than those which I had to complain of.

1897 Thomas Dwight Goodell

Female Porters

The principal city of Western Thessaly is Trikkala, of some fifteen thousand inhabitants in summer and eighteen thousand in winter, overlooked by a picturesque Turkish fort on the site of the ancient citadel. We intended to throw ourselves on the hospitality of a monastery that night, and made no stay at Trikkala; but while the train halted here a few minutes one painful scene burned itself into my memory. It was a group of women porters contending with one another for their burdens. By their skirts and hair, and their shrill, cracked voices, they must have been meant for women; but face and open bosom were so brown and withered, and they bent their backs under such enormous loads, it seemed that nothing feminine could have been left in those crushed and stunted wrecks of Heaven's handiwork. The Armenian porters of Constantinople stir one's pity sufficiently; to use a woman as *hammal* is too much. It was the only sight of the kind I saw in Greece, and was so un-Greek that I cannot but think of it as a sorrowful remnant of the blighting rule of the Mohammedans.

1898 Samuel J. Barrows

Tourists on Ladders

By the end of the nineteenth century, the travellers arriving at the Meteora were more properly "tourists", but they still had to face an adventure to gain access to the monasteries.

Trikkala is the second largest town in Thessaly. More picturesque is Kalabaka, at the western end of the road under the shadows of the great cliffs of Meteora. These cliffs are unlike any other formation in Greece. In our own northwest they would be called buttes. They are groups of pillared peaks, rising perpendicularly in lofty isolation on the plain. Seen from a distance, one of these groups might be taken for a vast cathedral with towers and turrets. Another group rises in detached pinnacles on the slope of the foothills. Upon this curious assemblage of peaks were built in the fourteenth century the famous Meteora ("mid-air") monasteries, originally twenty-four in number. It seems a curious adventure for religion to isolate itself on these lofty and almost inaccessible solitudes. But for the monks of those turbulent times a mid-air monastery served as a fortification as well as a temple. It protected them not only from the temptations of the world, but from the flesh and the devil in the shape of robbers and marauders. Of the twenty-four, but seven are now inhabited; the ruins of the others, like deserted eyries, crown these stern heights. As we stood under some of these perpendicular pinnacles the wonder was not merely that monasteries could be built upon them, but that any human being could have scaled them to begin with.

Procuring a local guide, we made our way to the foot of the Monastery of the Holy Trinity. There are two methods of ascent to several of these monasteries; one is by a rope-ladder with wooden rungs let down over the side of the cliff; the other is by means of a net, rope and windlass. We wished to try both methods, but as the windlass and rope were out of order, we were obliged to climb by the rope-ladder. Ascending first a flight of stairs of no difficulty, we passed along a narrow walk cut in the side of the cliff, the perils of which were only partly reduced by a rickety hand-railing. It showed us how much protection was needed and how little it could furnish. After winding round and up the cliff a considerable distance, we reached a ladder enclosed in a box hanging over the side of a cliff, and, ascending it, emerged into the monastery through a trap-door.

The view from the top was magnificent. Grand rocks rose on the other side of the chasm and grander mountains beyond. Red-roofed Kalabaka lay below, while through the plain wound the Peneius, more worthy of the silver speech into which Homer had coined it. We had seen it rushing through the narrow defile at Tempe, but here it leisurely uncoils its length in an ample bed on the plain. In the clear air above, an eagle was slowly circling, its wings almost motionless, as if deciding which of these deserted monasteries it would choose for its nest. The ten monks in the monastery were courteous and hospitable. When we saw the frayed-out rope and the "general flavor of mild decay" suggested by the windlass, - not, like wine, the better for age, - we felt that here, at least, the ladder was the lesser risk.

Descending the same way, we started for the Monastery of Saint Stephen, which stands much higher. By an easy bridle-path we climbed to the top of a cliff separated from that on which Saint Stephen stands by a deep abyss, spanned by a wooden draw-bridge. When robbers and brigands threatened the monastery the monks raised the drawbridge and rested in security. It was only after repeated knockings that we managed to make ourselves heard. An attendant opened the door and conducted us through a courtyard and upstairs into the reception-room of the Archimandrite Constantius, who received us warmly. Then we were shown to our rooms. We succeeded in getting a basin of water to wash in, but when I asked for a towel, the attendant smiled at such worldliness, and said they used towels in the village but not in the monastery. He informed me that there were ten monks, who employed forty-five workmen, some in the monastery and some on their farms below. I can easily believe that there were fifteen cats, for I saw eight. The servants set before us a supper of brown bread, fried eggs, cheese and wine. If these monks live high, it is not in their diet. After supper we took a walk round the cliff, and had a superb view of the Thessalian plain below, with the winding Peneius, the solemn gigantic masses of Meteora, and the lofty, snow-capped range of Pindus beyond. The abbot and the servant were communicative and not too high in the air to be remote from Greek politics. On these eagle cliffs nothing disturbed our rest, and Basil was not there to wake me for a daybreak service.

After a frugal breakfast, - it would not have been possible to get anything else, - we descended the cliff for a short distance, then made a sharp ascent, and skirted the edge of a deep ravine, where we had a fine view of the picturesque fantastic buttes which lay between us and the plain. Though we had left our heaviest bag at the railroad station, we still had too much to carry for a warm day; but the view repaid every sacrifice. Reaching at length the base of a cliff nearly two hundred feet high, upon which is perched the Monastery of Saint Barlaam, we shouted vigorously, until by and by a monk's head appeared at a window above. An attendant who looked small enough for a spider emerged from a hole in the cliff and descended spider-like on a long hanging ladder. He was not encumbered with much clothing, nor was he a devotee of soap; but when he learned that we were Americans, he was cordiality itself. We had had one experience with a ladder; we wanted now to try the net. The young man shouted to the monks above, and presently the rope descended with a heavy net on the hook. The young man spread the net upon the ground. Professor Tarbell courageously offered to try the experiment first. Accordingly, as directed, he sat cross-legged in the net. The meshes were drawn round him and fastened in the hook at the end of the rope. "Ready," shouted the Greek, and the monks above bent to the windlass and slowly lifted their catch. In spite of his constrained position, when he left the ground my friend preserved a semblance of humanity; but when he had gone a hundred and fifty feet, he seemed nothing but a suspended meal-bag, and I snapped my kodak at him with twinkling success.

It was my turn next. I felt something like a condemned criminal as I saw the rope and net descend. We are creatures of association. As a boy, I used to take in my hands the hook of a hoistway chain and swing back and forth from a platform thirty or forty feet from the ground; the exhilaration disguised the danger. Thousands of people every year ascend the Pilatus railroad or the cable road at Mürren, or go to the top of the Washington Monument in an elevator, or sleep on a railway train at the rate of fifty miles an hour. One soon becomes accustomed to experiences which are made safe simply because they are so dangerous. But to be bagged in a net, and drawn up on the outside of a cliff by a rope and windlass, rising as slowly and ignominiously as if you were a bale of merchandise, had in it elements of novelty, uncertainty, and unaccustomed danger.

The most trying perils are those which lack excitement. From experience I know that to join a cavalry charge is one of the most dramatic and exciting things in the world, and therefore requires but a small amount of courage, but to be suspended for four minutes in mid-air in a net affords unusual opportunity for reflection. A consciousness of your utter helplessness and the ridiculousness of your position alternates with speculations on the strength of the rope and the perfection of the windlass. I found, however, my courage slowly rising with the net. An advantage of ascending by net instead of by ladder is that the beautiful scenery opens gradually before you as you rise. A critical time is when you reach the top and hang poised for a few seconds opposite the door of the monastery. Two monks put out their hands at each side, and shouting "*Etoima*" to those at the windlass, pull you in and land you in a heap on the floor.

The Monastery of Saint Barlaam takes its name either from the saint of the fourteenth century or some hermit named after him. We had but time for a rapid view of the church. Tozer speaks enthusiastically of the Byzantine frescos and of the artistic grouping of one of the representations of the Virgin. Think of the sanctity of a monastery which no woman has ever entered! I can imagine what an exorcism, not of evil spirits, but of evil matter – the dirt of centuries - a few women from Broek might effect with their mops and brooms. We found but six monks and ten servants. All supplies had to be drawn up by the rope, for which there is a separate hoistway. The monastery bell was cracked. Considering the position of the church, one could not expect a very large number of church-goers, even if the bell had been sound. I saw here for the first time the semantron. This is a large plank suspended in the air and struck with a piece of iron. It is used in Lent instead of the bell. Its use is extremely ancient, and in Byzantine churches and monasteries long preceded the use of the bell.

We had tested the strength of the rope, the windlass and the muscle of the monks. There was but one critical moment in the descent. Into that moment seemed to be condensed half the peril the adventure. The net was spread on the floor near the hoistway and gathered up over my head and fastened in the hook, as before. Then there was a half turn at the windlass and I was pushed out from the landing. I felt the net settle and its cords become taut. It was literally a moment of suspense. My companions taunted me with the uncertainty of my position and wished they could photograph my expression. Fortunately, I had left my kodak below. The single moment was longer than the rest of the four minutes, which were comparatively agreeable. There was no need of distrusting the net. It was strong and big enough to hold two people. The monks do not like to haul up two men at once, but it is easier to let them down, and Professor Tarbell and Mr. Roddy ascended together. Just how they managed to braid their legs and arms I do not know, but they brought them all down with them and were safely disentangled at the bottom.

Wordsworth not inaptly called these monks fishers of men. Insulated in their lofty solitudes, they illustrated a strange conception of religion and life as remote from that of Homeric times or from the religion which built the Parthenon as it is from apostolic Christianity or the advanced spirit of our own age.

General View of Meteora (Baron von Stackelberg & Villeneuve)

Larissa

1802-09 Colonel William Leake

The Town of Turnavo

Turnavo contains 1500 families; of these only 70 are Mahometan, a number which compared with the six mosques still existing, shows how much the Turkish population has diminished. It is said that there were once 4000 houses, which the great number of those in ruins, or uninhabited, renders credible. The causes to which the depopulation is ascribed, are several successive years of plague, the first Russian war which brought the Albanians into Thessaly in great numbers, and lastly, the acquisition of the place by Aly Pasha, which has driven away the Turks. Turnavo, like Tzarltzena, is a name of Sclavonic origin, and shows that a colony of that race, perhaps from Turnavo in Bulgaria, was once settled here, of which no other trace than the name now remains. Another Illyric name is found at the lake and village Ezero, in Mount Titarus, between Tzaritzena and Rapsani. These are the more remarkable, as there are few if any others in the great eastern Thessalo-Macedonian range to the southward of Vodhena. Like Tzaritzena, Turnavo has been and is still indebted for its importance to the weaving and dyeing of the stuffs made of cotton, or of a mixture of silk and cotton called bukhasia and aladja, and to the dyeing of cotton thread, which is chiefly sold to the Ambelakiotes. Long towels in the Turkish and Greek fashion interwoven with gold threads, and shawls for the head and waist, are also made here. There are three dyeing manufactories; but the looms are all in private houses; these are reckoned to produce daily 1200 ... pieces of seven peeks each. There are only 200 working days in the year, so numerous are the Greek holidays. Ninety okes of thread are made every day in the town; the surrounding villages supply one third of that which is used in the looms, and all that which is dyed for exportation. Tzaritzena makes as many stuffs as Turnavo, but does not dye so much thread. As at Tzaritzena, Siatista, Kozani, and Kastoria, there are many persons here who speak German, and they were more numerous formerly; but as in the places just mentioned, those who have realized any property often prefer the secure enjoyment of it in Christendom, to the chance of increasing it here...

By the sacrifice of a sum of money to the Vezir, the Archons have procured an order forbidding the dancing boys from exercising their profession in that town; this has annoyed the people of Turnavo, by causing the boys to resort more frequently to that town, which attracts thither Turks and Musulman Albanians of the worst class, whom the Greeks are moreover often obliged to entertain. The Ayans of Larissa will not often permit the dancers to appear in that city; as it is generally attended with disturbances and drunken quarrels among the Janissaries, in which the boys themselves stand a chance of being murdered.

The Bishops' Debts

The metropolitan bishop of Larissa, who is now at Turnavo on a visitation, has been translated to this dignity from the see of Grevena since I met him last year at Ioannina. He paid sixty purses to the Porte upon this occasion, and finds the see burdened with a debt of 300 purses, bearing the customary high interest, which he finds the more difficult to pay, as the exportation of grain from Thessaly is forbidden to all but the agents of government, which disables the bishop's flock from contributing to the payment of his demands upon them, or at least supplies an excuse for withholding them. Almost all the Greek bishoprics are burdened in the same manner with debt; but like the public debts of other countries, they form a bond of union between individuals and the authorities, and in this country have the advantage of saving the former from the dangers of hoarding - the only alternative with those who are fearful of the risks of commerce. The necessity of being prepared to pay the interest gives the bishops also something more than a personal plea for enforcing the collection of their dues from the clergy and laity, in which they often find great difficulty. Aly Pasha's bishops are generally assisted by His Highness's buyurti, supported sometimes, especially in the case of the bishop of Ioannina, by a palikari or two, to ensure attention to it. It was by Aly's influence at Constantinople that the bishop of Larissa obtained his promotion, the Pasha finding it useful to the support of his influence in this part of Thessaly to have the chief Christian authority subservient to him, and in the hands of one who has long resided at his court.

The Ignorance of the "Higher" Classes

Sometimes the higher classes of Greeks show greater ignorance even than the peasantry. The master of the house in which I lodge, one of the richest men in the place, and who has resided in Germany, asks me for a herb to turn copper into gold, and learns, for the first time in his life, that the stream which flows by Turnavo is the same as that at Elassona, and that it has its origin in Mount Olympus.

Through the Vale of Tempe

Dec. 20.-From Ambellikia to Lit6khoro. The snows of Olympus had just received a golden tinge from the rays of the rising sun, when we began our descent into the strait, or narrowest part of the vale of Tempe. The direct distance is not more than half a mile, but the steepness of the hill and the bad condition of the winding kalderim, cause the descent to occupy half an hour.

At 3.30, Turkish time, we arrive on the river's bank, and soon afterwards pass the extremity of the root of Ossa, on the eastern side of the theatre-shaped site of Ambelakia, which, separated only by the river from a similar projection of Olympus, forms the commencement of the strait. After traversing a beautiful grove of planes, we arrive upon the rocks, where the space between the foot of the precipices of Ossa and the river is sufficient only for the road, which is about 20 feet above the water. Here a current of cold air issuing from a small cavern, gives to the place the name of Anemopetra. The wind proceeds, probably, from the channel of one of the subterraneous streams of water, of which there are many in the pass, rushing from the rocks into the Salamvria. The river flows with a steady and tranquil current, except where its course is interrupted by islands, or where dams have been constructed for intercepting fish.

After having passed some marks of chariot-wheels in the rock, we arrive at 3.55 at a spot where the bank is supported by the remains of a Hellenic wall, and at 4.8 at the ruins of a castle built of small stones and mortar, standing on one side of an immense fissure in the precipices of Ossa, which afford an extremely rocky, though not impracticable descent from the heights into the vale. Between the castle and the river there was space only for the road, nor is the level any wider between the opposite bank and the precipices of Olympus, where several caverns are seen, some of which retain traces of painting. They were once probably ascetic retreats; for one of them near the river side is still a church, dedicated to the Holy Trinity. It may formerly, perhaps, have been sacred to Pan and the Nymphs. As to the altar, or temple of Apollo Tempites, which once existed in Tempe, some of the circumstances attending his worship seem to require a more open situation than these narrowest parts of the strait, and Baba appears the most probable situation for it. The ceremonies performed there were commemorative of the purification of Apollo by order of Jupiter, after which he was said to have proceeded to Delphi, bearing in his hand a branch of bay gathered in the valley. Hence the victors in the Pythia were crowned with bay from Tempe, and the Delphi every nine years sent hither a Theoria, which, having approached the altar of Apollo in procession, sacrificed to the deity, sang hymns, and cut branches of bay. On other occasions, the inhabitants of the surrounding parts of Thessaly were in the habit of assembling in Tempe for sacrifices, symposia, and parties of pleasure, and some-times, according to Aelian, so numerous were the offerings, that the whole air was perfumed with the incense.

At 4.18 we leave the castle, and at 4.30 begin to ascend a root of Ossa, of which the slope is more gradual than before, but which terminating at the river's bank in a precipice, made it necessary that the road should pass over the hill. The traces of the ancient road, cut in the rock, and wide enough for carriages, still remain. In the beginning of the ascent, the rock on the right hand side of the road is excavated perpendicularly, and upon the face of it are engraved, in large letters much worn by time, and surrounded by a moulding of a common form, the words-L. Cassius Longinus Pro Cos. Tempe munivit. Here, again, on the opposite side of the river, the rocks meet the bank. After a halt of 5 minutes at the inscribed rock, we descend again on the other side of the ridge to the river side, and at 4.53 arrive at the end of the wolf's mouth, where a fine source of water, larger than any in the pass, rushes from the foot of the rocks into the river.

The walk of one hour and eight minutes from the foot of the mountain of Ambelakia to the eastern extremity of the pass, with a horse whose pace I have measured, will give a distance of about four miles and a half for the length of the road through Tempe. In this space the opening between Ossa and Olympus is in some points less than 100 yards, comprehending in fact no more than the breadth of a road, in addition to that of the river, which is here much compressed within its ordinary breadth in the plains, and not more than 50 yards across. On the northern bank there are places where it seems impossible that a road could ever have existed, so that the communication was probably maintained anciently as it is now, by means of two bridges, or by ferries. It is evident, at least, from the marks of wheels, and the Latin inscription, that the via militaris, or main route, was in the present track.

1809-10 Dr. Henry Holland

Larissa at the Beginning of the Nineteenth Century

We returned to Larissa while there was yet sufficient daylight to enable us to survey a part of the city. The only striking feature in its situation is derived from the Salympria; here a broad and deep stream, which; approaching the city through a tract of wooded valley, flows underneath a convent of Dervishes, two large Turkish mosques, and several groups of lofty buildings; and, passing the sombre enclosure of a Turkish burying-ground, again disappears among the woods. The extent and population of Larissa are very considerable; and the estimate I received of 4000 houses and 20,000 inhabitants, is probably not beyond the truth. The internal appearance of the city is mean and irregular; the streets are ill-built, narrow, and dirty; and in the houses and inhabitants alike; there, is a general indication of wretchedness. The bazaars, which form as usual the central part of the town, are indifferently supplied with manufactured goods. In walking through the streets in the suburbs of the city, I was surprised by observing the large amount of negro population, which was much greater than I have remarked in any other Turkish town. Many of these outer streets, from their situation, are exposed to the river floods of the Salympria, and about a year before our visit to Larissa, some hundred cottages are said to have been destroyed by this cause, the ruins of which were in rnany places still visible. The habitations in this quarter of the city are for the most part constructed of stones, wood, and clay, rudely compacted together.

Of the population of Larissa it is probable that three-fourths are entirely Turkish; the number of Greek, and Jewish inhabitants conjointly not exceeding a thousand families. A certain proportion of the Turkish residents possess lands in the surrounding country, and derive their revenue from this source; but the greater number are dependants on these landed proprietors, and live that life of unvarying indolence which is the habitual characteristic of the nation. This system of indolent dependence could not equally exist in a community where the habits and inventions of luxury and of civilization were more entirely formed; but the Turk (and perhaps it is true of other Oriental nations), while education and custom render him averse to all regular activity of life, and while he sleeps away much of his existence in listless apathy, is nevertheless singularly temperate in many of his habits; and if he creates little by his productive labour, it must be owned that it is but little he consumes. His diet is simple and moderate; the pipe, the baths, and the drinking of coffee are his principal luxuries as well as occupations; his garments, though costly, seldom require renewal; and general respectability in the scale of society is maintained with much less personal expence than in the communities of civilized Europe. It may be fair to add that this mutual patronage and dependence among Turks of different classes is probably influenced in part by motives connected with their religion; and the effect, though one but of partial and mistaken benevolence, is nït entirely to be removed from the rank of a national virtue. In its consequences, however, it is evidently injurious to the character and welfare of the community; to be aware of which, it is only necessary to contrast the exterior appearances of those towns where the lower class of population is Mussulmen, with others whcre the corresponding class is composed of Greek and Jewish inhabitants. Though the relative situation of the two people be that of masters and slaves, yet it will be found that all the outer signs of degradation belong in greater degree to the condition of the former. The Greek town presents in general the aspect of industrious and useful life; and unless when borne down by some of those circumstances of local oppression which are so common in the irregular government of Turkey, the population have an appearance of comfort in their dwellings, clothing, and in the various habits of life not much inferior to that of other nations in the south of Europe.

The Indolence and Ferocity of the Turks

At first sight, indolence and ferocity hardly seem to be compatible characteristics, but Dr. Holland is well able to sustain both his claims.

In the towns chiefly inhabited by Turks, the most striking circumstance is the air of uniform indolence and unbroken monotony which pervades every part of the scene. As you walk along the street, few sounds of the human voice come upon the ear. Reclining in his gallery, or on cushions before his door, the Turk is seen to repose in a silence and grave stillness of demeanour, which might for the moment sanction even idleness with the name of dignity: his only movement that of raising, or depressing, his long pipe; his only conversation, if any there be, an occasional brief sentence addressed in a low and deliberate tone to those who may be near him, and answered with the same formal apathy of manner. Or you may meet these people in their progress to the baths or the mosque, treading with a slow, stately, and measured step; scarcely deigning to notice the stranger as be passes them; and by demeanour alone drawing an involuntary homage of respect, which is little due to the intrinsic merits of the man. Elsewhere, ignorance is, generally noisy, or feeble; - among the Turks it is disguised from outward observation by a gravity or even propriety of manner, which are not the artifice of individuals, but the national habit of the people.

This universal aspect of indolence, however, is the circumstance which least offends the eye in a Turkish, town; and the matter it affords for speculation on the origin and variety of the national character, may reconcile it for a time to the mind of the observer. Its effects are more disagreeably seen in the appearances of neglect and decay which everywhere present themselves; houses falling for want of repair; the habitations of the lower classes wretched and comfortless; filth accumulating in the streets, without removal; and a general want of those circumstances which give order and propriety to social life. The stranger will be astonished, in a thousand instances, by the strangeness of the contrast between the exterior of the Turks and of Their habitations; and after following in the street a figure of dignified manner and splendid dress, will wonder to see him enter an abode where all is meanness and decay. This common character of the towns; where the population is principally Turkish, shews itself strikingly in Larissa, in various forms of nuisance and deformity. An active population might speedily reform these evils; but the inertness of the Turks cannot be roused into action even by personal inconvenience; and time is allowed to work its progressive changes without check or counteraction from the hand of man...

The Turkish inhabitants of Larissa are charged by the Greek with peculiar ferocity of disposition and hostility to the Christian religion. In a geographical work of some merit, composed in the Romaic language, they are characterized as ... "haters of Christ to the highest degree, and brutal"; and the same ill repute I have frequently heard extended to them in conversation with the Greeks of the country. With some exaggeration; there probably is a certain degree of truth in this; the irregularity of the internal government in Turkey giving rise to local varieties, which would otherwise seem improbable from the uniformity of the Turkish character. I had myself the opportunity of observing part the terror in which the Turks ïf Larissa are held by the Greek inhabitants of the place. The house of the Archbishop Polycarp resembled a prison, or a place of secret refuge; the gates conducting to it were always opened with a sort of suspicious anxiety, and an impression of alarm, and distrust was ever visible among the inhabitants of this mansion.. The Archbishop himself very rarely quits its precincts, influenced by the apprehension of insult if seen in the streets of the city. On the second day of our abode in his house, while sitting with him in his apartment, a Turk of surly and forbidding aspect, and evidently of the lower class, entered the room, seated himself unceremoniously on the sofa, filled his pi pe and took coffee from the attendants. The Archbishop was obviously embarrassed, but made no comment. After a short interval, he took a coin from his purse, probably a zequin, and put it silently into the hand of the Turk, who immediately disappeared. Our Tartar, too, was equally intrusive here, as he had been at Trikala; entering the apartment at any time smoking his pipe; and taking his part in conversation without restraint.

1830 David Urquhart

The Extreme Inquisitiveness of the Population

I suppose things are altered now - much for the better (course; but at the time of which I am writing, when Greece still was light-hearted and young, it was a hard thing for a man to keep his own counsel. At every turn of a passage, every every angle of a street, every furlong along the road, you were stopped at all times to have a long string of questions put to you... "Whence do you come?" "Whither are you going?" "What is your business?" How is your health?" "Where is to be seen your venerable paternal mansion?" "Which of the great allies has the honour of claiming you?" "What news?" - and this, be it observed, between perfect strangers. But when friends or acquaintances meet, and especially should one or both be women, then with the redoubled sigmas of Greek interrogatories, commences a sibilation which one might take for a dialogue of boa-constrictors. Your state, health, humour, are all separately asked for; similar enquiries are then instituted respecting all and each of your known relatives, horses and dogs. You must, in reply, present the appropriate compliments of the individual thus distinguished - thus: "How is the venerable archon, your father?" "He salutes you." "How is the valuable citizen, your brother?" "He kisses your eyes." - "How is the hopeful stripling, your son?" "He kisses your hand."

A Remarkable Economic and Social Experiment

Ottoman Greece is not noted as a place where manufacturing industry and commercial enterprise flourished; but this passage shows that under the right conditions, Greek industry could, for a time at least, reach the highest levels attained in Western Europe. Its demise, however, seems to have been due, at least in part, to that spirit of factionalism which was the curse of the Greeks, and to which there are many references in the accounts of travellers.

Am belakia was, perhaps, the spot, amid all the rich recollections of Thessaly, which I visited with the greatest interest; and, but for the lordly rnansions that still overlook the Vale of Tempe, the traveller might doubt the reality of a story which appears almost fabulous. I extract from Beaujour's *Tableau du Commerce de la Grece*," published at the commencement of this century, the details he has preserved respecting it, in as far as they were confirmed to me by the information I obtained on the spot.

"Ambelakia, by its activity, appears rather a borough of Holland than a village of Turkey. This village spreads, by its industry, movement, and life, over the surrounding country, and gives birth to an immense commerce, which unites Germany to Greece by a thousand threads. Its population has trebled in fifteen years, and amounts at present (1798) to four thousand, who live in their manufactories, like swarms of bees in their hives. In this village are unknown both the vices and cares engendered by idleness; the hearts of the Ambelakiotes are pure, and their faces serene; the slavery which blasts the plains watered by the Peneus, and stretching at their feet, has never ascended the sides of Pelion (Ossa); and they govern themselves, like their ancestors, by their *protoyeros*, (primates, elders,) and their own magistrates. Twice the Mussulmans of Larissa attempted to scale their rocks, and twice were they repulsed by hands which dropped the shuttle to seize the musket.

"Every arm, even those of the children, is employed in the factories; whilst the men dye the cotton, the women prepare and spin it. There are twenty-four factories, in which, yearly, two thousand five hundred bales of cotton yarn, of one hundred okes each are dyed (6138 cwts). This yarn finds its way into Germany, and is disposed of at Buda, Vienna, Leipsic, Dresden, Anspach, and Bayreuth. The Ambelakiote merchants had houses of their own in all these places. These houses belonged to distinct associations at Ambelakia. The competition thus established, reduced very considerably the common profits; they proposed, therefore, to unite thcmselves under one central administration.

Twenty years ago this plan was suggested, and in a few years afterwards it was carried into execution. The lowest shares in this joint-stock conlpany were five thousand piastres, (between 600*l.* and 700*l.*,) and the highest were restricted to twenty thousand, that the capitalists might not swallow up all the profits. The workmen suscribed their little profits, and, uniting in societies, purchased single shares. Besides their capital, their labour was reckoned in the general amount. They received their portion of the profits accordingly, and abundance was soon spread through the whole community. The dividends were, at first, restricted to ten per cent., and the surplus profit was applied to the augmenting of the capital, which, in two years, was raised from 600,000 to 1,000,000 piastres (120,000*l.*)

"Three directors, under an assumed firm, managed the affairs of the company; but the signature was also confided to three associates at Vienna, whence the returns were made. These two firms of Ambelakia and Vienna had their correspondents at Peste, Trieste, Leipsic, Salonique, Constantinople, and Smyrna, to receive their own staple, effect the return, and to extend the market for the cotton-yarn of Greece. An important part of their trust was to circulate the funds realised, from hand to hand, and from place to place, according to their own circumstances, necessities, and the rates of exchange."

Thus the company secured to itself both the profits of the speculation and the profits of the banker, which was exceedingly increased by the command and choice which these two capacities gave of time, market, and speculation. When the exchange was favourable, they remitted specie; when unfavourable, they remitted goods; or they speculated in Salonica, Constantinople, and Smyrna, by purchase of bills, or by the transmission of German goods, according to the fluctuations and demands of the different markets, of which their extensive relations put them immediately in possession, and by which the rapid turning of so large a capital gave them always the means of profiting.

"Never was a society established upon such economical principles; and never were fewer hands employed in the transaction of such a mass of business. To concentrate all the profits of Ambelakia, the correspondents were all Ambelakiots; and, to divide the profits more equally amongst them, they weere obliged to return to Ambelakia, after three years' service; and they had then to serve one year at home, to imbibe afresh the mercantile principles of the company.

"The greatest harmony long reigned in the association; the directors were disinterested, the correspondents zealous, and the workmen docile and laborious. The company's profits increased every day, on a capital which had rapidly become immense. Each investment realised a profit of from sixty to one hundred per cent.; all which was distributed, in just proportions, to capitalists and work men, according.to capital and industry. The shares had increased tenfold."

The disturbances which succecded to this period of unrivalled prosperity, are attributed, by Beaujour, with that provoking vagueness that suhstitutes epithets for causes, to the "*surabondance de richesse*," to "*assemblees tumultueuses*," to the workmen's quitting the shuttle for the pen, to the exactions of the rich, and to the insubordination of the inferior orders. To us it may, on the contrary, be a matter of surprise that such an association could exist, so long and so prosperously, in the absence of judicial authority to settle, in their origin, disputes and litigated interests, which, in the absence of such authority, could only be decided by violence. The infraction of an injudicious bye-law gave rise to litigation, by which the community was split into two factions. For several years, at an enormous expense, they went about to Constantinople, Salonica, and Vienna, transporting witnesses, and mendicating legal decisions, to reject them when obtained; and the company separated into as many parts as there were associations of workmen in the original firm. At this period, the Bank of Vienna, in which their funds were de-posited, broke; and, with this misfortune, political events combined to over-shadow the fortunes of Ambelakia, where prosperity, and even hope, were finally extinguished by the commercial revolution produced by the spinning-jennies of England.

Turkey now ceased to supply Germany with yarn: she became tributary for this, her staple manufacture, to England. Finally came the Greek Revolution. This event has reduced, within the same period, to a state of as complete desolation, the other flourishing townships of Magnesia, Pelion, Ossa, and Olympus. Even on the opposite heights of Olympus, across the valley of Tempe, Rapsana, from a thousand wealthy houses which tell years ago it possessed, is now, without being guilty of either "luxury" or "tumult", reduced to ten widowed hearths. But Beaujour's praise is as little merited as his censure is unjust. "Here," says he, "spring up anew grand and liberal ideas, on a soil devoted for twenty years to slavery; here the ancient Greek character arose in its early energy, amidst the torrents and caverns of Pelion (Ossa); and, to say all in a word, here were all the talents and virtues of ancient Greece born again in a corner of modern Turkey."

Had an old commercial emporium had a conveniently situated sea-port, or a provincial chief town, possessing capital, connections, and influence extended thus rapidly its commerce and prosperity, it would have been cited, and justly so, as a proof of sound principles of government; of public spirit, intelligence, and honour. What, then, shall we say of the character of the administration that has elevated an unknown, a weak, and insignificant hamlet to such a level of prosperity? This hamlet had not a single field in its vicinity - had no local industry - had no commercial connection-no advantage of position - was in the vicinity of no manufacturing movement - was on the track of no transit commerce - was not situated either on a navigable river, or on the sea - had no harbour even in its vicinity - and was accessible by no road, save a goat's path among precipices. Its industry receivcd no impulse from new discoveries, or secrets of chemistry, or combination of mechanical powers. The sole secret of its rise was the excellent adjustment of interests, the free election of its officers, the immediate control of expenditure, and, conseqnently, the union of intertests by the common pressure of burdens, and the union of sympathies by the smooth action of simple machinery...

Ambelakia supplied industrious Germany, not by the perfection of its machinery, but by the industry of its spindle and distaff. It taught Montpellier the art of dyeing, not from experimental chairs, but because dying was with it a domestic and culinary operation, subject to daily observation in every kitchen; and, by the simplicity and honesty, not the science of its system. It reads a lesson to commercial associations, and holds up an example unparalleled in the commercial history of Europe, of a joint stock and labour company ably and economically and successfully administered, in which the interests of industry and capital were equally represented. Yet the system of administration on which all this is engrafted, and the rights here enjoyed of property, proprietorship, and succcssion, - foundations of the political structure, - are common to the thousand halmlets of Thessaly, and to the Ottoman Empire. Here is to be sought the root, and found the promise, of the fuure fruits, the germ of which exist, although they lie inert in the bosom of those primeval inlstitutions which have not yet, in the East, been extirpated by legislation, or trodden down by faction.

1848-9 Edward Lear

The Storks of Thessaly

In my return to Larissa there is but just time to make one drawing of dark Olympus ere a frightful thunderstorm, with deluges of rain, breaks over the plain and pursues me to the city. It continues to pour all the afternoon, and I amuse myself, as best I can, in Hassan Bey's house. It is a large mansion, in the best Turkish style, and betokening the riches of its master. It occupies three sides of a walled courtyard, and one of its wings is allotted to the harem, who live concealed by a veil of close lattice work when at home, though I see them pass to and fro dressed in the usual disguise worn out of doors. I watch two storks employed in building on the roof of that part of the building. These birds are immensely numerous in Thessaly, and there is a nest on nearly every house in Larissa. No one disturbs them; and they are considered so peculiarly in favour with the Prophet that the vulgar believe the conversion of a Christian as being certain to follow their choice of his roof for their dwelling; formerly a Christian so honoured was forced to turn Mussulman or quit his dwelling - so at least they told me in Yannina, where two pair have selected the Vice-Consul's house for their abode. It is very amusing to watch them when at work, as they take infinite pains in the construction of what after all seems a very ill-built nest. I have seen them, after twisting and bending a long bit of grass or root for an hour in all directions, throw it away altogether. That will not do after all, they say; and then flying away they return with a second piece of material, in the choice of which they are very particular; and, according to my informants at Yannina, only make use of one sort of root. When they have arranged the twig or grass in a satisfactory manner they put up their heads on their shoulders and clatter in a mysterious manner with a sound like a dice shaken in a box. This clattering at early morning or evening, in this season of the year, is one certain characteristic that these towns are under Turkish government, inasmuch as the storks have all abandoned Greece (modern), for the Greeks shoot and molest them; only they still frequent Larissa, and the plain of the Spercheius, as being so near the frontier of Turkey that they can easily escape thither if necessary. This is foolishness in the Greeks, for the stork is most useful in devouring insects, especially the larva of the locust, which I observed in myriads on the plains near the entrance of Tempe; and I counted as many as seventy storks in one society, eating them as fast as possible, and with great dignity of carriage. That part of the roof of the harem which is not occupied by storks is covered with pigeons and jackdaws, a humane attention paid to the lower orders of creation being always one of the most striking traits of Turkish character.

A few days later, Lear had less reason to feel so positive about the storks.

The woes of Thessaly continued. In the middle of the night, the roof of Seid Effendi's house being slight, a restless stork put one of his legs through the crevice and could not extricate it; whereon ensued much kicking and screams, and at the summons came half the storks in Thessaly, and all night long the uproar was portentous. Four very wet jackdaws also came down the chimney and hopped over me and about the room till dawn.

1898 Samuel J. Barrows

A Walk through the Vale of Tempe

We reached the little khan of Baba at five o'clock, and after arranging for supper and lodging, had time to take a walk through the Vale of Tempe before sunset. This famous vale is, as its name signifies, a "cut" or pass in the mountains. The cliffs which form it belong on one side to the chain of Ossa and on the other side to that of Olympus. The vale is four and a half miles long. The cliffs rise with noble grandeur, and through the gorge the Peneius flows to the sea. Its banks are well wooded with the plane, elm, oak, willow, and wild fig. Some of the plane-trees are of great size. Especially impressive was a pair of twin trunks rising from a gigantic base. The rocks on each side were covered with hardy bushes and clinging vines. We were in the vale just in time for the fresh greenness of the leaves, the spring-tide of the river and the spring carols of the birds. Among them were the clear, fluent, bell-like tones of the nightingale. Is it more shy than most professional singers, or is it only coquettish? We hid ourselves in the bushes to get a glimpse of the *Meistersinger*, - for I dare not call a male song-bird a *prima donna*. I was surprised at the extreme plainness of the nightingale's dress; its plumage is of a reddish brown with a dull grey breast. In garb it is a sober Quaker among the birds, and if the members of that religious society were to hold a grove meeting in the Vale of Tempe, they would not have the heart to condemn the ravishing music of their feathered Friends. In the distance the horological cuckoo was measuring off his voice. The setting sun shone through the vale. As we advanced, the mountains came nearer together, until there was only room in the defile for the rushing river and the roadway beside it. Far up on the mountain-side was a small village, and, near it, fine cows - not very numerous in Greece - were grazing in the fields. The village on the terrace is Ambelakia, which, in spite of its remoteness in this vale, was famed in France and Europe for its dyeing and spinning, conducted on a co-operative plan.

We returned to the khan at sundown and had a meal as plain as the plumage of the nightingale. It was made up of brown bread, milk, and boiled eggs. The eggs were fresh, the milk sweet, and the brown bread wholesome. No animals disturbed our sleep except an inquisitive cat, which jumped in the window and then jumped out again, while cuckoos in the vale conscientiously counted the hours.

Larissa (Contemporary print)

Magnesia

1802-09 Colonel William Leake

The Houses of Volos

From Perivoli all ascent of near twenty minutes conducts me to the middle of the Greek town of Volo, under which name are comprehended also Perivolia, Kastro, and a detached suburb of Volo to the southward, called Vlakho Makhala. The houses of this town, so striking and attractive at a distance, hardly support, on a nearer view, the preconceived estimation of them. This is partly to be attributed to the general state of the arts in Turkey and partly to the insecurity even of this favoured district. Defence against hostile attack has been more considered than domestic comfort; not only against the robber, the pirate, the lawless Albanian, or Turkish soldier, or the extortion of neighbouring governors, but with a view also to intestine disputes, often ending in violence and open war, when the mountain is most secure against external enemies. Hence the houses are lofty and built in the form of towers. Glass windows are almost unknown; nor in other respects are the houses to be compared to those of the Vlakhiotes of Mount Pindus, or to those of some of the Greek towns of Macedonia. As an apology, the people of Volo remark, that being in the most exposed situation of the mountain, they have been less able to attend to luxuries than the securer inhabitants of Makrinitza or Zagora.

Greek Schools on Mount Pelion

One of their projects was to establish a college or academy on the mountain, which would quickly have attracted the youth of every part of Greece. They had even procured a firman from Sultan Selim, had obtained 800 purses, chiefly from some rich merchants settled in Europe, and had provided books and mathematical instruments, in all which they were greatly assisted by the Greek princes Ypsillinti and Demetrius Morusi, the enlightened supporters of learning at Constantinople; but a dispute having arisen in Magnesia resecting the town in which the academy was to be established, Makrinitza having claimed a right of preference which others contested, the principal persons on the mountain giving no encouragement to the measure, and the two Greek princes falling into disgrace at Constantinople, the project fell to the ground, soon after which the promoters of it retired into Christendom. There are now five schools on the mountain for teaching Hellenic; at Makrinitza, Dhrakia, Portaria, Zagora, and Milies. That of Makrinltza has generally about thirty scholars, a few of whom advance as far as Thucydides and Homer, the rest not beyond Aesop. When a little more instruction is thought desirable, the young men are sent to Constantinople. It is to be lamented that education has not met with better encouragement in this privileged and sequestered point in the centre of Greece; as it would soon have attracted many educated men as teachers or residents, and would have improved the native manners of the Magnesian peninsula, rendering it a centre of civilization and instruction for the Greeks, and ultimately for the other Christians of European Turkey. The Turkish government is no obstacle to such a proceeding, being too blind or too careless of distant consequences to oppose the education of its Christian subjects, and rather pleased perhaps to see them engaged in such peaceful pursuits, though in the end they may be the most formidable of any to the Ottoman power .

The Economy of the Mountain

Of the twenty-four villages of Mount Pelium, none but Argalasti, Nekhori, and Lekhonia, grow corn sufficient for their consumption; but all the lower part of the peninsula abounds in wine, silk, oil, cotton, pulse, oranges, fruits, and all the varied productions of the maritime climate of Greece. Those of the higher villages are almost confined to silk, wine, honey, and horticultural produce: none of them have many flocks or cattle. Volo and Makrinitza owning a part of the plain at the head of the Gulf, possess corn land in that situation; and the same towns, together with Portaria and Lekhonia, have some olive-trees on the heights. The lands of Makrinitza and Portaria produce a sufficiency of oil to admit of the sale of a small quantity in the alternate years. In all the higher villages silk is the staff of life; with this they procure provisions from Thessaly, enjoying plenty when there is a good crop of silk, and the reverse when the season is unfavourable. It is reckoned that landed property pays a fourth of its produce in taxes; and in case of dearth, as in the present year, there are many examples of severe distress on the mountain. Still they consider themselves fortunate in their privileges, in the protection which they enjoy from the unchecked extortion of provincial governors, and particularly in their exemption from the quartering of soldiers and the visits of Albanians. But they make a foolish use of their advantages. Internal discord divides every village into parties; a similar jealousy prevails between the principal towns, and each of them strives by bribery , intrigue, and the interest of their patrons at Constantinople, to injure its particular rival or adversary. The Turks are of course enriched, and the Greeks impoverished by these quarrels.

There are six or eight hundred looms in the mountain for the manufacture of narrow silken or mixed stuffs or towels; but the greater part of these fabrics belong to strangers from Aghia, Ambelakia, or Turnavo. Silken articles of a smaller kind, such as cords, girdles, and purges, are made by the women in some of the towns, particularly Volo, Makrinitza, and Portaria. The men work in leather, and make shoes, sacks, and valises. A weaver may earn 50 or 60 paras a day: a day labourer in the vineyards, olive and mulberry plantations, 30 paras, with bread, wine, and meat. The reapers in time of harvest in the plain receive 50 paras, with provision... Goat's flesh is the meat chiefly in use... The Magnesians, like the inhabitants of the coasts of Greece in general, derive little resource from the fish with which their seas abound.

Trikeri

Trikeri, called Bulbulje by the Turks, contains three or four hundred houses, constructed in the same manner as those of the district of Volo, and situated on the summit of a high hill at the eastern entrance of the gulf. The people live entirely by the sea; some of the poorer classes, as well as many of those in the southern villages of the Magnesian peninsula, cut sponges and catch starfish. The others are sailors, ship or boat-builders, and traders. The highest rank are ship-owners, or captains of ships. The richest lend money at a high interest upon maritime traffic, or make advances upon bills drawn upon Constantinople, where the cargoes which are chiefly of corn are generally sold. The Trikeriotes usually fit out their ventures in the same manner as the people of Ydhra, Spetzia, Poro, and many other maritime towns; that is to say, the owner, captain, and sailors, all have shares in the ship and cargo, the sailors generally sharing a half among them, which is in lieu of all other demands. During the scarcity of corn in France at the beginning of the Revolution a sailor's share for the voyage amounted sometimes to three purses, which at that time was equivalent to 150*l*. sterling.

The peninsula of Trikeri produces nothing but wood; this is brought to town by the women, who perform all the household work; while the men are employed entirely in maritime concerns. The women of some of the other towns of Magnesia are equally laborious, but it is said that none are to be compared with the Trikeriotes for strength, and for the enormous burthens of wood which they bring into the town spinning cotton on the way. Trikeri, although on the main land, is included in the Kapitan Pasha's government of the islands, and White Sea, as the Turks call the Aegean, and receives its orders from his interpreter, one of the four great Greek officers of the Porte. This arose from the circumstance of the old town having been on the island of Trikeri, the ancient Cicynnethus, from whence they were driven by the pirates.

Rivalries in Aghia

Soon afterwards we arrive in sight of Aghia, which stands on the foot of Mount Ossa, and half an hour before sunset arrive in the middle of the town at the end of a fifty minutes' ride from Dhesiani.

Soon after my arrival, a formal visit from the ... elders, is interrupted by the chimney catching fire – an accident that seemed alarming, as the house is chiefly of wood, and the fire burnt for some time with great fury; my visitors, however, considering it a matter of no consequence, or rather as a convenient substitute for sweeping, our discourse proceeds uninterrupted by the roaring flames. Aghia, which has now about 500 families, is said to have been considerably more populous before it fell into the hands of Aly Pasha. It was then governed by a voivoda appointed by the Sultana, to whom its revenue is assigned; and it enjoyed, as well as several other places in this neighbourhood similarly protected, among which the principal are Thanatu, Karitza, and Rapsiani, all now in the hands of Aly Pasha, the same advantages as the towns in the southern part of Magnesia. The upper c l asses at Aghia live upon the produce of their corn-fields and vineyards, or the culture of silk, and the manufacture of stuffs made of silk, called fitilia, or of silk and cotton mixed, named aladja, and of cotton towels. Out of 100 workshops, some of which have two looms, the cotton towels employ twenty. The fitilia are about twenty-five feet long; those called kaftanlik for making kaftans rather longer. The width is two feet, which is the usual breadth of a Thessalian loom. The measures in use at Aghia for their stuffs are a rupi, which is the breadth of the hand including the thumb: eight rupia make an endizia. A weaver earns forty paras a day. Labourers in the vineyards and mulberry grounds, and in the fields of corn and kalambokki receive twenty-five paras, and in the summer forty with provision; in the plain of Larissa sixty.

Aghia had begun to share in the commerce of dyed cotton thread with Germany, by which Ambelakia and Rapsiani have arisen to eminence, but the interruption caused by the war between Russia and the Porte, which has so much injured those two towns, has at Aghia almost annihilated the traffic with Germany. Enjoying a better soil and richer territory than Ambelakia and Rapsiani, it would have had a great advantage over those places had it not been more exposed by its situation to Albanian extortion. It is now 22 years since Aly first entered it as Dervent Aga; but it was not till a few years ago that he bought the malikhiane or farm for life from the Porte. He has been greatly assisted in his avaricious projects by the factious spirit of the inhabitants. By alternately encouraging each of the parties into which the place is divided, and by readily listening to their mutual accusations, he derives profit from every new complaint, and renders his power more secure in this quarter. At present the town is divided between the parties of two brothers, Alexis and George. The latter had held the post of hodja-bashi, and having been regular in his half-yearly visits to Ioannina with the aladjak, or collective payments from the town, accompanied by a present from himself, he had enjoyed for many years the undisturbed possession of a great part of his private property, together with the chief municipal power. In 1807 Mukhtar Pasha coming into Thessaly in pursuit of the rebel Papa Evtimios, listened to the persuasions of Alexis, who finding all other modes insufficient, openly accused his brother of having been in league with an Albanian Bolu-bashi, who is the Dervent Aga's agent at Aghia, to favour the flight of the bishop's niece, who had run away with one of the deacons; and of having received a bribe to connive at the elopement. In consequence of this accusation, both brothers were sent for to Ioannina, and have not yet been allowed to return home, though they have made great pecuniary sacrifices, both to the Vezir and to Mukhtar Pasha, and though Aly has at length declared himself satisfied that George had no share in the elopement. George's son, who had been at Vienna for his education, had not been twelve days in Aghia before the opposite tarafi accused him of having taken upon himself to act as a Gherondas, and of having raised money in that capacity without authority. He was forthwith sent for to Ioannina, where he still remains. Besides the brothers, some other branches of the family, to the amount of twelve or fourteen, are now there. The heads of the other chief houses are in Germany, so that the wife of Kyr. Ghiorghi seems now to be considered the chief person at Aghia.

The Turks of Velestion

In the town [of Velestinon] there are about 250 Turkish families, but the Turkish houses are much more numerous: such of the remainder as are tenantable are occupied by Greeks of Agrafa, or by Vlakhi of Mount Pindus. The chief profit of the Turks is derived from their gardens and mills, a sort of property they prefer, as it gives a good return without much trouble. The Turkish houses are built amidst gardens, which extend also beyond the houses to a considerable distance in the plain, the stream which flows from the fountain anciently called Hypereia furnishing an abundant irrigation, as well as the means of working numerous mills. All the surrounding villagers bring their corn here to be ground, and supply themselves with vegetables from a weekly market on Fridays. The Turks who possess corn land depend upon the Greeks for its cultivation. The former supply the seed, and a house for the farmer, who furnishes cattle and implements of agriculture, and takes half the crop after the deduction of the dhekatia; sometimes every thing belongs to the landlord, and the farmer is only a labourer, who receives a third of the nett produce for his own wages and the daily labour he may employ. The lower classes of Turks are shoemakers, tailors, barbers, butchers, bakers, cooks, menial servants, and labourers in the gardens but not in the fields. The Varusi, or Greek quarter, which once contained as many families as the present Turkish, now consists for the greater part of ruins or uninhabited houses, and a part of its site is converted into gardens or cornfields. The decline of the Greeks has been caused, like that of the Turks, as much by their foolish contentions as by the oppression of the government. The *farias*, or *tarafia*, into which they were divided, persecuted one another, intriguing with the Beys for this purpose, and lodging complaints against their rivals in the Turkish Mekheme; while the Turks found their interest in fomenting these disputes, and at Larissa, each Bey patronized some one or other of the principal Greek families.

Velestino was long noted for the savage disposition of its Turkish inhabitants, and for its lawless government, and it would then have been impossible for a traveller to make such a journey in Thessaly as I have done. Affairs are now altered. The Turks still retain their barbarous manners and their hatred of Christians, but they are kept within bounds by the fear of Aly Pasha, whose authority is unquestioned here, though he has not yet introduced one of his pedicular bolubashis to complete the humiliation of these insolent Osmanlis. On the fall of the nizam djedid and the elevation of Mustafa Bairaktar, they flattered themselves that Aly's influence at the Porte was at an end, and that they could resist his encroachments in Thessaly: he soon however sent twenty of his Derventli horsemen from Aghia to quarter upon the town, and did not withdraw them until their expenses, with the addition of a present, had cost the community eighty purses. Since that lesson his mandates have met with no resistance, and according to the lively expression of the Greeks, a dirty buyurti from Ioannina half the size of one's hand is of more effect than a firhman of the Porte three feet in length. By means of these "impressions of the lion's paw" the people of Velestino are robbed of twenty purses every year, without being saved thereby from similar imposts from the Porte when required by the necessities of war, or other causes... The mukata is in the hands of Seid Aga of Armyro, who is now in prison at Ioannina on the pretence of his having insulted one of the Vezir's tatars, for which he will probably atone by a heavy fine before he is allowed to return home.

The Bishop and the Greeks of Farsala

Fersala is an archbishopric, depending immediately on the patriarch of Constantinople. The present prelate had previously been a kalogheros in the patriarchate; and after having been employed as exarch upon several ecclesiastical missions, has been unable to obtain any better preferment than a see, of which the annual revenue is about 2000 piastres, or 130*l.* sterling. He has lately been sent by the patriarch to Ioannina upon the subject of the union of the metropolitan bishoprics of Arta and Ioannina, which the Vezir has now effected by his influence at Constantinople, and probably with advantage to both sees. The bishop confirms the favourable opinion of the Greek hierarchy as to the general conduct of Aly towards the Church, and states that on his late mission the Pasha said to him, "I never injured your Church and never will." He complains more of his holy brother of Larissa, who, he says, in spite of the patriarch, has torn from him four of the best villages of the plain, leaving only twenty in the archbishopric. Having found ninety piastres a year a rent too burdensome for his slender income, he has lately endeavoured to repair the palace, but has been obliged to confine himself to the ex pence of a few boards to save himself from falling into the stable through the floor of the only apartment which he inhabits, and in which some sheets of paper now supply the place of glass in the window-frames, while a few rugs on the divan and floor are the only furniture. The Greek church is severely burdened at present by an imdat seferi, or extraordinary war-tax, which the Porte has lately imposed upon the clergy, leaving them to repay themselves from their flocks as they can. The bishop, though conversant upon general subjects in consequence of his long residence at Constantinople, is totally deficient in ancient literature and history, and was even unconscious that the modern name, from which he takes his title, is but slightly corrupted from that which the city bore anciently during a long succession of ages. He supposes inscribed marbles to indicate hidden treasures; and of all the ancient names in this country Thessaly and Phthia alone seem to be known to him. He might easily obtain a little more information by means of the work of Bishop Meletius.

The ignorance of the history of their country, which the Greeks so generally betray, arises from the total neglect of Hellenic literature among them after they have acquired what is taught at school, or what is sufficient to qualify those young men for the church who are intended for that profession. But in this respect they might perhaps retort upon more civilized nations, and ask: "How many of you, after having spent several years of your youth in deciphering a small portion of the poets, orators, and historians of Greece, have ever bestowed a thought upon them; or how many of that superior class among ye, who have so many advantages over us, have any knowledge of the history or geography of Greece. Such knowledge ought undoubtedly to interest those most nearly who are born and live in the country, and speak the ancient language little changed. Nor will these motives fail to produce corresponding effects when education has made greater progress. The Greeks will then easily take the lead of all the nations of Europe in a familiar knowledge of their ancient literature.

1813 The Rev. Thomas Smart Hughes

An Artistic German Baron Captured by Brigands

Baron Stackelberg, responsible for many of the engravings used to illustrate this book, had the unfortunate experience of being kidnapped by brigands in this region.

We had not been long resident in Athens before an event occurred which created very general sensations of anxiety and sorrow. A letter received by Baron Haller from his accomplished and amiable friend Baron Stackelberg, stated that the writer had been taken by pirates as he was crossing the Gulf of Volo; that his most beautiful drawings had been torn to pieces before his face, his clothes carried off, and himself hurried along with these savages in their detestable enterprises, who forced him to sleep in the open air, and at last displayed instruments of torture for the purpose of terrifying him into the promise of a larger ransom. This they set at 60,000 piastres, and dispatched a messenger with the baron's letter to Athens.

A consultation was immediately held at the house of the French consul; but as this enormous sum was not only too great to be raised, but to be resisted upon every principle of policy towards others as well as the captive himself, the case required great delicacy of management, and only one person was thought to possess the qualifications requisite to conduct it happily. This was an Armenian merchant settled in Athens, named Acob, whose information in the languages, manners, and customs of different nations was unbounded, and whose honesty was unsuspected. He was unfortunately absent upon commercial speculations in Breotia or Phocis, and not expected to return in less than a month: but this obstacle did not long remain. After it had been determined that 12,000 piasters should be offered to the banditti, and the sum was raised, Baron Haller took charge of it and set out in quest of the Armenian.

This faithful friend scarcely rested day or night till he found Acob, and proceeded with him towards the haunts of the banditti: but as no reward could induce any person of the neighbourhood to undertake the office of mediator, they resolved to venture at once into the retreat of the horde; and having by some scouts obtained a knowledge of the station, they advanced thither boldly to the great joy of the poor captive, who was become extremely feeble from the effects of bad food, bad air, and a fever brought on by his sufferings. The conference was opened by Acob with singular address; he represented himself as the captain of a privateer in those seas, assured the pirates that they were mistaken in supposing their prisoner to be a man of fortune, since he was merely an artist labouring for his bread, whose prospects they had already injured by the destruction of his drawings; that if they rejected the offers now made of 10,000 piasters, he should depart, satisfied with having done his duty: finally he represented to them that a Turkish man of war was on the coast, as really was the case, to the commander of which, if they continued obstinate, he should leave their punishment: but the robbers, though they were somewhat abashed by the eloquence, confidence, and tone of authority which he used, suffered him to depart without coming to any conclusion.

Firmness was now necessary: this Acob saw and persevered notwithstanding the pain it might give both to the prisoner and to Baron Haller: that generous man however, unable to bear the anxiety which he suffered on account of his friend, stepped forward and urged the captain of the gang by every entreaty to release the prisoner, and to accept himself as an hostage until the other should recover. This noble offer, though rejected, was made in perfect sincerity of heart: the risk was great

The pirates were irritated - in all probability they would torture their prisoner for the purpose of succeeding better in their terms of ransom – and if they should chance to be pursued by the Turkish frigate, they would inevitably put all their captives to death and throw them overboard.

The disappointed negotiators returned to sleep at the nearest village; where about midnight they were awakened by one of the banditti, who came to propose 20,000 piasters for the ransom, which he gradually reduced to 15,000 at the lowest sum. Acob however, conjecturing that they were in some alarm, remained steady to his former determination, which soon brought the chief himself to their lodging, where the bargain was at last concluded for 10,000 piasters, and an additional present of one thousand to the captain. A shake by the hand was the seal of this negotiation, as sacred and as valid as the sultan's firman.

Next morning Baron Haller proceeded to the place appointed by the robbers, and being seated, like all the rest, cross-legged upon a carpet, he counted out the money in their presence. Baron Stackelberg was then shaved by one of the gang, a ceremony which is never omitted, and given over to his friends. They were all pressed much to stay and partake of a roasted lamb about to be prepared, but were too desirous of quitting such company, to accept their profferred hospitality. The robbers then wished them a good journey and expressed their hopes of capturing them again at a future time and pocketing some more of their cash.

The account given of these wretches was curious. They were composed of outlaws and villains from every part of Greece, the very dregs of society in a country where humanity is neither generally admired nor practised. They were mostly Mussulmen, but with a very imperfect knowledge of their faith; and in the hour of danger they had recourse to all kinds of superstition, though when secure they indulged in the most horrid blasphemies. In their bark a light was always kept burning before a picture of the virgin, and in storms they vowed wax-tapers to St. Nicholas, the Neptune of modern Greece, for a church dedicated to that saint which they sometimes visited; and these vows were religiously performed. In the daytime they drew their bark ashore and covered it with rushes, making their excursions at night. With regard to any capture, if it were money, they divided it immediately among the gang; if goods which were portable, they put them up to sale amongst themselves. For this purpose poor Baron Stackelberg, who saw his trunks rifled and emptied, was obliged to tell them the prime cost of every article, which was disposed of to the highest bidder. When they came to his firman, though they could not read it, they kissed and applied it to their foreheads in token of submission to the Sultan.

So great is the terror caused by these villains that they are seldom resisted: the unfortunate vessels which fall in their way eventually submit at once, or run ashore if they happen to be near the land, when the crew endeavour to effect their escape. An occurrence of this kind took place during Baron Stackelberg's captivity: a vessel, rather than be taken, ran aground, and the unfortunate sailors climbed the rocks to avoid their pursuers; but an old man less active than the rest being shot at and wounded, was captured and carried back for the purpose of slavery. One of the miscreants who was foiled in his pursuit of the others, as if to cool his thirst for blood, seized a poor goat that was quietly grazing near him, and cutting its throat with his *ataghan*, hurled the bleeding carcass down the rocks.

Central Greece

This part of Greece was liberated from Turkish rule and incorporated into the new kingdom of Greece during the War of Independence. Nevertheless, the proximity of the Ottoman border, and the failures of the early Bavarian and national governments to establish the infrastructure of a modern society outside the towns ensured that much of it would remain a lawless area for some considerable time after that date.

The City of Salona (G. Holland)

Akarnanias

1670s George Wheler

The Arrival of the Pasha of the Morea at Lepanto

We came in a very ill time to see this place: for the next day, so soon as it was light, all the barques were seized upon, to bring over the Basha of the Morea; who had received orders to come hither, and to Saint Mauro, to burn all the the galliots, or small galleys of the pirates he should find there. But they stayed not to be so complemented by him. The whole town was in a consternation at his coming; none stirred abroad, none opened their shops or doors. However we had the opportunity to see his reception, without stirring out of our chamber, it overlooking the harbour. The whole of his train was near five hundred persons, of which fifty Sclavonians were his guard. He crossed over from Vostitza, a town of the Morea, opposite to Lepanto. Before him in a boat came kettle-drums, others playing upon hautboys, and another stringed instrument, played on by a Moor; between which we could conceive no manner of harmony. Before him also was carried upon a pole, two horses tails, the marks of his dignity.

At his arrival, the Port saluted him with five guns, and the Veivode, Caddi, and other chief officers of the town, came to the gate at his landing, to kiss his feet, and receive him with all the respect they were capable to give him. So soon as he was landed, he mounted on horseback, and was conducted to the Veivode's House; the rest accompanying him on foot. The next day he clapped the Emir in prison, instead of his brother, who had murdered one of the town a great while ago. But he came off again for a sum of money; which was all the Basha desired. The next day after he demanded fifty horses of the Turks, fifty of the Hebrews, and thirty of the Christians; these being the least part of the town.

1802-09 Colonel William Leake

The Burdens of Taxation

Another disadvantage of which the Prodhromites, in common with the other small villagers of Acarnania, complain is, that although surrounded with pasture, they are unable to have any flocks, which all belong to the Vezir and his sons, or to rich Turks, or to other persons who pay the Vezir for permission to feed their flocks in this part of the country, all which are in the care of Vlakhiotes, or of Albanians from Mount Pindus. But even this oppression, or that which prevents the industrious man from employing his means in the most advantageous manner, or from carrying the fruits of his labour to the best market, is less grievous than the direct taxes and extortions which often deprive him at one blow of his scanty earnings. The *kefaliatiko*, or *kharatj*, is 7 piastres for every male above ten years old, in which is included half a piastre for the expenses of the Proestos of Tragamesti, the chief town of the district, or of the persons whom he sends here to collect it. The *vostina*, which is paid to the Spahi, is a capitation tax of 60 paras for every married, and of 30 paras for every unmarried man... [T]he dues, as the taxes are denominated collectively, amount at Prodhromo to near 500 piastres a year for each family, a large part of which consists of the share of an arbitrary imposition laid upon the village by the Proestos of Tragamesti in acquittance of the demand which the Vezir makes upon Karlili, to defray the expense of troops, or journeys, or wars, or upon any other pretence, and for the amount of which he is supposed to be accountable to the Porte, but does not account to anyone. The Hodja-bashis assemble and divide the burthen among the different districts, according to their population. Each of them afterwards adds to the sum the expenses which he himself incurs, or pretends to have incurred, in journeys to attend the Vezir, or for entertaining and lodging Turks and soldiers, or for horses in the public service, or upon any other plausible pretext. The imposition upon the village being as arbitrary as that of the Vezir upon the district, the Proestos enriches himself quickly, unless he should happen to be a man of extraordinary humanity, of whom there cannot be many in a country where honour and honesty are so little encouraged. In the territory of the Vezir they are particularly rare; for it is his usual policy to appoint the worst men to be primates, that he may make them disgorge when they are full of plunder; after which he often allows them to begin their extortions anew. In the smaller villages where the chief is styled *protoghero*, or chief alderman, he arranges in like manner the mode of payment of the khrei among the families, and generally in the Vezir's territories, or at least in those where his authority is firmly established, one person is charged with this office, or at most two in the large towns, whereas, in the Elefthero-khoria of Greece, it is the common custom for all the primati, or arkhondes, to meet and allot the taxes. If there be jealousy among them, as frequently occurs, so much the better for the great body of contributors, unless, which too often happens, one party complains to the Turkish authorities, and probably bribes them for the sake of the delightful advantage of triumphing over some hated opponent, and of acting the Turk over his fellow Christians.

But the most dreadful of all evils to the Acarnanian peasant is the *konakia*, or lodgings which he is obliged to give to the Albanian soldiers, although it is only upon such extraordinary occasions as the present progress of the Vezir that small villages situated so far out of the route as Prodhromo feel the inconvenience in its highest degree by the actual presence of the detested palikaria. Musta Bey, of Konitza, who was quartered upon Makhala, after having been supplied with provision and forage for himself and 250 followers, insisted upon a present of 100 piastres at departure, but was contented with 45.

A Village Struck by Sickness

We are informed by the people of Podholovltza that an epidemic disorder now reigning in Karlili has lately carried off six persons in the village. We therefore cross to Guria, which is situated about the same distance below the ferry that Podholovltza is above it. Here I find that the *loimiki*, as they call the sickness, was much exaggerated at Podholovitza, in order to frighten us away from thence, and that it has been worse here, though in neither place does it appear to be of a very malignant nature; for though hardly a Greek house in this village out of 30 or 40 has escaped it, two or three persons only have died. It is said to begin with head-ache and fever; but if the patient is blooded, which is almost their only remedy, he generally recovers in fifteen days. There are a few Turkish families at Guria, and a little mosque without a minaret. Below Guria the river spreads over a large space, and has some sandy islands in it. It then takes a long bend to the left towards the extreme point of the hills which slope from Stamna into the plain. In the opening between this point and some heights towards the mouth of the river, appears the village of Magula, on a small eminence in the plain, and Palea Katuna at the foot of the hills to the right. Katokhi is hid by a projection of them.

Albanians and Turks Compared

Our Albanian escort consists partly of Mahometans and partly of Christians, who are all from the country near Berat and Kolonia. Since we got rid at Makhali of a bolubashi who had persuaded some of the Mussulmans that it was beneath their dignity to march before *ghiaurs*, we have had no difficulties with any of them, and have kept them in perfect good humour by presenting them with a sheep or two every evening for their supper. Unlike the lazy, proud Turk, or the poor Greek peasant often deprived of all energy by the effects of continued misery and oppression, these Albanians are remarkable for their indefatigable activity. Every commanding height near the road I find occupied by one or more of them, by the time I come in sight of it, and it seems to be an object of emulation who shall arrive first. They answer all questions upon the topography with remarkable intelligence and accuracy, and permission to look through my telescope is an ample reward.

Nothing can be more dissimilar than the Albanian manners and those of the Osmanlis, the most indolent and phlegmatic of human beings, unless when roused by some extraordinary excitement. In one respect, however, the two people accord, namely, the love of gaming, though it is forbidden by the religion of Mahomet. As the Albanian soldier seldom burthens himself with provisions, he commonly solaces himself at a halt upon the road with a pinch of snuff and a draught of water. On arriving at a village, the first thing they generally do is to form a party at cards with heaps of paras, while those who do not play look on. A young man, who particularly distinguishes himself by his activity, named Alius, informs me, that in his younger days, like many of the Albanian soldiers, he attended cattle in his native mountains, and that at Arza, a place on Mount Trebusin, two hours from Klisura to the north-eastward, five hours from Tepeleni, and eight from Premedi, he was often in the habit of finding ancient coins of silver and copper.

The Hardiness of the *Kleftes*

Two years ago the Vezir took a famous Vlakhiote captain of robbers, Katz-Andonio, one of the greatest of the Kleftic heroes, and the subject of many a song. He ordered him to name the persons from whom he had received encouragement and presents. Andonio very coolly named all the Vezir's enemies, including the Russians, with whom the Turks were then at war. The Vezir knew that the robber was rich, and offered to spare his life for a share of his wealth, but without any effect upon him, as he knew Aly too well to trust to his promises. The Vezir then ordered his legs to be broken, which was done in the most cruel manner, in the midst of a crowd of Turks, whom Andonio abused all the while, saying they would not dare stand so near him if his legs were still whole, and joking with a relative who was suffering the same torture close by.

Down On the Coast

After dining at the mill we descend quickly with the wind and stream for about four miles, when a calm ensues, followed by a heavy fall of rain with furious gusts of wind at intervals. Our boat having grounded at the mouth of the river, we are conveyed in *monoxyla* to the island of Petala, which in the middle is separated only from the main land by a narrow channel connecting two harbours, both of which are well sheltered by the island, but have in no part a depth of more than six feet. The river of Trikardho discharges itself into the northern harbour: in the southern the boat is lying which I had ordered from Mesolonghi to convey me to Tragamesti; but such is the violence of the gale, that although the wind is quite favourable, the boatmen will not venture even to pass through the narrow channel uniting the two bays, still less to proceed to Tragamesti. We are obliged, therefore, to submit to be devoured by the fleas in the hut of Hassan Aga, son of Yussuf Arapi, the Vezir's Hasnadar, who commands sixty Albanians placed on the island by the Vezir to prevent its occupation by the Kleftes, who were in the habit of making incursions from hence into the neighbouring country. Hassan treats us hospitably as the friends of his master, giving us fish and lamb for supper, and excellent Ithacan wine which he has obtained by levying contributions of it from the boats which put in here.

His hut, dignified with the name of a *kula* or tower, is twelve feet square within, and serves for every thing but a kitchen, which among Albanian soldiers is generally *sub dio*. His *palikaria* occupy two other huts of the same size, but formed only of heaps of stones covered with branches, in which they all assemble when the weather is bad: when fine, they repose on the lee-side of skreens made of branches supported upon rough posts, and which may easily be shifted according to the wind. The Aga's hut alone is tiled. The men consider themselves in luxury, having fish from the harbour for the trouble of catching it, and bread *gratis* from the villages. Hassan complains that in summer the air is unhealthy, and the winged insects very troublesome; but adds, that gnats, the worst of all, are seldom seen after June, the place being too dry for them.

Petala consists almost entirely of rugged rocks, having small intervals of soil which are covered as usual in such situations in the winter and spring with a luxuriant growth of herbage, and a great variety of succulent or aromatic shrubs. On the summit are some velani oaks, and wild olives, and on the western side of the island a few fields which were cultivated by the Ithacans until Aly Pasha occupied the island.

A series of low swampy islets borders the main coast opposite to Petala, extending from a narrow stripe of low land which separates the marsh of Trikardho from the sea to the heights which rise from the northern side of the mouth of the .Achelous over against Kurtzolari.

Mistaken for *Kleftes*

April 8. – This morning, reinforced by Kyr K's guard of armatoli from Vonitza, and with others from Balim Bey, we proceed, between forty and fifty strong, to Ai Vasili, a village in a lofty situation on a northern slope of the mountain of Pergandi: the ascent to which from Balim-bey is through thick woods of oak: the distance one hour and a half. It happened, that when the armatoli stationed at Ai Vaslli first perceived our advanced Albanians, the latter were observed to be without capots, which, the morning being hot and the ascent steep, they had thrown upon the horses: some were seen driving two or three lambs, which we had purchased for them; others by accident were setting a large dog to pursue the cattle, all which circumstances were considered characteristic of kleftes. Taking us for thieves, therefore, the *armatoli* turned out, to the number of sixty, and without further ceremony fired a volley at the foremost of our escort, who, supposing it possible that the thieves might have got possession of Ai Vasili in the night, proceeded to act as against an enemy. They divided and crept through the woods in very good Yager style upon the flanks of the supposed enemy; and the firing continued for some time before the two parties recognized one another: the situation of the place was exactly calculated to render the scene interesting and picturesque, and a few wounded trees were the only casualties.

273

Kleftes on the Road to Vonitza

After remaining at St. Basil during the mid-day hours we set out for Vonitza. The captain of armatoli, on taking leave, wishes me a ... white face, a compliment borrowed from the Turkish. He has lately lost a son, killed in battle with the robbers, and is himself still suffering from a slanting gun-shot wound through the breast. We descend the mountain through a beautiful scene of corn-fields situated amidst copses of bay and groves of handsome oaks, and having passed the elevated valley above-mentioned, re-enter the forest, which here consists entirely of oaks. We fall into the lower road ... a little above the ancient foundations on the hill of St. Elias. Having again passed these, we descend into the valley, cross it, and arrive at Vonitza...

In the middle of the wood I saw the body of a horse which had been shot last night by the robbers: the owner, a poor man of Vonitza, who was going into the woods to procure some lambs for ... Easter-Sunday, was also killed by them. The same party robbed some men going to Lefkadha, but these escaped with the loss of their baggage and of 500 piastres in money.

1835 J. L. Stephens

An Unintended Visit to a Wrecked Town

It is clear from this passage that much of the devastation caused by the War of Independence was not repaired for some time.

On the evening of the - February 1835, by a bright starlight, after a short ramble among the Ionian Islands, I sailed from Zante, in a beautiful cutter of about forty tons, for Padras... There was hardly a breath of air when we left the harbour, but a breath was enough to fill our little sail. The wind, though of gentlest, was fair; and as we crawled from under the lee of the island, in a short time it became a fine sailing breeze. We sat on the deck till a late hour, and turned in with every prospect of being at Padras in the morning. Before daylight, however, the wind chopped about, and set in dead ahead, and when I went on deck in the morning, it was blowing a hurricane. We had passed the point of Padras; the wind was driving down the Gulf of Corinth as if old Aeolus had determined on thwarting our purpose; and our little cutter, dancing like a gull upon the angry waters, was driven into the harbour of Missilonghi.

The town was full in sight, but at such a distance, and the waves were running so high, that we could not reach it with our small boat. A long flat extends several miles into the sea, making the harbour completely inaccessible except to small Greek caiques built expressly for such navigation. We remained on board all day; and the next morning, the gale still continuing, made signals to a fishing-boat to come off and take us ashore. In a short time she came alongside; we bade farewell to our captain - an Italian and a noble fellow, cradled, and, as he said, born to die on the Adriatic – and in a few minutes struck the soil of fallen but immortal Greece.

Our manner of striking it, however, was not such as to call forth any of the warm emotions struggling in the breast of the scholar, for we were literally stuck in the mud. We were yet four or five miles from the shore, and the water was so low that the fishing-boat, with the additional weight of four men and luggage, could not swim clear. Our boatmen were two long sinewy Greeks, with the red tarbouch, embroidered jacket, sash, and large trousers, and with their long poles set us through the water with prodigious force; but as soon as the boat struck, they jumped out, and, putting their brawny shoulders under her sides, heaved her through into better water, and then resumed their poles. In this way they propelled her two or three miles, working alternately with their poles and shoulders, until they got her into a channel, when they hoisted the sail, laid directly for the harbour, and drove upon the beach with canvass all firing.

During the late Greek revolution, Missilonghi was the great debarking-place of European adventurers; and, probably, among all the desperadoes who ever landed there, none were more destitute and in better condition to "go ahead" than I; for I had all that I was worth on my back. At one of the Ionian Islands I had lost my carpet bag, containing my note-book and every article of wearing apparel except the suit in which I stood. Every condition, however, has its advantages; mine put me above porters and custom-house officers; and while my companions were busy with these plagues of travellers, I paced with great satisfaction the shore of Greece, though I am obliged to .confess that this satisfaction was for reasons utterly disconnected with any recollections of her ancient glories. Business before pleasure: one of our first inquiries was for a breakfast. Perhaps, if we had seen a monument, or solitary column, or ruin of any kind, it would have inspired us to better things; but there was nothing, absolutely nothing, that could recall an image of the past. Besides, we did not expect to land at Missilonghi, and were not bound to be inspired at a place into which we were thrown by accident; and, more than all, a drizzling rain was penetrating to our very bones; we were wet and cold, and what can men do in the way of sentiment when their teeth are chattering?

The town stands upon a flat, marshy plain, which extends several miles along the shore. The whole was a mass of new made ruins - of houses demolished and black with smoke - the tokens of savage and desolating war. In front, and directly along the shore, was a long street of miserable one-storey shanties, run up since the destruction of the old town, and so near the shore that sometimes it is washed by the sea, and at the time of our landing it was wet and muddy from the rain. It was a cheerless place, and reminded me of Communipaw in bad weather. It had no connection with the ancient glory of Greece, no name or place on her historic page, and no hotel where we could get a breakfast; but one of the officers of the customs conducted us to a shantie filled with Bavarian soldiers drinking. There was a sort of second storey, accessible only by a ladder; and one end of this was partitioned off with boards, but had neither bench, table, nor any other article of housekeeping. We had been on and almost in the water since daylight, exposed to a keen wind and drizzling rain, and now, at eleven o'clock, could probably have eaten several chickens apiece: but nothing came amiss, and as we could not get chickens, we took eggs, which, for lack of any vessel to boil them in, were roasted. We placed a huge loaf of bread on the middle of the floor, and seated ourselves around it, spreading out so as to keep the eggs from rolling away, and each hewing off bread for himself. Fortunately, the Greeks have learned from their quondam Turkish masters the art of making coffee, and a cup of this eastern cordial kept our dry bread from choking us.

When we came out again, the aspect of matters was more cheerful; the long street was swarming with Greeks, many of them armed with pistols and yataghan, but miserably poor in appearance, and in such numbers that not half of them could find the shelter of a roof at night. We were accosted by one dressed in a hat and frock-coat, and who, in occasional visits to Corfu and Trieste, had picked up some Italian and French, and a suit of European clothes, and was rather looked up to by his untravelled countrymen. As a man of the world who had received civilities abroad, he seemed to consider it incumbent upon him to reciprocate at home and with the tacit consent of all around, he undertook to do the honours of Missilonghi.

If, as a Greek, he had any national pride about him, he was imposing upon himself a severe task; for all that he could do was to conduct us among ruins, and, as he went along, tell us the story of the bloody siege which had reduced the place to its present woeful state. For more than a year, under unparalleled hardships, its brave garrison resisted the combined strength of the

Turkish and Egyptian armies; and when all hope was gone, resolved to cut their way through the enemy, or die in the attempt. Many of the aged and sick, the wounded and the women, refused to join in the sortie, and preferred to shut themselves up in an old mill, with the desperate purpose of resisting until they should bring around them a large crowd of Turks, when they would blow all up together. An old invalid soldier seated himself in a mine under the Bastion Bozzaris (the ruins of which we saw), the mine being charged with thirty kegs of gunpowder; the last sacrament was administered by the bishop and priests to the whole population, and at a signal the besieged made their desperate sortie.

One body dashed through the Turkish ranks, and, with many women and children, gained the mountains; but the rest were driven back. Many of the women ran to the sea, and plunged in with their children; husbands stabbed their wives with their own hands to save them from the Turks, and the old soldier under the bastion set fire to the train, and the remnant of the heroic garrison buried themselves under the ruins of Missilonghi.

Among them were thirteen foreigners, of whom only one escaped. One of the most distinguished was Meyer, a young Swiss, who entered as a volunteer at the beginning of the revolution, became attached to a beautiful Missilonghiote girl, married her, and when the final sortie was made, his wife being sick, he remained with her, and was blown up with the others. A letter written a few days before his death, and brought away by one who escaped in the sortie, records the condition of the garrison, "A wound which I have received in my shoulder, while I am in daily expectation of one which will be my passport to eternity, has prevented me till now from bidding you a last adieu. We are reduced to feed upon the most disgusting animals. We are suffering horribly with hunger and thirst. Sickness adds much to the calamities which overwhelm us. Seventeen hundred and forty of our brothers are dead; more than a hundred thousand bombs and balls, thrown by the enemy, have destroyed our bastions and our homes. We have been terribly distressed by the cold, for we have suffered great want of food. Notwithstanding so many privations, it is a great and noble spectacle to behold the ardour and devotedness of the garrison. A few days more, and these brave men will be angelic spirits, who will accuse before God the indifference of Christendom. In the name of all our brave men, among whom are Notho Bozzaris, I announce to you the resolution sworn to before Heaven, to defend foot by foot the land of Missilonghi, and to bury ourselves, without listening to any capitulation, under the ruins of this city. We are nearing near our final hour. History will render us justice. I am proud to think that the blood of a Swiss, of a child of William Tell, is about to mingle with that of the heroes of Greece."

But Missilonghi is a subject of still greater interest than this, for the reader will remember it as the place where Byron died. Almost the first questions I asked were about the poet, and it added to the dreary interest which the place inspired, to listen to the manner in which the Greeks spoke of him. It might be thought that here, on the spot where he breathed his last, malignity would have held her accursed tongue; but it was not so. He had committed the fault, unpardonable in the eyes of political opponents, of attaching to one of the great parties that then divided Greece; and though he had given her all that man could give, in his own dying words, "his time, his means, his health, and lastly, his life," the Greeks spoke of him with all the rancour and bitterness of party spirit. Even death had not won oblivion for his political offences; and I heard those who saw him die in her cause affirm that Byron was no friend to Greece.

His body, the reader will remember, was transported to England, and interred in the family sepulchre. The church where it lay in state is a heap of ruins, and there is no stone or monument recording his death; but, wishing to see some memorial connected with his residence here, we followed our guide to the house in which he died. It was a large square building of stone; one of the walls still standing, black with smoke, the rest a confused and shapeless mass of ruins. After his death it was converted into an hospital and magazine; and when the Turks entered the city, they set fire to the powder; the sick and dying were blown into the air, and we saw the ruins lying as they fell after the explosion. It was a melancholy spectacle, but it seemed to have a sort of moral fitness with the life and fortunes of the poet. It was as if the same wild destiny, the same wreck of hopes and fortunes, that attended him through life, were hovering over his grave. Living and dead, his actions and his character have been the subject of obloquy and reproach, perhaps justly; but it would have softened the heart of his bitterest enemy to see the place in which he died…

Moving on beyond the range of ruined houses, though still within the line of crumbling walls, we came to a spot perhaps as interesting as any that Greece in her best days could show. It was the tomb of Marco Bozzaris! No monumental marble emblazoned his deeds and fame; a few round stones piled over his head, which, but for our guide, we should have passed without noticing, were all that marked his grave. I would not disturb a proper reverence for the past; time covers with its dim and twilight glories both distant scenes and the men who acted in them; but, to my mind, Miltiades was not more of a hero at Marathon, or Leonidas at Thermopylae, than Marco Bozzaris at Misssilonghi. When they went out against the hosts of Persia, Athens and Sparta were great and free, and they had the prospect of glory and the praise of men, to the Greeks always dearer than life. But when the Suliote chief drew his sword, his country lay bleeding at the feet of a giant, and all Europe condemned the Greek revolution as foolhardy and desperate. For two months, with but a few hundred men, protected only by a ditch and slight parapet of earth, he defended the town, where his body now rests, against the whole Egyptian army. In stormy weather, living upon bad and unwholesome bread, with no covering but his cloak, he passed his days and nights in constant vigil; in every assault his sword cut down the foremost assailant, and his voice, rising above the din of battle, struck terror into the hearts of the enemy. In the struggle which ended with his life, with 2000 men he proposed to attack the whole army of Mustapha Pacha, and called upon all who were willing to die for their country to stand forward. The whole band advanced to a man. Unwilling to sacrifice so many brave men in a death-struggle, he chose 300, the sacred number of the Spartan band, his tried and trusty Suliotes. At midnight he placed himself at their head, directing that not a shot should be fired till he sounded his bugle; and his last command was, "If you lose sight of me, seek me in the pacha's tent." In the moment of victory he ordered the pacha to be seized, and received a ball in the loins; his voice still rose above the din of battle, cheering his men until he was struck by another ball in the head, and borne dead from the field of his glory.

Not far from the grave of Bozzaris was a pyramid of skulls, of men who had fallen in the last attack upon the city, piled up near the blackened and battered wall , which they had died in defending. In my after wanderings I learned to look more carelessly upon these things; and, perhaps, noticing everywhere the light estimation put upon human life in the East, learned to think more lightly of it myself; but then it was melancholy to see bleaching in the sun, under the eyes of their countrymen, the unburied bones of men who, but a little while ago, stood with swords in their hands, and animated by the noble resolution to free their country or die in the attempt. Our guide told us that they had been collected in that place with a view to sepulture; and that King Otho, as soon as he became of age, and took the government in his own hands, intended to erect a monument over them. In the meantime, they are at the mercy of every passing traveller; and the only remark that our guide made was a comment upon the force and unerring precision of the blow of the Turkish sabre, almost every skull being laid open on the side nearly down to the ear.

Phocis

1599 Thomas Dallam

Dogged by Murderous Turks on Parnassos

The 14th we departed from Zetoun, and having rode six or seven miles, we began to climb the hills of Parnassus, where we had all maner of ill weather, as thundring, lightning, rain, and snow, and our way was so bad as I think never did Christians travel the like. The mountains were huge and steep, stony, and the ways very narrow, so that if a horse should have stumbled or slided, both horse and man had been in great danger of their lives.

Also we were dogged, or followed, by four stout villains that were Turks. They would have persuaded our dragoman, which was our guide, to have given his consent unto the cutting of our throats in the night, and he did very wisely conceal it from us, and delayed the time with them, not daring to deny their suite; and so they followed us four days over Parnassus; but our dragoman every night give us charge to keep good watch, especially this last night, for they did purpose to go no farther after us, and our Turk, whom I call our dragoman, had permitted them that that night it should be done. Now, after he had given us warning to keep good watch, he went unto them and made them drink so much wine, or put somthing in their wine, that they were not only drunk but also sick, that they were not able to attempt anything against us to hurt us, for the which we had very great cause to give hearty thanks unto Almyghty God, who was our cheifest safeguard.

This night we lay in a little village under a wonderful high rock. Though that country be continually cold, yet the women there never wear anything on their feet; they are very well favored, but their feet be black and broad.

This man that was sent with us to be our drugaman, or interpreter, was an Inglishe man, born in Chorlaye in Lancashier; his name Finche. He was also in religon a perfect Turk, but he was our trusty friend. The next day, being the 17th, we came to Lippanta where our Turk revealed all this unto us, and these men we had seen, but never more than one at once, and he never stayed long in our company, for he came but to speak with our Turk about their villanous plot.

c.1800 Mr. Raikes

A Climb to the Corycian Cave

March 19. I quitted the village of Aracova at half past seven the master of the cottage in which I had slept undertook to guide us to the Corycian cave, with the situation of which he appeared acquainted. We left the road to Castri which continued to run along the narrow valley between the two mountains, and turning to the right began to ascend the slope of Parnassus by a steep road immediately from the village. The declivity was cultivated with an industry worthy of Switzerland. Every spot of vegetable soil was covered with low vines; and I remarked one attention to the value of productive ground which "occurred no where else in Greece. The shallow soil was sometimes interrupted by great masses of rock which reared themselves above the surface, and the careful husbandman unwilling to lose the corner on which he must otherwise have heaped the loose stones gathered from the rest of the field, had raised them in pyramids on these masses...

The vineyards were soon passed, and the ascent became more and more steep, until, in an hour's time from Aracova, I was surprised by entering on a wide plain of considerable extent, and under cultivation; where I expected to see nothing but rocks and snow. High above this wide level the ridges of Parnassus rose on the north and east, covered with snow and hid in clouds. The plain before me could not be less than four or five miles across; a large dull looking village was placed in the middle of it; a lake, with banks most beautifully broken, was on my left... The ground would have afforded pasture for their cattle, and some proportion of food for themselves, and the ascent to it was so steep and narrow, that it must have been defended by a very few men. The view to the southward from this spot was extensive and very striking; the mountain Cirphis on the other side of the valley of Aracova terminated in a flat table land like the recess in Parnassus, well cultivated, and studded with villages; but the greater height of both these plains raised them above the regions of spring, which we had left below; vegetation had not yet begun to appear, and the snow lay in patches over both of them. Beyond, the mountains of the Morea filled up the distance.

We rode across the plain towards the north, and leaving our horses at the foot of the ascent which bounded it, climbed up a steep and bushy slope to the mouth of the Corycian cave. I had been so repeatedly disappointed with scenes of this kind, they had so generally appeared inferior to the descriptions given of them, that I expected to meet with the same reverse here, and to find nothing but a dark narrow vault. I was, however, to be for once agreeably surprised; the narrow and low entrance of the cave, spread at once into a chamber 330 feet long, by nearly 200 wide; the stalactites from the top hung in the most graceful forms, the whole length of the roof, and fell, like drapery, down the sides. The depth of the folds was so vast and the masses thus suspended in the air were so great, that the relief and fullness of these natural hangings, were as complete as the fancy could have wished. They were not like concretions or encrustations, mere coverings of the rock; they were the gradual growth of ages, disposed in the most simple and majestic forms, and so rich and large, as to accord with the size and loftiness of the cavern. The stalagmites below and on the sides of the chamber, were still more fantastic in their forms, than the pendants above, and struck the eye with the fancied resemblance of vast human figures.

At the end of this great vault, a narrow passage leads down a wet slope of rock; with some difficulty, from the slippery nature of the ground on which I trod, I went a considerable way on, until I came to a place where the descent grew very steep, and my light being nearly exhausted, it seemed best to return. The encrustation of the grotto had begun to appear; but it was unbroken, and I was interested in finding this simple relic of the homage once paid to the Corycian nymphs by the ancient inhabitants of the country. The stalagmitic formations on the entrance of this second passage, are wild as imagination can conceive, and of the most brilliant whiteness.

It would not require a fancy, lively, like that of the ancient Greeks, to assign this beautiful grotto, as a residence to the nymphs. The stillness which reigns through it, only broken by the gentle sound of the water, which drops from the point of the statalactites … the dim light admitted by its narrow entrance, and reflected by the white ribs of the roof, with all the miraculous decorations of the interior, would impress the most insensible with feelings of awe, and lead him to attribute the influence of the scene to the presence of some supernatural being.

An inscription, which still remains on a mass of rock, near the entrance, marks that the cavern has been dedicated to Pan and the Nymphs…

1852 Edward About

A Contented Abbot

The monastery of Osias Loukas was to be a frequent haven for travellers crossing Parnassos.

I passed a very agreeable day at the monastery of Loukos, near Astros; thanks to the loquacious hospitality of the Hegoumenos or superior. On our arrival he was occupied with having his hands kissed by three or four rustics of the neighbourhood; he slipped away from their homage to run up to us, to bid us welcome.

He was a man of about forty-five, very fresh, very vigorous, with a fine beard and a good figure. He offered us, on dismounting, some tobacco of his own growth in pipes or handiwork; then, whilst Garnier and Curzon were making a water-colour sketch of his church, he did the honours to us of the house and garden. The house was rickety, but the garden was in a good state. "Here are our hives," said he, we gather honey, and you will tell me what you think of it; the honey of Hymettus has the perfume of thyme, the honey of Carysto smells of roses, but ours has a decided taste of orange-flowers."

"I suppose," I replied, "that the honey of your bees does not make up all your income?"

"No; we have two mills, a few corn-fields, and two ploughs; the peasants keep them going. Our olive trees give the greater part of our wealth. In good years we sell as much as 10,000 okas of oil (about 25,000 lbs.) We have got a few flocks hard by - our shepherds live in tents."

Whilst we were visiting together some Roman ruins near the monastery, the sheep-dogs came near us with an evident intention of tasting our skin; the Hegoumenos, notwithstanding his dignity, picked up some stones and defended his guest.

At the end of a quarter of an hour's conversation he entered on politics, and that lasted for a long time. He took in the "Age," a newspaper of the Russian party, published at Athens, and which, during ten years, has sown intolerance in Greece and insubordination in Turkey. I had no difficulty in seeing that my reverend friend was devoted soul and body to Nicholas, and that he cared for King Otho as much as for the Emperor of China.

When politics were exhausted, I brought him by degrees to speak to me of the labours and troubles of his condition.

"We have," said he, "little to do. When the services are ended, and we have chanted all that is prescribed by the canons, and made all the signs of the cross ordered by the Church, our task is finished. I have got a good chest as you see, and I sing very well for two hours together without tiring. As for the signs of the cross, which is a rather more tiresome exercise, I am not one-handed, thank Heaven! My stomach is used to the necessary fasts; and besides, I compensate myself on other days."

This good man talked of his Church as a trader of his shop, and of his prayers as a mason would of his trowel. The church bell rung, the evening service was going to begin. I conducted my host to his business, and he chanted the evening service while our supper was being got ready.

We had hardly sat down when the whole monastery entered tumultuously, the Hegoumenos at the head. We had before us a public of fifteen monks, who wished to see how the Franks take their food. The youngest of the apprentices had a roguish air, which reminded us of Peblo. All these importunate and serviceable people overpowered us with presents. They poured out the honey of their bees, the milk of their goats, the olives of their orchards, the fresh and salt cheese of their sheep, a resinous wine which Garnier appreciated, and two or three kinds of muscat wine in bottles – all of their own growth. The Hegoumenos refused to partake of our dinner. He had dined in his own circle; but he gave us his company, and the evening passed off gaily.

"And what are your pleasures?" I asked him...

He insinuated that, first of all, he enjoyed the purest pleasure which God has given to man - that of doing nothing. He added, that I had only to look at my glass and my plate, to see two other sources, from which, from time to time, he drew some satisfaction. He ended by declaring, that he had ceased lamenting those pleasures which his condition forbids him, but that he had round the monastery some leagues of forest and mountain, where he could hunt, run, and subject his body by fatigue. "Come and see me next year," said he, "spring or autumn, whenever you have leisure. We will go out hunting together, we will empty some of those old bottles, and you shall see, my son, that the profession of monk is a profession for a king!"

"Amen!" said the audience; and we went to sleep.

The little monks had deprived themselves for us of their room, their bed, and even of their coverlets; the poor little devils passed the night under a shed in the pale star-light.

Next morning at daybreak, Lefteri came to wake us; the horses were ready. We wished to wait till morning service was over, to take leave of the Hegoumenos; but he came out of the church, without respect for canons, and all the monastery left their prayers to come and say good-bye to us.

The hospitality you meet with at the convents is gratuitous; only it is good taste to give a dollar to the little monks, who never refuse it, and to drop an offering into the church-box; they take care to show it you.

1898 Samuel J. Barrows

A Young Monk

The situation of the monastery is simply exquisite. It is built on a mountain slope overlooking a fertile valley. Green barley fields contrast with dark underbrush, and here and there a grove of olives; beyond are sloping foot-hills and grander mountains. The birds were singing blithely, the sun was radiant, and the whole landscape, a beautiful combination of curve and colour, seemed vivified by the germinating warmth of a May day. St. Luke's long held the titles of "The queen of the monasteries and the glory of Hellas." It is dedicated not to the good physician whose name is affixed to one of the Gospels, but to a later Greek saint who distinguished himself by his piety a thousand years ago and around whose tomb the monastery was built. It contains two churches. The larger one has suffered much from pillage, earthquake and decay, but some of the better mosaics are still well preserved. There are forty-five monks in the monastery and thirty labourers. From their olive groves and vineyards they derive a good income. I was interested in the church, in the ground, in the hegoumenos, or prior, in the beautiful scenery, but most of all in Basileios.

Basil, as we called him for short, was a boy of thirteen. He was dressed in a monk's gown, but his ecclesiastical hat was not so high as that of his elders; it will grow with the boy. He was a monk in the opening bud; but the bloom of the boy was more exquisite than that of the monk. His eyes were a soft brown, even more expressive than his tongue. Through them you could read his guileless mind. He spoke Greek not with Athenian purity, but with a soft, winning accent. At first he spoke only in a whisper, as if the sanctity of the place would be broken if he talked louder. But after he knew me better he spoke with more ardour, and sometimes faster than I could follow. He went about bare-footed, and I envied him his freedom from shoe-leather. As I had come too late for service I confessed my wanderings to my brave little acolyte and said the Lord's Prayer to him in Greek.

Basil is an important element in the refectory. The monastery is not conducted on the communal plan. The hegoumenos lives by himself and takes his meals with another monk in a separate dining-room. Basil does the cooking. The meat for our dinner was cut into little pieces and spitted on an iron rod with a crank on one end. The monk basted the meat as the boy turned it patiently on the spit. I had a room to myself and plenty of books, but I found it more interesting in the cool of the evening to sit in front of the fire and watch the revolutions of the spit, looking now and then into my little monk's deep eyes and trying to win his smile by some attempted pleasantry. Basil reminded me of the lame boy I saw at Gastouri radiant with sunshine. Such faces I should like to look upon in some cloudy day in my life, to rekindle my hope from a shining heart.

About eight o'clock we sat down to dinner, consisting of meat and vegetables, bread and wine. We were four at the table, the hegoumenos, the other priest, Panagiotes and myself. The priests crossed themselves and said b*on appetit*. The hegoumenos piled my plate high; as for the rest they took little on their plates, but each with his fork hooked a piece from the general dish. There was a suggestion of New Testament communism and the paschal meal when they took pieces of bread on their forks and dipped them into the central platter.

In the evening I had a talk with the hegoumenos and with Panagiotes sitting on the veranda in the moonlight and looking into the moonlit valley below. W e talked about the Greek Church and about the monasteries.

"To become a member of the Greek Church" said the hegoumenos, "you must accept the faith of the church according to the Gospel."

"What do you think of the old philosophers, Socrates and Plato and the rest of them ?" I asked.

"Did they go to punishment or to heaven?"

"I don't know," he answered. He did not seem to have any sharp belief on questions of eschatology, but Panagiotes promptly suggested: "I believe a man who has lived a good life here will have a good life there, and a man who has been bad here will be bad there." I could not discover any anxiety as to the fate of the heathen, and the prior seemed more disturbed at the proposition in Athens to raise from the monasteries a fund from which to pay the priests. The Greek Church is not a missionary church.

It was just four o'clock the next morning when I heard a voice whisper in my ear. It was Basil. I dislike alarm clocks and did not wind him up to go off at that hour, but he seemed to take the responsibility of my religious education, and in his small still voice said that there were services in the chapel, and that it was the festival of the Holy Trinity. It was rain, not the service, that interfered with an early start, but the rain fell as gently as if it were a part of the ritual, and far more musically than the voices that intoned it. By half-past seven the shower had passed, the sun came out bright, and a fresh breeze blew over the hills. I said good-by to the monks and to Basil and started back to Delphi with my guide and his mule. Sometimes I walked for an hour and let Panagiotes ride, and often going up the hill we both walked and gave the mule a rest. My respect for this sturdy Greek increased the more I knew him. He could speak no language but his own, but he could read and write that, for I made excuses for testing him in both ways. He was remarkably intelligent. He knew the drift of Greek politics and the Scylla and Charybdis of Greek finance. "You ought to have gone to Parliament," I said.

"No," he answered, "I have not the education;" but it was perfectly clear that he had the brains. He is not without honour in his own town; he has represented the modern Delphi in the nomarchy and been president of the council. As we rode through the village of Distomo I asked him what it meant that so many men were lying round doing nothing. He reminded me that it was the feast of the Trinity and immediately repeated a passage from the creed. I am convinced that the Greeks have too many holidays and that the church calendar might profitably be reduced about one half.

1870-80s John Pentland Mahaffy

Out of their Time

A few hours brought us to the neighbourhood of the sea [at Itea]. The most curious feature of this valley, as we saw it, was a long string of camels tied together, and led by a small and shabby donkey. Our mules and horses turned with astonishment to examine these animals, which have survived here only, though introduced by the Turks into many parts of Greece.

The Monastery of Osias Loukas

(Contemporary engraving)

Fthiotidos

1745 Richard Pococke

A Shock in the Night

"When I came to Zeitoun I went to the kane, and chose for coolness, and to be free from vermin, to lay in the gallery which leads to the rooms. In my first sleep I was awakened by a terrible noise, and leaping up found a great part of the kane fallen down, and the horses running out of the stable; I did not know what was the cause, but my servant immediately said it was an earthquake, so that we were in the utmost consternation; the front and greatest part of the kane was destroyed, and we got out with much difficulty. A Turk who lay on the bulk before the gate was covered in ruins, but was taken out alive, and not much hurt. It was a moon shiny night; but so many houses had fallen down, and such a dust was raised that we could not see the sky; the women were screaming for their children and relations who were buried in the ruins of the houses; some of them were taken out alive, but several were killed: and going to the churches the next day I saw many laid out in them in order to be buried, their houses being fallen down. I got my things removed to a dunghill in a place most clear from buildings, and I felt near twenty shocks in about two hours time, some of which were very great: the next day it rained, and I got into a shed, but the people advised me to leave it; and every thing was attended with the utmost of distress, nothing was to be got, nor could I have horses till the afternoon; and when I crossed the plain I was shewn cracks in the earth about six inches wide, which they said were made by the earthquake. This calamity chiefly affected the Christians, whose houses were built only of stone and earth, but not one of the houses of the Turks fell down, which were strongly built with mortar. I observed as I travelled that the earthquake had thrown down many of the neighbouring villages, but did no great damage on the other side of the hills, which bound this plain to the south.

1802-09 Colonel William Leake

Caught "Between a Rock and a Hard Place"

When the thieves intend to attack a village, they usually take up a commanding position near it, from whence they send a letter to the Hodja-bashi, beginning probably with "My dear President," and inviting him to come and settle accounts with them. His answer most commonly is flight, in which he is followed by the principal inhabitants; when the robbers, no longer fearing any resistance, enter the village, burn a few houses, massacre the cattle, and carry off some of the women and children who have not, had time to escape, making choice of those whose release promises the highest ransom. The consequence is, that the villages in the neighbourhood of the haunts of the robbers generally find themselves under the necessity of satisfying their demands, and keeping on good terms with them. This, on the other hand, subjects them to the vengeance of the Dervent Aga, who imprisons their primates at Ioannina, and sends Albanians to quarter upon them. The greater part of the armatoli employed against the thieves by the districts adjoining Mount Othrys, namely, Zituni, Kokus and Armyro, and the same may be said of every other part of Greece infested by robbers, have themselves followed the same trade. If they ... voluntarily make their submission, they are always favourably received at the time, although perhaps marked out for future destruction; and unless they have given particular reason to the Vezir to suspect them, they are then employed as derventlidhes. As many of them have brothers or cousins among the thieves, there is generally a secret correspondence between the two parties; and the best mode of attacking a village is often pointed out to the robbers by one of their opponents, who, entering a village for the ostensible purpose of watching the motions of the thieves, lodges in a particular house for the sole object of examining his host's property, and of devising the best mode of plundering him, He then informs the robbers when and where to lie in wait for their victim, whose pleas of inability to pay ransom are met by evidences of a perfect knowledge on the part of the robbers of all the particulars of his possessions, These instances of treachery were more common before the extension of Aly''s power, who, by obtaining the government of a large part of Greece, has greatly narrowed the field of Kleftic ingenuity, In such a mountainous country, however, and on the borders of the districts governed by him, it is impossible entirely to suppress the robbers, Nor is he perhaps very desirous of this result, Security and tranquillity might be in excess if the benefit of his own services as guardian of the roads and passes were not sufficiently manifest to the Porte. Whether it be with a secret view of this kind, or as stating a real fact, he admits his inability to reduce the Greek mountains by his own troops alone, or to keep them ill a state of tranquillity but with the assistance of the inhabitants themselves.

1809-10 Dr. Henry Holland

A Night in a Poor Village

... [W]e pursued our route towards Leuterochori, where we designed to pass the night; a village situate among the heights of Oeta, and in the line of the only practicable route across this mountain-chain. From Thermopylae we ... skirted for a mile or two along the foot of the high cliffs, which are extended westward from the Pass, to form the southern boundary of the valley; and then began our ascent of the chain of Oeta, by a route equally singular and interesting, but difficult and not free from danger. At first we followed a path winding upwards along a deep and thickly wooded recess in the mountains, through which a stream flowed towards the sea. Turning then to the right, and rapidly ascending for nearly an hour, we came to the very edge of the cliffs which overhang the valley; lofty, precipitous and rugged, yet clothed with a rich profusion of wood. The view from this point of the plains of the Sperchius, of the bay, and of the chain of Othrys, was extremely magnificent; and interesting, as the last we obtained of the region of Thessaly. We now turned southwards, into the interior of the mountains; our ascent was rapidly continued, and before long; we saw only the clouds of a stormy evening rolling around and beneath us, disclosing at intervals the outline of loftier summits, entirely covered with snow. There was something of dreary wildness in our approach to Leuterochori, which may not easily be forgotten. Night was coming on, and we were enveloped by thick fogs, which now concealed all the great mountain forms that surrounded us. From the elevated situation of the place, the cold was very severe; and rendered more so by the snow and sleet falling upon us. We found the village to consist of 80 or 100 miserable cottages, scattered here and there over the rugged surface of one of the heights, and constructed rudely of mud, and stones which are found on the spot. As we entered the place we saw forty or fifty people assembled by the light of a few tapers in a wretched hovel, which we found to be the church; engaged in some of the religious ceremonies of the Christmas season. The habitation, which our Tartar selected as one of the best in the village, was scarcely accessible on horseback, from the precipitous ledges of rock, under which, as a shelter, it had been erected. It consisted of a single apartment, with naked mud-walls, and a flooring of the naked earth; one end of the room occupied by horses, the other inhabited by two large families; with no other furniture than a few wooden and earthen vessels, and the straw-mats, and woollen coats, which they used for their nightly covering.

Á large fire was lighted in the middle of the apartment; and all these poor people crowded around it, with an eagerness which seemed to show that even this was a luxury they did not always obtain. There was an aspect of meagre wretchedness and of absolute privation about them which I have seldom seen equalled. Our arrival, and the ferocious manner in which our Turkish attendants broke into the house, produced at first much alarm; the eldest daughter of one of the families, who in another sphere of life, might have been a beauty, was hurried away into a neighbouring hovel; in the faces and manner of those who remained, there was silently expressed an habitual expectation of ill-usage, which it was painful to the mind to contemplate... Some little presents we made the children, reconciled these poor people to us; and they shewed themselves grateful, when we saved the master of the family from the savage treatment of one of the *sourudzes.* When the Turks left the house at night, to sleep in an adjoining habitation, they became more easy, and to alarm succeeded a sort of familiar curiosity, much akin to that which belongs to savage life. The young woman who had been concealed at our first entrance, now appeared again, and formed one in the group of gazers who surrounded us. We all slept together round the embers of the fire; an assembly of fifteen people, nït to speak of six or eight horses, which had their quarters at the other end of the apartment. Our bedding excited much surprise and admiration; and we could not persuade any of the family to retire to rest on their mats and capotes, before they had witnessed every part of the preparation for our own repose.

c.1850 Henry M. Baird

An Attack upon a Village

Before leaving Stylida in the morning, we took care to procure a couple of caiques, which were, during the course of the day, to drop down the Gulf as far as the hamlet of Achladi. There we were to meet them, and be carried over to the opposite coast of Euboea. We again fell into a common foot-path, now leading through thickets of tangled bushes, and now through fields of wheat and barley. The soil appeared exceedingly rich, but less cultivated than almost. any other portion of Greece – a circumstance doubtless, due to the extreme insecurity of the entire region, and the impotence of the government to ward off from the unfortunate inhabitants the miseries of rapine and devastation. At a small village named Echinus we stopped to examine the remains of old Greek walls of regular masonry, and lunched at the village of Rachi.

We turned in at the house of the Papas, where a mat was spread for us; and, while we ate, he regaled us with a detailed account of an extensive robbery committed here a week before. Early in the morning, one of the band, in disguise, had found his way into the village as a spy, and made sure that almost the whole male population was dispersed in the distant fields, too far away to learn of the attack until it was too late. On his return, the miscreants, who, to the number of fifty-five, had been prowling in the outskirts, being satisfied that the way was clear, entered Rachi at about nine o'clock am. The first direction of Semos, the captain of the band, was to seize all the fire-arms in the village, and to place the inmates of the fifty houses - women and children almost exclusively - in close confinement, while the robbers searched for all that was valuable and portable. Money, however, was what most moved their cupidity. The numerous silver coins forming the most showy part of the head-dress, and ornamenting the person of the women, were of course the first to be laid hold of. But the ruffians were not so easily satisfied; and, even after their search, they suspected that much property remained hidden. As in Turkey, the Greeks and other *rayahs* are accustomed to conceal their wealth from the rapacity of the Mussulman, under the garb of poverty, so has the unsettled condition of this border country compelled almost every peasant to use similar precautions, Every dollar that can be spared is added to the hoard concealed in some hole in the ground. The process resorted to by the robbers for discovering the whereabouts of these hidden repositories was a cruel, but, as we should judge, a pretty effectual one. A kettle full of oil was set on the fire. If the unfortunate woman, who protested that she was ignorant where her husband had hid his treasure, relented in view of the coming torture, she was not molested. But if she persisted in her obstinacy, or really did not know where it was, the scalding oil was poured upon her neck, breast, and body. Five or six were subjected to this inhuman treatment; others were merely beaten; and one, whom we saw, boasted that, though the ruffians stabbed her in several places, she had not betrayed her husband's trust.

Notwithstanding all this suffering, strange to say, but one person was murdered, and that was a man against whom one of the robbers, himself a native of the place, entertained a personal grudge. A young man, who happened to be in the village, succeeded in creeping off to one of the neighbouring hills, where he discharged his gun as a signal. The country people soon came to the rescue. The band were thus, after a stay of two hours, compelled to abandon the village, though they had not ransacked one half of the houses. The mustered peasants, with a few soldiers, pursued the robbers; but though, after journeying five hours beyond the Turkish line, they came up with them, they recovered only some of the heavier goods that were dropped in the flight.

Our host, the priest, complained with bitterness of his own misfortunes. He said that until lately he had been *ephemerius*, or curate of Xerochori, in Euboea; but he had been tempted to leave it, by the promise of a larger salary and a more healthy situation. Fortunately for himself, he was absent at the time of the inroad; but his wife, the *papadia*, was beaten and ill-used, like the rest of the women. The priest estimated his loss at three hundred and seventy-seven drachms, and that of the entire village, according to the schedule which the chief magistrate of the district had drawn up the day before our arrival, could not be less than twenty thousand drachms (about $3350). When we rose to take leave, the papas begged us to speak to his old parishioners about him, and let them know of his misfortune. We fulfilled the commission, a couple of days after, at Xerochori.

Boeotia

1745 Richard Pococke

A Lake with Underground Connections

The plain in which the lake of Topolia lies seems to be about twelve miles long and six broad, that is, between thirty and forty miles in circumference... the reason why it is called at present a marsh rather than a lake, is, that in summer the water does not appear, all being overgrown with reeds, though it always has water and fish in it. There are several pools about the plain, which probably have a communication one with another, and in winter the water rises very much; all over it there are dry spots, which are improved, and also some villages; it is very observable in this lake, that though the Cephissus, and many streams fall into it, yet there are only subterraneous passages out of it, which are said to be sixty, and are seen about Topolia. Strabo mentions a subterraneous passage from it to Lake Hylica, it was a lake some distance to the north of Thebes, being about six miles over every way: it is probable that these lakes and morassy grounds had such influence on the air of Boeotia, as to affect the intellectual faculties of the inhabitants of this country, insomuch that a Boeotian genius for dullness became a proverb of reproach.

The Ruins of Thebes (E. Dodwell, 1834)

1740s Lord Charlemont

Stories about the Ancient Walls of Thebes

Part of the walls still remain of a construction which vouches their antiquity, together with two gates, both of them undoubtedly ancient. The one is arched, and considerable in its dimensions. The other is smaller, but of excellent workmanship, in style resembling the more ancient architecture of Delos. The inhabitants also have a tradition current among them that their town has been remarkable for a certain number of gates, which they mistaking for five, call it Pentapyli. Numberless ancient marbles bespeak the site of a magnificent city. Broken columns, capitals, and ancient inscriptions are everywhere to be met with. The impression made by the destruction of Thebes under Alexander is not yet effaced. The inhabitants still traditionally speak of it, telling a silly story of this Prince, who, as they pretend, caused the vanquished Thebans to be collected together in a small village about one hundred yards from the town, and there to be consumed by fire, from which supposed event the village is at this day called Pyra. They show the mounds of earth which were raised by Alexander for the assault, three of which, say they , were raised in one night; and indeed some traces evidently remain of this memorable siege, trenches and other marks of attack being clearly discernible on every side of the town.

Another whimsical tradition is current among the Thebans. They tell you that Alexander, in order that no trace should remain of Thebes, after demolishing that city, caused the stones, with which it had been built, to be transported by his soldiers to the sea. This however could scarcely have been accomplished unless Alexander had had in his army such a harper as Amphion.

1801 The Rev. Edward Daniel Clarke

Dinner with a Greek Archon in Livadia

We were conducted to the house of a rich Greek merchant, of the name of Logotheti, the archon or chief of Lebadea, a subject of the Grand Signior, since well known to other English travellers for his hospitality and kind offices.

His brother had been beheaded for his wealth, two years before, in Constantinople. In the house of this gentleman we had an opportunity of observing the genuine manners of the higher class of modern Greeks, unadulterated by the introduction of any foreign customs, or by a frequent intercourse with the inhabitants of other countries. They seemed to us much as they are said to have been in the time of Plato, and, in many respects, barbarous and disgusting. Their dinners, and indeed all their other meals, are wretched. Fowls boiled to rags, but still tough and stringy, and killed only an hour before they are dressed, constitute a principal dish, all heaped together upon a large copper or pewter salver, placed upon a low stool, round which the guests sit upon cushions; the place of honour being on that side where the long couch of the divan extends beneath the white-washed wall. A long and coarse towel, very ill washed, about twelve inches wide, is spread around the table, in one entire piece, over the knees of the party seated. Wine is only placed before strangers; the rest of the company receiving only a glass each of very bad wine with the dessert. Brandy is handed about before sitting down to table. All persons who partake of the meal, wash their hands in the room, both before and after eating. A girl with naked and dirty feet, enters the apartment, throwing to every one a napkin: she is followed by a second damsel, who goes to every guest, and, kneeling before him upon one knee, presents a pewter water-pot and a pewter bason, covered by a grillle, upon the top of which there is a piece of soap. An exhibition rather of a revolting nature, however cleanly, then succeeds. Having made a lather with the soap, they fill their mouths with it, and squirt it, mixed with saliva, into the bason. The ladies of the family also do the same; lathering their lips and teeth; and displaying their arms, during the operation of the washing, with studied attitudes, and a great deal of affectation; as if taught to consider the moments of ablution as a time when they may appear to most advantage. Then the master of the house takes his seat at the circular tray, his wife sitting by his side; and stripping his arms quite bare, by turning back the sleeves of his tunic towards his shoulders, he serves out the soup and the meat. Only one dish is placed upon the table at the same time. If it contain butchers' meat or poultry, he tears it into pieces with his fingers. During meals, the meat is always torn with the fingers. Knives and spoons are little used, and they are never changed. When meat or fish is brought in, the host squeezes a lemon over the dish. The room àll this while is filled with girls belonging to the house, and other menial attendants, all with their feet naked; also a mixed company of priests, physicians, and strangers, visiting the family. All these persons are admitted upon the raised part of the floor or divan: below the divan, near the door, are collected meaner dependants, peasants, old women, and slaves, who are allowed to sit there upon the floor, and to converse together. A certain inexpressible article of household furniture, called chaise percee by the French, is also seen, making a conspicuous and most disgusting appearance, in the room where the dinner is served; but in the houses of rich Greeks it is possible that such an exhibition may be owing to the vanity of possessing goods of foreign manufacture: the poorer class, whether from a regard to decorum, or wanting the means of thus violating it, are more decent.

The dinner being over, presently enters the *rhapsodos*, or Homer of his day, an itinerant songster, with his lyre, which he rests upon one knee, and plays like a fiddle. He does not ask to come in, but boldly forces his way through the crowd collected about the door; and assuming an air of consequence, steps upon the divan, taking a conspicuous seat among the higher class of visitants; there striking his lyre, and elevating his countenance towards the ceiling, he begins a most dismal recitative, accompanying his voice, which is only heard at intervals, with tones not less dismal, produced by the scraping of his three-stringed instrument. The recitative is some-times extemporaneous, and consists of sayings suited to the occasion; but in general it is a doleful love-ditty, composed of a string of short sentences expressing amorous lamentation, rising to a sort of climax, and then beginning over again; being equally destitute of melodious cadence, or of any animated expression.... the tone of the vocal part resembled rather that of the howling of dogs in the night, than any sound which might be called musical. And this was the impression always made upon us by the national music of the modern Greeks; that if a scale were formed for comparing it with the state of music in other European countries, it would fall below all the rest, excepting that of the Laplanders, to which, nevertheless, it bears some resemblance.

When the meal is over, a girl sweeps the carpet; and the guests are then marshalled, with the utmost attention to laws of precedence, in regular order upon the divan; the master and mistress of the house being seated at the upper end of the couch, and the rest of the party forming two lines, one on either side; each person being stationed according to his rank. The couches upon the divans of all apartments in the Levant being universally placed in the form of a Greek *n*, [i.e. *v*]the manner in which a company is scaled is invariably the same in every house. It does not vary, from the interior of the apartments in the Sultan's seraglio, to those of the meanest subjects in his dominions; the difference consisting only in the covering for the couches, and the decorations of the floor, walls, and windows.

After this arrangement has taken place, and every one is seated cross-legged, the pewter bason and ewer are brought out again; and again begins the same ceremony of ablution, with the same lathering and squirting. from all the mouths that have been fed. After this, tobacco-pipes are introduced; but even this part of the ceremony is not without its etiquette; for we having declined to use the pipes offered to us, they were not handed to the persons who sat next to us in the order observed, although the tobacco in them were already kindled, but taken out of the apartment; others of an inferior quality being substituted in lieu of them, to be offered to the persons seated below us. There are no people more inflated with a contemptible and vulgar pride than the Turks; and the Greeks who are the most servile imitators of their superiors, have borrowed many of these customs from their lords.

Costly furs are much esteemed by both, as ornaments of male and female attire; that is to say. if they be literally costly; as the finest fur that ever was seen would lose all its beauty in their eyes if it should become cheap. Their dresses are only esteemed in proportion to the sum of money they cost; changes depending upon what is called fashion being unknown among them. The cap of the infant of Logotheti consisted of a mass of pearls, so strung as to cover the head; and it was fringed with sequins, and other gold coin, among which we noticed some medals of the latest Christian Emperors, and Ecclesiastical coins. The dress worn by his wife was either of green velvet or of green satin, laden with a coarse and very heavy gold lace; the shoulders and back being otherwise ornamented with grey squirrel's fur.

There is yet another curious instance of their scrupulous attention to every possible distinction of precedency. The slippers of the superior guests are placed upon the step of the divan: those of lower rank, of the unfortunate, or dependant, are not allowed this honour; they are left below the divan, upon the lower part of the floor of the apartment, nearer to the door. At about the time that the tobacco-pipes are brought in, female visitants arrive to pay their respects to the mistress of the house, who, upon their coming, rises, and retires with the women present, to receive her guests in another apartment.

1813 Thomas Hughes

The Pleasures and Pains of the Road

I determined therefore to purssue my journey, and to fortify myself, imprudently took a strong dose of bark. We had less trouble in procuring horses than we had at Athens; for Mahomet here commenced the exercise of his authority, since the eagle of Epirus had stretched his wings from the mountains of Illyricum to the very confines of Attica: an Albanian tatar therefore was absolute in this part of the country.

We departed by the road which probably once ran through the gate Homoloides, near the temples of Jupiter and Ceres. The morning being uncommonly fine, and the sun glowing brilliantly, I at first felt refreshed and elated by inhaling the pure atmosphere and surveying the magnificent landscape which charms the eye during the first hour's ride from Thebes; Cithaeron, Helicon, and Parnassus forming the grand boundary of the horizon. These mighty and majestic features of nature, early impressed on the soul of man, when Greece was free, became as it were creating powers in the poetic talent which they excited: they themselves in return were celebrated by the genius which they had produced, whilst their groves and foothills were made the abode of those Graces and Muses to which they had given a fanciful existence...

Their lofty summits were now glittering in the resplendent garb of winter, though summer seemed still to linger on their verdant sides and bases.

In about two hours, passing through a defile, in some low hills, supposed to have been the station of the Sphinx, we entered upon the great plain of Topolias, and came in sight of the distant lake Copais on our right. Here we saw large flocks of bustards, a bird which amidst all the changes of human affairs seems to have kept undisturbed possession of this country since the days of Pausanias: they fled from us with great velocity, and though some of the party followed them at full gallop, they were unable to obtain a shot.

Soon afterwards I had a pleasant meeting with an old college friend, journeying towards Athens, from whom we received correct information of Buonaparte's great reverses; when those hopes of the liberation of Europe burst upon our minds which were soon to be so gloriously realized. Though I was at this time suffering great tortures, the incident relieved me by that powerful action which the mind seems sometimes to possess over the bodily frame: but when this excitement had subsided, my sufferings became so intense that I could with great difficulty sit on horseback: Messrs. Parker and Cockerell therefore kindly rode forward with the tatar to procure a lodging and the immediate attendance of the physician. When they had left us about an hour, we arrived in sight of a narrow defile, formed by a lofty mountain on the left hand and some low ridges extending into the plain on the right: as we approached this pass, the shrill signal sound of whistles echoed over the whole mountain and continued, with short intervals, during our progress. The suradgees in evident alarm exclaimed, "that the kleftes, or robbers, were at hand, and that we should all be murdered in the pass." The General, ignorant how these freebooters carry on operations, derided the intelligence and ordered us to prepare our firearms: but he replaced his pistols in their holsters when he learned that the banditti always fire from the shelter of the rocks, and that the best chance of safety lies in making the least show of resistance. Our pulses did not beat slower as we advanced toward the fatal gap. The General confessed that his sensations were much more unpleasant than when he first entered a field of battle: Antonietti cursed bitterly the villainous Greek, of whose character he had imbibed the utmost abhorrence, and bewailed the fate of his wife and family; the suradgees devoutly crossed themselves and vowed waxen tapers to a long list of interposing saints; the orderly sergeant stuck close to his officer without uttering a word; whilst I, writhing with pain, was almost careless of the event like a person sea-sick in a storm: at length we arrived at the terrific defile, the signal sounds became more shrill; we entered the narrow passage, put our beasts of burden on that side whence we expected the volley, marched on in solemn silence, and cleared it without a sound being uttered or a shot discharged. I can only account for this escape, from the circumstance of that part of the gang being absent whose station was at the pass.

The agony I endured now became so violent, that but, for the indefatigable exertions of the faithful Antonietti I must have lain this night upon the bare ground, to which I fell several times from my horse: yet even in these circumstances it was impossible to hear unmoved the novel and compassionate exhortations of the poor Greek suradgees, bidding me "take heart" in the words of a language that brought the picture of ancient times so strongly to imagination. Late in the evening we arrived at Livadia, where we found excellent accommodations, and the doctor in attendance.

This gentleman, a Cephalonian by birth, was much more intelligent than the ignorant person I had employed at Athens, and to whose injudicious treatment, restricting me to a very low diet after the fever had departed, this relapse was to be attributed. Livadia, from its situation upon the river Hercyna, is extremely subject to intermittent fevers, and on this account a good physician was a matter of primary importance: the present one was established there at an annual salary of 3000 piasters, or about one hundred and fifty pounds, for which he gave advice *gratis* to the poorer inhabitants.

An Unlucky General

Whilst our two friends were thus employed [seeing the archaeological sites], the General having no taste for antiquities, stayed at home. Here he had leisure to revolve in his mind the various indignities to which a British officer of high rank may be subjected on a Grecian tour; for having neglected to provide an English saddle and bridle, he was obliged to make use of those poor accoutrements which the country afforded; so that hitherto he had performed his journey upon a kind of hard wooden pack-saddle somewhat similar to that over which a baker's panniers in our own country are balanced; his feet were confined in stirrups similar in shape to large fire-shovels, the shortness of whose straps brought his knees nearly into contact with his chin, whilst a common rope-halter tied over the nose of his Rozinante left the choice of road very much to the discretion of the beast: add to this, that he was usually accommodated with the sorriest animal in the set, since he took the worst possible method of conciliating the tartar in the frequent ebullitions of an Hibernian temper, for which a Turk cannot be expected to make allowance: indeed it is scarcely possible to find a more independent high-minded set of men than these Ottoman couriers: faithful and devoted to their employers, ready to undergo any fatigue or encounter any danger in their service, whilst treated with civility, they are proportionably haughty and resentful if exposed to disdain or disrespect; and as the general was not included in the bouyourdee of the vizir, he was quite at the mercy of our conductor. This soon became manifest when he made known his determination of quitting the party and proceeding alone to the gulf of Salona, where a gun-boat was stationed under his orders: not a post-horse or a suradgee could be obtained ; nor could a guide be found who would venture to incur the displeasure of Ali Pasha's tartar. The General however persisting in his resolution to depart, even though he should march on foot, I exerted all my influence with Mahomet for an escort; which being at length involuntarily enough conceded, both master and man, though totally unacquainted with the country and ignorant of the language, set out with a determination of proceeding to Joannina and demanding the tatar's head from his master! The event however may afford a melancholy subject for the moralist: in three short weeks from this time we heard the cannon of Santa Maura firing over the General's own corpse!

A Soldier Bastinadoed in Livadia

From the mansion of the archon I proceeded towards the spot where the cavern of Trophonius is supposed to have existed... In passing ... near the gate of the serai, we saw an Albanian soldier undergoing the bastinado: the culprit being thrown flat upon his back in the street, his feet and legs were raised by a long pole, to the middle of which a cord was attached and tied round his ankles. 1,\"1) II\('\\ ~tuo(1 at each end of this pole, holding up his feet to receive the punishment,which two others inflicted with sticks of moderate size, beating alternately upon the sole of each foot. As the discipline was not intended to be very severe, his shoes were not taken off, nor were the blows laid on with a heavy hand; notwithstanding this he made outrageous cries, articulating the monosyllable boo, boo, boo, with astonishing rapidity: this affecting appeal however did not move a muscle in the face of the baloukbashee, who sat upon a large stone inspecting the operation and smoking his pipe with perfect indifference.

c. 1815 H. W. Williams

In the Home of a Wealthy Greek

Here we live with a Greek of high rank and authority, a gentleman in his manners, speaking Italian and French with ease and fluency. His house, for Greece, is rather handsome; nevertheless, I must confess, we find many things at variance with each other.

At dinner, we found a table with a cloth upon it, dirty and disgusting, and darned in a thousand places. A miserable rusty knife and fork were placed for each person. Before dinner the Archon washed his hands in our presence, the boy kneeling who held the ewer. His daughters and two Greek gentlemen dined with us. The eldest girl was about sixteen years of age, the youngest eight. Dinner came in dish after dish, and consisted of boiled rice and goat milk, with new cheese, lamb's-head, and paste in the shape of pancakes, kids bones stewed with onions, paste containing minced meat, and rice rolled in spinage, roast ribs of miserable lamb, and other parts of the animal laid together, liver, lights, and windpipe; eggs dyed and boiled hard.

During the whole time of dinner we had the same knife and fork, which were never wiped. Our Greek friends, men and girls, dispensed entirely with that convenience. The little miss ate enor mously, and took abundance of oil to her food. Her sister sitting squat on the divan or sofa, stretched over the table, and put the spoon with which she ate into every dish, licked it, and rolled the cheese about upon her palate, shewing it occasionally on the tip of her tongue, and looking as stupid and vacant as an idiot. Sometimes, too, she would put her hand into a dish and take out a bone, which she would gnaw without ceremony; the men did the same. All this:, no doubt, was perfectly compatible with Grecian politeness and good breeding. I only presume to observe, that it appeared a little odd to our British eyes and ears; our love at home for ease and freedom not being yet advanced so far. The servants retired backwards, and always left their slippers in the passage, which, by their constantly putting off and on, made a tiresome shuffling noise. When the servants were spoken to, it was generally in a low and whispering tone...

After dinner, a boy came with a porcelain basin and ewer, when each person washed his hands over the same basin, the boy kneeling and pouring water over them, and the water passing under a perforated cover. The young lady placed the basin before her, washed and scrubbed a considerable time, and used the same towel which the men had used! Pipes and coffee were presented immediately after dinner: strangers came in and joined in smoking, at which many were expert, returning the smoke they received in their mouths through their nostrils in puffs and suffocating streams: at this time there was little conversaiion.

In this predicament, there was nothing left for me but to look about, and knowing your insatiable curiosity, I shall attempt to describe the dining-room of the noble Greek. It is spacious, 80 feet at least in length, by 20 feet in breadth, surrounded by a sofa, covered with ornamented silk, very clean and safe to sit upon. The planks of the floor, are planed, and partly covered with a mat. The curtains are of white muslin, but wofully darned in the coarsest manner. In addition to the windows, which may be about the general height of those in England, there is a small oval opening over each, filled with a pane of glass, and the same are on the opposite side, and at the end, for the purpose of throwing a borrowed light into the adjoining rooms; so that the dining-room may be considered a reservoir of light. Then there hangs from the roof, which is impannelled with wood, a chandelier from a rich bouquet of flowers; the walls are also coated and..fancifully adorned with various carving, but not, as you may believe, in the purest taste. A mirror is hung at each comer. A few miserable chairs are placed for foreigners, and a table that may dine to the number of from eight to ten. No paintings, nor even prints of monks and devils.

In the evening we had cards, and three fat ladies made their appearance, and squatted on the sofa, their faces so much muffled up, that we could only see their eyes; how they contrived to breathe I do not know. When they moved, they rolled as it were from place to place, never spoke, nor were they spoken to. The ladies here seem ignorant and stupid. What a contrast to our charming women at home!

While we were engaged at cards, the servants came into the room (to the very boy who kneeled to us) to see the gentlemen play; even our own servant came and played a wretched tune upon the flute, to the great delight of all the party.

In the morning the girls innocently peeped in at the windows to see us dress, and absolutely came into the room while we were shaving. We breakfasted by ourselves, and the young ladies and female servants stood at the table to see us take our tea. I presume they had never seen a tea-pot before, as they were constantly examining it. We begged the girls to sit with us, hut they declined, nor would they taste our tea, on account of the milk which we put into it, this day being the beginning of their fast of forty days; they, however, received some in a paper, which they said they would take at some future time.

The Bridge of Livadia (William Walker, 1819)

1838 William Mure

Some Characters Observed in a Khan

At the outskirts of the town, by the road side as one enters, is the best - the only tolerable specimen of a khan it was my lot to meet with in Greece; a most fortunate circumstance for me, having been, as will appear, under the necessity of halting four whole days at this stage of my journey. As I found this establishment, its construction, and the humours of its inmates, a source of much entertainment, and a great means of enlivening the period of my durance within its walls, I shall venture here shortly to describe it. It is probably a very tolerable specimen, in point of structure, of thc better class of old Turkish khans, as represented in the descriptions and drawings of travellers in Turkey proper, or in Greece during the Turkish period... The building forms a quadrangle, enclosing a spacious open court, with a fountain-well in the centre. The gateway or entrance is in the middle of the front facing the road. This side, and each of the two contiguous, have an upper floor appronched by a wooden staircase or ladder, with a double flight of steps, constructed in the centre of the principal side of the building, in a position within the quadrangle corresponding to that of the gateway of entry from without. The ground floor of the same side of the square comprised the shop and dwelling of the khanjee, together with the accommodation for the agoghiates, and such other persons of the meaner class as may not desire separate quarters. The opposite side, which alone of the three had no upper story, was stable and cow-house. The ground-floor of the two flanks seemed to be chiefly used as magazines for farm produce, or goods in general. The staircase led up to an open gallery or portico of wood, running round the three principal sides of the court, and giving entrance to the various apartments of the upper flour. The two flanks, here as below, were for the must part granaries or storehouses. The front towards the street was subdivided into a row of small square rooms, or rather wooden boxes, the private apartments destined for the accommodation of the better class of guests, each with its separate door opening on the gallery, its windows - if a small square aperture in the wall, unglazed, with a wooden shutter, can deserve the name - and its alcove-formed fireplace, with projecting hearth... They had also their ceiling, or upper flooring of wooden boards, hiding the roof, but not protecting the space it covered from the rain, to which here, as elsewhere, the roof itself was so constructed as to allow a greater or less freedom or passage..

This four days' durance was also not without its value, as affording opporunity of some additional insight into the character and habits of the modern Hellenes, as exemplified in the persons of my fellow lodgers. Four of the small private apartments were occupied, besides my own; one by a leech merchant from Athens, who spoke bad though intelligible Italian, and was more civilized in appearance and manner than the other guests. He complained bitterly of the wet weather, which by raising the waters of the lake to an unusual height, prevented his fishermen from pursuing their comfortless avocation, and suspended his own business. The animals are caught by country people in his employ, who wade with bare feet and legs into the water, and seize them as they fasten on their skin. Another room was occupied by a couple of Argive cotton merchants, of rude demeanour, and uncouth ponderous persons, enveloped in a vast quantity of coarse white woollen drapery. A third was the quarter of two Albanian veterans, belonging to a party of irregular light infantry stationed in the town. These troops are distributed in detachments through the different provinces, as a sort of moveable armed police, liable to be called out to pursue brigands, or otherwise support the civil authorities or the regular gendarmerie. But from any thing I could learn or see, I was not led to form a high opinion of the value of their services; and their employment seemed generally to be considered as little better than an expedient to prevent them from relapsing into those habits of predatory life from which they had, most of them, been previously reclaimed. They were, like others of their cloth whom I happened to meet., wild, ferocious-looking fellows, and offensively dirty, in spite of their beautiful though soiled and greasy uniform, of native fashion but Bavarian colours, white and blue. Nicola was very amusing on the subject of his two countrymen, speaking of them with a mixture of compassion and contempt... He gave a moving account of the shabbiness of their pay, as well as of the filth and misery of their persons, quarters, and mode of life, which was indeed too self-evident to require any commentary. They seemed to be very much their own masters, and subjected to little either of discipline, duty, or authority, that I could perceive. One of them, a lean weather-beaten veteran, amused himself during a great part of the day in firing his musket around the Khan, a service which I found was performed on my account...

The other palikar, who seemed to be the man of the greatest consequence of the two, at least in his own estimation, a fine athletic fellow, with a fierce sinister countenance and a free and forward manner, paid me a visit on the second afternoon; and after shaking me cordially by the hand, uttered with much vehement gesture, a long and energetic harangue, scarcely one word of which I understood, but which I interpreted to convey certain anathemas against brigands and klephts, with offers of his protection and services in case of emergency, and an assurance of their value. My reason for putting this construction on his address, apart from the tenor of the few expressions I comprehended, was, that about the time of our arrival, reports had reached the place of a renewal or increase of brigandage in the neighbouring districts, especially towards Thermopylae and the Turkish frontier, always the more especial theatre of predatory warfare, and in which direction he supposed we were bound. These reports were in so far confirmed by the arrival of the post-rider from Talanta at the khan that forenoon, on foot, having been plundered of his horse, and stripped of every article on his person, with the exception of a few woollen rags scarcely sufficient to cover his nakedness. Nicola, on communicating this piece of intelligence, observed in his sarcastic way, that the travellers across the Turkish frontier, if they wished to ride in security, had better wait until the season was a little further advanced, when the government would probably send up Generals Church or Gordon, or some other of their commanders, to enlist the bands in their own service, and bestow commissions of colonel, major, or captain of light infantry, on their chiefs. I took this for a jest at the moment; but I afterwards found, to my surprise, that there was as much truth as satire in this remark, having been informed on high authority, that this strange method of encouraging the evil it was sought to check had in fact, been frequently resorted to, and to a considerable extent...

On retiring to their quarters at nightfall, these two heroes used to entertain themselves with chanting their native Albanian war-cries. Although neither air nor voices were very melodious, yet both combined the wild and martial with the plaintive character, in higher perfection than any other music of the kind I ever heard - and, mingling with the howling of the wind and the pelting of the storm through the courts of the building, and across the dreary ruins by which it was surrounded, came home with a singular effect of melancholy desolation to the fancy.

But the most curious inmates of the establishment were my own next-door neighbours, a party of students at the Academy of Livadia. They were five in number, brothers, or near relatives of each other; the eldest a fine tall handsome youth of about seventeen, the youngest a boy about twelve years of age. The cell they occupied was, like the others of the suit, of the same size as my own, the dimensions of which I ascertained by measurement to be about ten feet by eleven. In this apartment they studied, slept, fed, and cooked their victuals; the fire-place, at least, was destined for the latter purpose, but during the Greek Lent there is little scope for the exercise of the cullinary art; and their food consisted, like that of the population in general at this season, for the most part, of coarse bread, garlic, leeks, and preserved olives. Their room contained, as usual, no article of domestic furniture; but amends were made by four oblong wooden chests of such bulk as to cover the greater portion of its area. These were the repositories of their clothes, books, provisions and valuables of all kinds; and also served them as desks for writing their exercises, and for pillows when asleep. On the intermediate space, they reclined, squatted, romped, and reposed, upon their shaggy goat-skin cloaks or hair capottes, which protected them from the storm by day, and formed their mattress and bedding by night. They never undressed, much less changed their attire, during the period of my residence, nor probably in the course of the year, unless when the decay of the suit they wore, or the obligation of some great religious festival, might require its partial or complete renewal.

In the midst of all this filth and misery there was something exceedingly engaging in their temper and demean our. We were only separated by a thin partition of boards, full of chinks, through which each party could hear every thing, and see a good deal, of what was going on on the other side; and although, from daybreak until about nine or ten o' clock at night, with a short interval of absence at school hours, they kept up a perpetual chatter, swelling every now and then into boisterous screaming and romping, I never heard a cross word, or observed a symptom of quarrel or disagreement among them. Their lessons, which were all carried on in common - *viva voce* - and conjointly with their chattering and merriment, comprised, in as far as languages were concerned, the Greek, ancient and modern, and the Italian, but no Latin. One of their chief excercises was repeating and learning by heart portions of an Italo-Greek vocabulary. In the performance of this task, as indeed of all others imposed on them, they had instinctively resorted to the system of mutual instruction, rehearsing to each other in turns their separate allotments, every third or fourth sentence of which gave rise to a jest and peals of laughter. The older ones acted the part of tutors or monitors to their juniors, and occasionally assumed - though through-out palpably in jest - the functions of pedagogue, even to the extent of administering chastisement with the slipper, to this day as in ancient Greece. a common mode of infliction, accompanied with the proper amount of angry words on the part of the castigator, and of entreaties, expostulations, or lamentations on that of the chastised. They seemed all to be gifted by nature with a quickness of capacity, in the inverse ratio fortunately of the wretched means employed for its cultivation...

... [T]he elder one of the party ... informed me that two of them were his brothers, the other two his cousins, also brothers of each other. His father was a Papa of Distomo... He himself had been two years at the Academy, the others a proportionally shorter time. They had hired the room in the Khan as their permanent lodging. They visited the Academy at stated hours; but in other respects lived quite independently, subject to no apparent control, except an occasional visit from an old black-bearded papa of the town, who seemed to have, or rather fancy he had, some charge of them, either in the capacity of private tutor or religious instructor. The only perceptible effect of his presence was a certain addition to the additional merriment, of which he was not infrequently the butt, but always in the same spirit of good humour that pervaded their intercourse with each other... I enquired of the elder lad whether he and his brothers were intended for their father's profession. He replied that they were not unless it pleased them; that the object of their parents was merely to give them such an education as should qualify them to follow out any respectable career that might open up, whether civil, commercial, or ecclesiastical. Their appearance and mode of life bore sufficient evidence of their poverty, and by consequence both of the anxiety of the parents to cultivate the minds of their children, and of the inadequacy of the means at hand for the purpose...

1847-8 Bayard Taylor

Jealous Horses

The khan at Cheronaea was a mere hovel, where the only place for our beds was in the stable among the horses. Our hoofed friends were tolerably quiet, however, and nothing disturbed our slumber except the crowing of the cocks. But the landlord of this hotel demanded no less than three dollars for our lodging; and thereupon ensucd one of those terribly wordy battles in which Francois was a veteran combatant. Epithets struck and clashed against one another like swords; the host was pierced through and through with furious lunges, and even our valiant dragoman did not escape some severe wounds. Then some peasants, whose horses had been stalled for the night in our bedroom, demanded to be paid for the feed of the animals, because, they said, we had fed ours in the stable, which obliged them to feed theirs, unnecessarily. The Greeks believe, that if one horse sees another eat, without eating himself, he will fall sick, and perhaps die. Until I discovered this fact, I was surprised to find that when we reached a khan, all the horses were removed from the stable until after ours had been fed, when they were brought back again.

1870-80s John Pentland Mahaffy

Lake Copais

After the ridge, or saddle, is passed which separates the plain of Thebes from that of Orchomenus, the richness of the soil increases, but the land becomes very swampy and low, for at every half-mile comes a clear silver river, tumbling from the slopes of Helicon on our left, crossing the road, and flowing to swell the waters of Lake Copais - a vast sheet with undefined edges, half-marsh, half-lake-which for centuries had no outlet to the sea, and which was only kept from covering all the plain by evaporation in the heats of Summer. Great fields of sedge and rushes, giant reeds, and marsh plants unknown to colder countries, mark each river course as it nears the lake; and, as might be expected in this lonely fen country all manner of insect life and all manner of amphibia haunt the sites of ancient culture. Innumerable dragon-flies, of the most brilliant colours, were flitting about the reeds, and lighting on the rich blades of grass which lay on the water's surface; and now and then a daring frog would charge boldly at so great a prize, but retire again in fear when the fierce insect dashed against him in its impetuous start. Large land tortoises, with their highed-arched shells, yellow and brown, and patterned like the section of a great honeycomb, went lazily along the moist banks, and close by the water, which they could not bear to touch. Their aquatic cousins, on the other hand, were not solitary in habit, but but lay in lines along the sun-baked mud, and at the first approach of danger dropped into the water one after the other with successive flops, looking for all the world [like] a long row of smooth black pebbles which had suddenly come to life, like old Deucalion's clods, that - they might people this solitude. The sleepy and unmeaning faces of these tortoises were a great contrast to those of the water-snakes, which were very like them in form, but wonderfully keen and lively in expression. They, too, would glide into the water, when so strange a thing as man came near, but would presently raise their heads above the surface, and eye with wonder and suspicion, and in perfcct stillness, the approach of their natural enemy. The Copaic eels, so celebrated in the Attic comedy as the greatest of all dainties, are also still to bc caught; but the bright sun and cloudless sky made vain all my attempts to lure this famous darling of Greek epicures. We noticed that while the shrill cicada, which frequents dry places, was not common here, great emerald-green grasshoppers: were flying about spasmodically, with a sound and weight like that of a small bird.

1893 Charles Diehl

A Bad Review

A bad review is always more interesting to read than a good one, and few regions can have been given such consistently bad reviews as Thebes and Boeotia.

Amongst all the provinces of modern Greece, Boeotia is certainly one of the least attractive and the least visited. Travelling there is difficult, the inns are full of discomforts, and hospitality is anything but ready; while the scenery is rarely grand, and the ruins are never striking. In addition to all this, moreover, the very name of the county, in spite of the great memories of Pindar and Hesiod, of Epimanondas and of Plutarch, awakes an indescribable notion of heaviness, clumsiness and hopeless stupidity. from ancient times Boeotia has had a most unenviable reputation. The Athenians, like good neighbours, were never weary of jesting upon the stupidity and awkwardness and ignorance of the Thebans. Their slanderers were always ready to confuse 'Boeotian' with 'imbecile'. And indeed, when we cast up the intellectual balance sheet of Boeotia, and see that, with two or three exceptions, it has contributed nothing to Greek literature, and has never produced a sculptor, nor a great painter, we are inclined to think that its reputation is not undeserved.

The Ruins of Plataea (E. Dodwell, 1834)

Euboeia

1609-10 William Lithgow

A Discriminatory Burden

Hoisting sail from Dalamede, we set over to Nigroponti, being sixty miles distant, and bearing up Eastward to double the South Cape, we straight discovered two Turkish galleots pursuing us: Whereupon with both sailes and oares, we sought in to the bottom of a long creek, on the West side of the Cape, called Bajodi piscatori; whither also fled nine fisher-boates for refuge: The galleots fearing to follow us in, went to anchor, at a rocky islet in the mouth of the bay, and then within night were resolved to assail us. But night come, and every night of six (for there six days they expected us) we made such bonfires, that so affrighted them (being two miles from any village) they durst never adventure it. Yet I being a stranger was exposed by the untoward Greekes to stand sentinel every night, on the top of a high promontory, it being the dead time of a snowy and frosty winter; which did invite my Muse to bewaile the tossing of my toilsome life, my solitary wandering, and the long distance of my native sorie.

Upon the seventh day, there came down to visit us, two gentlemen of Venice, clothed after the Turkish manner; who under exile, were banished their native territories ten years for slaughter; each of them having two servants, and all of them carrying shables, and two guns apiece; which when I understood, they were Italians, I addressed myself to them, with a heavy complaint against the Greeks, in detaining my budgeto, and compelling me to endanger my life for their goods: whereupon they accusing the patrone, and finding him guilty of this oppression, belaboured him soundly with handy blows, and caused him to deliver my things, carrying me with them five miles to a town where they remained, called Rethenos, formerly Carastia, where I was exceeding kindly entertained ten days. And most nobly (as indeed they were noble) they bestowed on me forty chickens of gold at my departure, for the better advancement of my voyage, which was the first gift that ever I received in all my travels. For if the darts of death had not beene more advantageous to me, then Asiatic gifts, I had never beene able to have undergone this tributary, tedious, and sumptuous peregrination. The confluence of the divine providence allotting me means, from the loss of my dearest consorts gave me in the deepness of sorrow, a thankful rejoicing.

Nigroponti was formerly called Euboea, next, Albantes: and is now surnamed the Queene of Archipelago: The Turkes cognominate this isle Egribos. The Towne of Nigropont, from which the isle taketh the name, was taken in by Mahomet the second; Anno 1451. And in this isle is found the Amianten stone, which is said to be drawn in threads, as out of flax, whereof they make napkins, and other like stuffs; and to make it white, they use to throw it in the fire, being salted. The stone also is found here, called by the Greekes Ophites, and by us Serpentine. The circuit of this isle is three hundred forty six miles. It is seperated from the firm land of Thessalia, from the which it was once rent by an earthquake, with a narrow channel, over the which in one place there is a bridge, that passeth betweene the isle, and the main continent, and under it runneth a marvellous swift current, or Euripus, which ebbeth and floweth six times night and day. Within half a mile of the bridge, I saw a marble column, standing on the top of a little rock, whence (as the islanders told me) Aristotle leaped in, and drowned himself, after that he could not conceive the reason, why this channel so ebbed and flowed... This Ile bringeth forth in abundance, all things requisite for humane life, and decored with many goodly villages.

The chief cities are Nigropont, and Calchos. The principal rivers Cyro, and Nelos, of whom it is said, if a sheep drink of the former, his wool becommeth white, if of the latter coal black.

1674 Father Jacques-Paul Babin, S.J.

Chalkis in the Mid Seventeenth Century

The main town is two miles in compass, fortified with six very large towers, or rondells; the walls are high and thick with a dry ditch to the land, which is almost filled up with rubbish. To the south of the castle is a new platform with several very large guns, which carry some shot of about eighteen inches diameter; When I was there in the year 1676 a renegado was taken; He was a Greek born on the island of Candy; and turned Turk when the Vizier was at the siege of Candy; afterwards he married at Scio, and lived very well; but upon some discontent he made his escape from Scio, and got to the privateers of Malta, with whom he lived some years; and landing on this island, he with some others were surprised, and taken. His companions were condemned to the galleys, but his sentence was to be shot away, out of one of there great guns, which was accordingly effected.

None but Turks and Jews live within the castle, where are very spacious houses, and four which deserve the name of Seraglios: one for the Bailia , at the right hand coming into the Castle from the Port; one for his Lieutenant or Kidhja; a third belonging to Ibrahim Aga's Son (of whose Father we will speak anon;) and the fourth, to Muzlee Aga; which are very richly set out with carved work and painting.

At the latter I was very often entertained upon the following account. Muzlee Aga was taken a slave in. the year 1660, and sold at Legorne, where he continued several years, and served as a Porter about the Streets, paying his master daily what he got. He won the favour of Mr. William Mico (an English Merchant) who besides his due, would often give him some small matter, and recommended him to others of his friends. Muzlee Aga confiding in Mr Mico, imparts the circumstances of his present condition to him, telling him he had good friends, who would redeem him, and withall desired Mr. Mica to use his interest with his Patron, to be moderate in exacting his ransom, giving him a letter, to be sent to his friends at Negro Pont, but without his patron's knowledge. Mr. Mico, pursuant to his humble address, did obtain his ransom on easy terms. Soon after orders came from Muzlee Aga's friends to buy his ransom for five hundred pieces of eight, which they would pay at Smyrna. Which was short by two hundred of what was agreed for. Upon Muzlee Aga's obligation Mr. Mico frees him, and sends him to Smyrna to Mr. Richard Langly; in whose house he tarried, until the remainder of the money was sent him, which he paid, and went to his friends. I then lived at Smyrna with Mr. Langley; And now being at Negro Ponte, sitting in the coffee house one morning, I observed him to look very often on me, and rising from his place he came to me, asking me what country man I was, from whence I came, and whether I was going. I told him that I was an English man, come from Patras, and was going to Constantinople. Then, says he, you are the man I took you for, and I thank God, that I have an opportunity to requite the kindnesses, that I have received from your nation. He would often have me to eat with him. In the year 1679, I was here again, coming from Athens I was robbed by some Albaneses. Muzlee Aga gets me passage on a lundra (built in form like a galley, more for burden, and sailing than rowing) for Scio, sending aboard six hens, ten oakes (an oak is about two pound eight ounces English) of white biscuit, ten oakes of wine, a jar of olives, and a jar of pettmelli, recommending me to the reys (or master) saying, I recommend this man to you, when you see him, you see me, what you do to him, you do for me, and I will answer it, be it good or ill.

Notwithstanding their fine houses in the castle, the Basha has a very large house to the north-west of the Castle, near the galley haven. In the castle are two mosques; the one was a church dedicated to St. Mark, There are several wells, but most of the water which serves to drink is brought in with jars. About a furlong from the castle is the new town very well built (after the Turkish manner) with a large bazaar or market-place. Here are two mosques, and several Greek churches. The Christians here are thrice the number of the Turks, and Jews. The Jesuits have also a small chapel in their house; their care is to look after the slaves when the galleys are there. Between the castle and the town is their burying place, set out with many fine pieces of marble, most of which are brought from the ruins of Athens. The harbour is very secure against any wind, it may be said to be a port for above two miles, the main land being so near and the ground good anchor hold. It is secured from an enemy by the castle, which has above twenty good guns planted this way.

1847-8 Bayard Taylor

An Impressive Gorge

We now entered a deep, wide gorge, leading southward to the Euripean strait. Tall, dark pines feathered the mountain sides to the very summit, and abundant streams of water gushed down every rocky hollow. The road was a faint ,trail, difficult to find, and perilous in the extreme. ..

In some places it was a mere thread, notched along the face of a precipice, where one slip would have sent horse and rider down the awful gulf. With each one of these dangerous passes, the chances of our safety seemed to diminish; and when, at last, we reached a spot where the path was not more than four inches wide, resting on points of rotten-looking rock, Ajax and Themistocles turned back with the pack animals, the intrepid Francis dismounted, and the mare Erato stopped short. My nerves were in a tingle, but the sensation was more agreeable than otherwise. Come, Erato, said I, this is not much worse than those poetical chasms over which your divine namesake has often carried me. Francois went first, leading Boreas of the shaggy mane. I did not dismount, but dropped the reins on Erato's neck. As softly as a cat stealing upon a bird, she put out one paw, tried her foothold, then bracing herself upon it, brought forward the next foot and planted it in the same way, and thus, inch by inch, crept along. I sat perfectly still, keeping a just equilibrium, and looking at the path ahead-not for worlds into the yawning gulf. Millions of the finest needles were sticking into the pores of my skin; but when we reached the opposite side they fell out suddenly, and I felt as refreshed as if I had bathed in a tub of liquid electricity. Braisted followed in the same way; and after incredible labor, Ajax and Themistocles brought their horses around over the rocks. For an hour and a half more we descended the left side of the grand gorge, which gradually contracted, so as to form an impassable canon. The path was delightfully shaded with pines, ilexes, oaks, and laurels: and the air, filled with warm odors of scented leaves and the flowering gorse and ci8tus, was delicious to inhale. Finally, we reached the last knee of the mountain, which commands a wide prospect of the Euboean Gulf and the Locrian mountains beyond. A long upland terrace lay before us, and we rode for an hour and a half over its wooded undulations without seeing any signs of the port of Limni, our destination. The sun was setting in a bed of threatening vapors, and we were very tired and hungry, when at last the path led down a ravine to some fields of olive-trees near the sea-shore. But there were no signs of habitations: only some piles of sawed timber on the beach. We followed the windings of the indented coast for nearly two hours longer, before we came upon the wished-for haven...

c.1850 Henry M. Baird

Lost for Five Hundred Years

Baird records a remarkable archaeological find.

A curious discovery was made, a few years since, at Chalcis. A piece of the wall surrounding the citadel accidentally fell; and behind it there was perceived to be an opening. This being enlarged, proved to be a passage leading to a room, where were found a pile of coarse bags containing an enormous quantity of ancient armour. The articles were carefully transported to Athens by order of the king, and inspected by the historian Buchon. He pronounced them to belong to the first few years of the fourteenth century. He supposes that after the bloody battle fought at Scripu - the ancient Orchomenus in Boeotia - A.D. 1311, the defensive armour of those who had been slain was gathered together, and laid in this receptacle, from motives of reverence and curiosity. There it lay for five hundred and thirty years, until the casual falling of the wall brought it to light. This hypothesis, so interesting from its historical allusions, is fully confirmed by the variety noticeable in the style of the helmets, about one hundred in number. Some are of the kind worn by the Catalans; others resemble those of the Turcopole troops; while the majority seem to have belonged to the unfortunate Frank knights who fell in the marshy plain, and were overpowered by their opponents. All are rusty and battered, having evidently seen service; so that it does not appear that they were placed in this hidden chamber, as in an arsenal, for future use.

1879 Denton Jacques Snider

Chalkis in the Mid-Nineteenth Century

Snider observes that the stamp of the Turks upon this town was still evident some fifty or so years after Turkish rule had come to an end.

The town of Chalkis presented on that morning, which was market-day, a very mixed appearance. The Orient seems to be more strongly impressed upon this place than upon any other in Greece; yet it has also many a fierce reminder of the Occident; clearly it has been a point of conflict and of fluctuating possession in the old centuries. Its importance - for it commands the Euripus at the narrowest crossing – has always made it an object with conquerors. The traces of its various rulers and its checkered destiny are stamped everywhere upon its face, and at once possess the attention of the beholder. Here is a Gothic church with its pointed windows, dating from the Venetian occupation during the Middle Ages. It seems like a lost ghost, you salute it and ask it: How hast thou wandered hither from thy home in the dark foggy North? The lion of St. Mark is still seen over the gate of the castle; he yet has the hoary look of a crusader. Signs of Turkish occupation are noticed in the old mosques and towers, in the falling fortifications, in the careless construction of the walls. Wretched patchwork over great remains shows the Turk in Greece. Á few Mohammedans are said to linger still in Chalkis, the only place of the Prophet's worship in the kingdom is left here. Á few marbles built into the walls of the churches give a slight sprinkle of antiquity; but of the distinctive new Hellas the traveller seeks the signs in vain. But it will come, be not impatient.

The bazaar or market is on Monday; good fortune has landed me just at the right moment. The streets and particularly the public square are lined with small booths, everything which the Orient offers is for sale, mingled in admirable disorder with Western merchandise. Peddlers are here from all parts of Greece, hawking their wares; É see my man who fell into turbid Asopus, trying to sell a kind of carding comb; still the marks of the muddy waters fleck the white folds of his fustanella, as he dashes, all oblivious, through the surging crowd. Some American cottons and American cutlery can be noticed, but the English manufacturer possesses the market; for his success he has my best wishes at least, since he does not clamour for protection at home, while carrying his wares around the world. The most obstinate chafferers are the women who are selling, for no women appear as buyers; I am told that Greek women of respectability never go to market. What a bustling, bargaining, yet merry-making crowd! Dried figs I bought, good, yet enormously cheap; for five cents a peasant woman loaded me down, so that I had to leave part of my measure behind for want of transportation. I should have bought only a cent's worth

According to the rules of careful economy. My Wallachian shepherdess, too, I saw there, sitting among her curds and lambs, with wild luxuriant form now more fully revealed in the clear daylight; she greets me with another shower of sparkles and invites me anew to her mountain home. As I walked through one of the back streets, some Greek boys observing my foreign dress began to run after and mock the stranger; they were joined by others wherever we passed. I darted rapidly through an alley, but the crowd increased till a small mob was in pursuit. I turned back to the bazaar and lost myself from my tormentors in the throng. The boys did not mean anything except a little sport; but it was one of two acts of rudeness which I remember to have experienced in my journey through rural Greece. Postal matters seemed rather lax at Chalkis; two visits to the Post Office were not able to procure me an interview with the Postmaster or the sight of a postage stamp.

The Greek shops open with their whole fronts into the street, they always seem to be half outside in the free air. The shoemaker sits before his door and pegs away, the blacksmith's shop is next to the shoemaker's, his bellows can be blown by a person standing on the pavement. The artisans generally are working in the open air, or just across the threshold of the entrance. Public eating places are frequent; the kitchen is where the front window is in our houses; as you pass along the street, you can see the pot boiling and smell the oleaginous fragrance of its contents. If you wish, the keeper will hand you a spoon and a plate of lentils or beans with stewed mutton, and you can eat your dinner under the free blue sky of Hellas.

Thus the shops range close together down the street, like a series of pigeon holes, before which the active chattering folk is swarming. It is the gift of the climate: man can not endure to be housed up, though it be mid winter. The air invites, confinement within walls is painful, the glorious world is outside and the golden gifts of Helius. Yet just as the shops are open, free, unconfined, so the dwelling houses are close, walled-in, forbidding. There the women are, the family; the world must not be allowed to enter that sanctuary, nor must it come out into the world. I walked toward the suburbs through the more private streets, in the hope of catching a glimpse of some beautiful Greek shape. But there was not one to be seen, not a woman of the better class appeared any where…

… I went down to the bridge over the Euripus and looked at the flow of its waters. The first bridge is said to have been built by the Thebans during the Peloponnesian War; the building of it was one of the severest blows that Athens received, and according to Thucydides caused more terror than the defeat of the Sicilian expedition – doubtless one of the two exaggerations to be found in that coldest-blooded of historians. But look under the bridge at this strong current; it seems like a narrow stream dashing down a rocky bottom. Look at it longer; it is not as swift as it was, indeed t changes under your eye from a rapid torrent to a mild unruffled movement of slow waters. If you look a third time long enough, you will find that the current has wholly ceased, there is a complete calm under the bridge; nay, it begins slowly to move the other way, and soon increases to the swift dashing stream which you saw first, but in the opposite direction. This change takes place within a few minutes, and sometimes there are several such changes in twenty-four hours. On the whole this is the most capricious thing known of the sea. The cause is commonly said to be some mixed action of tides and winds along with the configuration of the land above and below. But I hold it to be an inherent principle of Greek water that it be able to run in one direction, then to turn around and run back again; true to the Greek character it sometimes has the capacity of being the opposite of itself. Enemies call this trait by the ugly name of lying or treachery; but let us call it versatility, the ability to turn about.

Spinning Cotton on Euboea (Baron von Stackelberg & C. F. Gille, 1831)

Athens and Attica

Athens under the Turks, often known in the West as *Settine* or *Settines*, was a provincial town, usually by-passed by Western travellers on their way to the East. Interrupted only by the destructive Venetian campaign of admiral Morosini in 1687-1688, Turkish rule in Athens seems to have been less ferocious than in other parts of Greece, with the exception of the governorship of the notorious Hadji Ali Haseki (1772-92). During the late eighteenth century it became a Mecca for aristocratic Philhellenes. Almost anyone who was anyone seems to have been in Athens in 1810. When Athens was designated the capital city of the new kingdom, in 1834, rebuilding began almost immediately. The Bavarian-Greek court was established, and the beginnings of the modern cosmopolitan city may soon be detected. With increasing Westernisation and sophistication, the city developed its own distinctive character and life-style based upon a compromise between the French style of the Second Empire and local traditions.

The Acropolis (Lantza,)

1672 Father Jacques-Paul Babin, S.J.

A Fallen City

The constant theme of Western visitors expressing disappointment that the modern city of Athens is an inadequate successor to its ancient reputation, is already evident in this first modern account of the city.

One can enter the city without crossing a gate, although I have noticed two or three gates which are never closed, since the city has no walls. Most of the streets resemble village roads. Instead of the superb buildings, the glorious monuments, and the rich temples which were once the ornaments of this city, you can see narrow unpaved streets, poor houses built from the ruins of ancient buildings, decorated with marble columns. These houses have only pieces of marble columns as decoration, sparingly built on the walls, and some marble steps with carved crosses which were once found on the doors and doorsteps of the now ruined churches. Nearly all the houses are of stone and not wood as in Constantinople. One can even find some beautiful ones, considering that this is a country in which luxurious houses are prohibited today.

The Christians turned [the Thiseion] into a church and dedicated it to Saint George. They assured me, however, that though the Turks refused to use this temple, for it was far from the centre of the city and their homes, they also prevented Christians from performing their worship in such a magnificent church. Its iron doors never open except on St. George's day using a silver key which Greeks offer to the Turks in return for their permission.

A lot of people confim that about 300 churches are preserved in Athens and its vicinity at a distance of a league. I would not believe it if I were not astonished at the great number of small churches, some of which were made of marble. I do not know the number of Turkish mosques, but it seems they do not exceed 8 or 9. They all have minarets...

The port of Athens is beautiful and is bigger and larger than the port of Marseilles... This port is called Porto Leone because of the white marble lion standing at the inner port near a lonely uninhabited house, built for storing merchandise before it was loaded on board the vessels, and also used by the customs officer. The lion, resting on its hind legs, is as high as a normal horse.

1609 William Lithgow

"The Great Cistern of Europe"

This city was the mother and wellspring of all liberal arts and sciences; and the great cistern of Europe, whence flowed so many conduit pipes of learning all were but now altogether decayed: The circuit of old Athens hath been according to the fundamental walls yet extant about six Italian miles, but now of no great quantity, nor many dwelling houses therein; being within two hundred the houses, having a castle which formerly was the temple of Minerva [the Parthenon]. They have abundance of all things, requisite for the sustenance of humane life, of which I had no small proof. For these Athenians, or Greeks, exceeding kindly banqueted me four days, and furnished me with necessary provision for my voyage to Creta; and also transported me by sea in a brigantine freely, and on their own charges to Serigo, being forty-four miles distant. After my redounded thanks, they having returned, the contemplation on their courtesies, brought me in remembrance, how curious the old Athenians were to hear of foreign news, and with what great regard and estimation they honoured travellers, of which as yet, they are no ways defective.

1676 George Wheler

The State of the City in the late Seventeenth Century

Athens, is situated in almost the middle of a large plain; so much as it wants in fruitfulness, is recompensed with health and beauty. The present town lieth not round about the castle, as anciently, but to the north-west side of it; being now spread on the plain under it in length, I believe, a mile and a half, in breadth somewhat above a mile; and esteemed four miles in circumference. It hath no walls to defend itself; in so much that they have been frequently surprised by the pirates from sea, and sustained great losses from them. Until some years since, they secured all the avenues into the town by gates, which they built anew, and made the outmost houses, lying close together, to serve instead of walls. These they shut up every night; and are by them reasonably well secured from these corsairs. The houses are very close built together, and the streets very narrow...

Athens is not so despicable a place that it should deserve to be considered only a small village, according to the report of some travellers, who, perhaps, have seen it only from sea, through the wrong end of their perspective-glass. For from the sea the castle is only perceivable; which hideth all the rest of the town, spread out upon the plain north of it. But if it be compared with the former state, those that thus consider Athens will find the scene quite changed; philosophers being now more rigorously banished thence by Fate, than they could ever be in old time by the ill humours of their governors. For the Athenians have had their share in the ill fortune of all those notable cities of the East; the fury of the destroyer having cast them also down, though not utterly extinguished them. Indeed I have seen but few towns in Turkey that have preserved themselves as well as this, nor that enjoy greater privileges under the tyranny of the Turks. True it is, some other cities, by trading, seem more rich than Athens. But I attribute this rather to the bad fortune of the place, than to want either of good harbours, or good merchandize, to export, or vend for such as may be imported.

Managing their Rulers

Their natural dexterity, in all the little matters they undertake, shews it self extraordinary; as in buying, selling, and all their domestic affairs; and not a little also in public, considering the circumstances they are in. For finding their Turkish governors were still too hard for them, and still imposing on them, notwithstanding the privileges they had capitulated for at their surrender, and dearly purchased afterward; they obtained the protection of the Kizlar Haga or Chief of the Black Eunuchs; who thereupon is become their patron, and whom they appeal to upon any difficulty, or abuse put upon them by the Turks. It is he, that orders whom he will to be their Veivode, their Caddi, and Haga of the Castle. The Veivode receiveth the revenue of Athens and payeth to the Kizlar Haga for his place thirty thousand crowns a year. The Christians endeavour to avoid the severe tribunal of the Turks as much as within them lies; and to that purpose have composed a little body politic among themselves. For having divided the town into eight quarters ... out of every one of these, one of the most substantial, and reverend ancient men is chosen, whom they call *epitropi*. These eight moderate all concerns in a friendly manner between Christians and Christians; and to these they commit all their public affairs of moment.

Although the little hope the Athenians have, of ever gaining their liberty from the Turkish tyranny constrains them to live peaceably under their government without running into rebellion against them, or fomenting any factions in the state; yet does their old humour of jealousy still continue: which, though they wisely moderate by reason so far as not to be transported thereby into any public mutiny against the Grand Seignior they now own for their emperor, yet they forbear not to show themselves sensible of the injuries committed by his ministers, and to complain of them and, with notable industry, to prosecute the vindication of their own right. An example of which, not unworthy of observation, happened about the time we were there...

The trade of Athens is but small at present, and consists mostly in little matters among themselves. But it would soon be greater, had they vent for their commodities. Tartans of Marseilles come often hither; but English ships seldom. Yet our consul expected one, when we were there; which came just as I parted thence. I saw it come into the Saronic Gulf: but did not believe, it came from England; otherwise I had laded more marbles on it than the consul did by my order.

The Manners of the Athenians

The Athenians, notwithstanding the long possession, that barbarism hath had of this place, seem to be much more polished, in manners and conversation, than any other of these parts; being civil, and of respectful behaviour to all, and highly complemental in their discourse. They still speak to one another in the third person, and never meet, without giving the time of the day, or using some good wish. Their wives go but little abroad, and their daughters never, as I could hear, till they go to the church to be married. Their wives come to church Sundays and holy-days. The most that I at any time saw, was on Easter Sunday, early in the morning, among whom were many seemingly handsome women, who looked very graceful in their manner of dress; but so horribly painted, that it was hard to conjecture what their natural complexion was, by reason of the thick vizard of paint they had on.

When a virgin is to be married, she is brought to the church, as richly attired as the fortune of her relations will bear; but her face is so bedaubed with gross paint, that it is not easy to determine, whether she be flesh and blood, or a statue made of plaster. She returns with a great crown of gilded metal on her head, accompanied by all the guests, and her near relations, with pipes, and hand-drums, and the best music they can make: whilst she, in the mean time, is conducted at so slow a pace, that it is scarcely perceivable, that she moveth. And so soon as she is entered into the house of her spouse, they throw sugar-plumbs out at the windows, upon the people, who are crowded and thronged at the door.

The Citadel

It was with great difficulty, we obtained the favour of seeing the castle of the Haga; who being newly come thither, and scarce settled in his place, knew not whether he might safely gratify us. But an old soldier of the castle, his friend and confident, for three okas of coffee, two to the governor and one to himself, persuaded him at last to give way; assuring him that it was never refused to such strangers, as it appeared that we were. The Haga hath for his garrison about an hundred Turks of the country, who reside there with their families; and are always on their guard, for fear of pirates, who often land there, and do a great deal of mischief; wherefore all night, a part of them by turns, go their rounds of the walls, making a great hallowing and noise, to signify their watchfulness.

The temple of Minerva [Parthenon] is not only the chief ornament of the citadel; but absolutely, both for matter and art, the most beautiful piece of antiquity remaining in the world. I wish I could communicate the pleasure I took in viewing it.

On the north side of the temple of Minerva we came to the temple of Erictheus. We could not have permission to go into the temple, to see it; because the Turk that lives in it, hath made it his seraglio for his women; and was then abroad.

The Monasteries of Mount Hymettos

After I had ... taken some of the prospects of the mountains, as the little time I had would permit, I made all the haste I could down (although very unwillingly so soon) for fear of being benighted: as Mr. Vernon was on the same account, and shut out of the town; putting the consul to a great deal of care and trouble for his safety, being gone out alone, afoot and without a guide. The first time I went forth with my companion and the consul, we losing our labour by reason of the snow that fell, returned down the nearest way we could, passing by three monasteries that lay on that side of the mountain. The first, in descending, is called Haghia Jani ho Carias. The second is now deserted, and they say the Italians had formerly a church there in common with the Greeks, called Hagios Georgios ho Koutelas. The third is called hagios Kyriani by the Greeks, and by the Turks Cosbashi; because of a sheep's head engraven on a marble sepulchre, now made use of for a cistern to the fountain arising there, whose stream falls into the Ilissos.

The convent is well-enough built for that country, where they do not strive to excel in stately buildings; but rather to hide themselves as much as they can in obscurity from the world. This mountain is celebrated for the best honey in all Greece, of which it makes a great quantity to send to Constantinople, where it is much esteemed for making sorbets. They use therefore to bring all the honey made hereabouts to be marked with the mark of this monastery of Cosbashi, to make it sell the better. We eat of it very freely, finding it to be very good; and were not at all incommodated with any gripings after it. This mountain was not less famous in times past for bees and admirable honey, the ancients believing that bees were first bred here, and that all other bees were but colonies from this mountain; which if so, we assured ourselves, that it must be from this part of the mountain that the colonies were sent, both because the honey here made is the best, and that here they never destroy the bees ... in taking away their honey.

The present abbot is called Ezekiel Stephanaki, who lives at Athens, and is a learned man for that country; understanding the ancient Greek very well, and Latin indifferently, with a little Italian. He understands philosophy too, so far as to be esteemed a Platonist; and notwithstanding that he is an abbot, yet he professes not to be a divine, but a physician. In my return to Athens I was daily with him; and of him I learned to read Greek according to the modern pronunciation. I found him to be really a good, discreet and understanding man; and what piques soever have been between the Benizuelos and him, peradventure, have proceeded rather from the emulation of the first, than from any real or just cause given by him. I easily perceived he was not over-fond of some of the Greekish superstitions; but for all that he seems to be both a good man and a good Christian; and whatever they talk of him otherwise, are but trifles, and perhaps undeserved. He hath some manuscripts, especially of St. John Damascene, which he offered to exchange with me for an atlas if I sent it him. But I have not yet had an opportunity to send it.

The rest of the convents about this mountain are called Asteri, Hagios Ioannes Kynigos, and Hagios Ioannes o Theologos. There is another convent near Mount St. George called Asomatos.

The Birth of a Monster

Portus Piraeus is called at present by the Greeks *Porto-Dracone*, and by the Franks *Porto-Lione*, by reason of a lion of marble, of admirable work, placed at the bottom of the bay, in a posture of sitting, but erected upon its forefeet. It is ten foot high, and by a hole pierced through it, answering to its mouth, appears to have been a fountain. There is such another in the way from Athens to Eleusis, in a couchant posture. Our French old and new Athens told us of a third in the castle, which we could have no account of, unless he took the fore part of an horse placed on the top of the northern wall, for a lion. By occasion of this, my comrade telleth a strange story, *viz.* of a monster, supposed to have been caused by an impression made upon the fantasy of the woman that bare it, by a sudden view of it. I do not remember that I was present at the relation, yet because I esteem the thing a matter of more than ordinary curiosity, I shall not pass it by.

It happened in the month of October, in the year of our Lord 1665, that a Turkish woman was delivered of it in the citadel after she had gone with it nine months, as of a child. So soon as it was brought into the world it leaped down on the ground began to go, and make a hideous noise, resembling somewhat the barking of a dog. It had ears standing upright like a hare's, and his chaps like a lion; its eyes sparkled, and had two great teeth sticking out of its mouth; its feet like a child, but the fingers of its hands rather resembled the claws of birds of prey; and its sex scarcely discernable. The veivode and caddi, hearing of it, came to make their inspection three days after its birth, and presently gave sentence of death against it; commanding they should dig a great hole in the ground, and throw the monster into it, and after that fill up the place again with stones; which was done upon the eight of October. A French surgeon, called Monsieur Fauchon, who lived then at Athens, desired to have the body, that he might embalm it, and send it to France. But it was denied him; the Turks affirming that it was a devil, and that the memory of it ought to perish with it, insomuch that he was forbidden to come near the place where it was buried.

A False Alarm

The following incident, which took place among the ruins of ancient Eleusis, demonstrates the strength of the omnipresent fear of pirate raids on the coast of the Bay of Salamis.

While my companion and I were thus busied, our curiosities were surprised on a sudden with the noise of two guns going off. I presently ran to the next convenient place to look down at, to see what the matter was; which I had no sooner done, but saw Mouratis, our dragoman, lie sprawling as killed. I quickly called my companion, and told him we were beset by the corsairs, or rogues. He thought I jested; but I assured him, I saw Mouratis lie killed as I thought. Where the consul was I could not tell; but we hasted to his rescue, either to save him, or lose our lives with him. So with all the expedition the rocks and ruins would give us leave, we ran to the place; where we found the consul rubbing Mouratis to bring him to life again: of whom, after we had shaken off our surprise, we understood the matter to be no more than being employed about providing us some meat. They started a hare just by them; which, as soon as they saw, our guide took my fowling piece, and Mouratis a short carbine, with a large bore, charged with four bullets, and shot at her. But the carbine, having been charged some days before, and perhaps with greater quantity of powder than was fit, in the discharge the piece recoiled, so that it felled him down backward, and struck all the breath out of his body. When he came to himself, it was a good while before we could learn of him what was the matter; and then he could hardly be persuaded, but that he had broken some ribs. But Jani, who had in vain run after the hare, returning, gave us a more particular account of the accident, and made us content that the poor hare had escaped us, as well as we the danger that we feared.

It happened at the same time, some Athenians coming that way from Corinth, hearing the guns go off, and seeing three or four men of us traversing those ruins, were frightened as much as we; and concluding us to be corsairs, lying there in ambush, to rob and do mischief, ran away as hard as they could drive, and hid themselves in the woods not far off; where, having stayed a pretty while, and beginning to doubt whether they might not be mistaken, and their fear groundless, sent a boy as their scout to discover what we were; who coming nearer to us, happened to know some of us; upon which he returned, and showed his company their mistake.

So having comforted Mouratis as well as we could, causing him to drink a large draught of wine; after dinner we set forward again on our journey, being very glad that we came off so well; and blessing God, that this once he suffered us *to fear, where no fear was.*

Turkish Fear of Corsairs

In the middle of the town [Megara], on the highest point of the rock, is a tower; where a veivode lived, until the corsairs came and took him away; which hath ever since so scared the Turks, that they durst no longer stay there. So that they are now wholly without Turks in the town. But the Christians that are, stand in great fear of the pirates, whether Turks or infidels pretending to be Christians, that upon the sight of every boat in the daytime, and but hearing their dogs bark in the night, they presently fall to packing up their few goods...

The Pendeli Monastery

The convent of Penteli is one of the most celebrated monasteries of all Greece... They consist of above a hundred caloiroes, and more than a hundred and thirty persons in number, having a considerable revenue belonging to them. They are under the protection of the Sultan's mother, of which they pay to the New Mosque she built, some years since, at Constantinople, yearly six thousand pounds weight of honey, and are obliged to furnish it with as much more at the price of five dollars the quintal. They seldom have less than five thousand stocks of bees, beside much arable land, and flocks of sheep and herds of cattle, together with large vineyards and olive yards, and want no other conveniences that the manner of their life requireth. The seniors of the house have all chambers to themselves, with novices to wait on them. Besides, I believe the situation of the place, especially in summertime, must needs be very agreeable; being between the ridges of the mountain, with divers curious fountains issuing out of it, which are received into pools to keep fish in, and turn their mills as they pass. They are shaded with woods of several sorts of trees, which moderate the heat of the summer, and furnish them with sufficient fuel against the cold of winter, which is sharp enough there; the top of the mountain being then still covered with snow.

They have not only provision for the body, but have also a library of good books to inform their minds, though I fear they make but little use of them. Their books are all manuscripts, and consist chiefly of the Greek fathers; most of which we found there...

The weather being very bad, snowy, rainy and windy, we were willing to spend that day there, being entertained by the good fathers with all the courtesy imaginable. They made us an excellent fire, which was but needful; for although there be no very great hard frosts in these countries, it is nevertheless sometimes extreme cold, especially when the winds blow over the mountains covered with snow, as then it happened to do over Pendelico, with such a force as we were scarce able to sit our horses, nor hinder the cold from passing through all the clothes we put on.

But this bad weather did not cool our curiosity so much, but that after we had refreshed ourselves we took a guide to go up and show us the quarries of white marble, with the other curious grottos of congelations. Some sparkle like walls of diamond; which being broken splitteth into talcum. Some show like scenes of trees and woods afar off. We crept down to one near twenty fathom, by a narrow way, on our hands and feet, to a fountain they say in summer is so cold, one cannot abide one's hands in it a *Pater noster*, which is a very short space of time, that work being usually despatched with great expedition as well in the Greek as in the Latin church. They hold that the ancient Christians used to hide themselves there in times of persecution.

1738 Lord Sandwich

An Unusual Method of Threshing in Megara

This city still preserves its ancient name of Megara, though it is now no other than a poor miserable village of about one hundred houses, or rather huts, none of them being more than one storey high. It is situated upon the side of a hill in the middle of a very fruitful plain; the inhabitants are an industrious people, employing themselves wholly in the cultivation of their lands, which answer their labours, affording them corn sufficient for their own use and for exportation.

At the time that we arrived at Megara they were threshing the corn, which is performed in a very peculiar manner. In the beginning of the month of August the inhabitants, men, women, and children, desert the village, and raising little huts of boughs of trees at some distance from the town, have no other habitation till their corn is all laid up in repositories. The use of the flail is unknown to them, instead of which they separate the corn from the ear in the following manner. They choose a piece of ground which must be very even, and the surface free from stones, or any other impediment; in the middle of this they drive a stake, to which they fasten four or five horses abreast, leaving between the stake and the nearest horse a space of about four yards. After this they lay their corn all round under the horses' feet, and then whipping them along keep them continually in a pretty good trot; which by trampling the corn under their feet make more expedition in separating it than five of the ablest threshers. After this they bury it all in wells dug for that purpose, where they let it lie till they have occasion for it, either for exportation or their own use.

1749 Lord Charlemont

Rural Piraeus

[H]ow pleasingly we were struck at our first landing at Piraeus, at the pastoral elegance of the shepherds and of their sheep.

A Vile Example of Turkish Tyranny

Walking one day, in company with some Athenians, on the Munychian promontory, a boat happened to pass us, which carried two prostitutes into banishment, to the island of Salamis, a punishment, it seems frequently inflicted on common strumpets. This circumstance gave rise to a conversation in which our companions bitterly inveighed against the Turkish governors for their horrid injustice and cruelty with regard to the maidens of Athens.

It has happened not infrequently, said they, that the Vaivode has privately conveyed some one of his wretched dependants into the house of some wealthy Greek, where there was a daughter of virtue and of beauty, on purpose that this wretch might be caught there by his officers, who were ordered to search the house upon an information lodged by some other of his creatures. In consequence of this detection the girl is supposed to be criminal, and is immediately seized upon, and sent to prison. The maiden in vain protests her innocence. Proofs are strong against her, and the villain, who was suborned to her ruin, confesses his own guilt, which includes hers. She has then no other means left but to claim inspection as a proof of her virginity, compelled thus to the sad necessity of injuring her modesty to secure her fame. Even this fails her, and the shocking, the humiliating, ceremony is gone through in vain. The matrons are bribed to declare her guilty, and the miserable victim is betrayed to ruin and to infamy! Nothing then remains to prevent her from being immediately sold for a slave, the usual sentence against girls of fashion who are proved to be criminal, but the purchase of her pardon by liberal gifts to the magistrate, and families are frequently ruined both in reputation and in fortune by this infamous and tyrannical practice.

Under such circumstances it is not at all strange that the people should be discontented in their present situation, which in itself is a bad one, but must appear wretched indeed if any idea of their former state should ever induce them to make the comparison. And in this respect the Athenians are far more unfortunate than the rest of the Greeks, inasmuch as they retain a stronger idea of their ancient splendour, and of consequence are more apt to repine at their present degradation. Many of them have brought tears into our eyes by asking us in the most pathetic manner whether there were not, in our more powerful and flourishing parts of Europe, some prince or people, who, reflecting on the ancient renown of Athens, and on its present wretched prostration, might be induced to seek by force of arms their deliverance from Turkish bondage.

1765 Richard Chandler

A Portent of Liberty

In the first year of our residence in the Levant, a rumour was current, that a cross of shining light had been seen at Constantinople, pendant in the air over the grand mosque, once a church dedicated to St. Sophia; and that the Turks were in consternation at the prodigy, and had endeavoured in vain to dissipate the vapour. The sign was interpreted to portend the exaltation of the Christians above the Mahometans; and this many surmised was speedily to be effected; disgust and jealousy then subsisting between the Russians and the Porte, and the Georgians contending with success against the Turkish armies. By such arts as these are the wretched Greeks preserved from despondency , roused to expectation, and consoled beneath the yoke of bondage.

The Dance of the Dervishes in the Tower of the Winds

The Tower of the Winds is now a *teckeh*, or place of worship belonging to a college of dervishes. I was present at a religious function, which concluded with their wonderful dance. The company was seated on goatskins on the floor cross-legged; forming a large circle. The chief dervish, a comely man, with a grey beard and of a fine presence, began the prayers, in which the rest bore part, all prostrating themselves, as usual, and several times touching the ground with their foreheads. On a sudden, they leaped up, threw off their outer garments, and, joining hands moved round slowly to music, shouting Allah, the name of God. The instruments sounding quicker, they kept time, calling out *Allah. Al illa All Allah.* God. There is no other God but God. Other sentences were added to these as their motion increased; and the chief dervish, bursting from the ring into the middle, as in a fit of enthusiasm, and letting down his hair behind, began turning about, his body poised on one of his great toes as on a pivot, without changing place. He was followed by another, who spun a different way, and then by more, four or five in number. The rapidity, with which they whisked round, was gradually augmented, and became amazing; their long hair not touching their shoulders but flying off; and the circle still surrounding them, shouting and throwing their heads backwards and forwards; the dome re-echoing the wild and loud music; and the noise as it were of frantic Bacchanals. At length, some quitting the ring and fainting, at which time it is believed they are favoured with ecstatic visions, the spectacle ended. We were soon after introduced into a room furnished with skins for sofas, and entertained with pipes and coffee by the chief dervish, whom we found, with several of his performers, as cool and placid, as if he had been only a looker-on.

The Orologion of Andronicus C yrrhestes (E. Dodwell,1805)

Private and Public Distresses

Our stay at Athens was prolonged by unforeseen obstacles. We encountered many a vexatious delay, and our residence became irksome ... from our detestation of Lombardi, who haunted our house, and, by his hateful presence, and by discourse which was impure, indelicate, and impious, in the highest degree, polluted, and poisoned every enjoyment.

Lombardi was said to have been a priest, and to have robbed the altars of the church. He had fled from his country to avoid the punishment of some crime of a most atrocious nature. He was acquainted with the Latin language, had some knowledge of medicine, and had lived with several bashas and great Turkish officers as their physician. He had signalised his courage and conduct in dangerous expeditions against *banditti* and insurgents; which services had been rewarded with money, horses, and garments lined with skins. He possessed uncommon address, eloquence, profligacy, hypocrisy. He had been a pretended proselyte to the Greek communion, and written a book in Italian, entitled *"Truth the Judge*, by Father Benzoni, a Jesuit and convert to the true Oriental Church...".". He had also composed a long and bitter invective against an archbishop of Larisa in Thessaly. He had been imprisoned at Athens, and had obtained his release with difficulty, by tears, entreaties, and the interposition of the Turks. Revenge was his highest gratification. He had employed the most unjustifiable means to compass the downfall, and even the deaths of his principal enemies. He was recently returned from Constantinople, and boasted, that by his intrigues there, he had levelled some proud archons at Athens, who had lately hoisted flags as consuls to European powers. He talked unconcernedly of the death of his elder and favourite son. Before our departure, he formally repudiated his wife, who was an Athenian; and renounced her children, a son and two daughters, who refused to relinquish Christianity. The Turks were offended at his want of natural affection, and pleaded in their behalf. He had espoused a young Albanian, and now cohabited with her; but a plurality of wives ranked among the least criminal of his various enormities.

A general disquiet of the people likewise contributed to render our situation not agreeable. Some exactions of the archbishop, who was to pay the money borrowed for the purchase of his see, made him unpopular. He had incurred also the displeasure of the vaiwode, and an open quarrel ensued. A scarcity of corn increased as winter advanced, until the distress of the people was so great that an insurrection was apprehended daily, and Achmet Aga, to appease the clamour, opened his granaries. Yet the vaiwode, to raise money for the purchase of his post for the ensuing year, sold a large portion of the future grain by contract, to Mr. Keyrac, a French merchant, who resided at Nauplia.

Lombardi fomented the public discord, working in private, like a mole underground. His zeal in persecuting the archbishop gave him influence with his enemies and with the vaiwode. He spirited up a mob to shout, "Barrabbas! Barrabbas!" on his coming from a church, in which the clergy had been assembled; and he used every method, which the most diabolical malice could suggest, to blacken his character. He laboured also to accomplish the ruin of other persons, at whom he had taken offence.

We were informed at Corinth, that soon after our departure from Athens, the archbishop had arrived there from Constantinople, and been reinstated in his see by officers commissioned for that purpose; that the bey or vaiwode had received him kindly, and ordered his musicians to attend him at his palace; and that a complete revolution had happened in his favour. Lombardi was greatly distressed and embarrassed, his intrigues defeated, disappointed in his views of revenge, unincluded in the general amnesty, fearing to return, and not knowing whither to fly.

A Waterspout in the Gulf

About the middle of October, while we resided at the [*Capuchin*] convent [*at the Monument of Lysikrates*], I had the satisfaction of seeing distinctly the phenomenon called a waterspout from the window of my apartment, which looked towards the sea. The weather had changed from settled and pleasant, and clouds resided on the mountains black and awful, particularly on Hymettus, whose side and tops were covered. About seven in the morning, when I rose, a cloud, tapering to a point, had descended in the gulf, between the islands of Aegina and Salamis. Round it, at the bottom, was a shining mist. After a minute or more, it began gradually to contract itself, and retired very leisurely up again into the sky. We had little rain this day, but at night pale lightning flashed at short intervals, and thunder, bursting over our heads, exceedingly loud, rolled tremendously, and it poured down as from open sluices. The quantity of water, which fell, was answerable to the long and visible preparation, but seasonable; seed time approaching...

The "Evil Stairway"

The name of the Scironian road is now (the robber being forgotten) Kache Scala, The bad way. In 1676 it was as terrible from the ambuscades of the corsairs as of old from the cruelty of Sciron. It has since been disused, and a road made over the mountain, on which the Turks have established a *dervene* or guard, with regulations to prevent the assembling or escape of robbers and banditti. The distance from Megara to Corinth, which is now computed at nine hours, was by the Scironian way only six; but on it the traveller was in continual peril.

We left our boats in the creek, and ascended to an arched cave in the rock, black with the smoke of fires kindled by travellers, who had rested there, or by mariners and fishermen who, like us, had declined venturing along so dangerous a coast in the night, or waited for favourable weather. We had from it an extensive view of the turbulent gulf beneath, and of the islands. We made a fire, and remained in it until morning. It then proved calm, and we re-embarked.

We coasted by the Scironian rocks, which are exceedingly high, rough, and dreadful. The way is by the edge of perpendicular precipices, narrow, and in many places carried over the breaks, and supported underneath, apparently, in so light a manner, that a spectator may reasonably shudder with horror at the idea of crossing. Wheler has mentioned it as the worst road which he ever travelled...

This "Scironian" road is the ancient predecessor of the two present coast roads between Athens and Corinth. The main autoroute is no less perilous today, due to wilfully reckless and incompetent drivers.

1788 "An Italian Gentleman"

Received by the Aga with Music and a Fool

We have paid a visit to the aga, or commander of the fortress. He was in his harem; he at least sent a message to this purpose, in order that we might dance attendance for sometime in what is called the antechamber. In about ten minutes he appeared. He is a handsome man, and for a domestic, has a very genteel and noble air...

He received us very politely, presenting us with coffee and sweetmeats, which we all tasted out of the same spoon. Some Turkish lords, and a fool whom he keeps for his amusement, were next served. This custom of keeping fools was formerly very much in vogue among the Europeans, and has been discontinued but very lately by our kings. This fool, which is very old and pale, like people of his character, was desired to counterfeit a philosopher; on which he trembled, became serious, then burst into a fit of laughter, and made a thousand contortions. The aga laughed, or rather smiled. We were then offered pipes, which we declined to accept.

The aga, however, very seriously began smoking with a pipe of a very singular construction, called a hookah, which is much used in the Levant. This pipe, which is about five feet in length, is made of brass wire covered with painted leather. It is terminated by a brass machine with two tubes, one of which is bent, and joins to its extremity; the other is perpendicular and filled with tobacco. These two pipes afterwards unite in one; and being placed in a crystalline vessel not quite filled with water, the smoke, as it passes through, occasions the water to bubble, and rising afterwards in clouds, is very refreshing. Smoking in this manner is not only pleasant, but even delightful, especially when rose water, which many employ, is used for that purpose.

The aga, for our amusement, entertained us with a concert, consisting of a cymbal, a flute, a mandora, and a paltry violin with three strings, accompanied by a voice still more disagreeable than all these instruments put together. While the Turks were rapt in ecstacy, our patience was almost exhausted; for even the pathetic appeared to us extremely monotonous and disagreeable.

This, however, might probably arise by our not being sensible of the variations; and because the music was in a style different from ours. A Frenchman who is settled here, and who is much attached to the Turkish customs, extols it to the skies.

1789 Lady Elizabeth Craven

A Frustrated Desire for "Marbles"

This is the first of several references in our selection to the desire for, and acquisition of, "marbles" as souvenirs by wealthy foreign visitors to Greece.

The temple of Minerva [*Parthenon*] in the citadel of Athens, was used by the Turks as a magazine for powder, which blowing up has flung downwards such a quantity of beautiful sculpture that I should be very happy to have permission to pick up the broken pieces on the ground – but, alas, sir, I cannot even have a little finger or a toe, for the ambassador who had been a whole year negotiating for permission to convey to Constantinople a fragment he had pitched upon, and thought himself sure of, will be sadly disappointed. The sailors were prepared with cranes, and everything necessary to convey this beautiful relic on board the *Tarleton*; when after the governor of the citadel, a Turk, had received us with great politeness, he took Mr. Truguet aside, and told him, unless he chose to endanger his life, he must give up the thoughts of touching any thing; that there was an intrigue in the Seraglio to displace him, and that if any thing was removed, that plea would be sufficient for him to get his head struck off. Chagrined and disappointed as Mr. De Truguet was, he could not with any humanity press the performance of the promise; and we returned to the consul's very much concerned at the excessive injustice and ignorance of the Turks, who have really not the smallest idea of the value of the treasures they possess, and destroy them wantonly on every occasion. For from one of the pillars of the temple of Theseus they have sliced a piece of marble to burn into lime for the construction of a Turkish fountain – and such is the fate of many a *chef d'oeuvre* of the best Grecian sculpture...

A Visit to the Baths

The baths here are very well contrived to stew the rheumatism out of a constitution, but how the women can support such heat of them is perfectly inconceivable. The Consul's wife, Madame Gaspari, and I went into a room which precedes the bath, which room is the place where the women dress and undress, sitting like sailors upon boards: there were above fifty; some having their hair washed, others dyed, or plaited; some were at the last part of their toilet, putting with a fine gold pin, the black dye into their eyelids. In short, I saw here Turkish and Greek nature, through every degree of concealment, in her primitive state, for the women sitting in the inner room were absolutely so many Eves, and as they came out their flesh looked boiled. These baths are the great amusement of the women, they stay generally five hours in them; that is in the water and at their toilet together; but I think I never saw so many fat women at once together, nor fat ones so fat as these…Few of these women had fair skins or fine forms – hardly any – and Madame Gaspari tells me, that the encomiums and flattering a fine young woman would meet with in these baths would be astonishing.

1794 John Bacon Sawry Morritt

"Marbles" By Any Means

Morritt exemplifies the ruthless attitudes of the aristocratic antiquities collectors of the period.

It is very pleasant to walk the streets here. Over almost every door is an antique statue or basso-relievo, more or less good though all much broken, so that you are in a perfect gallery of marbles in these lands. Some we steal, some we buy, and our court is much adorned with them. I am grown, too, a great medallist, and my collection increases fast, as I have above two hundred, and shall soon, I hope, have as many thousands. I buy the silver ones often under the price of the silver, and the copper ones for halfpence. At this rate I have got some good ones, and mean to keep them for the alleviation of Sir Dilberry's visits, as they will be as good playthings as the furniture and pictures for half an hour before dinner...

We have just breakfasted, and are meditating a walk to the citadel, where our Greek attendant is gone to meet the workmen, and is, I hope, hammering down the Centaurs and Lapiths... Nothing like making hay when the sun shines, and when the commandant has felt the pleasure of having our sequins for a few days. I think we shall bargain for a good deal of the old temple...

Goodbye for a moment. Scruples of conscience had arisen in the mind of the old scoundrel at the citadel; that is to say, he did not think we had offered him enough. We have, however, rather smoothed over his difficulties, and are to have the marble the first opportunity we can find to send it off from Athens. I, only being sensible of the extreme awkwardness of Grecian workmen, tremble lest it should be entirely broken to pieces on taking it out; if any accident happens to it I shall be quite crazy, as now there is nothing damaged but the faces and one of the hands. If I get it safe I shall be quite happy, and long to show it you at Rokeby.

When he had left Athens, Morritt found something else at Eleusina (the site of ancient Eleusis) to add to his collection in Rokeby, in Yorkshire:

You will laugh at me when I tell you that it had no head, and its arms were broken; however, it was a female figure, and the drapery and attitude pleased me so much that I took the trouble of packing it off on a mule for Corinth, and so to Zante. If I can get it well restored in Italy, it will figure in the Rokeby collection; and its greatest charm perhaps will be that I found it myself. At least, it was not expensive; for, giving half a crown to a priest that belonged to a chapel near it, we pretended to have a firman, and carried it off from the Greeks in triumph.

1801 Edward Clarke

The Destruction of the Parthenon

The "collection" of Greek statuary culminated in the removal of the Parthenon Marbles by Lusieri on behalf of Lord Elgin.

Some workmen were then engaged in making preparations, by means of ropes and pulleys, for taking down the metopes, where the sculptures remained the most perfect. The Disdar himself came to view the work, but with evident marks of dissatisfaction; and Lusieri told us that it was with great difficulty he could accomplish this part of his undertaking from the attachment the Turks entertained towards a building which they had been accustomed to regard with religious veneration and had converted into a mosque. We confessed that we participated the Moslem feeling in this instance and would gladly see an order enforced to preserve rather than destroy such a glorious edifice. After a short time spent in examining the several parts of the temple one of the workmen came to inform Don Battista that they were then going to lower one of the metopes. We saw this fine piece of sculpture raised from its station between the triglyphs: but the workmen endeavouring to give it a position adapted to the projected line of descent, a part of the adjoining masonry was loosened by the machinery; and down came the fine masses of the Pentilican marble, scattering their white fragments with thundering noise among the ruins. The Disdar, seeing this, could no longer restrain his emotions; but actually took his pipe from his mouth, and letting fall a tear, said in a most emphatic tone of voice, *"Telos!"* positively declaring that nothing should induce him to consent to any further dilapidations of the building.* Looking up we saw with regret the gap that had been made; which all the ambassadors of the earth, with all the sovereigns they represent aided by every resource that wealth and talent can now bestow, will never again repair. As to our friend Lusieri, it is hardly necessary to exculpate him; because he could only obey the orders he had received, and this he did with manifest reluctance: neither was there a workman employed in the undertaking, among the artists sent out of Rome for that purpose, who did not express his concern that such havoc should be deemed necessary, after moulds and casts had already been made of all the sculpture which it was designed to remove. The author would gladly have avoided the introduction of this subject; but as he was an eye-witness of these proceedings, it constitutes a part of the duties he has to fulfil in giving the narrative of his travels; and if his work be destined to survive him, it shall not, by its taciturnity with regard to the spoliation of the Athenian temples, seem to indicate any thing like an approval of the measures which have tended so materially towards their destruction.

* This man was, however, poor, and had a family to support; consequently, he was unable to withstand the temptations which a little money, accompanied by splendid promises, offered to the necessities of the situation. So far from adhering to his resolution, he was afterwards gradually prevailed upon to allow all the finest pieces of sculpture belonging to the Parthenon to be taken down; and succeeding travellers speak with concern of the injuries the building has sustained, exclusively of the loss caused by the removal of the metopes. One example of this nature may be mentioned; which, while it shows the havoc that has been carried on, will also prove the want of taste and utter barbarism of the undertaking...

In one of the angles of the pediment which was over the eastern facade of the temple, there was a horse's head, supposed to be intended for the horse of Neptune issuing from the earth, when struck by his trident, during his altercation with Minerva for the possession of Attica. The head of this animal had been judiciously placed by Phidias, that, to a spectator below, it seemed to be rising from an abyss, foaming and struggling to burst from its confined situation, with a degree of energy suited to the greatness and dignity of its character. All the perspective of the sculpture (if such an expression be admissible), and certainly all the harmony and fitness of its proportions, and all the effect of attitude and force of composition, depended upon the work being viewed precisely at the distance in which Phidias designed that it should be seen. Its removal, therefore, from its situation, amounted to nothing less than its destruction: - take it down, and all the aim of the sculptor is instantly frustrated! Could anyone believe that this was actually done? and that it was done, too, in the name of a nation vain of its distinction in the fine arts? Nay, more, that in doing this, finding the removal of this piece of sculpture could not be effected without destroying the entire angle of the pediment, the work of destruction was allowed to proceed even to this extent also? Thus the form of the temple has sustained a greater injury than it had already experienced from the Venetian artillery; and the horse's head has been removed, to be placed where it exhibits nothing of its original effect, like the acquisition said to have been made by another nobleman, who, being delighted at a puppet-show, bought Punch, and was chagrined to find, when he carried him home, that the figure had lost all its humour.

Yet we are seriously told … that this mischief has been done with a view to "rescue these specimens of sculpture from impending ruin"; then, why not exert the same influence which was employed in removing them, to induce the Turkish government to adopt measures for their effectual preservation…

The Ancient Wells of Athens

Having hired some Albanian peasants for the work, and obtained permission from the Waiwode, we began the examination of some of the wells. Mr. Cripps, in the mean time, superintended the excavation of a tumulus near the road leading to the Piraeus; but the difficulty of carrying on any undertaking of this kind, owing to the jealousy, not only of the Turks, but also of the Greeks, who always suppose that some secret hoard of gold is the object of research, renders it liable to continual interruption. After two days spent in opening the tomb, we had the mortification to find that it had been examined before; and we had good reason to believe that a knowledge of this circumstance was the sole ground of the easy permission we had obtained to begin the labour for the second time.

In the examination of the wells, we succeeded better; but our acquisitions were as nothing, compared with those which have since been made. The reasons which induced the author to suspect that the cleansing of an old well would lead to the discovery of valuable antiquities, were these: first, the wells of Greece were always the resort of its inhabitants; they were places of conversation, of music, dancing, revelling, and almost every kind of public festivity; secondly, that their remote antiquity is evident from the following extraordinary circumstance. Over the mouth of each well has been placed a massive marble cylinder, nearly corresponding, as to its form, ornaments, height and diameter, with the marble altars which are so commonly converted by the Turks into mortars for bruising their corn. A very entire altar of this shape is in the *Cambridge Collection of Greek Marbles*. These wells had no contrivance for raising water by means of a windlass, or even of the simple lever, common over all the north of Europe, which is often poised by a weight at the outer extremity. The water rose so near to the surface, that it was almost within reach of the hand; and the mode of raising it was by a hand-bucket, with a rope of twisted herbs. Owing to the general use of this rope, and its consequent friction against the sides of the well, the interior of those massive marble cylinders has been actually grooved all round, to the depth of two or three inches: in some instances, transverse channels appear crossing the others; obliquely, and to an equal depth. An effect so remarkable, caused in solid marble by its attrition with one of the softest substances, affords convincing proof that a great length of time must have elapsed before any one of those furrows in the stone could have been so produced; and that many ages would be requisite to form such channels in any number.

Having selected a dry well for our experiment, whose mouth was covered by a cylinder remarkably distinguished by this appearance, we removed a quantity of stones, old rubbish, and found at the bottom a substratum of moist marl. In this humid substance (the original deposit of the water when the well was used), the number of terra-cotta vessels, lamps, pitchers, bottles, some entire, others broken, was very great. We removed thirty-seven in an entire state, of various sizes and forms. They were chiefly of a coarse manufacture, without glazing or ornament of any kind; but the workmen brought up also the feet, handles, necks, and other parts of earthen vases of a very superior quality and workmanship: some of these were fluted, and of a jet black colour; others of a bright red, similar to those innumerable fragments of terra cotta found upon the site of all Grecian cities; especially in the outer Ceramicus, and in the sepulchres of Athens since opened, as well as those of Italy and of Sicily.

Straying Into Forbidden Territory

The following day was attended by a singular adventure. We had agreed to spend the greater part of this day with Lusieri, among the antiquities of the Citadel; and for the purpose, Mr. Cripps accompanied him to the Acropolis soon after breakfast. The author followed towards noon. About halfway up the steep which leads to the Propylaea, he heard a noise of laughter and of many clamorous voices, proceeding from a building situate in an area upon the left hand, which had the appearance of being a public bath. As it is always customary for strangers to mingle with the Moslems in such places without molestation, and as it had been the author's practice to bathe frequently for the preservation of his health, he advanced without further consideration towards the entrance, which he found covered with a carpet hanging before it. No human creature was to be seen without the bath, whether Turk or Greek. This was rather remarkable; but it seemed to be explained in the numbers who were heard talking within. As the author drew nearer to the door of the building, the voices were heard rather in a shriller tone than usual; but no suspicion entering into his mind, as to the sort of bathers which he would find assembled, he put aside the carpet, and stepping beneath the main dome of the *bagnio*, suddenly found himself in the midst of the principal women of Athens, many of whom were unveiled in every sense of the term, and all of them in utter amazement at the madness of the intrusion. The first impulse of astonishment entirely superseded all thought of the danger of his situation: he remained fixed and mute as a statue. A general shriek soon brought him to his recollection. Several black female slaves ran towards him, interposing before his face napkins, and driving him backwards towards the entrance.

He endeavoured, by signs and broken sentences, to convince them that he came there to bathe in the ordinary way; but this awkward attempt at an apology converted their fears into laughter, accompanied by sounds of "Hist! Hist!" and the most eager entreaties to him to abscond quickly, and without observation. As he drew back, he distinctly heard some one say, in Italian, that if he were seen he would be shot. By this time the Negro women were around him, covering his eyes with their hands and towels, and rather impeding his retreat, by pushing him blindfolded towards the door, whence he fled with all possible expedition.

As the sight of women in Turkey is rare, and always obtained with difficulty, the reader may perhaps wish to know what sort of beings the author saw, during the short interval that his eyes were open within the *bagnio*; although he can only describe the scene from a confused recollection. Upon the left hand, as he entered, there was an elderly female, who appeared to be of considerable rank, from the number of slaves sumptuously clad and in waiting upon her. She was reclined, as it is usual in all Turkish baths, upon a sort of divan, or raised floor, surrounding the circular hall of the bath, smoking and drinking coffee. A rich embroidered covering of green silk had been spread over her. Her slaves stood by her side, upon the marble pavement of the bath. Many other women of different ages were seated, or standing, or lying, upon the same divan. Some appeared coming in high wooden clogs from the sudatories or interior chambers of the bath, towards the divan; their long hair hanging dishevelled and straight, almost to the ground: the temperature of those cells had flushed their faces with a warm glow, seldom seen upon the pale and faded cheeks of the Grecian and Turkish women. Some of them were very handsome. Within the centre of the area, immediately beneath the dome, the black women and other attendants of the bath were busied heating towels, and preparing pipes and coffee for the bathers; according to the custom observed when men frequent these places.

The cause of this mistake remains now to be explained. This bath was not peculiarly set apart for the use of females: it was frequented also by the male inhabitants; but at stated hours the women have the privilege of appropriating it to their use; and this happened to be their time of bathing; consequently the men were absent. Upon such occasions, the Greek and Turkish women bathe together; owing to this circumstance, the news of the adventure was very speedily circulated all over Athens. As we did not return until the evening, the family with whom we resided, hearing of the affair, began to be uneasy, lest it had been brought to a serious termination; well knowing that of any of the Arnouts, or of the Turkish guard belonging to the citadel, had seen a man coming from the bath while the women were there, they, without hesitation, would have put him instantly to death; and the only reason we could assign for its never being afterwards noticed, was, that however generally it became the subject of conversation among the Turkish females of the city, their Moslem masters were kept in ignorance of the transaction.

We remained in the citadel during the rest of the day; not only to avoid any probable consequences of this affair, but also that we might once more leisurely survey the interesting objects it contains; and, lastly, have an opportunity of seeing from the Parthenon, the sun setting behind the Acropolis of Corinth; one of the finest sights in all Greece.

The Colours of Makronissos

We hired a pilot from Zia, for the Saronic Gulf; and left the harbour, with a fair wind, October the twenty-seventh, soon after sunrise.

We passed Macronisi, once called Helena, because Helen is supposed to have landed here after her expulsion from Troy; and we had such a glorious prospect of this island, and of the temple of Minerva Sunias standing upon the Cape [*the temple of Poseidon, Sounion, ed.*], together with other more distant objects, that we could recollect nothing like it: such a contrast of colours; such an association of the wonders of Nature and of Art; such perfection of grand and beautiful perspective, as no expression of perceptible properties can convey to the minds of those who have not beheld the objects themselves. Being well aware of the transitory nature of impressions made upon the memory by sights of this kind, the author wrote a description of this scene while it was actually before his eyes: but how poor is the effect produced by detailing the parts of a view in a narrative, which ought to strike as a whole upon the sense! He may tell, indeed, of the dark blue sea streaked with hues of deepest purple – of embrowning shadows – of lights effulgent as the sun – of marble pillars beaming a radiant brightness upon lofty precipices whose sides are diversified by refreshing verdure and by hoary mosses, and by gloomy and naked rocks; or by brighter surfaces reflecting the most vivid and varied tints, orange, red and grey: to these he may add an account of distant summits, more intensely azured than the clear and cloudless sky - of islands dimly seen through silvery mists upon the wide expanse of water shining, towards the horizon, as it were "a sea of glass": - and when he has exhausted his vocabulary, of every colour and shape exhibited by the face of Nature or by the works of Art, although he have not deviated from the truth in any part of his description, how little and how ineffectual has been the result of his undertaking.

1802 F. S. N. Douglas

Lamenting the Caryatids

One of the Caryatids, the six pillars of the Erechtheion in the form of maidens, was removed by Lord Elgin.

An illiterate servant of the Disdar of Athens. ..assured me that when the five other [maidens] had lost their sister, they manifested their affliction by filling the air at the close of the evening with the most mournful sighs and lamentations, that he himself had heard their complaints, and never without being so much affected as to be obliged to leave the citadel till they had ceased; and that the ravished sister was not deaf to their voice, but astonished the lower town where she was placed by answering in the same lamentable tones. We cannot refuse to acknowledge that the Athenians are not so indifferent as it has been sometimes represented to the wonders and monuments of their city.

1801-6 Edward Dodwell

Imprisoning the Disdar in a Box

Being aware, from the experience I had on my former visit to Athens, that the Disdar was a man of bad faith and insatiable rapacity, I made him a small present the first day, and begged the English agent to conclude a bargain with him for eighty piastres; in consideration of which I was to have free access to the Acropolis as often as I chose. In order to prevent the Disdar from exacting a larger sum, it was stipulated that the payment should take place after I had completed all my drawings and observations.

Many days however had not elapsed before he became impatient for the money, and asked me for a part of the promised sum: upon my refusal of which he prohibited my admission to the Acropolis. But when I returned, I succeeded in gaining an entrance, after enduring some insolent speeches from the soldiers, which I pretended not to understand. At length however I obtained their good graces by making some small presents to their children, who became so accustomed to this kind of tribute that they used to watch for me over the wall of the citadel. By throwing a few paras amongst them, I acquired the name of the Frank of the many paras, and for a small expense purchased the civility of the soldiers. The Disdar, however, became more and more impatient for the promised present; and in order to save time I frequently had my dinner sent up to the Acropolis; and with my artist employed the whole day in drawing. The Disdar watched the arrival of the dinner as eagerly as the children did the distribution of the paras, and seldom failed to drink the greater part of our wine; observing, that wine was not good for studious people like us.

After experiencing numerous vexations from this mercenary Turk, a ridiculous circumstance at length released us from the continuance of his importunities. I was one day engaged in drawing the Parthenon with the aid of my camera, when the Disdar, whose surprise was excited by the novelty of the sight, asked with a sort of fretful inquietude, what new conjuration I was performing with that extraordinary machine? I endeavoured to explain it, by putting in a clean sheet of paper, and making him look into the *camera obscura*; he no sooner saw the temple instantaneously reflected on the paper in all its lines and colours, than he imagined I had produced the effect by some magical process; his astonishment apparently mingled with alarm, and stroking his long black beard, he repeated the words *Allah, Masch-Allah*, several times. He again looked into the *camera obscura* with a kind of cautious diffidence, and at that moment some of his soldiers happening to pass before the reflecting glass, were beheld by the astonished Disdar walking upon the paper: he now became outrageous; and after calling me pig, devil, and Buonaparte, he told me, that if I chose, I might take away the temple and all the stones in the citadel; but that he would never permit me to conjure his soldiers into my box. When I found that it was in vain to reason with his ignorance, I changed my tone, and told him that if he did not leave me unmolested, I would put him into my box; and that he should find it a very difficult matter to get out again. His alarm was now visible; he immediately retired, and ever

The Upper Bazaar (E. Dodwell, 1805)

afterward stared at me with a mixture of apprehension and amazement. When he saw me come to the Acropolis, he carefully avoided my approach; and never afterwards gave me any further molestation…

The Destruction of the Parthenon Again

During my first tour to Greece I had the inexpressible mortification of being present when the Parthenon was despoiled of its finest sculpture, and instead of the picturesque beauty and high state of preservation in which I first saw it, it is now comparatively reduced to a state of shattered desolation. It is indeed impossible to suppress the feelings of regret which must arise in the breast of every traveller who has seen these temples before and since their late dilapidation. The whole proceeding was so unpopular in Athens, that it was necessary to pay the labourers more than their usual profits before any could be prevailed upon to assist in this work of profanation.

It is to be hoped that the ancient remains of Greece will for the future be preserved with more respect than they have hitherto experienced. The Constantinopolitan patriarch has been induced by the Greeks, who are fondly anticipating the regeneration of their country, to issue circular orders to all the Greeks not to disturb any ancient remains; and neither to assist nor connive at their destruction nor removal, under pain of excommunication.

1805-09 Colonel William Martin Leake

On Mount Parnes

The *Igumenos* of Aia Triadha, who came to St. Nicolas yesterday on hearing of my arrival, accompanies me to the summit of the mountain. The shortness of the days, and the uncertainty of the weather, making the most direct road preferable, we do not pass by Aia Triadha, but ascend the south-eastern slope of the mountain, in face of Kifissia and Mount Mendeli, crossing two or three *remata* which flow to the Cephisus. The lower part of the mountain is covered with pines; these, as we proceed, are mixed with holly-oaks and firs, and at length, towards the summit, the wood consists entirely of the last. Three years ago an accidental fire caught the fir wood, and consumed three quarters of it; such at least is the calculation of my companion the abbot; but one quarter perhaps would be nearer the truth. He says that the fire burnt four days, but that the greater part of the mischief was done in a few hours. Not much of the timber has been destroyed, but the dead and leafless trunks give a desolate appearance to the scenery, which before this accident must have been beautiful even in the present season: frequent rivulets and green ravines occur amidst the firs, and here and there a small space is cultivated with corn. With these exceptions the mountain is entirely covered with forests, and contains an inexhaustible supply of timber for the Athenians. It is to the manufacture of plank that I am indebted for the means of ascending the mountain on horseback by a tolerable road. Parnes still continues to supply Athens with charcoal, but the demand not being such as to cause any great consumption of wood in the manufacture of it, the people of Menidhi and Khassia … have no necessity at present to ascend very high in the mountain for their materials. The wild thyme, lentisk, myrtle, and other shrubs, produced in abundance upon Hymettus and the uncultivated parts of the *Pedeion* [plain, ed.], supply a sufficiency of wood for heating the ovens of Athens, and the *mangol* is not much used during the brief Athenian winter, when it is more the custom among the upper classes, all whose apartments have chimneys, to burn on their hearths some old olive or ilex, which has been overthrown by Boreas or Sciron. Both those trees make excellent firewood, but particularly the olive.

Mount Parnes still contains wild boars, as in the time of Pausanias, but bears are very rarely if ever seen. It abounds also in wolves, hares and partridges, and is covered with a good soil, better indeed than that of the now totally uncultivated plain which lies between it and Mount Pentelicum. Towards the top of the mountain, the rock makes its appearance on the most exposed ridges, but in general the firs reach to the very summit, and they impede in some directions the view, which is one of the most extensive in Greece. Attica, Boeotia, a part of Phocis, the southern portion of Euboea, the barriers of the Isthmus and the Saronic gulf, with the opposite coast of Argolis are ichnographically displayed. To the right of Mount Parnassus, rise the snow capped range of mountains on the borders of Aetolia and Doris, which extend to Oeta, to the right of which a long snowy ridge makes its appearance above the Boeotian mountains Ptoum and Hypatus, which I recognize for Othrys. In the northern portion of Euboea, the cliffs which border the coast between Politika and Limni are conspicuous…

A cross the Plain to Marathon

From Athens to Kifissia and Vrana. - At 9.55 pass through the Egripo gate: at 10.20 arrive at Ambelokipo, where are gardens and olive-grounds with small casini, situated along the Ilissus, for a considerable distance above the monastery of Petraki: from thence proceed along the south-eastern side of a ridge called Lule-vuno, the Ilissus remaining at a short distance on the right. By the road side are several round holes of great depth cut through the rock, belonging to a conduit apparently of ancient workmanship which still supplies the town, entering it at the north-eastern gate, which is vulgarly called Bubunistra, from the noise of the water in the conduit. At 11 on our left are the ruins of a Roman aqueduct on arches, crossing a valley, and which appears by its direction to have brought water from Mount Parnes. It was probably the same which was constructed for the Athenians by Trajan, and terminated by Antoninus Pius, as we learn from an inscription over the gate at Bubunistra. It is very possible that here, as at Eleusis, there was more than one source to the aqueduct; and that all the three mountains, Parnes, Pentelicum, and Hymettus, may have contributed water to the supply of Roman Athens. The work of Trajan was perhaps an addition from Mount Parnes, to the original conduit which was excavated in the rock, according to the mode customary in Greece before the time of the Romans.

We now enter the olive plantations which surround Kifisia and the adjacent villages. At 11.22 pass Kato Marusi, often called Logotheti, as belonging to the English vice-consul of that name. It contains only a pyrgo, a garden, and two or three cottages. At 11.25 cross a stream called Pispir, which originates near the monastery of Mendeli; it forms a considerable branch of the Cephusus. Having crossed several other smaller *remata*, and at 11.35 passed through Upper Marousi, we arrive at 11.56 at Kifisia, vulgarly pronounced Kifisha or Tjifisha. Here are several large pyrghi with good gardens, and a mosque, before which are a fountain and a beautiful plane-tree. The rare advantage in Attica of an abundance of running water in the middle of summer has rendered this place a favourite abode of the Turks of Athens; but the generality of the houses are in a ruinous condition, and all in the present season are empty. The Greeks are at work in the olive-grounds, cornfields, and vineyards; and the women, alarmed at the sight of an armed Albanian servant of mine, lock up their houses and hide themselves.

Having proceeded from Kifisia at 12.38, the olive-woods soon cease, and we enter upon the uncultivated root of Mount Pentelicum, which unites that mountain with Parnes. All the upper part of the plain of Athens adjacent to this ridge is covered with arbutus and stunted pines. At 1.25, having turned the end of the mountain, we are in a line between its summit and the pass of Deceleia, where the modern road to Egripo passes between two heights which are separated by a deep rema originating at a Kefalovrysi under Tatoy, a village, the territory of which is a narrow strip of cultivated land among the pine-woods. The torrent of Tatoy is a tributary of the Cephisus, but the fountains of Kifisia are the principal feeder of that river, though not the most distant, which is at Fasidhero, on the heights between Kifisia and Tatoy: this branch flows through the plain at no great distance to the west of Kifisia.

At 1.50 we pass the small village of Stamata in an elevated situation, surrounded by a few barren fields, among woods of pine. It was probably the site of a *demus*; but no fortifications or other remains are to be seen, although the position is important as being in the middle of the communication between the plain of Marathon and that of Athens. Several torrents flow through ravines on our right from Mount Pentelicum, and after uniting, enter the plain of Marathon at Vrana. We ascend through a barren mountainous tract studded with pines, until at 2.36, being at no great distance to the northward of the peaked summit of Mount Aforismos, an opening in the ridge commands a view of the plain of Marathon, the marsh, and salt lake, together with the channel and island of Euboea... Aforismos, though steep, has a very regular slope, and is beautifully clothed with pine-woods. It is probably the ancient Icarius. The descent from hence to Vrana is long, and we do not arrive there till 10.

1809-10 John Hobhouse

(Comparatively) Civilised Turks

Much greater hardships and perils than it can be the lot of any traveller in European Turkey to undergo, would be at once recompensed and forgotten on arriving at Athens - you there perceive an agreeable change in the aspect of all around you: the Turk, subdued either by the superior spirit of his subjects, or by the happy influence of a more genial climate, appears to have lost his ferocity, to have conformed to the soil, and to have put on a new character, ornamented by the virtues of humanity, kindness, and an easy affability, to which he attains in no other quarter of the Mahometan world. After having, in the course of your journey, been constantly on your guard against the outlaws of the land or sea, you feel that you may throw aside all unpleasant apprehensions, and, free from the cumbrous attendance of soldiers and servants, indulge in the contemplation of Athens.

The State of Athens at the beginning of the Nineteenth Century

Athens was in modern times so subject to the incursions of pirates and robbers, that it has been surrounded with a wall, about ten feet high; with apertures for the use of musketry. These walls, about forty years ago, were enlarged and repaired, and now comprehend a much wider space than when Chandler wrote, taking in two antiquities, the temple of Theseus and the arch of Adrian. The gateways to the wall, six in number, were formerly always closed at night, but the gates are now removed.

The open space between the walls and the city, one hundred and fifty or two hundred yards in breadth, is laid out in corn-grounds, and there are gardens attached to most of the principal houses. I walked round these walls at a brisk pace in forty-seven minutes - a circumstance which may suggest an idea of their circumference, and of the size of the city itself.

The number of houses in Athens is supposed to be between twelve and thirteen hundred; of these about four hundred are inhabited by Turks, the remainder by Greeks and Albanians, the latter of whom occupy about three hundred houses. There are also seven or eight Frank families, under the protection of the French Consul. None of the houses are well-built, nor so commodious as those of the better sort of Greeks at Ioannina or Livadia; and the streets are all of them narrow and irregular. In many of the lanes there is a raised causeway on both sides, so broad as to contract the middle of the street into a kind of dirty gutter. The bazaar is at a little distance from the foot of the hill, and is far from well furnished; but has several coffee-houses, which at all times are crowded by the more lazy of the Turks, amusing themselves with draughts and chess. It is formed by one street, rather wider than usual, intersecting another at right angles; and a little above where the two meet, is an ornamented fountain, the principal one in the town, supplied by a stream, which is brought in artificial channels or stone gutters, from a reservoir under Mount Hymettus.

The house of the Waiwode is of the poorer sort, though the entrance to it would become a palace, as it is between the columns of that antiquity distinguished by the name of the Doric Portico. That of the archbishop is the best in the town, containing within its precincts a spacious yard and garden. - There are only four principal mosques with minarets in the city, although there are eleven places of worship for the Turks. The number of Christian churches is out of all proportion to the Greek population; thirty-six are constantly open, and have services performed in them; but, reckoning the chapels which are shut except on the days of their peculiar saints, there are nearly two hundred consecrated buildings in Athens. The metropolitan church, called the Catholicon, is the only one of these that can be accounted handsome, and neither the temples of the Mahometans, nor those of the Christians, add any thing to the appearance of the town.

The Waiwode interferes but little with the management of the Christians, and generally contents himself with the receipt of the tribute, which is collected by the codja-bashees or archons - the immediate rulers, and, it should seem, the oppressors of the Greeks. The archons have been, until lately, eight in number; they are at present only five. I did not learn that the whole of these rulers ever assembled at any stated time, or have any regular system, for the transaction of business.

The regular tax transmitted from Attica to the Porte, is between seven hundred and seven hundred and fifty purses; but the codja-bashees, under various pretences, exact as many as fifteen hundred purses; and as they never give any account to the people of the manner in which their money has been disposed, do not fail to enrich themselves by the surplus amount. Threats, and sometimes punishments, are employed to wring from the peasants their hard-earned pittances; and such is the oppressive weight of the tyranny, that the murmurs of the commonalty have frequently broken out into open complaints; and even a complete revolution, involving the destruction of the archons, and an establishment of a better order of things, has been meditated by the more daring and ambitious among the oppressed...

The archbishop of Athens exercises an absolute authority over the whole of the clergy of his see, and has a prison near his house for the confinement of offenders, whom he may punish with the bastinade, or in any degree short of death. His place is purchased of the Patriarch, and is consequently the object of many intrigues, which not infrequently terminate in the expulsion of the incumbent, and the election of another archbishop. Popular clamour has also sometimes displaced such of these priests as have exceeded the usual bounds of extortion...

The families of Franks settled at Athens chiefly support themselves by lending money, at an interest of from twenty to thirty per cent, to the trading Greeks, and in a trifling exportation of oil.

They add, it must be supposed, considerably to the pleasures of a residence in this city, by their superior attainments and the ease of their manners. They have balls and parties in the winter and spring of the year, in their own small circle, to which the principal Greeks are invited.

Until within a few years, a journey to Athens was reckoned a considerable undertaking, fraught with difficulties and dangers; and at the period when every young man of fortune, in France and England, considered it an indispensable part of his education to survey the monuments of ancient art remaining in Italy, only a few desperate scholars and artists ventured to trust themselves amongst the barbarians, to contemplate the ruins of Greece. But these terrors, which a person who has been on the spot, cannot conceive could ever have been well-founded, seem at last to be dispelled: Attica at present swarms with travellers, and several of our fair countrywomen have ascended the rocks of the Acropolis. So great, indeed, has been the increase of visitants, that the city, according to a scheme formed by a Greek who was once in our service, will soon be provided with a tavern, a novelty surely never before witnessed at Athens.

The Climate

The winter in this country generally sets in about the beginning of January, and in the middle of that month the snows begin to fall. They were a little earlier in 1810, and, being accompanied with a strong north-east wind, made the cold rather unpleasant for two or three days, and drove large flights of wild turkeys and woodcocks into the plain close to the city. After the snows are down, which seldom are seen for more than a few days, except on the summits of the mountains, where they remain about a month, there are three weeks of fine weather, frosty and cold in the mornings and evenings, but with a clear sky and the sun shining hotly in the middle of the day. The natives then wear their warmest pelisses, and burn large fires of wood, brought into the city by the peasants who dwell on the sides of Mount Parnes.

The corn in the plain of Athens, which is cut in May, is very high at the beginning of March; and then also the vines begin to sprout, the olive-groves to bud, and the almond-trees, of which there is a great number in the neighbouring gardens, are so covered with their white and purple blossom, as to impart their varied hues to the face of the whole country.

The Plain of Athens

The region immediately to the north and north-west of the city, a plain of an irregularly oval shape, is interspersed with small villages, hidden in shady groves; and the modern Athenians, who are as fond as their ancestors were, of the luxury of a summer retreat, and who are induced, both by custom and temperament, to prefer vegetables and fruits to less cooling diet, reckon nearly a thousand gardens in the circuit of their small territory. To many of these are attached kiosks, or country-houses, ill-constructed indeed, being the lower part of them of mud, and the upper of badly jointed planks, but still capable of affording an agreeable shelter during the intolerable heats of summer. Some of these gardens are near villages, under the hills at some distance from the city, such as Kevrisha, the ancient Cephisia, at the foot of Mount Pentelicus, and Callandri, in the same quarter; but the large tract of them is in the long line of olive-groves which form the western boundary of the plain of Athens. The district watered by the Cephisus, in the neighbourhood of the site of the Academy, and the Colonus Hippius, about twenty minutes' walk from the gate leading to Thebes, is to the south called Sepolia, and to the north Patisia, and is divided into those extensive grounds which are particularly allotted for supplying the city with fruit and vegetables, and are for the most part not cultivated by their owners, but let out to the peasants of the villages.

The Cephissus, a sort of ditch-stream, almost dry in summer, and in winter only a torrent, passes through the extent of olive-groves and gardens, each of which it serves, by turns, to water. The watering is effected by raising a low mound round eight or nine trees, and then introducing the stream through dykes, so as to keep the roots and part of the trunks under water for the necessary length of time. Each owner waters his grove for thirty or forty hours, and pays a para a tree to the Waiwode, or to him who has farmed the revenue from that officer. During this period the peasants construct huts with boughs, and are mutually watchful, both day and night, neither to lose their own portion, nor to allow to others an unfair abundance of the valuable streams. I have several times seen their fires amongst the trees; and, as they watch in parties, andmix, as usual, much mirth with their employment, have heard the sound of their voices, and the tinkling music of their guitars, on returning to Athens from an evening's ride.

The village of Cevrishia [Kifissia] is the favourite resort of the Turks of Athens during the summer and autumnal months, and is alone, of all the villages of Attica, adorned with a mosque: it contains about two hundred houses. In the middle of it is an open space, where there are two fountains, and a large plane-tree, beneath whose overhanging branches is a flat stone, which is so carved into squares as to serve for a draught-table, and round which the Turks are seen sedately smoking, or engaged at their favourite pastime. This delightful spot still continues to answer the agreeable description given it by one who had here often wandered through the long and shady avenues, or rested by the side of the pure glassy stream, overflowing the margin of the marble baths in a thousand rills, which mingled their murmurs with the music of the birds. Even the modern Cephisia might be thought worthy the partialities of such an encomiast as Aulus Gellius.

1809-11 John Galt

Notes Composed in Stylish Lodgings

I have taken up my lodgings in the Capuchin convent, belonging to the Propaganda of Rome. The choragic monument of Lysicrates, which has been nicknamed the Lantern of Demosthenes, is attached to it and serves as a closet to the friar who has charge of the house. He has given me the use of it, and I have no less a pleasure, at this moment, than writing in one of the oldest and most elegant buildings in Europe.

My reception here, in consequence of the recommendation of Vilhi Pashaw, has been embarrassingly distinguished. The Governor sent me a couple of lambs and a dozen of fowls immediately on my arrival, and an offer of everything in his power during my stay in Athens...

On my return to my lodgings, and telling the friar what I had seen, he mentioned to me a curious practice of the young girls here when they become anxious to get husbands. On the first evening of the new moon they put a little honey, a little salt, and a piece of bread on a plate, which they leave at a particular spot, on the bank of the Ilissus, near the Stadium, and muttering some ancient words, of which the meaning has been forgotten, but which are to the effect that fate may send them 'a pretty young man' return home and long for the fulfilment of their charm. Above the spot where these offerings are made, a statue of Venus, according to Pausanias, formerly stood. It is therefore highly probable, that what is now a superstitious, was anciently a religious rite.

At first, as every traveller who comes to Athens must be, I was greatly vexed and disappointed by the dilapidation of the Temple of Minerva; but I am consoled by the reflection that the spoils are destined to ornament our own land, and that if they had not been taken possession of by Lord Elgin, they would probably have been carried away by the French.

The distant appearance of the Acropolis somewhat resembles that of Stirling Castle, but it is inferior in altitude and general effect. As a fortress, it is incapable of resisting any rational attack; the Turks, however, consider it a mighty redoubtable place; nay, for that matter, they even think frail old Athens herself capable of assuming a warlike attitude. At the proclamation of the present war against the Russians, they closed her paralytic gates in a most energetic manner. The following morning, Father Paul of the convent went at daybreak to take the air among the columns of Olympian Jove, and arriving at the arch of Hadrian, found them still shut: whereupon he gave them a kick, and the gates of Athens flew open at the first touch of his reverence's toe.

The baths and coffee-houses are the only places of public amusement which the Athenians of the nineteenth Christian century enjoy. Some time ago, a Savoyard, with a magic lantern, arrived in the town, and procured leave to exhibit. The exhibition excited the utmost amazement, for the showman also played hocus-pocus tricks, and vomited fire. Nothing was heard among the Turks but of the Magos; and the Greeks, little less astonished, abandoned themselves to the most mythological conjectures.

After dark every body who has occasion to go abroad must carry, or be accompanied with, a light. If found by the patrol without this flaming minister, the culprit is immediately taken to the guardhouse, and whipped on the soles before he is examined.

To the mere antiquary, this celebrated city cannot but long continue interesting, and to the classical enthusiast just liberated from the cloisters of his college, the scenery and ruins may often awaken enthusiasm and inspire delight, but to the traveller who rests for recreation, or who seeks a solace for misfortune, how wretched, how solitary, how empty is Athens!

The Corruption of the Greek Church

The town contains no less than thirty-nine parish churches, besides the metropolitan, and upwards of eighty chapels. The metropolitan is sometimes spoken of as a parish church, and it is usual to say, in consequence, that there are forty parishes. Athens is the seat of an archbishop...

In order to give you as full a notion as possible of the present state of Greek clergy, I will begin with the parish in which I reside. It is that of the Panagia Candili, or the Virgin of a Candle, or with a Candle, I cannot tell you which; and in it there are no less than ten chapels. The present incumbent bought the living on the condition of paying to the archbishop seven pounds ten shillings yearly. The ways and, means for raising this sum, and what is over for his own subsistence, consists of certain customary gifts at births, marriages, sicknesses, and deaths, thanksgiving for escapes, etc., etc. In cases of extreme danger, the high and efficient prayers of his Grace the archbishop may be obtained for the felonious sum of forty shillings.

The parochial pastors are removable at the will of the archbishop, and the offer of a better bonus is a good and valid reason for discarding any clergyman in Athens.

Considering the extent of the diocese, and the credulity of the people, the archbishopric of Athens should be a tolerable living; but the simony and corruptions of the Greek church are not limited to the inferior priesthood. Corruption, indeed, physical, moral, and political, always works upwards [*Ed. 'downward' surely!*]; and in Greece, as everywhere else, the general law prevails. The diocese is purchased for an annual stipend from the Patriarch of Constantinople, and the patriarchate itself is bought in a similar manner from the Divan; the Greek Church being in this respect little better than an excise on Christian souls for the emolument of the Ottoman state.

The nett income of the present archbishop of Athens may possibly exceed three hundred pounds sterling. His palace would, in Scotland, rank as a manse of the first class, and in England as a respectable parsonage. But the primate of all England does not exact a tithe of the reverence which is levied by this prelate.

The Charming of Serpents

Among the wonders of the east usually related by travellers, the charming of serpents, and rendering them harmless and familiar, is none of the least. If the art has not been before explained to you, I have it now in my power to communicate the secret, and you may make the experiment when you will. This morning a number of Albanian boys came to the gate of the convent, enquiring if the Inglesos would be pleased to see a tame viper, and having received permission to present themselves, they came up stairs with their show. It was a snake upwards of three feet long, twining round the arm of one of them in the true Laocoon gusto. The boy held it by the neck, between his finger and thumb. After exhibiting it for some time in this situation, he laid it down, and the others tormented it with their sticks to show off. Desiring Jacomo to enquire particularly how they reduced the serpent to so great a state of docility, I received the following account.

They found it asleep, placed a cleft stick across its neck, and giving it a bit of rag to bite, in order to exhaust its poison, they then dug out its teeth with a knife. Afterwards, in the way that Frederick the Great made stupid fellows alert soldiers, namely, by castigation, they reduced it to a proper state to be reviewed. The whole art seems to be no more than this: the vipers are deprived of their teeth, and rendered weak by a good beating. The movements they exhibit are evidently only their natural motions languidly performed.

Various Superstitions

To this worthy man, who, though a friar, is really liberal-minded, pious, and charitable, I am indebted for many curious and laughable anecdotes of the practice of his brethren to gain popularity with the old women of their neighbourhood. Women are the pillars of the church in all countries. I am also obliged to him for some information relating to the superstitions of the modern Athenians that I think will interest you.

One day he happened to take a child into his arms from its mother, as she passed the gate of the convent, and began to caress it, observing that he thought it the prettiest in all the town. The mother instantly, spitting in the poor child's face snatched it out of his arms in great terror; exclaiming, that what he had said was enough to cause the death, of her baby. I fancy the English of this is, that such praises might make her so proud, that Heaven would ... nip the life of the child in order to humble the pride of the parent.

When the Athenian women wash clothes, they are particularly careful to guard them from the moonshine, which they say never fails to produce sickness and melancholy to the wearers. If by accident the wet clothes fall within the glimpses of the moon, the washerwomen must spit three times over them, to neutralize the malignant property which it is supposed they have acquired. The rationale of this I cannot even conjecture.

The friar tells me that it is quite in vain to attempt to obtain a light or any fire from the houses of the Albanians after sunset, if the husband or head of the house be still a-field; This freat seems to be a police regulation of Nature's enactment, in order to obviate a plausible pretext for entering the cottages in the obscurity of twilight, when the women are defenceless by the absence of the men...

Four or five days after the baptism of a child, the midwife comes to the house, and prepares with her own mystical hands certain savoury messes, spreads a table, and places them on it; then departs, and all the house in silence retire to sleep, leaving the door open. This table is covered for the *Miri* of the child, an invisible being that is supposed to have the care of its destiny. In the course of the night, the *Miri* generally comes in the shape of a cat, or some other creature; and if contented with its charge, or, in other words, if the child is to be fortunate, partakes of the feast. If the *Miri* does not arrive, or does not taste the food, the child is considered as devoted to misfortune and misery, and, no doubt, the treatment it afterwards receives is conformable to this unlucky predestination.

When the mother feels the fullness of time at hand, the [midwife] is summoned. When called to the mysteries, she brings a three-footed stool in her hand, the uses of which the friar cannot well tell me, as they are known only to the initiated. The midwife having arrived, and being received by the matronly friends of the mother, proceeds, as the first part of the rites, to open every lock and lid in the house. At this ceremony, all the females who have not found, keys for themselves are, on analogical principles, excluded from the room. When this is done, those who remain must wait the conclusion, and none of them after the birth may be touched with impunity, as they are considered unclean, and requiring the purification of a sprinkling of holy water, and the benediction of an ecclesiastic.

These singular notions and practices induced me be more particular in my enquiries; and the friar having heard of others among the Albanians no less curious, we sent for an old woman, who is famous in the neighbourhood for her knowledge of simples, and the prognostications of disease, conceiving that the same sagacity which had enabled her to make the observations on which her skill is founded had also probably made her acquainted with the vulgar superstitions.

By her we were informed that the Albanians think that mankind, after death (observe I am not speaking of the religious opinions, but only of their vulgar notions) become *voorthoolakases*, and often pay visits to their friends, for the same reasons and in the same way that our country-ghosts go abroad. Their fashionable visiting-hour is also the same, viz. midnight. A *voorthoolakas* comes to reveal hidden treasures, to accuse murderers, and to a punish reprobates; to enforce the practice of honesty, justice, and, good-conduct, and, like our ghosts, the *voorthoolakases* uniformly vanish in a flash of fire.

But the *Collyvillory* of the Albanians is another sort of personage. He is one of your Pucks, that delight in mischief and pranks, and is besides a lewd and foul spirit, and therefore is very properly detested. Colly is supposed to be let loose on the night of the Nativity, with licence for twelve nights to plague men, or rather men's wives; at which time some one of the family must keep wakeful vigil all the livelong night, beside a clear and cheerful fire, otherwise this nasty abominable devil would make such an aqueous evacuation on the hearth, that never fire could be kindled there again.

The Albanians are also pestered with another species of infernal creatures, which seem to be of the self-same disposition as the Scottish witches and warlocks. These are men and women whose gifts are followed by misfortunes, whose eyes glimpse evil, and by whose touch the most prosperous affairs are blasted They work their malicious sorceries in the dark, collect herbs of baleful influence, by the help of which they strike their enemies with palsy, and cattle with distemper. The males are called *Maissi*, and the females *Maissa*. When they have resolved to bewitch a house or village with their spells, one of the *Maissi* rides three times round the fated place, screaming a prayer, the meaning of which is only known to the initiated, and the God Beelzebub.

These are undoubtedly curious national peculiarities; but there is another still more singular; and which interested me the more, as it resembles the well known mountaineer faculty of the second sight. The Albanians have among them persons who pretend to know the character of approaching events, by hearing sounds which resemble those that will accompany the actual occurrence .

Deception in Megara

Megara is entirely inhabited by Greeks who wear the Albanian dress, but have neither the simplicity nor the integrity commonly found under it. Among other things, we were informed that two bas-reliefs had lately been found by one of the inhabitants, and we went to his house to see them. The husband was not at home, but the wife told us that a priest, going his rounds, the other day, had blessed the house and sprinkled it with holy water; and that for this they had given him two marbles. A schoolmaster, who like an ancient philosopher under a portico, was giving lessons in an open shed to a dozen or twenty boys, overhearing our conversation, advanced and said that to his knowledge the sculptures were still in the house. After some altercation, it was at length agreed that we should be favoured with at least a sight of the antiques.

On making enquiry into the cause of this singular attempt, as it appeared to me, at useless concealment, I was informed that the governor of Corinth is building a fountain, and that, if he heard of the bas-reliefs, he would oblige the possessor to deliver them to him at Corinth, or, if he sold them, to pay him the money. The story of giving them to the priest had been invented in order to preserve them, because the Turks respect what belongs to the church, and regard whatever is set apart for its decoration or service with dread and veneration. Give me leave to tell you an anecdote by way of illustrating this tolerative superstition of the Turks.

Their indolence renders them hypochondriacal, and they are often ill of diseases of the imagination. An officer belonging to the garrison of Athens had lately a severe attack of this malady, and sent for a physician, a Frenchman of some humour. The doctor amused him with one dose of harmless trash after another, but without success. One morning happening to observe the head of a statue applied to some derogatory purpose in the Turk's house, both in order to get possession of the marble, and to divert the mind of the patient, he said to him "I have at last found out the cause of your disease, and I am only surprised that you are not worse." "And what is it, doctor?" asked the patient pathetically. "Nothing less," answered the doctor severely, "than a castigation of Heaven for the ignominy with which you treat one of our saints." "I!" exclaimed the Turk, "I certainly use no saint ignominiously, doctor." "Nay, but you do," answered the physician; "the saint is on the floor before you. Jesu, Maria! In what a condition!" "Oh!" replied the Turk, "how could I know that such a figure was a saint? "But" he added in a penitent tone, "I will order him to be washed, and immediately sent to church."

"There is no need for you to take that trouble," said the wily Frenchman, "I will carry him with me; and you will swallow this composing draught, and go to sleep comfortably." The officer obeyed with alacrity, slept soundly, and awoke perfectly recovered. The physician carried off the head, which, upon examination, proved of excellent workmanship, and a valuable fee. This story father Paul had from the doctor himself.

In Megara there are many inscriptions of no more value than the mortifications in your parish church. I observed in the street the trunk of a Venus, which, though terribly mutilated, still retained some traces of beautiful workmanship. I know not whether it is the effect of accident or design, that all the imperfect statues I have met with in Greece want the head, apparently broken off, but neatly cut. Pray is it quite ascertained that the Greeks were in the practice of making such tasteless things as busts? Possibly in many cases the statue may have been sacrificed in order to render the bust part easily transported.

The present town of Megara contains about one thousand inhabitants, who are chiefly employed in agriculture. A few of the cottages are neat; but the place on the whole is much inferior to the metropolis of Salamis. Being the midway stage between Athens and Corinth, it is often greatly harassed by the Turks and their horses. The citizens have, however, adopted an effectual plan to relieve themselves from accommodating the latter: they have made the doors of their cottages so low that no ordinary sized horse can enter them.

The inhabitants of the country round Megara are more military than those of Attica. They are, in fact, an organized militia, or rather I believe, they are domiciliated soldiers, appointed to guard the passes of the isthmus - and since they were settled there, Megara, which had become almost extinct, has risen to be again a very respectable village.

The house in which I procured lodgings was afflictingly infested with fleas, and a garrulous old man, who held with me a very edifying conversation to himself of several hours, but of which I did not literally understand one word: a few nods and winks, however, answered every purpose of speech on my side of the question; and he seemed to think me exceedingly conversible and jocose. When he went away, I should soon after have fallen asleep, but for the skipping multitudes that assailed me with beak and fang. Fleas, you know, like lions and tigers, and other bloody-minded beasts, are always most active during the night.

Next morning there was a great religious ceremony in the village; in its object pious and affecting, but rendered ludicrous by the circumstances which attended it. For a long time no rain has fallen, and the ground is quite parched. Last year the crop was deficient, and throughout the whole Ottoman empire great scarcity prevails at this moment. Another failure of the hopes of the husbandman must produce absolute famine. It is not therefore surprising that the people are alarmed, and seek to avert the calamity with which they are threatened.

At daybreak the whole town was afoot, men, women, and children, together with the inhabitants of several adjacent hamlets; forming in all upwards of two thousand persons. Being divided into three bands, they walked hand in hand towards the seashore, headed by the priests, and chanting a prayer suitable to the occasion. The first was called the company of God the Father, and carried a picture in which he is supposed to be delineated; the second was the company of the Son; and the last that of the Holy Ghost; each bearing suitable pictures. On arriving at the sea, the pictures were successively dipped in the water; and the procession then went to the village.

Praying for Rain in the Temple of Zeus

The drought still continues to parch, and the price of corn to rise. The distresses of the poor have become pressing and clamorous. The rumour from all parts, from Egypt, from Asia, and from Constantinople, is the progress of the scarcity, and the only enquiries are respecting the price of bread. The misery that threatens in individuals, renders the public calamity of the war but of secondary interest.

Last week, Hogia Murat, the governor, called together the chief Turks, and the primates of the city, and represented to them the necessity of adopting some measures for alleviating the distresses of the poor. He proposed a subscription for that purpose, and began it himself, with three purses, or seventy-five pounds sterling, a vast sum here. With the amount of this subscription, corn is to be imported, and sold at a reduced price.

Public prayers for rain are now ordered for nine successive days, and this morning they commenced. The first three are allotted to the Ottomans, the next to the Arabians and slaves, and the last three to the Christians. The ceremony began this morning, two hours before sunrise. The three principal emirs, with a boy before each of them, carrying the Koran on his head, followed by all the Turks of the city, with their male children, walked in procession to the place among the ruins of the Temple of Jupiter Olympius, which I have already mentioned; the emirs repeating, from papers which they held in their hands, the prayer for the occasion, and the Turks responsing "Amen" at the close of each sentence. After their arrival at the place of worship, the chief mufti delivered a sermon, sitting on the steps of the pulpit. His manner was simple, moderate, and slow, but impressive. The discourse lasted upwards of an hour and a half, and his auditors behaved as most Christian congregations do on similar occasions. Some listened with unaffected and sincere attention; others were so intent on making religious faces that I suspect they heard very little; and there were several young fellows who seemed to consider the whole a very tiresome affair. The boys were all for some time most exemplary in their deportment; but gradually, one by one, they began to move from place to place, and to throw pebbles and straws at each other. The governor, who is a really a good man, and gets tipsy every night, which, Father Paul jocularly observes, is the cause of his goodness, knowing the mufti to be rather long-winded, did not make his appearance till after the close of the discourse, but in time to assist at one of the most extraordinary ceremonies I ever witnessed or heard of.

A flock of ewes and lambs was driven together in the neighbourhood of the worshippers, and soon after the close of the sermon, the lambs were separated from their mothers, and all the Turks standing up began a loud and general supplication, in the most pathetic tones. The divided flock at the same time began to bleat. It is not easy to convey to you by words the effect of this simple and effective accompaniment, which infinitely, in my opinion, excelled the lead and leather popery of all the organs of Christendom. Viewing the dry bed of the Ilissus, and the blasted appearance of the grass, and beholding the sun, which at this moment arose from behind Mount Hymettus, red and arid, like a shield of polished copper, it seemed to me as if all nature, feeling the destructive thirst, seconded the supplication of man, and sympathized in his fears.

[*It is remarkable that these Muslims chose, as the place from which to supplicate Allah for rain, the site of the temple of Zeus, the rain god of the ancient Greeks.ed.*]

The Slave Trade at Piraeus

The Piraeus, as all the world knows, was the Wapping of Athens. It had a theatre for the sailors and their sweethearts; and, no doubt, it was a dirty blackguard place. The town no longer exists. A monastery, dedicated to St. Spiridion, and inhabited by three or four friars; a summer retreat and warehouses belonging to a Frenchman, who resides in the city in the double capacity of physician and merchant; and a custom-house, the collector belonging to which is a dealer in fruit and Greekish spirits; constitute the small beginnings of a new town. Poor states cannot afford to maintain their revenue officers independent of other employment: it is there fore expedient to let the revenue, as in this instance, to farmers. A few ports only, in all Turkey, can afford to pay their custom-house officers; but the commercial poverty is so extended, as not to admit of altering the general system of the empire for a few exceptions.

In the harbour, two ships were at anchor. One of them was destined to receive the spoils of the Parthenon; and the other had lately arrived with a cargo of human beings from the coast of Africa. The Athenians were always great slavemongers; and, at present, there are between two and three hundred in the city: they are chiefly females, the servants of the Turks, who have the reputation of being indulgent and kind-hearted masters. About a week ago, a black girl brought a duck to our convent for sale, and the friar asked her how she came to be made a slave. She gave a shrill ludicrous laugh, and said that she was taken by the catchers while she was at the well for water. She was born in Egypt, and caught in the neighbourhood of Alexandria.

The only trade at the Piraeus, besides the little that is done in the human commodity, is the exportation of the productions of, the Athenian territory, the principal article of which is oil.

An Unwelcome Excursion to the Marble Quarries of Pendeli

Of all the miseries of travelling, I do think that one of the greatest is to be obliged to visit those things which other travellers have happened to visit and describe. The marble quarry of Mount Pentelicus, from which the material for the principal edifices of Athens are supposed to have been brought, has become, it seems, one of the standing curiosities of Greece. This quarry is a large hole in the side of the hill; and a drapery of woodbine, which hangs fantastically like a curtain over the entrance, is the only thing worth looking at about it. The interior is just like any other cavern.

Knowing beforehand the sort of amusement which I had to expect, it is probable that I should not have been at the trouble of riding three hours over a vile breakneck road to see this curiosity; but Lord Byron and Mr. Hobhouse, with whom I happened to come from Gibraltar to Malta, being at present in Athens, and having chosen this as the object of one of their excursions, I was induced to accompany them.

We halted at a monastery at the foot of the mountain, where we got a guide, and ate fried eggs and olives. Dr. Chandler says, that the monks of this house are summoned to prayers by a tune which is played on a piece of an iron hoop, and on the outside of the church we saw a piece of crooked iron suspended, by which the hour of prayer is announced. What sort of a tune could be played upon this instrument, the doctor judiciously left his readers to imagine.

When we reached the mouth of the cave by the "very bad track," which the learned personage above-mentioned clambered up before us, we saw the little house which he made some use of in his description. This building the doctor at first thought was possibly a hermit's cell, but upon more deliberate reflection he became of opinion that it was designed perhaps for a sentinel to look out, and regulate, by signals, the approach of the men and teams employed in carrying marble to the city. This is a very sagacious notion. It is highly probable indeed that sentinels were appointed to regulate by signals the manoeuvres of carts coming to fetch away stones...

Having looked at the outside of the quarry, and the guide having lighted candles, we entered [*the cavern*] and saw what doctor Chandler saw, "chippings of marble." We then descended into a hole, just wide enough to let a man pass through it, and when we had descended far enough, we stopped, and, like many others who had been there before us, engraved our names, and crawled back again into the blessed sunshine.

If you have any desire to make an excursion equally instructive, find out an old dry subterraneous drain, then take half an ell of wax taper in your hand, and lying down on your belly like a worm, crawl into the drain. When you have got to a place where you have elbow-room, take out your penknife, with which scratch your name upon a stone. If in this operation the blade should snap, or, by shutting suddenly, should cut your finger, continue the work with the stump, or suck the wound, as the case may require. Having finished the inscription, turn your head a little askew to the left, if the place is large enough to allow you, and look at the engraving from the right corner of your dexter eye, for that is the proper position to admire such performances. This done, endeavour to get away from the scrape in the best manner you can. One word more by way of advice: if you happen to have a companion in the descent, and he goes out first, there is great reason to apprehend that he may give you a kick in the face. If he is behind, the chance is equal that you will kick him, which is the more agreeable way of the two for the accident to fall out. Therefore be sure to get out first, if at all possible.

1810 Charles Meryon

Piraeus and Some Friends

At daybreak on the 12th. of September we weighed anchor. The wind was fair, the day delightful, and by twelve o'clock we were at the entrance of the Piraeus.

The fame of Lord Byron's exploit in swimming across the Hellespont, from Sestos to Abydos, in imitation of Leander, had already reached us, and, just as we were passing the mole-head, we saw a man jump from it into the sea, whom Lord Sligo recognized to be Lord Byron himself, and, hailing him, bade him hasten to dress and to come and join us.

We sailed in, and anchored before a mean building at the bottom of the port, which served as a custom-house. There happened to be on the strand about a dozen horses, which had brought down part of the freight of a polacca lying at the quay to load. These were forcibly seized by our Tartar, and, laden with our baggage, sent off to the town, which is six miles inland. Lord Sligo himself set off on one of the horses of Lord Byron, who had now joined us, to send down conveyances for Lady Hester and the rest of us. It was evening before we entered Athens. Preparations had been made for our coming, and a house cleared of its tenants expressly for Lady Hester. Mr. A. and myself were lodged in a house which Lord Sligo had occupied some time previous to our reaching Greece. It had been tenanted by other English travellers, and the owners, who let it, were so far acquainted with Englishmen's wants, as to have procured some chairs and a table, furniture then seldom found in a room in Turkey...

While we were waiting on the shore, we had leisure to survey what was around us. The country immediately adjoining the port seemed bare and without verdure. Some remains of the quays, which once bordered the Piraeus, lay scattered at the water's edge, and a few ill-constructed boats, made fast by rush hawsers, showed how low the navy of Athens had declined. There were some Turkish women sitting on the bank, covered in every part excepting their eyes, who immediately walked away when we attempted to approach them. We were ignorant of the customs of the country, and Mr. A. made signs to them to stop, which excited greatly the anger of some Turks who were standing near us.

The horses arrived in about two hours. As we quitted the Piraeus the aspect of the country became more pleasing. Gentle slopes and hills, rising and sinking with a wavy line, gave a tranquillity and repose to the scenery, which few can understand who have not felt it in those countries.

While musing on the goodly prospect around me, on temples and demigods, on the Parthenon and Socrates, the cool Ilyssus and the shades of Academus, my reflections were interrupted by the loud smack of a whip, applied by Aly the Tartar to the back of a poor Greek, accompanied by a louder oath, which at once dissipated my vision, and brought me back to the reality of things around me.

Making Oneself at Home

I employed the first day in making my apartment tidy. I found my bedroom to be a white-washed chamber, having an unglazed window, with a shutter, which excluded light and let in the wind. There were large crevices in the floor, through which the dust and rubbish were swept, not by a long-handled broom, for I never saw one throughout Turkey, but by a hand-broom, upon these materials my servant had to go to work to make me a chamber. A mat was spread upon the floor, as being the coolest covering to the gaping chinks; my camp-bed was laid on boards, supported by two trestles; a piece of white linen formed a curtain to the window, and, my mosquito net being suspended on cross pieces of twine, I found myself almost as comfortable as if I had been lying upon an English four post bedstead. Lord Sligo and Mr. A., who seemed to despise luxuries in proportion as they had no means of enjoying them, made their beds on the floor, and all the servants slept in the open air. But, in this climate, to sleep under the cope of heaven is no cause of complaint...

The Boubounistra Gate (E. Dodwell, 1805)

341

The house occupied by Lady Hester was spacious and handsome, having a courtyard, a bath, and other requisites for comfort and quiet. None of the windows of the house had casemates, and, to ensure greater warmth, it was necessary to nail up some of them with old carpets, mats, etc. Her Ladyship was a great contriver of comfort, and I have known her transform a naked room, with holes in the walls, floors, and doors, into a snug apartment. The janissary sat at her gate, on a raised wooden couch, something like a kitchen table, with a railed back to it, which is generally to be seen at the doorways of most great persons in European Turkey, and upon which the master of the house will often place himself, to smoke his pipe, and to breathe the morning and evening air. The janissary acted as porter and guard.

I observed one morning that Aly, the janissary, had his feet swathed in old rags: on inquiring what was the matter, he pretended that they were covered on account of the cold; but I learned in the course of the day that he had been bastinadoed on the soles at the governor's, for riotous behaviour.

It was many days before we were settled and very many before we had surveyed the marvellous beauties of architecture and statuary which are left in this celebrated city. Our time passed most delightfully. The mornings were spent in examining the remains of ancient edifices, in rides, and in excursions into the environs; the evenings in the society of a few clever artists, who, enamoured of the spot, seemed wedded to it for the rest of their days...

Impression of Lord Byron

Lord Byron made one of the small society which collected every evening at Lady Hester's. What struck me as singular in his behaviour was his mode of entering a room; he would wheel

The Capuchin Monastery (C. Stanfield, 1811)

round from chair to chair to chair, until he reached the one where he proposed sitting, as if anxious to conceal his lameness as much as possible. He consulted me for the indisposition of a young Greek, about whom he seemed much interested.

1810 C. R. Cockerell

An Unfriendly People

This writer seems to have experienced some problems in getting along with the Greeks.

There is hardly anything that can be called society among the Greeks. I know a few families, but I very rarely visit them, for such society as theirs is hateful. As for the Greek men, in their slavery they have become utterly contemptible, bigoted, narrow-minded, lying, and treacherous. They have nothing to do but pull their neighbours' characters to pieces. Retired as I am, you would hardly believe there is not a thing I do that is not known and worse represented. Apropos of an act of insolence of the Disdar aga's (which I made him repair before the waiwode, the governor of the town), I heard that it was reported that I had been bastinadoed. This report I had to answer by spreading another, viz. that I should promptly shoot anyone, Turk or Christian, who should venture to lay a hand upon me. This had its effect, and I heard no more of bastinadoing. I do not think we are in much danger here. The Franks are highly esteemed by the governor, and the English especially.

The Return of the "War Heroes"

The other day we witnessed the departure of the old waiwode and the arrival of the new. Just as the former was leaving, the heroes from the Russian war arrived, brown and dusty. The leading man carried a banner. As they came into the court they were received with discharge of pistols, and embraced by their old friends with great demonstrations. I was very much affected. I heard afterwards that the rogues had never been further than Sofia, and had never smelt any powder but that which had gone to the killing of one of them by his companion in a brawl. So much for my feelings. The outgoing waiwode was escorted by the new one with great ceremony as far as the sacred wood.

Some "Franks" Suffer An Indignity

March 13 is the Turkish New Year's Day, and is a great festival with them. The women go out to Asomatos and dance on the grass. Men are not admitted to the party, but Greek women are. Linckh, Haller, and I went to see them from a distance, taking with us a glass, the better to see them. We were discovered, and some Turkish boys, many of whom were armed, came in great force towards us, and began to throw stones at us from some way off. Instead of retreating, we stood up to receive them, which rather intimidated them, and they stopped throwing and came up. We laughed with them, which in some measure assuaged them, and when some one said "Bakshish" we gave them some to scramble for, and so by degrees retired. Some of the Greek and Turkish women laughed at us for being driven off by boys; but it was a dangerous thing so to offend national prejudices, and I was very well pleased to be out of it. At best ours was an inglorious position.

The Theft of Some Other Marbles

I told you we were going to make a tour in the Morea, but before doing so we determined to see the remains of the temple at Aegina, opposite Athens, a three hours' sail. Our party was to be Haller, Linckh, Foster, and myself. At the moment of our starting an absurd incident occurred. There had been for some time a smouldering war between our servants and our janissary. When the latter heard that he was not to go with us, it broke out into a blaze. He said it was because the servants had been undermining his character, which they equally angrily denied. But he was in a fury, went home, got drunk, and then came out into the street and fired off his pistols, bawling out that no one but he was the legitimate protector of the English. For fear he should hurt some one with his shooting, I went out to him and expostulated. He was very drunk, and professed to love us greatly and that he would defend us against six or seven or even eight Turks; but as for the servants, "Why, my soul," he said, "have they thus treated me?" I contrived, however, to prevent his loading his pistols again, and as he worked the wine off, calm was at length restored; but the whole affair delayed us so long that we did not walk down to the Piraeus till night.

As we were sailing out of the port in our open boat we overtook the ship with Lord Byron on board. Passing under her stern we sang a favourite song of his, on which he looked out of the windows and invited us in. There we drank a glass of port with him, Colonel Travers, and two of the English officers, and talked of the three English frigates that had attacked five Turkish ones and a sloop of war off Corfu, and had taken and burnt three of them. We did not stay long, but bade them "bon voyage" and slipped over the side. We slept very well in the boat, and next morning reached Aegina.

The port is very picturesque. We went on at once from the town to the Temple of Jupiter [*of Aphaia*], which stands at some distance above it; and having got together workmen to help us in turning stones, etc., we pitched our tents for ourselves, and took possession of a cave at the north-east angle of the platform on which the temple stands - which had once been, perhaps, the cave of a sacred oracle - as a lodging for the servants and the janissary. The seas hereabouts are still infested with pirates, as they always have been. One of the workmen pointed me out the pirate boats off Sunium, which is one of their favourite haunts, and which one can see from the temple platform. But they never molested us during the twenty days and nights we camped out there for our party, with servants and janissary, was too strong to be meddled with. We got our provisions and labourers from the town, our fuel was the wild thyme, there were abundance of partridges to eat, and we bought kids of the shepherds; and when work was over for the day, there was a grand roasting of them over a blazing fire with an accompaniment of native music, singing and dancing. On the platform was growing a crop of barley, but on the actual ruins and fallen fragments of the temple itself no great amount of vegetable earth had collected, so that without very much labour we were able to find and examine all the stones necessary for a complete architectural analysis and restoration. At the end of a few days we had learnt all we could wish to know of the construction, from the stylobate to the tiles, and had done all we came to do.

But meanwhile a startling incident had occurred which wrought us all to the highest pitch of excitement. On the second day one of the excavators, working in the interior portico, struck on a piece of Parian marble which, as the building itself is of stone, arrested his attention. It turned out to be the head of a helmeted warrior, perfect in every feature. It lay with the face turned upwards, and as the features came out by degrees you can imagine nothing like the state of rapture and excitement to which we were wrought. Here was an altogether new interest, which set us to work with a will. Soon another head was turned up, then a leg and a foot, and finally, to make a long story short, we found under the fallen portions of the tympanum and the cornice of the eastern and western pediments no less than sixteen statues and thirteen heads, legs, arms, etc... and fragments of at least ten more), all in the highest preservation, not three feet below the surface of the ground. It seems incredible, considering the number of travellers who have visited the temple, that they should have remained so long undisturbed. It is evident that they were brought down with the pediment on the top of them by an earthquake, and all got broken in the fall; but we have found all the pieces and have now put together, as I say, sixteen entire figures.

The unusual bustle about the temple rapidly increased as the news of our operations spread. Many more men than we wanted began to congregate round us and gave me a good deal of trouble. Greek workmen have pretty ways. They bring you bunches of roses in the morning with pretty wishes for your good health; but they can be uncommonly insolent when there is no janissary to keep them in order. Once while Foster, being away at Athens, had taken the janissary with him, I had the greatest pother with them. A number that I did not want would hang about the diggings, now and then taking a hand themselves, but generally interfering with those who were labouring, and preventing any orderly and businesslike work. So at last I had to speak to them. I said we only required ten men, who should each receive one piastre per day, and that was all I had to spend; and if more than ten chose to work, no matter how many they might be, there would still be only the ten piastres to divide amongst them. They must settle amongst themselves what they would choose to do. Upon this what did the idlers do? One of them produced a fiddle; they settled into a ring and were preparing to dance. This was more than I could put up with. We should get no work done at all. So I interfered and stopped it, declaring that only those who worked, and worked hard, should get paid anything whatever. This threat was made more efficacious by my evident anger, and gradually the superfluous men left us in peace, and we got to work again.

It was not to be expected that we should be allowed to carry away what we had found without opposition. However much people may neglect their own possessions, as soon as they see them coveted by others they begin to value them. The primates of the island came to us in a body and read a statement made by the council of the island in which they begged us to desist from our operations, for that heaven only knew what misfortunes might not fall on the island in general, and the immediately surrounding land in particular, if we continued them. Such a rubbishy pretence of superstitious fear was obviously a mere excuse to extort money, and as we felt that it was only fair that we should pay, we sent our dragoman with them to the village to treat about the sum; and meanwhile a boat which out delay, and sent them on to the Piraeus, and from thence they were carried on to Athens by night to avoid exciting attention. Haller and I remained to carry on the digging, which we did with all possible vigour. The marbles being gone, the primates came to be easier to deal with. We completed our bargain with them to pay them 800 piastres, about 40*l*., for the antiquities we had found, with leave to continue the digging till we had explored the whole site. Altogether it took us sixteen days of very hard work, for besides watching and directing and generally managing the workmen, we had done a good deal of digging and handling of the marbles ourselves; all heads and specially delicate parts we were obliged to take out of the ground ourselves for fear of the workmen ruining them. On the whole we have been fortunate. Very few have been broken by carelessness. Besides all this, which was outside our own real business, we had been taking measurements and making careful drawings of every part and arrangement of the architecture till every detail of the construction and, as far as we could fathom it, of the art of the building itself was clearly understood by us. Meanwhile, after one or two days' absence, Foster and Linckh came back; and it then occurred to us that the receipt for the 800 piastres had only been given to the names of Foster and myself (who had paid it), and Linckh and Haller desired that theirs should be added. Linckh therefore went off to the town to get the matter rectified. But this was not so easy. The lawyer was a crafty rogue, and pretending to be drunk as soon as he had got back the receipt into his hands, refused to give it up, and did not do so until after a great deal of persuasion and threatening. When we fell in with him at dinner two days later he met us with the air of the most candid unconcern. It was at the table of a certain Chiouk aga who had been sent from Constantinople to receive the rayah tax. Linckh had met him in the town when he went about the receipt, and the Chiouk had paid us a visit at the temple next day and dined with us, eating and especially drinking a great deal. A compliment he paid us was to drink our healths firing off a pistol. I had to do the same in return. The man had been to England, and even to Oxford, and had come back with an odd jumble of ideas which amused us but are not worth repeating. Next day, as I have said, we dined with him and the rogue of a lawyer. He was very hospitable. Dinner consisted mainly of a whole lamb, off which with his fingers he tore entire limbs and threw them into our plates, which we, equally with our fingers, *a la Turque*, ate as best we could. We finished the evening with the Albanian dance, and walked up home to our tent...

We are now hard at work joining the broken pieces, and have taken a large house for the purpose. Some of the figures are already restored, and have a magnificent effect. Our council of artists here considers them as not inferior to the remains of the Parthenon, and certainly only in the second rank after the torso of the Vatican and other *chefs d'oeuvre*. We conduct all our affairs with respect to them in the utmost secrecy, for fear the Turk should either reclaim them or put difficulties in the way of our exporting them. The few friends we have and consult are dying with jealousy, and one who had meant to have farmed Aegina of the Captain Pasha has literally made himself quite ill with fretting. Fauvel, the French consul, was also a good deal disappointed; but he is too good a fellow to let envy affect his actions, and he has given excellent help and advice. The finding of such a treasure has tried every character concerned with it. He saw that this would be the case, and for fear it should operate to the prejudice of our beautiful collection, he proposed our signing a contract of honour that no one should take any measures to sell or divide it without the consent of the other three parties. This was done. It is not to be divided. It is a collection which a king or great nobleman who had the arts of his country at heart should spare no effort to secure; for it would be a school of art as well as an ornament to any country. The Germans have accordingly written to their ministers, and I have written to Canning; while Fauvel, who has a general order for the purpose from his minister, will make an offer to us on the French account. I had hoped that Lord Sligo would have offered for it; but our Germans, who calculate by the price of marbles in Rome, have named such a monstrous figure that it has frightened him. They talk of from 6,000*l* to 8,000*l*; but as we are eager that they should go to our museum, Foster and I have undertaken to present our shares if the marbles go to England, and I have written to Canning to say so. It would make a sensible deduction.

The whole matter is still full of uncertainties, for the Turks may give us a good deal of trouble. But one thing seems clear ... though we have agreed not to divide the collection, it may come to that if we cannot get away without; and if we can get them to England, even Foster's and my portions would make a noble acquisition to the museum.

Ignorant Rulers

One day I went to the waiwode on business. We had a long talk consisting mainly of questions about England, in which he displayed his ignorance to great advantage. ... [H]e asked what on earth we came here for, so far and at so much trouble, if not for money. Did it give us a preference in obtaining public situations, or were we paid? It was useless to assure him that we considered it part of education to travel, and that Athens was a very ancient place and much revered by us. He only thought the more that our object must be one we wished to conceal. I told him of the fuss made in London over the Persian ambassador, and that if he went all the world would wonder at him. At this he got very excited, and said he wished he had a good carico of oil which he could take to England, thereby paying his journey, and that once he was there he would make everyone pay to see him. All that he knew about England was that there were beautiful gardens there, especially one named Marcellias (Marseilles)! The man's one idea was money, and he kept on repeating that he was very poor. No wonder Greece is miserable under such rulers.

Veli Pasha, Governor of the Morea, passed through Athens a short time ago in a palankin of gold, while the country is in misery.

Greek Pride and Humility

The Greeks, cringing blackguards as they are, have often a sort of pride of their own. One of our servants, who received a piastre a day (1s.), has just left us. His amorosa, who lived close by, saw him carrying water and performing other menial offices and chaffed him, so he said he could stand it no longer and threw up a place the like of which he will not find again in Athens...

One morning by agreement we rose at daybreak and walked to Eleusis, intending to dig, but we found the labourers very idle and insolent; and after a few days, discovering no trace of the temple, we gave it up. The better sort of Greeks have some respect for the superior knowledge of Franks as evinced in my drawings; one man, a papa or priest, asked me whether I thought the ancients, whom they revere, can have been Franks or Romaics.

An Instance of Tyranny

An awkward incident occurred during our stay. We had in our service a handsome Greek lad to whom the cadi took a fancy and insisted on his taking service with him. The boy, much terrified, came and wept to us and Papa Nicola, with whom we lodged. We started off at once to the cadi, and gave him a piece of our mind, which considerably astonished and enraged him. He was afraid to touch us, but vowed to take it out of old Nicola, and the next day went off to Athens.

One night, the last of our stay, arrived a man from the *zabeti*, or police, of Athens to take up Nicola to answer certain accusations brought against him by the cadi. This soldier, who was a fine type of the genuine Athenian blackguard, swaggered in and partook freely of our wine, having already got drunk at the cadi's. He offered wine to passers-by as if it was his own, boasted, called himself *palikari*, roared out songs, and generally made himself most objectionable. He began to quiz a respectable Albanian who came in; and when the latter, who was very civil and called him "Aga," attempted to retort, flew into a rage, said he was a *palikar* again, and handled his sword and shook his pistols. I could stand it no longer at last, and said this was my house and no one was aga there but myself; that I should be glad to see him put his pistols down and let me have no more of his swaggering; otherwise I had pistols too, which I showed him, and would be ready to use them. I then treated our poor Albanian with great attention and him with contumely. This finished him and reduced the brute to absolute cringing as far as his conduct to me went. The wretched papa he bullied as before, and when he got up to go he and all the rest were up in an instant; one prepared his papouches, another supported him, a third opened the door, and a fourth held a lamp to light him out. But he had not yet finished his evening. Soon I heard a noise of singing and roaring from another house hard by, and received a message from him to beg I would sup with him, for now he had a table of his own and could invite me. The table was provided by some wretched Greek he was tyrannising over. Of course I did not go, but I moralised over the state of the country. Next day he carried off Nicola.

Another instance of the tyranny of these scoundrels was told me as having occurred only a few days before. A zabetis man had arrived and pretended to have lost on the way a purse containing 80 piastres. All the inhabitants were sent to search for it, and if they did not find it he said it must be repaid by the town - and it was. Among the people we met at Eleusis was a Greek merchant, a great beau from Hydra, at this time the most prosperous place in Greece; but away from his own town he had to cringe to the Turks like everyone else. On our way back to Athens we overtook him carrying an umbrella to shade his face, and with an Albanian boy behind him. When he saw our janissary, Mahomet, the umbrella was immediately lowered.

One Sows, Another Reaps

The population of Greece is so small now that large spaces are left uncultivated and rights to land are very undefined. In the neighbourhood of towns, there is always a considerable amount of cultivated ground, but although the cultivator of each patch hopes to reap it, there is nothing but fear of him to prevent another's doing it, so far as I can see. A field is ploughed and sown by an undefined set of people, and an equally or even less defined set may reap it. And in point of fact people do go and cut corn where they please or dare. We met a lot of Athenians on our way back, going to cut corn at Thebes.

1813 Dr. Henry Holland

The Approach to Athens along the Sacred Way

Crossing this long level, and leaving Eleusis to the right hand, we entered upon the Via Sacra, the road by which the great processions passed from Athens to the temple of Ceres at Eleusis. It conducted us first under the cliffs upon the shore; then by a rapid ascent between the hills Aegaleon and Corydalus, names long since familiar to the ear. We passed the picturesque monastery of Daphne, conjectured as the site of the temple of Apollo, which once stood in this pass; half a mile beyond, caught a view of the upper part of the plain of Athens; and a few minutes afterwards, in coming to a break in the hills, heard our Tartar shout with a loud voice, "Athena, Athena!" The intimation was needless. We already had the sacred city before our eyes; noble in its situation, noble in its ruins, and in the recollection it gives of ancient times and ancient men. It was now the latter part of the day, and the setting sun (the first setting sun of 1813) threw a gleam of light on the western front of the Acropolis, and on the splendid group of buildings which covers its summit. Already the Parthenon was discernible preeminent over the rest; the city of Athens was seen spread over a great extent below; the chain of Hymettus beyond; more immediately beneath us the great plain and olive-groves of Athens, conducting the eye in one direction to the lofty summits of Pentelicus, on the other to the Piraeus, to Salamis, Aegina and the other isles of the gulf, and to the mountains of the Peloponnesus in the remote distance. It is a landscape of the most extraordinary kind, such as might strongly interest the stranger, even without the aid of these associations, which every part of the scenery so amply affords.

We descended from the pass of the Sacred Way into the plain; traversed the venerable wood of olives which occupies its central part; crossed the small and divided stream of Cephissus, and at five o'clock entered the city by the gate, near to the temple of Theseus. The English, more than any other people, have cultivated the ancient, through the modern Athens, and one of the first persons we saw in approaching the place, was an Englishman, looking over an excavation which had been made for the purposes of research.

The character of the landscape around the city is very peculiar , even without reference to any of the features that have been described. There is a certain simplicity of outline and colouring, combined with the magnificence of form and extent, which contributes much to this particular effect. It cannot be called a rich scenery, for the dry soil of Attica refuses any luxuriance of vegetation; and, excepting the great olive-grove of the plain, little wood enters into the landscape. Yet one of its most striking features is a sort of repose, which may be derived from the form of the hills, from their slopes into the plain, and from the termination of this plain, in the placid surface of the gulf of Salamis; above all, perhaps, from the resting point which the eye finds in the height of the Acropolis, and in the splendid group of ruins covering its summit. In this latter object there is a majestic tranquillity, the effect of time and of its present state, which may not easily be described, so as to convey an idea of the reality of the spot. The stranger will find himself perplexed in fixing on the point of view whence the aspect of these ruins is most imposing, or their combination most perfect with the other groups which surround them.

The situation and outline of Hymettus add much to the beauty of the scenery around Athens, as well as the summits of the mountains of Pentelicus, which terminate the landscape towards

One of the many Fountains of Ottoman Athens (S. Pomardi, 1820)

the east. The three ports of the city are still perfectly distinct, and there are many vestiges of the town of the Piraeus ; but these objects are on too small a scale to detain the eye, which passes forwards to Salamis, Aegina, and the other isles of the gulf, and to the mountains of the Isthmus of Corinth, and of the Peloponnesus, in the remote distance.

Some part of the peculiarity of this scenery may perhaps be derived from the climate of Attica, which affords an atmosphere for the most part clear, dry, and temperate; very different from that which hangs over the low plains and marshes of Boeotia. The peninsular situation of Attica and the nature of the surface both contribute to this effect. The temperature at Athens is more uniform than in other parts of Greece, and the quantity of rain falling here below the general average of this country. It may certainly be supposed that the nature of the climate here has an influence on the aspect under which its scenery and ruins are given to the view. The state of the modern Athens does not appear, until lately, to have been generally known to the rest of Europe. Fancy has drawn for itself a wretched village, with houses scattered among the ruins of temples; and few before this time have looked for a large and flourishing town, well peopled, and containing many excellent houses, with various appendages belonging to the better stage of cultivated life. Yet all this will be found here; and on the identical spot which in old times was occupied by the sacred city of Minerva; the name preserved, and a multitude of other circumstances to add the impression which brings together ages thus remote in reality.

1812-14 William Turner

An Alternative View of the Removal of the Parthenon Marbles

The metopes of the peristyle of the pronaum are almost perfect. Those of the sides, thank heaven, are now in England, and those of the posticum are almost destroyed. I could not witness the progress which devastation has made here without wishing (however unpopular the doctrine) that Lord Elgin had carried off more. At all events, I think that Athens and England are both under infinite obligations to him for what he has saved. The very metal found inside the columns, for which the seller can procure thirty piastres, is a strong temptation to the barbarians, under whose custody the splendid ruins of Greece are now unfortunately placed...

Love and Marriage in Athens

After dinner I was asking the Consul why such pretty and agreeable girls as the Consulinas were not married; when he gave me in answer the following information as to the state of society in Greece. There seems to be no such thing as love among the Greeks. A disinterested love-match is a thing almost unheard of. If Helen were to revisit her country, no one would marry her without a dowry. This must amount to at least 10,000 piastres, part of which must be derived from landed property, or from at least 300 olive trees, which are worth from twenty to fifty piastres each: the whole wealth of the Consulinas consists, he told me, in sixty olive trees. On my reproaching the Greeks for their mercenary spirit, he said, that in this case it was justified by necessity, for that the Greek women (of Athens particularly) of all ranks were very expensive in dress, and excessively quarrelsome for precedence, about which the lower and higher orders would frequently quarrel in the bath till they beat each other very seriously about the head and breasts with the tin cups and wooden pattens used in it. That the Athenian women in particular were "cattivissime," being desperately given to gossiping, scandal, idleness, etc. in which they have not at all degenerated from their classical ancestors.

Spirit

The Greeks still seem to preserve some spirit in Athens. Four years ago, he told me, a Turk having murdered a Greek here, his countrymen all assembled in crowds, and armed, and blockaded the houses of the archons, whom they were with the utmost difficulty dissuaded from killing because they had not obtained justice for the murder from the waywode. After having sought for the murderer long and closely, but without success, they at length dispersed, to the great joy of the Turks, who had trembled before the momentary fury of the slaves whom they profess to despise. The murderer succeeded in escaping to Thebes, where he lived two years, and then returned to Athens, and bought his pardon with 600 piastres, which he paid to the wife of his victim. Soon after the same man murdered one of the primates of Athens, and again fled the city. To this last outrage he was supposed to have been incited (by money) by some Greek, who sought preferment by removing his rival. By a law of Athens, a Turk who murders a Greek is liable to a fine of forty purses (20,000 piastres) but even this miserable compensation the abject Greeks have scarcely ever the power to enforce.

Ancient Survivals

Many classically-educated visitors were eager to discover parallels between the manners and ways of the modern Greeks with those of their ancient ancestors.

Next to the pleasure enjoyed by the traveller in contemplating the ruins of Greece must be ranked that of observing the similarity of the manners of the present inhabitants with those of the ancients. In many of the ordinary practices of life this resemblance is striking. The hottest hours of the day are still devoted to sleep as they were in the times recorded by Xenophon, when Conon attempted to escape from the Lacedaemonians at Lesbos, and when Phrebidas surprised the citadel of Thebes. The Greeks still feed chiefly on vegetables, and salted or pickled provisions, and the women still seldom stir abroad, and when they do, conceal the face. The eyebrows of the Greek women are still blackened by art, and their cheeks, painted occasionally with red and white, as described by Xenophon, (*Memorabilia*, Book v) This latter custom in particular is universal in Zante among the upper classes. The laver, from which water is poured upon the hand previous to eating, (which is now of pewter among ,all classes,) appears by many passages in the Odyssey to have been a common utensil in the age of Homer, and something like the small moveable table (composed among the modern Levantines of a round plate of tin laid on a reversed stool) universally used in the Levant, seems to have been common among the ancient Greeks.

A Ride to Marathon

T. carried his gun with him, but was disappointed in his expectations of finding game, though hares and wildfowl are very plentiful in this favoured country. The ride would have been delightful, had it been only a ride; but it is easy to imagine what interest it excited, when it assumed the character of an excursion from Athens to Marathon. The only disagreeable circumstance it our jaunt arose from the excessive heat of the day. For three hours we rode along a most beautiful rich plain. We had Anchesmus to our right on leaving the city, and at a small distance from it, we saw some remains of Adrian's aqueduct to our left. In this plain we passed three small villages, whose gardens and olive groves (with which latter, indeed, the whole plain was covered) were in the highest possible state of fertility and beauty. In the second village was an enormous chestnut-tree, the largest I had ever seen, whose branches spread through a circle of from sixty to seventy feet. At the third village, we stopped a few minutes at a cottage, where water and eggs were the only breakfast they could furnish us, it being too early for the fruit-season, and their stock of wine not being sufficient to last through the year.

Leaving the plain, we mounted a slight ascent, and for two hours and a half continued along a steep rugged road, among moderate mountains overgrown with shrubs and fir-trees, which gave the scene an agreeable air of thorough wildness, and it was difficult to imagine oneself at only twelve miles distance from Athens. The scenery of Greece presents a variety that suits every taste: the lover of society may choose his residence in a port where European vessels are constantly touching; the antiquarian may fix himself where he sees from his window the most interesting monuments of her days of glory; and the advocate for solitude may find recesses in the mountains, where he may indulge in meditation even to madness. The rocks on the side of this road were all of Mica slate, which bore the colour and glittering appearance of silver; this made me think, that if the ground were dug, mines of that metal would be found, and I find that Chandler states, that he saw the site of silver mines near Athens. After two hours and a half riding along this wild solitude, I was surprised to find, that our road had been gradually and imperceptibly mounting, and .that we had now a very formidable and steep descent to encounter. From the top we had a fine view of the sea and the village and plain or Marathon.

We were half an hour descending, as the steepness and stony ruggedness of the road rendered a quick pace impossible. At the bottom of the mountain, we had to our left the cave of Pan, (who, by his part in the battle of Marathon, gave his name to panic fear,) which is a small natural excavation in the rock, and being now nearly choked up, and containing nothing to be seen, I spared myself the classic uncomfortableness of crawling down it on all fours. Near the cave and before the village runs a small and violent, but not deep, stream, on whose banks are a few fertile and well-cultivated gardens. The village is very pretty, being almost hidden by the foliage that surrounds it: it is very small, containing only thirty houses, of which not one is inhabited by a Turk. We stopped in it half an hour to dine; and on leaving it, we again crossed the stream (which has no name), and between two mountains rode about two hundred yards, till we came into the large plain, which has testified so strongly what man can do when he fights for, his home. Its smoothness justifies the remark of Herodotus ... that it was better adapted for the operations of cavalry, than any other part of Attica. Riding towards the sea, the first object we met was the monument of Miltiades, now reduced to a heap of loose stones: a little beyond this were the stones raised to the slaves and the Plataeans, which are now hardly perceptible, being covered with corn. The next object is the Tumulus of the Athenians, which stands near the sea, and is about forty feet high. It was once excavated by M. Fauvel, but he found nothing.

As we were sitting on it, enjoying the prospect from its top, an accident happened to Tupper which made us grateful to the Turks for the clumsiness of their manufactures. He was firing powder from the pan of his fowling-piece to clear it, and his pouch (a small gourd, containing a little more than half a pound of Turkish powder) being in his right waistcoat pocket, a spark flew into it and blew the whole up. The gun flew to a distance, his coat and waistcoat were more than half burnt, his shirt set on fire, and his right hand severely burnt. I, who was sitting close to him, escaped with the left skirt of my great coat being very much singed. It required all our wine (two bottles) to extinguish the fire in his shirt and clothes. He put his hand into his handkerchief made into a sling, and in five days it was quite recovered. This was the end of an accident which, if his pouch had contained English powder, might have gone hard with us.

We now rode to the west and saw the small columns (about three feet high) which were placed to the memory of the heroes who fell in the battle. Of these there are six standing, and six thrown down; one of the former has the appearance of an altar; near them are some stones which look as if they had belonged to some edifice. It is necessary to remark that these are not in their proper place, having been unclassically moved to make a tent for Lord and Lady Elgin, by the captain of the frigate which brought that nobleman from Constantinople to Athens.

1813 Thomas Smart Hughes

Vandalism

Next day Signore Lusieri had a shivering fit ... he was always thus attacked when an English or a French frigate anchored in the Piraeus. The young midshipmen are then let loose upon the venerable monuments of Athens, and are seldom deterred by religion or the police from indulging in the most wanton devastation of statues, cornices, and capitals, from which they carry off mementos of their Athenian travels.

I heard that this evil increased much afterwards from the great number of vessels which arrived at the port, and poor Philopappus lost his last leg by the hands or a mischievous young Frenchman. There may be some excuse for these youths, but what shall we say in defence of the captains of two English frigates who brought a tar-barrel on shore at Cape Sunium and bedaubed the white and brilliant columns of Minerva's temple with long lists of their own names and those of their officers and boat-crews, in this indelible material? This instance of barbarism we saw with a mixture of surprise and indignation: we only felt the latter sensation when we observed the accompanying signatures of a Sicilian crew. *They* cannot consider themselves entitled to any better claims for immortality. One of the reviewers of my first edition remarks pleasantly enough upon this passage that "an Englishman would not have been content to have been saved in Noah's Ark, without cutting his name in the timber."

Some Turkish Womenfolk Unveiled

This day the Orlando got underway and Lusieri recovered. He dined with us in the Pnyx, from whence we commanded a charming prospect both of town and country; nor did we find any pleasure more delightful than these Attic repasts which we made almost daily, varying the spot and enjoying the society of one or more intelligent friends. As we stood before the tent, a party of Greek women came up, anxious to look through our telescope and catch a last view of their husbands and relations then sailing out of the Piraeus: some Turkish ladies: also attracted by curiosity approached rather nearer than etiquette allows in general, but soon moved off as if the sight of a Christian were contagious. The face of a Turkish woman must not be seen in public: if a man meets one in the streets unveiled, he turns his face towards the wall till she has passed: so strong is the force of custom, that I one day saw the disdar aga turn his back upon his own daughter, a young girl of exquisite beauty, as she walked unveiled up the steps of the propylaea... Mr. Cockerell and Baron Haller performed the same evolution; but I had not yet learnt the forms of Turkish politeness.

Mr. Parker and myself were most vehemently abused, one day as we descended from the acropolis, by three Turkish ladies for daring to look at them. We certainly were attracted by nothing but their strange appearance; for they were so muffled up from head to foot in long white robes, with bandages covering the face and showing nothing but the eyes, that they looked exactly like a trio of Egyptian mummies going out to take the air.

These ladies however are not so squeamish when out of observation, as I afterwards discovered. Copying inscriptions one afternoon in the court of Lusieri whilst that worthy Don was enjoying his siesta, I heard a gentle knocking at the outer gates, which having opened I saw with surprise about twelve or fifteen Turkish ladies, covered with white mantles reaching from head to foot. Having let them in, they made me understand by signs that the object of their visit was to see a fine clock with musical chimes that Lord Elgin had presented to the city of Athens, as if to recall the despoiler of the Parthenon every hour to remembrance. They followed me slowly and silently to the temporary shed in which it was placed; but had no sooner entered than they began to giggle, and presently burst into a laugh: they then threw back their long veils as if by a preconcerted scheme to surprise me by that blaze of beauty which radiated from their large black eyes: I certainly never beheld so glorious a sight. I may have seen handsomer women than any individual among them, but never did I see such a combination of beauties, such beaming eyes and silken lashes, or such dazzling complexions: they appeared like a legion of houries sent expressly from the paradise of Mahomet. The lovely creatures seemed to enjoy my astonishment, and to triumph in the effect of their charms: encompassing me in a circle they gently pushed me towards the clock that I might show them its mechanism: this I had no sooner done, than with a shout of joy they seized the wires, and rang such a peal upon the chimes, that the Italian awoke from his nap, and running to the spot in his gown and slippers, began to chide them in so severe a strain that the laughter immediately ceased, silence was restored, the veils drawn again over their faces; and in the same slow and solemn step with which they entered, the whole party marched off the premises, leaving me in the state of a person just awakened out of a most extraordinary dream.

More Superstitions

Next day we pitched our tent in the great Stadium beyond Ilissus, whither we retired after having rambled over the district of Agrae, once sacred to Diana, and I viewed the fountain of the Ilissiades still called by its ancient name Callirhoe, with the ruins of a temple of Ceres, the site of the Lyceum, the Cynosarges, and the gardens of Venus below the monastery of Syriani; here an old stunted myrtle exists which is said to have outlived the empire both of men and deities, and serves at this day as an authentic record of the place: in a deep and shaded valley near the monastery, whose banks are fringed with the agnus castus, oleaster and willow, we found the stream of the Ilissus and a great number of Albanian women on its banks, employed in washing linen – picturesque enough in the mass, but possessing very few individual charms, The sides of Ilissus are marked by the foundations of buildings which in former times encroached upon its transparent stream, when the spreading plane-trees on its bank afforded a delicious retreat for the voluptuary or the philosopher. In the stadium, which was once coated with Pentelic marble by the generosity of Herodes Atticus, we observed, at the entrance of a passage cut through the hill, a small stone pedestal of modern workmanship; and sometimes used, as our guide informed us, for the purpose of propitiatory sacrifices: the goddesses to whom it is dedicated, strange to say! are the destinies or Fates; the worshippers are Athenian damsels who have arrived at the age of matrimonial despair, and the hierophant is an old woman. Early in the morning the parties repair hither, and having offered up their petitions to the presiding deities, leave upon the altar a frugal repast of eggs, honey, and a cake, though not of so rich a quality as that ancient bride-cake … which was offered to the divinities presiding over marriage, and from which our own custom may possibly be derived.

An Athenian friend of mine assured me that he made an excellent breakfast one morning upon these propitiatory offerings, having had his appetite well sharpened by a shooting excursion over the borders of Hymettus: to my inquiries whether these rites ever softened the hearts of the inexorable goddesses, he answered, that the priestesses of the altar, anxious for its reputation, always descant with such eloquence upon the charms and good qualities of its votaries, that they not infrequently succeed in removing every cause of complaint.

An Emissary from Constantinople

A few days after the messenger ... from Constantinople returned, with a confirmation of the vaivode's power for another year, and the papers of the haratch or capitation-tax. He was met near the city, and preceded by the disdar aga, his guard, and the college of dervishes, bearing their sacred axes and singing outrageously; whilst an immense crowd of horse and foot followed, firing off rockets, pistols, and muskets, till they came into the vaivode's court. The tatar rode all this time, though it rained hard, bareheaded, holding his high cap in one hand, and the firman of the Grand Signor in the other; and when he dismounted, he threw some handfuls.of paras amongst the people. As it was known that he had brought political news from the capital, the serai was besieged both this and the following day by crowds of Athenians ...

A Thief Exposed

[W]e were about to return into the Morea, when our plans were interrupted by one of those unlucky accidents to which all travellers are exposed: we were robbed of a large sum of money by our servant Giovanni Paximidachi whom we had engaged at Zante, Our suspicions were excited against this man by our friend Alecco Logotheti, who had seen him in Athens before, and who kindly assisted us in our investigation, which I shall detail for the benefit of any traveller who may be exposed to a similar occurrence. Having procured two men from the baloukbashee's guard, we stationed them at the door of our servants apartment, into which we entered for the purpose of instituting a search. For form's sake we began with Antonietti who emptied his trunks like an innocent man: but Giovanni, as if indignant at the very idea of suspicion, threw himself into a rage and his effects upon the floor, emptying out from a bag 200 dollars, which we had lately paid him for his wages, and desiring us in an impertinent manner to pick them up and count them. Taking no notice of his expressions for the present, we ordered him to replace his effects in his portmanteau, and then put a few questions to him relating to some dark hints which he had unwarily given to several persons, relating to his intentions. To one of these, addressed by Signore Logotheti, he answered with much insolence and menacing attitudes, that we clapped our hands for the patrol, who instantly came in and conveyed him to prison.

On this and the two following days he was examined before the baloukbashee; but though suspicious circumstances appeared, no positive proof came out against him: we then carried him before the vaivode assisted by the baloukbashee; old Logotheti, Signore Lusieri, and others; by whom many witnesses were examined, chiefly islanders, with whom he had associated in Athens; but all to no purpose. Both Turks and Greeks then exhorted us to extract a confession from him by torture: but it is scarcely necessary to add that we rejected such a methods of eliciting truth with firmness and indignation. Remanding him back therefore to prison, we continued our investigation; in the course of which we discovered a Greek woman with whom he had cohabited; and from whom the application of threats alone extorted a very important confession that Giovanni had boasted to her of his dexterity in cheating English travellers, declaring that ours was the last service he intended to enter; being determined this time to return home rich or return no more: profiting also by a hint from this modern Lamia, we opened his pillow; which, as Antonietti now recollected, he usually kept with jealous care: no discovery however was made till we arrived at the last corner, from whence we extracted a diamond ring, and a gold watch with its appurtenances of chain and seals; one of the latter bearing a coat of arms. Being again examined on the subject of this discovery, he seemed no ways abashed, but declared that the articles were left him by his father who had been a gentleman of Trieste; though at other times he had mentioned Malta and Candia as the places of his birth and parentage.

The methods by which he attempted to effect his release were curious and ingenious. One consisted in a threat of discovering to the voivode a plot into which he professed we had entered with Petri Revelachi to seize upon the government of Athens; but he succeeded only in terrifying the poor Athenian nearly out of his senses. He next declared that he would turn Turk and throw the perdition of his soul upon our heads: but hearing from the vaivode that he would be then irrevocably under his jurisdiction, and should be cut alive into small pieces, he changed his mind. At length chance had nearly done for him what his own cunning was unable to effect. The voivode cast an eye of desire upon the watch, which having by some pretext got into his possession, he declared he would not surrender till the right owner could be discovered: as for Giovanni, he no longer thought him worthy of being detained, but proposed sending him to Candia by a ship bound thither, which he said was lying in the Piraeus. To this arrangement however we made a determined resistance; and though I was at this time confined to my bed by a tertian ague, being roused by indignation I got up and forced old Logotheti to demand an audience of our upright judge, and express our determination of seeking redress at Constantinople unless the watch was restored. This threat produced effects more advantageous than we had foreseen: for he proposed sending the watch to Zante, under condition of its being returned to him if no owner could be found. To this we agreed, provided the thief might accompany it; which being granted, we drew up our case in detail, accompanying it with depositions under the seal of the British consulate, paid Giovanni his wages up to the day of departure, and sent him with the watch and ring, under custody of a tatar, to the Ionian government. After he had been gone about a week, several witnesses, relieved from their fears by his absence, gave us some important information: one of these had made for him a leathern girdle for the purpose of holding sequins; and another had changed for him 200 dollars, the exact sum of which we had been robbed, into that very coin: these depositions we forwarded immediately by a courier to Zante; but nothing could be elicited from Giovanni, though to the great disappointment of our honest vaivode, the watch was recognised by Mr. Foresti as the property of his son. At length by an ingenious contrivance of General Campbell the whole plot was unravelled: Giovanni was brought up for a last examination; after which he was informed that he might depart next morning: accordingly at that time, when he marched out of prison, decorated in his best apparel, he was again apprehended, and carried into a room, where every article of his dress was diligently examined. His coolness did not forsake him till they came to his shoes, which he kicked off his feet with an appearance of insulted honesty: these being handled, were found so much heavier and thicker than usual that it was judged expedient to cut them open; when lo! there were the Venetian sequins, all neatly arranged within the sole. As concealment was not likely now to benefit his cause, he made a general confession: the watch he had stolen out of the house of Mr. G. Foresti when he accompanied Dr. Holland to Joannina, and the diamond ring he had purloined from the trunk of that gentleman to whom it had been entrusted for conveyance to a friend by Mr. Pouqeville the French Consul: thus we had the satisfaction of restoring their property to these gentlemen, regaining our own, and frustrating the future machinations of this abandoned miscreant, who was sentenced to work for life upon the fortifications of Sant Maura. After the conclusion of this unpleasant business, I was confined by the fever to my bed for several weeks.

An Instance of Barbarous Justice

Next day we attended the court of the archbishop, who was chief magistrate of the Greeks, and whose assessors were the four primates with the Logothetes: I speak of these and other customs in the past tense; for of late years they have been interrupted and are very likely hereafter to be altered: to this tribunal the Greeks almost always brought those causes in which they themselves alone were implicated; they might indeed apply, or appeal to the Turkish governor, but in that case both parties generally suffered alike; besides they had an extreme aversion to the jurisdiction of their barbarous masters, which was made a matter of religious duty. Yet in this court of the archbishop no witnesses were examined upon oath; for when wished to have some evidence confirmed by affidavit in the affair of our robbery , it could not be effected, not one of the judges being acquainted with the formula. When a Turk and a Greek had a cause in hand, it was decided either by the cadi, or the vaivode with his assistance; and it is not difficult to guess on which side of the balance justice leaned. In affairs of criminal jurisdiction, the Turks took the law into their own hands, and the force of gold alone could arrest its progress. The power of the vaivode was nearly despotic, and he could cut off the heads of men as of poppies; it was however necessary for him to ascertain the strength of his interest at Constantinople, otherwise the Greeks might have removed him from his government; for a greater deference was paid to the remonstrancers of the Athenians than to those of any other Greek subjects of the Porte.

In their own families the Turks retain a species of patriarchal authority; and an awful instance of its execution occurred about a month before our arrival in Athens. The story was related to me of an aged venerable man whose long white beard had often caught my eye, as he sat at the entrance of the principal bath, of which he was the proprietor. The only daughter of this person was a woman of exquisite beauty, but faithless to her marriage vows: the impropriety of her conduct was frequently represented to her by her friends, but without avail; and her incontinence became a matter of public scandal: again the consequences to which such a course of life would lead were intimated to her; but this warning like the other was ineffectual.

Her father then determined upon the last dreadful expedient for obliterating so foul a stain from the honour of the family. Accompanied by his son, he entered the apartment of this unfortunate creature in the dead of night: the light of a solitary lamp showed to them the object of their visit in a tranquil slumber, beautiful as an angel, and apparently as innocent; the brother started back, and would have retreated, but was recalled by his father's stern command: this incident awoke the unhappy criminal, who immediately foresaw their intent and began to plead for mercy; she clasped the knees of her aged parent, and implored his forgiveness by the memory of her mother his beloved wife, but in vain; the fount of mercy was now closed: not a word either of pity or reproach was returned: she was thrown back upon the divan, and her last prayers for mercy were stifled by her executioners under the cushions of the sofa.

Of this action, though publicly known, no cognisance was taken by any authorities: the people were convinced of its equity, and the murderer of his child seemed to lose the feelings of remorse in the satisfaction made to violated honour.

Accommodation in Megara

After being absent nine hours from Corinth we arrived at Megara, the most miserable town of modern Greece; where a mud cottage many degrees inferior to an English cowshed was the best lodging we could receive.

c.1825 A Companion of HM Queen Caroline of Brunswick

Lonely Piraeus

On a delightful morning we mounted our horses very early, and leaving the city, took the road to the Phalereus. As we approached the sea, the coast gradually became more elevated, and terminated in heights, the buildings of which form, to the east and west, the harbours of Phalereus and Piraeus. On the beach of the Phalereus, we discerned traces of the walls that encompassed the port, and other ruins which were heaps of rubbish: these were, perhaps, the temples of Juno and Ceres. Near this spot, lay the little field and tomb of Aristides. We went down to the harbour, a circular basin, with a bottom of fine sand, capable of containing about fifty boats...

From the harbour of Phalereus we proceeded to that of Munychia, which is of an oval figure, and rather larger than the former. Lastly, turning the extremity of a craggy hill, and advancing from cape to cape, we reached the Piraeus. Our guide stopped in the curvature, formed by a neck of land, to show us a sepulchre excavated in the rock; it is now without roof, and is upon a level with the sea. By the regular flowing and ebbing of the tide, it is alternately covered and left exposed, by turns full and empty. At the distance of a few paces on the shore are seen the remains of a monument. It is the opinion of the learned, that in this place the bones of Themistocles were deposited. This interesting discovery is, however, contested. It is objected, that the fragments scattered around, are too fine to have been the tomb of Themistocles; and that, according to the ancient geographers quoted by Plutarch, this tomb was in reality an altar.

All travellers are astonished at the solitude of the Piraeus: we were much impressed by it. We had explored a desert coast, had surveyed three harbours, and in these three harbours had not perceived one single vessel. Nothing was to be seen but ruins, rocks, and the sea; and no sound met the ear, save the cries of the kingfisher, and the dashing of the surges against the tomb of Themistocles, producing an incessant murmur in this abode of eternal silence. Washed away by the billows, the ashes of the conqueror of Xerxes reposed beneath them, commingled with the bones of the vanquished Persians. In vain my eye sought the temple of Venus, the long gallery, and the statue emblematic of the people of Athens: the image of that inexorable people was for ever fallen, near the well, to which the exiled citizens repaired, to no purpose, to reclaim their country. Instead of those superb arsenals, those porticos whence the galleys were launched, and whence reverberated the shouts of the seamen; instead of those edifices, resembling the city of Rhodes in their appearance and beauty, we now saw nothing but a dilapidated convent, and a magazine in ruins. Here, in a wretched hut of wood, a Turkish custom-house officer sits all the year round, the lonely sentinel of the coast, and a model of stupid patience: whole months elapse without his witnessing the arrival of a single vessel. Such is the present deplorable condition of these once famous harbours. What can have destroyed so many of the stupendous monuments of the arts of mankind?

The port of the Piraeus forms a bow, the two ends of which approach so near to each other as to leave only a narrow passage: it is now called the Lion's Port, from a lion of marble, which was formerly to be seen there, but was removed to Venice by Morosini in 1686. The interior of the harbour was divided into three basins. You still see a wet dock, almost half filled up, which may possibly have been one of them. The historian Strabo affirms, that the great port of Athens was capable of holding four hundred ships, and Pliny swells the number to a thousand. Fifty of the brigs of modern Europe would completely fill it; and two of our frigates would not ride there at their ease, with a considerable length of cable. But the water is deep, and the bottom excellent; so that in the hands of a civilised nation, the Piraeus might even now become an important harbour. The only warehouse now to be seen there is of French origin, having been erected by M. Gaspari, formerly the Consul of France, at Athens. Thus it is not long since the Athenians were represented at the port of the Piraeus, by the nation which bears the nearest resemblance to them.

Having rested for a short time for refreshment at the custom-house, and at the monastery of St. Spiridion, Her Majesty returned to Athens by the road from the Piraeus. We perceived the remains of the long wall the entire extent of the way. We passed the tomb of Antiope the Amazon. We rode among the most beautiful of vines, as in Burgundy. We stopped at the public reservoirs, and under olive-trees; and I had the mortification to find that those precious remains of antiquity, the tomb of Menander, the cenotaph of Euripides, and the little temple dedicated to Socrates, no longer exist; or rather, as we may suppose, they have not yet been discovered. We pursued our way, and on approaching the Museum [*Museion or Philopappos Hill*], our guides pointed out to us a path winding up the side of a hill. This path, they informed us, had been made by a Russian artist, who every day repaired to the same spot to take views of Athens. If genius be no other than patience, as some philosophers have asserted, this painter must certainly possess a considerable share of that quality.

The Dervishes in the Temple of the Winds Again

The temple of the four Winds is an exquisite structure, in fine preservation; and the exterior is ornamented with the most beautiful sculpture, descriptive of the powers to which it was held sacred: this temple is at present, however, converted into a mosque, and here the dervishes perform their singular and most extravagant ceremonies. Never surely was any scene witnessed more extraordinary, more frightful!

In the outset of the ceremony, the premier or chief dervish sings or chants a kind of hymn, which the rest of the party repeat after him: they then seize him with seeming violence by the hand, and utter such incoherent and dreadful cries, that they appear to lose their breath, and actually seem on the very point of suffocation. Two of them then strip off their gowns, their shoes, and their turbans, beat their bosoms with an enraged air, tear up their dishevelled locks, like furies, from every part of their heads, shriek and cry out again till they are again out of breath, and then whirl and turn themselves rapidly round, until their eyes grow dim, and they fall to the earth. Afterwards there comes forward another·in the same way, with his hair wild and dishevelled, his dress half stripped off, and a dagger or knife grasped in his hand, which, after many horrid gestures, he plunges into his own bosom: the rest of this extraordinary group wipe up the blood with their hair; one of them takes a drop, and smears it on his face, and the others instantly lay hold of him, and toss him about violently among them, until he becomes senseless and falls. All then throw aside their turbans, the music commences a quick air, and they again spin or turn round as if distracted, kneel, kiss the earth, and rise again. The chief priest now holds a crown in his hand, and cries "Nolan la Mahomed, Nolan la;" and the rest repeat the same words, in different tones, and the most confused and incoherent manner. The priest next. places himself in the direction of Mecca, (where lies the tomb of their prophet) and in this portion bows repeatedly, and profoundly; in which salutations his example is followed by the others, who bow in the same manner, and turn rapidly round again to the sound of a sort of music, but which is indeed little better than the striking together of a pair of sandals. They at length conclude by embracing each other, and kneeling, with great seeming devotion, kiss the earth.

It is impossible, without witnessing this ludicrous and uncouth scene, to form a correct idea of the sensations which are called forth by it: at one moment it is difficult for one to repress laughter; at another, pity and dread powerfully contend for the mastery, I was myself so over-come by terror, that I involuntarily seized a native who was at my side for support, and trembled from head to foot in extreme agitation. It is forbidden to be a spectator of these horrible ceremonies, but Her Majesty had asked especial permission, and obtained it as a high favour.

The Finest View of Athens

Approaching Athens now on our return, after passing a deep defile, and as the hills opened at the other extremity towards sunset, such a prospect of Athens, and of the Athenian plain, with all the surrounding scenery, burst upon our view, as never has been, nor can be described. It is presented from the mouth, or gap, facing the city, which divides Corydallus upon the south; now called Laurel Mountain, from Aegaleon, a projecting part of Mount Parnes upon the north, immediately before descending into the extensive olive-plantations which cover all this side of the plain, upon the banks of the Cephissus. There is no spot whence Athens may be seen that

The Gate of the Market Place (Le Roy, 1755)

360

can compare with this point of view; and if, after visiting the city, anyone should leave it without coming to this eminence to enjoy the prospect here afforded, he will have formed a very inadequate conception of its grandeur; for all that nature and art, by every marvellous combination of vast and splendid objects, can possibly exhibit, aided by the most surprising effect of colour, light, and shade, is here presented to the spectator. The wretched representations made of the scenes in Greece, even by the best designs yet published in books of travels, have often been a subject of regret among those who have witnessed its extraordinary beauties; and, in the list of them, perhaps few may be considered as inferior to the numerous delineations which have appeared of this extraordinary city. But with such a spectacle before his eyes as this now alluded to, how deeply does the traveller deplore, that the impression is not only transitory as far as his own enjoyment, but that it is utterly incapable of being transmitted to the minds of others. With such reflections, we reluctantly quitted the spot; and passing downwards to the plain, crossed the Cephissus, and entered the olive-groves extending towards our left, over the site of the Academy. There are not less than forty thousand of these trees; the largest and finest of the kind we had seen in Greece. The most beautiful wood perhaps ever seen in England is that of the Athenian olive when polished. The air here is very unwholesome during the summer months, owing to the humidity of the soil, and perhaps principally to its not being properly drained. In the evening we arrived once more in Athens.

1818-19 Peter Edmund Laurent

Monastic Smugglers

The sounds of Attine, Atene, striking my ear , awoke me from my feverish lethargy; I leapt from the boat, and, in treading for the first time the Attic shore, felt as all must feel who have read the pages of Grecian history, but as few, very few, can describe - Where now are the superb temples which adorned this shore? Where the magazines; crowded with merchants? Where those streets, thronged with mariners of every nation? - All, desert and abandoned, reposes in the melancholy quiet of ruin. A few barks, with their long tops, bearing the furled sail at the mast head, were moored close to the land; on the shore stood a dirty hovel, dignified with the name of warehouse; a muddy marsh extended towards the left; there a few cranes, seeking their scanty food, interrupted now and then the dead silence with the steady flapping of their wings: on the right was seen the monastery of St. Spiridion; and the prospect was bounded on every side, by hillocks, which scemed, barely able to afford sustenance to a few squills, the only flower with which nature decks these barren rocks.

To reach Athens that evening was impossible, for it would have been necessary to send to town to procure mules; we proceeded, therefore, to the monastery, a stone edifice, with a wide entrance: it was built in a rectangular shape, and the small chapel of the fathers stood in the middle of the court: the loud barking of dogs greeted us at our approach, and, after some time, a *kaloieros* (or monk), made his appearance: he was a man of middle age; a thinset beard covered his pointed chin, and a dirty woollen cap shaded his face, the features of which bespoke the total absence of manly feeling: a long robe gathered with a leathern girdle, fell to his feet, upon which, he wore two rough-worked sandals. The *karavikyrios* who had guided us to the convent, carried the hand of this holy man to his forehead, and explained our want of a night's lodging; the monk viewed us with his sharp and diminutive eyes, shrugged his shoulders, and after a short pause informed us that the *egoumenos* or abbot was not in the convent; fear of the port miasmata had driven him: to Athens - there were no accommodations in the building - the society had no provisions left; -but the sight of a piece of gold soon overcame the numerous difficulties which avarice had raised; the father, holding in his hand a lighted torch of deal wood, conducted us by a wooden staircase erected on the outside of the building, to a long room, the walls of which were decorated with numerous inscriptions and many ugly faces; traced with charcoal and red ochre. A large mat of Spartan rushes was spread on the floor; upon this we extended ourselves; wrapped in our blankets, and having our portmanteaus for pillows: the wind whistled through, the partly untiled roof, the noise of which, joined to the fretfulness of sickness and the impatience of entering Athens, hindered me, from sleeping ere the dawn of day; then all in the convent was hurry and bustle: we looked from the windows, and saw the yard filled with mules and asses, loaded with skins of oil, which the muleteers and monks were busy pouring into casks ready for exportation. We afterwards learnt that the pasha of Euboea, under whose despotic jurisdiction the country of Themistocles now groans, had, for some trivial reason forbidden any oil to be exported from Attica except by certain monopolists; the inhabitants had, in consequence, to resort to smuggling: and the contraband goods were placed under the protection of Agios Spiridion and his monks, until they could be embarked aboard a French schooner which was expected in the port.

A Wedding

It was on a Sunday afternoon; the heat was excessive, and we were occupied in arranging our journal; my ear was struck with the monotonous sound of a Greek tambour, and the noise of people hurrying through the street. I followed them, and after turning through two or three lanes, came to the spot whence the sound proceeded. Some dirty musicians, with a tambour, a fiddle, and a guitar, were dancing, playing, and singing; after them came a Greek damsel, supported by two grave matrons, and followed by a long string of dames hoary with age: she was the bride, and notwithstanding the thermometer stood at 96 degrees, was covered with mantles and furs; her fingers' ends and joints were stained red; the lower part of her eyes was tinged with a blue colour; and her cheeks were ornamented with stars of black dye and leaf gold; a dirty urchin, walking backwards, held a mirror in such a manner that the young woman had her image constantly before her.

They moved literally at a snail's pace; the people threw from their windows and doors bottles of orange water, which perfumed the air, and the crowd, loud in their expressions of joy and congratulation, augmented as we advanced, hurrying round the bride, whose brow was never bent with a frown, and whose lips were never crossed with a smile during the ceremony.

The procession stopped at the house of the bridegroom; the bride was seated in an arm chair, and placed on the right of the house door; on the opposite side was seated her husband, his hairless head uncovered; by him stood a Turkish barber, holding in his hand a circular looking glass (similar to that with which Venus is represented) and other shaving instruments: the music continued playing, and the crowd shook the air with their shouts. Each, placing a few parats on the barber's looking-glass, sprinkled with orange water the face, of the bridegroom, and kissed him on the forehead and the eyes: the money thus collected was to procure a comfortable establishment for the young people; I subscribed my share, but preferred dispensing with the kisses. A Greek, an old man whose age was a sufficient excuse for the joke, pushed me towards the bride, whom I was consequently obliged to salute amidst the loud cheers of the assembly: - how the ceremony ended I cannot tell you, as the day fell, and I returned home ere all had embraced the bridegroom.

Vandalism Again

Hardly do any persons quit the Acropolis without clipping from its monuments some relic to carry back to their country. This rage for destroying has been carried so far that the elegant Ionic capitals, which I before mentioned, have nearly disappeared, and not one of the Caryatides now stands entire. The last time I visited the citadel, when taking a farewell view of the Pandroseon and the Hall of Erectheus, I was much displeased at seeing an English traveller, an officer of the navy (for such his uniform bespoke him to be) standing upon the base of one of the Caryatides, clinging with his left arm round the column, while his right hand, provided with a hard and heavy pebble, was endeavouring to knock off the only remaining nose of those six beautifully sculptured statues. I exerted my eloquence in vain to preserve this monument of art.

An Interesting Janissary at Kifissia

After three hours' ride, across the forest of olive trees, many of which seem to have stood centuries, we arrived at the village of Jevisa, formerly *Kefisia*: this place is much frequented by the Athenians in summer; many Turks have country houses there. In the middle of the village, round the trunk of a fine-spreading plane, is erected a brick platform, about three feet high, and covered with rush mat: this simple building answers all the purposes of a coffee-house. While we were here, refreshing ourselves and resting our steeds, we were addressed in tolerable Italian by a fine-looking Turkish janissary: his name was Housein: .he had been in the service of; the Princess of. Wales when she performed the voyage to Jerusalem: he had travelled with her in Italy and Germany. He was known in the suite under the name of Soleiman, and was handsomely rewarded for his services. But poor Housein having contracted among his Italian acquaintance too great an affection for billiards, was stripped of his fortune, and returned to his country in poverty. He now contents himself with offering his services to private individuals who stand in need of a janissary, one of the appendages generally taken with, supreme care by the British traveller, often too readily listens to the accounts of the ignorant and the prejudiced.

Housein was communicative, and gave us an amusing account of his travels, the effect of which seemed to have inspired him with the utmost contempt for his country and his comrades.

Working the Apiaries of Pendeli Monastery

The fathers had prepared for us a dish of good boiled rice, from which, sweetened with honey, we made an excellent, and certainly a most wholesome meal. A great quantity of honey is made yearly in the convent of Mendeli ; it is much yellower than that we see in France and England, and has an aromatic taste, by no means agreeable: the same observation applies to that of Mount Hymettus; the white is said to be the produce of young bees.

Athens is still celebrated for the honey produced in its territory: "Athenian honey" and "Syrian sugar" are the favourite delicacies of the Osmanlis. As honey is much used by the Turks, both in their cookery and in their beverages, apiaries are frequently seen in Greece; they are all conducted on the same plan, which I am told differs very widely from that adopted in England. We made many inquiries of the good monks of Mendeli concerning their mode of treating these industrious insects. I copy from my journal the following description , which was given me by one of the fathers...

The hives are placed on the southern declivity of a hill, in apiaries of one or two hundred hives, surrounded by a wall low enough to admit the free ingress of air, but, at the same time, sufficiently high to defend them from the beasts of the field. The hive is made of rushes, and resembles exactly, in shape and size, an English hamper; it is plastered with a mixture of dung and ashes, and is placed upon its bottom on a low stool; across the top are put twelve or fourteen twigs, to which the bees fasten their honeycombs; a conical roof of reed-straw is placed over the whole. When they wish to have any honey the bees are driven out by smoke, inserted under the roof, which is then taken off, and as many sticks, with the combs attached to them, as are wanted, are taken out; the roof is then replaced, and the bees are suffered to return. By dividing them early in the season, that is, by placing some of the combs in a new hive, the bees are hindered from swarming.

The fumigation is performed by a person whose hands are defended by a thick pair of gloves, and whose face is covered with a wire mask, similar to those, worn by fencers; a pot, with a sort of round chimney and a handle, is filled with burning cow dung, the smoke of which is dispersed in the hive. This operation is performed at midday.

1825 Count Pecchio

An Island of Refugees

During the War of Independence, travel and sightseeing on the mainland was sometimes impossible, and the visitors' attention was diverted to the Saronic islands, hich were also havens for refugees from the struggles in the Aegean and on the mainland.

At sunrise we were before Egina. The shaft of an old column, which is seen projecting from afar off; the beautiful plain reaching to the shore, covered with olive-trees, rich pastures, and cornfields; irregular mountains rising towards the south of the island, and bounding this beautiful view, made me wish that some accident might suspend our voyage. It became perfectly calm, and my wish was gratified. We went on shore to await the rising of the wind. I hastened to visit the solitary column (a fragment, possibly, of some temple); and thence, by the ruins of the ancient port of Egina, which are still visible in the sea - to Egina, which has arisen within these few years. The inhabitants had lived in a city built by the Venetians upon a mountain in the interior of the island; but the love of commerce induced them to prefer the seashore, and they accordingly chose the site of the ancient Egina.

The emigrations caused by the present revolution has assembled here a mixture of wandering Greeks from various parts; from Scio, Natolia, Zaituni, Livadia, etc.; the various dresses of the women presenting to the traveller a continued masquerade. The population now amounts to about 10,000 souls; amongst whom there are about 1000 Ipsariots, who, after the catastrophe in their own country, have sought an asylum here. The costume of the Ipsariot women is striking from its various colours, resembling that of Rome or the Swiss peasantry.

Now, however, a great part of them are dressed in mourning for their husbands and relatives, slain last year by the Turks. They wear on their heads a large turban, from which descends a corner of the handkerchief, which covers all their face except the eyes, and a band of hair which crosses their forehead. I cannot affirm whether this practice of covering the face is an imitation of the Turkish costume, or the continuance of that of ancient Athenian women.

The Ipsariot women are beautiful, courageous, and capable of the most heroic acts. Almost all of them can swim. The aunt of Captain Canaris, a strong woman of sixty years of age, saved her life at the taking of Ipsara by swimming three miles. The wealthiest families of Ipsara have taken refuge at Egina, and continue to follow maritime employment. Ipsara is an arid sterile rock. Egina, on the contrary, is fruitful, sunny, and under a delightful sky; nevertheless, the Ipsariots always sigh for their barren Ipsara. The government has offered them the Piraeus, as a compensation for the loss of their island; but the Ipsariots desire to suppress the illustrious name of the Piraeus, and to substitute that of New Ipsara. The mere name of country is an illusion dear to him who has lost the reality.

1825 James Emerson

Hydra

May 11th, (Tuesday.) - At ten o'clock this morning, after beating up against a strong head wind, which blows almost constantly during the morning from the N. E., through this strait, we came to anchor in the harbour of Hydra. The town, on approaching it from the sea, presents an extremely beautiful prospect; its large white houses rise up suddenly from the sea, along the precipitous cliffs which form its harbour; every little crag displayed the white sails of an immense number of windmills, and every peak was bristling with a battery. In the background, the rugged and barren summits of the rocks which form the island, with scarce a speck of cultivation or a single tree, are crowned with numerous monasteries. On one is stationed a guard to observe the approach of ships; and his lookout extending to an immense distance, the Hydriots, have, in general, the earliest intimation of any important naval movement. The streets, from the rugged situation of the town, are precipitous and uneven, but, to one arriving from the Peloponnesus, their cleanliness is their strongest recommendation. The quay, for the entire sweep of the harbour, is lined with storehouses and shops, which carry on the little external traffic that still remains, whilst their number shows the former extent of the Hydriot commerce.

The houses are all built in the most substantial manner; and, with the exception of their flat roofs, on European models. The apartments are large and airy; and the halls spacious, and always paved with marble. The walls are so thick, as almost to supersede the necessity of our sun-blinds in the niches of their deep-set windows. But, independent of the strength of the habitations, the neatness and extreme cleanliness of them are peculiarly remarkable, and speak highly for the domestic employments of the Hydriot ladies; who are still not entirely freed from the sedentary restriction so universal in the East. The furniture, half Turkish and half European, combines the luxury of one, with the convenience of the other, whilst its solidity and want of ornament show that it has been made for comfort, and not for ostentation.

The appearance of the population is much more prepossessing than that of any other class of the Greeks: the women are in general pretty; but an universal custom of wearing a kerchief folded over the head, and tied under the chin, destroys the fine contour of their features, and makes them all appear to have round faces. A short silken jacket neatly ornamented, and a large petticoat, containing an immense number of folds and breadths, generally of green stuff, bordered with a few gaudy stripes, complete their simple costume. The neat slipper so universal in the north of Italy, which so delicately shows the turn of the ankle and heel, is likewise worn by the Hydriot ladies; whose jetty hair and sparkling eyes, graceful figures, and beautiful hands, all enhanced by their half European manners, render them, if not the most beautiful, at least the most interesting females I have seen in the Levant.

The men are invariably athletic and well formed; their dress combining all the lightness of an oriental costume, with the grace of an European one; - their short jackets are covered with neat embroidery, and their only personal ornament is the handle of their ... stout knife, the sole weapon carried by an islander in Hydra. Their pantaloons, which reach merely to the knee, are the most singular part of their dress; being nothing more than a very broad and shallow sack of dyed cotton, with a swing case at the top, and two holes at each corner of the bottom, so that when drawn on, the superfluous folds fall down in a bag behind, whilst ample plaits above add considerably to the grace of the figure.

1827-8 Henry A. V. Post

An Inhospitable Island

To a person fresh from the filthy hovels of the Morea, the town of Hydra has an air of neatness and elegance, which, though real to a certain extent, is no doubt greatly enhanced by the contrast with other places. The streets, though narrow and precipitous, are tolerably clean, the houses, though deficient in architectural beauty, are many of them substantially and expensively built, and are generally furnished with glazed windows, a very unusual luxury in Greece. The gaudy little church belonging to the monastery of the Panagia, would be set down as one of the *videnda* even in the itineraries of France or Italy. Among its curiosities, are a pair of wax candles, weighing three hundred okas each, which were destined for Mecca as a present from the Sultan, but were captured on their way by a Hydriote vessel.

Hydra, superior as it is in many respects to the other, cities of Greece, is like nearly all the rest of them, totally destitute of inns or other establishments of the kind for the accommodation of travellers. The inhabitants are at the same time notorious for their aversion to strangers, and except in cases where they come particularly recommended to their hospitality, always regard them with suspicion and distrust. Jarvis found us quarters in the loft of a magazine, where, amid boxes and barrels, we partook of a sumptuous runner of caviari and olives, squatting *à la Turque* around a little circular board, raised a few inches from the floor, which is the species of dining-table most commonly met with in Greece.

The day of our arrival was the fete day of some saint, whose name I thought it not worth the trouble to inquire; the shops were closed, and nearly all the male inhabitants were parading up and down the quays, or amusing themselves about the coffee-houses in playing cards, smoking, and drinking punch and raki. Taken as a body, they are decidedly the most finely formed and athletic men I have ever seen; and are by the concurrent testimony of all travellers, the most uniformly well dressed population that is to be found in any city in Europe. Scarcely any appearance of poverty was visible - scarcely any of the ordinary miseries of war; to have seen them lounging about the cafes and bazaars, dressed in their holiday suits, quietly smoking their pipes, and twirling their rosaries, one would hardly have believed them to be at all interested in the calamitous events which had produced such frightful desolation among their brethren of the Morea...

The Hydriotes, I speak now of the lower classes, are distinguished by their pride and insolence towards strangers, no less than by the respectability of their appearance. For my own part, I had no reason to complain of any thing more than an occasional look of conscious superiority; but this is one of the accusations which are generally brought against them. They are likewise notorious for their lawless and unruly dispositions, and their fondness for noise and riot. During my short stay in their city, the streets were every night infested with drunken revellers, shouting, and singing, and firing their pistols, to the inconceivable annoyance and no small peril of the peaceably disposed inhabitants. Disputes and quarrels were very common, and not infrequently resulted in the shedding of blood. Discreditable, however, as these excesses are, it by no means follows, that the Hydriotes are naturally worse than other people. Let it be recollected, that the greater part of the population is composed of uneducated seafaring men; that the embarrassments which the war has thrown in the way of their occupations, oblige them to live in a great measure in idleness; that they are unrestrained by the authority of wholesome laws, and that their evil propensities may consequently be indulged with impunity; and we shall find far more reason to admire them for their moderation, than to censure them for their licentiousness. Let the maritime population of any civilized country in Europe or America be collected in a body - let them enjoy the same facilities, and be subjected to similar temptations, and we should see a state of society far more depraved than the world has ever yet seen in any Christian land. I had an opportunity of observing the contrast during a subsequent visit to Aegina, at a time when several English and Russian men-of-war were lying in the harbour; and it is a mortifying and disgraceful truth, that there was more drunkenness and debauchery, more noise and uproar, more frequent breaches of the peace, among the few hundred sailors that were let loose upon the town from the foreign men of war, than among the whole populace of Hydra, rioting, as they were, in the unrestrained licentiousness of newly acquired independence.

Sailors: Greek and American, Compared

After landing and securing the remainder of our cargo at Poros, I proceeded with a portion of it to the isthmus of Corinth, where great numbers of fugitives had assembled from different parts of the country, and were living in a state of the most shocking privation and distress. We hired for this purpose a small *martigo* [*vessel with a single, square rigged mast*] well supplied with arms, to resist any attack from pirates or the lawless soldiery, and manned with a dozen stout Poreotes, the most decent and respectable crew that I ever saw on board of any vessel...

While the scale of society is in general so much more elevated among the civilized nations of Europe, than in Greece, the Greek sailors are a much superior class of men to those of either England or America. They are not mere hirelings, who ship for a single voyage, and squander away their earnings, the first opportunity, in low and degrading debaucheries; they are frequently men of families, who have an interest in the vessel in which they sail, and to which they are permanently attached. There are many towns, such as Hydra, Spetzin, Tenos, Mykone, etc., inhabited almost entirely by the families of sea faring men. Though they are a good deal addicted to their light wines and raki, as their common strong beverage is called, they rarely roll into that excessive indulgence, which disgraces the seamen of other countries. An English or American sailor is a mere animal; he makes himself such by his vices, and is treated as such by his officers. He is placed at an awful distance below his captain, and kept under a useless and humiliating severity of discipline; he is spoken to like a dog, and fed like a pig. The Greek enjoys perhaps the opposite extreme of license and familiarity with his superiors, and, according to standard or good living which obtains among his countrymen, is fed better than the Frank; at all events, he is better clad. His principal food is bread, cheese, and olives, seasoned with an onion, and varied occasionally by a piece of salt fish, or plate of bean porridge; and there is certainly more refinement in a Greek crew, sitting cross-legged upon deck around their meagre table, than in an American mess, crowded into a dirty forecastle, and devouring their more substantial beef and pork, like swine out of a common trough. The American sailor is notorious for his profanity and contempt of things sacred; the Greek is devout or at least reverent in the observance of his religion, such as it is. Every Greek vessel is hallowed by a little picture of the Panagia, or Virgin, and sometimes of some saint, with a lighted lamp suspended before them; and a pot of burning incense is every evening carried round by the cabin boy, who officiates as priest, and smokes in turn every one of the ship's company, who all hold their caps over the purifying vapour, and piously cross themselves, while they pray the Panagia or St. Nicolas for a prosperous voyage. In point of skill and dexterity in the management of a vessel, the Greek sailors will bear a comparison with any in the world.

A Violent Affray

Shortly after our return to headquarters, the town was thrown into an alarming commotion, almost amounting to a civil war, by a trifle light as air, which would not be worth recording, but to illustrate the singularly inflammable state of the social elements in Greece. I was occupied in one of our magazines, when a soldier named Micheli, whom we had discharged from our service a short time before, came up to me decked out in the most extravagant style of *palikari* foppery, and made the modest demand of a barrel of flour. I at first treated his request jocosely, and asked him if it was upon the ground of poverty that he presented himself as a beggar. He answered very insolently that these supplies were sent out "for the nation," and that he, as one of the nation, was entitled to his share with the rest. Finding it impossible to get rid of his importunity by a civil refusal, I was at length obliged to eject him from the premises by a gentle application the hand to the back of his neck. His first impulse was to grasp his ataghan; but recollecting probably that I always carried a pair of pistols in my pocket, he thought proper to restrain his wrath for the present, and after a few commonplace imprecations, strode away muttering threats of vengeance.

Hydra in 1797 (A-L. Castellan, 1808)

It happened, unfortunately, that while his ire was yet in full and overflowing ebullition, he met an old *chamál* in our employ, accompanied by Francesco, one of our soldier-servants, bringing bread from the oven for the use of the hospital. Micheli seized this first opportunity for wreaking his vengeance, and snatching a loaf of bread from the tray, endeavoured to make off with his booty. But Francesco, true to his charge, laid fearlessly hold of the invader, and strove to rescue the captive loaf. He was overpowered and beaten by a friend of his antagonist, and chased through the street by Micheli himself with a drawn *ataghan* in his hand. A respectable shopkeeper of the town, indignant at the outrage, intervened in behalf of Francesco, and dealt retribution upon the man that had beaten him.

The affair soon became noised abroad, and a general uproar ensued. A large mob assembled about the scene of the affray, and two hostile parties were formed, one declaring for the Americans, the other for Micheli. In the midst of the confusion, the shopkeeper who had taken Francesco's part received a stab in the back from the knife of a fellow townsman, and almost immediately expired. It was now late in the evening, and Micheli and the murderer contrived to make their escape under cover of the darkness, and fled with precipitation from the island. It was a fortunate circumstance that the night closed in; in time to put an end to the quarrel before it had proceeded any farther; had it been otherwise, the most fatal consequences might have been the result. But it was too dark to fight, - and after a tumultuous war of words, during which an attack upon our hospital was loudly threatened, the contending parties at length gradually dispersed, and betook themselves to the coffee-houses, to drown their animosity in the fumes of tobacco and raki.

"Save us From Our Friends!"

A chapter of remarkable events had taken place at Poros during our absence. On new year's day the foreign officers of the fleet dined with the Lord High Admiral on board of his yacht, and several of them became gloriously intoxicated in honour of the joyous occasion. Among the number was Captain H. an Englishman, commander of the steamboat Enterprise, who, on returning to his vessel, began "in a merry mood" to belabour an old Frenchman that served under him in the capacity of armourer. The proud spirit of the Gaul could not passively endure a blow, and he accordingly returned the joke with great magnanimity. This roused the ire of Captain H. to a pitch of ungovernable fury; he staggered down into the cabin, seized a knife, and in seeking out the object of his vengeance stumbled over a Hydriote sailor who was lying asleep on deck, and in falling, plunged the knife into his body. The unfortunate man expired shortly after. The author of his death was sent to Aegina to be delivered up to justice; but the government declined having any thing to do with the affair, and he was set at liberty. He was, however, superseded in his command of the steamboat by Lieutenant K.; and it is a singular coincidence, affording a striking illustration of the licentious habits of the dissolute Franks who had come to seek their fortunes in Greece, that the new commander was also removed from the vessel very shortly afterwards, for killing a respectable citizen of Poros in a similar manner. He set out one evening, while in a state of intoxication, to pay a visit to one of his friends, but owing to the confusion of his vision, entered the wrong house. The owner, finding a stranger thus rudely intruding himself into his dwelling, took the liberty of inquiring his business, and receiving no answer attempted to dispute his passage; when the drunken Englishman immediately drew his sword, and unceremoniously ran him through the body.

369

The Ass Turned Rider

Athens was at this time in the hands of the Turks, and the great body of its population had taken refuge, as in ancient times, in the island of Salamis. A few days before, seven of the garrison had deserted, and crossing over to this island, had thrown themselves upon the generosity of their enemies. The Greeks not only allowed them to remain unmolested, but even received them into their houses and treated them with marked hospitality. Our own kind host had taken one of them under his protection. It was indeed a singular spectacle, to see a haughty Moslem supplicating the friendly offices of a poor Greek, whom a few years before he would have thought unworthy of any other notice than an insult or a blow, But the ass had now turned rider, and the long enslaved Greek held up his head and ventured to assume the look of a man, while the disdainful Turk unbent his pride, and professed the most unbounded friendship and admiration for the noble and generous Greeks! He said he was heartily sick of the war, and begged me very earnestly to take him along with me on my journey, and forward him to Jaffa, his native city; promising me in return the blessing of Allah and the Prophet. The reason, he said, which induced him and his comrades to desert, was the scarcity of bread under which they had long been suffering. Nearly a hundred others set out in company with them, but their courage failing them, they concluded to return, and to defer the execution of their purpose until they should ascertain by a signal concerted between them, whether the seven were favourably received. The appointed signal had been given, and his countrymen, he said, were no doubt looking for the first opportunity to effect their escape. Some days afterwards another party did in fact desert, and were at Aegina on my return to that island. They were merely deprived of their arms, and then permitted to circulate uncontrolled through the town. Two of them came one day into a coffee-house where I was sitting, when a Greek Captain, as if to vindicate the honour of his country, immediately ordered the *Cafegi* to furnish them with their favourite beverage. When the coffee was brought to them, and the individual who had sent it pointed out, the grateful Mussulmans laid their hands on their breasts and bowed their heads in acknowledgment, and seemed perfectly amazed at an act or generosity, so different from what they themselves would have shown towards an enemy under similar circumstances.

Wartime Spetses

Spetzia is, like. Hydra, almost exclusively inhabited by sea faring men, the most insolent and ungovernable of all the Greek islanders. Their dark and savage countenances, and the air of reckless ferocity with which they swagger along, ender them the most forbidding and repulsive of all the Greeks that I have met with. Cooped up in their barren island, deprived not only of their wonted means of subsistence, but of their favourite occupation upon the seas, which habit has rendered almost indispensable to their existence, and suddenly reduced to a life of idleness and poverty, they become restless and impatient, as might be expected, from so violent a change in their habits; their vicious propensities are suffered to grow rank and unrestrained, and produce the natural fruits of crime and disorder. Their commerce is gone, their navy is now scarcely more than a name, - and the gallant vessels which once wafted them riches with every gale that blew, are crowded together dismantled and deserted in the now silent and unfrequented harbour. Such of the inhabitants as have the means of indulgence spend their time in drinking and smoking, and gambling about the coffee-houses, and many of those who have not, will not scruple to obtain them by any mode which fortune may throw in their way. The consequence of this state of things is a degree of anarchy and insubordination, which makes it unsafe for a stranger to venture unprotected into the more retired parts of the town. I was walking one morning with my Mainiote companion, but a short distance from the bazaar, when were met by a friend of his who assured us that we were in great danger of being robbed and receiving personal injury if we proceeded any farther into the town. The same caution was afterwards repeated to us by an old priest. Such a state of society is to be lamented, but it would be unjust and unreasonable to censure men too severely for vices which have been entailed upon them, in a great measure, by their misfortunes; and we should be more especially careful in passing judgment upon these ignorant and unenlightened islanders, when the records of civilization afford such good reason to believe, that even our own countrymen, if placed in the same trying circumstances, with the same temptations to crime, and the same facilities for its commission, would be guilty of far greater excesses than have ever disgraced the populace of Hydra or Spetzia.

1828 Samuel Woodruff

Defence against Night Assault

Mr. E. and myself procured for each of us a substitute for a bedstead; made in the form of saw-jacks, and standing on eight feet. To prevent the ascent of vermin, we set the feet in tin cups partly filled with water. Thus fortified and entrenched, we expected to enjoy some repose. But we soon found that these outworks served only to secure us from the attack of bed bugs; while a nimbler race, like mounted cavalry, leaped our fosses, scaled the walls, and charged us in our citadels. We had, however, gained much, and were well compensated for our troubled expense.

1829 Thomas Alcock

Athens in Ruins

The few monuments of past grandeur standing amid a mass of ruin, as if saved by magic, - the wretched huts of some Albanian soldiers, - a paltry bazaar, - and five or six tolerable dwellings, in which the Bey and the chief officers reside, form the exact state of Athens in 1829...

Having, with some difficulty, clambered over large heaps of rubbish, we were amply repaid by a specimen of the most beautiful Corinthian order, the tomb of Lysicrates, better known as the lantern of Demosthenes. Its preservation seemed miraculous, but was owing to the protection of a monastery, in which it had been immured; and the revolution which destroyed the asylum happily spared the precious monument it contained. Under the impression that this, as well as other valuable remains, would, according to the assurance of the Turks, fall a prey to their vengeance before they left Athens, I ventured to ask the Bey if he would permit me to have it carried away, rather than suffer it to risk being destroyed; adding, that the stones were of no value, and that I could send him European articles of much more use to him. He replied, in the plenitude of his delight at the prospect I held out of presents, that I might have it, and that if it were worth millions still he should he happy it were so well disposed of. For the moment I was willing to entertain hopes that I might be able to rescue this beautiful ruin from entire destruction, and procure for the British Museum a specimen of Grecian architecture, such as it has not at present in its collection; but, on reflection, I found it would be difficult to remove, without material injury, a mass of about the weight of eight tons; and I was not anxious to incur the reproach of despoiling Greece of that which, perhaps, may still be an object of pride to her in her dawn of freedom, in spite of the determination of the Turks. I therefore abandoned this project, which, like many other resolves, gave a momentary delight in anticipation...

1829-31 E. C. Wines

An Unusual Method of Drinking

We saw two fellows drinking at a well [*near Piraeus*], and their *modus operandi* had for us at least the interest of novelty. One of them descended into the well, dipped up the water in his dirty red skull-cap, and handed it to his companion, who, in his turn, performed the same operation for the other.

1832-3 Christopher Wordsworth

The End of an Era - The Last Ramadan in Athens

The town of Athens is now lying in ruins. The streets are almost deserted; nearly all the houses are without roofs. The churches are reduced to bare walls and heaps of stones and mortar. There is but one church in which the service is performed. A few new wooden houses, one or two of more solid structure, and the two lines of planked sheds which form the bazaar are all the inhabited dwellings that Athens can now boast. So slowly does it recover from the effects of the late war.

Remaining here for a considerable period, we begin to regard Athens as a temporary home. Athens is now, which is of much consequence in the very troubled state of the country, not merely the most agreeable, but also the most secure residence in Greece.

We are lodged in a small house in that quarter of Athens which was once the inner Ceramaicus: our abode is the nearest building to the Temple of Theseus on the extreme verge of the modern town. There are few other buildings near it. At a little distance to the south a peasant is now engaged in ploughing the earth with a team of two oxen: the soil along which he is driving his furrows, was once a part of the agora of Athens.

There is not a single volume of any kind, ancient or modern, to be purchased here.

The bazaar or market of Athens is a long street, which is now the only one there of any importance. It has no foot-pavement; there is a gutter in the middle, down which, in this wintry weather the water runs in copious torrents. The houses are generally patched together with planks and plaster. Looking up the street, you command a view of the commodities with which this Athenian market is now supplied. Barrels of black caviar, small pocket-looking-glasses in red pasteboard cases, onions, tobacco piled up in brown heaps, black olives, figs strung together upon a rush, rices, pipes with amber mouth-pieces and brown clay bowls, rich stuffs, and silver-chased pistols, dirks, belts, and embroidered waistcoats, - these are the varied objects which a rapid glance along this street presents to the spectator.

The objects which are not to be found here, as well as those which are, ought not to be neglected in this description. Here there are no books, no lamps, no windows, no carriages, no newspapers, no post-office. The letters which arrived here a few days hence from Napoli , after having been publicly cried in the streets, if they were not claimed by the parties to whom they were addressed, were committed to the flames.

Such is the present state of Athens, as far as the streets speak of its condition. This city is still in the hands of the Turks. All the other continental towns of Greece south of Thermopylae are independent of Turkey. Strange it is that a distinction of this sort should have been reserved for Athens.

Such however is the case. The muezzin still mounts the scaffolding in the bazaar here to call the Mussulman to prayer at the stated hours; a few Turks still doze in the archways of the Acropolis, or recline while smoking their pipes, and leaning with their backs against the rusty cannon which are planted on the battlements of its walls; the Athenian peasant, as he drives his laden mule from Hymettus through the eastern gate of the town, still flings his small bundle of thyme and brushwood, from the load which he brings on his mule's back, as a tribute to the Mussulman toll-gatherer who sits at that entrance to the town; and a few days ago the cannon of the Acropolis fired the signal of the conclusion of the Turkish Ramadan - the last which will ever be celebrated at Athens.

Such alterations will probably have occurred within a few years that this description will then be perhaps considered as a chapter taken from a fabulous history of Athens, and its condition in a short period be as far removed from what it is at present, as from what it was in the most ancient times, under the old Cecropian monarchs, and at that obscure epoch, when its soil was trodden by the feet of the roving Pelasgi.

Perilous Condition of the Roads outside Athens

On setting out this morning from the gate of Athens on our way to the Piraeus, we were cautioned by our guides to delay our steps till we had formed a strong party to go with us. But a few days ago, two Greeks coming from the Piraeus in the evening were plundered and severely wounded on this road.

It would be regarded here as an act of incredible rashness for a traveller to venture on a ride from Athens to Acharnae. In the village of Menidi near Acharnae resides the Greek captain, Vasso. His soldiers, if they deserve the name, indemnify themselves for the pay of which they are defrauded, by seizing without mercy whatever falls in their way. By this system of depredation the whole of the province is reduced to beggary. Many of its villages are deserted; their population has quitted them, either to take refuge in the mountains, or to swell the numbers of these depredators.

Even the immediate neighbourhood of Athens itself is now in such a state, that unattended and leisurely excursions into its environs are difficult and dangerous. The delineation of a chart of Athens and its suburbs was lately commenced by two architects resident here. Their task has just been abandoned, on account of the insecurity with which they found that, even within sight of the walls of Athens, their researches were attended.

Carnival "at the Columns"

The spot, which from time immemorial has been chosen for its celebration, would alone give an unspeakable charm to this characteristic scene, independent of the invariable accessories of a cloudless sky and a brilliant sun, which the Greeks may at any time so confidently expect, that they wisely hold all their festivities in the open air. The fifteen majestic columns now alone remaining of the mighty temple of Jupiter Olympus, are usually abandoned to a solitude and stillness so intense, that there seems to hang around them a very atmosphere, of desolation, which singularly enhances the awful sublimity of these stately ruins; but on this day, before even the rising of the sun has been announced by the long shadows of the three lone pillars which stand apart from the rest, and have so long been as a gigantic sundial to that wide plain, the stern silence of this kingdom of the past is broken in upon by every sight and sound that can indicate life moot busy, stirring, and gay.

The whole population of Athens, men, women, and children, followed by their asses laden with provisions, carpets, and other indispensable luxuries, pour out of the town at this early hour, and assemble under the deserted columns: nor do they confine themselves to this spot alone, but spread in all directions along the myrtle-clad banks of the Ilissos, over the stadium, as entire in form to this day as when it shook with the roar of the wild beasts and the shouts of the combatants in those terrific games; and round the classic fountain of Calleroe, usually so still and quiet that the most timid of nymphs might use its limpid waters for her mirror, as the stars do every night.

Thus, clustering in groups that are almost always strikingly picturesque, they establish themselves for a long day of enjoyment; the little infants, strange-looking diminutive mummies; swaddled from head to foot, and with long streaming black hair, are laid among the green corn to sleep or scream as the case may be; the young girls arrange their little coquettish red caps to the best advantage, and look out from under their long eyelashes at the fierce cavaliers, who, with a self-satisfied air, and an incredibly small waist, keep continually careering at full gallop up and down, over rocks and stones in a reckless manner, more amusing to themselves than agreeable to their horses. Meanwhile the more sedate of the party seat themselves in a circle, and give their serious attention to one of their number, who either regales them unwearied for hours together with the most lamentable music produced by the rattling of a quill on the jingling wires of a sort of mandolin, or else chants, in a monotonous voice, a never-ending story, which, to my infinite delight, is generally word for word one of those we know so well in the *Arabian Nights*. Altogether it would be impossible to conceive a gayer or more animated scene, brightened as it is by the effects of the sunshine on the vivid colours of their dresses.

At noon a grotesque figure, representing the late carnival, is carried to his grave in procession, with a great deal of merriment and glee, where he is ignominiously decapitated and buried. From that moment the Greeks enter with all sincerity on the practice of the fast enjoined by their church..."

c.1833 N. Parker Willis

Recriminations Among the "Goths"

I was again in the Acropolis the following morning. Mr. Hill had kindly given me a note to Petrarches, the king's antiquary, a young Athenian, who married the sister of the Maid of Athens. We went together through the ruins. They have lately made new excavation, and some superb *bassi-relievi* are among the discoveries. One of them represented a procession leading victims to the sacrifice, and was the finest thing I ever saw. The leading figure was a superb female, from the head of which the nose had lately been barbarously broken. The face of the enthusiastic young antiquary flushed while I was lamenting it. It was done, he told me, but a week before, by an officer of the English squadron then lying at the Piraeus. Petrarches detected it immediately, and sent word to the admiral, who discovered the heartless Goth in a nephew of an English duke, a midshipman of his own ship. I should not have taken the trouble to mention so revolting a circumstance if I had not seen, in a splendid copy of the *Illustrations of Byron's Travels in Greece* a most virulent attack on the officers of the *Constellation*, and Americans generally, for the same thing. Who but Englishmen have robbed Athens, and Aegina, and all Greece? Who but Englishmen are watched like thieves in their visits to every place of curiosity in the world? Where is the superb caryatid of the Erechtheion? Stolen with such barbarous carelessness too, that the remaining statues and the superb portico they sustained are tumbling to the ground! The insolence of England's laying such sins at the door of another nation is insufferable.

For my part, I cannot conceive the motive for carrying away a fragment of a statue or column. I should as soon think of drawing a tooth as a specimen of some beautiful woman I had seen in my travels. And how I dare show such a theft to a person of taste, is quite as singular. Even when a whole column or statue is carried away, its main charm is gone with the association of the place. I venture to presume that no person of classic feeling ever saw Lord Elgin's marbles without execrating the folly that could bring them from their bright native sky to the vulgar atmosphere of London. For the sake of taste, let us discountenance such barbarisms in America.

The Erechthion and the adjoining temple are gems of architecture. The small portico of the caryatids (female figures, in place of columns, with their hands on their hips) must have been one of the most exquisite things in Greece. One of them (fallen in consequence of Lord Elgin's removal of the sister statuette) lies headless on the ground, and the remaining ones are badly mutilated, but they are very, very beautiful.

1835 George Finlay

The First Excavations

At Athens it was decided to excavate one half of the town in order to search for antiquities, though it was calculated by a French engineer that the expense would exceed the excavation of Pompeii; and it was said by Professor Thiersch himself, who knows something more about Greece and its antiquities there, than Armansperg, Maurer, Heideck, Abel.and Greinier, that working oxen were more wanted than the bull of Marathon itself in bronze or marble. The proprietors of the houses in the district marked out for the purpose of this excavation, were for two years prevented from completing them, even though some of them were half finished before the plan was adopted. At length, however, government changed its mind, and without any public communication, commenced building a large barrack in the middle of the ruins of Hadrian's library, exactly in the spot where excavation might have been attended with some success; and to cure its successors from a wish ever to repeat its own folly, it filled up that part of the enclosure near Lord Elgin's tower and nearly buried the church of the Megale Panaghia in which are many antiquities and some very curious paintings, with ten feet of additional rubbish...

1835 J. L. Stephens

The Parthenon from an Unusual Vantage Point

Once, under the direction of Mr. Hill, I clambered up to the very apex of the pediment, and, lying down at full length, leaned over and saw under the frieze the acanthus leaf delicately and beautifully painted on the marble, and, being protected from exposure, still retaining its freshness of colouring. It was entirely out of sight from below, and had been discovered, almost at the peril of his life, by the enthusiasm of an English artist. The wind was whistling around me as I leaned over to examine it, and, until that moment, I never appreciated fully the immense labour employed and the exquisite finish displayed in every portion of the temple.

The Threat of Modernity

The sentimental traveller must already mourn that Athens has been selected as the capital of Greece. Already have speculators and the whole tribe of "improvers" invaded the glorious city; and while I was lingering on the steps of the Parthenon, a German, who was quietly smoking among the ruins, a sort of superintendent, whom I had met before, came up, and offering me a cigar, and leaning against one of the forty columns of the temple, opened upon me with "his plans of city improvements"; with new streets, and projected railroads, and the rise of lots. At first I almost thought it personal, and that he was making a fling at me, in allusion to one of the greatest hobbies of my native city; but I soon round that he was as deeply bitten as if he had been in Chicago or Dunkirk; and the way in which he talked of moneyed facilities, the wants of the community, and a great French bank then contemplated at the Piraeus, would have been no discredit to some of my friends at home. The removal of the court has created a new era in Athens; but, in my mind, it is deeply to be regretted that it has been snatched from the ruin to which it was tending. Even I, deeply imbued with the utilitarian spirit or my country, and myself a quondam speculator in "up-town lots," would fain save Athens from the ruthless hand of renovation; from the building mania of modern speculators. I would have her go on till there was not a habitation among her ruins; till she stood, like Pompeii, alone in the wilderness, a sacred desert, where the traveller might sit down and meditate alone and undisturbed among the relics of the past. But already Athens has become a heterogeneous anomaly; the Greeks in their wild costume are jostled in the streets by Englishmen, Frenchmen, Italians, Dutchmen, Spaniards; and Bavarians, Russians, Danes, and sometimes Americans. European shops invite purchasers, by the side of eastern bazaars, coffee-houses, and billiard-rooms; and French and German restaurants are opened all over the city. Sir Pultney Malcolm has erected a house to hire near the site of Plato's Academy. Lady Franklin has bought land near the foot of Mount Hymettus for a country-seat. Several English gentlemen have done the same. Mr. Richmond, an American clergyman, has purchased a farm in the neighbourhood, and in a few years, if the "march of improvement" continues, the Temple of Theseus will be enclosed in the garden or the palace of King Otho; the Temple of the Winds will be concealed by a German opera-house, and the Lantern of Demosthenes by a row of three-story houses.

1836 Edward Giffard

The Acropolis Before its Denuding

Pursuing the road which winds round, as I have already said, between the Propylaea and the temple of Victory - the modern, and at present the only entrance to the Acropolis - we passed, on our left, the lofty tower before mentioned, raised on the south wing of the Propylaea by some of the Latin princes, who - for a long interval subsequent to the Crusades and before the capture by the Turks in 1456 - ruled this region, under the title of Dukes of Athens.

This Gothic, and comparatively modern tower, has lately received an ancient and illustrious denomination. It was pointed out to us, as the tower of ... Ulysses - not indeed him of Ithaca, but a modern Greek leader of the late revolution, who assumed this name from having been born in Ithaca, though of Thessalian parents; and who, after a strange variety of exploits, being suspected of practising the wily arts of his namesake and of some treachery to the patriot cause, was confined in this tower, whence he attempted to escape; but the rope by which he was descending broke, and the unhappy man was dashed to pieces, Such was the public version of the story; but there are not wanting some to believe, or at least to whisper, that he was thrown from the summit, as the readiest means of getting rid of a turbulent and troublesome, if not treacherous, rival.

This tower is in the rude style of the fortifications of Western Europe in the middle ages; and judging from all the views prior to the last year or two, the Franks had surrounded the whole summit of the Acropolis with walls and towers of the same character; so that, but for the pediments of the Parthenon peering above these works, the Acropolis must have looked like an old European fortress. In the progress of the labours, in which the present government is assiduously employed for clearing the Acropolis, all these Frank constructions, as well as those which the Turks superadded, have already, with the exception of this tower, disappeared.

The first persons we met on the Acropolis were parties of Greek labourers excavating and removing the rubbish, in order to bring the summit to its original levels. I say *levels*, for it is clear, both from what we could infer from the present aspect of the ground, as well as from ancient testimony, that the original surface was very unequal; even contiguous edifices not being on the same level. All the Frank and Turkish ramparts, which formed as it were a parapet to the fortress, having been already removed, the ancient temples now stand conspicuous down to their bases from quarters, (except on the westward, where the Propylaea intercepts the view) and the work-men, employed in the levelling, wheel their barrows to the very edges of the precipice, and empty their contents into the valley below.

I presume that the manner in which this is done has been duly considered, but it seemed to us that the Theatre of Bacchus, which lies at the south-east foot of the rock, had been already in part overwhelmed by the showers of rubbish, which not only obstruct its remains, but may also bury still deeper fragments which may have fallen from the Acropolis during the alterations it has suffered from the different conquerors. Great care is taken in carefully examining and sifting this rubbish *before* it is thrown down; and all relics, even the most apparently trifling, are removed to, and deposited in, a mosque which the Turks had erected in the interior of the Parthenon, forming a treasure, very different from that which the Opisthodomos of the ancient temple used to contain.

So very properly strict and jealous are the guardians of the works, that if a stranger stoops to pick up a piece of marble, even for cursory examination, he finds all eyes upon him; and I doubt whether he would be allowed to remove even a pebble from the sacred soil. We certainly had no intention to attempt any such spoliation, and on the contrary, felt the greatest pleasure at observing the care with which every fragment is preserved.

1836 Francis Hervé

"A Lark"

A short time before my arrival, a most interesting discovery had taken place, some frieze had been dug up of immense antiquity, having been found under the foundation of some part of the Acropolis. The subjects were in *mezzo relievo*, and remarkably fine; all more or less damaged, but not enough so to please the taste of some people, as a party of young midshipmen who had landed from an English frigate, having obtained permission to see these specimens of antique sculpture, one of them for a lark, no doubt as they would style it, broke off the nose from one of the figures. Signor Pittacki, the conservator, appointed by the Greek government, of these works of art, absolutely wept with vexation.

1836-7 Charles Bracebridge

A Modern Capital is Born

Many large houses have been erected within the last year, and buildings are going on with such spirit that the price of ground in good situations far exceeds the sum which could have been calculated on: £300 was lately given for about half an acre, and an adjoining piece has just been sold at the rate of £1200 or £1300 an acre. This at a distance from the commercial streets, where enormous prices are obtained for the square yard of frontage-ground. Three great streets have been some time since opened - the Adrian, Athena, and Aeolus Streets - all of which now assume a regular appearance; and though the dilatory system of some parties, and want of zeal and funds to overcome difficulties, have as yet prevented the opening of many of the minor communications, yet an attentive observer observes the huge masses of grey walls and rubbish disappear by little and little, crooked encumbered lanes become straight, and wherever two or three good houses are built, walls are thrown back, and a street of twenty feet wide appears. The style of building is rather modern German than anything else: neither the picturesque (and in this climate agreeable) Turkish house nor the Italian colonnade is seen; happily the English red brick is also absent. Many of the common houses are built after the Constantinople fashion - an upper story of woodwork filled up by dried bricks on a basement of broad stone walls.

On the whole, considering the necessary want of funds, taste, good practical architects, and workmen who have any knowledge of their art, the appearance of the new buildings is highly creditable. The walls of the old town were pulled down last spring, which gives the place a much better appearance. The town is now spread out in a fan-shape to the north of the Acropolis, and its diameters may be a mile and a half; the population probably does not yet exceed 10,000. One peculiarity of Athens is its churches, which are said to exceed 300; with few exceptions, they are in ruins. Such a fine opportunity for making open and planted squares will, I trust, not be lost when the dispute between the municipality and the government as to the right of property in these churches shall have been settled.

The supply of water brought into the town by the ancient aqueducts is abundant and excellent. When the town advances, no doubt many useful and beautiful fountains will vie with those of Rome or Naples. At present the Turkish fountains only are used.

I must not omit Piraeus, where several large houses have been built: some good streets, flanked by low but respectable dwellings, have already been completed. A large custom-house has been built, and a quay and lazaretto are in immediate contemplation; the population may be about 1,500. Though trade cannot be said to flourish at the Piraeus, still it has become a bustling place.

A change of ministers has lately taken place, and all the offices are not yet disposed of most of the employees are Greeks, and there is every reason to hope that a public system of business will be adopted, which may prevent intrigues and overcome jealousies which must injure this country. The great difficulty here is to obtain practical results rapidly; while some diplomats write 'rapports' and orders, the Greeks talk and promise; both seem equally averse from *doing...*

The modern buildings of Athens and other principal towns have, in spite of apparent want of capital, advanced rapidly. Extensive streets of ruins have been pierced by regular streets of respectable, if not very expensive, houses. The town (with its rising palace) has now become a modern capital, the fragments of the buildings of the last era form the exception to its general appearance, and seem left only as mementos of war and slavery, amidst the blessings of civilization.

1838 William Mure

A Night with a Camel in a Khan

It was our original intention to have reached Lipsina, the ancient Eleusis, that night; but the depth of the ground on the plains, and the snow on the mountain, had so far retarded our course, that we were obliged to halt at a khan, called Saint Vlasio, not far from the extremity of the valley - the poorest place of its class I had yet seen. It was, as usual, an oblong shed, but without subdivision or compartment of any kind. Three-fourths of the area were occupied by stabling; the remaining space, allotted for the accommodation of travellers, wanted the raised wooden platforms which we had hitherto found in similar establishments, and offered nothing but vacant extent of bare ground, slightly raised into a hearth in the centre, with the shelf of the khanjee in one corner, and the baggage of the travellers deposited along the walls on each side. The place was already occupied by several guests, and the number was swelled by the arrival of fresh parties every two or three minutes. There seemed to be many travellers on the road, and this khan had been selected by the majority as their halting-place for the night; I know not by what fatality, as it was but a halfway house from the capital in this direction. The wretchedness of this night's lodging, and of several others, equally comfortless, with which I was afterwards obliged to be satisfied, was amply compensated by the opportunity they afforded of witnessing scenes of a very curious description, and of obtaining an insight into the habits of the population, of which I should have been deprived, had I adopted the plan sometimes resorted to by travellers, of pitching my tent at each resting-place; the only one by which a tolerable degree of personal comfort can be secured in a tour through these regions.

The party within the khan consisted, on our arrival, of an Albanian chasseur, of the same class and equipment as my fellow-lodgers at Livadia, an Athenian barber, and his travelling companion, a substantial-looking person, who, from his excessive loquacity, in which he was only surpassed by his comrade of the razor, I presumed to belong to the same lively race. It was afterwards increased to fourteen men, and at least an equal number of horses and mules, by the arrival of new guests in rapid succession, each of whom, after tying up his beasts, took his place in the circle by the fire in the usual squatting position. I had secured on one side space sufficient for my mattress, and as I sat contemplating with dismay the rapid accumulation of animal filth in the midst of which I was to pass the night, I saw thrust through the entry the head and neck of a camel; which, however, after gazing wistfully around, first at the stable, and then at the fire, was withdrawn by its proprietor, convinced of the insufficiency of the passage to admit the residue of his person, which had remained outside during the reconnoitre. This apparition excited peals of laughter from the party within, who all united in good-humoured entreaties to the landlord of the khan to extend its hospitality to the poor foreigner. The thing, however, was found impracticable; and he was obliged to pass the night in the open air; meekly kneeling on all fours under an olive-tree, and munching a bundle of hay strewed on the ground before him.

These hovels have no chimneys of any kind - a rare luxury even in the better class of Greek cottages, the smoke being allowed to escape through the roof. This is very severe upon the eyes; but as the wood used is generally of a kind that emits but little smoke, and the open spaces between the tiles are not only quite sufficient to give it free issue, but even to afford a good view of the starry heaven above, one suffers less from the inconvenience than might be supposed. On the present occasion, indeed, there was some danger of a practical illustration of the old Greek proverb, - "Out of the smoke into the fire." The night was chill, and the flames were soon increased by an accumulation of dry pine and olive branches from the neighbouring forest, to a furnace of terrific heat and power, crackling and blazing most furiously to the very roof-tree of the hovel. This at first afforded much childish diversion to the rest of the circle, but great discomfort to myself, from the excessive heat and dazzling of the flames. I was besides in momentary expectation of the khan taking fire, when it would certainly have been burnt to the ground – a catastrophe which, with its consequences, would at least have supplied my journal-book with an important adventure. The khanjee, however, with several of his other guests, also soon became alarmed, and took effectual measures to reduce the flames.

Each man now pulled out his supper from his wallet consisting of brown bread, garlic, leeks, preserved olives, and other dried vegetables, with abundance of wine. Every traveller or party carries his supply of liquor in one or more large round wooden bottles, with flat sides, in form not unlike a lady's flat-sided smelling-bottle, with a short neck or spout at one end, and four little pegs or feet at the other, to admit of its standing upright. Glasses or mugs are dispensed with. The bottle, when common to a party, is handed round, and each sucks his fill from the spout in his turn. The practice of diluting with water, so universal in antiquity that drunkard and "bibber of unmixed wine" … were nearly synonymous terms, is now quite obsolete. The khanjee is expected to furnish little more than shelter, fireplace, and fuel. The remainder of the entertainment for either man or horse forms part of the traveller's baggage. Mine host has, however, generally a limited stock of the customary fare for a case of emergency. The dried olives chiefly belonged to his store; and I seldom failed in obtaining plenty of fresh eggs, or even a fowl from his hen-roost. On the present occasion, as there appeared a deficiency of bread, he set about providing a supply, in a mode which realized to the letter the scripture account of Sarah's baking. He "took quickly a measure of meal, kneaded it, and made a cake on the hearth." The loaf he produced was in fact a large round flat cake or bannock, of about twenty inches in breadth, and three in thickness. When properly kneaded and shaped, it was laid upon the hearth, completely embedded in a nest of fine embers deadened with ash, and was very soon ready for consumption. This was a common kind of loaf among the ancients, called Encryphias, or Pyriates, - and by other varieties of name in different provinces and dialects.

The conversation, in the mean time, became exceedingly animated, and would doubtless have been to me as interesting as to those who took part in it, could I have followed it out sufficiently, nor had I ever more reason to regret my imperfect familiarity with the modem Greek idiom. But although unable to keep pace with the voluble rapidity of the discourse, I made out from its general tenor, and the frequent recurrence of the word *klepht*, with some others of similar import, that the subject of one of the liveliest discussions was the "cursed law of witnesses," in connection with the robbery of the morning, and others recently committed in the neighbourhood under circumstances equally tending to evince the bad effects of the new statute. All agreed in reprobating so dangerous an innovation on old national custom, though not without a good deal of altercation on collateral points. Each man had his tale of predatory adventure to relate, in which, doubtless, not a few had been actors, as well as sufferers. From hence they proceeded to politics at large, and the state and prospects of the country. The principle orators were the barber and his fellow-traveller; the former, more especially, who harangued with surprising grace and fluency, and with all that air of conceit and authority which both his profession and nation entitled him to assume. His eloquence, though addressed to his antagonist or the company at large, I plainly observed, from his occasional side glances in my direction, at the moment of his most pompous periods, was chiefly intended to produce an effect on myself. He was a short, slight, compactly built figure, with lively black eyes, a swarthy complexion, and somewhat oriental cast of countenance; dressed, not like his neighbours, in the white fustanella or philibeg, but in loose jacket and levant trousers of a dingy olive colour, fastened at the knee round a stocking of the same hue; and as he sat, with his body bolt upright, his head crowned with his little conical scull-cap, and his legs tucked under him, sawing the air with his arms in energetic action, he put one very much in mind of an Indian juggler, or of one of those little squatting bronze idols, representing, I believe, the god Buddha, which became common in our mythological cabinets after the last great Burmese war. The Chimariote warrior and Nicola, who resembled each other a good deal in temper and manner, occasionally hazarded a few laconic or sarcastic remarks, indicating the mixture of amusement and of contempt excited by the garrulity of the Athenian; but scarcely any one of the party ventured formally to enter the lists with the two Attic orators. My Boeotian attendants said little or nothing; but with the characteristic phlegm of their race, turned their eyes from the one speaker to the other, as each took the lead in the argument, with looks, whether of indifference, or of admiration at their eloquence, it was not easy to distinguish; and during the heat of the discussion, their physical wants having been satisfied, they lay down and composed themselves to sleep.

As the debate began to flag, their example was followed by the rest of the company. The bed accommodation consisted partly of rush mats, of which the khan supplied a certain number, its only domestic furniture: partly of their own shaggy goatskin capottes; while those who affected the luxury of a pillow, used their wallets, corn sacks, or other articles of luggage best adapted to the purpose. Each man, as successively overpowered by the influence of the drowsy god, stretched himself out with his feet to the fire and his head to the wall, so that their arrangement might be compared to the spokes of a wheel, of which the hearth was the axle. The symmetry of this figure was, however, soon greatly disturbed. The space was but confined for so large a party, and when some of them, growing restless, began to turn or toss in their sleep, the spectacle that presented itself was as curious as it was degrading and offensive. Every here and there the figures were to be seen promiscuously blended, so as to render it difficult to distinguish to whom the splay feet, brawny legs and arms, and bushy heads sprawling over each other, belonged. The snoring too was deafening, and the animal stench, independent of the fumes of onions and garlic with which the air was previously impregnated, most overpowering. I had managed to keep my bed in a corner tolerably secure from the encroachments of the crowd; and, deprived of sleep by the assaults of my cruel enemies the fleas, amused myself, as I lay contemplating the scene, with the parody which offered itself on Homer's description of the bed of Ulysses among the seals, in the island of Pharos ...

> "A fearful couch was there, where smells unclean
> Salute the nose from garlic-fed Hellene."

Nor were we long in want of a Proteus to make up the fullness of the analogy; for in the midst of my Homeric reveries, I was startled, together with my sleeping companions, by a loud knock at the door, and on the latch being drawn up by the khanjee, in walked a *chorophylax*, or gendarme, in full accoutrement, with a country fellow behind him carrying a long gun upon his shoulder; a detachment of the party engaged in unsuccessful pursuit of the thieves. After reconnoitring with an air of official authority the groups around the fire, the gendarme enquired, in peremptory tone, who and whence we were, and insisted on each man giving an account of himself. The Albanian, and the stout Athenian, who seemed to be considered the principal civilian present became vouchers for the respectability of their fellow lodgers, explaining to the best of their knowledge, in answer to his queries, the character and profession of each, commencing with myself and suite; and all to his apparent satisfaction. His stern rigour of mien and language gradually thawed and after swallowing a draught of wine from the bottle next within his reach, and exchanging a word or two with his Albanian comrade, in which he described the inefficacy of their search after the robbers, he warmed himself over the embers for a few moments, and then taking his place in the circle with the remainder of the party, was soon fast asleep...

Harassed by my feverish state of wakefulness, I walked out to regale myself with the fresh air. It was a calm clear night. The rays of a brilliant moon playing through the silvery foliage of the olive groves, over the dark clustering tops of the pines, and lighting up the mountain glades and rocks which they clothed, made one feel oneself the more certainly in Attica, while they rendered the contrast between the splendours of nature, and the degraded condition of nature's lords in this fair desert, the more striking. On a piece of smooth greensward, hard by the door, under a large olive-tree, knelt the camel, in the same humble posture in which he had been left by his master five or six hours before. I made acquaintance with him by gathering and presenting him with a few fresh blades of grass, scratching his forehead, and other little marks of attention. I had serious thoughts of taking up my mattress and cloaks, and making my bed by his side. The air, however, though clear and tranquil, was damp and chill; and preferring present discomfort to the risk of catching a fever, and the consequent interruption of my journey, I returned for the few remaining hours of night to the warmth and stench of the khan.

In participating in such scenes as that here described, one was led to moralize on the vicissitudes of human affairs, by which the representatives of the most refined and polished race of the ancient world had been reduced, by many centuries of political degradation, and the adoption of the filthy habits of the successive races of barbarians by whom they had been overrun, not only to a complete ignorance of every thing that can be called domestic comfort, but to a state of squalid misery that places them nearly on a level with the brutes. A little further reflection, however, may suggest a doubt, whether it were fair to throw the whole blame of the present state of things upon either time or destiny, the Sclavonian, the Arnaut, or the Turk; and how far these very habits be not, among the middle and lower classes at least, an inheritance transmitted from the glorious days of their ancestors, I remember, indeed, to have heard a very learned friend on the other side of the channel, whose name occupies a high place in the annals of Hellenistic science, maintain, in talking over our respective travels in this country, that - in spite of the exterior dazzle of art, science, and literature, shed over the age of Pericles - there is much reason to believe, that the domestic manners which give such offence to those used to the higher standard of modern European civilization, were nearly the same then, among the class of society where they now prevail. To this extent I am not prepared to go; although, at first sight, there may appear something in favour of his view. I was indeed forcibly struck at the moment with the resemblance between the scene in this very khan, (besides others, which I afterwards witnessed in the private dwellings of the upper class of peasantry,) and the description given by Homer, in the *Odyssey*, of the routine of daily life in the cottage of Eumlpus. While viewing, by the dim light of the expiring embers, the architecture and furniture of the apartments and the brawny limbs of my fellow-lodgers scattered in picturesque groups around the hearth - derogatory as it may be to the dignity of a Homeric hero - I could not help figuring to myself the evening circle in the cottage of the hospitable swineherd, comprising, besides himself and his landlords old and young, four or five of his own subalterns, as presenting about the same hour of night a very similar aspect. The dwelling of the chief of one of the most important branches of the rural economy of the wealthy king, must have been, as in fact it is said to be, one of the best habitations of its class. Yet its interior seems to have been very little better fitted up than the khan of San Vlasio.

1839 Lord Carnarvon

A New Cosmopolitanism

There are several foreigners - amongst them some Englishmen and men of family - who have come to Greece for the purpose of investing their capital in land. Besides these settlers, if they may be so termed, persons of every nation are continually arriving at Athens, as at a common centre from which they severally diverge, some into the interior of the country, some to Constantinople, and some again into the more distant regions of Egypt and Syria. Of these some are either travelling for the sake of amusement, or have been drawn to Athens, fascinated by her magic name; some are journeying to the East, influenced by the political interest which now as ever attaches to these regions; or are prosecuting researches into some branch of oriental learning; or are accomplishing some practical object connected with archaeological or religious or missionary purposes. They often communicate to those around them a character of earnestness which is in some degree novel, and not altogether unpleasant.

Placed as we are at Athens, in the last fastnesses of the European world, we drink in with avidity every account of those Eastern regions on whose confines we stand, and we rejoice in the oriental character which almost every Athenian conversation ultimately assumes. Those, indeed, would be disappointed who might be tempted to spend a winter at Athens, expecting the tone of conversation and the intellectual attractions distinctive of the great capitals of Europe; but those who feel an interest in the actual condition, and the future prospects of that Eastern world which must hereafter force itself more and more upon the consideration of our statesmen, will find in the society of Athens much food for curious observation.

All is strange at Athens and full of striking contrast. The fragments of the old are jumbled with the elements of the new and as yet unformed society. Chiefs, respectable for their past exploits but who are disposed to lament that ever sons of theirs should read or write, jostle against their children, the disciples of young France. There seems as yet no principle of cohesion, not even a growing tendency to amalgamate; and even in the king's palace, the honest but slow and formal Bavarian sits side by side with the intelligent but less scrupulous Greek, with little courtesy on their lips, and with real aversion in their hearts.

Of such materials is Athenian society composed. The settler, the enterprising traveller, the missionary, the steady German, the Greek of the new democratic, and the Greek of the old feudal school, are simultaneously brought together on the narrow but varied stage of Athens.

1840 Edgar Garston

A Disproportionate Royal Establishment

The observation that style of the Bavarian monarchy established in Athens was out of proportion to the size and poverty of their kingdom, was one expressed by several travellers.

The new palace is a very extensive building, much larger than a King of Greece can require for his residence, or than his household can fill. It is an oblong square, about ninety paces by seventy. I have not seen the plans, but for the present it looks as if rather intended for a barrack than for a royal palace. It is generally stated that the cost of this building will be defrayed out of the private estate of the King; even if this be the case, it is to be regretted that a portion of the fund should not be otherwise applied. A smaller royal residence would have harmonized better with the extent of the kingdom, and have permitted the King to lend his aid to work of national utility in such a manner as to increase his hold upon the affections of his subjects.

1845, Felicia Mary Skene

A Court Ball

It is a gay scene, the first ball at court, which commences the Athenian winter, where the families who have not so much as heard of one another for the last six months meet once more to rejoice together that 'Les grandes chaleurs' are over at last. It is, however, a scene as peculiar as it is gay.

One of the most striking peculiarities of a residence in Greece at the present day, is the close proximity into which we are brought with its great Revolution, that noble struggle for independence. Among the gay, light-hearted throng which crowds the reception-rooms of the monarch, it is indeed singular to meet with the most prominent characters of that terrible struggle; and to see the old Palikars, with their iron hands, and their breasts all scarred with the wounds from which they escaped as by a miracle, quietly enjoying the amusement they derive from watching the dancers, and beating time to the merry tunes of waltzes and quadrilles. Indeed old Colocotroni, the sturdy, dauntless chief, whose fame has even reached England, had very nearly terminated his wild, stirring career within the walls of the dancing-room. He left it alive and well at midnight, and at two in the morning he was dead.

The capitani, or chiefs, are each a perfect picture, when dressed out in the full splendour of the Greek costume; and their wives and daughters, who, on such occasions, generally carry their

The Church of the Panaghia Gorgoepikoos (Du Moncel, 1846)

whole fortunes on their persons, sometimes wear their red caps, with the tassel, composed entirely of real pearls, while diamonds and jewels are lavishly disposed on the most conspicuous parts of their dress.

Preeminent amongst them all, the fair young queen is distinguished by the perfect grace of her movements and the sweetness of her smile; while the king is eagerly surrounded by all, for, despite of the continual reports to the contrary effect, he is beloved by his people, as he deserves, for his generosity and goodness of heart, though perhaps not even his own subjects have thoroughly appreciated his ceaseless toil and continued self-sacrifice for the good of the nation, or the patience with which he has continued, uncomplaining, in as difficult a position as a prince was ever placed in, without the aid of one person on whom he dared rely.

The diversity of languages to be heard on these festive occasions is quite singular, and on all sides may be heard the amusing mistakes resulting from the attempts of the natives of the different countries to understand each other; - an Englishman gravely conversing with the French ambassador on the state of the country, and observing that it must be very difficult to change the clothes of a whole nation, having substituted the word *habits* for *habitudes*, and a Greek whispering to an English lady, whose language he professes to have acquired at Corfu, that he does not think her partner "very good bred."

1849 Mark Twain

A Night Adventure

We arrived, and entered the ancient harbour of the Piraeus at last. We dropped anchor within half a mile of the village. Away off, across the undulating Plain of Attica, could be seen a little square-topped hill with a something on it, which our glasses soon discovered to be the ruined edifices of the citadel of the Athenians, and most prominent among them loomed the venerable Parthenon. So exquisitely clear and pure is this wonderful atmosphere that every column of the noble structure was discernible through the telescope, and even the smaller ruins about it assumed some semblance of shape. This at a distance of five or six miles. In the valley, near the Acropolis, (the square-topped hill before spoken of,) Athens itself could be vaguely made out with an ordinary lorgnette. Every body was anxious to get ashore and visit these classic localities as quickly as possible. No land we had yet seen had aroused such universal interest among the passengers.

But bad news came. The commandant of the Piraeus came in his boat, and said we must either depart or else get outside the harbour and remain imprisoned in our ship, under rigid quarantine, for eleven days! So we took up the anchor and moved outside, to lie a dozen hours or so, taking in supplies, and then sail for Constantinople. It was the bitterest disappointment we had yet experienced. To lie a whole day in sight of the Acropolis, and yet be obliged to go away without visiting Athens! Disappointment was hardly a strong enough word to describe the circumstances.

All hands were on deck, all the afternoon, with books and maps and glasses, trying to determine which "narrow rocky ridge" was the Areopagus, which sloping hill the Pnyx, which elevation the Museum Hill, and so on. And we got things confused. Discussion became heated, and party spirit ran high. Church members were gazing with emotion upon a hill which they said was the one St. Paul preached from, and another faction claimed that that hill was Hymettus, and another that it was Pentelicon! After all the trouble, we could be certain of only one thing — the square-topped hill was the Acropolis, and the grand ruin that crowned it was the Parthenon, whose picture we knew in infancy in the school books.

We inquired of every body who came near the ship, whether there were guards in the Piraeus, whether they were strict, what the chances were of capture should any of us slip ashore, and in case any of us made the venture and were caught, what would be probably done to us? The answers were discouraging: There was a strong guard or police force; the Piraeus was a small town, and any stranger seen in it would surely attract attention — capture would be certain. The commandant said the punishment would be 'heavy'; when asked 'how heavy?' he said it would be 'very severe' — that was all we could get out of him.

At eleven o'clock at night, when most of the ship's company were abed, four of us stole softly ashore in a small boat, a clouded moon favouring the enterprise, and started two and two, and far apart, over a low hill, intending to go clear around the Piraeus, out of the range of its police. Picking our way so stealthily over that rocky, nettle-grown eminence, made me feel a good deal as if I were on my way somewhere to steal something. My immediate comrade and I talked in an undertone about quarantine laws and their penalties, but we found nothing cheering in the subject. I was posted. Only a few days before, I was talking with our captain, and he mentioned the case of a man who swam ashore from a quarantined ship somewhere, and got imprisoned six months for it; and when he was in Genoa a few years ago, a captain of a quarantined ship went in his boat to a departing ship, which was already outside of the harbour, and put a letter on board to be taken to his family, and the authorities imprisoned him three months for it, and then conducted him and his ship fairly to sea, and warned him never to show himself in that port again while he lived. This kind of conversation did no good, further than to give a sort of dismal interest to our quarantine-breaking expedition, and so we dropped it. We made the entire circuit of the town without seeing any body but one man, who stared at us curiously, but said nothing, and a dozen persons asleep on the ground before their doors, whom we walked among and never woke — but we woke up dogs enough, in all conscience — we always had one or two barking at our heels, and several times we had as many as ten and twelve at once. They made such a preposterous din that persons aboard our ship said they could tell how we were progressing for a long time, and where we were, by the barking of the dogs. The clouded moon still favoured us. When we had made the whole circuit, and were passing among the houses on the further side of the town, the moon came out splendidly, but we no longer feared the light. As we approached a well, near a house, to get a drink, the owner merely glanced at us and went within. He left the quiet, slumbering town at our mercy. I record it here proudly, that we didn't do any thing to it.

Seeing no road, we took a tall hill to the left of the distant Acropolis for a mark, and steered straight for it over all obstructions, and over a little rougher piece of country than exists any where else outside of the State of Nevada, perhaps. Part of the way it was covered with small, loose stones — we trod on six at a time, and they all rolled. Another part of it was dry, loose, newly-ploughed ground. Still another part of it was a long stretch of low grapevines, which were tanglesome and troublesome, and which we took to be brambles. The Attic Plain, barring the grapevines, was a barren, desolate, unpoetical waste — I wonder what it was in Greece's Age of Glory, five hundred years before Christ?

In the neighbourhood of one o'clock in the morning, when we were heated with fast walking and parched with thirst, Denny exclaimed, 'Why, these weeds are grapevines!' and in five minutes we had a score of bunches of large, white, delicious grapes, and were reaching down for more when a dark shape rose mysteriously up out of the shadows beside us and said 'Ho!' And so we left.

In ten minutes more we struck into a beautiful road, and unlike some others we had stumbled upon at intervals, it led in the right direction. We followed it. It was broad, and smooth, and white - handsome and in perfect repair, and shaded on both sides for a mile or so with single ranks of trees, and also with luxuriant vineyards. Twice we entered and stole grapes, and the second time somebody shouted at us from some invisible place. Whereupon we left again. We speculated in grapes no more on that side of Athens.

Shortly we came upon an ancient stone aqueduct, built upon arches, and from that time forth we had ruins all about us — we were approaching our journey's end. We could not see the Acropolis now or the high hill, either, and I wanted to follow the road till we were abreast of them, but the others overruled me, and we toiled laboriously up the stony hill immediately in our front - and from its summit saw another — climbed it and saw another! It was an hour of exhausting work. Soon we came upon a row of open graves, cut in the solid rock - (for a while one of them served Socrates for a prison) - we passed around the shoulder of the hill, and the citadel, in all its ruined magnificence, burst upon us! We hurried across the ravine and up a winding road, and stood on the old Acropolis, with the prodigious walls of the citadel towering above our heads. We did not stop to inspect their massive blocks of marble, or measure their height, or guess at their extraordinary thickness, but passed at once through a great arched passage like a railway tunnel, and went straight to the gate that leads to the ancient temples. It was locked! So, after all, it seemed that we were not to see the great Parthenon face to face. We sat down and held a council of war. Result: the gate was only a flimsy structure of wood — we would break it down. It seemed like desecration, but then we had travelled far, and our necessities were urgent. We could not hunt up guides and keepers — we must be on the ship before daylight. So we argued. This was all very fine, but when we came to break the gate, we could not do it. We moved around an angle of the wall and found a low bastion — eight feet high without — ten or twelve within. Denny prepared to scale it, and we got ready to follow. By dint of hard scrambling he finally straddled the top, but some loose stones crumbled away and fell with a crash into the court within. There was instantly a banging of doors and a shout. Denny dropped from the wall in a twinkling, and we retreated in disorder to the gate. Xerxes took that mighty citadel four hundred and eighty years before Christ, when his five millions of soldiers and camp-followers followed him to Greece, and if we four Americans could have remained unmolested five minutes longer, we would have taken it too.

The garrison had turned out - four Greeks. We clamoured at the gate, and they admitted us. (Bribery and corruption.)

We crossed a large court, entered a great door, and stood upon a pavement of purest white marble, deeply worn by footprints. Before us, in the flooding moonlight, rose the noblest ruins we had ever looked upon - the Propylae; a small Temple of Minerva; the Temple of Hercules, and the grand Parthenon...

As we wandered thoughtfully down the marble-paved length of this stately temple, the scene about us was strangely impressive. Here and there, in lavish profusion, were gleaming white statues of men and women, propped against blocks of marble, some of them armless, some without legs, others headless - but all looking mournful in the moonlight, and startlingly human! They rose up and confronted the midnight intruder on every side - they stared at him with stony eyes from unlooked-for nooks and recesses; they peered at him over fragmentary heaps far down the desolate corridors; they barred his way in the midst of the broad forum, and solemnly pointed with handless arms the way from the sacred fane; and through the roofless temple the moon looked down, and banded the floor and darkened the scattered fragments and broken statues with the slanting shadows of the columns.

What a world of ruined sculpture was about us! Set up in rows - stacked up in piles - scattered broadcast over the wide area of the Acropolis - were hundreds of crippled statues of all sizes and of the most exquisite workmanship; and vast fragments of marble that once belonged to the entablatures, covered with bas-reliefs representing battles and sieges, ships of war with three and four tiers of oars, pageants and processions - every thing one could think of. History says that the temples of the Acropolis were filled with the noblest works of Praxiteles and Phidias, and of many a great master in sculpture besides - and surely these elegant fragments attest it.

We walked out into the grass-grown, fragment-strewn court beyond the Parthenon. It startled us, every now and then, to see a stony white face stare suddenly up at us out of the grass with its dead eyes. The place seemed alive with ghosts. I half expected to see the Athenian heroes of twenty centuries ago glide out of the shadows and steal into the old temple they knew so well and regarded with such boundless pride.

The full moon wag riding high in the cloudless heavens, now. We sauntered carelessly and unthinkingly to the edge of the lofty battlements of the citadel, and looked down - a vision! And such a vision! Athens by moonlight! The prophet that thought the splendours of the New Jerusalem were revealed to him, surely saw this instead! It lay in the level plain right under our feet - all spread abroad like a picture - and we looked down upon it as we might have looked from a balloon. We saw no semblance of a street, but every house, every window, every clinging vine, every projection was as distinct and sharply marked as if the time were noonday; and yet there was no glare, no glitter, nothing harsh or repulsive — the noiseless city was flooded with the mellowest light that ever streamed from the moon, and seemed like some living creature wrapped in peaceful slumber. On its further side was a little temple, whose delicate pillars and ornate front glowed with a rich lustre that chained the eye like a spell; and nearer by, the palace of the king reared its creamy walls out of the midst of a great garden of shrubbery that was flecked all over with a random shower of amber lights - a spray of golden sparks that lost their brightness in the glory of the moon, and glinted softly upon the sea of dark foliage like the pallid stars of the milky-way. Overhead the stately columns, majestic still in their ruin — under foot the dreaming city — in the distance the silver sea - not on the broad earth is there an other picture half so beautiful!

As we turned and moved again through the temple, I wished that the illustrious men who had sat in it in the remote ages could visit it again and reveal themselves to our curious eyes - Plato, Aristotle, Demosthenes, Socrates, Phocion, Pythagoras, Euclid, Pindar, Xenophon, Herodotus, Praxiteles and Phidias, Zeuxis the painter. What a constellation of celebrated names! But more than all, I wished that old Diogenes, groping so patiently with his lantern, searching so zealously for one solitary honest man in all the world, might meander along and stumble on our party. I ought not to say it, may be, but still I suppose he would have put out his light.

We left the Parthenon to keep its watch over old Athens, as it had kept it for twenty-three hundred years, and went and stood outside the walls of the citadel. In the distance was the ancient, but still almost perfect Temple of Theseus, and close by, looking to the west, was the Bema, from whence Demosthenes thundered his philippics and fired the wavering patriotism of his countrymen. To the right was Mars Hill, where the Areopagus sat in ancient times, and where St. Paul defined his position, and below was the marketplace where he 'disputed daily' with the gossip-loving Athenians. We climbed the stone steps St. Paul ascended, and stood in the square-cut place he stood in, and tried to recollect the Bible account of the matter...

It occurred to us, after a while, that if we wanted to get home before daylight betrayed us, we had better be moving. So we hurried away. When far on our road, we had a parting view of the

Parthenon, with the moonlight streaming through its open colonnades and touching its capitals with silver. As it looked then, solemn, grand, and beautiful it will always remain in our memories.

As we marched along, we began to get over our fears, and ceased to care much about quarantine scouts or any body else. We grew bold and reckless; and once, in a sudden burst of courage, I even threw a stone at a dog. It was a pleasant reflection, though, that I did not hit him, because his master might just possibly have been a policeman. Inspired by this happy failure, my valour became utterly uncontrollable, and at intervals I absolutely whistled, though on a moderate key. But boldness breeds boldness, and shortly I plunged into a vineyard, in the full light of the moon, and captured a gallon of superb grapes, not even minding the presence of a peasant who rode by on a mule. Denny and Birch followed my example.

Now I had grapes enough for a dozen, but then Jackson was all swollen up with courage, too, and he was obliged to enter a vineyard presently. The first bunch he seized brought trouble. A frowsy, bearded brigand sprang into the road with a shout, and flourished a musket in the light of the moon! We sidled toward the Piraeus - not running you understand, but only advancing with celerity. The brigand shouted again, but still we advanced. It was getting late, and we had no time to fool away on every ass that wanted to drivel Greek platitudes to us. We would just as soon have talked with him as not if we had not been in a hurry. Presently Denny said, "Those fellows are following us!'

We turned, and, sure enough, there they were - three fantastic pirates armed with guns. We slackened our pace to let them come up, and in the meantime I got out my cargo of grapes and dropped them firmly but reluctantly into the shadows by the wayside. But I was not afraid. I only felt that it was not right to steal grapes. And all the more so when the owner was around — and not only around, but with his friends around also. The villains came up and searched a bundle Dr. Birch had in his hand, and scowled upon him when they found it had nothing in it but some holy rocks from Mars Hill, and these were not contraband. They evidently suspected him of playing some wretched fraud upon them, and seemed half inclined to scalp the party. But finally they dismissed us with a warning, couched in excellent Greek, I suppose, and dropped tranquilly in our wake. When they had gone three hundred yards they stopped, and we went on rejoiced. But behold, another armed rascal came out of the shadows and took their place, and followed us two hundred yards. Then he delivered us over to another miscreant, who emerged from some mysterious place, and he in turn to another! For a mile and a half our rear was guarded all the while by armed men. I never travelled in so much state before in all my life.

It was a good while after that before we ventured to steal any more grapes, and when we did we stirred up another troublesome brigand, and then we ceased all further speculation in that line. I suppose that fellow that rode by on the mule posted all the sentinels, from Athens to the Piraeus, about us.

Every field on that long route was watched by an armed sentinel, some of whom had fallen asleep, no doubt, but were on hand, nevertheless. This shows what sort of a country modern Attica is — a community of questionable characters. These men were not there to guard their possessions against strangers, but against each other; for strangers seldom visit Athens and the Piraeus, and when they do, they go in daylight, and can buy all the grapes they want for a trifle. The modern inhabitants are confiscators and falsifiers of high repute, if gossip speaks truly concerning them, and I freely believe it does.

Just as the earliest tinges of the dawn flushed the eastern sky and turned the pillared Parthenon to a broken harp hung in the pearly horizon, we closed our thirteenth mile of weary, roundabout marching, and emerged upon the seashore abreast the ships, with our usual escort of fifteen hundred Piraean dogs howling at our heels. We hailed a boat that was two or three hundred yards from shore, and discovered in a moment that it was a police-boat on the lookout for any quarantine-breakers that might chance to be abroad. So we dodged - we were used to that by this time - and when the scouts reached the spot we had so lately occupied, we were absent. They cruised along the shore, but in the wrong direction, and shortly our own boat issued from the gloom and took us aboard. They had heard our signal on the ship. We rowed noiselessly away, and before the police-boat came in sight again, we were safe at home once more.

Four more of our passengers were anxious to visit Athens, and started half an hour after we returned; but they had not been ashore five minutes till the police discovered and chased them so hotly that they barely escaped to their boat again, and that was all. They pursued the enterprise no further.

We set sail for Constantinople today, but some of us little care for that. We have seen all there was to see in the old city that had its birth sixteen hundred years before Christ was born, and was an old town before the foundations of Troy were laid - and saw it in its most attractive aspect. Wherefore, why should *we* worry ?

Two other passengers ran the blockade successfully last night. So we learned this morning. They slipped away so quietly that they were not missed from the ship for several hours. They had the hardihood to march into the Piraeus in the early dusk and hire a carriage. They ran some danger of adding two or three months' imprisonment to the other novelties of their Holy Land Pleasure Excursion. I admire 'cheek.' But they went and came safely, and never walked a step.

1852 Edmund About

A Fine Sight

I set out for Aegina with an architect of the Academy of Rome, my friend Garnier, who was then undertaking that beautiful restoration which was admired a few months ago at the Palace of the Fine Arts. Aegina is only six leagues from Athens; but the roads are as bad, the lodgings as uninhabitable, the feeding as desperately bad, as in any district of Greece. We had landed at the village, which is the chief town of the island; our boatman had taken us to the most comfortable tavern in the place - comfortable is a word which has no equivalent in Greek. We had supped in the midst of the populace, who examined with curiosity our clothes, our faces, and the omelette which our servant was getting ready for us; at last we had slept in a shed on the mattresses we had brought with us. Will he nill he, the traveller is like the sage - he must carry everything with him. Next morning we set out for the Temple of Aegina, which Garnier was to draw and measure at his leisure; all our baggage went with us. We intended to hire a cot near the temple, and establish ourselves there for a fortnight or twenty days. The architect had got ladders, drawing-paper, and sketching apparatus; we had in common two mattresses a very few inches thick, two coverlets, rice, sugar and coffee, potatoes, and some other superfluities only to be found in the capital.

At break of day the people of Aegina were present at a fine sight. We had got two baggage-horses; one was blind of an eye, and carried the ladders; the other enjoyed the whole of his equine advantages, and to him we had confided the mattresses and provisions, the hopes of all our days and nights. He was proud of his charge, and walked with a jaunty step. But the bearer of the ladders, either surprised at being so laden, or from jealousy of his companion less laden than himself, or from the effect of that prejudice which makes us despise humble though useful functions, only aspired to getting rid of the burden which our confidence had committed to him. He ran against the houses, the walls, the passers-by, the ladders foremost: his master followed close behind, sometimes goaded him with a magnificent blue umbrella, Sometimes dragged him back by the pole of the ladder, or pushed him right and left - handling the ladder like the tiller of a boat. Two donkeys, intended for our riding, guessed at an early hour that the road would be difficult; they took advantage of the disorder to escape, bolt into a house, and barricade themselves inside so well, that they were left there. Our band was thus reduced to seven persons; two of them horses. Each animal had its pilot: such is the custom; he that hires the beast, has the man into the bargain. The ladders went first, the baggage after, then Garnier with his long pike, then myself with my gun; lastly, the servant with our sketch books and papers. At each turn of the road, the vicious one-eyed animal played one of his tricks; his companion, indignant at this, refused to move; the blue umbrella did its work; the guides uttered a kind of nasal howl to encourage their animals; the village dogs, unaccustomed to see caravans, barked their loudest, the women ran to their doors, the girls to their windows, and laughed at us to our faces. Thanks to the zeal of our guides, we were not more than half an hour in traversing the town, which is of the size of the Rue de Poitiers; but the inhabitants will long remember a day so fruitful in emotions; and if ever Aegina has a history, our passage through it will be an event in it.

The Joys of The Road

The village we were leaving is two hours from the temple on foot; if on horseback, rather more time is required. Judge from that if the roads are good! But this road is so varied, that one would walk on it a whole lifetime without being wearied of it; at one time it follows the slope of a rough and scarped mountain, at another it descends into deep ravines, clothed with trees of every kind, and large wild-flowers which our gardens might well envy. Some enormous fig-trees twist their thick arms amidst the almond-trees with their slender foliage; here and there are to be found a few orange-trees of a dark green, pines scathed with winter, cypresses of capricious forms; and at certain distances, the king of trees, the palm, raises its beautiful dishevelled head; gild this landscape with a ray of sun; scatter here and there ruins of ancient and modern times - churches on all the elevations, Turkish houses on all the slopes, square-like towers crowned with terraces, all cleanly white-washed with lime; on the roads little troops of donkeys carrying whole families; in the fields flocks of sheep; goats on the rocks; here and there a few lean cows lying down and staring at the traveller with their large astonished eyes; and everywhere the song of the larks, who rise into the sky as if going to reach the sun; everywhere the saucy chattering of the blackbirds rejoicing at the budding of the vine, and hundreds of birds of every kind disputing for a drop of dew that the sun had forgotten to drink up. I have seen it again often, that charming road; and although I stumbled over the stones, slipped among the rocks, and got my feet wet in the water of the streams, I would wish much to wander over it again.

The Cult of the Garden

Greece is in want for necessaries; she consoles herself with superfluities.

For many years, not a house has been built in Attica without the addition of a small pleasure-garden. Private individuals, the poorest and the most in debt, allow themselves the pleasure of cultivating a few orange-trees and a few flowers. Never in their gardens do they leave a space for the cultivation of kitchen vegetables; they would think themselves dishonoured, if they discovered behind their house a stealthy onion, or a sneaking cabbage. With them vanity is stronger than self-interest and want.

A garden, however, costs a good deal. Shrubs, one with another, cost two drachms each at the Greek nursery gardens, or the Genoese Bottaro. If vegetable mould is required, it must be bought; if one wants to water the trees (and the trees all want to be watered), a conduit must be bought for two hundred drachms a year, which the municipality sells without warranting it, for the peasants turn off the water from the aqueducts for the benefit of their own fields; or else a Maltese must be paid two drachms and a half a day to draw water from the well.

The trees often require renewing: the heat decimates them regularly every summer; it would seem as if they were subject to fevers like men. The owner must cultivate his garden himself, or have it cultivated by day-labourers, for the servants of the house are not to be reckoned on. One says, "I am a valet, and not the gardener;" another, "You took me to clean your pipes, and not the garden walks;" a third does not complain, but is so clever at spoiling whatever he touches, that he is soon forbidden to touch anything.

But the possession of a garden is a pleasure which consoles for many vexations; from the beginning of January till the middle of May, happy is the man who can live in his garden! If care has been taken to raise against the north wind a barrier of tall cypresses, one may, nine days in ten, walk about sheltered from cold. The lemon-trees open in the very first days of the year their buds of white tinted with violet; the pepper-trees, like weeping-willows which have not lost their leaves, let fall in confusion their long branches; the pines, arbutus-trees, lentisks, and twenty other kinds of resinous trees, offer to the eye a soft gloomy shade, of which one never wearies. The sycoids form here and there thick green carpets; stunted cactus, crouching in corners, or arranged in hedges, raise in confusion their thorny limbs; hedges of rosemary flower all the winter, and draw down by their strong perfume the winged artists that labour on Hymettus; the narcissus shows itself in February; the anemones and daffodils in March; at the end of April there are flowers everywhere. Then the melias adorn themselves with their violet bunches; the chilly orange-trees bud without fear; the vine plays with the almond-trees; jessamine and passion-flowers twine together along the walls; the clematis stretches its long arms around the arbour, and the climbing rose-trees delight to spot with red the old palisades.

We had in our garden three uncultivated plots where a few handfuls of seeds of all kinds had been thrown in once for all. Everything flowered in April; poppies, camomile, sainfoin, fumatory, wild poppies. During a whole month the flowers, the bees, butterflies, lizards, beetles, and the birds which hid their nests in the long grass, were mixed together, tumbling one over the other in wild confusion; and beneath, the dull earth seemed to become animated with a swarming life. Above all this humming tangle floated a strong luscious scent of honey, which gladdened the heart.

Let us think no more of it; for indeed all this luxury faded on the 1st of June, to make way for myrtles and oleanders, which retired in July before the dust and the grasshoppers.

The Queen has, without comparison, the finest garden in the kingdom. Good and bad years together, fifty thousand drachms are expended there - a twentieth part of the civil list. If there is anything worth envying in the little kingdom of Greece, it is the possession of this great garden. I say great, on account of its extent and not on account of its design – It is an English garden full of winding paths without one avenue of tall trees. A gardener of the time of Louis XIV would be shocked at it, and would exclaim that the king's majesty compromised itself in alleys of this sort. No offence to the good Le Notre; the Queen's garden is a pretty thing, and M. Bareaud, who made it, a clever man.

No doubt, it might perhaps have been better to leave the ground as it was naked, untilled, burned up, and tangled here and there with wild plants. Theophile Gautier was indignant at grass having been sown in such a picturesque spot, and that such fine rocks had been spoiled. But the Queen wished to surround herself with shade, perfumes, bright colours, and the song of birds - what she asked for has been given her.

Those who have passed three summer months in Greece, know that the most precious good, and the one most worthy of being sought for, is shade - in the royal garden there are thickets where the sun never penetrates. The King's dining-room is a room under the open sky, surrounded by open galleries; the sides and the roof are of climbing rose-trees, crowded together, entwined and matted like the work of a basket-maker.

By one of those pieces of good luck which only happen to the fortunate, the Queen found, whilst laying out her garden, the remains of a Roman villa - something like two hundred square yards of mosaic. Part of this precious work was restored, the rest destroyed, and the Queen is in possession of a large gallery and five or six delightful chambers, the pavement of which is supplied by the Romans, the decorations by camelias, and the walls by passion-flowers. The principal charm of this garden for travellers from France is, that in it you see in the open air plants in flower, which we rear by the side of a stove. The orange-trees of the Luxembourg and the Tuileries are always rather like those curly trees which are given to children on their birthday, with six sheep and a shepherd. The Queen has a small orange grove which are really trees and not toys. She has palm-trees larger than those of the Jardin des Plantes, growing in the middle of a green lawn. What costs the most is the lawn, not the palm-trees. Nobody will ever know how much care, labour, and water, is necessary for keeping turf alive at Athens in July. It is a really royal luxury. To water her grass, the Queen has confiscated a certain number of water conduits, which were going in a vulgar way to carry their water into the town to give drink to the citizens. Her Majesty has taken them into her service - the Athenians are the worse for it, but the grass finds itself all the better.

The ruins of the temple of Olympian Jupiter rise from the plain a little below the garden. Adrian had no idea that he was constructing this gigantic temple to embellish an English garden, and to please the eyes of a princess of Oldenburg.

The Queen likes her garden such as it is, but she would like it better if the trees were higher. She aspires to a high grove, but she will not obtain it, and will never console herself for this. Vegetable mould is too scarce; the roots of the trees do not extend to a sufficient depth; the winds that blow over Attica are too violent. I have seen cypresses a hundred years old upset in a second by the north wind. The Queen does not give in; she obliges her gardeners carefully to prime the trees, to allow them to grow higher. After each storm the labourers find two or three hundred trees with their roots in the air; they replant them as best they may, and set to work again to prune them.

The Queen's garden is public - it is fair enough that those who pay for it should have the right of walking in it. But as the Queen walks there too, and does not like meeting her subjects face to face, the public is only admitted after the time that their Majesties go out riding until nightfall. In summer, the Queen goes out sometimes at half-past seven in the evening, so that visitors have just the time to go in and come out again. If by chance the Queen does not go out before night, the garden remains closed all day. The soldiers who watch at the gates show an accommodating disposition towards their countrymen, and often allow them to enter before the stated hour. But, on the other hand, it often happens that they cross their bayonets before an ambassador at the hour when everybody may go in. The regulation is so well drawn up and so cleverly carried out that the garden has nothing to fear from a crowd, and no one will ever be suffocated in its walks.

Capital Punishment Greek-Style

The most horrible of all punishments inflicted by justice is in every country the easiest of application. One escapes prison and the galleys, there is no escape from the tomb, and a man is soon dead.

It is not so in the kingdom of Greece, and the application of capital punishment was impossible there till 1847.

The Government sought for an executioner in the country; it found none. It had two or three brought from abroad; it saw them massacred by the people. It thought of making use of soldiers as executioners; the Senate did not allow it. At last they found a man sufficiently starved to lend his hand to the sad work of human justice. This wretched man lives alone, far from Athens, in a fortress where he is guarded by soldiers. He is brought in a vessel clandestinely the evening before the execution; he is hastily reconducted as soon as he has performed his work; before, during, and after the exercise of his functions, soldiers surround him to protect his life. When the Minister of Justice was fortunate enough to find an executioner, there were in the prisons thirty or forty under sentence of death, who were patiently waiting for their turn. These arrears were liquidated one way or other.

The guillotine is erected at a few paces from Athens, at the entrance of the grotto of the Nymphs. The scaffold is of the height of a man, and the horror of the spectacle is increased by it; it seems to the spectators that they have only to stretch out their hands to stay the knife, and they feel as if they accomplices in shedding blood. But that which adds to the interest of this legal tragedy, is that the patient defends his life. The law ordains that he shall walk freely to punishment, and that his hands shall not be bound. Now the greater part of those that are sentenced, brigands by profession, are vigorous men, who never fail to struggle with the executioner. Every execution begins by a duel, in which justice always has the upper hand, for she is armed with a dagger. When the culprit has received eight or ten wounds, and has lost all his strength with his blood, he goes freely to execution, and his head falls. The people return to the town asking themselves how they could best assassinate the executioner. This is the morality of this tragedy.

Some of the Courtiers of Athens

This is an example of the needlessly offensive comments which made M. About notorious.

The Marshal of the palace is the highest dignitary of the kingdom; it is through his intervention that ambassador an audience of the King. He walks first after the King in all solemnities. The organization of the Court festivities belongs to him by right; he is at the same time grand-master of the ceremonies. By a singular caprice of politics, the grand-master of the ceremonies, Marshal of the palace, was, during the latter years a little old man from the Morea, who does not know French, who has not at all a courtly appearance, and who only needs a ring in his nose to resemble a redskin. This is the great man Colocotronis.

The Marshal of the palace and the King's aides-de camp put on for ceremony the richest costume imaginable. It is a coat of cloth of gold, which brings to mind certain dresses of the time of Francis I. Embroidery is profusely lavished over them so as to dazzle the eyesight. This coat, when of silver, costs three thousand francs; if gold, it must cost more than ten thousand. It is true that it does not wear out, that the fashion never changes, and that the garment may last for many generations.

The Outdoor Life

Do you wish to see the Greek people in their true light ? walk in the streets. In all times, the Greeks have lived in the open air. The Romans, it is said, were very fond of the public squares; and it is asserted that they detested their homes. I defy them ever to have ever hated them like the Greeks, for it rains at Rome ten times more than at Athens.

When one examines what remains of the ancient town, one is struck with the smallness of the houses, which have all left their traces on the soil. It would never be believed, if history had not confirmed it, that such dens had been inhabited by men. The Abbé Barthélemy has drawn in his book the plan of an Athenian dwelling. I would undertake to give a ball to fifty Athenian houses in the house of the Abbé Barthélemy. These huts, which we can measure with a cane, were not endurable in the daytime; it was as much as could be done to eat and sleep there. The day was passed in the marketplace, in the street, or on the parade. Such is the practice to this day, although the houses are more convenient and more spacious than in the time of Pericles.

It is always difficult to cross the space in the centre of the town, at the branching off of the streets of Aeolus and Hermes. It is there that the citizens, sitting before the coffee-houses, or standing up in the middle of the street, discuss the questions of peace and war, and, smoking their cigarettes, alter the map of Europe.

Whilst the statesmen are professing in the open air, the students, collected in groups before the University, debate tumultuously; the *papas* before their churches raise some point of orthodoxy; the townspeople fill with their argumentation the shops of the grocer, the barber, or the chemist. These three kinds of establishments are the drawing-rooms for the use of the people; the chemist in particular brings together the elite of the tradespeople and middle classes; the talkers do not fill up the shop; they prefer standing on the threshold, one foot on the pavement, and one ear in the street to catch the news which circulates.

The bazaar is perhaps the most frequented part of the town. In the morning, all the people of the town, of what ever rank, go themselves to market. If you wish to see a senator carrying kidneys in one hand, and salad in the other, go to the bazaar at eight in the morning. The maidservants Landernau will never be able to gossip so unceasingly as these right honourables making their bargains. They walk from shop to shop, getting information as to the price of apples and onions, or giving an account of their vote the day before to some money-changer, who stops them as they go by.

The money-changer has, as formerly, his shop in the marketplace. The ancients called him *trapezitis* - the man with the table, He has changed neither his name nor his occupation nor his table, since the days of Aristophanes; only, thanks to the progress of civilisation, he has covered his table with an iron trellis-work, which protects his gold and silver coins,

At eight o'clock in the evening, in summer, the bazaar has really all enchanted aspect, It is the hour when the workmen, the servants, the soldiers, come to buy their provisions for supper. The more dainty divide among seven or eight a sheep's-head for sixpence; the frugal men buy a slice of pink watermelon, or a large cucumber, which they bite at like an apple. The shopkeepers, from the midst of their vegetables and their fruits, call the buyers with loud cries; large lamps, full of olive oil, throw a fine red light on the heaps of figs, pomegranates, melons, and grapes. In this confusion, all these things appear brilliant; discordant sounds become harmonious; you do not perceive that you are paddling in black mud, and hardly smell the nauseous odours with which the bazaar is infected...

A foreigner who should arrive at Athens about midnight in July, would not be a little surprised at finding the streets covered with cloaks. If he thought that these had been strewn to do him honour, and if he advanced carelessly through these old clothes, he would feel the ground move, he would see arms and legs coming out of the earth, and would hear a concert of energetic grunts.

The people have the habit of sleeping in the street from the middle of May till the end of September. The women sleep on terraces or on the roofs, provided that the roofs are flat.

It may have been observed that the women occupy little space in this chapter; it is because the women occupy very little space in the streets. They go out rarely, and only to return as quickly as possible. They never go to the bazaar. The men have preserved this privilege since the Turkish rule, or rather since the highest antiquity.

The highway is the drawing-room and bedroom of the Greeks of the stronger sex; why, then, is their room so badly swept? Why is their room never made tidy? Constantinople perhaps is the only large town which could dispute with Athens the palm of dirtiness. Here you meet in the streets a dead crow, there a crushed fowl, further on a dog in a state of decomposition. I believe, in truth, that if a cab-horse should die before the Beautiful Greece coffeehouse, the Tortoni of Athens, that the care of removing it would be let to the vultures.

The police allow individuals to dig great lime-pits in front of their houses ... It allows large pools of water to remain in the streets; no one has ever thought of covering over the great ditch which traverses the finest quarter of the town. More than this, the bridge which joins the two shores of this sewer, in front of the printing-office, lost eight years ago one of the wooden crossbeams, and nothing is easier than to break one's leg there. The missing plank might be replaced for two drachms; but no one has ever given it a thought.

The streets are lighted with oil, except on the nights on which the light of the moon is reckoned on. If the almanac is wrong, or if the moon hides itself, all Athenians are allowed to break their necks.

Transport in Mid Nineteenth Century Athens

Carriages are not scarce at Athens, and plenty are to be found for the town or the country. I have before said that the country extends to four leagues from the town. Nothing is more shabby than these poor hackney-coaches of Athens, rickety, dirty, and in bad repair; they seldom have window glasses, and I do not know if they have always got four wheels.

They are all to be found together in a muddy place called the square of the carriages; it is not easy to make a choice, one is so pulled about and besieged by the coachmen. An agreement is made with these gentry, the police has not established a tariff. One may go to Piraeus for one drachm and a half, or for sixty drachms, according to the occasion. I have seen flies hired for sixty drachms, eight days beforehand, for a ball at the Piraeus; on the same day I have got one for two drachms. The carriages rise and fall, like the public funds in other places, without one's always knowing the reason why.

There has been some talk of establishing omnibuses between Athens and Piraeus. The traffic is very frequent; the carriages are dear. The business appears, at first sight, an excellent one; it is a very bad one, and would be ruinous. The omnibuses could not charge less than fifty lepta for a run of two leagues; now the Greeks find means of going to Piraeus for twenty-five lepta...

The Promenade to Patissia

When you have traversed the whole of the street of Aeolus, turning your back on the Acropolis, and on the Tower of the Winds, you see before you a dusty road, a good mile in length, and at the end a little village. This village was, under the Turks, the residence of a pasha. The name of pasha, or padishah, has remained a little corrupted it is true; the Athenians call it Patissia.

The road to Patissia is the turf of Athens. If I said it was an agreeable promenade, I should be as false as a Greek historian. The road is badly kept up, and would not hold its rank among our country roads. The trees, with which it has been attempted to line it, are dead, or dying, or sickly; the four or five wine shops which stand on the right and left hand of it, are not Parthenons; the barley fields or uncultivated land which it passes through, do not constitute a terrestrial paradise.

Yet the promenaders who crowd together on this road, can see, when the dust permits, one of the finest panoramas of the world. They have before them Mount Parnes, split with a wide yawning gap; behind them Athens and the Acropolis; to the right, Lycabettus; to the left, the sea, the islands and hills of the Morea. The sight is less fine at the Bois de Boulogne.

The fashionable world of Athens has for its principal diversion, in summer as in winter, this walk on the road to Patissia. People come there on foot, in carriages, and especially on horse-back. Every Greek who can manage to borrow three hundred drachms, makes haste to buy a horse; every Greek who has three drachms in his pocket, devotes them to the hire of a horse. The shopkeepers in the Rue Vivienne may do their best; they will never be such great riders as the hairdressers and shoemakers of Athens on Sundays.

The young officials who gain more than two thousand drachms a year, the townspeople who have enough to live on, the cavalry officers, and sometimes the members of the diplomatic body, make the pride of the Patissia road. The jockey club of Paris is represented there by a very good rider, Baron Roger de la Tour-du-Pin, attaché to the French Legation. The *chargé d' Affaires* of one of the German courts, rides there every day in thorough jockey costume. The pretty women of the society of Athens, who almost all of them are good riders, risk themselves there from time to time. I have often met Ianthe, who used to leap the ditches on a splendid white horse. She was the best rider in the town; when she went out, followed by a company of friends, she had such a grand appearance, that the boys ran up more than once to shout on her passing by: they took her for the Queen. The Queen will never forgive her those mistakes.

The public has no other established promenade than the Patissia road. People show themselves there in winter, from three to five; in summer, from seven to nine. In winter, the only days on which it remains deserted, are the days when the north wind blows; it would be almost impossible to walk against the wind as far as the village. It is a strong current, which I have sometimes amused myself by stemming, after carefully wrapping myself up: arrived at Patissia, you have only to turn your face to Athens; the wind will be sufficient to carry you there.

On going out of the town, on the right hand of the road, extends a bare open space, the soil of which is a kind of natural macadam: the only ornament of this place is a little wooden rotunda, which can shelter twenty persons. It is under the roof of this modest edifice that the band takes its place every Sunday. The people stand round in a ring to listen; the King and Queen come into the middle of the ring, to give a show to their subjects.

This music is a weekly fête for the whole population of Athens. The weather must be fright-fully bad for a Sunday to pass without music. It is at the band that one may see collected together all classes of society, from the members of the Court down to the ragged and begging poor. At three o'clock in winter, and six in summer, a picket of soldiers comes to the place. The musicians in military uniform come not long after; they go and take their places under their kiosk of white wood. Soon after, the white plume of Colonel Touret makes its appearance. The musicians would never consent to play if the colonel was not there. He takes his stand on the road, in front of the little bridge which connects it with the parade; it is there that he waits for their Majesties, making his horse caracole; it has never more than two feet on the ground at once. The prefect of police, in Palikari dress, comes next, with a cudgel in his hand. His officials, whom one would not like to meet in a corner of a wood, are around him; each of them carries a stick, on which is written, to reassure the public: "Strength of the law". Upon an order of the colonel, the picket of soldiers scatter themselves in such a way as to describe a large circle round the musicians. Behind them the carriages take up a position; behind the carriages, the pedestrians and riders walk up and down. The shopkeepers of Athens walk about with their wives and children, in all their finery. The head of the family twists between his fingers a large chaplet, which is not a religious implement, but a pastime, a plaything for grown-up persons, the beads of which they amuse themselves by counting mechanically and without thinking of it. This gentle exercise ends by becoming a necessity for those who have acquired the habit, and I know some very clever Frenchmen who have left Greece several years ago, who have serious occupations, a busy and agitated life, and who are no longer masters of themselves, when they have not got this chaplet between their fingers: so much has the habit bewitched them! I have seen in Greece the president of the Senate directing a stormy discussion without ceasing for a moment to count the beads of his chaplet.

A certain number of women are to be met with at the band, who put their noses out of doors only once a week. Their husbands take them ready dressed out of a box, of which they have got the key; they just brush them a little, and expose them to the open air till the evening. After the band, they go back again into the chest, which is shut up again hermetically.

These ladies are *en grande toilette*. Dress is one of the cankers of Athenian society. An official in the receipt of twelve hundred francs buys for his wife a pink or white watered-silk gown, which is to be seen every Sunday dragging in the dust. These sad dolls advance majestically with an embroidered handkerchief in their hands. It is the only pocket-handkerchief in the house; men of all classes blow their noses with their fingers with great dexterity; the rich townspeople make use of their handkerchiefs afterwards. The high society uses the handkerchief in the European manner, and is not any the prouder.

In a corner out of the way, along a wall, the maidservants, work-women, Albanian women, and all the poorer classes of women, are crowded together. It is amidst this confusion of arms and legs that one discovers the finest profiles, and the noblest countenances. I have seen maidservants come from Naxos or Milos, who would have eclipsed all the women of Athens, if they could have been soaked in running water for six months.

At the hour appointed for the beginning of the ceremony, the colonel, who might give the sun lessons in punctuality, makes a sign to the orchestra; they play quadrilles, waltzes, polkas, and all other kinds of composed music. The public listens to these varied noises with all the attention they deserve, that is to say, pretty ill. Towards the second or third piece, one sees the colonel's horse carried away as if it had wings. By this symptom one perceives that the King is coming.

The King and Queen enter the ring at a gallop; their suite stops at the entrance. It is usually composed of an aide-de-camp, one or two orderly officers, a maid of honour, and the Queen's groom - a good fat German, who trains her horses, and takes the freshness out of them a little in the morning, when she is going out riding in the evening. The picket of cavalry, which follows their Majesties at a distance of twenty-five paces, goes and places itself on the other side of the ring.

Those Frenchmen who have frequented the circus of the Champs-Elysées, or have attended the representations of the Hippodrome, are suddenly brought back to their recollections, when they see these strange evolutions performed to the sound of this loud music. The King and Queen have halted side by side, and are occupied with holding in their horses, listening to the noise of the brass instruments, contemplating their people; and smiling at one another. The Queen's dress has often something theatrical about it. From time to time the King amuses himself by marking time, like an absolute monarch who has placed himself above laws and rules.

At the end of the piece, their Majesties, followed by their Court, cross the ring; the citizens take off their caps; the riders of the escort spur their horses, and the Court is lost in a cloud of dust. Do not cry; it will come back again. I have seen the King come back as many as four times in the same afternoon; the musicians were not tired of blowing, nor the citizens with bowing.

c. 1850 S.S.Cox

Threshing at the Columns

Like many American writers, S.S.Cox seems to have been primarily concerned to make unfavourable comparisons with the USA. Evidently, such writers had something to prove.

Now as I look at its remains, the eye finds its area covered by great stacks of wheat, in the process of threshing. Men are superintending. This process was peculiar. Imagine three cultivators, or corn harrows, with teeth turned backward; these chained together, and a man ... one on each; drawn by horses trampling the straw, while men were engaged in stirring it up, and you have a very unscientific description of the threshing process. Women were riding the horses, and stirring the straw, assessing the work. A motley group that, in the Temple of Jupiter! Why so much straw here ? It is a ridiculous law, that every farmer shall bring his wheat or grain into the point fixed by the officer, there to be threshed in his presence, so that government may take its toll! American farmers! how would you like that? Jupiter Olympus! would you not upset such a government in a jiffy?

c. 1850 Henry M. Baird

The Blessing of the Waters

On the morning of the festival of Epiphany, a singular ceremony took place at Piraeus analogous to the marrying of the sea practised by the ancient doges of Venice. At an early hour the Archbishop of Athens, attended by a large company of ecclesiastics, repaired to the margin of the harbour. A vast throng, especially of boatmen, gathered around while he proceeded to bless the waters according to a formula provided for such occasions. At the same time he cast a small cross into the waves. By the contact, the waters of the bay are presumed to be hallowed, and the shipping in some measure insured from shipwreck and other perils of the deep. From the annual repetition, it would seem that the blessing is sufficient only for a single year; and were it not renewed, it would be almost impossible to persuade a Greek sailor to embark upon the unsanctified element. Scarcely had the cross disappeared from sight before a crowd of boatmen plunged in to find the glittering prize. And then began a strife in the deep water, until one, more fortunate than his competitors, emerged, clutching the cross in his hand, Amidst the congratulations of his friends, he now hastened home. Having equipped himself with his best suit of clothes, he next rode to Athens and presented himself with his cross at the palace. It is customary for the king to make the finder the handsome gift of one hundred or more drachms. The ministers of state, and then all others, follow the royal example; and, even before the day has closed, it not infrequently happens that the boatman's gains amount to a hundred dollars.

A Contentious Block of Marble

This passage illustrates both the continued appetite of foreign visitors for "marbles", and the contempt of the Greek archaeological service at the time for any remains other than those of the ancient period.

[A]n amusing incident occurred at Piraeus. A young American lieutenant had long been desirous of procuring a block of genuine Pentelican marble, to serve as a pedestal for the bust of his father-in-law, a warm admirer of Greece. In the garden of a friend in Athens, he found a piece that exactly suited his purpose. The owner cheerfully presented him with it, and had it neatly enclosed in a box. One evening, after a call in the city, the officer placed it in his carriage and rode down to Piraeus, expecting to find one of the ship's boats in waiting. It was late, however, and none were to be found; but there were other boats at hand, and he deposited himself and his prize in one of these. On reaching the frigate he stepped on board, telling the boatmen to bring his box on deck. Instead of doing so, they demanded an exorbitant fare, and when he refused to pay it, quietly shoved off; and put back to shore. The lieutenant, who was on deck and unarmed, was unable to stop the rogues; and retired to his state-room for the night, as may be imagined, considerably vexed at the occurrence. Early the next morning, application was made for the arrest of the dishonest boatmen. They were readily identified, and in their house was found the box, which they had conveyed thither with no little trouble, and had broken open to discover its contents. They had evidently been deceived by its great weight; and doubtless their chagrin was considerable, when instead of a small treasure in gold or silver, they found inside nothing but a worthless block of stone.

But for an unlucky discovery, the box would now have been restored to its owner. The marble had once been embedded in some church or chapel, as was manifest from a large Byzantine cross rudely carved on one face. The custom-house officers declared that this cross was old, and that the stone came under the category of antiquities, whose exportation is prohibited by law. There was no use in arguing the matter with them. The only resource was to send up to the city for Mr. Pittakes, the General Superintendent of Antiquities; who, on his arrival, laughed at the simplicity of the officials, and readily granted permission to export that block, and as many more such as could be procured.

A Walk on Hymettos

Hymettus is the nearest mountain to Athens, its base being scarcely two or three miles distant to the southeast. One day in January, I seized the opportunity of a fair sky to visit the lower parts of the mountain; and after an hour's walk across the plain, commenced the ascent. The dry season was scarcely over, for the first winter rain had fallen in December, after the annual drought of summer; but the fields already began to look green, and the ground was covered with the common anemones of every shade, from white and blue to red. An olive grove was the first sign of our approach to the Monastery of Syriani, or Cresariani. It contains several buildings for the monks. As usual in the cloisters of Greece, the entrance to the rooms is by means of half-decayed verandas and staircases running up on the side of the building that faces the court. Here, also, is a church, over the door of which I noticed a painting of the Presentation of the Virgin at the Temple, which was striking for its simplicity. Anna sits upon a step of the building representing the Temple of Jerusalem, towards whose entrance the child Mary advances; while the angels who are placed around proclaim the event to the universe. It is quite in contrast with Titian's grand conception of the same subject at Venice.

The monastery has sadly fallen from its pristine glory. The fraternity is represented by a single abbot, who lives here quite alone. I afterwards learned that he is a man of hospitable disposition and agreeable manners, and regretted that I had not made his acquaintance. His is a remarkable history, and yet one that has been often paralleled in Greece. Previous to the Revolution he officiated as a parish priest; but having drawn the sword at the time of the war, and killed some Turks, the strict canons of his Church obliged him to cease from his ministrations. Under similar circumstances, many others of the clergy have become soldiers, lawyers, or politicians. This man, however, preferred a retired life, and settled down here. He came near losing his life subsequently by an act of imprudence. A noted *kleft* – this occurred but a few years since - had been infesting Hymettus, and levying contributions on the peasants even within sight of Athens. The abbot gave notice to the government of his lurking-place on the mountain; and the robber hearing of it, vowed to take revenge on the informer. At the same time, with that species of frankness which is not inconsistent in the breast of the brigand with the greatest amount of cunning, he sent a letter to his enemy apprising him of this intention. Fortunately for the latter, the *kleft* himself was murdered by an emissary of the government. A peasant was hired to join the robbers, and put himself under the command of the criminal, whom, on the first favourable opportunity, he shot. It is reported that this peasant, in his turn, became a *kleft*, and was killed in an affray with the soldiery.

One part of the worthy abbot's duties seems to be to watch over the miracle, which annually occurs on the festival of some one of the saints, and which twenty thousand persons congregate to witness. As the wonder consists in a sudden rise of the water in a certain fountain to an unusual height, and the pipe that feeds it comes from within the enclosure, it must be allowed that his task can scarcely be considered very difficult.

1850 Walter Colton

The Condition of the Clergy

The condition of the clergy is an important topic for consideration. Like most other topics, to a general view it has a dark as well as a bright side. The priest, or *papas*, it is true, has not necessarily sundered, by a prescribed celibacy, all the ties that serve to unite him, in sympathy and affection, with his spiritual flock. In fact, many of the parish priests are married men; nor is this circumstance considered in the least discreditable. There is, however, this restriction: the aspirant for orders must marry, if at all, before becoming a deacon; and so it happens that while a priest may be a married man, yet a priest is prohibited from marrying.

Although the priest's tenure of office does not depend, as has been asserted, at least in Greece, upon the life of his wife, he can not marry a second time without forfeiting his priestly character. Happily, neither law nor public opinion place any obstacles in the way of his retiring. There are not a few curates who have renounced their sacerdotal functions from this cause; while a much larger number who took up arms in the Revolutionary War, and imbrued their hands in blood, are on that account incapacitated from officiating.

The ignorance and degradation of the clergy forms the gloomier aspect of the picture. Springing from the lowest class of society, they are notoriously illiterate and immoral. So deeply rooted has the notion of their debasement become in the popular mind, that when a boy is unruly, and his parents have failed in persuading him to learn some honest trade, they frequently consider the Church their last and only resource. This idea is embodied in a current proverb, which may be rendered in English by the couplet,

> "Vicious and ignorant, gluttonous beast,
> Nothing remains but to make him a priest."

But when the fact is known, that until lately there has been no provision for their education, beyond schools where they might learn to read and write, such a state of things will scarcely excite surprise. It is even asserted that a few ecclesiastics may still be found, unable to read their service, and consequently relying either upon their own memory or upon the assistance of others. I have myself met with several who gloried in the scantiness of the opportunities for instruction enjoyed by their order, asserting that a more liberal education had the effect of making atheists of the youth. Unfortunately this is not far from being the case in Greece. I have known several deacons and others in the university that were sceptics even as to the truth of religion, and would gladly cut off their long hair, (letting the hair grow long is considered indispensable to the exercise of any of the priestly functions) and lay aside their sacerdotal robes, could they be sure of gaining a livelihood by some other profession than that they had embraced. The monks are even more ignorant and degraded, while they display an inveterate hostility to every measure tending to enlighten and elevate the people.

Corruption is, unhappily, equally common in Church and State. It is notorious that no one can obtain the appointment of Greek Consul for the more frequented ports - such as Trieste, Marseilles, or Odessa - without first obtaining the influence and support of some important man near the king's person, by means of a costly present. A similar practice holds good with respect to the ordination of priests. So flagrant is this system of bribery in every department of the Church, that in a "letter-writer" published at Athens, not many years ago, and now lying before me, a number of forms are given for such occasions as the following. In one, the writer beseeches a bishop not to grant a divorce in the case of his daughter, and accompanies his petition with a present of 5000 piastres - a little more than $200. Another is an application to a prelate for a dispensation to permit a man to marry a third time.

It will be remembered that a third marriage is an abomination in the eyes of the Greeks, and is considered criminal unless the previous permission of the Patriarch be obtained. The applicant states that the prelate's agent, to whom he had addressed himself, had demanded the sum of three thousand piastres; and he therefore begs not to be compelled to pay anything more than that which is customary .The character of the transaction is more frequently veiled under the appearance of a gift. The Patriarch of .Jerusalem grants plenary pardon to all that devoutly visit the Holy Places: but the pilgrim must first gratify his avarice by a present of some two hundred dollars. Having satisfied his conscience at so cheap a price, the *Hadgi*, as he is now called, returns to his own country, with a store of acquired righteousness so ample, as to be quite sufficient, both in his own estimation and in that of his neighbours, to cover all his future sins.

He rarely fails to make large drafts on this imaginary deposit. "As bad as a *Hadgi*," has become a proverbial expression to denote the most abandoned of characters.

1857-8 Bayard Taylor

The Proliforation of Holidays

The festivals of the Greek Church are fully as numerous, if not even more so, than those of the Latin. About every third day is an *eorti*, or holy-day of some venerable unwashed saint, or company of saints, whose memory is duly honoured by a general loafing-spell of the inhabitants. The greatest benefit that could happen to Greece, and to all Southern Europe, would be the discanonization of nine-tenths of those holy drones, who do enough harm by sanctifying indolence, to outweigh a thousand times the good they may have accomplished during their lives. God's Sabbath is enough for man's needs, and both St. George, the Swindler, and St. Polycarp, the Martyr, have sufficient honour done them in the way of chapels, shrines, candles and incense, to forego the appropriation of certain days, on which no one thinks particularly about them. Not only are the labourers idle and the shops generally shut, on everyone of these festival days, but the university, schools and public offices are closed also. The Greeks are very zealous professors, and would exhibit much more progress as a people, if they did not make a millstone of their religion, and wear it around their necks.

My Greek teacher, who was a student of law, insisted on being paid by the month, and turned his agreement to profit by rigidly observing every saint's-day.

Vanity

He was indebted to the lessons he gave me for the means of buying an overcoat, and always came into my room half frozen from his fireless chambers; yet, with that inordinate vanity which characterizes the Greeks of all classes, he declared that he was not obliged and did not wish to teach, but condescended to do so for the pleasure of visiting me! Next door to us there was a small, one-story house, inhabited by a poor family. The daughter, a girl of twelve or thirteen, attended the Arsakeion, or Seminary for Girls, a gift of Arsakis to the Greek people, just across the street. The ridiculous little chit must have a servant to carry her two books those thirty paces, and we sometimes saw her, when the school was over, waiting behind the door, not daring to appear in the street with books in her hand. Nearly all the girls who came to the Arsakeion (some two hundred day-scholars) were similarly attended, yet they were mostly from families of moderate means.

1861 Dr. Corrigan

A Cure for Hydrophobia on Salamina

In concluding my notice of this fete and fair [*at the monastery of the Panayia at Salamis*], I must mention that the convent has acquired great celebrity for the cure, or more strictly speaking, the prevention of hydrophobia. The monks make no secret of the remedy or the process; and were kind enough to give me, not only the mode of using their remedies, but specimens of the medicines. The process adopted is this - the patient, on being bitten, or as soon after as possible, is brought to the convent. The wound is then cauterized with boiling oil. A small brass saucer, containing oil, and a brazier, containing some live charcoal, were brought into the room to show me the manner of doing it. The saucer containing the oil was laid upon the burning charcoal; and on the oil acquiring a boiling heat a piece of wool, twisted hard, was soaked in it, and this is applied to the wound until the wound, and parts immediately around it, are hardened and cauterized. This, the ancient mode of cauterizing a poisoned wound, is probably a better mode of arresting the passage of the poison into the circulation than our modern application of caustic, for the boiling oil by its heat solidifies all the fluids and tissues of the part, and effectually prevents all absorption and circulation, while modern caustic can act only on the surface, or as far as its chemical action extends. The patient is then given every second or third day, for two or three weeks, about five grains of a powder composed of one part of a powdered fly of the nature of cantharides, and two parts of the powder of a root which grows wild around the convent. The fly is somewhat larger than the Spanish fly, used for blistering, and is named scientifically the "Mylatais Graeca." It is gathered on the plain, and kept dried for use. I have obtained preparations of it, and of the root, for the museum of the King and Queen College of Physicians. The plant is *Cynanchum Erectum*. By some, the preventive powers of this medicine are firmly believed in, by others not. The power of prevention is always a difficult matter to ascertain, because of several persons bitten very few may imbibe the poison. The poisonous saliva may be exhausted after several bites; or, what is more to be relied on, bites through clothes rarely carry poison. The cloth or linen through which the tooth passes wipes it clean. I have seen some deaths from hydrophobia; and in all the bite was on the face or hands - unprotected parts. The serpent has a tube running through its tooth into a poison bag at the root of it; and having first inserted the tooth the serpent then discharges the poison along the tube as a bullet is sent along a gun barrel; but the dog's tooth can only carry with it the poisonous saliva which happens to lie along its surface, and if the tooth be wiped by passing through clothes, there is very little, if any, risk to be apprehended. If a rabid dog attack you wrap the hands in skirt or coat, guard the face, and you need have little or no fear.

There can scarcely be a doubt that some time or other a cure for hydrophobia will be discovered, for the disease is purely a functional affection of a portion of the nervous system; and it is well I think to collect all the information we can, and specimens of the preventions or remedies which have acquired any reputation.

1872 Charles K. Tuckerman

The New City

If, from the thickly-settled and business quarters we proceed to the newer parts of the city, things wear a more attractive look. The streets are wide, the side-walks cleanly, and but for certain nuisances which force the pedestrian to take to the street, would be worthy of any city. Balconies protrude from even the meanest edifice, and are regarded as a desideratum by all households, for the accommodation of the ladies of the family, who sit thereon in passive enjoyment of the street view during the long summer afternoons and evenings. The dwellings are built very much on the same model, and are mostly intended for two families; having one entrance through a gate and courtyard to the first floor apartments, and another front door conducting to the suite of rooms above. The walls are constructed of large cobble stones, roughly cemented, and are substantial enough for a fortress; but the enemy they are intended to provide against is more subtle and powerful than the armaments of war. Earthquakes are not infrequent in Greece, and have been attended with great loss of life and property. In Athens, however, they have never exceeded a slight *tremblement*, sufficient to awake the sleeper at night, but not endangering even a chimney-pot.

The dwelling-houses are generally furnished with great simplicity, and there is an absence of that comfortable home look which the abundance of drapery and furniture gives to an English parlour or French salon. Even in the best houses, carpets are sometimes deemed superfluous, or are visible only in the shape of rugs before the sofas, or a square of tapestry in the middle of the floor. But the nakedness below is atoned for by the gorgeousness above. Every ceiling, from dining-room to bedroom, is decorated with coloured designs, and the salon is sometimes so gay with arabesque, as to suggest the idea that the carpet has been spread by accident on the ceiling instead of the floor. The sofa is the seat of honour, and on it the guest is invited to seat himself. Two rows of chairs are generally seen at right angles to the sofa, which, when duly occupied, give rather a formal appearance to a social gathering. Black coffee or sweetmeats are invariably offered to visitors in many of the Greek families, as in the days of the Turkish regime.

Each dwelling-house in the better portions of the city has its garden in the rear. Thick and high walls may hide it from the passing gaze; but there it is, a ceaseless pleasure to the occupants, and often an evidence of their cultivated tastes. In very many of the gardens, or in the court yards of private dwellings; the visitor notices small fragments of ancient sculpture set up against the wall, or inserted in it; portions of vases, bas-relieves, a trunkless head, or a headless trunk, inscriptions, etc., which were discovered for the most part on the spot where they are now seen, having been turned up in the excavations during the progress of the building. The removal of antiquities from the country is now forbidden by law; but the discoverer is permitted to retain them as his personal property. During the litigation and delays which occurred while the plan for the new city was being matured, and which contemplated the entire abolishment of the narrow, crooked lanes which deformed the old Turkish town, the owners of many of the lots became impatient, and erected dwellings on the old sites. The result of this is, that the broad, regular thoroughfares were commenced after a large part of the present city was erected, and there is no doubt but that beneath the soil in the older parts of the city are concealed many precious archaeological remains, which would otherwise have been brought to light.

1870-80s John Pentland Mahaffy

Vandalism Continued

... [A]ll these buildings [The monument of Lysicrates, the Temple of the Winds, Hadrian's Arch, etc.] are either miserably defaced, or of such late date and decayed taste as to make them unworthy specimens of pure Greek art. A single century ago there was much to be seen and admired which has since disappeared; and even today the majority of the population are careless as to the treatment of ancient monuments, and sometimes even mischievous in wantonly defacing them. Thus, I saw the marble tombs of Ottfried Muller and Charles Lenormant - tombs which, though modern, were yet erected at the cost of the nation to men who were eminent lovers and students of Greek art - I saw these tombs used as common targets by the neighbourhood, and all peppered with marks of shot and of bullets. I saw them, too, all but blown up by workmen blasting for building-stones close beside them. I saw, also, from the Acropolis, a young gentleman practising with a pistol at a piece old carved marble work in the Theatre of Dionysus. His object seemed to be to chip off a piece from the edge at every shot. Happily, on this occasion, our vantage ground enabled us to take the law into our own hands; and after in vain appealing to a custodian to interfere, we adopted the tactics of Apollo at Delphi, and by detaching stones from the top of our precipice, we put to flight the wretched barbarian who had come to ravage the treasures of that most sacred place.

The Ancient Olive Groves of the Kefisos

But amid all the dusty and bare features of the view, the eye fastens with delight on one great broad band of dark green, which, starting from the west side of Pentelicus, close to Mount Parnes in the north, sweeps straight down the valley, passing about two miles to the west of Athens, and reaching to the Piraeus. This is the plain of the Kephissus, and these are the famous olive woods which contain with them the deme Colonus, so celebrated by Sophocles, and the groves of Academe, at their nearest point to the city. The dust of Athens, and the bareness of the plain, make all walks about the town disagreeable, save either the ascent of Lycabettus, or a ramble into these olive woods. The river Kephissus, which waters them, is a respectable, though narrow river, even in summer often discharging a good deal of water, but much divided into trenches and arms, which are very convenient for irrigation.

So there is a strip of country, fully ten miles long, and perhaps two wide on the average, which affords delicious shade and greenness and the song of birds, instead of hot sunlight and dust and the shrill clamour of the tettix without.

I have wandered many hours in these delightful woods, listening to the nightingales, which sing all day in the deep shade and solitude, as it were in a prolonged twilight, and hearing the plane-tree whispering to the elm as Aristophanes has it, and seeing the white poplar show its

The Military Hospital, Makriyanni(1836)

silvery leaves in the breeze, and wondering whether the huge old olive stems, so like the old pollarded stumps in Windsor Forest, could be the actual sacred trees, the *moriai* under which the youth of Athens ran their races. The banks of the Kephissus, too, are lined with great reeds, and sedgy marsh plants, which stoop over into its sandy shallows and wave idly in the current of its stream. The ouzel and the kingfisher start from under one's feet, and bright fish move out lazily from their sunny bay into the deeper pool. Now and then through a vista the Acropolis shows itself in a framework of green foliage, nor do I know any more enchanting view of that great ruin.

All the ground under the dense olive trees was covered with standing corn, for here, as in Southern Italy, the shade of trees seems no hindrance to the ripening of the ear. But there was here thicker wood than in Italian cornfields; on the other hand, there was not that rich festooning of vines which spread from tree to tree, and which give a Neapolitan summer landscape so peculiar a charm. A few homesteads there were along the roads, and even at one of the bridges a children's school, full of those beautiful fair children whose heads remind one so strongly of the old Greek statues. But all the houses were walled in, and many of them seemed solitary and deserted. The memories of rapine and violence were still there. I was told, indeed, that no country in Europe was so secure, and I confess I found it so myself in my wanderings; but when we see how every disturbance or war on the frontier revives again the rumour of brigandage, I could not help feeling that the desert state of the land, and the general sense of insecurity, however irrational in the intervals of peace, was not surprising.

There is no other excursion in the immediate vicinity of Athens of any like beauty or interest.

1878 James Albert Harrison

A Summer's Evening at Faliron

Yesterday evening after dinner we went down by the train to Phalerum and attended the open air theatre there... The road was built by an English company, is about four miles long, and rides smoothly and agreeably. This is the great promenade of Athens: take a ticket for Phalerum, stroll up and down the lovely beach, and then sit for an hour or two under the stars listening to Greek or Italian music. Modern Greek music is singularly nasal and monotone. There is something wild and wailing in it. I have heard vocalization and choral chants of great beauty in the Russian church, but the music of a Greek Easter, for example, is like a seasick Gregorian chant.

The beau-monde was out in force at Phalerum this evening. I was glad to find the seats numbered, enabling one to get up and go out in the intermezzos. The play was a little Italian operette (Sappho), and the music was really charming. .. There was a graceful ballet, at which the Athenians for some inscrutable reason hissed, for there were no legs and no indecency. Of course the dresses were wonderfully scant, and there was an exhibition of feminine gymnastics, as in all ballets, but I cannot believe the nation of Lais and Phryne so prudish as to object to legs, especially when the national costume seems so particularly to ignore them. Possibly there may have been something objectionable in the characters of the dancers. At any rate there was vehement applause as well as vehement hissing.:. The music and the mise-en-scene this special evening were singularly appropriate. Hardly a flutter of breeze, cloudless tranquillity above, the gentle ripple of the Aegean on the shore, the rich mountain outlines gradually withdrawing themselves in purple obscurity, the gleam of multitudinous stars, the fragrance of the salt sea and scented gardens, all blending with the classic subject and the delightful music to make an almost antique picture

The programme or libretto was in Greek interspersed with Italian songs. There was no richness in the costumes or special virtuosity in the orchestra; and yet the whole dwells in my memory as a scene to be remembered...

I made the mistake of getting two tickets instead of one, not being sufficiently acquainted with colloquial Greek to rectify the error after I had discovered it. The incessant talking and humming of people all around me prevented a full enjoyment of my first musical evening in Greece.

Phalerum Bay is peculiarly beautiful. An English ironclad was lying at anchor in the offing, and several of her tars with- their wide-awake, upturned straw hats assisted at the play. There are delightful baths, to which the languid Athenians continually resort. Fifty lepta for a bath, one drachma for the theatre, and one for the return ticket, make up an evening's amusement that is extremely cheap and popular. The water is shallow. There are several pretty villas on the shore, and the usual series of *xenodocheia*, *ostiaria*, and brassieres along it. A gay multitude sat in front of them, enjoying the balmy air, the view, the invariable cigarette, and the tiny cup of coffee, preparatory to the play. An evening at Phalerum is almost the only summer amusement the Athenians have. One would think these beautiful mountains, like those in the neighbourhood of Rome, would be covered with villas; but such has been the insecurity of the country that there are none. Little villages here and there - Patissia, Colonos, Ambelokipos, Kalandri - are gown over the plain; but they all hover in sight like a hen and her chickens. I notice in the hotel this precautionary placard: "Gentlemen on the point of making excursions will please inform the proprietor twenty-four hours beforehand." This is for the purpose of letting the authorities know of the intended journey in case an escort should be needed, or to keep them on the lookout.

A Surprising Use for Archaeological Sites

Besides the leprous-looking coffee-houses that have sprung up at the feet of Olympian Jove and desecrate the place, the peregrinating Greeks make these splendid columns a sort of undressing-room. It is the same with the tomb of Themistocles, the prison of Socrates on the Museum Hill, the excavations in the Kerameikos, and every accessible monument a little with-drawn from the public gaze. Travellers in Italy will remember the same practice of the Italians. The habit is an heirloom of immemorial antiquity, and goes hand in hand, I suppose, with the filth of Martial and the foulness of Athenaeus. The Campanile of Venice, and even the roof of the Cathedral of Milan, are made hideous by these things.

1879 Denton Jacques Snider

Retsina in Halandri

Threading my way through the vineyard, I came to the small village of Chalandri. The church is the most important edifice of the village; next to the church is the wineshop, which is the only house open to the stranger as a resort or resting-place. All the dwellings are walled in, and seem to be hermetically sealed; there is no friendly opening of porches and of doors toward the street, as in an American town. The domestic abode turns away from the outside world which is suspected and repelled; one walks through the lonely streets enlivened nowhere by children at play or by housewives sewing at the front door; he feels as if shunned and rejected by his kind, condemned beforehand by some unjust suspicion. Oriental seclusion of the family is suggested, perhaps too readily, to the mind of the traveller.

The wineshop has the only open door or window in the town; there I enter. It has no floor; good mother earth takes my wearied feet upon her bare bosom. There is no ceiling overhead to hide the naked rafters which give support on the outside to the boards on which the tiles are laid. The place has a rather a dark, cave-like appearance, forbidding, I should say, were it not for the huge hogsheads which are disposed in a long row on one side of the room, and which contains infinite joys. My hearers will probably think that I had learned enough for one day about the Greek wine-god; but the thirst for knowledge of Greek divinity was not yet stilled. At my call the youth in attendance brought a clear yellow liquid with a slight sparkle, for which he charged me at the rate of one cent a glass...

The taste of the wine becomes like the taste of pitch, or, as some say, of sealing-wax. At the first effort to drink this wine nature revolts, sometimes revolutionizes; only after much preliminary training and chastising does the rebellious palate suffer this fluid to pass its portal. As it was my rule to eat and drink, or learn to eat and drink what the people of the countries I visited ate and drank, I began with recinato shortly after my arrival at Athens. In two or three weeks I no longer noticed the pitchy taste in the wine, except by a special effort. Other kinds of wines are obtainable in the city, but in the country nothing else but recinato is to he found; hence the necessity of a previous training to this drink, if one wishes to travel in the provinces, for he can not do it on water. The reasons given for treating wine in this way are two mainly: to preserve it from spoiling in the hot climate of Greece, and to make it more healthy. The ancients also had this method of treating wine, as appears from Pliny...

This is an Albanian town, and the youth at the bar informs me that here within five miles of classic Athens, Albanian is the language of the inhabitants. But let there be no further delay; rest and refreshment have attached fresh wings to the body, the pedestrian will fly into the street, bound for Pentelicus, now rising up cloud-wrapped before him - in real clouds, I mean, and not in wine-fumes, as you might suppose. Women in their white smocks - not a nightdress here – dart shyly through the streets without looking at him, or taking special pains to glance in the opposite direction while he is passing. Folded over their forehead above, and over their chin and mouth below, is a linen covering, intended to hide the grateful portion of the face from the curious eye of the male. The enlightened traveller will again curse the custom as a relic of the oriental seclusion of women. They are mostly stockingless, their bare feet are slipped into a sort of loose sandal; over the smock is sometimes worn a white woollen cloak. On the whole they seem lightly clad for midwinter; but their white forms moving along in the distance through the clear mild air give a joyous Greek impression to the landscape, as if it were dotted with statuary.

Here comes a maiden, on her shoulder bearing water to the village from the spring in a vessel like the ancient amphora. She turns out of the road, looks away from me, and adjusts more closely the wrappage around her chin and forehead; still I peer into her face. Wild irregular features I caught a glimpse of, burnt to dark brown by the sun of the plain. It is manifest from this and other glimpses that Helen is not here at Chalandri, nor is she to be found among the Albanian race. These people, usually considered of Slavic origin, are said to have come into Greece at various times during the Middle Ages, and they still preserve unmixed their blood, their language, their customs, and their physical characteristics.

Thus one trudges forward, leaving the houses behind, and passing by the spring, from which the maiden came who was carrying water to the village. Washers too are here, women with large undraped limbs, standing in the cold stream snow-fed from the mountains; there they twist and writhe in deadly conflict with soiled garments. A momentary glance the traveller will cast at them for the sake of antique, and then modestly turn away.

Stood Up by a Soldier in Kifissia

So, in musing mood, accompanied by the declining sun I walk over he fields to the road and soon enter the village of Kephissia. It was famous in antiquity for its pleasant rills and agreeable air, and it is still a great resort during the summer; the diplomatic body generally adjourn hither from the intolerable heat of Athens. It is dusk, I pass through the main street, which always leads to that shining beacon of the Greek village, the wine-shop. The hunger and thirst of the weary traveller can here be stilled. This was my first Greek lunch in the country, so it may be of interest to tell you what it was composed of. Recinato, of the best quality and in the greatest abundance at the smallest prices; dark bread, coarse, of unbolted flour, but well-baked and good such were the two staples, bread and wine. For something by way of luxury I called for goat's cheese. This cheese is brought in little granulous balls which easily crumble and then it looks like our dry hand-cheese. It is made by the shepherds on the mountains in a not very tidy way; one ingredient is often found scattered through it, the reason for which I never learned - namely, the goat's-hairs. I always picked them out of mine, thinking that they had no business there, but it must be confessed that they are pretty generally included in this cheese and seem to share in the very idea of it.

Butter, in the occidental sense of the word, is not to be found in Greece; yet I am always afraid that you will think of the pun, and will try to confute me by pointing triumphantly to oleomargyrine. But this last article I do not think has yet come into Greece, even though it may sometimes have come out of it. Butter-eating Thracians, certain barbarians were anciently called with contempt, in contrast to the oil-consuming Greeks, civilized men. To be sure there are a few cows here; Boeotia and Euboea have fine cattle. But the small picking from the mountains will not produce butter; only goats and sheep yield milk from such slender nourishment. For sheep are milked in Greece, and their milk is made into various products of the dairy. Nothing will better illustrate the extreme economy of this country than the fact that sheep are milked. The American farmer has never heard of such a thing, and sheep's cheese and butter, brought into an American market might possibly be sold as rare curiosities.

There is quite a detachment of soldiers stationed in the town, for the purpose of guarding the road to Marathon lest timid excursionists get a fright. As it is a holiday, the most of the soldiers are gathered into the wineshop, and are quite merry. They are singing Romaic songs with that jolly whine peculiar to Greek music. All the talk is about the treaty of Berlin, the new boundary of Greece, the prospect of war with the Ottoman. The keeper of the wineshop is flourishing a huge knife, showing the manner in which he is going to sever the Turkish head from the Turkish body, should he only get a chance. Patriotic exhilaration does indeed prevail, but there is no drunkenness, according to the American conception of the word and the deed. The Greek certainly deserves his reputation of being the most temperate of men; for he is not intemperate even in his temperance.

A soldier observing me sits down on the bench at my side and talks with me; He speaks Italian well, and, as it seems to me, likes to show off his beautiful acquirement to his astonished comrades. He is a good patriot, not a grumbler; he is willingly serving out the time of his conscription, though with privation and pecuniary loss as he affirms, and as one may well believe. But his dear Hellas can have his time and his life, if necessary; he is full of her glories, though he deeply laments her weakness and her small territory. Still he thinks that she has performed wonders of progress during the short period of her independence, and he believes that she is destined to be the bearer of light and liberty to the East. She is to rule the Orient once more, her goal is Constantinople.

Thus thinks the common soldier, representing, in my opinion, the average intelligence and character of the Greek. For in his character there is still a high aspiration, an ideal striving after improvement, although the reality may be discouraging. I hail him as a comrade, and tell him that I too was a soldier and give him a short bit out of my campaigning. He ends by inviting me to bunk with him that night in his quarters - an invitation which I gladly accept. I wanted to see how the Greek soldier fared; I felt perfectly able to endure whatever quarters he had to bestow, even down to sleeping on the feathery side of a board, though I confess that I have been a little enervated in recent years by the luxury of a bed.

The bugle blew, my soldier had to go to roll-call; he said he would return in fifteen or twenty minutes, and conduct me to my place of repose for the night. But he did not come back so soon; I was sleepy and tired, and could not wait; accordingly I went off to a large hotel which has been built here for the purpose of accommodating the high guests of the summer; but at the present season it has only an excursionist now and then from the city. I need not say anything about this hotel except that when you enter it, you step out of Greece into Western Europe. You will get there a fair bed and a fair meal in quite the same fashion as in other parts of the world. It is arranged on the principle of causing the traveller to live quite in the same manner that he lives at home; so that in this way he may travel over the whole world without experiencing anything of it, substantially without going out of his own house. My regret is that I did not get to bunk with that soldier, and to take a little glance at the inside of things in his quarters, all of which would help to fill up the picture of Greek life. In return for which I can now only tell you that I obtained a bed and a beefsteak - both of them doubtless old acquaintances of yours that need not be fully described.

1886 John Edwin Sandys

An Excursion to Cape Sunion and the Mines of Lavrion

At 3.30 we left for Laurium by the new railway, stopping on our way at several very unpretentious stations. Over one of these, which was only a small shed, I saw the name of Liopesi, a village on the site of Paeania, the deme of Demosthenes. It lies at the foot of the north-eastern end of the range of Hymettus, where the mountain terminates in a rugged and precipitous cliff. While our train moved slowly on, we had fine views of Pentelicus, and afterwards of the wild country in the south-east of Attica.

The name of Laurium, which in ancient times was applied to the mining district in general, is now given to the modern mining village, which also bears the name of Ergasteria. The modern Laurium, at which we arrived after six o'clock, is a dreary little place, with a number of small houses on the four sides of an open space of bare and dusty ground. After finding our inn, the Hotel de l'Europe (where some very unpalatable tea was served us in two tumblers of thick glass), we called at about seven o'clock on M. Serpieri, who gave us a most kind and cordial reception. He would gladly have put us up for the night, had we not already taken a room at the wretched little inn - a dirty place, where it proved almost impossible to sleep. He at once arranged for his brother-in-law and partner, M. Ernest Pellissier, to meet us early the next morning, and drive us first to Sunium and afterwards to the mines.

April 2. - At half-past seven in the morning, we started for Sunium in an open carriage drawn by three horses, in company with M. Pellissier, who, as we soon found, had spent some time at Newcastle, and was very fairly familiar with English. Even the road to Sunium had been constructed by the French company, who are very public-spirited people and apparently do a great deal that in other countries would be done at the public expense. The wild flowers by the roadside, and the bright little bays of blue water which we passed on our left, added much to our enjoyment. After a rapid drive of about an hour, followed by a short walk, we reached the famous ruins of the temple of Athene with its radiant columns, not mellowed with hues of amber like those of the Parthenon, but standing in stainless glory in a magnificent situation on the breezy height at the end of the headland... The most conspicuous part of the ruins is the row of nine lofty columns that give to the cape its medieval and modern name of Cape Colonna...

It was not without some regret at the unavoidable shortness of our stay that we hastened back to the carriage and returned to Laurium, which we entered before ten. After being hospitably entertained by M. Serpieri, we started off again with M. Pellissier at half past eleven and drove inland towards the works of the French company, through some wild and rugged scenery, with rough hillsides partly covered with low brushwood. On our way, we passed through the small village formed by the company for their work-people, with the two churches which they had also built, on two opposite heights, one for those of the Greek, the other for those of the Roman communion. After about an hour's drive we reached the mines, which are connected with Laurium by special lines of railway. As I wanted to see something of the works themselves, I was introduced to the chief engineer, a particularly pleasant young fellow, who made me put on a blouse and a small leather helmet in preparation for the descent. I went in his company down one of the shafts, the one that was named after M. Serpieri himself, and, on alighting, traversed several of the long galleries, where I was shown the far narrower and less regular passages worked by the miners in ancient times. These passages, I was told, were found to be frequently of a spiral form, and sometimes hardly left room, enough for a man to crawl through. Old tools and water-jugs and niches for lamps have occasionally been found, but I saw none of these myself. A "small museum" of these finds is mentioned in Baedeker's excellent guidebook, but I could discover nothing about it on the spot; on my return to Cambridge, however, I learnt from Professor Middleton that its contents had gone to the Louvre. It is sometimes supposed that the modern miners confine themselves to extracting, by means of improved processes, the large amount of lead ore and the very small quantity of silver that still remain in the ancient refuse. This is not the case, at any rate with the French company, who have extensive mines, excavated by themselves, which it would take, I was told, several days to traverse. They export their lead mainly to Newcastle, and their zinc to Swansea and Antwerp. On leaving the works we were presented with a large number of beautiful specimens of galena, aragonite, and other minerals; and after a most interesting visit, were driven back to our inn, where we had more than an hour to spare before the 3.35 train which brought us back to Athens at 6.10, much delighted with the kind and hospitable reception we had met with on this our last excursion in Attica.

1888 Thomas D. Seymour

Bed-linen at Lavrion

The *Hotel d'Europe,* at Laurium, had three rooms for guests. These were stuffy and dusty. The bed linen certainly had not been ironed, and the suspicion arose that it had not been washed. The host himself was the cook as well as the porter. But these were sumptuous accommodations compared with what may be found in many places.

1898 Samuel J. Barrows

A Modern Diogenes

In a corner of the Odeion of Herodes Atticus is an enormous earthenware wine jar, a vessel which still goes by its ancient name of pitkos. One day, as Professor Dorpfeld was concluding his lecture to a group of archaeologists in the ruins of the old theatre, they were suddenly startled by seeing a head thrust out of the jar which lay on its side. Then shoulders, body and legs slowly emerged. Inquiry showed that a half-witted man, driven about by the persecutions of a rabble of boys, had taken refuge in the old wine jar and had lived there most of the time for two weeks. A kind woman had brought him food and covered the mouth of the jar with a curtain. The poor wretch sadly lacked the wisdom of Diogenes and was more in need of merciful than of honest men. This modern Greek duplication of the life of the old cynic I offer in evidence against the scepticism of those who maintain that the philosopher could not have found a jar big enough to live in; and I have no doubt that if we could have got at the philosophy of this second Diogenes we should have found it sufficiently cynical.

It is in this way that old customs, words, ideas and traditions keep popping up and emerging from the human pottery in which they have been bottled. When you examine them you find that they are not dead; they have not even been hermetically sealed; though a little wrinkled or a trifle rheumatic, they are living and breathing and frequently venture out in public.

Prayers For Business

The modern church is close enough to the modern market, but the pious merchant does not always content his soul with going to church; he gets the church to come to him. One day I stepped into a photographer's to see about some work. There behind the counter stood a priest; before him were various symbols of his religion, and a saucer in which incense was burning. Prayer-book in hand, he was going through a portion of the liturgy. The photographer and his son were apparently paying no attention to him or his prayers, but busied themselves in arranging pictures. Nor did the priest appear to be greatly interested in his service. He went through it as if it were a matter of business; and so it was. The next day I asked the photographer what it all meant. "It means," said he, "that my mother is a pious old woman, and she likes to have the priest come round on the first day of the month and pray that business may be good." He smiled sceptically himself and confided to me that he thought the best way to help his trade was to do good work. I am glad to say that he lived up to this practical precept.

My Goats

I am the owner of seven goats. I own them just as I own the Parthenon, the Areopagus, Lycabettus, or Pentelicus. They are mine because I have appropriated them, - not their milk, their hair or their skins, but the whole goat, horns, beard, hoof and all. I do not mean gastronomically, but optically. Cows in Athens are rare, but goats and donkeys are numerous. I will not say that the goat's milk flows like water, for that would be to cast doubts upon the honesty of the milkman; but it flows in sufficient quantity to return a good revenue of coppers to the herdsman. One of the commonest sights in Athens is that of six or eight sober-looking goats marching through the streets, driven by a goatherd, who carries the milk measure in his hand. He has a regular route morning and afternoon. When he comes to the house of a customer, he milks one of the goats, receives the milk in his measure, and pours it into the servant's pitcher .There are a few cow stables; but goat's milk is the fashion in Athens, and, in fact all over Greece. It is no new fashion, but, like many other customs of this people, goes back through centuries.

On the opposite side of the street from my room was a small garden, with a wall about four feet high, made of nicely fitted slabs of stone surmounted by an iron railing. Twice a day the goats solemnly came down the broad street, crossed to the other side and ranged themselves along this garden wall. During the winter they served as a semi-diurnal clock, and also as a zoological thermometer. When I looked out of my window of a morning and found the goats there, I knew it was seven o'clock. If they hugged the wall closely, I knew it was windy; if one of them wore a blanket, I knew it was cold. In milder weather, one or two of them might venture into the middle of the sidewalk; but they were seldom more than a foot or two from the wall, and most of them stood against it as closely as if they were posing for a Parthenon frieze. One of their peculiarities was that they never faced all the same way. It was most natural for them to halt with their heads in the direction toward which they were going, which was always toward Lycabettus, but two and sometimes more of them always turned round and faced the Acropolis. Whether this was for artistic or archaeological reasons, or whether it was because goats are often more adversative than conjunctive, I did not discover; but I never found more than six heads facing the same way, and usually but three or four.

There are some advantages in driving the herd of goats to the customers. The milk is fresh. There is no danger of getting yesterday's draft instead of today's, or of getting a skimmed chalky fluid instead of milk with a roof of cream on it. The milkman is not obliged to carry cans. Each goat transports her own supply. No horse or wagon is needed... One milkman in Athens is too lazy to walk with his herd. He always rides ahead on a small donkey; seven goats follow, and a dog brings up the rear. Occasionally, a milkman may be seen with his cans strapped over the back of a donkey, while his cows or goats are left at home; but no such thing as a milkman's wagon is found on the thoroughfares.

Speedy Dispatch of a Suicide

One morning, just as they [the milkman and his goats] made their usual call, and ranged themselves against the garden wall, a man came out on the lower roof of the house behind it and shot himself. The fact that he had held a prominent position in a bank, and was the victim of this sudden impulse in a moment of depression, did not serve to delay his funeral. The stigma attached to suicide cannot be removed. In fact, in the longer catechism of the Greco-Russian Church suicide is said to be "the most criminal of all murders. For if it be contrary to nature to kill another man like unto ourselves, much more is it contrary to nature to kill our own selves" The funeral of a suicide is always held as soon as possible. In this case the man was buried without a priest at four o'clock the same afternoon, and of course in unconsecrated ground. Two of my friends had left that morning on an excursion for Marathon. They started after breakfast, and got back to a seven o'clock dinner. When they left, this man was living, when they came back, he had been buried three hours.

The Cyclades

Following the seizure of Constantinople by the Venetians in 1204 the islands of the Archipelago were divided among various adventurers to hold as hereditary fiefs of the Serene Republic. Following the fall of Constantinople most of these dynasties lost their power, as the Turks gradually extended their control over the Sea. During the following centuries some islands were taken and retaken by the Venetians and Turks several times as each struggled for influence in the area. Tinos withstood Turkish attacks completely for five hundred years, not falling until 1714. During the Russo Turkish War of 1770-1, many islands came under Russian control for a few years. Some islands had considerable Catholic populations, and stood aloof during the War of Independence, Syros in particular profiting from the devastation of trade rivals Chios and Psara. Most were immediately made part of the new kingdom of Greece.

The City and Island of Syra

(Choisieul-Gouffier & J. B. Tillard)

1596 Fynes Moryson

A Voyage through the Archipelago

The next morning early, being the one and twenty of December, we set sail, and the same day we sailed close by the island Zantorini, more then one hundred miles distant from Candia. They report, that this island, and another of the same name (both of little circuit) were in our age cast up in the midst of the sea, with an eruption of flames and of brimstone, and that they are not inhabited, but are commonly called the Devil's Islands, because many ships casting anchor there, and fastening their cables upon land, have had their cables loosed by spirits in the night, and so suffered shipwreck, or hardly escaped the same.

The night following we sailed in the midst of many islands which made that channel very dangerous, and for my part I was more afraid of the danger, because our Candian merchant growing acquainted with an harlot in the ship, was not ashamed to have the use of her body in the sight of the mariners that watched, and much blamed him for the same. Upon Wednesday the two and twenty of December, we sailed by the island Paros, celebrated by poets for the fine Marble growing there, and so we came to the island Naxos, two hundred miles distant from Candia. Naxos and the adjacent islands had their own duke of old, but now are subject to the Turk, as the other islands be for the most part. And our mariners dwelling in this island, and landing to see their wives, we also landed with them, where I did see upon a hill like a peninsula near this chief village, two marble images erected to Theseus and Ariadne. Here I observed, that when any stranger or inhabitant lands, the beggars flock to the doors of the houses or inns where they eat, and having formerly observed in the Greek Church at Venice, that when they gave their alms to beggers, they not only suffered them to touch their garments with their lousy rags, but also took them familiarly by the hands, I knew not whether I should attribute this fashion to their charitable affection in time of their bondage, or to their seldom feasting, and the multitude of beggars.

c.1609 William Lithgow

An Island of Partridges

From Milo I came to Zephano in a small boat, an island of circuit about twenty miles, and ten miles distant from Milo. The inhabitants are poor, yet kind people. There are an infinite number of partridges within this isle of a reddish colour, and bigger than ours in Brittaine. They are wild, and only killed by small shot. But I have seen in other islands flocks of them feeding in the fields, and usually kept by children. Some others I have seen in the streets of villages, without any keeper, even as our hens do with us.

Sleeping in a Chapel

From thence I embarked, and arrived at Angusa in Parir. This isle is forty miles long and six miles broad; being plentiful enough in all necessary things for the use of man.

In Angusa I stayed sixteen days, storm-sted with Northerly winds. And in all that time I never came to bed, for my lodging was in a little chapel a mile without the village, on hard stones, where I also had a fire and dressed my meat. The Greeks visited me oftentimes, and entreated me above all things that I should not enter the bounds of their sanctuary, because I was not of their religion. But I, in regard of the longsome and cold nights, was enforced every night to creep in, in the midst of the sanctuary to keep myself warm; which sanctuary was nothing but an altar hemmed in with a partition wall about my height, dividing the little room from the body of the chapel.

These miserable islanders are a kind of silly poor people; which in their behaviour showed the necessity they had to live, rather than by any pleasure in their living.

From thence I embarked on a small bark of ten tonnes, come from Scithia in Candy, and laden with oil; and about midday we arrived in the isle of Mecano, where we but only dined, and so set forward to Zea.

1670s M. de la Guillitiére

A Mutual Regard

Not far off we saw a vast number of sea-hogs, or, (if you will have them under a better title) dolphins following our ship, and ranged, according to their custom, two and two, a male and a female, and the male always behind. They did not swim quietly as the other fishes do, but were still leaping up and falling down again into the waters, which our seamen interpreted as an infallible prognostic of ill weather. I never saw so many dolphins as in that place ... nor flatter heads, which is the beauty of that sort of fish. It is easy to distinguish which of them were most handsome. Several of them had long heads, which were not so comely, but all of them threw their noses in the air; and gave us our choice. Our seamen would have it that they throw up their heads in that manner the better to hear the word Simon, which they roared out as loud as they could, supposing they followed them thereby. I think they did it for more convenient respiration, for the dolphin is a soggy fish, and almost stifled if it lies long under water without air.... I will not meddle with the secret sympathy which renders this fish naturally kind to man and ... it so easily to our kind. Such problems as these are the rocks of Reason upon which the curious do frequently split. Our virtuosi (being full of their learned ideas, and lying as it were to catch for anything that might give new light to their old notions) proposed themselves an experiment about these dolphins. They resolved to take two or three of them with their harping irons; and if they took one they might take a hundred, their amity one for another not suffering them to part. The design was to dissect a female, and examine the form of her belly ... that if possible we might find out whether in the structure and fabric of this fish there might not be some secret analogy with the inwards of a man, to which (for want of a better reason) we might ascribe their kindness and strange inclination to our sex. But we discovered that the inclination of man was more powerful to them, for the Italian mariners would not endure that we should do them any mischief, calling them the companions of their voyage, and the faithful sentinels, who by their leaping and playing upon the waters, do give them constant notice of any tempest approaching, and by these means our experiment was lost.

1687 Bernard Randolph

The Island that Exploded

Calogero lies between Andros and Scio. The greatest part of which, about thirty years ago was blown up, and the inhabitants destroyed. I have heard several merchants say that there at Smyrna most of the plate and money was turned blackish when the island was blown up, and many of the stones were cast upon the islands of Tine and Andros. A very small part of the island is now remaining.

Andros

1811-12 C. R. Cockerell

Mutinous Sailors and the Dog Down a Well

The wind falling light, we anchored in a small bay - and landed, and there we made fire in a cave and cooked our dinner. It was most romantic. After touching at Scyros, we put into Andros. While our ship was lying here in the port our sailors became mutinous. They began by stealing a pig from the land, and then went on to ransack our baggage and steal from it knives, clothes, and other things. All this happened while we ourselves were on shore, but our servants remonstrated, whereupon the scoundrels threatened to throw them overboard. There was nothing for us to do but apply to the English consul for protection. He sent for the chief instigator of the troubles, but he, as soon as he got ashore, ran away and was lost sight of. Under the circumstances, what we did was to deduct from the captain's pay the value of our losses and shift our goods from on board his vessel into another boat, a small one, in which we set sail for the island of Tinos.

We slept at San Nicolo on the bare ground, having made ourselves a fire in a tiny chapel. Fop, my dog, fell into a well and was rescued with great difficulty. One of the peasants, who had never seen anything like a Skye terrier before, when he saw him pulled out took him for a fiend or a goblin, and crossed himself devoutly.

1883-4 James Theodore Bent

The Towers of Andros

At Menites we were first introduced to the towers of Andros, a peculiarity of the island which arose from a constitution which it alone seems to have possessed. Until quite recent years the Andriotes were divided into two classes, the archons and the tillers of the soil: the former generally traced their descent from Venetian families, and each of them built a square tower in the middle of his land, and was a person of authority. There was a curious custom among these archons, that the first son who married always inherited the tower and the estate whilst the others entered monasteries, became schoolmasters, or sought employment in foreign parts: hence Andros is especially rich in monastic establishments, several of which are still in existence.

These square towers form a curious feature of the landscape. Originally they were entered at an upper storey by a ladder, which drew up and secured those inside from invasion. To the lower storey there were no doors or windows, but it was entered by a trap door from above and served as the family storeroom. Round the top of the towers were overhanging niches out of which the besieged could pour boiling oil and shoot their assailants; but thanks to the quiescence of modern times, the gloomy aspect of these towers is much ameliorated. Stone staircases have been fitted on outside to serve as approaches instead of ladders; windows have been opened, and in most of them an air of comfort now reigns.

But the family pride of the archons is by no means extinct, although under a different *régime* their power is greatly modified. They are exceedingly strict about marriages, and if the son of an archon demeans himself by wishing to marry beneath him, the paternal wrath is at once aroused: the young man's father will say that the girl has used magic to attract her lover, love philtres and potions, such as they have plenty of in Andros, but which are discountenanced by the Church as emanating from the devil. In the face of accusations such as these the young man can hardly continue his suit for shame. Many of these little artifices are attributed to the girls of Andros, such as sewing something on the sly into the coat of the object of their desire, or stealing his handkerchief and shuffling it in some mysterious way as they mutter incantations. These are harmless enough, but they know more intricate ones than these, which are brought into requisition if the simpler ones fail, and which are not very pleasing to recount.

Silly Andriote women think, too, that by treading on their husband's foot during a certain portion of the marriage service they will command in the household. We were shown one day, as an instance of this, a young woman who had lately married and tried this method; and so outraged was her newly acquired husband that as soon as they returned from church he gave her a good beating, and now she looks as humble-minded a helpmate as any man could wish to have.

An Uncomfortable Sojourn in a Monastery

The monastery is built on a fearful spot under the rocks of a mountain ridge to the south of the vale of Andros, so that it faces due north, and in the winter months gets no sun, and is exposed to every chilling blast. As seen from below, it is like a village a wall all round it, of dull brown stone, and with a whitewashed church rising up in the midst. There were quantities of leafless mulberry trees around it, and a rushing stream, which was swollen by the melting snow above. Inside, it was just like the nunnery of Tenos - intricate lanes and alleys full of pigs and fowls, leading into a sort of agora before the church, where in summer time the monks meet to chat; but now nothing could equal the chilliness of the spot. Evening had come on before we arrived; huge mist clouds rolled down us from the mountains, and everything we touched about the place felt clammy and damp. We were conducted down endless lanes and passages to the room of the prior Gregory, a tall, gaunt man of very ascetic appearance, which inspired awe. Our comfort not enhanced by the presence of a madman, who frequently told us that he was king of Andros, and that was his favourite palace. Superior Gregory apologised for him by saying that there were no asylums in Andros, that when a man is too dangerous to be at large he is taken by a monastery out of charity. Then again the lay brother, who acted as servant to the superior, had no chin - a most repulsive object to look upon. His duties are to wait on the superior, ring the bells, light the candles in the church, and say, 'Kyrie eleison' as fast he can at the proper time; and to fulfil these offices the good monks always chose a man whose deformities would unfit him for shining in any other rank in life.

Though I have visited many monasteries in Greece this was the first time I had passed the night in one, and I must say my curiosity was blended with awe at the appearance of those around me. Superior Gregory looked very cross at us from time to time, and presently I heard that our servant had suggested that, as we were tired and hungry, we should cook a portion of our lamb for our evening meal. 'Unheard of thing!' I heard him say. 'Why, to cook flesh in our monastery during the first week in Lent is against the canons of the church;' and feeling that we had imposed our society on them we felt it only right to offer no remonstrances, though, when dinner time came our hearts sank within us. Our bill of fare was as follows – First course, a soup of rice boiled in water, and tasting chiefly of the latter ingredient. Second course a soup of lentils and onions, more substantial than the last, but horribly unsatisfying to hungry travellers. Superior Gregory then graciously permitted us to eat some of our own caviare, and even went to the length of producing red caviare, such as the Greeks rejoice in, and *kalvas*, a Turkish sweet-meat made of sugar, flour, and sesame oil. Such was our meal, which we washed down with generous wine, and as the meal went on, the stern Gregory thawed a little.

Our next fear was about sleeping arrangements, and here again, our worst apprehensions were realised: we were to occupy a damp cell, no sheets on the bed, only coarse, home-spun rugs, and those dripping with wet.

'Matins will be at four o'clock tomorrow morning,' said Gregory as he somewhat sarcastically wished us a good night.

'Must we be there? asked I humbly; our tyrant considered a little, and then told us that we might remain in bed if we wished, being heterodox and travellers.

It was the first Friday in the great fast, so matins in the morning would last four hours. 'Should I go?' thought I; and when, at four o'clock, I was sleepless and heard the *semantron* sound, I decided that bed offered no charms and went.

The Greek *semandra* are curious inventions for making a noise. Each monastery has gener-ally two, one of wood and one of metal; the former is a planed of timber, made often of maple wood, about three long and nine inches wide. This is hung up outside the church, and the ringer produces his noise by striking it with a wooden mallet. As a rule, the wooden one only is sounded at dawn, but today, being a great Lenten service, the iron one was sounded: it is a semicircular which produces a noise not unlike a cracked gong. I have heard that these *semandra* date from the days when the Turks refused to allow the Christians to use bells. In the dead of night it was a curious noise, and as I issued forth into the chilly morning air and saw the monks, lanterns in hand, hurrying to church, I seemed to be wafted back into centuries long gone by; the wind howling and driving large snowflakes against our faces, and on this occasion I learnt the word for 'I shiver,' a specimen of Andriote patois which I will never forget.

Silkworms, and Naked Women on the Rooftops

J. Theodore Bent was in idefatigable collector of folk customs, and he visited every inhabited island in the Cyclades in search of them. But few could have been as much of a surprise to him as this one.

Until a few years ago Andros produced a large quantity of silk, and still a great number of mulberry trees are scattered over the plains and the hills; and one is surprised to find many houses of the poorer class in the town so large and commodious: it is because once upon a time they were constructed with a view to the manufacture of silk. Fifteen years ago disease attacked the worms and numbers of fine mulberry trees were cut down and lemons planted in their stead; with the fruit of those that are left they make a disgusting potent drink called mouroraki, much drunk at feast time, and the cause of many a bloody brawl in Andros.

In those days the Andriotes were very superstitious about their silkworms, and a woman who wished to secure a good crop of silk believed it a sure plan to appear stark naked on her flat roof at the early dawn of May morning. This curious custom is luckily not considered necessary for the success of the lemons, and hence it is abandoned; but it reminds one, oddly enough, of that lively picture drawn by Terence, in his 'Adriana' of the women of Andros, which does not credit them with an abundant stock of morality.

Tinos

1609-10 William Lithgow

An Unconquerable Island

The next isle of any note we touched at, was Tino. This island is under the Signory of Venice, and was sometime beautified with the Temple of Neptune. By Aristotle it was called Idrusa; of Demostenes, and Eschines, Erusea: It hath an impregnable Castle, builded on the top of a high locke, towards the East end or promontory of the isle, and ever provided with three years provision, and a garrison of two hundred soldiers, so that the Turks by no means can conquer it. The island itself is twenty miles in length, and a great refuge for all Christian ships and galleys that haunt in the Levant.

1812-15 William Turner

The Catholics *en fete*

This evening there was a great crowd of Catholics at the convent celebrating the festival of the *Corpus Domini*, which they carried in procession to the church. After the ceremony, the bells in the churches were rung, and all the cannons, guns, and pistols in the town were repeatedly fired in honour of the occasion. And the Consul told me that all the Catholic villages in Tino, of which there are above twenty, contend which shall fire the most powder on this occasion.

The north-wind still continued most violent: indeed it is much more so here than elsewhere, owing to two immensely high mountains overhanging the town, between which it pours down in such a torrent that many people told me they wanted very much to go to the villages above, but dare not climb the mountains for fear of being blown down by the wind, which has frequently happened to peasants.

1926 Paul Wilsach

The Pilgrimage to the Virgin of Tinos

The perpendicular line was the main street, seldom more than twenty feet wide, which led from the shore about a mile up to the hilltop where stands the shrine. This is the Sacred Way of Tinos. Over its stones the penitents approach, candles in hand. Up its length the sick and dying are wheeled and carried in expectation of a miracle at the shrine. Often in supplication and often in thanksgiving, the devout drag themselves the entire length on their knees or on their hands and knees. There were, however, none of these manifestations on that morning before the dawn of the feast. The Sacred Way at that hour was packed tight with thousands of pilgrims moving slowly in both directions with an eye rather for the secular aspect of things about them.

The inclined street is lined with low buildings, none of which rises more than two stories. Its whole length was narrowed, and made into a continuous bazaar, by carts and tables and booths along both sides, where all sorts of objects, sacred and profane, were offered for sale: lace made by the peasants, heaps of golden oranges, gaudily painted toys, glassware, rugs, peanuts, naively burned amphorae and bowls of strange shapes, thick black coffee, embroideries, candles of all sizes and colours and decorations at frequent intervals, toys ships, crude crosses, religious lithographs, icons stampéd in rather raw colours or stamped entirely in a metal resembling tin, Turkish delight at some tables, Greek sweets at others, conversation beads, booths of fried fish with pots of boiling oil hissing behind them, tables loaded with notions of all varieties, heaps of fresh bread again in the shape of hollow circles, odd objects in bead work, cheap jewellery, bright hued necklaces, walking sticks, postcards, ashtrays made of lobster shells with a gaudily painted Madonna in the bowl, and other objects of seemingly infinite variety.

A goat's carcass hung before one door and people waited in turn to buy their slices, which they took to the nearest boiling oil, and ate fresh fried between hunks of broken bread. At the rate of activity at that hour the butcher must have sold a whole herd during the week.

Near by was a pleasanter sight, where four Greek nuns stood behind tables selling crosses of wood or beaded work, which for months before they had been making with their own hands. Their handiwork was crude and uninteresting, but not so themselves. They were robed entirely in black, without the slightest relief of the Western nuns' snowy linen. Their heads were half wrapped and half draped with soft cloths in precisely the convention of the women of Old Testament art.

At somewhat frequent intervals were tables loaded with ex-votos; small objects fashioned from wood or stamped in cheap metal; so that he who had been saved in a storm might hang a ship in the shrine, and those who by their prayers had recovered their sight or hearing or had been spared a hand or a foot, might leave there imitative memorials of their cures.

As usual the better part of such an occasion as this one was the people. There had been little colour in the dress of those aboard the ship from Piraeus, but they were town folk. Here, however, were congested the simpler folk who had sailed to Tinos in small boats from the island villages, and their finery illustrated the traditional costumes of many neighbourhoods. All sorts of brilliant colouring and bold patterns went into the skirts and jackets, the aprons and capes and shawls. There were undoubtedly rare specimens of that Greek island embroidery which is hunted so hard for collections. There were colour combinations without number, but the simpler favourites, because more numerous, seemed to be gold on black and white on blue.

The men showed themselves a fraction the more splendid figures, in spite of the insignificance of the shallow embroidered disks or caps which they wear at impossible angles, and which defy any explanation of how they stay on. The splendour came rather from their embroidered vests and flowing white sleeves, from their full pleated white petticoats, from the fuzzy spheres large as oranges on the toes of their long shoes, and from their hooded coats of heavy white sheep's wool slung diagonally across the shoulders.

It became increasingly evident, as we neared the church, that there are sick who come to Tinos to seek no other cure than that of an empty pocket. There were beggars under one's feet right up to the gate of the sanctuary. None seemed, as beggars elsewhere, merely poor or aged. They were of all ages, but principally young, and nearly all men and boys, and they made such a display of twisted limbs, of stumps of legs and arms, of sores and swellings, as one could scarcely credit. The crowds were generous, and paper as well as pennies flowed into the palms and cups and caps and baskets which they held up for the offering. It was said that these beggars, in common with the small merchants, photographers and showmen are part of a caravan which turns up in every island to capitalize each feast and pilgrimage in its turn.

At the head of the Sacred Way, across a plaza, the church is approached through an arched gate in the wall of the great rectangular enclosure. It rises opposite, across a marble paved courtyard some hundred feet wide and not less shallow. Around the inner sides of the wall are built a double tier of colonnaded galleries, behind which are tiny rooms (mere cells) to house the pilgrims. Many hundreds could be sheltered there, but not more than an inconsequential fraction of the thousands present...

In the darkness the colonnades seemed deserted, but their pavements were actually carpeted with sleepers. Other sleepers lay huddled along the walls in every direction. They were apparently oblivious of the crowds which strolled or stood about the court and packed the two marble stairways and the arcaded porches before the church above. There was perfect good nature in the mass of humanity that pushed and pressed its way up the steps inch by inch toward the central doorway, but outside the church itself there was scarcely any order.

At the door, sailors from the warships guarded the way, and from time to time allowed a few to pass in, as the word was signalled from a side door that an equal number had passed out in that direction. From the time I started up the steps it was nearly an hour before I reached the guns which barred the entrance. The final enforced delay at the doorway gave a comprehensive view of the interior.

The Evangelistria has the rectangular shape of most Greek orthodox churches. It is not large, or it is at least so broken by columns, and it is so thickly hung with ex-votos and banners, that the open space between the door and the altar screen seems little more than that of a chapel. Votive lamps and chandeliers cluster so close that the roof is almost invisible, and the hangings themselves form a kind of ceiling, as it were, of silver stalactites. Attached to the walls, to the columns, and pendent lamps, are ex-votos of silver, or of a metal in imitation of silver, and it need not have been surprising that nearly every one of these was in the form of a ship as became an island people whose life is on the water, whose great friend and terrible foe is the sea, and who in treacherous winds and sudden tempest turn for security to this island shrine.

There were candles everywhere. The soft flames lighted not more than a limited radius near them, and only added to the obscurity behind the low arches and above the swinging ceiling of lamps. If the decorations were crude or garish they did not appear so, for the tapers softened everything, so that the scene was one of Oriental and theatrical splendour.

The shrine was filled with pilgrims, but it was not crowded. The first object of curiosity and devotion to every one as he entered was the miraculous icon, which was saluted with a fervent kiss. It rested, near the door, on a richly embroidered desk surmounted with a canopy blazing with lights and jewelled votive offerings. The painting is enclosed in a golden frame measuring about eighteen by twelve inches. It is covered with a richly figured plate of silver, set with precious stones in such a way that only the faces of the Virgin and the Gabriel may be seen...

There was a curious mixture of piety and commerce even inside the church. Every one who brought a candle lighted it at the shrine and left it there, and there were candle venders for those who came without or who wished to burn more than they had brought. As fast as the candles were lighted and put in place, and the donor was out of sight, they were blown out, removed to make room for others, and resold, so that a candle brought its price many times into the church treasury.

In every part of the sacred edifice stood priests, sombre in their black gowns, and with their long black hair and beards, holding a small cross in one hand and a contribution plate in the other. The pilgrims went from one ecclesiastic to another kissing the cross, as the priest muttered a blessing, and adding a mite to the currency on the plate. The priests interrupted these devotional acts only long enough to empty the money into their pockets, but it accumulated so fast that they retired often to relieve their pockets.

The three doors of the iconostasis stood open and each one framed a vested priest. An unbroken line of communicants filed past. The priest in the centre placed a morsel of blessed bread in each mouth. The priests in the two other doorways administered a spoonful of holy water in the same way. These devotional acts, like all others here, were accompanied by a contribution to a convenient plate or basket. It is believable that, as was said, this is one of the richest churches in Greece.

The sick are brought in great numbers on the pilgrimages to Tinos. The floor along the inner wall of the church was lined with them. Pale and silent, ragged and wan, crippled and twisted, they lay with their eyes closed, elbow to elbow, in solid files. They had been there all night, some perhaps for several nights, and would remain until the culminating ceremony on the morning of the feast itself. These night-long vigils of the sick awaiting a miracle are the distinguishing characteristic of this shrine...

The scenes in the church are repeated below in the Chapel of the Well, and in the long corridor that leads to it; shuffling crowds, reclining sick, priests, candles, shimmering ex-votos, contributions and sales. Here the principal points of devotion were the spot where the icon of Saint Luke had been found and the now sacred well itself. Earth from the former place is supposed to have miraculous properties in curing afflictions of the eyes. One priest scooped up the dirt here and sealed it in tiny packages which another priest distributed gratis. But no one accepted such a packet and failed to leave an offering of money in the inevitable salver. Although I saw no cures at Tinos, it was generally insisted eight or ten of the so-called miracles were worked every year. The greater wonder seemed to be that the wretched sick lying along the cold stone floors survived an hour , much less a night, in the density and odours of this unaired place...

The procession was finally heralded by the sailors clearing a path along the quay to the pavilion. Into the clearing friends carried helpless sick and laid them on the cobbles directly in the path of the priests. Such poor wretches hope the priests bearing and accompanying the icon will touch them as they pick their way over them, for in that way it is believed a miracle is assured. But the crowd was badly handled, and it seemed as if the sick on the pavement would be crushed to death before the icon came, unless they anticipated the miracle, and got up and ran away. But the crowd was badly handled, and it seemed as if the sick on the pavement would be crushed to death before the icon came, unless they anticipated the miracle, and got up and ran away.

The procession as a whole was scarcely imposing, but the pale countenances of the bearded priests and bishops, under their black conical bonnets, and wrapped in splendid copes, made a brave display. A bishop, distinguished by the veil which hung from his bonnet, carried the sacred picture, but the chief personage of the procession was the Archbishop of Syra inside a pyramid of cloth of gold all jewelled over, a domed crown of gold on his head, and in his hand a *rabdos*, or gilded crosier of entwined serpents, which, at a pilgrimage of anticipated cures, seemed not a little suggestive of the staff of the antecedent Aesculapius, Greek god of health...

His Grace of Syra gave a blessing with the icon and preached a sermon to which few listened and only those within a few feet of him could have heard. The sense of finality was already on the festival. When the clergy and their escort later returned toward the hilltop shrine the attention paid them was as nothing compared to the devotion of the crowd to the business of getting back to their boats. It was not later than noon when the vessels began to file out, picking their way among the sailing boats whose lateens were already scattered in all directions like winged gulls foraging over the waters.

Mykonos

1628 Rev. Charles Robson

An Island of Women

At this Mycona we stayed three days by reason of the extremity of weather: a barren island of small extent some fifteen miles in compass, wholly inhabited by poor Greeks, having but one, I cannot tell whether to call it, village or town of the same name with the island, subject to the dominion and spoil of the Turks. In all my life I never saw a place better peopled with women; their number exceeding the number of men five for one: the barrenness of the isle is much helped with the industry of the people, forcing corn out of the rocky mountains, scarce passable for men: yet they continue so poor by reason of the Turk's pillages, that unless they were merry Greeks indeed, any would wonder what delight they could take in living, in continual fear, in continual and extreme necessity.

A Priest who Could Not Read the Bible

Here (as Travellers use to do) the first thing I visited was one of their churches: where by chance I found their Septuagint, and an old man nothing differing in poverty or habit from the rest, there conning his lesson, I took the Bible and red in it; he stood amazed at it, and offering to kiss my hand spoke to me in the common Greek, which is so degenerate from the true and ancient, that there is either none or little affinity betwixt them. I answered in the learned, but I percieved he understood me as much as I did him, which was scarce a word. Then I thinking that though he understood not me he understood the Bible, I spoke my mind to him by pointing out sentences in the Bible, but he understood them as much as he did me. I wondered at this ignorance, and Gods Justice: and relating this story to one of the merchants that had lived some time amongst them at Sio, he told me that none of their Colieroes (priests) but that read the Bible in the learned Greek, their liturgy being in the same, but scarce

Woman of Mykonos
(Baron von Stackelberg, 1825)

425

one of a hundred could understand it. I did not wonder at this, calling to mind the history of our Mass-mumbling priests in Queen Mary's days. In all their churches, fairer then their ordinary houses, scarce either fairer or larger then ours, they have painted, but no carved images.

1680s Bernard Randolph

A Nest of Pirates

Micone keeps its name, lying to the SE of Tine, about twelve miles distant, being nearly forty miles about. It has but one town bearing the name of the island, which is at the NW part, without any fortification. It is a large town, having many Greek churches, and one Latin church, which serves when any privateers come; for here are very few other than the Greek religion. Most of the inhabitants are privateers, who serve with the Legorneses and the Malteses, leaving their women to their own discretion, and the civility of strangers. The chief product of the islands is wine, corn and fruit. The Venetians usually in time of peace come with their ships, and provide themselves with wine. But the greatest of their profit is from privateers. The women here are very beautiful, and want not for husbands. Those who go to sea are the younger sort of their men, and when they have well-stocked themselves with gain, come and spend it here.

This island is very near the road from Constantinople and Egypt, and seldom is it free from privateers. Great complaint has been made to the Port and every year the Capedan Basha did threaten them; but the crafty old men (whom they call the Vecchiardi) used to meet the Basha at Scio, in a sad condition, complaining that they must leave the island in case the Capedan Basha did not allow them a castle and a garrison; pretending that they could not command in their own houses, while the privateers were there; and representing their condition in a most deplorable manner. For several years they prevented the Capedan Basha from coming to visit them, enjoying their time in the best manner they could.

In the year 1680 in the month of September, one Anzelo Maria takes a Saik, which came from Alexandria, very richly laden, which Saik he carries to Micone, where he divided the prize amongst his companions, letting the Reys (or master who was a Greek of Metelino) have his freedom to depart.

The Reys pretended he would go for Venice and to have passage thither he would pass to Tine, telling Anzelo Maria that he had no money to defray his expense, and so desired his charity. Anzelo Maria gave him ten dollars, with which he departed for Tine, where he found a boat ready to sail for Scio, upon which he embarks and arrived next morning. Here he finds the Capedan Basha ready to go for Constantinople. To him he runs, giving him an account of the loss he had sustained from Anzelo Maria, whom he left but two days before at Micone.

No sooner had the Capedan Basha notice, but immediately he gives the signal for departure. About midnight he sails from Scio, and the next day about noon came before Micone. The weather being rainy and thick, he was not seen by the Miconiotes till he was almost in the haven; but comes into the harbour to the south-ward of the town, and immediately landed two thousand Levents (soldiers of the galleys) to take possession of all the boats and other vessels that were in the harbour before the town.

While Anzelo Maria was at dinner with his friends, news was brought to him that the Capedan Basha was arrived at the back side of the town, and had landed his Levents; upon which he immediately went to a point of land where was a small fisher boat, in which he and another man put to sea, and notwithstanding the seas run very high, they passed over to Delos in sight of all the galleys; the wind being so strong as none of the galleys could get out to pursue him, and most thought it impossible he could escape drowning.

We leave him to his fate and come back to Micone, where the scene is strangely altered since morning, when all had their best attire on, singing and dancing in every house. Now they had all unstripped themselves, seeking places to hide their fine clothes, and husbands, whose singing was turned into weeping and wailing. The Vecchiardi were sent for, to whom the Capedan Basha said, "Bring me Anzelo Maria immediately, or I will hang you up at the galley-yard. The Capedan Basha's name was Kaplan Basha; he was a man of great resolution and subject to passion. The Vecchiardi summoned all the inhabitants, ordering the priests to excommunicate all those who should conceal Anzelo Maria, or any of his companions, and not bring them before the Capedan Basha.

Ten of his intimate companions were found and carried aboard the Basha's galleys. None of these knew of Anzelo Maria's escape, nor did value their lives to save his. Most of them were Venetians or Sclavonians. The Basha ordered them to be put in irons till next morning, and that night every house in the town was searched, not a chest but what was emptied and the vaults in the churches opened to look for privateers, so as that night above two hundred men were clapped in irons. The wife of Anzelo Maria and her mother were put in charge of the Kiahja that night. Next morning the Capedan Basha sent again for the Vecchiardi, threatening to hang them if they did not produce Anzelo Maria. They told him that he was certainly got out of the island in a small boat, and without question must have perished in the sea.

Then he ordered the ten men who were comrades of Anzelo Maria to be brought before him. To the first, he said, "Confess if you know where your captain is, and you shall have your liberty. To which he boldly answered: that he knew not, and if he did know, he would sooner lose his life than discover him. Again says the Basha, if you do not discover to me where he is immediately, your head shall be separated from your body. He answered boldly, "I am in your power; you may do with me what you please; and if I might have my choice, I had rather die than be your slave. He was immediately beheaded in the presence of his companions, thereby to terrify them. A second came, to whom the Basha offered as to the first, but he was in the same tune with his companion. Then says the Basha, "Upon my word" (taking his beard in his hand) "if any one of you discover to me where Anzelo Maria is, you shall have your liberties and money to carry you out of the country. But they were all of the first man's resolution. At last the Basha resolved to carry away all their lives, but upon mature reflection, he only condemned them to the galleys.

After these was brought a surgeon who had often cured Anzelo Maria of his wounds. He was laid down and thrashed on the feet with small sticks one hundred blows; then he was brought to the Basha, who ordered the executioner to be present, threatening to have his head taken off if he did not find out Anzelo Maria. The surgeon told him he had not seen him in above three days. He was then laid down again, and received two hundred stripes on the buttocks, two hundred on the belly, and being in a swoon, he was carried away. Thus he was used for three days. I saw him before he was perfectly cured, and from his mouth and several of the Vecchiardi I had this account.

The wife of Anzelo Maria and her mother, to make them confess, were served as follows: They were stripped and put into two pair of Greek breeches, which were drawn up above their knees, the upper part tied above their breasts, and their hands tied up to a post. Into each pair of breeches was put a young kitling, which were beaten with small sticks, which made them leap up and down in the breeches, and exercise their claws upon the women's bodies. Thrice were they thus served.

For a week did the Basha continue in this island, and carried away with him what riches he could find (pretending they belonged to Anzelo Maria) with one hundred young men that had been with the privateers. He threatened the Vecchiardi, that if he heard they had received Anzelo Maria, or suffered the privateers to come upon the island, he would hang every one of them, and make their children slaves.

About a fortnight after the Basha's departure, Anzelo Maria came with six brigantines, ordering his wife to go over to Tine and reside there. The poor Greeks did not presume to oppose him, or any other privateers, so miserable is the condition of this poor people.

1682 George Wheler

Seagoing Women

"The greatest part of the inhabitants are pirates, and this place is a great staple for their prey: here they keep their wives, children and mistresses. The greatest part of the town seems to consist of women; who deservedly have a greater reputation for beauty than chastity; the men being, most of them, abroad seeking their fortune. Our captain had here a seraglio of them when he was a corsair in these seas, as I before mentioned. But those being now antedated, he was for new game at his coming hither; and therefore found out a pretty young virgin for his mistress, which he bought of her brutal father, as provision for his voyage to Constantinople.

The history of the taking her I will not let pass without relating it, because I was by accident at the rape of this fair Helena. The admiral of our little fleet, unexpectedly hoisting sail, before he had brought her aboard, he sent his long boat to fetch her away, by some of his trusty servants: I having left something ashore where I lodged, begged leave of the captain to go with the boat; which I obtained with some difficulty, not imagining the reason of their putting ashore at that time. They went straight to the captain's house, while I went to fetch my things: when I returned back to them I found them very merry, drinking with some other women the captain had formerly kept; and also some pirates, who had been of the captain's comrades, esteemed stout men. One, I remember, was extremely civil to me, and offered me many favours, I knew not how to accept of; and withal assured me, that if he had the fortune to meet me at sea, that he would treat me with all civility imaginable; for which I thanked him, hoping never to have any need of his kindness.

Those sent by the captain went straight to the house of this young one; who with weeping and great seeming unwillingness, suffered herself to be carried to the boat; whilst her mother put the rest of the town in an uproar; who in multitudes followed her to the waterside. The mother stood raging on the shore as if she had not known what her husband had done; whilst some stood to look, and others (I judge) to be looked on: for along the shore I believe, above a hundred girls, from ten or eleven to fourteen or fifteen years old, stood with their coats as high as their middle (I guess to signify that they were ready to accompany her, so soon as the occasion offered).

Thus she was conveyed aboard, and a cabin built for her, where the captain could retire to her himself, and oblige the rest of his friends. He kept the next day a feast, inviting the officers to his nuptials, and had her dressed in a very fine Venetian habit.

1718 Joseph Pitton de Tournefort

A Persistent Vampire

We were present at a very different Scene, and one very barbarous, in the same Island, which happened upon occasion of one of those Corpses, which they fancy come to life again after their interment. The Man whose Story we are going to relate, was a Peasant of Mycone, naturally ill-natured and quarrelsome; this is a Circumstance to be taken notice of in such cases: he was murdered in the fields, no body knew how, or by whom. Two days after his being buried in a Chapel in the Town it was noised about that he was seen to walk in the night with great haste, that he tumbled about Peoples Goods, put out their Lamps, griped them behind and a thousand other monkey Tricks. At first the Story was received with Laughter; but the thing was looked upon to be Serious, when the better sort of People began to complain of it; the Papas themselves gave credit to the Fact, and no doubt had their reasons for so doing; Masses must be said, to be sure: but for all this, the Peasant drove his old trade, and heeded nothing they could do. After diverse meetings of the chief People of the City, or Priests and Monks, it was gravely concluded, that 'twas necessary, in consequence of some musty Ceremonial, to wait till nine days after the Interment should be expired.

On the tenth day they said one Mass in the Chapel where the Body was laid, in order to drive out the Demon which they imagined was got into it. After Mass, they took up the Body, and got every thing ready for pulling out its Heart. The butcher of the town, an old clumsy fellow, first opens the belly instead of the breast: he groped a long while among the entrails, but could not find what he looked for; at last somebody told him he should cut up the diaphragm. The heart was pulled out, to the admiration of all the spectators. In the mean time, the corpse stunk so abominably, that they were obliged to burn frankincense; but this smoke mixing with the exhalations from the carcass, increased the Stink, and began to muddle the poor peoples' pericranies. Their imagination, struck with the spectacle before them, grew full of visions. It came into their noddles, that a thick smoke arose out of the body; we durst not say it was the smoke of the incense. They were incessantly bawling out "Vroucalacas!" in the chapel and place before it: this is the name they give to these pretended redivivi. The noise bellowed through the streets, and it seemed to be a name invented on purpose to rend the roof of the chapel. Several there present averred, that the wretch's blood was extremely red: the butcher swore the body was still warm; whence they concluded, that the deceased was a very ill man for not being thoroughly dead, or in plain terms for suffering himself to be reanimated by Old Nick; which is the notion they have of a vroucolacas. They then roared out that name in a stupendous manner. Just at this time came in a flock of people, loudly protesting they plainly perceived the body was not grown stiff, when it was carried from the fields to church to be buried, and that consequently it was a true Vroucolacas; which word was still the burden of the song.

I don't doubt they would have sworn it did not stink, had we not been there; so amazed were the poor people with this disaster, and so infatuated with their notion of the dead's being reanimated. As for us who got as close to the corpse as we could, that we might be more exact in our observations, we were almost poisoned with the intolerable stink that issued from it. When they asked us what we thought of this body, we told them we believed it to be very thoroughly dead: but as we were willing to cure, or at least not to exasperate their prejudiced imaginations, we represented to them, that it was no wonder the butcher should feel a little warmth when he groped among the entrails that were then rotting; that it was no extraordinary thing for it to emit fumes, since dung turned up will do the same; that as for the pretended redness of the blood, it still appeared by the butcher's Hands to be nothing but a very stinking nasty smear.

After all our reasons, they were of opinion it would be their wisest course to burn the dead man's heart on the seashore: but this execution did not make him a bit more tractable; he went on with his racket more furiously than ever: he was accused of beating folks in the night, breaking down doors, and even roofs of houses; clattering windows; tearing clothes; emptying bottles and vessels. 'Twas a most thirsty devil! I believe he did not spare any body but the consul in whose house we lodged. Nothing could be more miserable than the condition of this island; all the inhabitants seemed frighted out of their senses; the wisest among them were stricken like the rest: 'twas an epidemical disease of the brain, as dangerous and infectious as the madness of dogs. Whole families quitted their houses, and brought their tent-beds from the farthest parts of town into the public place, there to spend the night. They were every instant complaining of some new insult; nothing was to be heard but sighs and groans at the approach of night: the better sort of people retired into the country.

When the prepossession was so general, we thought it our best way to hold our tongues. Had we opposed it, we had not only been accounted ridiculous blockheads, but atheists and infidels. How was it possible to stand against a madness of a whole people? Those that believed we doubted the truth of the fact, came and upbraided us with our incredulity, and strove to prove that there were such things as vroucolacasses, by citations out of the *Buckler of Faith*, written by F. Richard a Jesuit missionary. He was a Latin, say they, and consequently you ought to give him credit. We should have got nothing by denying the justness of the consequence: it was as good a comedy to us every morning, to hear the new follies committed by this night-bird; they charged him with being guilty of the most abominable sins.

Some citizens, that were zealous for the good of the public, fancied they had been deficient in the most material part of the ceremony. They were of opinion, that they had been wrong in saying Mass before they had pulled out the wretch's heart: had we taken this precaution, quoth they, we had bit the devil, as sure as a gun; he would have been hanged before he would ever have come there again: whereas saying mass first, the cunning dog fled it for a while, and came back again when the danger was over.

Notwithstanding these wise reflections, they remained in as much perplexity as they were the first day: they meet night and morning, they debate, they make processions three days and three nights; they oblige the papas to fast; you might see them running from house to house, holy-water-brush in hand, sprinkling it all about, and washing the doors with it; nay, they poured it into the mouth of the poor vroucolacas.

We so often repeated it to the magistrates of the town, that in Christendom we should keep the strictest watch a-nights upon such an occasion, to observe what was done; that at last they caught a few vagabonds, who undoubtedly had a hand in these disorders: but either they were not the chief ringleaders, or else they were released too soon. For two days afterwards, to make themselves amends for the Lent they had kept in prison, they fell foul again upon the wine-tubs of those who were such fools as to leave their houses empty in the night: so that the people were forced to betake themselves again to their prayers.

One day, as they were hard at this work, after having stuck I know not how many naked swords over the grave of this corpse, which they took up three or four times a day, for any man's whim; an Albaneze that happened to be at Mycone, took upon him to say with a voice of authority, that it was to the last degree ridiculous to make use of the swords of Christians in a case like this. Can you not conceive, blind as ye are, says he, that the handles of these swords, being made like a cross, hinders the devil from coming out of the body? Why do you not rather take the Turkish sabres? The advice of this learned man had no effect: the vroucolacas was incorrigible, and all the inhabitants were in a strange consternation; they knew not now what saint to call upon, when of a sudden with one voice, as if they had given each other the hint, they fell to bawling out all through the city, that it was intolerable to wait any longer; that the only way left was to burn the vroucolacas entire; that after so doing, let the devil lurk in it if he could; that 'twas better to have recourse to this extremity, than to have the island totally deserted. And indeed whole families began to pack up, in order to retire to Syra or Tinos. The magistrates therefore ordered the vroucolacas to be carried to the point of the island St. George, where they prepared a great pile with pitch and tar, for fear the wood, as dry as it was, should not burn fast enough of itself. What they had before left of this miserable carcass was thrown into this fire, and consumed presently. It was on the first of January 1701. We saw the flame as we returned from Delos. It might justly be called a bonfire of joy, since after this no more complaints were heard against the vroucolacas; they said that the devil had now met with his match, and some ballads were made to turn him into ridicule.

All over the Archipelago they are persuaded, that only the Greeks of the Grecian rite have their carcasses reanimated by the devil: the inhabitants of the island of Santorini are terribly afraid of these bulbeggars. Those of Mycone, after their visions were clearly dispersed, began to be equally apprehensive of the prosecutions of the Turks and those of the bishop of Tinos. Not one papas would be at St. George when the Body was burnt, for fear the bishop should exact a sum of money of them, for taking up and burning a corpse without permission from him. As for the Turks, it is certain that at their next visit they made the community of Mycone pay dear for their cruelty to this poor rogue, who became in every respect the abomination and horror of his countrymen. After such an instance of folly, can we refuse to own that the present Greeks are no great Grecians; and that there is nothing but ignorance and superstition among them?"

The Practice of Medicine

The physicians all over the Levant, are generally Jews or natives of Candia, old nurselings of Padua, who dare purge none but such as are upon the mending hand. The whole science of the Orientals, in matters of distempers, consists in giving fat broths to such as are in a fever, and in reducing their diet to next to nothing; that is to say, for the first fifteen or sixteen days of a continual fever, happen what will, they will not suffer the patient to take anything but a slender panade twice a day, or two doses of rice-water. These panadoes are bread crumbed, and boiled in broth not made of flesh meat: they let a certain quantity of crumb of bread soak in warm water, and then boil this water till the crumb is almost dissolved; sometimes they add a little sugar at last. This food agrees better with the constitution of Carthusian monks than laymen, who must be blooded or purged at certain times, in order to prevent such accidents; as without such precaution would be the death of them. Thus fares it with these poor Greeks, whom the slightest fever (with their way of managing) reduces to skin and bones, and they are whole years in recovering. Hippocrates, the learnedest of all the Greek physicians, has reason good to condemn this outrageous way of dieting, and prescribes purgatives as soon as ever the symptoms sufficiently appear.

If the patient grows light-headed, he is presently looked upon as possessed by the devil; the physicians and surgeons are strait dismissed, and the papas sent for; who after they have extolled the sage conduct of his parents, fall to repeating I know not what prayers, and almost drown the patient with holy water: and so torment him with exorcisms that, instead of abating his deliriousness, they add to it. At Mycone they called us madmen, for proposing to the relations of a woman of quality to have her blooded in the foot, to settle her head. The Papas were going to ring us a peal: What could we say to people that won't hear reason? Not content with splitting her brains two or three days under pretence of driving the Devil out of her body *nolens volens*, they carried the poor woman to Church, and threatened to bury her quick, if she did not declare the name of the demon that possessed her; could we but learn his name, quoth they, we'd soon make him know his Lord God from Tom Bell. For want of this, they were sadly at a nonplus, for they knew not how to speak to him. The papas were in a muck-sweat upon it, and as uneasy as if they trod upon thorns: at length the sick party, whose distemper was a most malignant fever made her exist in such strong convulsions, as frightened everybody. The whole art of the papas terminated in making the bystanders sensible of the violence of the conflict between the devil and the patient, who for not making a vigorous defence, these doctors said should not be put in consecrated ground; and accordingly they carried her from the church to the country, whereas others are brought from the country to the church. Whenever any one recovers after so tragical a scene, the people cry a miracle, and the papas go for wonder-workers.

1738 Lord Sandwich

Some Particularly Insulting Observations about the Islanders

Having passed time, we soon came to anchor in the road of Mycone, which defended us from the rage of a violent northerly wind, and it detained us here for the space of ten days. This isle has preserved its ancient name uncorrupted to this day; and is at present in greater prosperity than when Greece flourished. The inhabitants of it being in those times famous only for their poverty, and address in insinuating themselves to great men's tables, which rendered the name of Myconian almost synonymous with parasite…

It has at present no more than one village, situated near the seashore, the inhabitants of which are in pretty good circumstances, which is entirely due to their own industry; they being reputed the best sailors of all the Archipelago, and owning several vessels of burden, with which they carry on a very advantageous trade. In the village you will meet with above five women to one man, they being most of them employed in the ships, which seldom lie idle, especially in the summer; at which time there is to be seen in Mycone scarce anything but old men, women, children and fat hogs.

1746 Lord Charlemont

Temporary marriages

In many of the smaller islands, as well as in this of Micone, the following singular custom is commonly practised… If a stranger should wish to enjoy anyone of the young unmarried women, he addresses himself immediately to her parents, and demands the girl in marriage. The bargain is presently struck, and the couple are brought before a magistrate, where they swear mutual fidelity during the man's residence in the island, the bridegroom engaging himself to pay at his departure a great sum of money, as well as a present advance, and, in case the lady should prove with child, a still larger sum. This money is set apart in the girl's portion, and with this, upon the departure of her consort, she soon procures herself a real husband among her countrymen, who esteem her not a whit the less for this previous connection, deeming her a widow to all intents and purposes. The parents warrant the damsel to be a maid, and the price is fixed according to her beauty and accomplishments, being seldom however less than one hundred sequins, about fifty pounds, a sum large enough to preclude travellers from profiting as much as they would wish of this convenient institution, as the short stay they usually make at each of the islands would by the frequency of its repetition, render this species of gallantry rather too expensive, especially as these islands, in which it is practised, are unluckily, in every other respect, the least worthy of a traveller's notice...

...Wheler informs us that in his time the greater part of the inhabitants of Micone were pirates, and that this island was one great staple for their prey; that there they kept their wives, children, and mistresses, and he goes on to relate how the Captain of the ship, on board which he then was, purchased here a girl from her father as a provision for his voyage to Constantinople. Now it appears to me by no means improbable that these corsairs have left behind them some traces of their manners, and that the custom above mentioned may be derived from that system of life which they had established. Indeed this island, as well as many of the smaller islands in the Archipelago, is still much molested by pirates, who, as we may naturally suppose, being now what they ever have been, a set of dissolute wretches, carefully keep up a usage so well suited to their manners, and prevent any possibility of the people being reclaimed. It must however be allowed that the women of Micone are in general very handsome, in spite of their monstrous dress, which is, if possible, still uglier than any we have yet seen... They are moreover, in comparison with their circumstances, very expensive in this article.

1789 "An Italian Gentleman"

An Early Reference to Plate Smashing

We passed a large house in which we heard a great noise, and from which the people within were throwing plates through the windows. We asked if it were a mad house, and were told that it was the place of the archon, that is, of a prince, for this is the title still assumed by the richest and noblest of the Greeks); and that they were making merry, which occasioned the noise; and that at these feasts archons are accustomed to break plates as a proof of their magnificence.

1809-10 John Galt

The Island of Poetesses

In this island the women are undoubtedly the superior sex. Their complexion if of an English fairness, and many of them are very beautiful. But it is in their intelligence and address that their superiority consists. They not only possess a persuasive eloquence of manner, highly interesting, but are habituated to close reasoning, and the discussion of matters of business. In legal disputes among their husbands, they are the advocates before the magistrates; and I am told that there are women in the town, who, on important occasions, have displayed wonderful powers, of argument and illustration. They are almost universally improvisatorè; and in their occasional dirges at funerals, often display a felicity of conception that would do credit to studied efforts. I have myself been a witness to their, performance in this way, and had the good fortune to obtain an accurate explanation of their expressions, as they occurred. A young woman, who was much esteemed in the town, died in childbed and her female acquaintances, to the number of several hundreds, all dressed in their gayest apparel, attended the funeral. While the corpse was conveying to the church, a chorus sang, in praise of the beauty and good qualities of the deceased. One began the verse; another, at the pause, took up the strain; and when a stanza was thus finished by several, the whole singers repeated it together. The' young woman's mother was in the- procession, and her distress excited universal pity. One of the singers exclaimed: "She embraced her child, and died of the joy of being a mother." The mother, taking up the verse, cried, "O my Child! my child! where is now the joy of her that was thine!" This simple and pathetic apostrophe produced an effect that can only be imagined, not described. After the obsequies, all the women returned to the house, and began their regular dirge. Unlike poetesses in general; the women of Myconos are very good housewives, and remarkably industrious. They knit large quantities of stockings, which they send as adventures with their relations and husbands to the markets of Smyrna, Constantinople, and, during peace, even as far as the Russian ports of the Black Sea.

A Disputed Abbatial Election

I must now let you into a secret. The abbess is always chosen from the poorer sisterhood, that she may not have presumption enough to infringe the freedom of the superiors. Sister Theophila is in figure the reverse of her brother, being a tall, manly-looking woman, a very Hecate, and as I have said, a great humorist. On our arrival at the convent, she informed us that there were strong symptoms of a schism in the conclave. The nun pitched upon by Sister Theopila was declared, by one party, to be a simpleton; and they were resolved to call to the vacant dignity another who possessed more energy of mind, and who was better suited to the exigencies of the times. But the sister was resolute, and expressed her determination to carry the business through with a high hand. This assurance was highly satisfactory to the secular powers. To me it was delightful, and I became greatly interested in the result. On returning to the monastery we found On our arrival we found sister Theophiphila all in a bustle, preparing with the assistance of two of her nieces, very pretty girls, lemonades and sweetmeats to regale the bishop and the visitors. Every other moment she suspended her labour to tell us what an arduous task she was engaged in with the schismatics, who were resolved on extremities. In the midst of her discourse notice was given that the bishop was coming: she instantly went to receive him, and all the nuns being summoned to attend, they were drawn up in equal rows at each side of the portal, Sister Theophila standing majestically on the steps. The bishop was seen, coming up the hill: before him a priest carried the pastoral staff, and a gaily dressed train of seculars followed. Among the train I happened to observe several country lads with tall sticks in the one hand, and large nosegays in the other; and I was just beginning to philosophize on the generality of the taste of all bumpkins for tall sticks and large nosegays, when one of the nuns ran from the ranks, and prostrated herself on the ground before the bishop's horse. In less than the time of an amen sister Theophila also darted forward, seized the nun by the arm, and giving her three most undignified thumps on the back, flung her off to a distance. It was exceedingly provoking to the sister to see all her arrangements thus destroyed. Matters were however irretrievable - order was gone - and the bishop was received in a tumultuous manner, and amidst profane shouts of laughter. The poor nun, it seems, is a little crazy, and the marvellous splendour of the bishop's appearance, had transported her to this untimely display of zeal.

The bishop, having alighted, walked to the church. The nuns successively came forward, and kneeling with their foreheads to the ground, kissed his feet. The two contending parties then presented their respective candidates. A dispute ensued, which sister Theophila ended by seizing her opponent's arm, and pulling her from the presence of the bishop, in manifest violation, however, of the freedom of election. The bishop being in the secret, immediately accepted the candidate chosen by our party, and entered the church to consecrate her. But when summoned, to appear she was not forthcoming. Dreading a turbulent reign, she shrank from the offered dignity. But our leader was not about to be trifled with. Bouncing from her stall, she grasped her protegèe by the hand, and compelled her to receive the benediction. The nuns then one by one, knelt before the new abbess, and proffered their obedience and allegiance. The leader of the opposition being still somewhat refractory, instead of kneeling, began to remonstrate something like a protest against the proceedings, which sister Theophila; with her characteristic promptitude and decision, cut short, by giving her a push on the back of the neck that laid her reverentially at the feet of the abbess.

In less than half an hour after the consecration, order was restored to the sisterhood; we enjoyed lemonade and sweetmeats in tranquillity: the nuns resumed their knitting, and I have since heard that the schism, is now entirely healed.

1828 Henry A. V. Post

A Tendency to Baldness

Mykone is in general an extremely arid island, and contains a great deal of uncultivated land; it yields however an abundance of barley, figs, and wine, and with respect to the latter, sustains the reputation which it anciently enjoyed. The quantity usually produced at the beginning of the last century was from twenty-five to thirty thousand barrels a year. The island abounds with partridges, quails, woodcock, and a variety of other birds. From some unknown cause it is still remarkable, as in ancient times, for the early age at which the inhabitants become bald. The town is about as well built as many of the small towns of France and Italy, and contains at present a population of five or six thousand souls, of whom the greater part of the men have their home upon the seas. Its convenient situation, lying, as it does, upon the great thoroughfare of the Archipelago, rendered piracies at one time very frequent in its neighbourhood, when so many of its mariners were thrown out of employ by the sudden interruption of trade consequent upon the breaking out of the revolution. The security of commerce was however in a great measure restored in the Tenos and Mykone passage, as it is called, by the energetic measures resorted to by Capt. Hamilton of H. B. M. frigate *Cambrian*, and Capt. Kearney of the US sloop of war *Warren*. The latter, by his prompt and spirited interference, succeeded in, recovering the cargo of the American brig *Cherub*, which was robbed in the vicinity in the year 1827.

Delos

1627 Sir Kenelm Digby

The Thirst for Marbles

With half my ship went to Delphos, which is a very good port, and there I spent my time taking in some marble stones and statues. ..Because idleness should not fix their minds upon any untamed fancies (as is usual among seamen), and together to avail myself of the convenience of carrying away some antiquities there, I busied them in rolling of stones down to the seaside, which they did with such eagerness as though it had been the earnestest business that they came out for, and they mastered prodigious massy weights: but one stone, the greatest and fairest of all, containing four statues, they gave over after they had been, three hundred men, a whole day about it.

1674 Father Jacques-Paul Babin, S.J.

Open House

The ruins are carried away by all ships who come to anchor there, so as part are in England, France, Holland, but most at Venice.

Statue of Apollo, Delos (S. Devries, 1673)

Amorgos

1718 Joseph Pitton de Tournefort

The Cliff-Face Monastery

The best places in Amorgos belong to the Monastery of the Virgin, whither they come from afar to assist at mass; for all extraordinary situations strike devotion into the populace. Three miles from the burgh, at the edge of the sea, is built a large house, which at a distance resembles a chest of drawers fixed towards the bottom of a hideous rock, naturally perpendicular, and exceeding in height that of La Sainte Baume in Provence. The chest of drawers does however afford convenient lodging to a hundred caloyers; but there is no entering it without very good recommendation, and by a small opening contrived in one of the corners of the building, the door of it covered with iron plates. Within is a guardroom furnished with huge wooden clubs like that of Hercules, fit to knock down an ox at a blow: there did not seem to be much need of this precaution; for with a kick of a foot they might easily turn off a man from the top of the ladder by which they ascend to this door. The ladder has a dozen wooden rounds, without reckoning some stone steps against which it rests. After this, you pass up a very narrow staircase; but neither the cells nor the chapel are cut in the rock, as hath been reported. The religious assured us that their house was built by the Emperor Comnenius, who likewise handsomely endowed it; I am not slack to believe as much; Anne Comnenius, his daughter, takes notice that the mother of that Prince had caused him to be bred up in a monastery till the day of his marriage.

Those of Amorgos give out, that this foundation was occasioned by a miraculous image of the Virgin painted on wood, which they keep in their chapel for a mighty relic; pretending that this image being profaned in the isle of Cyprus, and broke in two pieces, was conveyed in a supernatural manner by sea to the foot, of the rock of Amorgos, where the two pieces joined themselves again; that the same hath wrought, and does still work, divers miracles. The image seemed to us to be altogether smoke-dried, and of a very imperfect design: the caloyers that keep it, are very slovenly; their house has the savour of a nasty guardroom, and this convent looks more like a harbouring-place for highwaymen, than a religious retreat. As there is no departing handsomely from a monastery without bestowing something by way of benefaction, we dropped them a few pieces, and the monks regaled us with a plate of grapes, the bunches whereof were about a foot long; each berry almost oval, fifteen or eighteen lines long, whitish green, exceeding sweet, and of an exquisite taste. This convent having nothing about it but the sea and frightful rocks, I could not forbear asking the monks whence they had such fine fruit; they answered, from another part of the island near a chapel where was preserved that famed urn which at a certain time of the year fills itself with water, and then empties itself again.

A Modern Oracle

For many visitors the chief curiosity of the island was a still-functioning oracle.

Christianity has not altered the fabulous disposition of the Greeks. On the morrow we went to the chapel, to satisfy ourselves concerning this prodigy, and to eat of those fine grapes. St. George Balsami, so is the chapel called, is four miles off the town, on the left of the West Port, close to an orchard of fruit trees terraced, at the further end of a kitchen-garden watered with a small spring, among a parcel of cultivated vineyards: a charming abode, as we thought, for a papas. Though the chapel is no more than fifteen foot long, and ten broad, yet it is divided into three naves with good walls, as if it were a large church; but the side-naves are so narrow, that but one person can pass in front. You enter the chapel by a corner of the nave on the left, and we presently spying a spring of water over against the door; judged that this pretended miracle was not difficult to be explained. This spring, which is a very little one, is restrained in a conservatory five foot four inches long, two foot eight inches broad; the water was not then above a foot deep. Six paces from it, below a closet wrought in the same nave, is buried, even with the surface of the earth, the so much celebrated urn, which is consulted as the oracle of the archipelago. It is a vessel of marble almost oval, about two foot high, sixteen inches broad; the opening of it, which is round, and eight inches diameter, is covered with a piece of wood fastened by an iron bar placed crosswise.

The closet is more carefully shut, and they never open it till you have given them some money towards saying masses. We were not short in our respects of that kind, and so had the pleasure to see the urn uncovered and to measure the water, which was seven inches nine lines deep: but they would not let us search further, nor examine the bottom of the urn, which is covered with mud. The papas only told us it was the ordinary depth of the water: we prayed him then to explain to us the secret of this mighty miracle. It consists, said he, in that the water rises and sinks several times in the year. 'Twas answered, that the overplus of the conservatory, which is close to it, might more or less pass through the earth, and be insensibly imbibed by that marble, which was no more than an inch thick, and perhaps cracked at the bottom. This place is very dark, and the urn must be emptied e'er it can be well searched into; for Father Richard asserts, that the bottom of this vessel is nothing but white clay. The papas thought it enough to tell us it was a great miracle.

We desired him to tell us, whether 'twas true that the urn was filled sometimes in the space of half an hour, and emptied itself visibly several times a day in the same space; whether it was true, that in a moment it was so full as to run over, and the next moment so dry, as if there never had been a drop of water in it. The good man, distrusting us, and not being so great a fool as he seemed to be, answered, that we needed but to tarry a little time to have ocular demonstration; that as for himself; he had never seen it either quite full or quite empty, but that it was the effect of a miracle, and of the virtue of the great St. George; that such as came to consult the urn, before they undertook any business of importance, miscarried if the water was lower than usual; that as for us, we ought to rejoice it was otherwise when we came. We tarried about two hours in the neighbourhood of the chapel, to make draughts of plants or eat grapes; detaching from time to time some one of us, with a wax-candle in hand, to go and see whether the water rose or fell: but it constantly answered our plumbline, which was a stick gauged a seven inches nine lines deep. In fine, we thought we could not do better than abide by the explication given us of it by our servant; he was a lad of good sense, and perceiving we were under some perplexity concerning this mystery, without recurring to the transpiration of the water through the earth and marble, without naming St. George or the Virgin Mary, told us with great indifference that the pappas, to make his own pot boil, had the art to empty and fill this urn out of the conservatory, with his pot-ladle, whenever he met with such as were willing to be imposed on, as are for the greatest part those who hunt after miraculous things.

This blunt speech made laugh. We took our leaves of the pappas, who judging by our behaviour that we wanted faith concerning the urn, came in haste after us, to tell us a convincing story of it.: A certain Greek bishop, said he, with his pockets full of gold, was going to Constantinople, to purchase some more considerable dignity, and by the way had a mind first to consult the urn, as to the success of his voyage, but he found it almost empty. Mortified at this, he spent four or five days in prayer and lamentation: the papas seeing him so dispirited piously resolved to pour a good pot-full of water into the urn, but to his own great surprise, when he brought the bishop to visit it, he found the water just as low as before. They redoubled prayers to the great St. George; nay, they went to the principal convent, to conjure the Panagia to send water. Would ye think it, gentlemen, (continued our pappas with an air of assurance) the water one fine morning was found there in great plenty. The bishop departed, after returning a thousand thanks, and was no sooner arrived at Paros, than he was informed to his exceeding great comfort, that while he was at Amorgos, that is, while there was a failure of the water, the sea was covered with corsairs; who meeting with no prize, had sailed away, some to the Morea, others towards the Gulf of Thessaloniki. Furthermore, added he, our holy urn favours the privateers, whether they be Christians or barbarians. They make us mad when they come to consult the great St. George, who is the true general of the heavenly militia and not St. Michael of Serpho, as is pretended by the caloyers of that island After this fine discourse, which we made no other reply to than bowing our heads, we took our leaves, very well satisfied with each other: the papas, that he had related to us his story, and we with discovering the frauds of the monks, and the credulity of the people who are thus abused in all the countries of ignorance and superstition.

An Alarm

As we were going in search of samples, to our great surprise we saw our sailors coming down front the mountains, so scared that they knew not whether their saik was carried off by Maltese, Barbarees or banditti. This adventure concerned us a little: but we soon learnt at the consul's house, that the vessel was in the port, that the seamen had quitted it to get ashore, at sight of one of M. Cintray's galliots; and that in short, M. Tourtin, who commanded it, being informed the goods on board belonged to Frenchmen, set it at liberty .One is subject to these petty alarms in the Archipelago, where one can't pass from one isle to another but in boats with two or four oars, which never go except in calm weather. It would be still worse to make use of large vessels, which, though they are secure from the banditti, yet they wear out one's patience in staying for a wind.

These banditti, who are dreaded in all parts of the Archipelago, are a parcel of villains, who are forced by indigence to lay hold on the first vessel they light of, and lie in wait for others at the turn of some cape, or in some creek. These wretches, not content with plundering people, throw 'em overboard with a stone about their necks, for fear of being seized, upon the complaints of those they have ill used. We understood afterwards, that M. de Cintra had made a prize of two vessels belonging to these banditti who were carrying off a ship laden with timber, and eighteen Turkish passengers.

1883-4 James Theodore Bent

Easter on Amorgos

I do not propose to narrate the usual routine of a Greek Easter-the breaking of the long fast, the elaborately decorated lambs to be slaughtered for the meal, the nocturnal services, and the friendly greetings; of these everybody knows enough – but I shall confine myself to what is peculiar to Amorgos, and open my narrative on a lovely Easter morning, when all the world were in their festival attire, ready to participate in the first day's programme.

First of all I must take the reader to visit a convent dedicated to the life-saving Virgin, the wonder of Amorgos. It is the wealthiest convent in Greece next to Megaspelaion, having all the richest lands in Amorgos, and the neighbouring islands of Skinousa and Karos belong exclusively to it, besides possessions in Crete, in the Turkish islands, and elsewhere. The position chosen for this convent is most extraordinary. A long line of cliff, about two miles from the town, runs sheer down 1,000 feet into the sea; a narrow road, or ledge, along the coast leads along this cliff to the convent, which is built halfway up. Nothing but the outer wall is visible as you approach. The church and cells are made inside the rock. The whole, as Tournefort aptly expresses it, resembles a chest of drawers. This convent was founded by the Byzantine emperor Alexius Comnenus, whose picture existed until lately, but they suffer here frequently from rocks which fall from above, one of which fell not long ago and broke into the apse of the church and destroyed the picture of the emperor.

We entered by a drawbridge, with fortifications against pirates, and were shown into the reception room, where the superior, a brother of the member for Santorin, met us, and conducted us to the cells in the rock above, to the large storehouses below, and to the narrow church, with its five magnificent silver pictures, three of which were to be the object of such extraordinary veneration during Easter week.

The position of this convent is truly awful. From the balconies one looks deep down into the sea, and overhead towers the red rock, blackened for some distance by the smoke of the convent fires; here and there are dotted holes in the rock where hermits used to dwell in almost inaccessible eyries. It is, geographically speaking, the natural frontier of Greece. Not twenty miles off we could see from the balcony the Turkish islands, and beyond them the coast of Asia Minor. In fact the Turkish island of Astypalaea seems scarcely five miles away. The Greeks say it ought to belong to them, but when the boundary line was drawn by the representatives of the Powers in conference, they had such a bad map before them that it was assigned to Turkey. Our friendly monks looked too sleepy and wanting in energy to think of suicide, otherwise every advantage would here be within their reach.

Three of the five silver ikons in the church were to be the object of our veneration for seven days to come. One adorns a portrait of the Madonna herself, found, they say, by some sailors in the sea below, in two pieces, in which condition it was washed all the way from Cyprus, having been treated profanely there. It is beautifully embossed with silver and gold, as are also the other ikons. This fashion of fulfilling a vow by putting a silver arm or limb on a sacred picture has had a bad effect on the general appearance, and reminds us of the statue mentioned by Lucian which Eucrates had in his house, and had gilded the breast as a thank offering for recovery from a fever. A second is of St. George Balsamitis, the patron saint of the prophetic source Amorgos, of which more anon; and another is an iron cross, set in silver, and found, they say, on the heights of Mount Krytelos, a desolate mountain to the north of Amorgos, only visited by peasants, who go there to cut down the prickly evergreen oak which covers it, as fodder for their mules.

We were up and about early on Easter morning; the clanging of bells and the bustle beneath our windows made it impossible to sleep. Papa Demetrios came in, dressed exceedingly smartly in his best canonicals, to give us the Easter greeting. Even the demarch was more condescending to his wife today. At nine o'clock we and all the world started forth on our pilgrimage to meet the holy icons from the convent. The place of meeting was only a quarter of a mile from the town at the top of the steep cliff, and here all the inhabitants of the island from the villages far and near were assembled to do reverence.

I was puzzled as to what could be the meaning of three round circles, like threshing floors, left empty in the midst of the assemblage. All round were spread gay rugs and carpets and rich brocades; everyone seemed subdued by a sort of reverential awe. Demetrios and two other chosen priests, together with their acolytes, set forth along the narrow road to the convent to fetch the icons, for no monk is allowed to participate in this great ceremony. They must stop in their cells and pray; it would never do for them to be contaminated by the pomps and vanities of so gay a throng. So at the convent door, year after year at Easter time the superior hands over to the three priests the three most precious icons, to be worshipped for a week. A standard led the way, the iron cross on a staff followed, two icons came next, and as they wended their by the narrow path along the sea the priests and their acolytes chanted monotonous music of praise. The crowd was now in breathless excitement as they were seen to approach, and as the three treasures were set up in the three threshing-floors everybody prostrated himself on his carpet and worshipped. It was the great panegyris of Amorgos, and of the 5,000 inhabitants of the island not one who was able to come was absent.

It was an impressive sight to look upon. Steep mountains on either side, below at a giddy depth the blue sea, and all around the fanatical islanders were lying prostrate in prayer, wrought to the highest pitch of religious fanaticism.

Amidst the firing of guns and ringing of bells the ikons were then conveyed into the town to the Church of Christ, a convent and church belonging to the monks of Chozobiotissa, and kept in readiness for them when business or dissipation summoned them to leave their cave retreat. Here vespers were sung in the presence of a crowded audience, and the first event of the feast was over.

Elsewhere in Greece on Easter Day dancing would naturally ensue, but out of reverence to their guests no festivities are allowed of a frivolous nature, and everyone walks to and fro with a religious awe upon him.

The Oracle in the Late Nineteenth Century

By the time that Theodore Bent arrived on Amorgos, the method by which the oracle was divined seems to have changed.

On entering the narthex Papa Anatolios still demurred much about opening the oracle for me, fearing that I intended to scoff; but at length I prevailed upon him, and he put on his purple stole, and went hurriedly through the liturgy to St. George before the altar. After this he took a tumbler, which he asked me carefully to inspect, and on my expressing my satisfaction as to its cleanness he proceeded to unlock a little chapel on the right side of the narthex with mysterious gratings all round, and adorned inside and out with frescoes of the Byzantine School.

Here was the sacred stream, the *agiasma* , which flows into a marble basin, carefully kept clean with a sponge at hand lest any extraneous matter should by chance get in. Thereupon he filled the tumbler and went to examine its contents in the sun's rays with a microscope, that he might read my destiny .He then returned to the steps of the altar and solemnly delivered his oracle."

Syros

1801 Edward Daniel Clarke

The Well as a Social Centre

The modern town of Syra probably occupies the site of the ancient Acropolis. The island has always been renowned for the advantages it enjoys, in the excellence of its port, in its salubrity, and its fertility. It is on this account extolled by Homer. It produces wine, figs, cotton, barley, and also wheat, although not so plentifully as barley. We saw an abundance of poultry, and a very fine breed of pigs; but the streets of the town are as dirty and narrow as they probably were in the days of Homer. If the ancient Persians have been characteristically described as the worshippers of fire, the inhabitants of Syra, both ancient and modern, may be considered as the worshippers of Homer. The old fountain, at which the nymphs of the island assembled in the earliest ages, exists in its original state; the same rendezvous as it was formerly, whether or love and gallantry, or of gossiping and tale-telling. It is near to the town, and the most limpid water gushes continually from the solid rock. It is regarded by the inhabitants with a degree of religious veneration; and they preserve a tradition that the pilgrims of old time, in their way to Delos, resorted hither for purification. We ... saw, however, a pleasing procession, formed by the young women of the island, coming with songs, and carrying their pitchers of water on their heads, from this fountain. Here they are met by their lovers, who relieve them from their burdens, and bear a part in the general chorus. It is also the scene of their dances, and therefore the favourite rendezvous of the youth of both sexes. The Eleusinian women practised a dance about a well which was called Callichorus, and their dance was also accompanied by songs in honour of Ceres. These "Songs of the well" are still sung in other parts of Greece as well as in Syra.

The Ceremonies of the Vintage

Among other ancient customs still existing in Syra, the ceremonies of the vintage are particularly conspicuous. Before sunrise, a number of young woman are seen coming towards the town, covered with the branches and leaves of the vine; when they are met or accompanied by their lovers, singing loud songs, and joining in a circular dance. This is evidently the orbicular choir who sung the *Dithyrambi* and danced that species of song in praise of Bacchus. Thus do the present inhabitants of the islands exhibit a faithful portraiture of the manners and customs of their progenitors; the ceremonies of ancient Greece have not been swept away by the revolutions of the country...

1828 Samuel Woodruff

A School

Went on shore this afternoon; called on Dr. I. and spent two hours with him in his school. The more I see and learn of the Greek children, the more I admire their vivacity and docility. Where could American charity be better bestowed than by sending the gospel, religious tracts, and other schoolbooks, for the benefit of these children!

I was much pleased at the method used by Dr. I. with his youngest class, - ten or fifteen boys, from six to nine years of age. Arranged on one side of their sanded table, with their wooden pencils, their attention was directed to a painted board elevated in front of them, on which was presented one of the letters of the alphabet. The head of the class pronounces the name of the letter aloud, which is responded by each of the class. They then use their pencils, forming the letter in the sand. These lessons are continued from day to day, until the class are able to form every letter and character of the alphabet. They then proceed with monosyllables, and onward to long words knowledge of reading and sentences. Thus the pupil acquires the knowledge of reading and writing simultaneously. Might not this mode be profitably adopted in all our infant schools?"

Late 1840s Aubrey de Vere

An Interrupted Journey

Pride ... will have a fall. The second day, we had passed several islands, among others Zea and Thermia, and were rapidly approaching Syra when we went down to dinner. A little before the end of our meal, the captain, to our no small astonishment, sent us word that we must make haste, as the boat was waiting to land us on the island! It was in vain that every one who had taken his place for Constantinople produced his ticket, and declared that he had no curiosity to see Syra. Nothing further could we make out than that the vessel we were in was not going to Constantinople - that the captain had taken us to Syra for our own good - that our fares to Constantinople had been accepted out of deference to general principles - that during the night we were to be lodged like princes in the Lazaretto - and that, the next morning, the vessel, which was really proceeding to Constantinople, would have the honour of waiting on us, and would be but too happy to take us to the end of our voyage.

Where there is no alternative, a man's deliberations need not cost him much time. Gloomily and silently we descended the ship's side - a motley, many-coloured company - and seated ourselves in the little boat. The captain stood at the side of the ship, took off his hat, smiled, and made us a short speech, apparently very obliging, and particularly satisfactory to himself; but the splashing of the oars drowned his parting words...

Before we had done ruminating dark fancies, and chewing out the luxury of a grievance, we discovered that those who complain about trifles are not left long without real cause for complaint. Close to the shore, where our boat grated against the sand, were ranged a dozen dens (for they were not good enough to be called hovels), built of pebbles and mud. "There live the fishermen of Syra," I remarked: "poor men, I suppose they are out just now providing our supper." "On the contrary," replied the steersman, "there you must live yourselves for a little time: but, courage! you will be as comfortable as possible: the sea never comes in." Thinking ourselves in a strange dream, we landed, and bent low enough to look into one of these kennels, in which there was neither floor nor ceiling, nor yet chair or table. There it stood-four walls - an abode in the abstract - no particular house - a place stripped of impertinences, and free from conventionalities. In consternation we recoiled, fully resolved to get on board the boat again, and insist on being received in the ship. Already, however, the sailors had pushed off at the command of their steersman, who took his cigar out of his mouth, and remarked that the lazaretto seemed faulty from what it lacked rather than from what it possessed!

Three of these dens being vacant at the time of our arrival, I was able to select one, in which I had but two companions. They stuck a tallow candle against the earthen wall, resolved that if the fleas devoured them before morning, at least they would "perish in the light." Down they lay, contented, low-minded Greeks, without self-respect enough to consider themselves as men aggrieved, and were asleep in a few minutes. I found it less easy to reconcile myself to my lot, but hit upon an expedient not sufficiently appreciated, that of conquering vexation with fatigue. Accordingly, leaving my companions to their dreams, I sallied forth, and walked for hours up and down beside the still and gleaming sea. I have seldom seen a more picturesque spectacle than the town of Syra presented on that occasion. It is placed on a crescent-hill, which rises from the waterside, just opposite the little island on which the lazaretto stands. The whole of this crescent, and also a steep mound on its summit, is covered with houses ranged one above another, stage beyond stage, like the steps of an amphitheatre. In the town there is not one single shutter, the consequence of which was that nearly every light was visible from our prison. The illumination was reflected in the water, and could not easily be exceeded in brilliancy. At an early hour in the morning weariness crept over me, and I retired to rest. I was awaked by the joyful acclamations of my fellow-sufferers, who had already discovered the arrival of the second French steamboat. In a few minutes we had tumbled our luggage into a boat, each man rushing to the landing-place with a portmanteau on his shoulder, and rowed along side. At the bulwarks stood the captain and several officers, all very like each other, and all very ugly, smiling, nodding, and bowing to us, and whispering to each other. Up rose every man in our boat, which swayed about till I thought it would have upset-Greek, Turk, Jew, and Armenian, and chattered vociferously for about three minutes, each in his own language, making a confusion of tongues in which not one word was intelligible. The captain listened with much politeness and answered, when the hub-bub had subsided, "Mais, messieurs, certainement!" Distrusting so general an assent, I got up in my turn, and stated our case to him, requesting him to take us on to Constantinople. "Impossible," was his reply. We were in quarantine, and so should he be if he meddled with us. "But you are going to Constantinople, the city of the plague." " No matter," was his reply. "The ship which had brought us thus far came from Alexandria: the plague at Alexandria differed from that at Constantinople, and far exceeded it in virulence." "But we had been given tickets to Constantinople." " No matter; it must be confessed that it was an imprudence to have given them." I made one more desperate effort in an oration full of sublimity and pathos, insisting on the law of nations, the honour of the French flag, insult to the English nation, and the rights of man; - in the midst of which the vessel steamed off, splashing us all over with the spray from her paddles, the captain and his officers taking off their hats, shrugging their shoulders, and lifting up their eyebrows into arches steeper than the "Bridge of sighs" ... The last words which I caught were "pauvres diables," from the captain, and "enfin c' est egal" from the officer next him. Nothing remained but to row back to the lazaretto, which accordingly we did, the Greeks tossing back their heads with scornful laughter, the Armenians and Jews gesticulating with rage, while a solemn Turk who said nothing, evidently thought the more, twisting his beard in his hand, glancing after the ship with lurid eyes, and no doubt wishing for a sword!

On returning to the lazaretto, the first thing we discovered was that, during our brief absence, a hundred and fifty pilgrims, on their way to a saintly shrine in a neighbouring island, had taken possession of our dens. There we stood, a group for a painter, with our portmanteaus on our shoulders, our bags in our hands, bitter indignation swelling in our hearts, and our eyes fixed in jealous amazement upon the strangers who had contrived to rob us of our hitherto detested homes. In reply to our enquiries and reproaches, the authorities told us that there was still one small room unoccupied at the top of the lazaretto, into which we might pack ourselves if we pleased; on the other hand, we were equally free, if we preferred it, to squeeze ourselves into our old kennels. We cast another despairing glance at their new occupants, who were crammed so tightly together that a cat or a dog could hardly have found room among them; nor would a cat which preserved a remnant of self-respect have made the attempt. These pilgrims were, most of them, beggars, and apparently had not been washed since the battle of Navarino, if indeed they had ever been washed in their lives. There could be little doubt that they were covered with vermin of every sort; and in the East there are nine different kinds of bugs alone. A brief consultation was quite sufficient to determine us; and we desired the guardians to place us where they pleased, provided they removed us from the present company. We were marshalled accordingly to our upper chamber. Having taken possession of it, and deposited our luggage on the floor, we sallied forth again to an open court, where we passed the day, meditating on the interesting chances which befell travellers, and the knowledge of the world which they are sure to pick up on their way.

Late in the evening it grew cold, and I was obliged to take refuge within the walls of our dungeon. I found my companions already there, squatting tailor-wise, each man upon that carpet with which the eastern traveller is generally provided. All were talking at once, and each in a different language, laughing and telling stories, until my brain went round like the brain of a dancing Dervise. As it grew later, and the cold increased, each of them pulled up the four corners of his carpet and knotted them over his shoulders, nothing remaining outside the pyramid thus formed except his head and red night-cap. A strange spectacle they presented, squatting there like so many wretches whom an Evil Genius of Africa had immersed in leathern bottles and left for a season. Every moment their volubility seemed to wax fiercer, and I had given over all hopes of sleep, feeling indeed as much stunned as if I had been hanged by the heels from the topmost story of the Tower of Babel, when all at once there came a pause; - the imprisoned spirits wavered in their circle, lay down, or rather tumbled over, with one accord, and in another moment were snoring. There was but one exception, an Armenian merchant, who continued for more than two hours to recount a series of stories for his own amusement, accompanying them with furious gesticulations. He also, however, at last ceased, - brought to a standstill in a moment, like a child's top when it has hit against the wall, upset, and joined the rest of the sleepers.

The next day was fortunately the last of our quarantine, and thenceforward we were to enjoy the freedom of the island. Great was our alarm, however, on descending into the court, lest any of the more-recently arrived travellers should touch us, as such an accident (a thing of frequent occurrence) would have consigned us to another imprisonment of fourteen days. So nervous did this prospect make me, that long after I was set free, I could not help, while walking about Syra, instinctively holding forth my stick between me and anyone who approached very near. I had still to wait five days for the arrival of another packet.

With the assistance of the English Consul I succeeded in making out the Secretary of the French packet office, and insisted on receiving a clearer explanation than I had yet been favoured with of the singular fact that although I had taken my place in a steamer bound for Constantinople, that vessel had notwithstanding proceeded to Alexandria instead, dropping me at Syra. Mr. Secretary, in reply, commenced a long harangue, dividing the subject into different heads, each of which he counted on his fingers as he proceeded. Three of these heads he had already disposed of, when, perceiving that he had ten fingers at his command, and that the question would therefore necessarily divide itself into ten heads, I interposed, stating that he had convinced me already, and that I would give him no further trouble, except to refund the money I had paid. This demand astonished him very much, shocked him not a little, and would have pained him yet more had he not obligingly attributed it to my ignorance of the world and of business. Here, however, I was resolute; and after a tremendous discussion, during which he snatched off his spectacles and put them on again more than a dozen times, I confuted him in argument, and he repaid me my money, with the exception of the fare as far as Syra, assuring me, however, to the last, that he did so out of politeness, not out of justice, "casualties being," as he remarked, "part of the order of nature."

Early 1850s Captain Adolphus Slade, R.N.

Some Curiosities Observed

The first object that attracted my attention on landing, was a man on the beach, the half of his legs and his feet red with blood; in Rome I might have taken him for a cardinal: he was undergoing the vernal depletion universally practised by the Greeks. The second was an auction in the open street by inch of candle: the auctioneer held a candle in his hand, and as long as it burned the bidding continued. The third was our consul, a Greek, not the steadier for his bottle. He insisted on sharing my company at the table d'hote, the daily resort of a good quantity of villainy; then on signing my passport, to show me, I suppose, that he could write, his signature being no more necessary than that of the Great Mogul. He was a reasonable specimen of a class of persons scattered over the Archipelago, styled British officers, who disgrace the flag that waves over their dwellings. I mean the consuls of the different islands, some honorary, some with inadequate salaries. Chiefly Greeks - such Greeks as the most staunch Philhellenists, whose hearts bound at the name, who believe that Themistocleses and Miltiadeses are still to be seen in every province, would object to - they are found at Pera ready for any service, according to their several necessities, under the title of protected Rayas, which they enjoy through the means of one ambassador or other, and thereby are not regarded by the Porte as direct subjects. And thus it frequently happens that a person scarcely owned by any country, whose only recommendation consists, perhaps, in having been domestic to an ambassador, in or out of doors, is appointed all at once agent for a great nation; as, for example, M. Vitalis held a menial office in a consul's house at Pera previous to his own consular appointment at Syra. The piratic trade, (graeco, free trade,) by which Syra, as its emporium, taking no part in the war of independence, rose from insignificance to prosperity, received no check at his hands. He became rich. Deeply will the cut-throat population of Syra lament (should the time arrive) when a good blade and a swift bark cease to be riches to him who can wield the one and steer the other. During the height of its illegal career the bazaars offered a singular contrast. English cottons, French jewellery, Turkish silks, might all be seen *pele mele* selling for mere trifles. I once bought there, in the same shop, Pope's works (for eighteen-pence) and a Koran; the former, of course, was part of the plunder of an English merchant-vessel; the latter, of a Turkish vessel, conveying pilgrims on their way to Mecca.

1856-57 Herman Melville

Some Impressions

Some old men looked like Pericles reduced to a chiffonier - such a union of picturesque and poverty stricken. All round barren tawny hills, here and there terraced with stone. View of the islands - little hamlets, white, half way up mountains. - The azure of the sea, and ermine of the clouds, the Greek flag (blue and white) seems suggested by the azure of her sky and ermine of her clouds. The wharf, a kind of semicircle, coinciding with the amphitheatre of hills. - In December tables and chairs out of doors, coffee and water pipes. - Carpenters and blacksmiths working in the theatrical costumes.

The crowds on the quays all with red caps, looking like flamingos. Long tassels - labourers wear them, and carry great bundles of codfish on their heads. - Few seem to have anything to do. All lounge.

1883-4 James Theodore Bent

Religious Rivalries

One afternoon I strolled up the hill, to inspect the town of "Upper Syra", as it is now called, where the medieval Roman Catholic settlement still exists; here everything is old world, and the inhabitants seem utterly unconcerned about the busy life in the lower town, The houses are like steps, one above the other; and the steep narrow streets, foul with refuse and tenanted by pigs lead up in spiral fashion to the convent and church of Saint George, which crowns the hill. From the terrace in front of the edifice a fine view is obtained over the sea, dotted with Cyclades as far as the eye can reach; to the right is a brown stony valley, characteristic of Syra, and on the brow of the opposite hill a newly-fledged Greek convent seems as if it looked with contempt on the Roman Catholic town, as much as to say that its reign is over. Between the Eastern and Western church there is no kindly feeling. On my way down to the lower town, I met some girls who had strolled upwards to take the air. They asked me my intention on seeing me enter a Greek church, and on my inquiring if they were Westerns or Orthodox, they affirmed so eagerly that they belonged to the latter persuasion, that I was constrained to question them further on their knowledge of the relation between the two creeds.

One of them, who said she was a niece of Canarios, one of the great heroes of the war of independence, regretted loudly that shortly she was to marry a rich Roman Catholic; her principal objection being, from what I could gather, a current belief that when a Roman Catholic has received the last sacrament and shows symptoms of recovery, the priest goes back and strangles him with a rope, for after this sacred event no one is permitted to live. She was a young lady of considerable sentiment I imagine, for she carried in her hand a pretty flower which grows on the hills under the acanthus bushes, called "patience" by the Greeks… "For when I look at it: she concluded, "I feel strengthened to bear my lot patiently."

Traditional Euthanasia for the Old Folk

We saw hardly any signs of habitation on our way until we came to a low whitewashed cottage, where lives, high up on the mountain-top, a tottering old man ninety-five years of age. He looks after a small garden, and whenever he wants anything he walks into Hermoupolis to do his shopping. Our muleteer called him out, and he came to welcome us: he was full of stories about the wonderful changes he had seen during his long, eventful life; how he had fought for his country's liberties; how he had assisted in building the first houses for the refugees down by the harbour. When we left him, I asked our muleteer if people frequently lived to be so old at Syra. "Yes," was the reply, an old woman died at one hundred and thirty only a short while ago; in former years people lived so long that they had to be thrown down a mountain cliff which is still called Geronsi. This tradition of longevity in Syra is curious, and more especially so in connection with the slaughter of the aged. On the neighbouring island of Keos it is well known that the old and useless members of society were obliged to swallow hemlock when a certain age was reached. The Abbé della Rocca, one of the Roman Catholic brethren in Syra, writing a century ago, tells us of the same tradition existing then about the great age and general healthiness of the Syriotes.

447

Paros

1883-4 James Theodore Bent

Into The Ancient Underground Quarries

Every credit is due to the enterprise of the Belgian company which have lately contracted to supply the world with Parian marble. Down by the harbour they have erected costly works, and have got all the latest improvements in machinery; but unfortunately first when they attacked the marble quarries on Mount Marpessa they worked at a wrong vein, so that a new shaft had to be opened; and only now, after the expenditure or a vast amount of toil and money, have they at last got into the vein of genuine *lychnites* - that brilliant sparkling marble so prized by the ancients for statues and sculpture of every sort.

It would have been a long ascent on muleback to the convent of St. Minas, close to which are the various holes into the bowels of Mount Marpcssa; as it was, we were only an hour in making the ascent, and had a very pleasant journey. Not that Paros is in the least degree pretty - on this northern side it is almost the ugliest of the islands - but it was pleasant to sit and enjoy the ever-changing distant views, and see the shepherds run out of their *mandras* and gaze with eyes and mouth wide open at the terrible innovation which has actually found its way to the Cyclades. We saw quantities of beehives, too, constructed in the sloping ground - just rows of holes, lined with slabs, where the bees fix their combs; for there is no need here of straw hives or our cunning northern appliances for keeping them warm in winter. Yet it was cold enough up by the quarries: a biting wind was blowing from the north, which made us glad to dive into the shafts, and made shiver when we came out again. There is much debris of marble before the mines, and there are several holes into the mountain side, all of which were opened in ancient times. Into one of these we descended by a steep shaft, by the aid of miners' lamps. Very soon we were able to recognise the old chisel-marks, and in pursuing this shaft it was that the modern Parian Marble Company made their great mistake. To the right of us and to the left of us we passed various channels which the ancients had worked and exhausted the vein, and when we came to the depth of over two hundred feet we saw a huge block of marble just as they had left it ready to be hauled up. Their plan undoubtedly was to work all round the block they wished to get up, making it just small enough to pass up the shaft, and up which they must have dragged it by an arrangement of pulleys and props which we do not understand now. In many parts the shaft has fallen in, for the pillars left to support it have given way, owing to the weight above them. All these things were put to rights by the modern company at an outlay of much money, only to find when they reached the bottom, and got all the rubbish cleared away, that the vein they were following was all but exhausted; so they had to sink another shaft, and at length their efforts have been crowned with success. By a difficult passage lately constructed these two shafts have been joined; along this we crawled, and came up by the other one. The manager told me that, according to his calculation, the vein of good marble extends one hundred and fifty metres into the mountain.

Thirty years ago, when Ross went down the mine with King Otho and Queen Amalia, he said they had to crawl on their hands and knees to get down a very little way, and his majesty had to take off his epaulettes to enable him to proceed at all; the queen, as she squeezed her way through, loosened some stones, which came upon her and terrified her exceedingly. On hearing her screams the king hurried back, and in this dark mine the bystanders were witnesses of a royal embrace of the tenderest nature.

There is a third shaft parallel to the other two which appears to have been of considerable importance in ancient times, for close to the entrance is the well-known bas-relief presented, as the inscription tells us, by Adamas to the nymphs: it is a wedding scene carved on the bare rock, the human banquet is going on below, whilst in the upper storey the gods are having another, at which Bacchus is presiding. Some Vandals, of - happily for themselves - unknown nationality, have removed the central figures from the lower banquet; so the manager of the mines, with commendable discretion, has had the whole bas-relief carefully covered over with wood to protect it, which he kindly ordered to be removed for our inspection.

The descent into the bowels of Mount Marpessa and the subsequent climb were productive of an appetite of considerable dimensions; so, before starting on our mule ride to Leukis, we lunched at a shanty the manager of the mines has built for himself close by – pleasant enough I dare say, in summer, but miserable, with the four winds of heaven howling around, in winter.

"The Gem of Paros"

Leukis is considered the gem of Paros, and before going there we heard glowing accounts of its beauty. It lies under the shadow of Mount Elias, the highest summit of Paros; there are plenty of olives, oranges, and lemons about it, and it is decidedly the largest place on the island; for, as in Naxos, these central valleys have escaped from the inroads of pirates and others in search of wood. The entrance to the valley at the top of which Leukis is situated was protected by two other villages with medieval fortresses, Kephalo and Kosto, the former of which was the last stronghold of the Venier family, and which Barbarossa only conquered by cutting off the water supply.

But Leukis is by no means a bright white place… as its name indicates; it is dirty and black ill in the extreme, the only white thing about it being a hideous new church with all elaborate marble *tempelon*, a marble throne, and a marble pulpit - not that they want pulpits one bit in Greek churches as far as I could see. In former days they used to read the prophets, epistle, and gospel from the *ambon*; now they do this on the *soleas*, or steps outside the sanctuary, and do nothing in the pulpit. Over the entrance door outside is a curious marble slab on which is sculptured a portrait of the worthy man who founded this edifice in 1830: he is depicted as a regular islander, with his wide baggy trousers and the ... pointed fez, on his head; and in one corner of the slab is the hand of God pointing out of a cloud in the direction of the meek but beneficent-looking old man. From the churchyard the view over the sister isle of Naxos, with its lovely fantastic peaks, was very charming, far surpassing anything to be seen on Paros.

We had a pleasant walk that evening with the demarch, who showed us with pride the orange and lemon groves and the numerous wells of flowing water which make of Leukis the most favoured spot on Paros.

No one dares to draw water after dark out of these wells, for the waters slumber, they think, like human beings, and if they are disturbed the genius of the place will bring evil on the intruder. In common with other Greeks of the mountainous districts, the people of Leukis are highly superstitious; witches they have in quantities amongst them, which haunt the caves and rocks on the mountain side: they arc old men or women, past a hundred, who go by the name of *stringlai*, not unlike the Harpies of old, for they can turn into birds at will, and have sometimes women's heads and the bodies of birds; and about these witches the people of Leukis have lots of legends which they tell, one of which relates how an evil woman haunts the neighbourhood, eating all the men she can find, until a prince shall come and conquer her, like Theseus and the Cromyan Sow. At night sometimes, says the legend, these witches come to houses, cut out the heart of a man, and have a feast; from dangers such as these the hero of the legend is generally saved by some extraordinary interference. Unbaptized babes are, however, their favourite food, and for this reason children wear phylacteries around their necks.

Here in Leukis we heard a good deal more about those Kalkagàri of which Naxos had provided us with so much information; children born during the days between Christmas and Epiphany are generally supposed to grow into these unpleasant hobgoblins. It was close upon the time now, and expectant mothers were growing nervous lest their progeny should appear at this season. "We know of several Kalkagàri in Leukis, said the demarch solemnly, children who have been born at this unlucky epoch." And then he told us stories of how these unfortunate youngsters would walk in their sleep and torment their friends. "We know of them," he concluded, "but we do not talk about them; for their parents do not like to have the fact alluded to. The only way of averting the disaster is to place a blessed palm branch over the door at the time of birth."

That evening we had another of those festive gatherings which our island hosts loved to improvise for us, and a wild shepherd boy, clad in skins, came to play music for the dancing. He was a primitive musician in very truth; his instrunment the much-loved *sabouna*, just a lamb's skin fastened at the head and feet, a big reed with two smaller ones stuck inside at one end of the skin, and a cow's horn to bring out the sound at the other. And to the music of this they danced the *syrtos,* with some local acrobatic variations which made us realise why the island doctors recommended this dance for torpid livers and indigestion.

Greek Dance on Paros (J. B. Hilaire & P. Martini, 1782)

Antiparos

c.1825 A Companion of HM Queen Caroline of Brunswick

A Queen into the The Cave

Her Majesty now determined on an excursion among the numerous islands of the Grecian Archipelago, in order to visit and inspect any natural curiosities or interesting remains of antiquity which they may contain. Among the extraordinary and beautiful productions of nature, probably nothing in that part of the globe can exceed the exquisite beauties of the natural grotto of Antiparos, so called from the island of that name, about forty leagues from Athens. After a short and pleasant trip we landed upon the barren island of Antiparos, and were conducted by the governor to a small village. Here we found a few inhabitants, who were described to us as the casual legacies of different vessels, and principally Maltese, taken by corsairs, and left on shore to shift for themselves. Some of them provided us with mules, ropes, and candles for the grotto, which is situate near the summit of the highest mountain of Antiparos, in the south part of the island. As we rode along, our beasts were terrified by the attacks of the gadfly, an insect which infests everyone of these islands.

Having reached the top of the mountain before mentioned, we came to the mouth of this most prodigious cavern, which may be described as the greatest natural curiosity of its kind in the known world. The entrance to it exhibits nothing very remarkable; but no book of travels ever did or ever can portray the beauties of the interior. The mode of descent is by ropes, which, on the different declivities, are either held by the natives, or they are joined to a cable which is fastened at the entrance around a stalactite pillar. In this manner we were conducted, first down one declivity, and then down another, until we entered the spacious chambers of this truly enchanted grotto. The roof, the floor, the sides of a whole series of magnificent caverns, are entirely invested with a dazzling incrustation, as white as snow. Columns, some of which were five-and-twenty feet in length, pended in fine icicle forms above our heads. Fortunately, some of them are so far above the reach of the numerous travellers who, during many ages, have visited this place, that no one has been able to injure or to remove them. Others extend from the roof to the floor, with diameters equal to that of the mast of a first rate ship of the line. The encrustations of the floor, caused by falling drops from above, have grown up into vegetable forms. The last chamber into which we descended surprised us more by the grandeur of its exhibition than any other. Probably there are many other chambers below this, yet unexplored, for no attempt has been made to penetrate farther; and if this be true, the new caverns, when opened, would appear in perfect splendour, unsullied in any part of them by the smoke of torches, or by the hands of intruders.

1826 Charles Swan

Fireworks Underground

Everywhere hang huge masses of one shape or other; those from the roof are principally pointed, with a drop of clear water appended. On the lower part arise pillars, rounded at the top like a pineapple, and fretted in a similar manner. In some places the stalactite has partitioned off a portion of the cavern, making cells, whose roofs become ornamented with a broad and sloping stalagmite, something of the pattern of a fish's fin. We fired a couple of ship's blue lights from one of the higher parts of the cavern. The effect was uncommonly fine. They showed the whole place to perfection, and gave a magnificent tinge to the opaque bodies of the pendent stalactites. I brought off several specimens.

In this cavern, AD 1673, according to M. Tournefort, the Marquis de Nointel, French Ambassador to the Porte, had the folly or the vanity to continue 'the three Christian holidays'. He caused high mass to be celebrated upon a piece of stalactite, which still retains the name of the altar. 'Men were posted from space to space, in every precipice from the altar to the opening of the cavern, who gave the signal with their handkerchiefs, when the body of our Lord was lifted up; at this signal fire was put to twenty four drakes, and to several patereroes that were at the entrance of the cavern: the trumpets, hautbois, fifes and violins, made the consecration yet more magnificent.'

1883-4 James Theodore Bent

A Unique Christmas Midnight Mass

Bent provides more details about his remarkable event.

This vast hall which we had now reached, right in the heart of the mountain ... resembles some lovely cathedral, sparkling with gems, the dome of which is supported by pillars of exquisite workmanship. Stalectites surround the edifice like statues of saints in niches... It is not surprising that the idea of sanctity was suggested to the minds of the first modern travellers who . descended here. At one end of this vast temple, screened off by stalectites, is a natural sanctuary with a ready-made altar... Two pillars in front of this were broken off by M. de Nointel to serve as a table for the celebration of his midnight mass in 1673...

M. de Nointel was the French ambassador at the Porte, and a great archaeologist... Out of some strange caprice he chose to pass three Christmas holidays in this grotto, accompanied by five hundred persons - his domestics, merchants, corsairs, timid natives who were bribed by largesses - any, in fact, who were willing to follow him.

It must have been a most impressive sight, that midnight mass in the bowels of the earth. A hundred large torches of yellow wax and four hundred lamps burning night and day illuminated the place, and men posted in every available space, on stalactites and in crevices all the way to the entrance, gave notice by the waving of their handkerchiefs one to the other of the moment of the elevation of the host, and at the given signal explosives were let off at the entrance of the cavern, trumpets sounded, to herald the event to the world.

M. de Nointel passed the three nights in a small chamber close to the altar, whilst his friends scattered themselves about. The great difficulty was to provide food and water for so many individuals... Luckily for them a spring of clear water was discovered inside the cavern; how they provided food for such a multitude we do not know. The suite doubtless found it exceedingly difficult to pass the time in this imprisonment, so we are not surprised to find that they amused themselves by writing their names on the walls and on the pillars with firebrands. It is curious to see how fresh and clear these names have remained after the lapse of more than two centuries.

A further but uninteresting descent of about eighty feet can be made beyond this hall, where all the most energetic travellers have penetrated and written their names, and amongst others, Otho, the first king of the Hellenes.

Naxos

1718 Joseph Pitton de Tournefort

Fighting for Christianity in the Aegean

The Turks did not dare to appear much abroad in there islands before the departure of the French Privateers, who would often go and take them by the beard, and away with them on board ship, where they made slaves of them. Our privateers have been sometimes more successful in the preservation of Christianity, than the most zealous missionaries: witness the following example.

Some years ago, ten or a dozen families of Naxos embraced the Mahometan religion: the Christians of the Latin communion got them snapped up by the privateers, who carried them to Malta. Since which, no one has thought it worth while to turn Mahometan at Naxos. The famousest corsairs of the Archipelago had nothing odious but the name of corsair. They were men of quality and distinguished valour, who only followed the mode of the times they lived in. Did not Messieurs de Valbelle, Gardane, Colongue, come to be captains and flag-officers of the King's fleet, after they had cruised upon the infidels? How many Knights of Malta do we see supporting in the Levant the Christian name under the banner of religion? These gentlemen minister justice to such as address themselves to them...

The Grand Seigneur never need to fear any rebellion in this island; the moment a Latin stirs, the Greeks give notice to the Cadi, and before a Greek opens his mouth, the Cadi knows what he meant to say before he has shut it...

Relics of a Lost Nobility

The Turks use all these gentlemen of both sorts, just alike. At the arrival of the meanest Bey of a galliot, neither the Latins nor the Greeks ever dare appear but in red caps, like the common galley slaves, and tremble before the pettiest officer. As soon as ever the Turks are withdrawn, the Naxian nobility resume their former haughtiness: nothing is to be seen but caps of velvet, nor to be heard of but tables of genealogy; some deduce

The Gates of the Temple of Dionysos
(Henry Wright & Elizabeth Byrne)

453

themselves from the Palaeologi or Comnenii, others from the Justiniani, the Grimaldi, the Summaripas.

The ladies here are most ridiculously vain; you shall see them return from the country after the vintage, with a train of thirty or forty women , half on foot and half upon asses, one carries upon her head a napkin or two made of cotton, or a petticoat of her mistress, the other marches along, holding in her hand a pair of stockings, a stone kettle, or a few earthen plates; all the furniture of the house is set to view, and the mistress sorrily mounted, makes her entry into the city in a kind of triumph at the head of this procession. The children are in the middle, and the husband usually brings up the rear.

1789 Lady Elizabeth Craven

Bad Taste

The town of Naxos is a poor place; we waited near four hours to see a Naxiote maiden dressed in her holiday clothes – which are neither decent nor pretty – A short shift reaching to her knees served as a petticoat – her vest was fantastic beyond conception, pearls, feathers, beads, sowed on, in various forms – and two wings, like those of a butterfly, stuck between her shoulders, added to the strange appearance – Her head and neck were adorned with gold, chains, pearls, stones, ribbands – In all my life I never saw so bizarre a figure We took our leave of her, making excuses for the trouble we had given her, and sailed for the small island of Antiparos.

1801 Edward Daniel Clarke

A Very Primitive Way of Life

The little creek in which our vessel found shelter is called, by the islanders, the bay of Panormo; and there are some insignificant ruins upon the rocks above it, which they call Panormo Castle. The only inhabitants we saw were parties of men leading uninterruptedly a pastoral life, without paying any tax, either to the island or to the Turkish government: we found them tending their sheep and goats in this wild part of Naxos, like a race of primeval shepherds. They brought us some sheep soon after our arrival; descending the rocks with their bare feet, and wearing upon their legs the *cothurnus*, in its most ancient form made of the undressed skins of their goats, with the flair on the outside. Whence they came, or who they were, we could not learn; for they said they had little connection with any of the village of the island, nor any settled place of residence; that they had neither wives nor houses; sleeping at night behind some bush, in the open air, and labouring merely for subsistence, without a thought of riches. They had all the same kind of clothing: it consisted of a woollen jacket, and short trousers, of their own manufacture, partly concealing the *cothurnus* of goat's hair upon their legs. They cover their head with a red skull cap, which is manufactured at Venice. Reckoning their goats and sheep together, these independent shepherds have five or six hundred animals in each flock. They shear their sheep twice a year; putting the rams to the ewes in May, and removing them when the latter begin to lamb. They speak the modern Greek language; and perhaps recruit their numbers from the race of Albanians which is scattered over all Greece. They told us that they made three or four hundred piastres annually, out of a flock of five hundred sheep and goats; and this sum they spend in the few necessaries and indulgences they may require. We killed and dressed one of their sheep: the mutton had a very bad flavour.

1883-4 James Theodore Bent

The Village of Thieves

After our meal the priest came out with us to show us the lion. Philoti is a large village, crowning twin heights, with an ugly new Greek church in the declivity between. As we were climbing up one of the heights, we heard terrible language issuing from a shed where some women were grinding corn with simple but quaint hand mills, namely two heavy round stones, the upper one of which works on a pivot attached to a stick a yard and a half long, which is fixed into a wooden fork in the wall so loosely that it can be revolved with ease by pressing on the stick. The women hall stopped their grinding, and were listening with awe to the declamations of an old grey-haired hag, who was telling a pitiful tale of how robbers from Apeiranthos the night before had broken into her yard and tried to steal her pigs, which squeaked so loudly that she woke, and frightened the robbers away, but not before one of her pigs had been slain. Nothing would satisfy the old woman but that we should return with her to her house, view the scene of the intended robbery, and lay her case before the authorities on our return to the capital.

Everywhere in Naxos they have a bad word for the people of Apeiranthos; a village of robbers, we were told it was, away in the mountains. It was to be our next halting place after leaving Philoti, so we were concerned at all the evil reports we had heard; for, say they, a man of Apeiranthos is clever enough to steal the sole off your boot, or the hat off your head, without your knowing it; and the facetious Naxiotes tell an ill-natured legend about these people with great gusto, namely, that Apeiranthos was a Cretan colony; that Barabbas was a Cretan ; and that after his delivery from prison he returned home, where he behaved so badly that the Cretans drove him away: so he came to Naxos and founded the colony of Apeiranthos.

By the time we got to the old woman's house we were almost out of breath, for she lived at the extreme summit one of the heights in a funny desolate cottage, with furniture of a primitive kind, absolutely nothing worth stealing except her pig. However we saw here for the first time a speciality of Philoti, namely, a siphon with which wine is drawn out of the large jars in which they keep it. After the wine is put in they cover the jars over with a coating of clay into which a siphon is stuck, so constructed that you can fill it by suction; you then pour it out of the hole you have sucked and use the end that has been introduced into the jar for a handle.

The following morning (for a wonder!) was beautiful, and at earliest dawn the inhabitants of Philoti appeared on their flat roofs. I thought they must all be mad at first, for they were occupied in kicking about what appeared to me to be the marble pillars of some ancient temple; but I soon discovered that each roof was provided with a round marble roller, and that every woman was kicking hers about to press the mud roof, which the late rains had disturbed.

Today with a prospect of fine weather we determined to make the tour of Mount Jupiter - Mount Zia, as they call it now. Naxos in former ages was called Zia,

And on a large stone on the northern slope of the mountain we read the following inscription in ancient characters: "the mountain of Milesian Jupiter". It is a peaked conical mountain, only 3,290 ft in height, but as it rises almost straight from the sea-level it appears exceedingly lofty. Its slopes are rugged and covered with the holly oak (*Ilex aquifolium*), with the prickly leaves of which the peasants feed their cattle. We first climbed up to a steep cave, which goes deep into the heart of the mountain: at its entrance is an altar called "the church of Zia," where a priest goes once a year in the summer time and holds a liturgy for the mountain shepherds; around it are a few incense pots and bits of wood which have been sacred pictures in days gone by. At this altar a shepherd is accustomed to swear to his innocence if another charges him with having stolen a sheep or a goat. An oath by the altar of Zia is held very sacred by the mountaineers, and is an earnest of innocence. It is curious still to find the actual word *Zeus* existing in this form, and the idea of a supreme God has been transferred from Zeus to the present religious tenets. "God is shaking his hair," say the peasants when there is an earthquake, as if he were the Olympus-throned Zeus of the *Iliad*. This cave and the mountain of Jupiter, I have little doubt, had much to do with the ancient worship of Jupiter. The old myth related how the king of the gods was brought from his birthplace in Crete to Naxos, where he was brought up, from whence he re-moved to take up his kingdom on Olympus. We have seen the above-mentioned inscription, the cave with the altar still in it; is it not highly probable that this is the cave in which Zeus was supposed to have spent his youth? It runs a very long way into the rock, and we had it lighted up for us by brushwood, but it contains nothing remarkable, save a spring of hot water, which in ancient times may have given rise to superstition. A local tradition says that once upon a time all the inhabitants of Philoti took refuge here from Saracen marauders who followed them, and by making a fire at the mouth of the cave they suffocated them all.

Leaving the peaky summit of Mount Zia to our left – for as midday came on clouds began to gather around the summit, and it was useless to make the ascent - we joined a path which leads from Philoti to Panormos, just close to a well of excellent water, shaded by a plantain tree... The tower "of the winter torrent" is on this road to Panormos: it is round and of white marble, and is principally worthy of notice from its spiral staircase, but is in no way so perfect as those of Andros and Amorgos. Having seen this we returned by another road to Philoti, thus making the entire circuit of Mount Zia.

Next morning we started for that dreaded haunt of robbers, Apeiranthos. The road led over a spur of mountains which joins Mount Jupiter with Mount Koronon, and divides Naxos into two districts – the bright and sunny vales of Drymalia and Trajaia on one side, and the bleak northern villages of Apeiranthos, Komiake, and Bothro on the other. As we descended on the village Barabbas is supposed to have found we could not help thinking that, for nefarious purposes, he had chosen well, being, as it is, far off from the haunts of men, and overlooking from a rocky eminence a fairly fertile valley, by which the sea could easily be approached.

Apeiranthos is a large village of romantic aspect, with houses built on the edges of precipices, and above it towers Mount fanari... The houses are for the most part yellow with a peculiar lichen. The streets are tortyous and narrow, so constituted that when pirates came the inhabitants could baffle anyone who attempted to enter their labyrinths.

We had a letter of introduction to the chief functionary of the place, the demarch, or, as our friends in Naxia said, "the chief robber"; so we thought we should at all events be in good quarters in this den of thieves. Whilst this letter was being delivered we stood in the little agora with our eyes firmly fixed on our luggage. "The reports are true," we thought as we looked around us; for never have I seen a wilder, more forbidding set of people than the men of Apeiranthos as they gathered round and stared at us. The town is high, faces north, and is extremely cold; so each man had on a huge brown greatcoat, with hair outside and a rim of red inside; some had their hoods pulled over their heads; others had their cloaks hanging loosely around them, and show-ing a powerful physique. Altogether they resembled conspirators in a chorus, and made us regret having ventured amongst them. Another curious and marked type of these men was their large noses, which they screwed up when they laughed, and which increased their sinister appearance.

Our misgivings were soon dissipated by the kindness of the demarch and his brother, whose hospitality knew no bounds; yet we could not help noticing that the windows were closely barred, and that when they went out with us they gave special instructions to the women to look after our things.

"You see," said the demarch, "there are some bad people amongst us, who live by piracy, though of late their number has been greatly reduced. But it will be long before we lose the name of being the worst people in the island. Everywhere the Naxiotes have a bad name, and you have come amongst the worst of the Naxiotes." He laughed at this confession, and I think we felt our confidence entirely restored by his frankness.

The Apeiranthiotes are thrifty and well-to-do; they have comfortable houses, far better than the other Naxiote villagers. Many of them have made money abroad, and returned to spend it in their mountain home. They have quantities of lovely red silk embroidery amongst them, Cretan work, which points to their origin; for doubtless there is this much truth in the Barabbas story that Apeiranthos was colonised by Cretans at the time of one of the numerous revolutions which have driven away so many from there, and the ill-will, and perhaps jealousy, or their neighbours – for nowhere in the Cyclades are the Cretan refugees popular - have invented the tradition about Barabbas...

There is much that is quaint about this people: they speak a marked dialect, with ancient forms and words, which we met with nowhere else; they use the ancient form of the plural; and the shepherds of Apeiranthos wear a wonderful garb, which ... rather resembles two sacks of flannel fastened together than trousers; their shoes are sewn together with strings of goat's hide, round their waist they wear a cotton vest wound round and round their bodies, and skin caps on their heads...

As for hospitality, these people are unequalled, and our host was desperately insulted at any hint of any remuneration for his kindness; as we rode away they filled our pockets with nuts and figs, and gave us a bottle of delicious *raki* to warm us on the road; and we wanted it too, for about two hours after leaving Apeiranthos our road ascended almost to the summit of Mount Fanari, where we were exposed to the hail and a biting wind, and were lost in a mist. The Naxiote mountains in winter are anything but enjoyable - wild and desolate, with just a few eagles soaring in the air now and again...

Human Hibernation (Male Only)

[W]e retired to rest on Christmas Eve, little dreaming what a store of storm and rain was being prepared for us by Jupiter the Rainy. For nearly a week Naxos and her mountains formed the centre of a sort of cyclone. Torrents would fall for hours, and then a gleam of sunshine lead us to hope that it was past, but it returned again with equal vigour, going round and round the lofty mountains. In our house we suffered severely; the miserable flat roofs covered with pressed mud soon began to leak; our sitting room was a lake, and then it came into our bedroom, so that we were forced to sleep under umbrellas and waterproofs. Never was the intense idleness and apathy of the Naxiotes more apparent than during this weather. No mules from the country villages, for nobody thinks of travelling when it rains; consequently no brushwood was brought in, and the stock of fuel was soon exhausted, the result being that there was not a fire in Naxia at which to cook a meal - not that this mattered much, for there was nothing to cook...

Men stay in bed all day on these occasions, murmuring, "Winter, winter!" when my thermometer outside our window never fell lower than 55 degrees Fahrenheit. It was the misery of damp and inactivity from which we suffered, during those weary days, not from cold; and those wretched pasteboard houses, where rain pours from window and from roof...

Ios

1692 "Mr. Roberts"

Taken by Corsairs

. I was cast away June 12 1692 in the haven of Nio, in his Majesties hired Ship, the *Arcana* galley, which sank, as it was there careening. Having lost a considerable value in her, I was in hopes to get part of my loss again, our ship being sunk in but 17 foot water: so I stayed behind, but most of our men went away in a French prize we had taken. The next day I agreed with a Greek to carry me for Scio, from whence I could get passage for Smirna, and so transport my self home again. But the third day being June the 15th, I was frustrated of my design; for a crusal or corsair coming into the harbour, he immediately sent his boat ashore, where meeting with five more of our men, who were also left behind, he soon with fair words got them on board; who presently told him of me. So ashore they came, in search of me; and one of them being a genius, soon found me. Upon our meeting, he saluted me with a kiss, and called me by my name, having learned it of our men; for I never saw him in my life before. He invited me to drink, which I refused, as partly knowing his design; and I had heard how miserably men lived in a crusal. Seeing therefore that all his wits would not take, he left me. In the evening came to me an English man, who had sailed in her eight years, his name was Dawes, he was a native of Saltash in Cornwall, whom we had taken out of this crural, before our ship was lost: but he, like a dog returning to his vomit, went on board again; where he yet remains, for ought I know.

Then came a Dane, and he strove to wheedle me: after him a Livornese with a letter from the captain, promising me great rewards, if I would come on board and be his gunner; all which I utterly refused and denied: so that June the 16th, coming to the waterside to embark for Scio, there came out of the rocks twelve rogues, whereof this Dawes was one, laid hold on me, and carried me on board on the starboard side; where I no sooner ascended, but came a fellow and clapped a chain on my leg, and no one spoke to me one word. Neither did I see any captain in five days time, but then he called to me, and asked me to serve him, which I utterly denied: Whereupon he called me dog, and said he would make me leave my Lutheran bones in the Archipelago, for pretending to go to Turkey to betray him. I answered, I had no such thoughts, neither knew I how to go about it; but I knew that the Greeks traded with the Turks daily, and could give them intelligence; and that for my part, I had never been in Turkey in my life, but all my pleading was in vain: For he knew that in these poor distressed isles was no more justice to be had than what his accursed self would allow, so that I was forced to remain there. Money he offered me to the value of ten dollars, but them I was advised to refuse, by a friend who assured me, if I took none he would in a short time let me go: So to sea we went, where he knocked off my chains, and ordered me to cunn the Ship, in which station I continued for three months. Crusal is a word mistakenly used, for corsair; which in English signifies a privateer; wherein we acted our part, not in taking Turkish vessels but Greek saicks, or any small ships that came in our way. When I had spent three months in this unpleasing traffic, I was preferred forsooth to be Mr. Gunner, but God knows it came upon me by compulsion; for the Captain having first beat the old Livornese gunner severely, who was a man of sixty years of age, he commanded me into the gun-room, to take the charge of what was there; which with an unwilling willingness I did, and continued there till I made my escape; before which I shall give a little account in the mean time, of my manner of living.

The first three months I eat with the lieutenant, and afterwards with the captain, it being the Italian custom in all ships; who while I was gunner, would often tell me, I should have all the patereroes we took, which was really my due; though for thirty-five patereroes and seventy chambers, I never had any more than two dollars, and seven ryalls, being all the money I ever saw for my sixteen months service. In the mean while to make my captivity (as I may say) as easy as I could; I always employed my self to study, and having a Greek boy allowed me, that spoke Turkish, Greek, and Italian, (of the latter whereof, I was almost master ere I came here) I did by the boys means, get an insight in the other two: Besides which, my way of living was such, that I always took great notice wheresoever I went, of the Isles …

The manner of punishing persons for petty crimes, viz. for staying or going ashore without leave, and returning again of their own accord, etc. is as follows, They are brought before the capstan, and seized fast with a crow of iron at their heels. Then a slave beats them with a rope of two inches thick, on their bare backs, until the captain bids him leave off: And when the slave can lay on no longer, who is all the while egged on by a renegade Greek that looks after the slaves, the other takes him in hand. And then the captain next belabours him with his cane, who if he finds they do not perform their work authentically, canes them all three without mercy.

They use the same method for him that is at topmast head; for if those that are above deck see a sail (which, by reason of the high land, they often do before him that is aloft), then he is relieved and brought to the capstan; and his due, according to the rigour, is five hundred blows, but he seldom escapes with less than the best half.

1718 Joseph Pitton de Tournefort

A Disappointed Visitor

There remains no footstep of antiquity in Nio. The inhabitants have no notion of anything but the pence; they are all thieves by profession, and therefore the Turks call it Little Malta. It is a harbouring-placc for most of the corsairs of the Mediterranean.

Thera (Santorini)

1674 Father Jacques-Paul Babin, S.J.

A Haunted Island

Nio, Nampho, St. Erino (or St. Torino) and Policandro are good islands, but they are continually plagued with privateers so as all that their land doth produce, will but serve to pay their taxes. If any can be said to have the preeminence, it is St. Erino, here being several merchants, who have some power amongst the Maltese, and drive a smart trade; buying up prize goods, they carry them, and sell them at Scala-nova, and other places in Asia, bringing for returns cotton, which is here wrought into dimitys, and which are the best in all the Archipelago. Great quantities go yearly to Candia, Zante, and other places. These Merchants also agree at Constantinople for the tribute of the whole island.

Most strangers are given to understand the whole island is enchanted; such terrifying noises are sometimes heard, and the ships' moorings to the shore being often loosed. A Dutch ship being in the Venetians' service came to anchor in the bay, making a hawser fast to one of the rocks, and having understood how other vessels were used to be served, the master had two men ashore to watch lest any should cut his hawser. In the night there came a cat to the water-side. One of the Dutchmen flings a stone at the cat, hit it, and imagined that it was dead. Immediately came down certain overgrown cats, and so plagued the Dutchman that they called their ship for help, upon which the boat came to shore, to carry the man aboard; but before they could come, one of the men was almost dead. Many such things the Venetian mariners give an account of, having had the cables very often cut close to the ship, which may yet be done in the night by a man swimming from the shore.

1883-4 James Theodore Bent

Sailing into the Caldera

On entering the basin of Santorin one experiences directly the pleasant impression of seeing something utterly new. To the left we were swiftly borne past a white line of houses perched along the edge of blood red rocks which form the northernmost point of the island. This is Epanomeria. Further on the red promontory Scaros juts out into the basin, and on it are the crumbling ruins of the medieval fortress; above this, on black rocks, is perched the white village of Meroviglia, 1,000 feet above the sea, which commences a long line of white houses, nearly two miles in extent, which blends itself with Phera, the present capital of the island.

The steamer stopped in front of a nest of houses, clinging to the cliff, which forms the little port. And what astounding houses they are! For the most part only holes chiselled in the soft volcanic rock, and faced with a fronting of stone, in which there is a door, a window above it, and perhaps one on each side. Half the inhabitants of Santorin, in spite of the encouragement given by government to the building of regular houses, prefer to live like rabbits in the ground. The capital and one or two of the principal villages now boast of handsome houses properly built, but some of the remote villages are still mere rabbit warrens excavated in the pumice-stone rocks as they have been for centuries.

The wall of rock is ascended by a newly-made path, which joins Phera and her port 950 feet beneath her - which 950 feet are composed of countless layers of volcanic eruptions in contorted lines of black and sides by a tiny white church which crowns a pinnacle of black lava, rising a thousand feet straight out of the sea.

Below Meroviglia the red rock on which Scaros is built juts out into the bay; on the top of it is the castle of the mediaeval rulers, and around cluster the old houses which were abandoned only twenty years ago because they were falling into the sea; and the last inhabitant, an old woman, had to be dragged away by main force, so attached was she to the home of her ancestors...

The Vineyards

On the following morning we set off for a long walk to explore the slopes of the island, which gently lead down to the outer sea. The aspect of the place is ugly enough in winter, and resembles a brown flat plain covered with hampers, for at santorin they always weave the tendrils of their vines into circles, the effect in Winter being that each vineyard looks as if hampers were placed all over it in rows and at intervals of every two yards. The Santoriniotes treat the vine differently to the other islanders, for here they plough their vineyards instead of digging them, and, contrary to the biblical injunction, I have often seen a bullock yoked to a mule in so doing.

For the first two or three years after planting a vine, they cut off most of the shoots, leaving only a few trailing on the ground, after which they weave them into the above-mentioned baskets, which in summer are quite hidden with leaves and fruit. This hamper increases in size year by year, until after twenty years it is cut off and the vine is left with only a few branches, of which some are trailed round in circles and others left lying on the ground, This work is done yearly...

The wine of Santorin is certainly most excellent, and is drunk largely in Russia; much, too, finds its way via France, to England under the name of claret; but a cunning wine-maker has christened a certain brand "Bordeaux'" and hopes by this artifice it may sell in England without passing through a French cellar, which entails considerable reduction in profits. But the best wine in the island is a white one called "of the night" because the grapes of which it is made are gathered before sunrise, and are supposed to have a better aroma for this cause. They make more wine here than anywhere else in Greece; they have seventy different types of grapes, the best of which are chosen for making that abominably luscious production called "vino Santo". The grapes are exposed on the roofs in the sun for fourteen days before they are pressed; hence sweetness and consistency are acquired.

Without her vineyards Santorin would be a desert. There is not enough barley grown to support a quarter of the inhabitants. There is not nearly straw enough for the mules, which deficiency is supplied by giving them the soft shoots of the vines to eat, whereas the extraneous branches are given to the hens. Even the branches and old hampers which are despised by the mules and the hens are not sufficient to supply the inhabitants with wood enough for their cooking purposes. Every article of clothing and every household utensil come from without; even water in years of drought has to be fetched from the neighbouring islands; and as we toiled through the basket-covered fields, the thin soil of which made walking such an exertion, we regretted that it was January, and not July, when all those baskets would be green and the grapes would hang temptingly around.

Everywhere we passed cisterns excavated in the ground and coated with cement. Some of them thirty to forty yards in circumference, for Santorini is almost waterless except for that collected in these cisterns. Every house has its own cistern, and public ones are kept at the expense of the community at fitting intervals along the roadsides, and provided with a pail for drawing up the water, and troughs for the mules to drink out of.

Only three natural springs exist on the island, and are in that part which is not volcanic. One of these, called the "life-giving stream," and has the curious anomaly of flowing more plentifully in drought; on the same formation four wells have been dug; the rest of the island depends entirely on its cisterns. Considering that the water collected into these reservoirs flows from all sides, from courtyards and alleys, the property of pigs and dogs, I felt rather chary about drinking it; but in reality it is most delicious water, the pumice-stone apparently purifies it; it is clear as crystal, and cool, produces rather than allays thirst.

Cave Dwellings

The cave dwellings were once among the most characteristic features of life on Thera, and many are still in use.

[M]idday brought us to the curious village of Gonia, of which from a distance all that can be seen is the two churches, for most of the houses of the village are excavated in the pumice-stone rock.

In one of these we lunched... The house was composed of two rooms, both in the rock; the outer one the family occupied by day, with a door opening into the street, a window over it and one on each side; the inner room the family occupied by night, and into this a ray of sunlight never penetrates.

These excavated houses ... are the subject of special legislation in Santorin. Those dwelling in them have no actual right to the land over their heads, but then nobody can make a vineyard or a reservoir without the consent of the householder below.

The next village we passed through is called Bothro, or Trench, and is a yet more perfect specimen of these Santorin rabbit warrens: the village occupies the bed of one of those chasms or watercourses, and not a sign of habitation, except the church, can be seen until you are in the midst of it. The construction is thus. The bed of the torrent forms the street; on either side are lovely gardens, for in this sheltered spot everything flourishes; luxuriant prickly pears and geraniums flower all the year round, and vines hang in festoons from trellisses. The houses on either side of the street are in the rock, each house has been chiselled out, and presents only a front wall with doors and windows. People say they are healthy; in fact, epidemics are exceedingly rare in Santorin. They are cool in summer and warm in winter, but they are damp; and, curiously enough, though water is so scarce, the inhabitants of Santorin suffer more from damp than anything else, for the moisture created by the sea air is not absorbed by the dry earth and gets into other things. Bread becomes mouldy directly, and so do boots, salt is always damp, tools rust in twenty-four hours, and those strings of beads with which the Greeks delight to play, get wet as if they had been dipped in water. Books decay as if from worms, and in an empty house you see spiders' webs hanging and sparkling with moisture in the sunshine. I never was more surprised than when I found mosquitos abundant in January here - they have them all the year round - and not a duckpond on the island.

A Shoemaker-Singer-Poet

This is a rare example of the survival of a popular oral tradition of petic composition and performance into nineteenth century Europe.

At Bothro we went to visit a shoemaker renowned for his songs. He was hard at work in his excavated house, which consisted of only one large room: he had two sabounas hung over his bed, and he was hard at work with his apprentices at his craft. The songs, as sung by our friend the shoemaker, were very pleasantly illustrative of Greek village customs. A talented man such as he is recognised as the village bard; he not only sings the songs he learnt from his elders, but he is deputed to make songs, like a poet laureate, about the passing events of life. These he teaches to his apprentices whilst they are at work; and so, like the tales of Homer, they are transmitted from generation to generation. He sang one about a woman of Santorini who two years before had murdered her husband. For greater effect he shut his eyes whilst singing, and now and again, when he felt hoarse, he took a pull at the mastic bottle which an apprentice held ready for him. But his masterpiece is a song about the eruption of 1866-70. It is very long and lasted nearly three quarters of an hour, always in the same monotonous, jerky key; but all listened intently, and so did I, for he articulated his words with surprising distinctness; and if the poetry was indifferent the facts were there, for he began:--

> In one thousand eight hundred and sixty-six,
> On the seventeenth of January,
> On Tuesday, at four o' clock,
> Haephestus commenced his eruption

and proceeded to describe each event minutely - how professors and steamers came from afar; how Thera was the wonder of all the earth - and now and again before a pause, and as a hint that he wanted a pull at the mastic bottle, he broke his narrative with a refrain :-

> O Thera! loveliest isle of Greece,
> Our peaceful, happy home,
> Will this great dread be overpast,
> Or waste wilt thou become?

At Bothro we visited many of these dug-out houses, and found their inhabitants prosperous and sharp-witted. From what I saw, I quite think the Santoriniotes are the sharpest Greeks I have ever met...

Mad about Cheese-Pies

Thera clearly led the way in developing what is today a characteristic dish throughout the country.

Amongst other delicacies peculiar to Santorin is *tyropita*, which, literally translated, means cheese cake. It is a curious composition, the first ingredient being a curd of sheep's milk, then some eggs, cheese, barley, cinnamon, mastic, and saffron. The impression left upon us when tasting it was that it was horrid, but the Santoriniotes are wild about it, and at Easter time, sooner than be without his cheesecake, a peasant will go through any privation. At this time they bake as many as fifty or sixty for each family, and what they cannot eat, when it is the consistency of a poultice, they dry and soak in their coffee on other feast days.

Folegandros

1883-4 James Theodore Bent

"An Enchanted Shore"

A string of island rocks almost joins Sikinos to Pholygandros - fantastic barren rocks, which sparkle in the sunshine, and of which we got to know every form and shape during that long day of patient tacking, accomplishing our sail of twelve miles in the same number of hours. Of all the islands of the Aegean Sea, Pholygandros can boast of the most majestic coastline: in fact, I doubt if it can be equalled anywhere. A precipituus line of rocks, in places rising 1,160 feet above the sea, forms the north-eastern bulwark. As we approached it the sun had set, and the sky was lurid with that red strange light which astonished the world, particularly the superstitious Greek world, in the winter of 1883-4. The water was almost transparent, and its depths looked wonderfully mysterious as we glided in amongst the rocks, some of which were white and looked like Nereids come to drive us from an enchanted shore. Such scenes as this make one realise how easy it has been to imagine the phantasies of the Odyssey and of modern folklore.

When I saw the spot again by daylight we wondered exceedingly how we had been able to climb up on hands and knees; it is known as the Plaka, a flat rock which slopes down into the sea at an angle of fifty degrees, and which is slippery in winter with running water; after scaling which we had a tremendous scramble in the dark up to the town, which is built on the edge of the cliff, 750 feet above us; and the path in winter up this side of the island is little better than a waterfall.

"Inside" and "Outside"

A string of island rocks almost joins Sikinos to Pholygandros - fantastic barren rocks, which sparkle in the sunshine, and of which we got to know every form and shape during that long day of patient tacking accomplishing our sail of twelve miles in the same number of hours. Of all the islands of the Aegean Sea Pholygandros can boast of the most majestic coastline; in fact I doubt if it can be equalled anywhere. A precipitous line of rocks, in places rising 1,160 ft above the sea, forms the north-eastern bulwark; as we approached it the sun had set, and the sky was lurid with that red strange light which astonished the world, and particularly the superstitious Greek world, in the winter of 1883-4. The water was almost transparent, and its depths looked wonderfully mysterious as we glided in amongst the rocks, some of which were white and looked like Nereids come to drive us from an enchanted shore.

Such scenes as this make one realise how easy it has been to imagine the phantasies of the *Odyssey*, and of modern folklore.

When I saw the spot again by daylight we wondered exceedingly how we had been able to climb up on hands and knees; it is known as the Plaka, a flat rock which slopes down into the sea at an angle of fifty degrees, and which is slippery in winter with running water; after scaling which we had a tremendous scramble in the dark up to the town, which is built on the edge of the cliff, 750 feet above us; and the path in winter up this side of the island is little better than a waterfall.

On reaching habitations we inquired where the demarch lived. "Outside" was the stoical reply. "Outside what?"' we asked. "Not Inside," was the angry rejoinder; and no further information could we get out of the man. We pursued our way in search of a more intelligent informant, until at length we discovered that Pholygandros boasts of only one town, which is walled, and called "Inside" (mesa), and of a colony outside this wall, of better-class houses, which is called "Outside", (exo); and a Pholygandriote knows of no other names but these.

Island Politics

Our new host was a very different man from our last. He was horribly modern in all his ideas; seventeen years ago he had travelled and gone as far as Paris, and since then he had lived with but one object - namely, that of modernising his island and rooting out superstitions. He had been in office as demarch for ten years, and boasted greatly of his improvements: how he had made a good road from the town down to the southern harbour, where we should have landed if the wind had been favourable; how he had encouraged education and new ideas in agriculture: and concluded by saying, "You will find our island a little Paris after Sikinos."

No one can realise the power a demarch possesses in these far-off islands in the Aegean Sea, especially in one like Pholygandros, where the steamer does not touch, and where sometimes in winter they are weeks without a post. He is a sort of king, or rather president of a small republic, elected every three years; and at these elections party spirit is most fearfully strained; for every Greek is a politician, and talks politics at his cafe, at his social gatherings, and everywhere, just as his forefathers did before him.

The Pholygandriotes do not care one jot about the Government at Athens; they have two joint members with Melos and Kimolos and three other islands; but they do not care a bit about their election - it is in the election of a demarch that they throw all their interest. For Athens, a king, and a parliament seem such miles away to them, it does not matter much what they do; the demarch is elected by them, and is theirs alone, and in his rise or fall all the local interest centres.

Of course there are two parties in Pholygandros: one is an aristocratic party, headed by one Venier, of an old Venetian family, and seconded by Themistocles Mavrojenes, one of the great Pariote family, who once could boast of a *hospodar* of Wallachia as one of their members; and then there is the democratic party, headed by our new host the demarch, which just now is in the ascendant. At the last election they had a furious contest; blood had not been spilt or murder committed, as was the case at Siphnos on a similar occasion, but party spirit ran so high, and still continues so, that Dr. Venier and the democratic demarch are not yet on speaking terms. One day, during our stay, our hostess came, in grief, to ask our advice about her father, who was very ill and at the point of death, she feared, so that the day before they had given him the "prayer oil"...; but still he refused to have Dr. Venier called in - his hated political rival. "He would rather die," she said, "unattended by a physician than have that man in his house."

The Folegandros Style of Dying

It was evident that nothing could be done for the old man, whose days were numbered; so we tried to change the subject from the hated Venier, as the name seemed to raise our hostess' ire exceedingly and tried to console her about her father, and to find out about their customs in Pholygandros at funerals. "Well," said she, "we shall be busy when the old man passes away. No one is more respected than he, and such a lot of people would have to be invited to the "grief table"; whereupon she was asked to explain what this meant. It appears that in this island when a death has occurred cooking is not deemed correct in the house for two or three days, so the relatives and friends bring food – "bitter food" … as they call it - and spread a "grief table" in the house of mourning. They hang the rooms with black, and remove the inevitable crochet from the sofas for a season. I felt an inward desire that, if the old man must die soon, he might die whilst we were there, that we might hear the lamentations and see the customs; but he did not die, and again we were told to put off our funeral enquiries till we got to Mykonos.

The prayer oil was administered to the old man, as we had been told; so I asked our hostess to explain the ceremony. "Here in Pholygandros we generally have five priests to perform the ceremony: a table is set in the sick man's room, on which is placed a dish of wheat, and a vessel on the wheat, into which the oil is poured; five pieces of stick with cotton tied round them are stuck into the wheat; the gospel is laid on this, and the five priests stand round with their chasubles … on, and sing tropaea, and read the suitable portions of Scripture whilst the censer is waved in the room. At the end of all this the chief priest dips a twig into the oil and makes a sign of the cross on the sick man, who kisses at the same time the proffered Bible, and then is left to die in the odour of sanctity."

The Golden Grotto and a Frightened Mayor

It was a most enchanting day that we chose for a visit to the Golden grotto of Pholygandros. Out of politeness the demarch determined to go with us; he had never been inside it he said; and I feel convinced that our rebukes urged on this energetic but misguided man to undertake a task for which by reason of increasing years he was totally unfitted.

We rode down the demarch's newly paved mule road to the southern harbour, and there beheld the maritime importance of Pholygandros as compared with Sikinos. They have four caïque belonging to them, and lots of fishing-boats, and the harbour, though small, shallow, and exposed to the south, is deserving of the name. A small colony of fishermen's huts forms the port, and here we noticed a clever little contrivance which they fasten to their nets in rough weather so that they may know where to find them. A bell is hung from two bent reeds, which form a little dome built on some flat reeds, and around the bell hang stones which strike it when the sea is rough.

Here, as elsewhere, we were struck by the universal use of the gourd for all domestic purposes. A gourd with a long handle they will put on the table for a decanter; small gourds cut in half serve as wineglasses; gourds with handles are used by every fisherman for baling water out of his boat; they are used for floating nets, and likewise for sieves through which milk is passed: a hole is made at one end, and a piece of the equally useful brushwood is stuffed into it, then the milk passes through the brushwood and is strained. Gourds properly prepared are used almost exclusively for the carrying of wine on a journey, and replace bottles in a country where the wine is quite a secondary consideration; for you pay threepence for your bottle and perhaps a halfpenny for the wine that is in it.

We got into a small boat at the harbour, and were rowed all along the wonderful line of cliff to where the grotto is; a cliff which rises 1,160 feet straight out of the sea without a break or a ledge to catch the eye, is by no means a common sight, and this cliff extends thus for nearly two miles. The formation is limestone streaked with iron, and here and there a few tufts of green relieve the monotony, the whole contrasting wonderfully with the indigo colour of the sea under its wide-spread shadow. Arato, an old writer, tells us that Pholygandros was once called "Iron", and that its second name was taken from a son of Minoa, of Crete; it well deserves the name Iron, for this wall of cliff is like a band of rusty iron coming out of the sea. We were rowed close up to the grotto, the entrance to which is about thirty feet above the sea, and thirty feet of apparently horizontal rock.

It was much easier to tell why it was called the golden grotto than to get into it, for the iron in the surrounding rock makes it look like a black picture set in a frame of gold; but our climb to it was fearful and the energetic demarch won our infinite respect by ultimately accomplishing it. Anciently this grotto was approached by steps from above, which are now worn away; they led up to the old town on the cliff, and their existence was discovered in 1837 by Kyrios Latre; but now the only way of reaching the grotto from the land side is by being let down by ropes for unpleasant distances.

Inside the grotto is curious and adorned with stalactites, like cathedral stalls, but nothing worthy of admiration after one has seen the grotto of Antiparos; inside, however, it has some ancient cisterns, which interested us, still full of water, and the haunt of countless pigeons. There are three of them - one round, one square, and one semicircular – and appearances point to its having been a place from whence the inhabitants in times of siege could get their water; also it appears to have been used as a cemetery, for rows of tombs have been found here and marble statuettes. We turned the thin sandy soil with which the bottom is covered and found quantities of ancient broken bits of pottery of a coarse description; and it struck me as a place that might repay a little excavation.

It was all very well to have climbed up – the descent was quite another thing. I would almost warrant that the demarch had never been so terrified in his life as he was then; our two sailors helped him down slowly by steadying his tottering steps and finding footholds for them. Beads of perspiration stood on his brow when he reached the boat, and if future travellers visit the golden grotto of Pholygandros, I feel confident that he will not attempt to accompany them, but remain prudently in the boat below.

A Third-Rate Chapel for an Inefficient Saint

Pholygandros is an island of most extraordinary shape, and if we had not Arato's authority for deriving its name from Minoa's son we might be tempted to speculate that it had something to do with a polypus, for the *h* is only a modern innovation, From the central height of the island legs stretch out into the sea in every direction, and this central height divides Pholygandros into two parts, one of which is a perfect wilderness of stones and the other very fertile, possessing smiling valleys and mountain slopes cultivated up to the very summit.

Of course the highest mountain is called Mount Prophet Elias, and close to it is the summit of St. Eleutherios, with a little church dedicated to that saint at the top. When there is a drought all the Pholygndriotes with the priests and the sacred pictures or Madonna walk in procession first to the top of Mount Prophet Elias, where they kneel around his shrine and pray for rain; after which they go and do likewise at the shrine of St. Eleutherios. "There is quite a little historical interest associated with our Church of St. Eleutherios." Old Themistocles Mavrojenes said to me that evening. "Seventy years ago there lived a pirate who annoyed the Pholygandriotes excessively. They prayed and prayed to St. Eleutherios for his death, and vowed a church to the saint's honour whenever that event should take place. The pirate, however, would not die, and for many years continued his depredations, until at last, at a ripe old age, he was gathered to his fathers; and our townspeople, who evidently think that no limitations can be brought to bear on the answering of a prayer, felt in duty bound to erect a church. It is a wretched little concern, however," concluded Mavrojenes apologetically; "if he had been more prompt in his succour St. Freedom would have had a better temple erected in his honour."

Skyros

1718 Joseph Pitton de Tournefort
A Sacred Debt-Collector

There's but one village in all Skyros, and that on a rock running up like a.sugar-loaf, ten miles from the port of St. George. The monastery, which bears the saint's name, makes the finest part of this village, though it has not above five or six caloyers, who carefully preserve an image of silver, on a very thin leaf, on which there is a coarse representation of St. George's miracles. This leaf, which is about four foot deep and two broad, is nailed on a piece of wood which has a handle to it like a crucifix, and which they carry as they do a banner. They pretend this image escaped the fury of the iconoclasts, and also performs great miracles daily, exercising particular severities on such as neglect to fulfil the vows made to St. George. There are not greater imposters in the world than the Greeks. Hear what they would have Father Sauger believe concerning this matter.

"This image" says he, "painted bunglingly on a log of wood, is placed over the great altar of the cathedral dedicated to St. George, and served by schismatics. When the church is full of people, the image is seen to move of itself, and notwithstanding its heaviness, will transport itself through the air into the midst of the assembly; among whom, if there chances to be one that has failed to perform his vows, the image singles him out, squats itself on his shoulders, where it sticks close, and plies him with furious buffetings, till he pays what he owes to the Church. The cream of the jest is, the image is not only endued with this virtue within the narrow limits of the Church, but generally throughout the whole island, where it will go and unkennel a man in the secret lurking-place. It goes its rounds in an extraordinary manner. A blind monk carries it on his shoulders; the image all the while, by an occult impression, directing him where he shall go. The debtor, seeing 'em coming, makes off, you may be sure, as fast as he can; but all to no purpose. Let him dodge and play at bo-peep as much as he pleases, the monk is steady in his pursuit, ascends, descends, passes, repasses, enters all places. Soon as ever he finds his man, the image leaps on his neck to rights, and so belabours him, that some have told me they thought the poor wretch would be murdered."

Without having recourseto magic, as does Father Sauger, the best way is flatly to deny the Fact, as we did, when they would have paumed their iImpertinences on us. A very honeft gentleman in company with us, had a mind to convince himself of the thing, and promised St. George ten crown-pieces, with an intention never to pay him. On our return back, we went to the church, to see if the blind image-porter with his burden would come and claim his promise, or knock him down for non-performance; but Heaven be praised, both image and image-bearer happened to be out of the spleen that day:

Father Sauger was likewise misinformed as to the nature of the image. It is not painted, but only carved on a plate of silver, which the more surprised us, because such sculptures are an Abomination to the Greeks. The chapel where it is kept is very small, adorned with gildings after the Greek mode. The convent is very nasty; but we drank admirable red wine there. It is certain we did not smart for our curiosity, and the monks, seeiong by our countenances, that we were not overburdened with credulity, only laughed at our questions...

Kea (Zea)

c. 1680 Bernard Randolph

Strong Women

Here I saw a woman that went into the fields to gather Velania, big with child, and another in her arms. In the field she was delivered, and brought both her children well home.

1801 Edward Daniel Clarke

Hospitality By Trickery

An amusing adventure befell us the next day, in our search for medals. We have before had occasion to allude to the hospitality of the Greeks, to their love of festivity, and to the sort of sensation excited by the arrival of strangers among them; but perhaps the following anecdote may exhibit their national characteristics in a more striking manner than has been hitherto done. The Consul having sent his mules to the harbour, we went to visit him, as we had promised to do, and despatched messengers about the town in search of medals and gems. Towards the evening, as we were preparing to take leave of our host, a little girl arrived; who said, if we would follow her, she would conduct us to a house where several antiquities would be offered to us for sale. Being conducted towards the spot, we were surprise to meet a young lady, very splendidly dressed, who offered us some medals, and said, if we would accompany her, she would take us to a house where the owner kept a collection of such rarities. Presently we met a second female, nearly of the same age, and similarly habited; who addressed the first, laughing, and then literally seized one of us by the arm, bidding her companion seize the other: and in this manner we were hurried into a crowded assembly, where many of the inhabitants had been collected for a regular ball. The dancing instantly began; and being welcomed with loud cheers into the midst of the party, there was no alternative but to give up all thoughts, for the rest of the evening, of returning to our caique, and contribute to the hilarity of those by whom we had been thus hospitably inveigled. Our conductors proved to be two of the daughters of the *idioproxenos*, who thus honourably entertained, after the manner of his forefathers, two private strangers, whom he was never likely to see again, and from whom he could reap no possible advantage. Every species of Greek dance was exhibited for the amusement of his guests; from the bounding hornpipe and rigadoon, to the more stately measures of the orbicular brawl, and the "thread-my-needle" of the modern *Roméka*. The whole night passed in one uninterrupted scene of the most joyous vivacity. To us it seemed to exhibit a moving picture of other times; for in the dances we actually beheld the choirs of the ancient Greeks, as originally they were led around the altars of Delos, or amidst the rocks of Delphi, or by the waters of Helicon, or along the banks of the Eurotas. When morning dawned, we retired; but we left them still dancing; and we heard their reiterated songs as we descended through the valley towards the shore.

1817-18 Peter Edmund Laurent

A Theft and a Restoration

As the part of the island wherein we landed was uninhabited, we were obliged to proceed immediately to the town, which was about six miles distant; no inquiries were made as to whence 'we came, and consequently we were not subjected to the irksome laws of quarantine: some mules were immediately procured, and they brought our luggage to the town; where we remained that night. The British vice-consul offered us the use of, his boat to cross the gulf to Athens. We accepted his offer; and, having bargained with the ... captain of the bark, for the passage, we departed early on the following morning...

On our return to the shore we were not a little surprised to find that all had been stolen. We were, in consequence, of this robbery, obliged to protract our stay in the island several days. Gratitude binds me to acknowledge (and with sincere pleasure do I fulfil that duty) the active exertions of the vice-consul, by whose means we re-obtained possession of our stolen goods. The theft had been committed by three persons, one of whom was the abbot of a convent in the island. It is an assertion which many travellers have made, and I believe with justice, that hardly ever is any crime ,committed in modern Greece, the instigator and mover of which is not a minister of religion; nay, strange as it may appear, the hordes, of Maniote pirates have each their priest, who invokes the assistance of the Almighty in their sanguinary expeditions, and pronounces a holy benediction upon the head of the ruthless adventurers.

We experienced great hospitality during our second stay here; all, but more particularly the women, pitied our state; thus destitute and at such a distance from home; they were ever ready to render us little assistances, which spoke the feelings of their bosoms - were we sitting near a peasant's cottage, fruits and refreshments were brought to us; were we climbing the rocks between the town and the port, all who met us greeted us with words of consolation and expressions of pity; in short, during our endeavours to re-obtain our lost effects, we witnessed more than enough to convince us, that although ignorance and depravity may impel some individuals to disgrace the country by their crimes, yet these islanders possess the foundation of all the social virtues - humanity.

1883-4 James Theodore Bent

Island Folk-Lore

...the distant parts of the island are dotted over with tiny cottages called "stables" where many families live entirely – consequently the children remain uneducated, and the parents teach them their superstitions. Some of these stables are congregated together and form hamlets nearly large enough to be provided with a Government school, when matters will be changed; but, as it is, the inhabitants of these outlying hamlets learn nothing, and, perhaps, only visit the town once or twice a year – generally if they can on September 11, the day of the raising of the cross – and then they bring with them a bundle tied up in a white handkerchief. This they hang on the tripod, on which the tray for holding the cross is put, and they do not take it off again until the cross is raised. This handkerchief contains corn, barley, beans, two roses, figs, garlic, cotton, cocoons, flax, and a little bees' wax. When the time for sowing seed has come they yoke their oxen, and rub a bit of the garlic on their foreheads, and, as they do so, say, "May you, my oxen, and may you, my family, be strong! May the fruits of the earth be blessed!" After this they throw all that the handkerchief contained into the earth, being careful to observe a strict fast on this day.

On September 1 the owner of one of these "stables" (rightly, indeed, so called, for they are more fitted for beast than man) has a duty to perform: as soon as he wakes in the morning he must go out of his house and fetch a stone. This he throws into the house, saying, at the same time, "May my family be healthful, and may money, like this stone, be thrown into my house."

The Nereids of Kea

When [the mists] cleared away we had a glorious day, and we simply revelled in the lovely scenery of Keos after, bare, ugly Thermià. The road winds along very high ground; on either side are deep, dark valleys leading down towards the sea, with fantastic rocks and full of oak trees; in the dim morning these great oaks, with their huge stems and stretching arms, looked weird enough. No wonder the superstitious Keotes people them and their cliffs with Nereids; somehow in Keos these mystic beings seem to be brought into closer union with humanity than elsewhere. "They often," says the housewife, "steal her clothes, her sheets, and bed linen, but they nearly always return them." Very often the Nereids have children by human men, for the most part malicious, evil-disposed children. "Charon must have been your sponsor and a Nereid your dam," is a frequent expression of abuse to naughty children. For those who are supposed to have been struck by the Nereids when sleeping under a tree the following cure is much in vogue. A white cloth is spread on the spot, and on it is put a plate with bread, honey, and other sweets, a bottle of good wine, a knife, a fork, an empty glass, unburnt candle, and a censer. These things must be brought by an old woman, who utters mystic words and then goes away, that the Nereids may eat, undisturbed, and that in their good humour they may allow the sufferer to regain his health.

More interesting even than this relic of the offerings the Athenians once made to the Eumenides on the slopes of Areopagus is another custom the Keotes have of treating children who are supposed to have been struck by these Nereids. In Keos St. Artemidos is the patron of these weakling, and the church dedicated to him is some little way from the town on the hill slopes; thither a mother will take a child afflicted by any mysterious wasting, "struck by the Nereides," as they say. She then strips off its clothes and puts on new ones, blessed by the priest, leaving the old ones as a perquisite to the Church; and then if perchance the child grows strong she will thank St. Artemidos for the blessing he has vouchsafed, unconscious that by so doing she is perpetuating the archaic worship of Artemis, to whom in classical times were attached the epithets *paidotrophos, kourotrophos, philomeirax*; and now the Ionian idea of the fructifying and nourishing properties of the Ephesian Artemis has been transferred to her Christian namesake. We found traces of the worship of Artemis having existed in Keos along with that of Apollo in ancient times, for Barba Manthos had a little image of the Ephesian Artemis in his collection, which he had found in a temple at Karthaia. There is yet another remedy for a sickly boy, peculiar, as far as I know, to Keos, but probably a branch of the same system to which I have alluded at Melos and elsewhere.

An Old Character

As the wine flowed freely the old man became exceedingly talkative, and Barba Manthos for our benefit drew him out to tell us the adventures of his long life, some of which were calculated to make the females present awkward if it ever entered into their minds to feel shy.

"And then I became a monk," said the old man at the conclusion of his narratives, "that is to say, I light the lamps of the church, sweep it out when it is dirty, and live in a cell."

"Are not you afraid of living here all alone in this remote corner of the world?" I asked.

"Nothing would harm an old man like me," was his reply; but Barba Manthos privately told me that nobody in the whole island had seen such wonderful hobgoblins as he, for he it was that had made them open old Manetas' grave two years after his death by saying that he had met him in the road, and, sure enough, they found no body in the tomb, so they got the priest in hot haste, who poured oil into it and set fire to the oil. At this ceremony the old man declared he saw a blue flame go straight up to heaven, and that he had never seen old Manetas since.

"I heard strange music in my stable the other day," said the old man musingly, and, sure enough, next day my little granddaughter fell ill. I knew it was the Nereids who did it. Not long after, whilst digging in my field, I found a stick like a cross; this I put upon her bed at night, and, sure enough, next day she was well." He then told us his firm belief in the evil eye affecting cattle and trees; for had not three or his healthiest goats sickened and died last year just because a man with the evil eye had admired them?" "The best thing possible for the evil eye," he said in conclusion, is to throw salt into the fire, and let an old woman say some magic words, whilst all gape over the fire with open mouths; and then the priest can do a good deal by reading the proper liturgy for the evil eye, only they have in their ignorance and folly abandoned this good practice of late years."

Our old friend tottered about with us on his stick, jabbering the while, only too glad get some one to listen to his stories. He is a type of the Greek of the old régime, a character that will not be found in another generation in all the realm of Hellas.

The Miltos Mines

As we rode along in the direction of the ancient miltos mines Barba Manthos told us how in his day the sea had made many encroachments on the northern coast, and how the land was constantly slipping in this part. Curiously enough Pliny tells us that a great piece of the island once fell into the sea, swallowing up men, villages, and all, and Barba Manthos pointed out as we went along a spot where thirty years ago a field with some oak trees had slipped down to a much lower level. It is the same story over again; motions of the crust, upheavals, and subsidences are common in every island, and in former days they must have been more frequent and more tremendous than now, for the evidence of earthquakes, which now are seldom felt in the Cyclades, are numerous, whilst at Chios, and in the Sporades generally, earthquakes are of annual occurrence; and mythology, with wonderful tales of the appearance of islands and the disappearance of towns; according to the caprice of the gods, corroborates the evidence of nature.

The miltos mines are deep holes chiselled in the side of a mountain, about an hour's ride from the town, to the north of the island, and are known as the "caveholes" by the inhabitants. The chiselled rock has a very bright, rich colour and is strongly impregnated with iron; the marks of the ancient tools are still plain, and numerous lamps have been found inside. It appears that the Athenians produced their much-prized dye by subjecting the stones to heat. About half an hour's ride below the mines is the harbour of Otzia, where there are traces of an ancient mole and of ancient buildings. Doubtless the miltos was shipped from here, and probably many a boat in ancient days here painted its bows and became, as Homer expresses it, "a red-cheeked ship".

Kythnos

1718 Joseph Pitton de Tournefort

Mistaken for Pirates

From Syra we direded our course to Thermia, another island, 25 miles from Syra from cape to cape... The nearness of Thermia to Zia suffers us not to doubt that Thermia is the island of Cythnos...

We arrived at Thermia the night between the 30th and 31st of October, and were forced to lie in a chapel, where we were like to have our throats cut. Some Turks of Negropont, who were in a large caicque near ours, seeing our sailors stripping off the skins of a couple of sheep we had bought at Syra, went and raised the town upon us, as if we were banditti, come to plunder the port. Upon this, the country people took to their arms: but as good-fortune would have it, the consul of France, M. Janachi, whom they raised out of bed to go along with 'em, enquiring what sort of figure these pretended banditti made, and being told that four of 'em wore hats, rightly concluded they could not be banditti, who seldom have so much as a thrum-cap to their pates. He therefore prayed the townsmen of Thermia to go home again, assuring them that they were merchants, Frenchmen belike, come to buy corn and silk. For all that, they made him dispatch away two of his domestics to go and get intelligence of us. We were surprised about three in the morning, to see entering the chapel two persons, who with their carbines cocked, demanded who we were, and all that: when we had satisfied them, they told us that had it not been for the prudent remonstrances of the consul of France, we had gone to pot, every mother's son of us. Being recovered from our fright, we waited on the consul to thank him: there we had the mortification to see, among our accusers, a Turk whom we knew Waivod at Serpho, and who was more alarmed than any other, becaufe he had packed up and was carrying off his ill-gotten treasure. He begged us a thousand pardons, and recommended us earnestly to the consul's favour and protection.

The Economy of the Island

The island of Thermia, unlike most of the islands of the Archipelago, is not steep. Its soil is good and well-improved, it affords little wheat, but a great deal of barley, and a sufficiency of wine and figs, scarce any oil at all. The silk of this island is said to be as good as that of Tinos ... which brings confiderable profit to the country; for they make there above 1200 pound weight of that commodity. Their other trade lies in barley, wine, honey, wax, wool; their cotton manufacture is only for their own use. They make a pretty sort of gauze or yellow veils, w hich the women of the island wear about their heads. Thermia likewise affords plenty of provision; there is such a prodigious quantity of partridges, that they export cages full of 'em to the neighbouring islands, where they sell 'em for three pence a-piece. The place has few rabbits, and no hares at all. As for wood, they have none to speak of, so they burn nothing but stubble.

Serifos

1883-4 James Theodore Bent

Buried in the Fields

The village of Livadhi, by the harbour, is small but tidy, and we there partook of refreshments in a clean fisherman's cottage off a table rudely carved with all sorts of fish designs. The ceilings of the houses are here all made of canes placed crosswise; on the top of this ceiling they put seaweed, and on the top of the seaweed mud, which is carefully pressed and rolled, and forms the roof of the one-storeyed houses; a very treacherous roof indeed, in wet weather, as we often experienced.

The tiny plain down by the harbour is a pattern of fertility. There is a well in each field; pomegranates, figs, and almond trees abound; another feature peculiar to Seriphos at once caught the eye: every proprietor has his grave in his own field, built like a little shrine, and if he sells his field special provision in the articles of sale have to be made for the non-disturbance of ancestral bones. This custom is not carried on in any other of the Cyclades, and reminded us of the days when an Athenian possessor of land left directions in his will to, be buried in his private ground. Frequently, too, the graves, as at Seriphos now, were by the roadside. The family sepulchre of Isocrates was near the Cynosarges, that of Thucydides by the Melitic Gate.

A Loquacious Guide

We climbed up the steep ascent to the town on foot, as did the rest of the population, who had come to see the steamer arrive: women carrying their babies tied to their backs with string; fishermen with their baskets full of fish, now in great request, for the ante-Christmas fast had just set in; and, by our side our new host, Captain George, trotted; pointing out each object of interest we passed. "This is the tomb of So-and-so, who died of so, and was the father of Maria So-and-so. This is the Church of St. Isidoros, where is a spring of warm water, reckoned excellent for the health, where a yearly panegyris (a festival) is held; and it was built by Sophia Makri, who was asleep and dreamt she was caught by her neck by St. Isidoros and commanded to go and build a church on this spot. When she awoke she had it built. Come in and have a glass of water; there is iron in it." So Captain George rambled on. I followed him in, drank some exquisite water, and recognised why it was dedicated to St. Isidoros, because *sideros*, iron (according to modern pronunciation) suggested one of those ecclesiastical puns in which the Eastern Church loves to indulge.

Captain George here paused awhile to rest, and as I scrutinised our new acquaintance I felt I did not like him; he was a little thickset man with an evil countenance, but sparkling with intelligence. Afterwards I learnt that he was well known in these seas as an expert smuggler, who would have been a pirate if he had lived fifty years ago. He had just got a nice new caïque painted green, and his plan was to offer us hospitality and to persuade us to take his boat at a price which would pay him better than smuggling.

We went on a little further.

"Here is the Church of St. Tryphon," said Captain George, "the protector of agriculture." Not knowing much about St. Tryphon I questioned further, and found that he is in great repute here. On his day no one works or cleans out his house, because they think he has power over rats and all animals hurtful to agriculture, and on St. Tryphon's Day the Church has offices and prayers for the special supplication of this saint to ward off blight. St. Tryphon must, I thought, be a descendant of Apollo Smintheus, who was worshipped in the neighbouring isle of Keos.

Captain George's house was a new one, at the lower end of the town, really quite a mansion for the islands. You enter the one sitting room with the divan, and off this are several little boxes, about eight feet square, entered by gates four feet high, the upper part being open: these are bedrooms. Ours had a thin gauze blind across the opening, which afforded us only a sorry attempt at seclusion.

Captain George's wife was a chattel, and a very uninteresting piece of furniture, too; for he hounded the poor thing about until she looked like a scared mongrel. She waited upon us at meals and never took a part in them. She cooked, she swept, and she slaved whilst the captain made merry with his guests. The wife of a lower class Greek is a pitiable object, much as she was in Hesiod's time, who, in his *Works and Days* shows us a wife's condition then, and considered it the worst possible feature of a bad wife to wish to sit at meals with her lord and master.

The Dirtiest Town in the Archipelago

After the usual slight refreshments of coffee, jam, and mastic, we were joined by the demarch, a priest, and a schoolmaster, and taken forth to see the town. Of all towns in the Greek Islands, Seriphos will remain fixed in my mind as the most filthy. The main street is a sewer into which all the offal is thrown; and it is tenanted by countless pigs - for each householder has liberty to keep three. What the nuisance must have been when the number was unlimited I cannot think. Furthermore this street is like a ladder of rocks, and the pigs in their movements are as nimble as goats, most dangerous to the peace of mind of the pedestrian. Sometimes the street is not two feet wide, sometimes it is expanded to six feet, but always an inch deep in mire, often more.

In one of these narrow streets on the Tuesday after Easter the maidens of Seriphos play their favourite game of the swing…. They hang a rope from one wall to the other, put some clothes on it, and swing, singing and swinging, one after the other. Aware of this the young men try to pass by, and are called upon for a toll of one penny each, a song, and a swing. The words they generally use are as follows; - "The gold is swung, the silver is swung, and swung, too, is my love with the golden hair;" to which the maiden replies, "Who is it that swings me that I may gild him with my favour, that I may work him a fez all covered with pearls?" Then, having paid his penny, he is permitted to pass, and another comes on and does likewise.

The houses opening on to this street were mere black holes, where sat families shivering round charcoal fires on which pots ... were boiling for the evening meal. They seemed hospitably inclined towards us, for one woman ran out with a branch of myrtle and some basil, which she handed me for good luck; rather a nuisance, indeed, for the ascent demanded all one's care. The summit of the hill, and the castle crowning it, were at length reached, and here the schoolmaster showed us a niche in which, he said, once stood a statue of a king of Seriphos, which the English had taken away. I asked for further particulars about this, to me, unknown royal house of Seriphos, but the schoolmaster's genius for invention would lead him no further. He had not the face to tell me that it was a statue of King Polydectes. Over the gateway to the castle was a coat of arms, and 1433 over it; so I felt convinced that the schoolmaster alluded to a statue of one of the Latin dukes who ruled in Seriphos. But, though the English have been great robbers in Greece in their day, I question if anyone ever burdened himself with the statue of a Crispi or a Sommaripa.

Island Husbandry

Next morning we started on an expedition with the object of visiting a convent dedicated to the Archangel Michael and a remote village called Galene (peace). Captain George was to be our guide. He had nothing to do, he said, and if we would pay for a mule for him nothing would give him greater pleasure than to do the honours of his island. There is much that is pretty in the steep slopes of Seriphos, though the island, except near the town, is bare; for at this time of year the vineyards were brown, and the long, straggling vines, which in the islands are trained along the ground to get what protection they can from the summer winds, do not in winter present a very lovely appearance. Seriphos is noted for its wine, and it is one of the chief industries of the place. Each vineyard has its winepress in it … these are just whitewashed tanks out of which the juice of the grapes when trampled on flows into a lower tank; all round were thrown the remnants of stalks and skins from the late vintage and the hard matter which had been extracted from the compressed pulp. After extracting the juice in this manner they boil it for a month before it is considered fit to drink; and the day of St. Minas, in November, is considered as the proper one on which to stop boiling the wine… ; and on this day all the well-known wine-tasters of the place repair to the vats and expect a present of wine straight out of them as an incentive to approve.

In July, when the first fruits of the vintage are supposed to be ready, they throw a bunch of grapes into their houses, thinking thereby to rid them of rats and other vermin, saying, as they do so, "The black grape will sicken, the black grape will poison. Out with you, fleas and rats!" And on August 6, when the vintage begins, the Church has special offices and prayers for the success of the same.

In connection with the planting of vineyards they have quite a Bacchic festival in Seriphos. On one of the many feast-days of the Virgin after matins are over the man who desires to plant a new vineyard calls together fifty or more men, according to the size of the field which he intends to plant. To each man he hands a spade, and then he fills skins with wine, and has joints of goat's flesh, which have been roasted for the occasion, brought out, and the company start off in high glee, singing a they go and preceded by a standard-bearer holding a white banner. During their interval of rest they consume the goats and the wine, and then work till the vineyard is planted - for it must all be done in one day - and in the evening they return home, with their spades, their hoes, and the wineskins empty, somewhat the merrier for having imbibed the contents. At a spot called Panagia, before the Virgin's Church, the white standard is set up, and the Seriphiotes enjoy a dance, that evening in which the vineyard-planters join.

A somewhat similar cooperation is customary in Seriphos when the first rains of October fall. All the husbandmen meet together to assist one another at the forges in preparing their implements of husbandry for the coming season. They come with their spades, their ploughs, and their mattocks, and they come prepared, too, to have a festive gathering; and every evening until the work is done they have drinking parties, regular symposia…

Another custom connected with husbandry still in vogue in Seriphos is that on September 14, the Day of the Cross. Farmers take a little of the grain which is about shortly to be sown and a rose with them to church. These things are blessed in the liturgy. The rose is broken up and scattered about in the first field which is sown that year as a sure emblem of abundance and success. This is a trace of the ancient … sacrifices before the sowing of seed, to ensure a productive harvest.

The "Transfiguration Basket"

Captain George was most communicative about the ways of his country, as were also the muleteers who accompanied us, and supplied any knowledge in which captain George was wanting. One of them, a stalwart fellow with grizzled hair, suddenly put me a question which puzzled me not a little.

"Did you ever hear of the transfiguration basket, sir?"

The man was difficult to understand, the Seriphiote dialect being full of obscure words; and not until Captain George had come to my assistance did I comprehend what was meant. And he put it as follows into intelligible Greek for my benefit.

"On the day of our Saviour's transfiguration all faithful Seriphiotes believe that a basket is let down from heaven, full of all manner of good things, for the man who is lucky enough to be the first to see it; but he must be very quick in asking for what he wants, for the basket is immediately drawn up again, and the gift is not forthcoming."

As a confirmation of this story, the muleteer went on to relate how a shepherd had once seen this basket descending, and, thinking hurriedly in his mind that money would be the best thing to have, he cried out in all haste "Two thousand (*chilia*)," and was going to add florins, when two jars, called here *cheilia* ... fell from the basket at his feet.

This story ought to be a warning to the Greeks generally to alter their pronunciation; for when nearly all the vowels and diphthongs are pronounced like *e* ... other people are puzzled who are less hurried visitors than the heavenly basket.

The Monastery of the Archangel

By this time we were nearing the convent of the archangel. From a distance it looked like a fortress; around it is a high wall with battlements, and a terrace inside, from which in those old troublous times the monks could fight. Beneath the terrace are the cells, and in the centre of the square is the church. There are four towers at each end of the walls, one of which is now converted into a dovecote. The entrance is exceedingly low, only about four feet high, at the top of a flight of steps, which have been added since the days of pirates. Formerly it was approached only by a wooden staircase, which could be drawn up. In the door is a most extraordinary bolt and wooden key, being a long bit of jagged wood, which is shoved into the bolt, and fits itself with a jerk into the required place; but it requires practice to work these locks. The ceiling of the porch was all crisscross reed work, like the houses, and from it were hung the scales, with which they weighed the produce of the fields let, out to husbandmen.

The church is old and interesting, being round and vaulted, evidently much earlier than the date over the door, 1447, which was of marble, and with rudely carved grape tendrils, with leaves painted green, stalks painted brown, and the background yellow, climbing up the jambs, above which were two birds on two poplars and an inscription describing the might of the archangel.

Inside the church was beautifully frescoed, having round it a frieze of saints, full length, over a dado of drapery. The vaulted roof was covered with biblical scenes, and on the entrance wall was the usual terrible fresco of St. Michael, and on the left those awful representations of hell so common in Byzantine churches. There is the fiery river with its inscription on a scroll ... kings, bishops, etc. are engulfed in a dragon's mouth; the proud man ... is hung by his feet from a tree; the evil speaker... is dragged by his feet, whilst a demon follows him, shoving a spear down his throat; the glutton is being slapped by two demons at the same time on the stomach and on the mouth; the drunkard is head downwards to let the wine run out; those who cannot get up for early mass on Sundays are lying in bed like dead men, with elegant coverlets over them; and the tortures of the woman who has nourished a foreigner are horrible to behold: a fitting subject for contemplation in these lands, from whence the female population has gone, at one time or another, to the Turkish towns as servants or to fill the harems.

The poor old monk who accompanied us was in a great state of grief that his superior was absent; however we satisfied him by promising to look in again on our return from Galene. He was such a queer old wretch, with bare legs, baggy blue trousers, blue cotton jacket lined with filthy fur, and a black cap on his head, by which alone we knew him to be a monk. His poor head was all on one side, and surrounded by a large crop of unkempt grizzled hair. Most of these monks are little above peasants; they go into the monasteries, instead of the workhouse, when too old and infirm to work, and take a vow to observe celibacy and let their hair grow.

In Greece, as with us, the proverb is common, "When the devil grows old he becomes a monk." They till the ground belonging to the monastery and do all the menial offices, carrying out thereby the advice of an Egyptian father who taught that a labouring monk was tempted but by one devil, whilst an idle one was exposed to the devastation of a legion.

The Nereids of Serifos

No sooner had we spoken of Nereids than demarch's daughter, a woman of fifty or more, at on developed a desire to talk and tell her story as to what had happened to her as she was staying in Constantino with a cousin of hers who had just had a lovely child which had become ugly owing to the influence of the Nereids; so the mother was determined to take child and lay it on a marble monument in St. George's Church. Having done this she laid it on a grave for, a while and took Miss Kousoupis with her without telling her anything about it. The child was left for five minutes on the grave, and then the mother gave it to Miss Kousoupis to carry; and as they went away, owing to the mother having given Miss Kousoupi no notice of what she was doing, she looked round, and the child died, in a fortnight, and she herself suffered from headaches giddiness, and general wasting, and was brought back to Seriphos in a dying state. So her mother took her to the monastery of the archangel, where we had just been and there they lived for forty days until she recovered; but even now she said she was liable to fits of faintness and giddiness. Here in one story we have two ancient ideas combined: the baneful influence of the Nereids on the young, and the prevalent idea that illness can be cured by lying in churches. The vividness of the narration and the excitement of the narrator quite convinced me that she believed that what she was telling me was true.

Seeing we were interested in this subject, the demarchos sent for an old woman popularly believed at Galene to be one hundred years old. Her sobriquet was Plyntes, for in her youthful days she had been employed in washing out the wine-vats after the process of treading the grapes was over. Such a wrinkled piece of goods I never saw. She had on a white cap drawn forwards over her eyes, so that only the nose and chin could be seen *en profile*. Over this was a shawl tied round her chin; she had on a snuff-coloured short petticoat, stockings to match, a fur jacket, and over it a wide coat of brown Dutch carpet. She hobbled in, and seemed terrified of us, crossing herself lest we should cast on her the evil eye. She would not speak a word at first, in spite of the demarch's assurances that our intentions were peaceable.

"She almost shrieked when he spoke about Nereids, started up, and prepared to hobble away, but was persuaded to return. Again when the question was put she asserted, "I know nothing," shut her eyes, and groaned, and then, turning to our, by no means juvenile, host, she murmured, "My little boy, what are they going to do to me? "Thereupon everyone set to work to console her and stroke her, assuring her that the English meant no harm; so she at length told her tale in a low voice, which had to be translated to me from the dialect.

"Years ago Michael Kappazacharias was digging in his vineyard near St. Cyprian's Church." Here she grew frightened again, and crossed herself violently before continuing, "Well, it was a very calm, still day, when suddenly a whirlwind came and carried him to some distance; and as he was being borne along he felt the firm grip of the Nereids. Shortly afterwards he was found lying senseless, and carried in that state to the village." In this story we had the Nereids of the storm, like the Harpies of old, who carried off the daughter of Pandareos from the halls of Olympus in a rushing wind, such a wind as Penelope longed for to carry her away to get relief from the troubles which surrounded her.

The Life of the Pirates (Baron von Stackelberg & C. F. Gille, 1831)

Sifnos

1718 Joseph Pitton de Tournefort

How to Avoid Work Island-Style

About fifty Years ago there came to Siphanto some Jews, by order of the Porte, to examine into the lead-Mines; but the burghers fearing they should be constrained to work 'em, bribed the captain of the galliot that had brought over those Jews, to sink his vessel, which accordingly he did by boring holes in it while the Jews were aboard with a cargo of ore consign'd to Thessalonica. This officer saved himself in his chaloupe, the rest went to the bottom. After this, some other Jews came over on the like errand, but made no better a hand on't. The Siphantines. to get rid of 'em at once, gave a sum of money to a corsair of Provence, who was at Milo, and who cannonaded a second galliot laden with Jews and lead-ore: so that the Turks and Jews both gave over the enterprise.

1883-4 James Theodore Bent

The Spirits of Place

The Siphniotes are industrious and well-to-do; they have a fertile island, olives grow to any extent, and every Greek knows that "an olive with a kernel gives a boot to a man." They have mines, too, and though the richer inhabitants complain that the existence of mines makes labour and provisions dear yet there are two sides to this question. A French company has started mining operations at Kamara, a place so called from, the vaulted chambers cut by ancient miners in the cliffs, (Italian, *camere*) close to the sea. We visited them one day, and saw there an interesting cave with the inscription over it, "the temple of the nymphs", cut in the rock. Here we have an old centre of nymph worship, and here we still find wonderful stories of Nereids and *genii loci* associated with the spot. Travellers who cross a certain stream close to here, more especially at midnight or midday, are exposed to the danger of being possessed; and to cure such cases it is customary to prepare and place at a spot where three roads meet, or hang in the wells, some bread wrapped up in a clean napkin, and some honey, milk, and eggs, to appease the nymphs. The *genii loci*, too, haunt certain well-known trees and cliffs, and are like our old friends the hamadryads. Woodcutters fear to lie or sleep under a big old olive tree called Megdanos; and when they have to cut down a tree that they suppose to be possessed they are exceedingly careful when it falls to prostrate themselves humbly and in silence lest the spirit should chastise them as it escapes; and sometimes they put a stone on the trunk of the tree so as to prevent its egress.

At the wells we find another kind of sprite called by the peasants Arabs, and sometimes even piously inclined sprites haunt churches; these are rarely evil-doing; if they are, they do not live in the church, but in a cave hard by, so as to prevent people from going there to worship. And not unfrequently we hear stories of the prowess of the patron saint – how he has driven them off and rendered the place safe again.

Some Giddy Nuns

On our return journey we visited what was once a celebrated convent for nuns, dedicated to St. John the Theologian. Captain Prokos told us some sorry tales about the goings on of these ladies when he was young, for generally before they were placed in this convent they had been guilty of some misconduct at home; and the Convent of St. John the Theologian before it was disestablished by the present Government was the favourite rendezvous of all the gallants of Siphnos. Captain Prokos lead us to infer that he had been there more than once, at which speech his wife administered a sharp reprimand, for she was not the down-trodden squaw our late hostess had become. Now these giddy nuns are scattered to the wind, and the tottering walls of their convent are inhabited by two very ancient females whose duty it is to clean the church and keep the lamp burning. The Siphniotes call it the Convent of **Mongou** amongst themselves. The name was curious, and excited my curiosity. A tradition, on which is based the origin of this name, says that a pious Siphniote built it years ago, and his wife objected to the money he had spent upon it; whereat he replied, in French, "J'ai fait mon gout" and the name has stuck to it ever since. It is curious what a lot of western words have crept into the Siphniote dialect. Pigs they call francesi (Frenchmen) because a traveller of that nation exclaimed on hearing a pig grunt, "Voilà une langue que je comprends"! The schoolmaster of Siphnos rejoices in the name of **Gion**. "Mine is a family of French origin," he said; "the name was formerly spelt Jean." Probably the mines had something to do with this and the family who ruled Siphnos in the Venetian days, the Da Corogna, of Spanish extraction: this family provided princes for Siphnos for a century and a half, and then, in 1456, the heiress of this family married one Nikolas Gozzadini, who became lord of Siphnos; not until 1617 was the last of this family cast out by the Turks. There still live on the island of Santorin another branch of the Da Corogna family.

Greek Sailor
(Baron von Stackelberg
& B. Consorti, 1825)

Kimolos

c. 1790 "An Italian Gentleman"

A Small Island at the End of the Eighteenth Century

This island is not far distant from Milo, and is only eight miles in circumference. The port, which is small, is not deep enough to admit ships of burden. The country is mountainous, ... and almost barren. There is none but cistern water, and very little of that. The small portion of land laid out in agriculture or vineyards produces scarcely sufficient for the support of its inhabitants; so that they eat the grapes and are obliged to get wine from Milo. The island grows likewise a little barley and cotton; but nature, which never bestows everything, has denied in trees what it has given it in silver. There is a great deal of terra Cimolia, to which the ancients, among other properties, attributed that of curing the rheum. It is a sort of white chalk, fatty and soapy, heavy, tasteless and friable, used at present as it was in the days of Pliny, to whiten linen. I am told that in the baths of Smyrna they rub the skin with it. Game, on account of the multitude of sportsmen, is not plentiful. We have met with some partridges and hares, however. I shot at them with my usual skill, and you may guess that I missed them. The village contains at most three hundred souls. The houses are small and wretched, resembling rather cottages. The churches and chapels, which are very numerous, re better built. There is not a single Turk here, but there is French consul, who does not omit every morning to display his flag...

These people are all sailors, and the greater part excellent pilots. Beside their own language, they speak Italian, French, and even English. The women knit cotton stockings with which they supply the neighbouring islands. Their natural sprightliness, added to a desire of disposing of their commodities, made them so familiar that several of them took us by the arm and proposed us to go home with them. This behaviour has given rise to a report that their virtue is not proof against seduction, which indeed I understood to be so far true, when they are enabled by the sale of it to procure the price of an absolution, the refusal of which they consider a great calamity.

1883-4 James Theodore Bent

Laying Vampires

Their belief in vampires here in Kimolos is very firm... If a dying man curse himself, or any enemy of his shall curse him when at the point of death, that man will become a vampire. The earth cannot dissolve his body; he will wander about at night strangling men and beasts and sucking their blood. There is no peace for him in Hades, no peace for his relatives, for he returns to his home and "feeds on his own," as the expression goes; he brings with him plagues, typhus, cholera; the grass dies near his grave, the flowers wither, and are eaten by worms, ruin comes on the herds, and dogs wander ominously about the streets howling in the night.

If there is a suspected case of vampire they go to a priest ... he accompanies them to the grave of the supposed ghost, and on bended knee they supplicate the All-Merciful to have compassion on this wretched being... and on the grave the priest pours some boiling water and some vinegar. After this ... it is generally observed that the ghost stops his wanderings; many affirm that whilst the service is going on they hear the rattle of the bones as they settle in the grave.

Melos

1687 Randolph, Bernard

A Warm *Rendez-Vous*

It has a very fair harbour, large, and secure against all winds. Here privateers do usually come to make up their fleets, and it is most commonly their rendezvous, at their first coming into the Archipelago ...Here are several hot places for men to sweat, at the side of hills, which in some places are so hot as to roast an egg, if put between the hollow of some stones. All the whole island is esteemed to have fire under it, which is thought to consume the stones, which are very like to honeycombs, being all hollow.

1738 Lord Sandwich

Thick Legs

The dress of the women in this country is very peculiar; their petticoats coming no lower than their knees, in order to show (what with them is reckoned the greatest perfection) their thick legs. This is a fashion so much in vogue among them, that it is a common thing to see them with seven or eight pairs of stockings on, besides bandages round the small of the leg, which render them more deformed than nature intended them.

1813 Colonel William Leake

The Economy of the Island

Oct. 10. - Light adverse winds or calms, accompanied with rain having continued to prevail, it is not until this morning that we enter the port of Milo, and anchor near the head of the bay. Land, and visit the hot springs: the hottest is on the sea-beach, a mile from the old town. The ground around them is impregnated with sulphur, as appears by a yellow crust on many of the stones. In the side of a little rocky height above is another hot source in a cavern, and a vapour issuing from the fissures so hot that the water appears less so than it really is. A thick crust of salt is formed on the rocks around, and flakes of salt float on the surface. Turks from the neighbouring continent sometimes come here to take a course of bathing. To the south-east of this height are some salt-pans, and a marshy level, in which, towards the hills, stands the khora, or town, once containing 16,000 inhabitants, but now not more than two hundred families. There are twenty-five Greek and two Latin churches still remaining. The ruins and the naked valley surrounded by white rocky heights, and with scarcely any vegetation except a few meagre date-trees, give the place a most dismal appearance. The air is said to be very unhealthy. In the afternoon I proceed to the village called Kastro, which is situated on a peaked rocky height above the northern side of the entrance of the bay, and lodge in the house of the English vice-consul, Mr. Peter Mikhelis, who with many of his relations, and all the richer Miliotes, gain their livelihood as pilots for the Aegean sea. At the highest point of the village they have a lookout room, where some of them are always on the watch for ships making signals for pilots. They are well supplied with English telescopes, and have good boats, with which they sometimes meet vessels at a distance of 12 or 15 miles from the island. The rule is, that whoever first discovers a ship has a prior right to offer himself as pilot. Milo has now not more than between two and three thousand inhabitants, who, in addition to the productions consumed by themselves, raise for exportation, in tolerable years, 2000 kila politika of wheat, and 12 or 14000 of barley, 2 or 300 kantari of cotton, and 1500 barrels of wine. The island would derive also a considerable profit from its mines of alum and sulphur, if the fear of the Porte did not prevent the inhabitants from working them. The mines are on the eastern side of the island, near a height which emits smoke, and has every appearance of having been a volcano.

The oil produced in the island is seldom sufficient, even in good years, for its consumption. They depend upon their neighbours for cheese, and import a few European articles of household furniture. The men are all dressed in the white cotton cloth made in the island, with the exception of a few of the more opulent, who wear striped cottons from Turkey. The dress of the women is also of Miliote cotton, generally with a red edging or fringe of flaxen lace, which is also home-made.

There are a few looms in the island for the making of a coarse woollen cloth. They have few sheep, and oxen only for tillage. The soil is not in general good, the cotton pods are small, and the wheat and barley, though sometimes returning ten to one, supply only a dingy disagreeable bread. The island is capable of producing excellent wine, as some specimens prove, both sweet and dry, but little care is observed in the making, and water is generally mixed with the wine before it is offered for sale. The island suffers often from drought; potherbs are very scarce, and there is no fruit of any kind. At the present season grapes are brought for sale from Sifno.

1831-2 J. E. Dekay

Taking on a Pilot

At three o'clock, a part of the town and harbour of Milos came into view. The chief town was formerly situated near the water, but its unhealthiness caused it to be abandoned, and the inhabitants clambered up to the top of the hill in the vicinity of the new town, which is composed entirely of white houses, and has a very singular appearance when seen from the ship. The houses are clustered round the sides and cover the summit of a peak one thousand feet high, and resemble more in appearance a rookery or pigeon house than the residence of human beings...

It is now primarily celebrated for its pilots, which are esteemed the best in the Archipelago. Shortly after firing a gun and hoisting a flag, a small sail-boat was seen making its way out of the harbour towards us. While lying-to for this boat, we had an opportunity of witnessing its manoeuvres; and as we had rather elevated ideas of the cleverness of the Greek islanders in this particular, it was with surprise that we found them unseamanlike and lubberley. There were three persons in the boat, and when, after much scolding, and pushing, and rowing, they were fairly alongside, two of them jumped on board, and in tolerable English offered their services as pilots; each produced large tin boxes filled with certificates from the various ships in which they had exercised their craft, and it appeared from these documents that they had at different times been on board the ships of every naval power in the world. The eldest was a sallow-faced beetle-browed man of few words and quiet deportment. His companion was a hale, handsome, black-eyed fellow of about thirty, decorated with a pair of jetty mustachios, which he twirled about with infinite complacency, while answering the interrogatories of the captain. He was, according to his own story, a man of various accomplishments, speaking no less than six languages, that is to say, English, French, Italian, Turkish, Illyrian and Greek. "I speks sis lankishes, and all so good as Ingleesh" was the phrase in which he conveyed this information.

Desirous of using my college Greek upon this descendant of Leonidas, I gravely addressed him in a set speech, of the accuracy of which I could have no doubt, as I had selected it from a Romaic vocabulary. The man stared, and upon repeating my phrase, he asked me what language I was speaking. Like the Englishman who puzzled Scaliger by talking Latin with a cockney accent, I felt rather annoyed by this question; and taking the vocabulary from my pocket, I asked him if he knew that language. He assured me that it was good Greek, but that (begging my pardon) I had spoken it as if it had been English. I was perfectly aware that there were important differences in grammatical structure between the ancient and modern Greek, but I was now for the first time to learn that the pronunciation taught in all our colleges was so decidedly burlesque and *outré* as to excite laughter whenever it was heard in Greece.

1830s "An officer of the US Navy"
A Ride across the Island

Passing Cithera, we held our course for Milo, - and soon came to anchor in its well sheltered harbour. The first sentiment that occurred to me, in looking at the form and aspect of this island, turned to the injustice which has been done to it, in the purposes which it has been compelled to subserve. It appeared as if from some motive of curiosity it had merely looked up out of the wave, to see what was going on in this strange world - had been caught in that situation and detained, as an adventurous traveller peeping into an Arab encampment, is sometimes held there in lawless bondage. Yet there is no cast of grief or violence upon it; indeed it seems as cheerful as if it never had endured a compulsory servitude; though so far from having escaped the ignoble task of contributing to the maintenance of man, it has at one time sustained a population of twenty thousand upon its own resources...

In the recent struggle between the Greek and Turk, this little isle saved itself from Moslem vengeance by its peaceful demeanour: and better served the interests of humanity in thus becoming a partial asylum, where the oppressed and despairing might recover strength and resolution. It is now what it was in earlier times - a sort of resting place for the mariner. In weariness and storm, he has only to drop around into this quiet harbour, and then he may tune his reed, or traverse his deck, and let the tempest without rave till it frets itself to rest.

But our object here was not to shelter ourselves from a gale, but to procure the aid of those whose knowledge of the intricate passes of this sea might perhaps save us from that last disaster which sometimes befalls a ship. The skill of the pilot here, though, is very much confined to occasions when there is the least necessity for it. It is to be relied on when perils are distinctly visible, - but when storm and wave and night mingle in conflict, the Greek pilot has no resource but to fall on his knees and supplicate the assistance of the blessed Virgin. Could that sweet saint send out the light of those stars which once lighted her solitary path in Judea, it would be eminently wise to invoke her aid. Far be it from me, however, to quench the hope and trust which even a delusive confidence may awaken. Yet in a storm, I would sooner trust to a strong cable, or a good offing with a close reef, than to any miraculous preservation within the power of the compassionate Madonna. But enough of these heterodox sentiments.

Mounting some little stunted ponies, which were but a trifle larger than goats, we went in quest of some of the natural curiosities of the island. A short ride brought us to the tepid springs, which rise quite up the harbour near the water's edge. These springs are strongly impregnated with sulphur, and are much frequented by those afflicted with scrofulous diseases; - maladies which are often met with here, and which are ascribed to a noxious property in the honey with which the Cyclades abound. So there is no sweet without its bitter - no rose without its thorn. But nature sometimes, as in the present case, furnishes an antidote for the ills which she brings. Would that man could do the same, but his wrongs strike so deeply, that a reparation is frequently not within his power. A broken heart can never be revived and restored; it may perchance smile again, but its smiles will be like flowers on a sepulchre.

From the springs we rode to a singular cave near the entrance of the harbour. After winding down a narrow and difficult passage, we found ourselves in a large hall, beautifully vaulted with crystallized sulphur. This mineral in the hands of man, has a bad name, and a worse association; but left to nature, she converts it into brilliant gems, with which she studs the glowing domes of her caverned palaces.

Here was one of her halls in which even an Egeria might have dwelt, and sighed for nothing earthly, unless it were the footsteps of her mortal lover. And perhaps it was in other times the abode of some sweet romantic being, whose devoted love flew the crowd, to cherish in solitude and silence its fondness and trust. For there is something in the spirit of this mysterious passion which takes the heart away from the empty bustle and prattle of the multitude. It is this which sanctifies the private hearth, and garlands the domestic altar with flowers that can never die. One that looks away from the companion of his bosom, for solace and delight, has mistaken the path to true happiness and virtue.

But I am again on a theme that has little to do with the present fountains and grottoes of Milo. We were struck on riding over the island, with the number and variety of its caverns, and with the beautiful results of the chemical operations, which are constantly going on in these natural laboratories. These singular results are produced from rich mineral substances, abounding in the hollow hills, dissolved and sublimated by the agency of a volcanic flame, which appears to live in the heart of the island. Let this isle alone; - it needs no forge, retort, blowpipe or galvanic battery, to aid its chemical experiments. To its lectures Pliny listened, and thousands since have wisely imitated the docility of his example. We observed in our rambles the constant occurrence of excavations, which were once immense reservoirs for the reception of rain water - there being no fresh springs in the island, and which, though now neglected and partially filled by falling fragments, attest the former denseness of the population.

We spent some time among the catacombs, the most perfect of which are just being opened, and may be found near the site of the ancient capital. These chambers of the dead are cut in the soft rock, being eight or ten feet square and as many in height, with narrow cells opening around them, in which the bodies were deposited. In the cells are discovered the jewels and ornaments of the deceased, and in the chambers lachrymatory vases, in which the bereaved preserved their tears, as sacred to the memory of the departed. Among the ornaments a massive ring was recently discovered, which was purchased here for fifty pounds, and subsequently sold for five hundred. The vases are some of them of glass, brilliantly coloured in the material; others of an argillaceous substance, pencilled with a delicate and unfading force. They are now searched for and sold by the natives to the antiquary, or any one who may feel or affect all interest in the arts and habits of the ancients. How every thing in this world tends to ruin and forgetfulness! We are not only to die - to be placed in the earth - but the violets are to be plucked from our graves - these narrow mounds perhaps to be levelled down to gratify the pride of a village and furnish a promenade for the gay - and then as if this were not enough, should the place of our burial in after ages become known, our ashes may be disturbed and though the tearless grief of our friends may save the search after lachrymatories - yet our very dust may be sifted in search of a gainful trinket. What has been will be; for "there is nothing new under the sun." Then let me be spared all mockery of grief - all eulogies written and forgotten by the same individual - let my resting place be unknown.

1883-4 James Theodore Bent

Decline

Tournefort tells us that when he visited Melos twenty years later all the productions of the island were of incomparable excellence, and Consul Brest stated that his father had told him that when he was ,young Melos was most fertile, and had upwards of 20,000 inhabitants. But the invention of steam, and disease have combined to destroy Melos: owing to the former ships do not find it necessary to stop at Melos, and the corsairs' fair has been long since abandoned; and owing to the prevalence of the latter, at the beginning of this century, the inhabitants thought the island was under a curse. The old capital was abandoned, numbers fled; and if it were not for refugees from Crete, Melos would be now almost uninhabited. Only 7,000 are now left, and many houses in the Kastro are falling into ruins. There is lack of energy nowadays in Melos, for Syra monopolises all the trade that once came here, and the Cretan exiles refuse to cultivate as they ought the fertile centre of the island, for they are only awaiting a favourable turn in events to return to their own island. Even the fishermen complain that the fish have left the port, owing to the unscrupulous use of dynamite of late years as an easy means to kill the fish. If only Melos could have been chosen as the centre of commerce how much better would it have been than Syra! The harbour is excellent, and then ballast could be taken of sulphur, salt, and millstones, the products of Melos, whereas on bare Syra they can get nothing but common stones.

Our Lady of the Sea

Mr. Photopoulos, in full uniform, took us out for a walk after breakfast; and we directed our steps up towards the citadel, and were at once struck with the great

feature of Melos; namely, the quantity of churches and miracle-working pictures. This is easily accounted for by the numerous plagues which have swept over the island.

First we visited my Lady of the Sea, the pilots' church, high up on the hillside, where the Madonna has taken the place of Aphrodite. Years ago this church, which is of good Byzantine style, was falling into ruins, when the smallpox broke out badly, and a pious Meliote dreamt he saw my Lady of the Sea, who bade him build her church anew.

Over a side door are the arms and initials of John Crispi, 1553, one of the last dukes of Naxos; inside there is a richly carved *tempelon* of doves plucking vine-tendrils; the women's portion of this church, which is on one side overlooking the sea, has a lovely view, which must be distracting to the female prayers if they have any soul for beauty in them. Here they have an altar all to themselves, and can hardly see into the body of the church. In former years the seclusion of the fair sex was more stringent than it is now. St. Basil, so runs the legend, once detected a woman winking at an officiating deacon, and for her offence her sex was doomed to be veiled off from the males: this veil is now altogether abandoned, but is usually replaced by a screen of trellis-work.

Dancing Among the Tombs of the Dead

As we wandered amongst the villages near the Chora, we found many interesting objects for observation. At Trypete, so called from the holes, or rather ancient tombs, cut in the rock close to, we found them hard at work dancing this same Sunday evening. What inveterate dancers these Greeks are! There, in a small room about fifteen feet square, they were performing the syrtos. The children of the family had been piled on the bed, boxes and articles of daily use had been roughly shoved away into corners. Crowds of people were looking on, yet the charmed circle was well kept, and the dancing, though not so good as what I saw elsewhere, was fair enough, and some of the local steps were pretty. The people of Trypete owe a debt of gratitude to their dead ancestors, for the tombs in the rocks make excellent stables for their mules, pigsties, and offices.

Islanders' Beliefs

There is another village close to called Nychia, from the idea that giants have clawed the volcanic rocks with their nails. This is supposed to be a very ghostly place, where many people have been seized by uncanny Nereids, as also are the valley of Plathena and Pheropotamos, a clayey spot, when women have been known to disappear altogether in the mire. Fishermen say they hear women singing about here, and stones are hurled at their boats, which cause them great trepidation. I am convinced the reciters of these stories thoroughly believe in them themselves, for they will tremble as they relate them and cross themselves vigorously.

Another village close to the Kastro is called Plaka, and here is a church dedicated to the "Virgin of the Rushes", for a black picture of her was found amongst some reeds not far from this spot. They took it to the then capital of the island, Zephyria, but a pestilence broke out, and they were obliged to bring it back and build a church for it here. A short distance beyond Plaka is a tiny little church dedicated to the manifestation of the Virgin, where a very curious custom is still observed, not, however, so frequently as it used to be, for it is against the law. When a child becomes emaciated they say it is struck by the Nereids, who dance in the dry bed of a river close to this church. If no physic benefits the little sufferer it is an obvious case of Nereid disease, and the only cure for this is to take it, strip it naked, and leave it on the cold marble altar of this little church for a season. To effect a radical cure the child should remain there all night, but the mother is afraid of detection, so dare not leave it there so long. If the babe survives this treatment it is not struck by the Nereids, and the parents' peace of mind is restored; but if, on the contrary, as often happens, this treatment is fatal, the parents are content to think that God has willed that their darling should fall a victim to those evil spirits. The little church is a quaint spot. The high altar on which they place the children rests on a fluted pillar of ancient date, for the spot is just over the ruins of the old town and the vale of Klima, which we decided to visit at the end of our stay in Melos; for, as the weather looked favourable again, we thought it best to take advantage of it to visit the deserted western horn of the island.

Crete

Crete remained under Venetian rule after the Turkish conquest of the mainland, and experienced something of a renaissance as refugees from Constantinople gathered there. Yet the islanders always resented foreign rule, and there were many revolts. Crete was also hard-pressed by the Turks, but it was only in 1669, after the twenty-one year siege of Candia, that they could establish control over the island, bringing to an end over four hundred years of Venetian rule. The fierce islanders appreciated Turkish rule no more than that of the Venetians, and during the nineteenth century revolt after revolt was suppressed with brutal savagery. After the insurrection of 1821, Mehmet Ali, the able viceroy of Egypt, was authorised by the Porte to suppress the rebels and take over the government of the island himself. But it was 1840 before he could claim success. Even then sporadic revolts continued, as the indomitable population sought to expel their foreign rulers. In 1898 the Great Powers intervened to place the island under the control of Prince George of Greece, acting as a High Commissioner, and at last, in 1913, Crete became part of the kingdom of Greece.

Bridge to the east of Rethmynos (W. Turner, 1834)

1551 Roger Bodenham

A Warlike People

Bodenham describes the islanders' response to a threat from the Turks.

There are in that island of Candia many banished men that live continually in the mountains. They came down to serve to the number of four or five thousand. They are good archers. Every one was armed with his bow and arrows, a sword and a dagger; and had long hair, and boots that reached up to the groin, and shirt of mail hanging, the one half before, the other half behind. These were sent away as soon as the army was past. They would drink wine out of all measure.

1596 Fynes Moryson

Offending the Sailors

... [I]n the evening we came to the Cape of S. John the first Promontory of the island Candia, distant some one hundred and fifty miles, (I always understand Italian miles, being now amongst the Italians) from Modon, the foresaid city of Morea, and these high mountains of Candia were yet covered on the top with snow. We sailed on the South side of Candia, and towards evening passed by the middle part of the island, and the thirteenth day by nine of the clock in the morning, we sailed by the Cape of Salomon, being towards the East the furthest part of Candia...

At this time our mariners, as well Greeks as Italians, were greatly offended with one of our French consorts, a layman, because at dinner time, according to the negligent fashion of the French, he turned the clean side of his trencher upward: for of all men the mariners and of all mariners the Greeks and Italians are most superstitious; and if any thing in the ship chance to be turned upside down, they take it for an ill sign, as if the ship should be overwhelmed. Otherwise I never observed, that either the chief or inferior mariners ever used the least disrespect to any passenger, being rather loving and familiar to them in conversation. And I remember that my brother Henry using to walk upon the highest hatches, the Patron, and Scrivano, and others, did with smiling observe his fast walking and melancholy humour, yet howsoever it was troublesome to them, did only once, and that courteously reprove him, or rather desire him that he would have respect to the mariners, who watched all night for the public safety, and were then sleeping under the hatches. Always understand that a man may not bee so bold in another man's house as in his own, and may yet less be bold in a ship of strangers; and that an unknown passenger must of all other be most respective. And whereas Mariners are held by some to be thievish, surely in the haven at the journey's end, (where thieves easily find receivers), it is good to be wary in keeping that belongs to you: but at sea no place is more safe then a ship, where the things stolen, are easily found, and the offenders severely punished.

1609 William Lithgow

Crete at the Beginning of the Seventeenth Century

Candy is a large and famous city, formerly called Matium, situated on a plain by the sea side, having a goodly haven for ships, and a fair arsenal wherein are 36 galleys. It is exceeding strong, and daily guarded with 2000 soldiers, and the walls in compass are about three leagues.

In this time there was no viceroy, the former being newly dead, and the place vacant, the soldiers kept a bloody quarter among themselves, or against any whomsoever their malignity was intended, for in all the time I stayed there being ten days, it was nothing to see every day four or five men killed in the streets: neither could the rector, nor the captains help it, so tumultuous were the disordered soldiers, and the occasions of revenge and quarrellings so influent. This commonly they practise in every such like vacation, which otherwise, they durst never attempt without death, and severe punishment; and truly me thought it was as barbarous a governed place for the time, as ever I saw in the world; for hardly could I save my own life free from their dangers, in the which I was twice miserably involved...

In all my travels through this realm, I never could see a Greek come forth of his house unarmed: and after such a martial manner, that on his head he weareth a bare steel cap, a bow in his hand, a long sword by his side, a broad ponard overthwart his belly, and a round target hanging at his girdle. They are not costly in apparel, for they wear but linen clothes, and use no shoes but boots of white leather, to keep their legs in the fields from the pricks of a kind of thistle, wherewith the country is overcharged like unto little bushes or short shrubs which are marvellous sharp, and offensive unto the inhabitants; whereof, often a day to my great harm, I found their bloody smart: The women generally wear linen breaches as men do, and boots after the same manner, and their linen coats no longer then the middle of their thighs, and are insatiably inclined to venery, such is the nature of the soil and climate...

The Candiots are excellent good archers, surpassing all the oriental people therein, courageous and valiant upon the sea, as in former times they were; and they are naturally inclined to singing: so that commonly after meat, man, wife, and child of each family, will for the space of an hour, sing with such a harmony, as is wonderful melodious to the hearer; yea, and they cannot forgo the custom of it of the state for his passage, which was wine and biscuit-bread: Thereafter, I embarked him for Venice in a Flemish ship, the Master being a Scotsman, John Allen, born in Glasgow, and dwelt at Middleborough in Zeland.

Four Drunken Friars

Here I stayed in Canea twenty five days before I could get passage for the Arch Islands, being purposed for Constantinople but gladly would not have left the Monastery of these four friars, with whom I was lodged, if it had not been for my designs; in regard of their great cheer and deep draughts of Malvasey I received hourly, and oftentimes against my will. Every night after supper the friars forced me to dance with them, either one gagliard or other: Their music in the end was sound drunkenness, and their syncopa turned to spew up all, and their bed converted to a board, or else the hard floor, for these beastly swine were nightly so full that they had never power to go to their own chambers, but where they fell, there they lay till the morn. The cloister itself had two fair courts, the least of which might have lodged any King of Europe. The church was little, and among the four friars, there was but one mass-priest, being a Greek borne and turned to the Roman faction: his new name was Pattarras Matecarras, Pater Libenter, or Father of free will; indeed a right name for so sottish a fellow, for he was so free of his stomach to receive in strong liquor, that for the space of twenty days of my being there, I never saw him, nor anyone of the other three truly sober. Many odd merriments and jests have I observed of these friars of Candie, but time will not suffer me to relate them, only remitting the rest to my private discourse, a fig for their folly.

Kindnesses Repaid

Being frustrate of my intention at Candy, I was forced to return to Canea the same way I went: when come, I was exceeding merry with my old friends the Englishmen. Meanwhile there arrived from Tunis in Barbary, an English rungate named Wolson, bound for the Rhodes: where after short acquaintance I with his natives, and understanding what I was, he imparted these words: "I have had my elder brother," said he, "the Master (or Captain) of a ship, slain at Burntland in Scotland by one called Keere; and notwithstanding he was beheaded, I have long since sworn to be revenged of my brother's death on the first Scotsman I ever saw or met, and my design is, to stab him with a knife this night, as he goeth late home to his lodging desiring their assistance. But Smith, Hargrave, and Horsfeild refused, yet Cooke and Rollands yielded. Meanwhile Smith knowing where I used sometimes to diet, found me at supper in a ... soldier's house, where acquainting me with this plot, the host, he, and three Italian soldiers conveyed me to my bed, passing by the arch-villain, and his confederates, where he was prepared for the mischief: which when he saw his treachery was discovered, he fled away, and was seen no more here.

Remarking the fidelity and kindness that Smith had twice shown me, first in freeing me from the danger of galley-slavery, and now in saving my life, I advised to do him a good deed in some part of acquittance, and thus it was: At his first coming to Venice, he was taken up as a soldier for Candy: where, when transported, within a small time he found the Captain's promise and performance different, which enforced him at the beginning to borrow a little money of his Lieutenant. The five years of their abode expired, and fresh companies come from Venice to exhibit the charge, Smith not being able to discharge his debt, was turned over to the new captain for five years more, who paid the old captain his money; and his time also worn out, the third captain came, where likewise he was put in his hands serving him five years longer. Thus having served three captains fifteen years, and never likely able (for a small trifle) to attain his liberty, I went to the captain and paid his debt, obtaining also of the rector his licence to depart...

Robbed!

This aforesaid Carabusa, is the principal fortress of Creta, being of it self invincible, and is not unlike to the Castle of Dunbertan, which standeth at the mouth of Clyd; upon which River the ancient City of Lanerke is situated. For this Fort is environed with a rock higher then the walls, and joineth close with Capo Ermlco. Having learned of the thievish way I had to Canea, I advised to put my money in exchange, which the Captain of that strength very courteously performed; and would also have dissuaded me from my purpose, but I by no persuasion of him would stay. From thence departing, all alone, scarcely was I advanced twelve miles in my way, when I was beset on the skirt of a rocky mountain with three Greek murdering renegadoes, and an Italian bandido: who laying hands on me, beat me most cruelly, robbed me of all my clothes, and stripped me naked, threatening me with many grievous speeches.

At last the respective Italian, perceiving I was a stranger, and could not speak the Cretan tongue, began to ask me in his own language, where was my money? To whom I soberly answered, I had no more then he saw, which was fourscore bagantines: which scarcely amounted to two groats English. But he not giving credit to these words, searched all my clothes and budgeto, yet found nothing except my linen, and letters of recommendations I had from divers Princes of Christendom, especially the Duke of Venice, whose subjects they were, if they had been lawful subjects; which when he saw, did move him to compassion, and earnestly entreated the other three thieves to grant me mercy, and to save my life. A long deliberation being ended, they restored back again my pilgrim's clothes, and letters, but my blue gown and bagantines they kept. Such also was their thievish courtesy toward me, that for my better safeguard in the way they gave me a stamped piece of clay as a token to show any of their companions, if I encountered with any of them, for they were about twenty rascals of a confederate band that lay in this desert passage.

Leaving them with many counterfeit thanks, I travelled that day seven and thirty miles, and at night attained to the unhappy village of Pickehorno: where I could have neither meat, drink, lodging, nor any refreshment to my wearied body. These desperate Candiots thronged about me, gazing, as though astonished to see me both want company and their language, and by their cruel looks, they seemed to be a barbarous and uncivil people. For all these highlanders of Candy are tyrannical, bloodthirsty and deceitful. The consideration of which and (the appearance of my death, signed to me secretly by a pitiful woman) made me to shun their villainy in stealing forth from them in the dark night, and privately sought for a secure place of repose in a umbrageous cave by the seaside, where I lay till morning with a fearful heart, a crazed body, a thirsty stomach, and a hungry belly. Upon the appearing of the next aurora, and when the welkin had put aside the vizard of the night, the stars being covered, and the earth discovered by the sun, I embraced my unknown way, and about midday came to Canea.

Assisting an Escapee at Chania

In my first abode in Canea, being a fortnight, there came six galleys from Venice, upon one of which there was a young French gentleman, a Protestant, borne near Monpeillier in Langadocke; who being by chance in company with other four of his countrymen in Venice, one of them killed a young noble Venetian, about the quarrel of a courtesan; whereupon they flying to the French ambassador's house, the rest escaped, and he only apprehended by a by a fall in his flight, was afterward condemned by the senators to the galleys enduring life. Now the galleys lying here six days, he got leave of the captain to come a shore with a keeper, when he would, carrying an iron bolt on his leg; in which time we falling in acquaintance, he complained heavily of his hard fortune, and how because he was a Protestant, (besides his slavery) he was severely abused in the galley; sighing forth these words with tears, "Lord have mercy upon me, and grant me patience, for neither friends, nor money can redeem me." At which expression I was both sad and sorrowful, the one moving my soul to exult in joy for his religion: the other, for his misfortunes, working a Christian condolement for intolerable affliction. For I was in Venice, at that same time when this accident fell out, yet would not tell him so much. But pondering seriously his lamentable distress, I secretly advised him the manner how he might escape, and how far I would hazard the liberty of my life for his deliverance, desiring him to come ashore early the next morning. Meanwhile I went to an old Greekish woman, with whom I was friendly inward, for she was my laundress; and reciting to her the whole business, she willingly condescended to lend me an old gown, and a black veil for his disguise. The time come, and we met, the matter was difficult to shake off the keeper; but such was my plot, I did invite him to the wine, where after tractall discourses, and deep draughts of leatick, reason failing, sleep overcame his senses. Whereupon conducting my friend to the appointed place, I disburdened him of his irons, clothed him in a female habit, and sent him out before me, conducted by the Greekish woman; and when securely past both guards and gate, I followed, carrying with me his clothes; where, when accosting him by a field of olives, and the other returned back, we speedily crossed the vale of Suda, and interchanging his apparel, I directed him the way over the mountains to a Greekish convent on the south side of the land, a place of safeguard, called commonly the Monastery of Refuge; where he would kindly be entertained, till either the galleys, or men of war of Malta arrived; it being a custom at their going, or coming from the Levant to touch here, to relieve and carry away distressed men. This is a place whereunto bandits, men slayers, and robbers repair for relief.

And now many joyful thanks from him redounded, I returned keeping the high way, where incontinent I encountered two English soldiers, John Smith, and Thomas Hargrave, coming of purpose to inform me of an imminent danger, showing me that all the officers of the galleys, with a number of soldiers were in searching the city, and hunting all over the fields for me. After which relation, consulting with them, what way I could come to the Italian Monastery Saint Salvator, for there I lay; (the vulgar town affording neither lodging nor beds), they answered me they would venture their lives for my liberty, and I should enter at the eastern (the least frequented) gate of the city, where three other English men were that day on guard, for so there were five of them here in garrison. Where, when we came, the other English accompanied with eight French soldiers their familiars, came along with us also. And having past the market place, and near my lodging, four officers and six galley soldiers, ran to lay hands on me: whereat the English and French unsheathing their swords, valiantly resisted their fury, and deadly wounded two of the officers. Meanwhile fresh supply coming from the galleys, John Smith ran along with me to the monastery, leaving the rest at pell mell, to intercept their following. At last the captains of the garrison approaching the tumult, relieved their own soldiers, and drove back the other to the galleys. A little thereafter the general of the galleys come to the monastery, and examined me concerning the fugitive, but I clearing my self so, and quenching the least suspicion he might conceive (notwithstanding of mine accusers) he could lay nothing to my charge: howsoever it was, he seemed somewhat favourable; partly, because I had the Duke of Venice his passport, partly because of mine intended voyage to Jerusalem; partly, because he was a great favourer of the French nation: and partly because he could not mend himself, in regard of my shelter, and the Governor's favour. Yet nevertheless, I detained my self under safeguard of the cloister, until the galleys were gone.

The Plain of Suda

Being here disappointed of transportation to the Archipelago, I had advised to visit Candy: and in my way I past by the large haven of Suda, which hath no town or village, save only a castle, situated on a rock in the sea, at the entry of the Bay. The bounds of that harbour may receive at one time above two thousand ships and galleys, and is the only key of the island: for the which place, the King of Spain hath oft offered an infinite deal of money to the Venetians, whereby his Navy which sometimes resort in the Levant, might have access and relief; but they would never grant him his request; which policy of his was only to have surprised the kingdom.

South-west from this famous harbour, lieth a pleasant plain surnamed the valley of Suda. It is twenty Italian miles long, and two of breadth. And I remember, or I descended to cross the valley, and pass the haven, me thought the whole planure resembled to me a green sea; and that was only by reason of infinite olive trees grew there, whose boughs and leaves over-top all other fructiferous trees in that plain. The villages for loss of ground are all built on the skirts of rocks, upon the south side of the valley ; yea, and so difficile to climb them, and so dangerous to dwell in them, that me thought their lives were in like peril, as he who was adjoined to sit under the point of a two handed sword, and it hanging by the hair of a horse tail.

Trust me, I told along these rocks at one time, and within my sight, some 67 villages but when I entered the valley, I could not find a foot of ground unmanured, save a narrow passing way wherein I was, the olives, pomegranates, dates, figs, oranges, lemons, and pomi del Adamo growing all through other, and at the roots of which trees grew wheat, malvasie, muscadine, leaticke wines, grenadiers, carnobiers, melons, and all other sorts of fruits and herbs, the earth can yield to man; that for beauty, pleasure, and profit it may easily be surnamed, the garden of the whole universe, being the goodliest plot, the diamond spark, and the honey spot of all Candy. There is no land more temperate for air, for it hath a double spring-tide; no soil more fertile, and therefore it is called the combat of Bacchus and Ceres; nor region or valley more hospitable, in regard of the sea, having such a noble haven cut through its bosom, being as it were the very resting place of Neptune.

1700 Joseph Pitton de Tournefort
Into an Ancient Labyrinth

This spot near ancient Gortyn, was much visited and considered by many to me the labyrinth constructed by Daedelus, inhabited by the Minotaur, and from which Theseus famously escaped. Today scholarly opinion is that it is nothing more than an ancient quarry.

The first of July, after we had furnished our selves with flambeaus at the archpriest's, we set forward to see the Labyrinth. This famous place is a subterranean passage in manner of a street, which by a thousand intricacies and windings, as it were by mere chance, and without the least regularity, pervades the whole cavity or inside of a little hill at the foot of Mount Ida, three miles from Gortyna.

The entrance into this Labyrinth is by a natural opening, seven or eight paces broad, but so low, that even a middle-sized man can't pass through without stooping. The flooring of this entrance is very rugged and unequal; the ceiling flat and even, terminated by divers beds of stone, laid horizontal one upon another. The first thing you come at, is a kind of cavern exceeding rustic, and gently sloping: in this there is nothing extraordinary, but as you move forward, the place is perfectly surprising; nothing but turnings and crooked byways. The principal alley, which is less perplexing than the rest, in length about 1 200 paces, leads to the further end of the Labyrinth, and concludes in two large beautiful apartments, where strangers rest themselves with pleasure. Though this alley divides itself, at its extremity, into two or three branches, yet the dangerous part of the Labyrinth is not there; but rather at its entrance, about some thirty paces from the cavern on the left hand. If a man strikes into any other path, after he has gone a good way, he is bewildered among a thousand twirlings, twinings, sinuosities, crinkle-crankles, and turn-again lanes, that he could scarce ever get out again without the utmost danger of being lost. Our guides therefore chose this principal alley, without deviating either to the right or left. In traversing this alley we measured 1160 good paces. It is from seven to eight foot high, ceiled with a stratum of rocks, horizontal and quite flat, as are most beds of stone in those parts. And yet there are some places where a man must stoop a little: nay, about the middle of the route, you meet with a passage so very strait and low, that you must creep upon all four to get along. Generally speaking, the grand walking-place is broad enough for three or four to go abreast: its pavement is smooth, not many ups nor downs. The walls are either perpendicular, or made of stones which formerly choked up the passage, and which are disposed with a studied regularity; but so many alleys offer themselves on all sides, that you must take the utmost care how you proceed.

Being beforehand resolved to make the best of our way out of this subterranean maze, our first care was to post one of our guards at the mouth of the cavern, with order to fetch people from the next town, to come and help us out, in case we returned not before night. In the second place, each of us carried a large lighted flambeau in his hand. Thirdly, at every difficult turning we fastened on the right hand scrolls of paper numbered. Fourthly, one of our guides dropped on the left bundles of thorns, and another scattered straw all the way on the ground. In this manner we got safe enough to the further end of the Labyrinth, where the grand walk divides itself into two or three branches, and where there are likewise two rooms or apartments, almost round ... cut in the rock. Here are divers inscriptions made with charcoal; such as Father Francisco Maria Pesaro, capuchin... In the grand walk there are also great numbers of cyphers and other marks... We observed the following dates: 1495, 1560, 1579, 1699. We too wrote the year of the Lord, 1700 in three different places, with a black stone.

Having taken these precautions, it was easy enough to find our way out: but after a thorough examination of the structure of this Labyrinth we all concurred in opinion, that it could never have been ... an ancient quarry, out of which were dug the stones that built the towns of Gortyna and Gnossus. Is it likely they would go for stone above a thousand paces deep into a place so full of odd turnings, that 'tis next to impossible to disentangle one's self? Again, how could they draw their stone through a place so pinched in, that we were forced to crawl our way out for above a hundred paces together? Besides, the mountain is so craggy and full of precipices, that we had all the difficulty in the world to ride up it... It is likewise observable, that the stone of this Labyrinth was neither a good hue, nor a competent hardness. It is downright dingy...

It is therefore more probable that the Labyrinth is a natural cavity, which in times past some body out of curiosity took a fancy to try what they could make of it by widening most of those passages that were too much straitened... The reason why they meddled not with that narrow neck was perhaps to let posterity know, how the rest were naturally made; for beyond that place the alley is as beautiful as on this side... The ancient Cretans, who were a very polite people, and strongly devoted to the fine arts, took a particular pleasure in finishing what had been but sketched out by Nature. Doubtless some shepherds having discovered the subterranean conduits, gave occasion to more considerable people to turn it into this marvellous maze, to serve for an asylum in the civil wars, or to screen themselves from the fury of a tyrannical government. At present it is only a retreat for bats and the like...

I forgot to tell that at Brices we lodged with an old papas, very zealous for his way of worship, and wretchedly ignorant. He would have persuaded us in his balderdash Italian, that there was an ancient prophecy wrote on the walls of the Labyrinth, importing that the Czar of Muscovy was very soon to be master of the Ottoman Empire, and deliver the Greeks from the slavery of the Turks; adding that he very well remembered, when the siege of Candia was carrying on, a certain Greek assured the Vizier Cuperli that he should take the place, according to another prophecy of this same Labyrinth. Whatever scrawlings are made upon the walls of the labyrinth by travellers, these simpletons swallow down for prophecies.

Two Forms of Execution

When a wretch is to be impaled, they lay him naked on the ground, his face downward, his hands tied behind his back, on which they place a pack-saddle. Astride of this sit two of the execution servants to keep the criminal from stirring, while a third, with his hands squeezing the nape of his neck, keeps him from turning his head. A fourth officer thrusts a stake in at the fundament. This stake or wooden pike, after he has shoved as far as he can with his hands, is leisurely driven up with a beetle or mallet till the stake comes out at the shoulder or breast. Then they are tied upright to posts fixed in the highway, and so left.

If they chance not to die immediately, the Turks that are most zealous for the Government come about them, not to exhort them to turn Mussulmans, i.e. believers, but to rail and call them a thousand names. The Turks are fully persuaded that a man who commits any great crime is unworthy to become a Mussulman, that when a Mussulman is condemned to die, nobody will assist him in the least, because they believe his crime has rendered him Gaour, that is to say, an Infidel and a Christian.

The Gaunch is a sort of estrapade, usually set up at the city gates. The executioner lifts up the criminal by means of a pulley, and then letting -go the rope, down falls the wretch among a parcel of iron flesh-hooks; which give him a quick or lasting misery, as he chances to light. In this condition they leave them. Sometimes they live two or three days, and will ask for a pipe of tobacco, while their comrades are cursing and blaspheming like devils.

A bashaw passing by one of these places in Candia, an offender that was hanging on the gaunch calls out to him with a sneer, "Good my Lord, since you are so charitable according to your Law, be so good as to shoot me through the head, to put an end to this tragedy."

The Island Horses

Though the Candiots live a slothful life, yet they are often on horseback a hunting; they have no notion of hunting afoot: The great men have for the most part Barbary horses, exceeding beautiful, and which will hold out much longer here than, in France, where the damps that fall after sunset, together with the hay, make them short-winded and subject to defluxions. The horses of the island are fiery little tits, finely chested and long-tailed: most of them are so gaunt-bellied, the saddle won't keep on their backs. They are stone-horses, and have such a way of clinging to the rocks, that it is amazing to behold how swift they will climb the steepest heights. In the most hideous descents, which are frequent enough in this island, they tread firm and sure but then you must give them their head, and trust entirely to their management. They never miscarry when they are left to themselves, any more than when they bear burdens almost twice the weight of a man: when they fall, it is generally occasioned by their riders holding too strait a rein, for then their head being raised too high, they can't see how to place their feet. Whenever I happened to be on the edge of a precipice, instead of pretending to regulate my horse's motion, I shut my eyes, that I might not see the danger, or else alighted with my friends to search after samples.

1730s Richard Pococke

Burying Caiaphas

About a quarter of a mile to the west of the town [Knossos] there is a building near the road which is ten feet square within, the walls are six feet thick, and cased with brick inside and out; it seems to have been some ancient sepulchre; the people say it is the tomb of Caiaphas; and the most modest account they give of it is, that he landed at this place, where he died and was buried, that his body being found above ground, they buried it again, which happened seven times, and at last they built this strong fabric above it, which, they say, prevented its rising again, to which they add many other circumstances equally ridiculous. I mention this only to show that the people of Crete now have as great a genius now for spreading fables, as they had in the times of paganism.

Buying a Slave

When I was at Retimo I heard of a German slave, a native of Silesia, who was taken in the wars with the emperor, and I agreed for him with the Turk his master for $200; every thing being concluded, the property of him was transferred to me by kissing the feet of his old proprietor, and then of his new master. I proposed to give him his choice either to remain with me as a servant, or to be given up to the priests at Constantinople who redeem captives, on their returning me the money. The love of his native country made him choose the latter, and I delivered him up into their hands about a year afterwards.

1811-12 C. R. Cockerell

Into the "Labyrinth" with a Madman

On the second day we started on our expedition to visit the Labyrinth...

At night we reached Schallous, a small village, and passed the night in the house of an old Greek. Both he and his wife were terrified at first, as we were in Turkish dress, and they had suffered terribly at the hands of the Turks. He told me afterwards that his son, after an absence of five years, had come home, and the very first night some Turks had broken into the house, eaten and drunk all they could lay hands on, and finally murdered the poor youth.

Next day, by Hagiospiliotissa to the convent of S. Georgio. Our janissaries here gave us a sample of the tyranny of Turks by preparing for us and themselves a magnificent repast, and getting drunk and insulting the papades. Three hours more of hilly country, commanded at intervals by fortified towers brought us to the foot of Ida...

In a steep part of the hill looking towards the plain is an inconspicuous hole in the rock, - unmarked by any architectural or structural feature. This is the entrance to the Labyrinth. We had brought a quantity of string for a clue, which we rolled on two long sticks, then lit torches and went in. At first one enters a vestibule out of which lead several openings. Two of the three, perhaps four, dark entrances are blocked up, but one remains open. This we followed, and for three mortal hours and more we groped about among intricate passages and in spacious halls. The windings bewildered us at once, and my compass being broken I was quite ignorant as to where I was. The clearly intentional intricacy and apparently endless number of galleries impressed me with a sense of horror - and fascination I cannot describe. At every ten steps one was arrested, and had to turn to right or left, sometimes to choose one of three or four roads. What if one should lose the clue!

A poor madman had insisted on accompanying us all the way from Candia. He used to call me St. Michael; Douglas, St. George; and Foster, Minos. We knew him as Delli Yani. Much against our will he persisted in following us into the cavern, and when we stopped, going off with a boy who had a lantern. Conceive our horror when we found suddenly that he had disappeared. There in that awful obscurity he might wander about till death relieved him. We sent back two men along the clue with torches to shout for him, and listened anxiously, but the Turks were quite unconcerned. God, they said, takes care of madmen. We went on, and sure enough after about an hour Delli Yani turned up with the boy, who was horribly frightened. We entered many chambers; in some were Venetian names, such as 'Spinola'; in another, 'Hawkins 1794', , 'Fiott' and other Englishmen, and many names of Jews. All the culs-de-sac were infested with bats, which were very annoying, and rose in thousands when one of our party fired a pistol. In one place is a spring. Here and there we saw some lichen, and there were occasional signs of metallic substances, but not enough to support the idea of its having been a mine. The stone is sandy, stratified, and easily cut, the air dry, and it appears to me that the most probable purpose of this wonderful excavation was as a secure storehouse for corn and valuables from the attacks of robbers in the days of Minos. The work was plainly all done with the chisel.

The passage is always eight or ten feet wide, and four, five, six, eight, or ten feet or more high. In many places it had fallen in. The peasants tell all sorts of stories about it. They told me that in one place there are reeds and a pool, and that the hole goes right through the mountain for three miles; that a sow went in and came out seven years after with a litter of pigs; and so on.

1833-34 Robert Pashley

The Cave of Skulls

… and, a little below it, the entrance of a cavern. Our progress in this passage is suddenly arrested by a perpendicular descent of about eighteen feet: the cave has every appearance of extending to some distance in this direction, but not having a ladder we cannot explore its recesses. The stalactites a little before us in this part, to which we can approach no nearer, hang down in a great cluster as much as thirty feet below the level on which we are standing. Returning hence to the entrance cavern, we turn, at its north or rather north-eastern extremity, along another passage: after continuing for about ten feet, it enlarges into a kind of room twenty-seven feet long, at the further end of which we again enter a narrow pass the length of which is thirteen feet. On emerging from this passage, which we do with considerable difficulty, by clambering round the rock, and letting ourselves down, as well as we can, into another apartment, we find before us a view the grandeur and beauty of which surpasses all that we have hitherto seen. On looking back at the hole in the rock, through which we have just emerged, and where one of my attendants is standing with a lighted taper, the effect is very striking. The apartment in which we have now arrived is about 150 feet long, and varies greatly in width: its height is pretty nearly uniform, and is considerable. Between twenty and thirty feet from the mouth of the pass by which we entered, is a great stalagmite, which rises up and forms a column reaching to the top of the cave, while the stalactites on each side hang in the most beautiful order: near the great central mass the bones and skulls of the poor Christians are so thickly scattered, that it is almost impossible to avoid crushing them as we pick our steps along. On the south-western side of this apartment a complete range of stalactites separates it from a good sized passage; after walking along which we enter a much smaller one, only eight feet long, which leads into a very little room, where we find water and many earthenware vessels. They were already firmly and almost inseparably attached to the ground by means of the deposit left by the constant dripping of the water. In the course of a century it would wholly have embedded them in stalagmites. My Greek companions, with great difficulty, succeeded in rescuing these utensils from the grave which was beginning to swallow them up. Going on from this chamber, we traverse a passage so low and narrow that we are obliged to crawl on our hands and knees, and descend into a small room, the ground in which is literally covered with bones and skulls: in its centre is a columnar stalagmite, which reaches from the ground to the rocks about eighteen feet above our heads. There are also some other considerable stalagmites in the room. A narrow passage leads, by a steep descent, from this chamber to another nearly under it, also small; and on entering which about a dozen skulls, and a proportionate number of bones, are seen spread over the ground. This then was the furthest point to which the unhappy refugees could flee, and here the last of them perished.

The want of a sufficient number of lights, on our first visit, prevented my examining the cavern as I wished: I therefore returned to it on the Sunday morning, having first obtained, from the Papas of Melidhoni, a supply of wax candles, of his own manufacture, The above account is the result of both my visits.

Religious Attitudes in Crete

The cathedral church of the Archbishop, which is close by his residence, is highly adorned with silver ornaments and with paintings. Here, as well as in the other Greek church of the city, there is a latticed gallery, with a separate entrance for the women, so that the devotions of the male assembly are never disturbed in the way in which they always may be, and frequently are, in civilized Europe.

The practice thus observed by the Oriental church had become so general in the time of Constantine, that it is mentioned of his mother, the Empress Helena, that even she had always to pray with the women in their part of the building. The latticed galleries within which they are concealed at the present day, are precisely the same sort of place which old ecclesiastical writers describe as appropriated to them: the existence of a separate entrance in ancient times is also distinctly stated.

I know not whether miraculous legends are told of any of the pictorial ornaments of this cathedral. In the mountains of Lasithi, a short day's ride to the east-south-east of Megalo-Kastron, is found a picture which is believed to have come spontaneously and unaided, through the air, from Constantinople...

The Greek tradition respecting the wonderful self-directed journey of the Virgin's picture to this island will justify the mention of Roman Catholic legend, the alleged scene of which was the cathedral church of Megalo-Kastron. At the celebration of mass, as soon as the wafer had been consecrated, it rose up in the air, eluded the priest's attempt to recover possession of it, and flew into the hands of Pasquale Cigogna, the pious Duke of Candia.

When we reflect upon the manner in which the population of Crete has become half Mohammedan at the outbreaking of the Greek revolution, we need hardly wonder that, in this island, the credulity and superstition of the Mohammedans should closely resemble those of the Christian population. Thus any supposed apparition of the Panaghia, in a particular spot, draws even Moslem devotees to implore her aid; and, in this city, the devout Mohammedan women burn incense every Friday, and some of them suspend bits of rag, and similar votive offerings, to honour an ancient statue... The tradition current among them is that the saint was an Arab, to whose dress the ancient robe of the statue bears some resemblance, and that he greatly distinguished himself during the famous siege of the Kastron. The reason for his transmutation into stone is also assigned. The social and religious position of the Cretan Musulman is certainly curious. We have already seen how the Musulman population of the island had been introduced, like that of Albania, by the apostasy of its Christian inhabitants, and without any influx of strangers to the soil: We have also noticed some of the peculiarities of the Cretan Mohammedan's position: for instance, his becoming, not infrequently, the spiritual father of his Christian neighbour's child, and his most un-Musulman habit of drinking the excellent wine which is produced in his native island, Another characteristic of their social position should also be pointed out: they have been very generally in the habit of taking as their wives Christian maidens, who retained their own faith, but all whose children were ordinarily brought up as followers of the prophet...

Although marriages of Christian women with Mohammedans have been common in Crete, and also elsewhere, yet, no doubt, many men among the Greeks would submit to death rather than marry a woman who had not been duly baptized. And, with respect to their daughters, there are alliances, their aversion to which is almost insuperable: for instance those contracted with members of the Roman Catholic church. With the Greeks, as with the Mohammedan, the heretic is more hateful than the infidel: and the follower of the Prophet is preferred as a son-in-law to the bondman of the Pope.

Not half a century has passed since a Patriarch of Constantinople, regarding, as perhaps became the subject of an absolute monarch, his sovereign, the Turkish Emperor, in the light of God's Vicegerent on earth, even congratulated his Christian world, on the favour shown them by the deity in raising up the powerful nation of the Turks, *to insure the spiritual salvation of his elect people*, by protecting them from the heresies of the western churches.

I learnt, from M. Godebout and other persons, that the Greek Archbishop adopted, on a recent occasion, a practice of the ancient Greeks and Romans, which is seldom observed by Christians, though of common occurrence at the festive entertainments of Mohammedan gentlemen. In order to enliven a party, at which the Pasha, and Osman-bey, as well as the consular agents and the principal Cretans of the city, were present, the Prelate procured the attendance of a number of dancing-girls.

The Metropolitan might have defended this practice, not only by the powerful argument of its antiquity, but even by the authority of Socrates. In the *Symposion* of Xenophon, the great Athenian sage, who is said by Cicero to have brought down philosophy to the earth, to arbitrate on the ordinary social relations and affairs of mankind, is described as having made the varied and agile motions of a dancing girl the basis of a philosophical lesson, which he bestowed on his disciples.

I suppose that, at the present day, such an exhibition of the free and easy motions of such females, cannot be of ordinary occurrence in the palaces of Christian Prelates, either in the oriental or in any other church. But we have the high and conclusive authority of a General Council, as evidence that this convivial usage of the ancient heathens was adopted and enjoyed by members of the Christian priesthood…

A Modern Pardoner

Soon after leaving this monastery we meet an itinerant monk, who had, what I, at first, took for a bible, in his hand. It turns out to be a little case of relics of several distinguished saints. Amongst them were Haghios Gheorghios, Haghios Dionysios the Areopagite, Haghios Panteleimon, the Saint and Martyr Demos of Smyrna, Haghios Ioannes Eremites, and others. The monk belonged to the monastery of Haghios Antonios, called Pezanes, near the plain of Messara. The Revolution has destroyed most of their olive-trees, and his journey is intended, by the aid of God, and through the means of these holy relics, to obtain eleemosynary contributions in aid of their impoverished convent.

I need hardly say that my Greek attendant devoutly kissed the sacred contents of the case. Each of us gave his mite towards restoring the monks to the enjoyment of the comforts of the good old times.

A Massacre of Christians

The history of Crete sometimes seems little more than a succession of massacres.

I stayed some time in this village after descending front the Rhoka. The inhabitants of these parts of the island, where the Mohammedan population is numerous, and which are near the chief city, did not join the Greeks of western Crete in their attempt to shake off the Turkish yoke till more than a year after the outbreaking of the revolt. A very tragical scene occurred at Kani-Kasteli, while it was still inhabited only by a few Mohammedans, and a peaceful and submissive Christian population.

On the morning of Good Friday, in the year 1822, the Greeks of Kani-Kasteli assembled to celebrate the usual religious service of the day, in the church of their village. Two *papadhes*, a father and son, officiated. Three Mohammedans of the village thought the occasion too good to be let pass, and went well armed to the place of Christian worship. Since the Greeks of the district of Temenos, at that time, had none of them joined their correligionaries of Sfakia and the western parts of the island, they were all unarmed. One of the three Mohammedans took his post outside the church-door. The other two entered it and shot thirty men dead on the spot. Five others were wounded but recovered. Two women also received severe wounds, inflicted by accident, for the Mohammedans meant only to massacre the men, One of these women died the next day. The young papas escaped through a window behind the altar. It would seem as if, from the moment when the partial insurrection of the mountaineers in the west took place, the Mohammedans had perpetrated every cold-blooded atrocity and cruelty that was likely to drive all the Christians of the island to make common cause with the Sfakians, who, if they died, at all events did so with arms in their hands, and were not butchered like sheep, as any Christian might be in all the other parts of Crete.

Popular Methods of Dating

It being now almost sunset I thought it prudent, instead of going on to Haghio Vasili this evening, to turn off to the left soon after passing the fountain. After going about a mile to the southward, we arrived at the village of Sykologo. The chief produce of its fields is corn, although it possesses wine and oil enough for its own consumption.

Many coins were brought to me: they were almost all Venetian. Out of a party of half a dozen Greeks not one knows the year, or has any idea of an era. They reckon neither from Christ nor Mohammed; but tell me that they believe in Christ. On my asking who he was, they answer, "How should we know ? We are ignorant peasants, and only know how to cultivate our fields and vineyards." Scarcely any Cretan Greeks, except some of the Pateres in the monasteries, have ever heard of the Christian era; but they all date events one by another. Thus, in Crete, the year of the great earthquake; the time when Khadji Osman-pasha was governor of Khania; the outbreaking of the Greek revolution; the peace of Khusein-bey; the war of Khadji Mikhali; and the final submission to the Egyptians, are the principal epochs to which all the events of the last five-and-twenty years are referred.

The Village which had Never Seen a "European" Before

Finding, on my return to Kyriakusalia, that I had not time to reach Fre, the principal village of Apokorona, by sunset, I proceeded only to Rhamne, a little hamlet, situated on the lower ranges of the White Mountains, to which a Greek undertook to show Our Highnesses the way from Kyriakusalia. My stupid Turk knew neither the road nor any thing else. A very short ride, chiefly through groves of olives brought us to Rhamne. The Proestos of this village had such indifferent accommodation to offer, that he took us to the house of a friend, where however we certainly did not fare sumptuously, and had to sleep in the same room with our horses. The people were most anxious to do all they could for us: the Proestos spent some time himself in searching the village for eggs, which at last he found: the only addition to them consisted of olives, black barley-bread and plenty of excellent water. The evening meal of my host and his wife was a dish of wild herbs, on which the Cretans seem chiefly to live: they boil them, and then serve them up in oil; bread, olives, and sometimes cheese, completing the meal. On this occasion our accommodations were certainly most indifferent, and the people were fully aware of it. "What a difference there must be, said they, between Londhra and this place." They had never seen an European before. We found it cold in spite of our host's exertions to keep up a good fire: the snow was lying on the mountains down to within fifty or sixty feet of the level of the village. The daughter of the Proestos of Rhamne was taken prisoner, by the Mohammedans, during the war, and was sold as a slave at Alexandria, where she remained twelve years. On obtaining her freedom, a few months ago, she immediately returned to her native village, speaking both Turkish and Arabic nearly as fluently as her mother-tongue. The party of Mohammedans, which carried off this young woman from Rhamne, fell in with my host's father on the same occasion. In conformity with their general custom, they put him to death. At the same period of the struggle the Christians used invariably to slay even their female prisoners: this was done to avoid, what was regarded as a still deeper crime than murder, improper familiarity between their own warriors and any woman who had not received Christian baptism.

Character of the Lakiotes

The Lakiotes acted a most conspicuous and honourable part in the war. This was partly owing to their active habits, caused by the mountainous nature of their country; but still more to their having been accustomed to the use of firearms, both for the chase on their neighbouring mountains, and for less innocent objects; which, in so wild and savage a state of society as that which existed in Crete, before the outbreaking of the Greek revolution, used constantly to offer themselves.

In those times they used often to have petty wars with the Turks: that is, a Lakiote would cut off a Turk who had given him what he thought a just cause of offence, and, if the perpetrator of the crime was found out, the Pasha would come to the village with a sufficient force, and burn his house, etc. If he was not found out, a heavy fine was imposed on the village. Old Nikoludhes, my host, the proestos or headman of Laki, had his house burnt in this way no less than three times: it was also twice confiscated by the Pasha, along with all the property of his uncle and relations. In these petty wars Nikoludhes received nine gunshot wounds, three of which, since his vest and shirt were open, the day being very warm, I saw on his breast the moment I first spoke to him.

In the same good old times, if anyone had an enemy and had also a Sfakian friend, he used to avail himself of the latter, in order to get the other put out of the way. It was simply necessary to intimate his wish, and to make at the same time a suitable present, and the Sfakian would at once watch for his opportunity, and soon give the desired proof of his friendship.

Venetian Treachery

When the Turks conquered Crete they were at first welcomed by many Cretans, despite being Muslims. Some of the folk memories of the people concerning the cruelties of Venetian rule go a long way to explaining this attitude.

Krustogherako in Selino, and some villages in the immediate neighbourhood of Laki, were the scene of atrocities, while Crete belonged to the Most Serene Republic, such as in all probability have never been perpetrated by any Pasha in any part of the Turkish Empire. The following account of the proceedings of Venetian nobles, and of the public representatives of Venice in the island, is drawn from the manuscript account of a Venetian writer, who plainly approves of the atrocities which he describes.

From the time of the great revolt in the year 1363, the island remained tranquil, under the Venetian government, till the beginning of the sixteenth century. At that time, however, the Greeks of Selino, Sfakia, and the Rhiza, including, some villages situated almost on the very plain of Khania, united together and refused to obey the representatives of Venice. Their leaders were George Gadhanole, a native of Krustogherako, the Pateropuli of Sfakia, and some other families of the Archontopuli, as they were called. Gadanhole was elected Rector … of these provinces. Each department of the new administration was filled by its proper officers, all appointed by the Rector. Thus duties and taxes were now paid, not to the Venetian, but to the Greek authorities; and two independent powers coexisted for some time in the island. At length the Greek Rector suddenly presented himself at the country house of Francesco Molini, a Venetian noble, in the neighbourhood of Khania, and asked his daughter in marriage for Petro, "the most beautiful and the bravest of all his sons;" and in whose favour the Rector declared his intention of resigning his office, on the celebration of the marriage. The alliance was agreed on; the "Rettore" gave his son a massive gold ring, and the betrothal at once took place. The youth kissed his future bride, and placed the ring on her finger: the wedding was to be solemnized the next

Sunday week, at the Venetian's country house, a few miles out of Khania. Molini was merely to send for a notary and a few friends, and Gadhanole, with his son, was to be accompanied by a train not exceeding five hundred men. The Greeks left the country-house of the Venetian gentleman without for an instant suspecting that he meditated any foul play.

The following morning Molini visited the Governor of Khania, and obtained his promise of co-operation in an attempt to obtain, for the supposed indignity, a satisfaction "which might serve as an example to posterity In order, however, to prevent any suspicion of his good faith, Molini despatched tailors to his country-house, to prepare new dresses for the wedding, and also sent presents of fine cloth to his future son-in-law. During the next few days, the Governor of Khania assembled about a hundred and fifty horsemen, and seventeen hundred foot-soldiers, within the city.

On the day before the wedding, Molini went from Khania to his house at Alikiano, accompanied by about fifty of his friends, to be present at the marriage on the morrow. He gave orders for roasting a hundred sheep and oxen, and for making all due preparations to celebrate the nuptials with becoming splendour. The Greek Rector arrived, accompanied by about three hundred and fifty men and one hundred women, on the Sunday morning, and was delighted at all that he witnessed. He was received by Molini with every demonstration of kindness and affection. After the marriage ceremony, the day was naturally spent in festivity and rejoicing. The Greeks ate and drank, and danced and sang. The Venetian sedulously plied his guests with wine, and the intoxication which was pretended by the Venetian nobles present, all of whom were parties to the plot, really overcame the whole host of the unfortunate and too confiding Greeks. Some time after sunset, a rocket thrown up at Khania gave notice, to the Venetians, of the approach of the troops to consummate their design. The Greeks, overpowered by wine and sleep, were all dispersed about the palace. As soon as the military force arrived, most of the destined victims were at once bound hand and foot, but were suffered to sleep on till near sunrise. At daybreak Molini and the Public Representative of the Most Serene Republic hung the Greek Rector, the unfortunate bridegroom, and one of his younger brothers. Of the family of the Musuri three were shot, and the rest hanged on trees. Of the Kondi, sixteen were present, eight of whom the Venetians hung, and sent the others to the galleys in chains. All the rest of the ill-fated prisoners were divided into four parties: not, however, with any intention, on the part of their ferocious and treacherous foes, of mitigating the penalty to be exacted from them, for an equally merciless fate awaited them all. The Venetians hung the first division of them at the gate of Khania, the second at Krustogherako, which village, the birthplace of Gadhanole, was also razed to the ground; the third at the castle of Apokorona, and the fourth on the mountains between Laki and Theriso, above Meskla, to which village Gadhanole had removed from Krustogherako.

"Thus," says the Venetian Chronicler, who proves himself a worthy reciter of such barbarities of hill countrymen, "they were annihilated, and all men who were faithful and devoted to God and their Prince were solaced and consoled."

The Senate at Venice, however, did not think the consolation it thus received sufficient; but elected one Cavalli as Proveditor, giving him the fullest authorities for extirpating the seditious Greeks. In executing these instructions he marched out of Khania a little before midnight, and surprised the village of Fotigniaco, near Murnies, and about four miles from Khania, accompanied by all his troops. They surrounded the place, and dragged all its inhabitants, men, women and children, out of their houses. They then set on fire every dwelling in the village, and, at daybreak, the orders of the Venetian Senate began to be fully accomplished. Twelve of the Greek Primates were hanged, and, "to cause still greater fear," Capelli sought out the pregnant wives of four of the principal persons of the place, and "cutting open their bodies with large knives," tore forth their unborn children" an act which truly inspired very great terror through the whole district. This was the deliberate proceeding of a high public functionary of the Venetian Senate! "It is true," adds the Chronicler, "their crimes merited a severer punishment, and such also followed." For all the captives were conducted into the city, with their families, and great numbers of them were there put to death: the rest were transported from Crete to the three islands, so that the wicked race was thus eradicated." Five or six individuals alone escaped, at the moment when Cavalli arrived, like a midnight murderer, and found refuge in the villages of Murnies and Kertomadhes.

Cavalli, after so satisfactory a commencement, pressed onward in his course, and next required all the Greeks of Kastel-Franko, Apokorona, Sfakia, Selino, and Kisamos, "to appear in the city, and make their submission. Some of them ventured to do so, but the leading families, and the mountaineers, could not trust themselves to the word or mercy of persons, by whom all ordinary principles of justice and humanity were wholly disregarded. Their property was therefore declared confiscated, their lives forfeited, and a price was set on their heads. The life of any inhabitant of the several proscribed districts could only be redeemed on a condition, which is perhaps more revolting to the common feelings of mankind, than any other savage act of these unchristian rulers. Pardon was promised to anyone of the proscribed, on condition that he produced, in Khania, "*the head of his father, or brother, or cousin, or nephew.*" This generous humanity was extended even further: each additional head which one man might bring into the city, would entitle him to demand from the governor the forfeited life of another relation. It is painful to learn, that the lives of many of the unfortunate objects of this barbarous and inhuman persecution, were thus redeemed by the deaths of their dearest relatives.

At length a priest, of the family of the Pateri-Zapa, entered the city, accompanied by his two sons, and by two of his brothers, each individual of the mournful party carrying in his hand a human head. We know, from the terms of the Venetian law, how near and dear those who had thus heroically died, must have been to the five survivors, whose lives could only be rendered secure by this dreadful sacrifice. The wretched men placed their bleeding offerings before the Signor Cavalli, and the other representatives of Venice, and with the bitterest tears stated whose heads they were. The facts were duly established by witnesses: even the Governor, who had been sent to Crete, in order "to extirpate" the seditious Greeks, was moved: and the law was at length abolished.

A Modern Crusade

As we passed along Manias described to me, at great length, the disastrous flight of the Mahommedans through this pass, at the very outbreaking of the revolution: he even pointed out spots where individuals, of whom he spoke, had fallen: and the whitening human bones, which were still seen in some of the places, were a painful proof of the faithfulness of his story. I heard the same facts described by many other persons before I left the island, and the following is the sum and substance of what I learnt.

The Pasha determined, in August 1821, on penetrating into Sfakia, and accompanied by an immense host of Cretan Mohammedans, made good his passage to Askyfo. All attempts to withstand the advance of the enemy were vain, and the Sfakians were obliged to retire to the loftier mountains of the West.

The Mohammedans encamped in the plain of Askyfo, expecting to receive, ere long, the submission of the rebels. The Greeks, however, in no wise dispirited by the overwhelming numbers of the enemy, employed diligently that evening, and the ensuing night, in summoning aid from all the neighbouring villages, and, most of all, in sending intelligence of what had happened to Malaxa, an important post, where nearly a hundred Askyfiotes were stationed, along with other Greeks. Thus, by daybreak, the Christian force assembled at Xerokampos, about two miles west of Askyfo, was between four and five hundred strong.

On advancing towards the plain, they saw that it was covered by the Turkish tents and troops, which, since a breathless calm prevailed, were more than half concealed from their view by the smoke of their villages, which were already sacked and in flames. Russos accompanied by a small party, approached his own house, the highest on the side of the mountain, though little more than a musket-shot from the edge of the plain: on entering it he found that a large earthen vessel of wine had escaped the notice of the Mohammedans, This was soon distributed among his followers, who, descending a little nearer the plain, opened their fire from behind some low walls; and many other Sfakians, who had already occupied the villages of Petres, and Stavrorakhi, situated a little to the south of the station of Russos, and on the same western slope, began their attack at the same time. These simultaneous volleys caused no little astonishment and rage among the Mohammedans, who, on seeing the Greeks approach, supposed them to be coming to submit, and that they should have no more trouble in putting down what they called the Sfakian revolt.

The action thus commenced soon after sunrise: for full seven hours the Mohammedans constantly kept up a heavy fire of musketry, and directed, as well as they were able, against the redoubts of the Greeks, three field-pieces, which they had brought with them. During this time also considerable execution was done in the Turkish ranks by the less noisy fire which was directed against them, with a far surer aim, by the Greeks. By about two hours after midday, the Sfakians, were nearly nine hundred strong, numerous reinforcements of small parties having arrived during the morning, A considerable body of the mountaineers now took possession of the wood immediately above Kares, at the north-western extremity of the plain, and opened a destructive fire on the Turkish column which was already engaged at that village. The Mohammedans, engaged there, on finding themselves exposed to this unexpected attack, wavered for a moment, and then commenced a precipitate retreat.

The plight of this division immediately caused a panic throughout their whole host, and the rout became general. The Greeks pursued their enemies across the plain, and harassed their rear as they retreated along the path which conducts to the district of Apokorona.

As soon as the Mohammedans reached the very commencement of the descent, where the glen begins to contract in width, the Greeks detached from their main body a party, who, making a rapid circuit over the hills on the north-west, arrived on the left flank of their fleeing foes at the narrowest part of the gorge, about three hundred paces from its opening, and when the foremost of the fugitives were only just passing the spot. This party of Sfakians immediately opened, on the dense retreating column, a deadly fire, of which every shot told. The Mohammedans, with more courage than prudence, attempted for a moment to make a stand; but soon found, that the fearful advantages possessed by an enemy, who was almost entirely concealed from their view, left them no chance of safety, except in a rapid flight. Many of the horsemen at once abandoned their steeds, which, when they had to traverse the rugged paths of Sfakia, only impeded their escape, and betook themselves to the mountains on the eastern side of the defile.

Before the last of the fugitives emerged from the glen, heaps of dead bodies lay on the road all the way from this narrow path to the entrance above Krapi: and those who have experienced the intolerable stench produced, under the burning summer-sun of this latitude, by the decomposition of a single dead body, lying exposed to its putrefying beams, will readily believe the Sfakian who says that for weeks afterwards they were unable to pass even near the spot...

The traveller who visits Sfakia, as I do, thirteen years after the event, still sees by the roadside the bleached bones of many of those who fell: memorials of mortal strife, which, in these regions, are but too frequently met with.

When the main body of the Mohammedans had at length passed out, and found themselves on the open barren mountains about Krapi, the rear continued to be harassed by a steady pursuit, to avoid which numerous parties made their escape to the mountains. The Sfakians pursued the flying enemy as far as Armyro, near twelve miles from Askyfo, harassing his rear, and cutting off everyone who was not active enough to keep up with the main body in their disorderly flight.

At Armyro sunset and the shades of night gave the Turks that protection which they might have found in their own numbers, had their leaders been but once able to rally them when they had reached the plain.

But, though the main body of the Turks was thus unmolested by any further pursuit, their numerous stragglers had other and greater horrors to endure. Those of them who were wounded were unable long to continue their flight; and, with no friend to aid them, sunk down and died. Even the strongest and most vigorous were scarcely better able to escape; for most of them lost their way in the mountains, or were intercepted by parties of Sfakians, who, for the next two or three days, according to their own accounts, hunted these unhappy stragglers "like so many wild-goats."

A solitary Mohammedan entered a Sfakian village at midday: all its male inhabitants happened to be absent: the women (who were unarmed, while he had arms) at first treated him kindly; but only till they found an opportunity of dispatching him. When I visited Nipro, my host said, that, two or three days after their great victory, "a Mohammedan came here, and fell on his knees a few paces from my door, imploring a draught of water." And what did you do? "I took my tufek - and shot him." We must make some allowance, in estimating the morality of such conduct, for the provocation received by the Christians of Crete, during more than a whole century; and, most of all, for the feelings so recently excited by the butchery of the Patriarch at Constantinople; of the Bishop of Kisamos at Khania; of the Metropolitan and five other Christian Prelates at Megalo-Kastron, and of nearly *a thousand* unarmed Greeks in various parts of this island.

Corpses not stripped of their arms, when occasionally found by Sfakian shepherds for months afterwards, sufficiently indicated that others had died from absolute want and exhaustion. Some, after skulking under the trees in the daytime, and vainly endeavouring to find their way towards Rhithymnos by night, unable to withstand the stern behests of those imperious tyrants, Hunger and Thirst, at length, as their only chance of preserving life, entered a village, and, throwing themselves at the feet of the first Greek they found, implored mercy and a draught of water. Perhaps the reader may suppose that such a prayer would be granted if he does, he knows not the Sfakian, whose hatred of the very name of Mohammedan makes him even proud of recounting such atrocities as these massacres of unresisting and helpless suppliants.

A word more, and the history of this disastrous flight will be concluded. As if it had been destined, that all modes of escape should prove equally unavailing, many parties of Mohammedans, who fled in bodies of from five or six to eighteen or twenty men, were intercepted by the mountaineers: one was thus destroyed at Limni, and another at Gonia, between Kalikrati and Polis: a third, more numerous than the other two, had got right across the mountains to Skalote, when at length they were observed, were attacked by a superior force of the active and warlike mountaineers, and were cut off to a man.

The Mohammedans are said to have lost, on the occasion, nearly nine hundred men, as well as many mules laden with military stores, and their three field-pieces. The loss of the Christians was quite insignificant.

It may easily be imagined how so signal a victory would elate the spirits of those who had already a strong religious feeling on the subject of the war: who now believed themselves to he under the special guardianship of the Deity, to whom they wholly ascribed their success: who were fighting for the body and blood of the Lord Christ: whose every banner was accompanied by a priest, often one of the bravest combatants: who celebrated, with an unheard of frequency, the most solemn ordinances of their religion: and who were thus raised to so exalted a pitch of religious fervour and enthusiasm, that, in their zeal for God's honour and service, they could, one and all, subdue even their dearest affections, when they believed that, by indulging them, they would be rendered unworthy champions of the holy cause which they had espoused.

The Christian husbands of Crete, on thus becoming soldiers of the Cross, shrunk from the caresses of their wives, as from a pollution, which would most probably be punished by their falling in the next engagement. This singular piece of religious self-denial lasted, with most of them, for the greater part of the first year. I believe this feature is one of several peculiar to the war in Crete. The religious principle was certainly stronger here than elsewhere.

A Mountain Village

An ascent of about forty minutes from Krapi, brings us to the highest point of the path, and, in a few minutes more, we see the plain of Askyfo, spread out before and below us. We are rather more than a quarter of an hour in descending to it. The villages classed together under the common name of Askyfo, are situated in a plain of about three to four miles in circumference, so surrounded by lofty mountain-summits, that it has somewhat the appearance of a large amphitheatre.

Manias being still unmarried, his mother keeps house for him: we find, however, that the door of his dwelling at Askifo is closed, the old lady not having yet come up into Sfakia, from their winter residence at Dhramia. I therefore lodge with a neighbour and nephew of Manias. My host's wife is extremely beautiful: she was born at Anopolis, and never left her native place until she married, three years ago: since that event she has not stirred out of Askyffo, except once to visit her mother at Anopolis.

The difference in temperature between the plain of Apokorona this morning at ten, and these lofty summits even at two in the afternoon, is very considerable. There is always an agreeable breeze here in the hot weather, and the evenings and mornings are delightfully cool, even in the months of July and August. I suppose Askyfo to be more than fifteen hundred, perhaps nearly two thousand feet, below the highest summits of the Sfakian chain of mountains, and to be somewhere between four and five thousand feet above the sea-level… The present number of families at Arkyfo is about one hundred and sixty, They are Christians, without a single exception, as is the case throughout Sfakia.

The town of Sfakia is the chief winter residence of the Askyfiotes: many families, however, not having any dwelling except at Askyfo, make the necessary provision for remaining here through the winter, and are ordinarily confined to their houses, for several weeks, by the snow.

Soon after arriving at my present quarters I asked for a glass of water. My host, instead of saying "your health" to me, in the usual way, after I had swallowed it, exclaimed, "Christ is risen," to which I, of course, replied, "Truly he is risen." This Easter salutation is now *alone* used, even when a man sneezes, "Christ is risen," are the words by which he is addressed.

Several of the, villagers come to my host's house to see and talk with me. One of them is an uncle of Manias', and brother of Buzo-Marko, who fell at Grabusa. Of the seven Sfakians who were executed by the Pasha last December, four were of Askyfo, and only one of them had been present in the assembly at Murnies. The other three of the seven were of Nipros, Komitadhes and Haghios Ioannes: two of the Askyfiotes, and the other three Sfakians, were arrested and executed in this village in the following manner.

When the Pashas had established their headquarters at Fre, and their army was dispersed through the villages of Ipos, Prosnero, Alikampo and other places in the plain of Apokorona, they at length sent to Askyfo Ali-effendi, the Turkish President of the Council of Sfakia, accompanied by a bimbashi, (colonel), with a battalion of regular troops and about one hundred and fifty Arnauts. On their arrival the President and the Colonel professed to be the bearers of letters, both from the Pashas in the plain below, and from the Viceroy, Mehmet-Ali-pasha, to the inhabitants of Sfakia. They therefore despatched messengers to each of the villages of the whole Sfakian district, requesting that two or three of the principal persons of every place would come to Askyfo, in order to be present at the reading of these letters. The wary Sfakians suspected some treachery, and came but slowly; so slowly that the Turks waited no less than six days before they executed their real intention. They never read any letters from the Viceroy or Pashas, but, on the evening of the sixth or seventh day of their stay, about two hours before sunset, they arrested five of their destined victims, and immediately wrote to the Pasha, telling him the names of those whom they had secured.

The sensation produced in the village may be easily conceived. These hardy mountaineers, who had maintained a contest with the Turks, with but little intermission, for a period of ten years; and who, however closely pressed by superiority of numbers, had always found a refuge in the fastnesses or on the summits of their native mountains, were not likely to stand tamely by, and see their innocent fellow-villagers and relations arrested and conducted down to the headquarters at Fre, probably to be executed in cold blood by these Egyptians, whom everyone hated as bitterly as the old Turks.

Now the villagers of Askyfo and Nipros, not an hour distant, would supply a body of full two hundred men: they would also be able to obtain a reinforcement from Asfento, so that probably they would muster about three hundred, nearly all of whom could arm themselves in an instant. The leading men among them held a secret deliberation, and felt satisfied that daybreak would see their fellow-villagers marched off under a strong escort, of perhaps a hundred men, to the Pashas. They therefore determined to go in two parties so as suddenly to enclose them as they passed the narrowest part of the defile. "We will then demand their prisoners, and we will have them either dead or alive." Happily, however, for the tranquillity of Crete, and, perhaps, for the Sfakians themselves, the messenger sent to the Pashas returned in the silence and darkness of night, and communicated his orders to the President and Colonel. When the Sfakians were on the look out, at the very earliest dawn, to see what the Turks were on the point of doing, the first sight that met their eyes was the five bodies of the unfortunate prisoners, one or two of whom had been despatched by the bowstring, and the rest had been bayoneted by the Arabs, in the house where they were guarded.

The Askyfiotes around me, three of whom, in their height and muscular strength, are such men as one sees only in these mountains, sigh as they repeat the tale, and point out to me, in the group which surrounds me, a young woman, dressed in the garb of mourning, who lost her father during the war, and whose brother was one of the victims thus recently sacrificed. His orphan, a child of four years old, is standing by her. The Sfakians doubt whether they did not do wrong, in thus remaining quiet, and think that their best course would have been to have taken their arms, and once more occupying the most inaccessible of their mountains, thence to have waged and suffered a war of extermination with their foe.

I inquire whether any Askyfiote remembers the events of the Russian invasion of the Morea in 1769, when nearly a thousand Sfakians left their homes to fight against the Turks, and when the Cretan Turks, taking advantage of their absence, exacted a heavy penalty from those whom they had left behind them, for the part they took. I am told that, among the five men seized and massacred here, there was an old man, Andhrulios Papadhakes, who was one of Lambro's Capitanei, and still possessed, at the time of his death, Lambro's pistols and some of his clothes. He was mentioned in the Greek song which celebrated Lambro's exploits. The poor old man, whose extreme age, for he had lived nearly a whole century, might alone have protected him, even if he had taken some part in an assembly where thousands met together, had never been present at Murnies. But he was distinguished from olden times, and even among the inhabitants of these mountains, for his hatred of the Turkish rulers of his country; and the reputation which he thus acquired was probably the cause of his death, and certainly entitles him to be regarded as one of the patriots, who were celebrated by our poet before the outbreaking of the Greek revolution.

Vampires

When at Askyfo I had asked about the vampires, or *katakhanadhes* as the Cretans call them, of whom I had heard from Manias and others of his fellow-countrymen, and whose existence and ill-deeds form a general article of popular belief throughout the island. Of course this belief is very strong in the mountains.

If any one ventures to doubt it, undeniable facts are brought forward to silence the incredulous. At Anopolis I am on ground which has long been haunted by them, and is celebrated in numerous stories, some of which are amusing enough, in which their exploits are recorded.

I subjoin one of these stories in the very words in which it was communicated to me. The account is peculiarly worthy of credit, since I heard it in many places, and all the relations given to me agreed in every material point. The following is a translation, and, even without comparing it with the original, the reader will see, from its very style, that it is a close, though somewhat condensed, version of the words of the Sfakian peasants,

Once on a time the village of Kalikrati, in the district of Sfakia, was haunted by a *katakhanas*, and people did not know what man he was or from what part. This katakhanas destroyed both children and many full-grown men; and desolated both that village and many others. They had buried him at the church of Saint George at Kallikrati, and in those times he was a man of note, and they had built an arch over his grave. Now a certain shepherd, his mutual *synteknos*, was tending his sheep and goats near the church, and, on being caught by a shower, he went to the sepulchre, that he might he shaded from the rain, Afterwards he determined to sleep, and to pass the night there, and, after taking off his arms, he placed them by the stone which served him as his pillow, crosswise. And people might say, that it is on this account that the *katakhanas* was not permitted to have his tomb. During the night, then, as he wished to go out again, that he might destroy men, he said to the shepherd: "Gossip, get up hence, for I have some business that requires me to come out." The shepherd answered him not, either the first time, or the second, or the third; for thus he knew that the man had become a *katakhanas*, and that it was he who had done all those evil deeds. On this account he said to him, on the fourth time of his speaking, "I shall not get up hence, gossip, for I fear that you are no better than you should be, and may do me some mischief: but, if I must get up, swear to me by your winding-sheet, that you will not hurt me, and on this I will get up." And he did not pronounce the proposed words, but said other things: nevertheless, when the shepherd did not suffer him to get up, he swore to him as he wished. On this he got up, and, taking his arms, removed them away from the monument, and the *katakhanas* came forth, and, after greeting the shepherd, said to him, "Gossip, you must not go away, but sit down here; for I have some business which I must go after; but I shall return within the hour, for I have something to say to you." So the shepherd waited for him. And the *katakhanas* went a distance of about ten miles, where there was a couple recently married, and he destroyed them. On his return, his gossip saw that he was carrying some liver, his hands being moistened with blood: and, as he carried it, he blew into it, just as the butcher does, to increase the size of the liver. And he showed his gossip that it was cooked, as if it had been done on the fire. After this he said, "Let us sit down, gossip, that we may eat." And the shepherd pretended to eat it, but only swallowed dry bread, and kept dropping the liver into his bosom. Therefore, when the hour for their separation arrived, the *katakhanas* said to the shepherd, "Gossip, this which you have seen, you must not mention, for, if you do, my twenty nails will be fixed in your children and yourself." Yet the shepherd lost no time, but gave information to priests, and others, and they went to the tomb, and there they found the *katakhanas*, just as he had been buried. And all people became satisfied that it was he who had done all the evil deeds. On this account they collected a great deal of wood, and they cast him on it, and burnt him. His gossip was not present, but, when the *katakhanas* was already half consumed, he too came forward in order that he might enjoy the ceremony. And the *katakhanas* cast, as it were, a single spot of blood, and it fell on his foot, which wasted away, as if it had been roasted on a fire. On this account they sifted even the ashes, and found the little fingernail of the katakhanas unburned, and burnt it too.

This supposed vampire's habit of feeding on the human liver, may perhaps account for an exclamation of a Cretan mother, recorded in the travels of Tavernier: "I will sooner eat the liver of my child."…

The Sfakians also generally believe that the ravages committed by these night-wanderers, used, in former times, to be far more frequent than they are at the present day; and that they are become comparatively rare, solely in consequence of the increased zeal and skill possessed by members of the sacerdotal order!

1851-3 Captain T. A. B. Spratt

Idolatrous Muslims

The bus of a Roman statue at a fountain within the town, that is figured in Pashley, and which, according to Antonio Belli, a Venetian writer on Crete, came from Ierapetra, is similarly decorated and paid, reverence to by some Turkish devotees every Friday (the Mussulman's Sabbath), besides having a lamp with oil or incense set before it also. This is the only indication of image-worship which I have ever observed amongst Mohammedans; and I was informed that it is due to a belief amongst the superstitious, that it is the petrified remnant of the body of a sainted Ethiopian Mussulman who was killed in the war, and whose head and lower members were cut off by the Christians, but who is destined to rise to life when the Ghiaour are to be exterminated from the island.

Mermaids

Whoever has crossed the deeps of the Aegean Sea on a calm sunny day can never forget the intensity of its ultramarine blue, as it combines the azure reflected from the firmament above, with the blue hues arising from its own crystal-clear transparency and profundity beneath. And if he so crosses this landlocked bowl, this bath of the Sirens (as we may fairly call the deep pool in front of Aptera), and is reflective, imaginative, he might pass from an admiration of the scene around, and of the submarine tints below, to such a reverie as the voyagers of past times doubtless did when slowly sailing over it with the fable in their minds, and at last might figure to himself the attempted flight of the Sirens at the moment of their defeat, and their plunge, with now plumeless pinions, into the clear blue waters - or perhaps even see them again, as mermaids, or nereids, returning to its surface for pastime, and scattering the pearl-drops from their tresses, as gems fall before the footsteps of a fairy. And if he had seen what I and many others saw in these very waters, in this very bay, as doubtless the ancient Cretans or the navigators to its shore often did, and had not modern science and experience to guide him and settle his judgment, he might have believed in mermaids and sea-nymphs too.

Early one calm summer's morning, when we were lying at anchor off the Tuzla Scala, at the head of Suda Bay, and the surface of the bay was like a mirror, the officers and men then on board were suddenly attracted by something unusual that was seen splashing and apparently sporting upon the surface of its waters at no great distance from them, and to naked eyes looked remarkably like a human head and neck, with long flowing tresses, which, from its action, the creature seemed to be occasionally throwing and tossing about from side to side, or beating upon the surface of the then calm bay, as if to free them from their entanglement, or from the matted weed they had caught up from the rocky recesses of the deep whence the strange creature had come. A mermaid, truly might easily have been the exclamation and belief of many who saw it, had they lived a century or two earlier.

And what was this phenomenon? Is the natural inquiry. Merely a common seal that was disappointing a Cretan gentleman of a delicacy of the deep; for it was breakfasting upon a huge octopodia, or species of eight-armed sepia or cuttlefish, with which it had risen from the bottom and come to the surface to free itself from the long tenacious arms which the strong and muscular creature had entwined round the head, face, and shoulders of the amphibian; and as these arms are each provided with large cup-like suckers, the octopodia's strength of hold is such that it could easily drown a man with two or three of them only, if the rest were firmly attached to a stone or rock at the bottom. Hence the seal's struggles and splashing to detach them.

When the seal had tired out by wounding, or half-drowned its victim in the air by remaining sufficiently long at the surface, it then leisurely and apparently playfully tossed and turned it over and over as a cat does a mouse; and thus represented to a distant observer all the fanciful attitudes of a mermaid in sport, or in the act of clearing her tresses from entanglements.

What more is wanting to explain the origin of mermaids, or perhaps even that of the fable of the Sirens of Aptera, over whose bath or pool we have been induced for a moment here to pause and to contemplate?

A Sleepless Night

At length they departed; and I arose also to prepare my bed in my own way, as I had preferred my own meal; for to work well a man must sleep well, and to sleep even at all, under the hospitality of a Cretan village's resident, one must have either a coat of mail for outside skin, or be buried in a sort of sack, or slung in a hammock, as partial aids to this requirement, I came, therefore, provided with both the latter, as I brought no tent, the season being advancing towards winter, and I expected to find it very cold at this elevation; for to hope for rest and sleep, unprovided against such companions as a Cretan's house contains, is out of the question, as I have often experienced when duty or the pleasure of travel has thrown me, as it too frequently has, into the company of legions of those tormentors of the human frame and mind, the flead, and, alas! Too, of those troubled spirits that haunt the long, long Levantine night, when they are present, with their trumpeting – a song that never ceases, but trumpets the louder the more they are thwarted and disappointed in their attack - and with snouts also that, in one's dozy, dreamy state of combat and resistance, the victim is led to compare to the bill of a snipe or the probe of a vampire which is endeavouring to bore into your flesh.

And then there is that other enemy of the thin-skinncd man, the "B flat" to use a delicate name often applied to distinguish it from the first-named, the "F sharp"), and yet an unmusical fellow, too, who steals upon you without sound, and generally without crawl or even touch that can be felt to warn you of its approach, but from some part of the clothes nearest you, under or over, as the case may be, probes or bites with head erect or bent backwards from his fat body, and with the mouth only just reaching you. Thus this cunning fellow, then and from there, sends the unfelt but yet penetrating probe into you, and sucks his full from the sweet veins he has reached, and, as a return for the nectar he has drawn, deposits an irritant something as a memento of his feast, that soon sets blood and skin in a blaze of fever and of certain torment for full forty-eight hours afterwards. And even through sheet or shirt the stealthy and silent "B flat," as also his trumpeting companion of the night, the mosquito, will bite and sting the tender-fleshed novice and traveller. At least they do so in the East, and Crete is no exception; for they dropped or hopped into my hammock from the floor and rafters of my hospitable Cretan's hovel at Khadra in dozens, and in desperation or delight as disappointment or success met their attacks. It is somewhere stated that the Hindoos, to surpass in charity the Mahomedans, never destroy a maimed or sick animal, have established hospitals for animals of all kinds, and even for the creatures I have here named; and thus the poor native traveller who calls for a lodging or food is fed at this great house of charity on one condition only, viz. that he feeds the fleas, etc., in return, by sleeping for a night in the apartment especially kept for them. What dilettante repose they must enjoy; if they can feel! And surely the Levantine has a kindred charity when he revels in the myriads of fleas, &c., that are known to abound there. Oh, the penalty of research and travel in these lands! The feather-bed reader little knows how dearly the fruits are sometimes won.

The morning dawn consequently made me wish to be away from such enemies of rest and repose, my pellicle not being equal to its continuance or repetition; so with the rising sun I was off to the top of an adjacent mountain to rid myself of some of my friends, and to finish my observations for the topography of this part, after heartily thanking my host and hostess for their kindness and hospitality, although we paid liberally for them in blood and coin.

A "Haunted" Sarcophagus

It having come to my knowledge that two sculptured sarcophagi had been recently found near the theatre at Ierapetra, the trustees of the British Museum, being informed of it by me, were induced to become the purchasers of them from the Greek family it in whose property they were found. The purchase having been effected, their removal was effected also by the officers and crew of H.M.S. " Medina," during the latter part of December 1860 and the beginning of January 1861, but with considerable labour and difficulty, in consequence of the exposed position of the anchorage of Ierapetra at that season, and the great weight and the situation of the tombs.

As the largest of these tombs weighed nearly seven tons, a very substantial pier had to be made upon this open sandy coast before it could be embarked; and as it had to be removed some distance, over heavy ground or sand, to the most sheltered part of the bay, the operation was both slow and tedious. This duty, however, was performed with great zeal by the shore party under the direction of Messrs. Wilkinson and Drew, and its shipment by Mr. Stokes, master, aided by our chief boatswain's mate and perfect seaman John Douglas: and as the larger tomb was an interesting as well as a fine specimen of art, although much mutilated and cracked, great care was taken to preserve it, as far as possible, from further injury during its removal; and to prevent it being injured wantonly or by local enemies (there being a party there who were opposed to our removal of the relic), Mr. Wilkinson thought it advisable to sleep inside the tomb until it had arrived within the walls of the town: yet it did not wholly escape mischief; for some wanton hand destroyed what remained of the face of Hector.

The sarcophagus having thus been brought to within a few yards of the land gate of Ierapetra, upon the top of which a Turkish sentry nightly walked his solitary watches, when from time to time he called the hours, with his face towards his post and therefore turned away from the town, his eyes looked directly down upon these tombs of the dead, which, after many centuries of repose, were now being transported from their hallowed resting-place by the rude hand of strangers.

It was a subject for reflection to a meditative mind, even though he were but Turkish sentinel. The midnight hour, too, favoured the mind's play in phantom spectres and ghosts, more especially on that night, as the moon's light was dimmed by heavy clouds that hung over the adjacent mountains, and there was lightning and thunder, and a storm of wind now and then swept over the town. Whether our sentinel was meditative, or whether he had previously any apprehension of the ghosts of the men whose tombs were being so ruthlessly removed by the hands of infidels, I cannot tell; but I can aver that as he thus had his eyes upon the two marble sarcophagi, and had commenced his occasional call of "All's well," to quiet the fears and alarms of the slumbering natives within, those eyes were suddenly fixed, as they beheld a tall figure, enshrined in a winding-sheet, and white as a spectre, suddenly rise out of one of the tombs. The words of the affrighted Turk stuck in his throat before they were half uttered, as if grasped by a vice; and then, as if struck by an unseen hand, he as suddenly dropped down from his post behind the thick screen of walls and gates of the city; and neither he nor any other sentry of that guard ever ventured to mount to the summit of that gateway again whilst the tombs were there, nor was the gate opened by the sergeant of the guard until broad daylight had appeared to ensure them from another vision of the spectre, the ghost of the tomb.

The account of that sight has no doubt since been often repeated in the barrack by the sergeant and his party on guard during that eventful night. Many a tale of terror and legend, regarding ghosts and spectres, has arisen from a circumstance or circumstances as explicable and simple, if explanation had been sought for at the time; and that the ghost of the hero who was buried in the tomb some twenty centuries before had not appeared to the sentry on that night it would probably be as hard to convince them, or their many subsequent hearers at their distant homes, as to disabuse people of their belief in the stories told of ghosts in some benighted parts of our own land.

Taking the Sun for Religion's Sake

But, before reaching this valley, we passed near a somewhat substantial but solitary building upon the ridge-brow leading up to Iuktas from Phortetsa, and which my guides pointed out as being a Turkish monastery for a certain sect of dervishes, accompanying the communication with a muttering of some word of contempt, and with a curse upon the race. In turning off the road into a path that leads to the monastery, which, in spite of my guides' disinclination, I was desirous of approaching, we came suddenly upon three young dervishes, who were seated in a secluded position under a rock, and apparently where they could receive the full force of the sun's rays upon their features during a devotional reverie, - the principal object of which, however, seemed to be to enable them to obtain that tanning of their features and skin for which the mendicant dervish of the East is remarkable. It thus was apparently a part of their training or education for the obtaining a complexion of the skin, as a professional requisite to the exercise of their craft and calling; and I frequently observed afterwards, during my stay in Crete, one of the three so sitting at the hottest time of the day, under the hottest wall, in the hottest part of the town, with breast and face bared to the sun's bronzing influence, and with composed features, indicative of the most perfect absorption, and the most enthusiastic devotion of mind and aim; nothing distracted him. "Allah is great, and Mahomet is His prophet, and I am his devout disciple," seemed to be the all-absorbing sentiment on these occasions. And thus as the young dervishes faced the mountain that had been so venerated in the days of Paganism, as well as the midday sun, the idea could hardly help arising in my mind, that the situation of the monastery might have been chosen from some tradition of its sacredness relative to the tomb of the God of gods.

Places of religious sanctity, of any time and people always retain a certain special interest attached to them; and thus it is natural that the superstition of one creed should in some degree become absorbed in the superstitions of another that succeeds it, especially such as those of some of the sects of Mahomedan dervishes. Hence some are disposed to recognize in their religious dance a relic of the "Pyrrhic dance" of the Greeks. And this reminds me that the Pyrrhic dance was called the Cretan dance, so also the worship of Zeus and other deities has frequently been changed, in those localities, to that of the prophets or saints of the Greek church; and thus the chapel replaces the shrine, or the church the temple. And it appears from Pashley's research in reference to the Tomb of Zeus, that it continued to be venerated in Crete until the Theodosian persecution of the heathens, in the fourth century, put a stop to the worship of the old deities by the Cretans.

Lack of Cleanliness

[S]ome hospitable Greeks ... lodged me for the night; they were a young married couple, whose first child was not yet born, but nigh unto its birth, judging from the appearance of the good-looking hostess. The house was low and large compared to many others, but irregularly built, and consisted of two compartments, one for general use, the other for their mule and cows, with old stores and stock in one of its corners.

But the part inhabited was a specimen of primitive contentment: - a mud floor full of pits; a long bench, on the inner side, half mud and half masonry, as the, bedstead or couch; a fireplace in a niche; and a chimney just through the roof, with a broken water-jar as the chimney-pot; one low door, and a small window like a scuttle in the innermost part, served for ingress and light to the dwelling. As the room was low and wide, its roof was supported along the centre by two crooked trees ornamented with sacks, seeds, lamps and earthen pottery, either stuck upon nails or upon some branches, but all black together like the roof above. Yet here was a tolerably well-to-do young Cretan's house of the eastern uplands; a more comfortless hovel one can hardly conceive amongst a race professing to possess some amount of civilization. What a contrast to the clean habitation of a Bulgarian or Wallachian peasant! Where, upon a vast expanse of mud and clay, and simply out of that clay, with chopped straw and cowdung, the cleanest and neatest cottages are constructed; whilst here, where all is dry naturally, both soil and climate, and where they are surrounded by stone for lime, and abundance of fuel to make it, the peasant takes no pains to render his habitation much better than that compartment which is appropriated to his beast.

Is not this one of the many illustrations of the different effects resulting from the force of habit and example being made permanent by blind prejudice or indolence? Or how can it be accounted for among an intelligent race such as the Cretans, that their habitations are so inferior to those in the neighbouring islands of Caso, Carpatho, and Rhodes, where the interior as well as exterior of the houses has an air of neatness as well as cleanness, as an evident necessity in connection with the domestic requirements? The idea of order and arrangement of the various utensils for effect is also apparent in the latter islands; but in the Cretan villages it is wholly wanting. No whitewash is used for cleanness, dirt is hidden by darkness, and discomfort by apathy.

But, on the other hand, how often is the passion for cleanliness carried to excess when the mind is allowed no further expansion, and where the force of example has established it! He who has had a fidgety, over clean housekeeper, or lodged with an ever-washing Dutch landlady, in a sort of perpetual swamp, will readily understand the idea.

In the one case it is torturing a habit or necessity into an inconvenience and nuisance, and in the other maintaining in perpetuity primitive discomfort and uncleanliness, simply because natural causes have not rendered the cleansing processes habitually necessary for health and comfort, as they have among the inhabitants of the swampy flats of Wallachia or the humid lowlands of Holland; and thus the benefit of a simple coating of whitewash is not considered or appreciated, either for cleanliness or neatness, although so easily obtained and applied. But natural as well as artificial life is made up of such strange contrasts.

Moreover the upland Cretan's desire and hope is ever diverted into another direction than that of the improvement of his social comfort and condition; he sighs to shake off the hateful rule of the foreigner. Alas! He has so sighed and struggled for national independence ever since it was first lost to the Roman Martellus, and yet he is not convinced that it is more likely to be obtained by a development of moral improvement and influence, through civilization, than through petty intrigue, dogged apathy, or premature war.

A Couple of "Quacks"

Gonies is situated high up on the western ridge bounding this enclosed valley leading to the gorge; the valley for the most part consists of poor soil, and is surrounded by disturbed shaley or schistose rocks and serpentine, which has protruded here and much discoloured and distorted the rocks in contact with it. We travelled over a mass of this serpentine for more than a quarter of a mile, when passing through the valley at the foot of Gonies hill.

Gonies contains about thirty houses. Beyond it, at the head of the valley to the north-west, we hear of a small hamlet called Kamirotis, and by striking out of the "vasiliko dromo," as this mountain-track is called, from being the most frequented road between Candia and Retimo or Rhithymna, we reach it in a quarter of an hour. Selecting a level spot in one of the adjacent terraces for the tent, we soon had it erected, and were at leisure to enjoy the scenery surrounding this romantic little spot. We were now above the slaty rock", and in the midst of the broken up and detached limestone crags that overlie them, with narrow cultivable ledges beneath, descending like a series of steps down their crumbling sides; and upon a few of those in the immediate vicinity of our tent were a variety of fruit-trees flourishing in the irrigation of a copious spring that issued from beneath a neighbouring crag, where we heard again the homely blackbird singing its vespers before retiring to roost.

This was the bright picture of a romantic little mountain location. Now turning to look at the village and its inhabitants, I found a sorry contrast. Four miserable hovels were all that were inhabited out of the twenty-five that belonged to it before the revolution. Of these four, one was occupied by a poor woman widowed since May last, from the inner recess of whose hovel proceeded, as I approached it, the piteous cries of a poor little girl, her only daughter, who, I found on inquiry, was at that moment suffering from a severe paroxysm of fever and ague, recently caught whilst gleaning a few handfuls of corn amongst the fields in the plains of Candia.

Shortly after my arrival, there came also to this hamlet two important looking travellers in Frank dresses, although one bestrode a jaded mule, and the other a donkey. They, however, proved to be an itinerant Ionian quack doctor and his servant, belonging to Khania, but both natives of Cergo; and they were now travelling together, dispensing advice and medicine among all the mountain-villagers, wherever there were unfortunate dupes sufficiently afflicted and able to pay for them.

Their object in coming here, however, was simply to obtain a night's lodging, having arrived too late to proceed to a more populous village. But as the male population of the hamlet were absent, and did not return from their labours till after dark, they were patiently waiting their coming, near the widow's hovel, since none of the wives nor the widow dared to offer them lodgings in the absence of any of the male part of the community, the poor woman, however, was induced to appeal to me for some medicine for her sick daughter, at the south of which request the itinerant quack pricked up his ears and approached; but as poverty was so unmistakeably stamped within and without the cottage, he shrugged up his shoulders and walked away, neither revealing his mission to her nor uttering a word of sympathy. I had thought of offering him room in my tent, had he failed to obtain a sleeping-place at one or other of the houses of this small hamlet; but this severed our intended friendly acquaintance as fellow travellers, mid, taking upon myself to prescribe for the poor girl, gave a few quinine pills from my own stock, and recommended some absinth tea, as I found that they possessed the herb on the adjacent hills, and knew it, but not its tonic properties.

A Former Slave's Story

It is frequently forgotten that in parts of the Mediterranean it was still possible for someone living peaceably in his own village to be captured and sold into slavery during the early years of the nineteenth century.

My mules were ready with their baggage soon after daylight on the following morning, when we proceeded westward, and in a quarter of an hour crossed the pass in the mountain above the hamlet separating the torrents or streams which flow down this root of Ida into the Melavisi on the east and the Mylopotamo on the west side. A sea of ridges stretches before us to the westward for several miles, enclosed between the northern face of Ida and the lofty-pinnacled root of it, which here bends round parallel to the northern shore, and thus, branching round from the eastern base of the celebrated mountain, embraces in its sweep the rich and wooded district of Mylopotamo, formerly called the Avlopotamo.

The height of this pass must be at least 3000 feet above the sea. Descending from it into the head of the Mylopotamo valley immediately after crossing the pass, we asked every passer-by or peasant for information respecting the situation of the villages before us, and of any spot where ancient ruins of any kind existed; for I found that our guides, or rather muleteers, knew only the direct road down the valley to Retimo, and were useless when out of this track.

We at length accost an old woman on a donkey, journeying eastward. Belonging to the village of Anoya, not far distant, she proved of service in directing me to it, as neither of my guides had ever been there; and finding it a large village of 200 houses, I expected that it would prove to be an ancient site also, although the old woman, who said she had been born there, and had also lived there for ten or twelve years since her release from slavery, assured me that she had never heard of such a thing, adding that the only Hellenic places in the neighbourhood were Tylisso and Axo. As she was somewhat more than usually communicative and intelligent, I was led to inquire into the history of her slavery, when she commenced a tale of woe respecting the afflictions she had sustained in the early part of the revolutionary struggle for independence, between 1820 and 1830. Pointing to her wrinkled features, she said, "These furrows are not the effect of age, but of my griefs. I am not old, although I look it." She appeared seventy, but was only a little over fifty. "My husband was killed by the Turks; my four sons were taken from me to Alexandria, whither also I and my only daughter were taken and sold as slaves. My four sons are still in Egypt. I was myself bought from the Turks by the Austrian consul at Megalo Kastron, and lived with him there for seven years afterwards as his servant, as a recompense for the purchase-money. My only daughter also was released, got married, and joined me in my native village; but the husband proved a vagabond, and ran away, leaving her with three children to maintain, and with hardly any means; and I am now going to some acquaintances and friends to beg for them a little bread till the time of the olive-picking!"

The narrative was irresistible; and the manner in which it was related disarmed doubt, especially as I knew that it was a tale not uncommon in Crete of afflictions resulting from the revolution. Thanking the poor dame for her information, and receiving from her the accustomed prayer or benediction and expressions of gratitude and thanks, we parted. Following her directions, we crossed the narrow valley, and fell into a zigzag path leading up the steep side of a ridge of reddish-brown slaty strata; in twenty minutes we reached the village, perched upon the upper edge of the cultivable territory lying on the northern flank of Ida, where the cultivation is chiefly carried on upon narrow terraces along the sides of innumerable narrow ridges, that here, like the fibrous roots of a large tree, shoot out from the base of the mountain.

In the Cave of Skulls - a Century after the Slaughter

We pass between Kastri on our left (hearing that it was only a middle-age or Venetian fortress) and Melidoni within the mountains on the right, where exists the celebrated grotto in which nearly 300 Cretans were suffocated by smoke and fire during the civil struggle for independence between the Turk and Greek. Pashley has fully described this event, and the nature of the cavern; and therefore, although I have been within its deep and dark retreat, and seen the skulls and bones of those that perished there, I shall add nothing to his pages relative to the horrible and barbarous deed. But it is perhaps of some interest to record here, whilst referring to this cavern, that when I visited it, not a quarter of a century after the event, the skulls and bones were in some parts already becoming firmly fixed in the floor by a satalagmitic incrustation resulting from the occasional dripping of water from the calcareous roof; and I thus notice it as a caution to cave-explorers upon the fallacy of conclusions as to age deduced from the depth or amount of successive stalagmitic strata in calcareous caverns. I consider, also, that the stalactites of this cavern are far superior to those in the much extolled grotto of Antiparos.

A Community of Turkish Seafarers

Off the north end of the peninsula of Spina Longa, and close under the squally heights there rises abruptly from the sea a small but high and cliffy islet, upon which the Venetians built a strong fortress, serving both to defend the entrance to the anchorage behind it and also to be a secure garrison for the command and subjection of the natives of the Mirabella; for the Venetians, in spite of its inconvenience, made this the chief trading-port of the eastern part of Crete.

The fortress of Spina Longa was several times attacked by the Turks; but, being of the form and character of Gibraltar on a small scale, and, moreover, well fortified for the period, and also being wholly insulated, it remained in the hands of the Venetians long after the island of Crete had become subject to the Turks. Its fortifications are at present much fallen into decay; but it contains about eighty Turkish families, the town being situated on the western side of the rock, as the eastern face is quite precipitous, like that of Gibraltar. Its inhabitants are chiefly sailors, who carry on some trade in seven or eight schooners that belong to them, as well as possessing ten or twelve coasting felluccas, or caiques, for local trade, or for making summer voyages to the neighbouring islands for wood, grain, and melons, in their several seasons; for Crete, although so capable, does not produce sufficient of either to meet the consumption of its larger towns.

...a church built by the Venetians at the south end of the town... is now used as a mosque; and there are some large cisterns at the north-east end of the town, that supply the garrison with water, of detestable odour and flavour from stagnation and neglect.

It is singular thus to find in Crete a community of Turks whose occupation is exclusively the sea! And some of them are excellent sailors. And I am told that a few years since they had a fine brig also, which they had the confidence to send with a cargo to England, as she was commanded by one of their most enterprising and skilful skippers, whose great repute and skill as a Levantine navigator had thus induced them to venture her on a voyage to our difficult seas and shores, where, unhappily, fate or fortune frowned upon their temerity; for both captain and crew and their fine vessel were lost together.

The trading ambition of the little community received a serious check in this loss, from which it is perhaps not likely to recover; for they have not ventured to build another to replace her. "Kismit" (i.e. fate) settled it; so they are now content to trade at home, instead of venturing upon distant voyages.

A Mahomedan community of sailors and traders on a barren rock adjacent to a fertile island, recalls to mind the community of Christian sailors and sponge-divers who inhabit the barren rocks of Castelorizzo, Symi, and Khalki, as well as others in the Levant.

The reason of such a location or occupation was perhaps in some degree identical, viz. the preferring to seek a livelihood from the sea to the risks and discord of a life in association with their neighbours the Christians of the Mirabella, and very probably from their knowing the deep-rooted hatred formerly felt against them, as participators in the tragic events connected with the cave of Melato, which rendered return to their mountain-villages imprudent, if not impossible. Besides, they are also the appointed gunners to the island-fortress at the present time.

1857-58 Bayard Taylor

Two Very Different Monasteries

In the morning, the horses were brought to us at an early hour, in charge of Hadji Bey, a jolly old officer of gendarmes, who was to accompany us. As far as the village of Kalepa, where the Pasha was then residing, there is a carriage-road; afterwards, only a stony mountain path. From the spinal ridge of the promontory, which we crossed, we overlooked all the plain of Khania, and beyond the Dictynnaean peninsula, to the western extremity of Crete. The White Mountains, though less than seven thousand feet in height, deceive the eye by the contrast between their spotless snows and the summer at their base, and seem to rival the Alps. The day was cloudless and balmy; birds sang on every tree, and the grassy hollows were starred with anemones, white, pink, violet and crimson. It was the first breath of the southern spring, after a winter which had been as terrible for Crete as for Greece.

After a ride of three hours, we reached a broad valley, at the foot of that barren mountain mass in which the promontory terminates. To the eastward we saw the large monastery of Agia Triaaa (the Holy Trinity), overlooking its fat sweep of vine and olive land; but as I wished to visit the glen of Katholiko, among the mountains, we crossed the valley to a large farmhouse, in order to procure a guide. The sun shone hot into the stony and dirty courtyard, surrounded by one-storey huts, and not a soul was to be seen. There was a little chapel at hand, and a carved piece of iron suspended to an orange tree beside it, in lieu of a bell. Hadji Bey shouted, and Francois beat the sacred metal with a stone, until a gray-bearded native and two young fellows, with hair hanging in a long braid down their backs, made their appearance. What was our surprise, then, to see the doors open and a number of women and children, who had previously concealed themselves, issue forth! We were now regaled with wine, and Diakos, one of the long-haired youths, mounted his mule to guide us. In the deep, dry mountain glen which we entered, I found numbers of carob-trees. Rocks of dark-blue limestone, stained with bright orange oxydations, overhung us as we followed the track of a torrent upward into the heart of this bleak region, where, surrounded by the hot, arid peaks, is the monastery of Governato.

A very dirty old monk and two servants were the only inmates. We were hungry, and had counted on as good a dinner as might be had in Lent, but some black bread, cheese, and an unlimited supply of water were all that we obtained. The monk informed us that the monastery was dedicated to St. John, and was celebrated for the abundance of its honey; but neither honey nor locusts could he give us. Behind the chapel was a vault in which they put the dead monks. When the vault gets full, they take out the bones and skulls and throw them into an open chamber adjoining, where their daily sight and smell furnish wholesome lessons of mortality to the survivors. Francois was so indignant at the monk's venerable filthiness and the Lenten fare he gave us, that he refused to pay anything "to the Church," as is delicately customary.

We descended on foot to the monastery of Katholiko, which we reached in half an hour. Its situation is like that of San Saba in Palestine, at the bottom of a split in the stony hills, and the sun rarely shines upon it. Steps cut in the rock lead down the face of the precipice to the deserted monastery, near which is a cavern 500 feet long, leading into the rock. The ravine is spanned by an arch, nearly 50 feet high, at one end of which is a deep, dark well, wherein refractory monks were imprisoned. The only living thing we saw was a shepherd-boy, who shouted to us from the top of the opposite cliffs. Of St. John the Hermit, whom the monastery commemorates, I know no more than I do of St. .John the Hunter, who has a similar establishment near Athens.

At Agia Triada, we found things different indeed. As we rode up the stately avenue of cypresses, between vineyards and almond trees in blossom, servants advanced to take our horses, and the hegoumenos, or abbot, shouted, "Kalosa orizete!" (welcome) from the top of the steps. With his long gown and rotund person, he resembled a good-natured grandmother, but the volumes of his beard expressed redundant masculinity. We were ushered into a clean room, furnished with a tolerable library of orthodox volumes. A boy of fifteen, with a face like the young Raphael, brought us glasses of a rich, dark wine, something like Port, jelly and coffee. The size and substantial character of this monastery attest its wealth, no less than the flourishing appearance of the lands belonging to it. Its large courtyard is shaded with vine-bowers and orange trees, and the chapel in the centre has a facade supported by Doric columns.

A Frustrated Engineer at Rethmyno

Towards evening we received a visit from Mr. Woodward, the English engineer who had charge of the new road. He had been a year and a half in Crete, and seemed very glad to get a chance of speaking his own language again. His account of the people went very far to confirm my own impressions. They are violently opposed to improvement of any kind, and the road, especially, excited their bitterest hostility. They stole his flagpoles, tried to break his instruments, and even went so far as to attack his person. He was obliged to carry on the work under the protection of a company of Albanian soldiers. The Cretans, he stated, are conceited and disputatious in their character, to an astonishing degree. His greatest difficulty with the labourer on the road was their unwillingness to be taught anything, as it wounds their vanity to confess that they do not know it already. They even advised him how to use his instrument!. If a stone was to be lifted, every man gave his advice as to the method, and the day would have been spent in discussing the different proposals, if he had not cut them short by threatening to fine every man who uttered another word. Their pockets are the most sensitive portion of their bodies, and even vanity gives way to preserve them. The law obliged the population of each district, in turn, to work nine days annually upon the road, or commute at the rate of six piastres a day. This was by no means an oppressive measure, yet men worth their hundreds of thousands were following the ranks of the labourers, in order to save the slight tax. Some of the villages were just beginning to see the advantage of the road, and, had a few miles been completed, the engineer thought the opposition would be greatly diminished.

Scandalised Caterpillars

We now commenced ascending the northern spurs of Ida, and the scenery was of the wildest and grandest kind, though dreary enough in the pelting rain, which increased every hour. All the steep mountain slopes, far and near, were covered with vineyards, which produce the excellent red Cretan wine. There are fortunes to be made by some one who has enterprise and skill enough to undertake the business of properly preparing and exporting the wines of Crete.

The vines, I learned, are much more exempt from disease than in Greece and the Ionian Islands. They are subject, however, to the ravages of a caterpillar, for the expulsion of which, when all other means have failed, a singular superstition is employed. The insects are formally summoned to appear before the judicial tribunal of the district, in order to be tried for their trespasses, and the fear of a legal prosecution, it is believed, will cause them to cease at once from their ravages! If this be true, caterpillars are the most sagacious of vermin. In some parts of Crete, a not less singular remedy is applied. It is one of those peculiar customs which most travellers, like the historian Gibbon, express "in the decent obscurity of a learned language;" but I do not know why I should not say that the remedy consists in an immodest exposure on the part of the women, whereat the worms are so shocked that they drop from the vines, wriggle themselves into the earth, and are seen no more.

A Medieval Relic

The arsenal is one of the most curious relics of the Middle Ages which I have ever seen. It is a massive stone building in the Palladian style. One side was thrown down by the earthquake, and the other walls cracked in many places from top to bottom, but fortunately not beyond the possibility of repair. It is completely stored with arms of all kinds, heaped together in great piles and covered with rust. Scores of cannon, with their carriages, lean against the walls; great haystacks of swords rise above on's head; heavy flails, studded with spikes, lances, arquebusses and morning-stars are heaped in dusty confusion along the length of the dark hall. In the upper story is a space evidently devoted to trophies taken in war. To every pillar is affixed a wooden shield with a Latin motto, around which are hung helmets, pikes, rapiers, and two-handed swords. There are also a multitude of tents, cordage, and kettles of balsam, which was used in making plasters for the wounded.

Everything appears to be very much in the same condition as it was left by the Venetians, two centuries ago. The officers gave me leave to select an arrow from the sheaves of those weapons, cautioning me, however, not to scratch myself with the point, as many of them were poisoned. The Metropolitan's secretary, who longed for a Christian relic, secretly slipped one of them up his sleeve and carried it off.

1868 Edward Postlethwaite

An Abandoned Town

On entering, we passed a nice-looking church; the best-looking I had seen in Crete. Whenever I pass these edifices, I feel a secret sense of comfort, telling as they do of heavenly hope, and spirits made proof by this, against the trials and ills of life. But how! Has the plague been here? Where are the people gone to ? Echo asks where!

Ere entering, I had doubts of finding accommodation in the place; but on entering, we find more houses than men; of some the doors are looked; of others, taken away. Cats steal about amongst them mewing for remnants; but all other living creatures - men, mules, dogs – of these there is seen nothing.

After wandering and waiting for a certain time, we were accosted by the proprietor of the house I have spoken of – who had probably heard of our coming-and offered us accommodation for a limited time within his dwelling – limited because he had left it himself, and was locking it up, as had done the rest of the inhabitants, in fear of Moslem visitation. We gladly, however, availed ourselves of even this brief shelter from the blazing sun; and spreading our blankets in the well-known upper room, reposed there through the sultry hours of the day. About noon, suddenly summoned by Appleton, I went to the window, and thence beheld sailing majestically past us, scarce a musket-shot distant, the flagship of Omar Pasha, with soldiers on deck, and the imperial standard flaunting astern. It was followed by four or five other steamers, making a goodly show.

He forbore to fire at the town, probably knowing it was abandoned, or because he had resolved on its occupation (which took place a little later) by his own troops.

This parade of his naval force was simply entertaining to ourselves, but was watched with different feelings by the former denizens of the deserted town. And where were they? Yonder, reader, on the mountain's brow, far above their homes, knowing full well the parade was the precursor of invasion and attack, which, consisting as the encampment did of women and children (as well as men), was of course matter of serious consideration to them. They must have suffered much hardship in their present position from want of water and difficulty of procuring provision. For the *Arcadi* (at this time the saviour craft to Crete), swift as it was, could not be every where at once; and while some communities were being supplied by her, others starved. This difficulty was aggravated to them by their present withdrawal from the coast, and the strictness with which the enemy enforced the blockade.

But the Sphakians are the hardiest of the Cretan tribes; they have never been entirely subjected, and seem determined not to be so now, at any rate, with the political status so generally favourable to their cause. And, in troth, a more favourable juncture for a successful rising this people can never have had: their nearest neighbour, Hellas, of the same stock, free and sympathetic; Russia energetically this latter, for every motive that could actuate her; Italy the same, from having passed, and successfully, through a similar ordeal; France, from its chivalrous sentiment and Philhellenic bias, instinctively relied on; and England, ever a source of hope, although not now an operant friend, yet certain never to prove an active enemy. Well armed themselves, served) by auxiliaries both by land and sea, there never was a time apparently so propitious to their object – of achieving at last their emancipation; the only condition on their own part - *concord*.

The inhabitants of Sphakia, I say, were posted on the heights overlooking their city, now utterly abandoned, save in one particular quarter, less exposed than the rest to the enemy's shot. Here some forty or fifty volunteers, chiefly Greek, had taken lodgment, postponing considerations of safety to that of comfort. They were chiefly, if not all, from Hellas, and all brave soldiers – their seemingly sole point of uniformity; for, in other respects - in character, social status, ways and means, dress and address – there was as great a diversity as there well could be. They were armed with *fusils* of ordinary length; and clad in close-fitting vestments, to my mind neither so sightly nor commodious as the Cretan garb.

Lodged too, in this same quarter was Captain -, whose acquaintance we had made on our first visit here, and who again received us with much amiability. But I am anticipating a little, being still recumbent on the floor of our first lodging. Appleton enters, and quoth he – "Our friend – has come to shut up his house, and we must shift our quarters, as we are the only two people left in this part of the town.

There is no difficulty in finding tenements in Sphakia; and my dragoman, I learned, had chosen one for us among his friends the Greek volunteers, to which we presently repaired, after heartily thanking our last host as he locked his door.

Our new abode belonged to an empirical physician of Anopolis (the place where I lay ill after the sunstroke). His mansion consisted of a room of the ordinary size, with a closet at the end; and for furniture had (rare redundance here) a tressel to sleep on, a kitchen table to cook on, and a settle to sit on. But the place was ankle-deep in dirt, and void of all utensils, even a besom.

Such as it was, however, we needs must take and make the best of it. The time did not admit of being dainty; and, lo! there in the midst is our host himself, ready to do the honours. The Cretan empirics are persons who, possessing some natural acumen, and giving their minds that way, in cases of wounds or pestilence bestow their best attentions on those who may have a fancy for them.

Our host was probably a fair type of his class - a portly man of forty, whose countenance seemed to indicate the possession of much intelligence: had there been any doubt of such possession, the keen super-sapient glance with which he favoured me would have dispelled it in the minds of most; whilst his speech, oracular and spare, would have riveted their faith in his proficiency.

Setting down my bag and repairing my tressel bed (which secured me by eighteen inches from the dirt around), for some time we sat, he on his settle and I on my couch, holding a silent conference; when he arose, and with a shake of the head equally impressive and unintelligible took his departure.

1886 Charles Edwards

Inside a Leper-Colony

I have been spending an hour with the hapless lepers of Canea. People talk of the danger of intercourse with those who are leprous, but without the predisposing state of health I do not believe there is the least likelihood, or even possibility, of becoming a leper from contagion. Father Damien, in the Sandwich Isles, may in time fall a victim to his position;* but it will be due to many influences which do not concern the man who sits with a leper for an hour or two merely.

There are nearly a hundred of these poor people here. They are banished from the city, of course, though they get as near to it on the banks by the roadside as the authorities will permit. The same rule of hardness holds here as in Cyprus. Let a man, woman, or child in town or village show but the faintest mark of the leper, and the neighbours hale the "suspect" before the demarch or mayor of the district. The poor creature is then examined. The neighbours bring all the condemnatory evidence they can against him: he has been torpid for some time previously, complaining of fatigue without due reason, sleeping badly at night, subject to shivering fits, etc. These are the monitory symptoms; and when the small circular spots of a darkish hue come out on the flesh, they will tolerate the sufferer no longer. And once let the authorities determine that they have been right in believing such an one to be tainted, the victim is expelled from his home as ruthlessly as if he were the vilest of criminals.

Mothers and fathers thus part with their children; or their children with their parents. The leper must go and live apart with the other lepers: though "live" is hardly the word, for he may not work for his bread (who would employ him?); he must beg halfpence that he may buy bread to drag him through the miserable remnant of his days. Think of it for two minutes, and you will be less in charity with this Moslem rule, which knows nothing, or next to nothing, of true humanity.

The dusty road from the western gate of the city soon brings one to the reddish earth-banks and refuse-heaps, which are the daily couch of those of the lepers who get nearest to Canea. They are swathed in rags or clothes in fair condition, according to the time that has elapsed since their expulsion from their homes. Some are dressed decently enough, therefore. But others are half-naked, women as well as men, and, taking the cue from their relatives, they have become so callous that they expose their diseased bodies for hours at a time. Nothing can be more unsightly than the blotched and bloated copper-coloured face of a badly-stricken leper; add to this the vague and even mechanical stare of appeal in the eyes, and you will wonder the less that few good Cretans pass the lepers' quarters without contributing a coin to one or other of the petitioners. I felt thoroughly ashamed of my own health in the midst of these poor creatures, all crying out for "Pity! Pity! and a little help."

But it is not often that the leper's face is so deformed out of human semblance. Usually, the limbs are the affected parts. Legs and arms swell, go a deep purple or copper colour, become scaly; and this slowly spreads to the trunk, and saps the strength of life. I saw one young woman of perhaps eighteen or twenty years of age, beautifully shaped, with a winning expression of face, and large tender eyes. She sat with the rest on the bank, her left hand supported in the right, the palm upwards; but she looked steadily before her, and said not a word. The tip of a bandage on one of her feet showed where the evil had touched her; but it seemed a cruel shame that such a girl should be relegated to such a life as incurably leprous.

"Nothing can be done," said a local doctor, to whom I talked on the subject." It is due to the salt-fish they eat, and the quantity of olive-oil they take with everything, because it is so plentiful. This thins their blood. It is hereditary, too, and the child who has put his father among the lepers may always fear it himself."

This is all very well as a tradition, but it does not commend itself as very reasonable. Our good Western doctors must put an end to such weak doctrines of surrender. According to the great Moses Chorensis, Constantine the Great had a touch of leprosy. In his days a bath of warm blood drawn from the bodies of little children was thought to be the best possible remedy. The little children were therefore selected, and as good as doomed, when it happened that the king dreamed of a better remedy still. He was a Pagan; but in his dream he was bidden to become a Christian, and see what would then become of his leprosy. Thus he was cured. This tale may have satisfied Moses Chorensis, but of course it will not be recorded in a dictionary of therapeutics. In Crete it is the Christians who suffer most; the Moslems seem to find a safeguard in free-living, lethargy, and a plurality of wives.

A little way from the city the road bifurcates, and the point of bifurcation is the apex of the triangular hamlet of the Canea lepers. Twenty or thirty square white houses (like big bandboxes) line the adjacent sides of the two roads for about a hundred yards. The houses are of a uniform size, and contain but one room, a cell about twelve feet square. They are of earth and stones, cemented and whitewashed, with walls of good thickness, but dirty indeed, and naked of furniture. For a chimney some of them use an ancient water-jar turned upside down, with its bottom knocked out. Here, in these huts, the lepers congregate, and find what comfort they can in a society which knows nothing of social grades, and where the richest man is he who has picked up most halfpence during the last twelve hours. I found a veritable family in one hut-father, mother, grown daughters, and little children. They herded together like cattle in a stall; and yet, as far as I could ascertain, the children were not tainted. Their parents had married in the community, been blessed by a Greek priest, and given birth to them with this fearful sentence upon their heads. But, for the most part, the houses are inhabited by solitary individuals, who lie out in the roadway, begging alms, while it is daylight, and creep into their dens for the watches of the night.

On the pretext of a light for a cigarette, I entered one of these houses. The occupant was a fine fellow of about forty, with curly hair, but a woebegone expression. He was so much astonished when I asked if I might come in that he stared and said nothing; but he understood when I pointed at my cigarette. He was crouching over a tiny earthen fireplace, boiling some coffee, but got up at once and offered me his seat, with a very saddening look of gratitude in his face. It would have done you good, however, to see how simply he was made happy with a few cigarettes, one of which he consented to light and smoke with me.

I asked him if he lived alone.

"Malista" (yes), said he, with pitiful shaking of the head. He pointed to his leg, as if to tell me that, conditioned as he was, he was likely to be alone, always. The leg was swollen, and the foot too; but otherwise he was a strong, hearty-looking man.

Of course we could not talk much, but my few Greek words of inquiry soon made him prattle away. He talked slowly, too, the better to let me understand him. There was a diminutive shrine in one corner of the room, over the pile of discoloured clothes and sacking upon a heap of olive-boughs which served him for a bed, and he nodded towards the picture of Maria. I fancy the poor fellow was telling me that he found his consolation in the picture, and I hope it was so. Besides the bed, there was little in the room. I sat on an old pot; he on a low stool. A water-jar hung on a nail from the wall; a tin lamp of ancient design stood on a rude shelf: and a bottle of oil by the lamp. The floor was of native earth trodden hard. Four or five halfpence lay by him, representing his accumulated store; when these were spent he would have to join the others on the bank, crying, "Pity! pity!" all the day long. And a lump of barley-bread was at hand, ready to be eaten when the coffee was made. From the open doorway we looked at a hedge of aloes, five feet in height, on the other side of the road; but the mountains shone through the dark green leaves. A circumscribed area, and a circumscribed life! With the coming of the stars, the leper would throw himself, dressed as he was, on the uncleanly heap in the corner, there to sleep until the beggary and tedium of a new day dawned upon him! At parting, I gave Constantinos (as my leper was called) a shake of the hand that seemed to surprise him as much as my apparition in his house had surprised him at the outset.

One need not suppose that the average leper suffers much acute pain, for, with all their disfigurement and poverty and degradation, they are not a morose community of people. I heard not a little hearty laughter while I was resting with them. Constantinos complained of a heaviness in his diseased leg - if I understood him rightly, he spoke of it as a dead limb - he stamped on the ground with it and lifted his eyebrows, shaking his head negatively, as if to imply that he felt nothing from the shock; and this numbness is probably the sensation which ordinarily goes with the malady.

Incorporated with the lepers' village is a tiny paddock where the grass grows high under the shade of a knot of trees which stand by one side of it. This is the cemetery which is destined to receive them all. They have it always before their eyes; but it is not an obtrusive burying-ground; four humbly upright stones among the grass are its sole monuments.

Wise Women and Politics Cretan-Style

And how do we pass the time when it is not daylight, and when, therefore, no one who does not desire a broken neck or leg thinks of stumbling about the dark streets of Candia? Indeed, it might have been a weary business, were I not with a man who can play cribbage and has gained a thorough knowledge of the Cretans, and is willing to say what he thinks about them. Speaking for himself, Mr. Almond likes the hill-Cretans well enough; but he is inclined to say that this is because they like him, and treat him more hospitably than they would treat a prince, if any such cared to invade their lairs. At times he has to go into very wild and sequestered parts of the country to make an inspection of the cables under his control; but when the word is passed that he is coming (and the signal goes as it was wont to go thousands of years ago-by tongues and quick legs), the clansmen choose out a fat lamb from their flocks, kill, skewer, and roast it, so that he may eat crisp chops a few minutes after he sets foot in their midst. They give him their best house, wine, etc., and will take no money; and they do it all with gay cordiality.

But, on the other hand, they have still a measure of lawlessness in their blood; and therefore they are superstitious, as well as hot-tempered and revengeful. They adore the old hag of their community, who has got a sound reputation as a seer, wise woman, healer, etc. She it is that they fly to when any actual ills assail them. The priest is very well as a mere ritual-monger; otherwise he has to find his level among them as best he may, on the strength of his particular endowments as layman. And, to complete the circuit of ancient error which has these people in its thrall, the very priest himself has as much regard for the wise woman of the village as any other of the villagers have. I was even told of a worthy ecclesiastic who hastened miles across the mountains to procure a charm from one of these old and ugly dames, that he might hang it round the neck of his daughter, who was sick. A muscular Cretan, who would not delay to tackle three or four Turks if it were required of him, would be ready to die of dread of a vampire if he saw an inexplicable shadow in the night, and would be for digging up this or that corpse in the neighbouring churchyard, to see if the flush of blood in its normally pale face indicated it as his unholy assailant in the quiet hours. Death-feuds, moreover, are perhaps as common in Crete as in Corsica; though, as the more quarrelsome parts of the island are not within easy ken of the officials who register births and deaths, and far from the editorial office of the one little newspaper which Canea issues for the pastime of its contributors, such tragedies do not come, duly recorded, before the public. They go from tongue to tongue, however, and a European who visits the hills, has their goodwill, and is able to talk with them in their own language, is soon informed by these stout-hearted rogues of the various little events of the kind which give a zest to high life far from civilized influences.

This very week a body of the Mount Ida men set law and liberty at defiance in a very remarkable way. The election of members for the Cretan National Assembly is at hand, and even here the course of politics does not run smoothly. It seems that a certain measure was in project by certain candidates for election, which measure was not in accord with the wishes of the gentlemen of the hills. These hill men said as much when they paid their visits to Candia, previous to the appointment of the day of election. They may have threatened also - but that would probably be put down to a spirit of mere bombast, of which their haughty carriage is generally very suggestive. At any rate, no regard was paid to their protests, menaces, or adjurations. The day of nomination arrived. Then, to the astonishment of Candia, Governor-General, officers of the five or six thousand Moslem soldiers who occupy the town, and all save a few of the citizens, it transpired that these obnoxious aspirants for Parliamentary honours had been seized and carried off to the mountains, where they were likely to be held until the election was ended. Straightway soldiers were ordered to this ravine and that, to yonder village in a romantic hollow near a mountain-top, and to this suspected valley where it was known that some of these unscrupulous politicians had their dwelling. But in vain. All that can be gathered is this - that the candidates will be kept imprisoned in the uplands until the National Assembly has got its complement of members. And as the election takes place tomorrow, the rascals will be sure to have it all their own way. I have no doubt the Governor shrugs his shoulders and smiles.

In a Taverna

The scene inside the tavern was a pretty one. The house was new: the clean state of the long bamboos and rushes of its ceiling showed this. Water-skins hung from the ceiling, and a mandoline or two, which their owners would begin to twang when the stars were out. And these same proprietors, with a dozen or more of other villagers and soldiery, were seated about the room at little tables, playing cards in a very spirited manner, with their legs as far away from them as possible, and a fine rakish air over them all. It needed as much assurance in a stranger to disturb these splendid fellows at their game as to pay his first visit to his first clubhouse. Hovering round their more dissipated elders were several cherubic little boys in blue cotton smocks, who were early being initiated into the charms of fast life.

When I say that this scene was a pretty one, you must understand that its prettiness was due to the rich sunlight upon the vivid colours of the dress of these country Cretans, quite as much as to the dramatic grouping of the people. In rude category, I might enumerate the details in this fashion: yellow bamboo stalks; black goatskins hanging therefrom; whitewashed walls; earth floor; tables set irregularly in the ground; counter with flasks of red and white wine thereupon; Cretans in grey silk vests, short much-be-buttoned ,jackets, scarlet and white sashes, blue breeches of the bag type, and long yellow leather jackboots, with very low heels - all having white-handled knives in their waistbands, and jewels, green, blue, or ruby red, in the hafts of their knives; soldiers in scarlet, with the arrowhead embroidered on their sleeves; boys in blue; two or three grey-beards smoking chibouks, and talking with a good deal of gesture; a dog, yellow and mangy, stretched by one of the tables, now and again lifting his nose to smell a Queen of Diamonds or a King of Spades just torn asunder and pitched among the thick heap of other cards similarly destroyed. To give a little rough variety to the picture, you must rip open the vest and white-frilled shirt of one or two of the younger men, and expose their strong chests, matted with black hair; and you may let one of them thrust his hands into the poll of his head when the cards are peculiarly unkind, and say something so very unparliamentary that all the others for one moment look up from their own play and laugh a deep free laugh, and even the cherubic boys who have watched hitherto in silence, smile or maybe blush a little in a cherubic fashion, as they look slyly at each other, and immediately look somewhere else when they find that the impulse has been one common to them all. In a polite way, I believe we were much cursed when we appeared, as a quite irresistible distraction to this hot gambling. And it was with no very winning expression that gallant after gallant pitched down his cards, tilted round his chair, and, sinking fully into it, with his legs straight in front of him, and his arms folded across his swart breast, demanded to know who we were and what we wanted in Mesoghia. .However, when the questioning had subsided, the men returned to their cards.

1890 The Rev. Henry Fanshawe Tozer

Suppressing a Protest

In forty minutes we reached the dilapidated village of Murnies, the decay of which was somewhat softened by the fine orange trees and other cultivation in its neighbourhood. This is a place of melancholy memories, for it was the scene of one of the worst of the many acts of treachery of which the Turks have been guilty in the island. As far as the circumstances can be summed up in a few sentences they were as follows. At the conclusion of the Greek War of Independence, during which the Cretans had struggled vigorously for freedom, and seemed on the point of forcing the Mahometans to leave the country, it was decided by the Allied Powers that Crete should be annexed to the dominions of Mehemet Ali, and assurances were given to the inhabitants by the British Government of the system of order which that potentate would introduce. In the summer of 1833 the Viceroy of Egypt visited the island, and immediately after his departure a proclamation was published, which tended to make a great part of the landed estates throughout the country his property. To protest against this, several thousands of the Christian population assembled at Murnies, which from its position close to the foot of the Rhiza and in the neighbourhood of the capital, has frequently been the scene of such meetings on the part of the mountaineers. After some delay, promises of redress were given, and the assembly, which had throughout been peacefully conducted, dispersed with the exception of a few hundred men. When, however, an Egyptian squadron arrived, and the authorities felt themselves in a stronger position, they proceeded to Murnies, and arrested thirty-three of the people who had remained there, ten of whom were subsequently hanged, while at the same time, in order to strike terror into the Christians, twenty one other persons were seized and executed in other parts of the island. Who can wonder, after this and similar atrocities, if an insurrection in Crete is almost an internecine struggle?

Ruin and Desolation

At first our route lay along the shore, on which the huge waves were plunging violently; but after a time we were forced to make a detour inland to reach a bridge over the river Platanios, which it was impossible to ford at the usual point. The meadows on the further side of this stream presented a spectacle of rare beauty from the anemones with which they were covered. For size, number, brilliancy, and variety of colour I have never seen such a show. Every tint was to be seen-crimson, rose pink, faint pink, purple, light mauve, and white. If, according to the ancient symbolism, these flowers represent the blood of Adonis and the tears of Aphrodite, both must have been abundantly shed here. The name for them in the country is   Malakanthos. At this point we turned southwards, and ascended gradually over one of the most fertile districts in the whole of Crete; on every side the slopes were covered with olive plantations, while the orange and the fig grew in the neighbourhood of the villages, and in the first of these that we reached - called Ardeli - we saw a fine palm-tree.

It was here that we first began to realise how terrible had been the results of the last insurrection (1866-9). Every village that we passed through, and all that we could see along the hillsides, had been plundered, gutted, and burnt; nothing but ruins met the eye; it was as if a horde of Tartars had swept over the face of the country. A few of these belonged to Mahometans, but the great majority were Christian; and on our arrival the miserable inhabitants - those, that is to say, who had not emigrated –emerged from the lower storey of their houses, which they had temporarily repaired, half-clothed and half-starved. To add to their misfortunes, for the last three years the olive crop, on which they mainly depend, had failed, and the great severity of the winter had reduced them to the last extremity. This state of things we subsequently found to prevail throughout the island; along our whole route not a single village was standing; and what distressed us most was to find that many of those who were in this lamentable condition were persons of some position and very fair education. Another thing, also, we gathered pretty plainly, viz. that they would rise in insurrection again when the next opportunity presented itself; and this was hardly to be wondered at, for they had nothing to lose, and could scarcely be in a worse plight than they were in at that time.

The Ruins of Arkadi Monastery

The convent of Arkadi, which was once regarded as the largest and richest in Crete, having an income of about £1000 a year, was at this time a mass of ruins. The siege of this place by the Turks, and the massacre that followed, from its tragic character, did more than anything else to attract the attention of Western Europe to the Cretan struggle. Only two or the survivors, a monk and a boy, were now residing within the walls; indeed, the rest or the Fathers perished at the time of the siege, and its present occupants had come from other monasteries.

The Superior was a most ignorant man; his conversation consisted almost entirely in saying "it drips, it drips" a remark that was suggested by the pitiless rain, which penetrated so constantly the patched-up roof of the room we occupied, that to avoid it we were frequently obliged to shift our position, and it even dropped on to our beds at night. At Retimo we had been told that the monastery had been rebuilt, and that we should find good accommodation; but the truth was that only two or three rooms were habitable, or which ours was the best. Throughout our tour in Crete we had to carry our provisions with us, for the natives could not supply us even with bread; wine, however, was to be had, and this was excellent. The buildings form a single quadrangle, in the middle of which stands the church; this had been repaired, as also in some measure had the western facade of the monastery; but neither of them shows any trace of Byzantine architecture, being in a debased Renaissance style, and the whole convent, at its best period, must have presented a striking contrast to the lordly structures of Mount Athos. A few tall cypresses in the court did their best to relieve the dismal desolation.

The following morning, at our request, the monk who had been present at the siege conducted us round the building and described to us the harrowing details. It took place on November 19, 1866. The Christians who defended it had assembled there some days before, and for greater safety had brought together the women, children, and old men from the neighbouring country within the walls. The Turks approached from the side of Retimo, and at first their commander offered the defenders terms of capitulation, but these were refused, because his soldiers were irregulars, and the Christians knew from experience that they would neither obey orders, nor suffer anyone to escape. A cannon, which the besiegers had dragged hither with some difficulty, was at first planted on a neighbouring height, but as it produced but little effect on the walls, and in the meantime the attacking parties suffered greatly from the fire of the besieged, on the following day it was brought up in front of the monastery, so as to command the entrance gate, which they blew in. After a fearful struggle, they forced their way in at the point of the bayonet, and commenced an indiscriminate massacre, in which 300 souls perished. The court ran with blood, our informant said, and was so piled with bodies that it was impossible to pass from one side to the other. Simultaneously with this attack in front, another band of Turks made an assault from behind, where there was a postern; but close to it the powder magazine was situated, in a chamber over which numbers of monks and women and children were congregated together. As soon as the besiegers were close to the postern, the Christians set fire to the powder, and blew up all this part of the building, involving their friends and their enemies in common ruin. Large pieces of the shattered wall remain outside the new wall, and though most of the Turks were buried where they fell, yet the bones of others might be seen lying on the ground. In the midst of the massacre six-and-thirty Christians took refuge in the refectory, but they were pursued and all killed, and their blood still stained the walls. About sixty others collected together in a corridor, and begged for quarter, as having taken no part in the insurrection, and the lives of these were spared. The monastery was then fired, and many sick and helpless persons perished in the conflagration. The horrible narrative told by an earwitness on the spot carried our thoughts back to the Suliotes and their destruction by Ali Pasha. It is fair, however, to remember that this same convent was the scene of a great massacre of Mahometans by Christians at the time of the first insurrection. Barbarity is the order of the day in Cretan warfare.

A Remarkable Story

Gradually the Bay of Messara opened out before us, with the headland of Matala beyond, to the eastward of which appeared a depression in the hills which border the coast, marking the site of the "air Havens." At the same time the red sunset tints, seen through a dip in the dark mountains to the west, gave cheering signs of a change in the weather. At nightfall we found ourselves at the village of Apodulo, on the mountain-side, and here we determined to pass the night. While our dragoman was enquiring for tolerable quarters for us among the ruined dwellings, we rested at the first cottage we came to, which consisted of one long ground-floor room blackened with smoke, with a clay floor and a large kitchen range, beds and a few old rude articles of furniture, while in one corner a sheep was tethered. Its occupants were three sisters, remarkably handsome girls, who were dressed as ordinary peasants, and were engaged in cooking and other domestic occupations, but from their acquaintance with a purer idiom of Greek than the native language were evidently superior to their present position. They were perfect Italian madonnas, having oval faces and oval eyes fringed with fine lashes and surmounted by arched and well-marked eyebrows, the upper lip short, and the nose well-cut and slightly aquiline. Besides an upper dress, they wore the usual dress of Cretan women, white trousers reaching nearly to the ankle, a short petticoat, and a handkerchief on the head. Shortly afterwards the mother entered, wearing a curious cape of woollen stuff, which hung from the head and covered the back and sides; and she again was followed by the old father, who carried a sort of crook, and looked a truly patriarchal old man. The parents only spoke the ordinary Cretan dialect. The Turks had destroyed all the property of this family during the insurrection, and this accounted for the reduced circumstances in which we found them living; but one of their relations, at all events, was on the road to fortune, and from his case we learnt how rapidly an intelligent Greek can make his way in the world. After a little conversation the old woman produced a large photograph, framed and glazed, representing a good-looking gentleman in a Frank dress; and this person we learnt was one of her sons, who had emigrated at the conclusion of the war, and now held an excellent mercantile appointment at Marseilles.

We were destined, however, to a more startling surprise. Great was our astonishment when we found that the old man's sister had married an English gentleman, and was still living in Scotland. It is a very curious history. At the time when Crete was under the dominion of Mehemet Ali, a boy and girl of the Psaraki family (for that is their name, though in Cretan it is pronounced Psaratch) were carried off with many others as slaves to Egypt. Mr. H-, who was then in that country, saw this female slave exposed for sale, and being struck with her beauty, bought her and married her. In the course of time the brother also obtained his freedom, and became a travelling servant (our dragoman was acquainted with him, having met him on several occasions); and in that capacity he once accompanied his sister and her husband on a tour on the Nile. Subsequently the married couple returned to Crete, and established themselves at Apodulo. There Mr. H- built himself a house, which was made over to his wife, since he being a foreigner could not hold it in his own name, and at a later period, when they left the country and took up their residence in England, it passed into the hands of one of Mrs. H-'s brothers, the old patriarch with whom we were conversing. This dwelling was assigned to us as our abode for the night, and in its half-ruined state a most dismal habitation it was, for our room, which partook of the nature of a cellar, was fearfully damp, possessed no door, and was partly tenanted by rabbits, which seemed to have discovered the secret of perpetual motion. Of the other children of the Psaraki family, besides those whom I have mentioned, one son is the priest of the parish, while two boys live at home and attend the village school, where they get their education gratis, having only to provide their books.

These schools are regulated by the Demogerontia, an institution peculiar to the Cretan Christians, which consists of a representative council for a certain area of the country, under the presidency of the bishop, and superintends the administration of certain properties, makes provision for widows and orphans, and directs education. It is now arranged that about a quarter of the revenues of all the monasteries shall be handed over to the Demogerontiae for the support of the schools. The Psaraki boys were quick children, and, like the girls, understood our Romaic much more readily than the parents did. The brother in Marseilles, Alexander, was anxious that one of them should come out to him to make his fortune, and the boy expressed himself ready to go, but his mother was unwilling to part with him.

1926 Paul Wilsach

East and West in Iraklion

The minarets along the coast of Crete are only traces of the recently departed Moslems. In the towns at least the followers of the prophet seem to be near even if they are never in sight. Evidences accumulated during nearly three centuries of occupation are not destroyed in a dozen years of impoverished independence. Candia especially is Oriental, with balconies closed in with grilles, and with tiny cubicles of Shops entirely open on the street. Some particular reaches of a street are devoted to a single trade, so that the bazaar effect of the East lingers on. The Turks at one time began to dig a moat around the town, but before it was finished they abandoned it. Time, however, has been kind to the scarred precipices, and now they are green, and the bottom of the ditch is a succession of market gardens.

Inasmuch as every Moslem was sent across to Anatolia in the recent exchange of nationals which has brought the Christian Greeks back within their own borders, the fez as such is rarely seen in Crete, except as worn by the Christians, crushed back, out of shape, so that it more nearly resembles the Greek's ancient Phrygian cap of liberty.

Candia is indeed a curious town; Venetian at the port, reminiscently European on the rise of the street ascending to the city, but truly Levantine in the tangled mass on the plateau. The people are like that, too – a motley of many races. One can not rightly speak of the Turks and Greeks of Crete, for neither blood is pure here, and when repatriation was imposed the political line did not separate races as much as the followers of Christ from the followers of Mahomet.

But the silent minarets, the grilled balconies, the bazaars and battered fez are not the only survivors of the departed Mussulman, for there was no repatriation of the dead. On many hillsides just beyond the towns are little cemeteries lapsing into ruin. Headstones, often as not topped with a chiselled turban, in the Moslem manner, totter about in the bramble of neglected overgrowth, as if struggling vainly to drag their marble feet in search of the departed friends of the sleepers they were left to guard. For so simple a people, not the least tragedy of repatriation must have been this forced separation of the living from their dead. What thoughts wing their way back from the new homes in Asia? And over there, under the crescent, are other God's-acres, though not of another God, where the Christians sleep beneath their black crosses, which totter, too, doubtless victims of the same unwilling fate-imposed neglect.

One can at times believe that the most distinctive Western influence in Crete is gasoline. It is not expressed, however, in motor-cars, of' which there are scarcely any, nor in stationary gas-engines, of which there must be many tucked away in odd corners, but in the abundance of rectangular five-gallon tins. Long after their contents have exploded, these containers live on in an accumulation which is in evidence on every hand. At the fountains they appear as modern metal amphorae on the head or shoulders of the water-carriers. Cut in half, with wire handles, they appear as waste jars alongside the washstands in the hotels. One glimpses them as flower-pots edging paths in the gardens of courts seen through arches, on balconies above the street, and even on the roofs where their contents make the skyline bloom.

The heart of Candia presents itself as a maze of bazaar-like streets filled with donkeys and cigarette-boys, and the Portico of the Barbers. There is a fragment of a Venetian palace and a quaint fountain, too, but these, as well as some slight fraction of the whole number of donkeys and cigarette-boys, might be elsewhere. That open air barber shop, however, is Candia's own. Three steps lead up to four columns which support the roof of a paved portico. Simple, small, wooden chairs are scattered about with a pleasant informality. Two or three packing-boxes serve as tonsorial altars for blades and bottles. The only system of running water was a particularly slow menial who brought a bucketful occasionally from the nearest fountain, and rested during intervals in the haze of cigarette smoke and his own meditations.

The barbers were mere boys in their early teens, and one was so short that he was obliged to stand on a stool to reach the top of the customer's head. The proprietor was surely the swarthy senior of leisurely airs whose business seemed so entirely social. His curly hair was raven black, and before one ear he wore a red rose, and above the other an ivory-white comb. That comb was merely a decorative touch, or, at most, mere professional insignia, for he seemed never to officiate in his own temple except as the recipient of small moneys and as the dispenser of the grand manner.

His portico seemed quite as much club as shop. It was usually crowded, though not entirely with customers. Visitors came in to see their friends under the ministrations of razor and Scissors, but if that diversion was denied them they remained to chat and smoke or thumb their conversation-beads. It was, indeed, quite a gossip forum, where small talk ran along to the accompaniment of snipping scissors, razors beating on straps, and the friendly hello of passers-by. If there were not chairs enough for all it made small difference for the idlers lolled against the columns or made a chaise-longue of the angle of the floor and wall, and with their endless cigarette smoke might have been offering incense in this temple. The shop was apparently without union hours, for it was not least busy at night. Then it was made even more picturesque by the pale efforts of four cotton wicks which gave off more smoke than flame, and seemed to create less light than shadow. But, day or night, it was the one genuinely social touch to a drab town.

An "Arab" Village

A large Arab village of between 2000 and 3000 souls has recently risen on the sandy shore just outside of the fortress on [the eastern] side [of the Bay of Chania], the inhabitants of which have ... come from Egypt and Cyrenaïca... They are chiefly boatmen, porters, and servants; and it may be said to be the only Arab settlement in Europe where their habits of life and habitations are fully retained in every respect as in a pure Arab village; and the most arid and sandy part of the shore is selected, apparently as most resembling their own African coast and its associated desert. It is a perfect little African community and village in all its features, having also a sprinkling of Bedouin tents adjacent, in which dwell families of the purest Bedouin race and colour, most of whom fled from the Cyrenaïca during some recent famine.

The Eastern

Aegean Islands

Lying as they do, close to the shores of Anatolia, the islands of the North-Eastern Aegean were early occupied by the Turks, suffering varied fates. Thus Chios was privileged to enjoy great freedom from Turkish interference, while Samos was entirely depopulated for many years. Some islands were temporarily occupied by the Russians during during the Russo-Turkish War of the early 1770s. They played a prominent role in the War of Independence, again bringing upon themselves the most diverse responses from the Turks. Chios was devastated and its population massacred, while Samos was granted local autonomy. They were finally liberated by the Greek warfleet during the Balkan Wars of 1912-13.

c.1609 William Lithgow

A Race of Remarkable Swimmers

The inhabitants of the smaller islands off the coast of Anatolia were long famous for their extraordinary abilities as swimmers.

Continuing our navigation, I saw the little isle Ephdosh, where the Turks told me that all the islanders were naturally good swimmers, paying no more tribute to their great Lord the Turk, save only once in the year there are several men and women chosen by a Turkish captain who must swim a whole league right out in the sea, and go down to the bottom of the waters to fetch thence some token they have got ground. And if they shall happen to fail in this, the island will be deruced again to pay him yearly rent.

This I saw with mine eyes whilst we were becalmed, there came a man and two womwn swimming to us, more than a mile of way, carrying with them (dry and above the water) baskets of fruit to sell, the which made me not a little to wonder. For when they came to the ship's side, they would neither board nor boat with us, but lay leaning, or as it were, resting themselves on the sea upon their one side, and so sold their fruits; keeping complements and discourses with us for about an hour.

Contenting them for their ware, and a fresh gale arising, we set forward, accoasting the little isle of Samothracia.

Thasos

The Rev. Henry Fanshawe Tozer

Government from Egypt

Before starting for the interior of Thasos I paid my respects to the Bey, who is the representative of the Khedive of Egypt. It seems strange at first sight that a district which forms an integral part of the dominions of the Porte should be practically in the possession of a vassal potentate; but the arrangement dates from the time of Mehemet Ali, and arose from his connection with this part of Turkey, for, as I have already stated, he was a native of Cavalla. Among the inhabitants it is reported that he began life as a sailor in this island; but, whether this is true or not, it is certain that he cherished a strong affection for it: and when he rose to power, he obtained it as a gift from the Sultan. The same privilege has ever since been continued to his successors. In consequence of this the natives enjoy a considerable amount of independence, for, with the exception of the retinue of the Bey and a few soldiers, there are no Mahometans resident among them. They are also lightly taxed; for there is no capitation tax, nor are they burdened by duties on live stock and other products, like the inhabitants of other parts of Turkey: in fact, the customs duties, which go to the Sultan, are the only impost. Hence, though the island is poor owing to its natural resources not being developed, the people are well contented with the government.

Village Coinages

Another arrangement which is peculiar to Thasos, and which it is well for the traveller to be acquainted with before visiting the interior, is the system of local currency. Strange as it may seem, every village has its own peculiar coins, and these do not pass current outside the area of that village, except at Limena, which forms a general emporium for the island. In this respect the inhabitants have outdone even the ancient Greeks, among whom, though every city had its special coinage, the money that came from elsewhere was freely received. The pieces that are used are the copper, or rather brass, coins, which were current in Turkey until about ten years ago, when they were called in by the government; on these each village imprints its private stamp before they can be put in circulation. The stamp in every case consists of four letters, placed within the limbs of a cross, two of which denote the name of the commune, the other two the dedication of the village church. Thus - to take one specimen out of several which I possess - the coins of the village of Vulgaro are marked with the letters[standing for] "District of Vulgaro: Repose of the Virgin". This exclusive system is believed to be of ancient date. The disadvantages of it are apparent to every one; what its advantages may be, I leave to political economists to determine.

A Journey Across the Interior

Having hired three mules, which were accompanied by a young muleteer called Petro, I started at 11am, in the enjoyment of brilliant sunshine and fresh invigorating air. Our course lay due south, in the direction of the pyramidal summit, which I have already mentioned as being conspicuous from Limena, and when we had reached the head of the plain, we entered a lovely valley filled with pine-trees. It was not long before I discovered what are the principal products of the island. For first there met us a mule laden with two large pigskins full of oil, on its way to the port, and shortly afterwards we passed a long row of beehives, which were ranged by the side of the road in a solitary place, where no dwelling seemed near. The hives were cylindrical baskets of wickerwork, with a covering of earth, and a large stone on the top of each. In addition to timber, oil and honey are largely exported from Thasos. At the head of the valley there followed a long ascent toward the shoulder of the mountain behind; and when this was reached, a beautiful view broke upon us or a bay on the eastern coast, flanked by wooded heights, with a wide plain in front covered with olive-trees. On the western side rise the loftiest summits of the island, culminating in the central peak of Hagios Elias, which reaches a height of more than 3000 feet; and all along the face of these the rocks descend, first in steep precipices, and then in gentler slopes, towards the plain. The path now wound gradually downwards, and at the end of two hours from Limena we reached the village of Panagia, which was formerly the residence of the Bey. The four hundred houses of which it is composed are clustered irregularly within a theatre-formed valley, in the midst of scenery truly Alpine in its grandeur. The traveller has no need to enquire into the employment of the inhabitants, for the whole place reeks of oil, and the numerous clear streams that rush through the streets are doubtless utilized in the service of the oil-mills. An hour's further descent brought us to another village, Potamia, where we rested for our midday meal.

At this point a pass commences, which leads over the flank of Hagios Elias into the interior of the island. To reach the summit three hours are required, and during the latter part of the way the ascent is so steep that our baggage mule required frequently to rest. Altogether it is a remarkable mountain route, and the material of which the road is composed is everywhere white marble, though the rocks frequently appeared black from weathering. All about the lower slopes numerous violets were in flower, but after a time the only blossoms that remained were the blue squills, and owing to the elevation and the steepness of the ground, the pine-trees became very sparse along the declivities. Behind us in the distance the great plain of the Nestus and the mountains of Thrace were very imposing, but in the opposite direction a far more beautiful sight awaited me. When we had crossed the ridge, which must be more than two thousand feet above the sea, there opened out a wide view over the southern part of Thasos and the open Aegean beyond: this was divided in two by a lofty mountain immediately, facing us, and the spaces of blue water enclosed between this and the nearer heights on either hand presented to the eye two exquisite vignettes, in one of which the conspicuous object was the colossal peak of Athos, in the other the massive Samothrace, whose snow-capped summits rose above the mist that obscured its base.

From the ridge a long descent leads to Theologo, which is the chief place in the centre of the island, and was at one time its capital. It is hard to say why the site which it occupies should have been chosen for a village, for the valley in which it lies is a marble wilderness, the slopes on either hand being covered with nothing but bare blocks of stone. The houses are roofed with slabs of this material in place of tiles. Perhaps the position may have been selected because it is intermediate between two spaces of arable ground in the upper and lower parts of the valley, bordering on the stream which intersects it. The inhabitants appeared poor, but, notwithstanding this, there is a large school of recent construction. I was conducted to the *Konak* or official residence, a crazy building of unpromising exterior, in which, however, a clean room, which formed the bureau of the Subashi, was placed at my disposal.

That officer, who was a Mussulman from Crete, was most polite in his attentions. Not the least acceptable of these was, that he provided me with a *mangal* or Turkish brazier for charcoal, for notwithstanding the warmth of the sun by day, the nights were cold owing to the elevation at which the village stands.

The following day (April 1) I devoted to a visit to the quarries at Alke, from which in ancient times the Thasian marble was obtained. This place is situated on the southern coast; and as our muleteer Petro was unacquainted with the road, I engaged a native of Theologo as guide for the day. We were accompanied also by a guard, whom the Bey at Limena had pressed upon me with so much polite insistence that I could not well decline to accept his company, though aware that he was intended to watch my proceedings, and to prevent excavation or the removal of antiquities. I have often found that Turkish guards, though they may not be wanted for defence, are willing to make themselves useful in helping one's travelling servant, and doing various little services; but my present attendant was wholly indisposed towards any such offices. He was an Albanian from Monastir in western Macedonia, and possessed most of the faults which are found in his race. Lazy and overbearing, he endeavoured to make everyone else act as his servant. As the baggage mule was not required for my use this day, he took it for himself to ride; but in the steeper parts of the road, where he dismounted, he expected another of the company to lead it. When he wanted water, he despatched one of the country people to fetch it for him. He walked delicately in his moccasins in true Albanian fashion, and was too proud to enquire his way for fear of betraying his ignorance. Petro designated him as "ballast"… that is to say, "good-for-nothing stuff;" and this was a fair description of his character.

Leaving Theologo, we crossed the stream, in the neighbourhood of which grow enormous plane-trees, and ascended the opposite mountain-side. This was so stony that there was practically no track along it, and a way had to be extemporised over the rocks. At the head of this desolate region we reached the pine-forest, and for a long time continued to wind in and out of most beautiful dells at a great height above the sea. The scenery of this part is not inferior to that in the north of the island, for behind this enchanting foreground the peak of Athos, here thirty miles distant, rises from the Aegean to the height of 6400 feet, white with snow on its northern face; and from its foot the peninsula of the Holy Mountain, and the neighbouring coast as far as the mouth of the Strymon, extend along the horizon. In the western part of Thasos, which from this point we overlook, the most striking object is the wooded summit of Hagios Matz, the name of which is a corruption of Asomatos, i.e. the Archangel. This district I did not propose to visit, because it contains no objects of interest. At the end of an hour and a half's riding we crossed the ridge, and came in sight of a vast expanse of the open sea, with the islands of Lemnos, Imbros and Samothrace. The turf beneath our feet was here sprinkled with the delicate blue flowers of dwarf forget-me-nots. A breakneck descent now commenced over steep broken rocks, where riding was impossible; and when the foot of these was reached, for two hours more the way led over gentler declivities, until at last the strange peninsula of Alke came in sight beneath us. It resembles a long and narrow island, lying parallel to the coast and close to it, but is joined to the mainland by an isthmus near its eastern extremity. The little bay thus formed, which is conspicuous from above with its clear green water, provides a commodious harbour for ships which come hither to fetch timber for exportation. At the time of my visit a vessel of some size was lying moored to the shore.

Samothrace

1890 The Rev. Henry Fanshawe Tozer
Cardboard Money

The money that is in use in Samothrace is hardly less curious than that of Thasos. In default of small Turkish money, a paper currency has been established, consisting of small squares of thin cardboard, on which are printed the name of the island with that of the principal church, and the value of the piece. Some of these notes, or tickets, have been sent from Constantinople, but others are made in Chora itself. The smallest, which are about an inch square, are equivalent to ten *paras*, or a halfpenny. I doubt whether the Austrian Tyrol in its most advanced days of paper currency ever equalled this.

Ibex

Another curiosity, besides some specimens of these which I bought away with me, is a native stool formed of a rough slab of wood, 18 in. long by 8 in. wide, which has been placed on the arch of a pair of ibex horns, so that the whole thing forms a tripod, supported by the root and the extremities of the horns. The seat is fastened on by strong iron nails, which have been ruthlessly driven through the wood into the curving horns. The horns measure three feet in length, and are capable of supporting a great weight. The ibexes are found in the desolate mountains in the eastern part of Samothrace, and are perhaps of the same kind as those which exist in the Taurus in Asia Minor. The kids are sometimes captured by the natives, and are carried to Constantinople as pets by the Turkish governors when they quit the island; but I am not aware that they have attracted the attention of any naturalist. Not having seen the animal myself, I am unable to say whether it resembles a Cretan ibex.

The Byzantine Harbour, Mytilene (Illustrated London News, 1867)

Lemnos

1669 Dr. John Covel

The "Sealed Earth"

For many centuries the main attraction of Lemnos was the source of the "terra sigillata" or "sealed earth", probably originally a substance of volcanic origin, widely believed to have impressive properties.

On the side hills, on the contrary side of the valley, directly over against the middle point betwixt this hill and Panagia Kotzinatz, is the place where they dig the terra sigillata. At the foot of a hard rock of grey hard freestone inclining to marble is a little clear spring of most excellent water, which, falling down a little lower, looseth its water in a kind of milky bog; on the east side of this spring, within a foot or my hand's breadth of it, they every year take out the earth on the sixth of August, about three hours after the sun. Several papas, as well as others, would fain have persuaded me that, at the time of our Saviour's transfiguration, this place was sanctified to have this virtuous earth, and that it is never to be found soft and unctuous, but always perfect rock, unless only that day, which they keep holy in remembrance of the Metamorphosis, and at that time when the priest hath said his liturgy; but I believe they take it only that day, and set the greater price upon it by its scarceness. Either it was the Venetian, or perhaps Turkish policy for the Grand Signor to engross it all to himself, unless some little, which the Greeks steal; and they prefer no poor Greek to take any for his own occasions, for they count it an infallible cure of all agues taken in the beginning of the fit with water, and drank so two or three times. Their women drink it to hasten childbirth, and to stop the fluxes that are extraordinary; and they count it an excellent counter-poison, and have got a story that no vessel made of it will hold poison, but immediately splinter in a thousand pieces.

1849 Robert Curzon

Eaten Alive

We had a long row in the hot sun along the sheltered coast till we landed at a rotten wooden pier before the chief city or rather the dirty village of the Lemnians. I had a letter to a gentleman who was sent by a merchant of Constantinople to collect wool upon this island; so to him I bent my way, hooted at by some Lemnian women, the worthy descendants, probably of those fair dames who have gained a disagreeable immortality by murdering their husbands. [From a story in Herodotus] Here it was that Vulcan broke his leg.

And no wonder, for a more barren, rocky place, no one could have been kicked down into. My friend of the wool packs, who was a Frenchman, was very kind and civil, only he had nothing to offer me beyond a bare house, like the consul's Jew at the Dardanelles, so I walked about and looked at nothing, which was all there was to see, whilst my servant hired a little square-rigged brig to take me next day to Mount Athos.

After dinner I made inquiries of my host what he had in the way of bed. His answer was specific. There was no bed, no mattress, no divan; sheets were unknown things, and the wool he did not recommend. But at last I was told of a mattress which an old woman next door was possessed of, and which she sometimes let out to strangers; and in an evil hour I sent for it. That treacherous bed and its clean white coverlet will never be forgotten by me. I laid down upon it and in one minute was fast asleep — the next I started up a perfect Marsyas. Never until that day had I any idea of what fleas could do. So simultaneous and well conducted was their attack that I was bitten all over from top to toe at the first assault. They evidently were delighted at the unexpected change of diet from a grim, skinny old woman to a well-fed traveller fresh from the table of the embassy. I examined the white coverlet - it was actually brown with fleas. I threw away my clothes, and taking desperate measures to get rid or some myriads of my assailants, out of the room and put on a dressing-gown in the outer hall, at the window of which I sat down to cool the fever of my blood. I half expected to see the fleas open the door and march in after me, as the rats did after Bishop Hatto on his island in the Rhine; but fortunately the villains did not venture to leave their mattress. There I sat, fanning myself in the night air and bathing my face and limbs in water till the sun rose, when with a doleful countenance I asked my way to a bath. I found one, and went into the hot inner room with nothing on but a towel round my waist and one on my head, as the custom is. There was no one else there, and when the bath man came in he started back with horror, for he thought I had got that most deadly kind of plague which breaks out in an eruption and carries off the patient in a few hours. When it was explained to him how I had fallen into the clutches of these Lemnian fleas, he proceeded to rub me and soap me according to the Turkish fashion, and wonderfully soothing and comforting it was.

1890 The Rev. Henry Fanshawe Tozer

Staying at the School House

At the end of four hours' riding from Kastro I reached the village of Atziki, which is situated in the middle of the plain. Here I obtained night quarters in the schoolhouse, a place of abode which is often available in these islands, for the building is the property of the community, and there is usually a vacant apartment in addition to the school-room and that occupied by the master. After I had settled in, some of the inhabitants hospitably offered to provide me with a more comfortable lodging; but I was too well satisfied with the position of my humble quarters at the extremity of the village, and the independence which I thus enjoyed, to be persuaded to leave them. One of the chief men, however, who was desirous of showing me a bas-relief of Byzantine workmanship which had lately been discovered, conducted me to his house, and I was surprised at the appearance of its neatly furnished rooms, which were altogether superior to what is usually found in Greek villages. The young schoolmaster was a favourable specimen of a class of men who have contributed more than any other, perhaps, towards the advancement of the Greeks. Though occupying a single room, which contained little more than a bed, a table, a few chairs, and his books, he was an intelligent man, and had received his education at Athens.

The Expiration of a Very Ancient Custom

Tozer has an exhaustive study of this long-lasting and curious phenomenon.

In visiting this part of Lemnos I had two objects in view; first, to investigate the spot from which the "Lemnian earth" is obtained, and to gather any information which could be discovered relating to it; and secondly, to explore the site of the ancient city of Hephaestia. These are situated in the same neighbourhood, near the head of the northern inlet, the bay of Purnia, from one to two hours distant from Atziki. The following morning (March 25) I proceeded in this direction, together with the schoolmaster, who at the last moment offered to accompany me; his scholars, who had already assembled, were dismissed with the welcome news of a holiday. The continuance of north-east wind and drifting rain rendered the weather "melancholy" ... indeed, during the whole of my stay in Lemnos I hardly saw the sun, and the impression of the outward aspect of the island which I carried away with me was a gloomy one. As we crossed the low heights at the back of the village, we soon reached a point where both the remarkable inlets are visible; that of Mudros is by far the deeper of the two, and is distinguished by its windings, and by the numerous small headlands which project into it from either shore. At last we descended to the hamlet of Kotchinot, in the innermost recesses of the bay of Purnia, where a number of shops ... have been erected on the seashore; in the neighbourhood of these stand the remains of a considerable mediaeval castle... While we were there we were overtaken by a guard, who had been sent by the Pasha to serve as an escort. I dismissed him with compliments and thanks, since perfect security reigned in the island; but on the following day two others met me when returning from Atziki to Kastro, and accompanied me on the way. I shrewdly suspected that they were intended to spy out my proceedings, for at the present day every traveller from Western Europe is regarded by the Turks as entertaining designs for excavation, which is strictly forbidden unless specially authorised by the government; and this I found to be the view taken by the natives of my military escort.

As the scene of the digging for the Lemnian earth is near to Kotchino, I now enquired for some one who could conduct us to the place; and I was fortunate in securing the services of an old man who had passed his life in this neighbourhood, and was consequently familiar with the traditions respecting it; also, being a potter by trade, he was accustomed to make vessels of this material. Notwithstanding his years, he was an excellent walker, and he afterwards accompanied me to the site of Hephaestia. I found that he had visited Mount Athos, and was acquainted with several of the monasteries. Under his guidance we now made our way to the spot. Before proceeding further, however, in my narrative, it may be well for me to give some account of this earth, to which an extraordinary interest attaches owing to the permanence of the belief in its medicinal qualities, and of the customs which have been associated with it. There is the more reason for dwelling on the subject now, because within a few years the local knowledge of it is doomed to extinction.

The principal ancient writers who have given an account of the Lemnian earth are Pliny, Dioscorides, and Galen: but the two former obtained their information at second-hand, while Galen, in a truly scientific spirit, investigated the matter for himself; and voyaged to Lemnos in order to make his enquiries on the spot. So great was his interest in it, that after failing in his first attempt to reach the place on his way from Asia Minor to Rome - the captain of the vessel in which he sailed having landed him at Myrina, and refusing to wait while he visited the interior of the island -he included Lemnos in his return journey, and on this occasion directed his course to Hephaestia, in the neighbourhood of which city he was informed that this material was found. By Dioscorides it is called simply , "Lemnian earth"; but Galen and Pliny apply to it the names of "Lemnian red earth" ... or "Lemnian seal" … the latter of these terms being derived from the stamp which was impressed upon it, and without which it was not allowed to be sold. The three writers mention a great variety of disorders for which it was a remedy, but they all agree in regarding it as an antidote to poison, and as a cure for the bites of serpents... It was both taken as a medicine, and employed in external applications.

Galen, who lived in the second century after Christ, has left us a circumstantial account of the place from which the earth was taken, of the ceremonies observed on the occasion, and of the mode of its preparation as a drug. He describes the hill on which it was found as having a burnt appearance, from its surface being of the colour of ochre, and destitute of all vegetation. On certain occasions (and one of these coincided with the time of his visit) the priestess of Artemis came to this spot, and after performing a number of rites, the chief of which consisted in casting offerings of wheat and barley, as a compensation, into the cavity from which the earth was dug, carried off a cart-load of it to the city. That which was thus removed was considered sacred, and might be touched by no other hand than hers; but she mixed it with water, kneaded it, and then strained off both the moisture and the gritty particles: after which, when it had assumed the consistence of soft wax, she divided it into small pieces, and impressed upon them the seal of Artemis. Dioscorides affirms that goat's blood was mixed with it; and Galen tells us that his anxiety to discover whether this statement of his predecessor was true was his chief motive for enquiring thus minutely into the origin of the drug. When, however, he interrogated the most intelligent of the inhabitants on the point, their only answer was a burst of laughter, which satisfactorily settled the question.

The exportation of this earth and its use in pharmacy must have continued throughout the Middle Ages, for we find its reputation undiminished at the expiration of that period. In the sixteenth century it was in so great request as an antidote to the plague, to dysentery, and to other disorders, that ambassadors, when returning from Constantinople to their native countries, were wont to bring pieces of it as a present to distinguished men. When Lemnos was regained by the Turks from the Venetians in the year 1657, Mohammed Kiuprili, who commanded on that occasion, sent word to Adrianople to the Sultan that he had won the island where the "sealed earth" was found. A further proof of the value which was attached to it is given by its being largely counterfeited. Belon speaks of some kinds as being "sophistiquées"; and Thevet in his Cosmographie du Levant (date 1554) remarks "Les Juifs la falsifient beaucoup, quand ils la vendent a ceux qui ne la connoissent." In Western Europe it was known from an early period as *terra sigillata*; but the original Greek term *sphragis* also found its way into the pharmacopoeias of the West, where it appears in such corrupt forms as *lempnia frigdos*, and even *lima fragis*.

We are fortunate in possessing, for the sixteenth century, a description of the digging of the earth, and of the circumstances attending it, from the pen of a writer not less observant than Galen was in his time. This was the French traveller, Pierre Belon, whose name has been already mentioned, and who, like the Greek physician, came to Lemnos with the express purpose of investigating this subject. Then, as now, the locality was a hill in the neighbourhood of Kotchino, which place he names, though he was under the mistaken impression that the castle there formed part of the ruins of Hephaestia. On the hillside were two fountains, of which the one on the right hand of the ascent was perennial, while that to the left dried up in the summer time. No trees grew upon it, except a carob, an elder, and a willow, which overhung the perennial spring; nevertheless, the corn nourished which was sown upon it. This last statement is in direct contradiction to that of Galen on the same point; but it is quite conceivable that in the course of so many centuries a covering of mould may have formed there. The earth was dug from the upper part of the hill, but this took place only on one day of the year, the sixth of August, in the presence of the Turkish governor of the island and a large concourse of people. The ceremony commenced with a mass, which was said by the Greek priests and monks in a little chapel at the foot of the hill; and at the conclusion of this they mounted the declivity, and the soil was removed by which the opening in the ground, leading to the peculiar vein of earth, was closed. This entrance was so deep, that from fifty to sixty men were required to clear it. When the medicinal earth was reached, the monks filled a number of sacks with it, and made these over to the Turkish authorities, after which the soil which had been removed was once more replaced. The greater part of the earth was despatched to the Sultan at Constantinople, but a certain portion was sold to merchants on the spot, and those who took part in the digging were allowed to carry off a small quantity for their private use. In no case, however, was any one allowed to sell it until it was sealed. It was made into small cakes, and of these Belon saw numerous specimens of various shades of colour, but the prevailing tint was dull red. In his book he gives representations of the seals that were used.

Let me now describe the place which I saw, and the observances of which I received an account. The excavation to which I was conducted by my local guide is situated on a small space of nearly level ground, somewhat below the summit of a hill about two hundred feet above the sea, and less than a mile to the southward of Kotchino. At the foot of the last ascent before it is reached there is a spring called Phtelidia, over which an ogive arch of stone has been cut at the point where it issues from the rocks. When I enquired whether there was another fountain in the neighbourhood, my informant mentioned one called Kokala, which rises on the opposite side of the hill. The ground is everywhere clothed with turf, but is otherwise devoid of vegetation. The cavity from which the "sacred earth", as it is universally called by the Greeks, is taken, is an insignificant hole, about fifty feet in circumference and ten feet deep, the bottom of which is now filled up with dry stalks of thistles. The sacred earth is found at a depth of three feet below this. In the neighbourhood there is another spot which seems to have been excavated, and it is believed that the vein extends for some distance below the soil. The earth, however, is not the same as that which Galen and Belon describe; for while they speak of it as red in colour, the specimens which were shown to me resembled ordinary clay: either the original vein has been exhausted, or they no longer dig deep enough to reach it. As in Belon's time, it can only be dug on the sixth of August; and unless this takes place before sunrise all its efficacy is lost. It is also confidently believed in the island (I heard it both at Kastro and at Atziki) that when the ground is opened, the sacred earth wells up of its own accord – "leaps up", "boils up", were the expressions used; but when I questioned my local authority, who had often been present, on this point, he replied much in the same way as Galen's auditors did to his enquiries about the admixture of goat's blood in the drug. His account of the customs observed on the occasion, which continued in full force until five or six years ago, was as follows. On the appointed morning the governor or his representative proceeded to the spot, accompanied by the Mahometan khodjas and the Christian priests, both of whom took part in the ceremony: the former of these offered a lamb as a sacrifice, of the flesh of which they afterwards partook, while fish was provided for the Christians, who were prohibited from eating meat at that season, owing to its falling in the fast of fourteen days which precedes the festival of the Virgin. Tradition, he said, affirmed that sometimes two or three thousand persons were present, and in his father's time as much as seven mules' load of the earth was carried away, to be sent to Constantinople. It was there made into pieces of the size of tablets of soap, and was stamped with the government seal.

The locality which I have mentioned is evidently the same which Belon visited, and probably corresponds to that described by Galen. The resemblances between the ancient and the modern customs and beliefs are also very striking. The sacred character attached to the earth and the religious auspices under which it was removed, the offerings made on the occasion, the guarantee of genuineness provided by the seal, and the confidence which was placed in its efficacy as a medicine, are features common to the earlier and the later accounts, and seem to point to an unbroken tradition. To these one more may be added, which is not the least curious, I have mentioned that the ancient authorities agree in regarding it as an antidote to poison - At the present day small bowls are made on the spot of this material, and are bought by the Turks, who believe that a vessel made of this clay neutralises the effect of any poison that is put into it. I purchased several of these from the potter, and each of them is stamped in - five places with the government seal, which bears in Arabic characters the same inscription which Belon mentions as being used in his day - *tin machtum*, i.e. sealed earth.' This seal, he informed me, was obtained for him from Constantinople twenty years before by an exiled Pasha, who desired that a number of these bowls might be made for him.

Notwithstanding the long duration of this timeworn belief it is evident from the neglect into which it has lately fallen, that ere long it will be a thing of the past. For several years the Turkish governor has ceased to attend, and, following his example, first the khodjas and then the priests absented themselves, and no lamb is now sacrificed. Last year only twelve persons were present. Though the tablets were to be bought in chemists' shops in Kastro at the time of Conze's visit to the island in 1858, I enquired in vain for them; and neither the existing governor, nor any persons of the younger generation, had heard of this remedy. In the eastern parts of Lemnos, however, it is still in use for fevers and some other disorders, for the women possess nuts of it, which they string like the beads of a rosary; these they grate in case of illness, and take a teaspoonful of the powder in water. Not long ago the proprietor of the hillside applied for leave to plough over the spot and sow it with corn; and though for the time this was not allowed by the government, yet, when the annual celebration has come to an end, the prohibition will safely be ignored, and from that time forward the locality itself will be forgotten. This sudden eclipse of what was once an important medicine is partly due, no doubt, to the progress of medical science even in these remote regions; but perhaps it may also have been caused by the discovery that it is devoid of efficacy. That this is the case at the present day has been proved by an analysis of its component parts. Whether it was so with the original ... we have no means of learning.

Taking Provisions to Earthquake Victims, Mytilene (Illustrated London News, 1867)

Lesbos (Mytilene)

c. 1610 Sir George Sandys

Sponge Fishers as "Noble Savages"

The reader might be forgiven for wondering whether the sponge-fishers themselves would have waxed quite so lyrical about their enjoyment of the "simple life".

On the one and twentieth day of September, the winds grew contrary... we entered the Gulf of Colonus. They hoping to have some purchase about a ship cast there away but a little before, divers of them leaped into the sea, diving into the bottom, and stayed there for so long as if it had been their habitable element. And without question, they exceeded all others in that faculty, trained thereunto from childhood. And the excellentest among them can best perform it. Inasmuch that although worth nothing, he shall be proffered in marriage the best endowed and most beautiful virgin of their island. For they generally get their living by these sponges gathered from the sides of rocks about the bottom of the straits, sometimes fifteen fathoms under water. A happy people that live according to Nature, and want not much in that they covet but little. Their apparel no other than linen breeches, over that a smock close girt unto them with a towel, putting on sometimes when they go ashore long sleeveless coats of homespun cotton. Yet their bodies need not envy their bellies: biscuit, olives, garlic and onions being their principle sustenance. Sometimes for change they will scale the rocks for sampier, and search the bottom of the less deep seas for a certain little fish, if I may so call it, shaped like a burr, and named by the Italians riceio. Their ordinary drink being water, yet once a day they will warm their bloods with a draught of wine, contented as well with this as those that will take the rarities of the earth do pamper their voracities... When they will, they work, and sleep when they are weary; the bank that they row upon, their couches, as ours was the poop; hardened by use against heat and cold, which day and night interchangeably inflicteth. So cheerful in poverty that they will dance whilst their legs will bear thcm, and sing till they grow hoarse; secured from the cares and fears that accompany riches.

1745 Richard Pococke

An Island at the Mercy of Brigands

The following passage illustrates how easily even a significant island could fall into the hands of a small but well-organised and aggressive band of criminals.

"...[A]bout three years ago a troop of banditti Christians from the Morea and other parts, to the number of about fifty, came into the island well-armed, raised money in all the villages, murdered several people, and among them the Christian aga. Some galleottes were sent against them, and they were dispersed, except about twenty, who submitted to the government, and pretend to have a liberty to carry arms; and in reality govern the island in every thing, in which they are pleased to interfere; they marry themselves by force to the richest parties, and being dispersed through he villages do what they please, and have a captain at the head of them, maintaining themselves by the money they have raised. And this small number of men render the island very unhappy, the Turkish governors themselves standing in awe of them, and no one has the courage or resolution to oppose them."

1746 Lord Charlemont

The Land Where the Woman "Wear the Trousers"

Despite the appalling state of law and order in the island, as evidenced by the testimony of Richard Pococke above, the young Lord Charlemont was concerned chiefly with the women of the island of Sappho, a subject which was to monopolise the attention of subsequent visitors.

The women here seem to have arrogated to themselves the department and privileges of the men! Contrary to the usage of all other countries the eldest daughter here inherits, and the sons, like daughters everywhere else, are portioned off with small dowers, or, which is still worse, frequently turned out, penniless, to seek their fortune. If a man has two daughters, the eldest, at her marriage, is entitled to all her mother's possessions, which are by far the greater part of the family estate, as the mother, keeping up her prerogative, never parts with the power over any portion of what she has brought into the family, until she is forced to it by the marriage of her daughter, and the father also is compelled to ruin himself by adding whatever little money he may have scraped together by his industry .The second daughter inherits nothing, and is condemned to perpetual celibacy .She is styled a *calogria*, which signifies properly a religious woman or nun, and is in effect menial servant to her sister, being employed by her in any office she may think fit to impose, frequently serving her as waiting maid, as cook, and often in employments still more degrading. She wears a habit peculiar to her situation, which she can never change, a sort of monastic dress, coarse, and of dark brown. One advantage however she enjoys over her sister, that, whereas the elder, before marriage, is never allowed to go abroad, or see any man, her nearest relations only excepted, the *calogria*, except when employed in domestic toil, is in this respect at perfect liberty .But, when the sister is married, the situation of the poor *calogria* is rendered still more humiliating by the comparison between their conditions. The married sister enjoys every sort of liberty. The whole family fortune is hers, and she spends it as she pleases. Her husband is her first domestic. Her father and mother are dependent upon her. She dresses in the most magnificent manner, covered over, according to the fashion of the island, with pearls, and with pieces of gold, which are commonly sequins, while the wretched *calogria* follows her as a servant, arrayed in simple homespun brown, and without the most distant hope of ever changing her condition. But the misfortunes of the family are not yet at an end. The father and mother, with what little is left them, cïntrive by their industry to accumulate a second little fortune, and this, if they should have a third daughter, they – are obliged to give to her upon her marriage, and the fourth, if there should be one, becomes the *calogria*, and so on through all the daughters alternately.

Whenever the daughter is marriageable, she can, by custom, compel the father to procure her a husband, and the mother, such is the power of habit, is foolish enough to join in teasing him into an immediate compliance, though its consequences must be equally fatal and ruinous to both of them. From hence it happens that nothing is more common than to see the old father and mother reduced to the utmost indigence, and even begging about the streets, while their unnatural daughters are in affluence; and we ourselves have frequently been shown the eldest daughter parading it through the town in the greatest splendour, while her mother and second sister followed her as servants, and made a melancholy part of her train of attendants. The sons, as soon as they are of an age to gain a livelihood, are turned out of the family, sometimes with a small present or portion, but more frequently without anything to support them. They either endeavour to live by their labour, or, which is more usual, go on board some vessel as sailors, or as servants, remaining abroad till they have got together some competency, and then they return home to marry and to be henpecked. Some few there are who, taking advantage of the Turkish law, break through this whimsical custom who marry their *calogrias*, and retain to themselves a competent provision; but these are accounted men in singular cast, and are hated and despised as conformists to Turkish manners, and deserters of their native custom; so that we may suppose that they are but few indeed, who have the boldness to depart from the manners of their country, and to brave the contempt, the derision, and the hatred of their neighbours and fellow-citizens.

Of all these extraordinary particulars I was informed by the French Consul, a man of sense and veracity, who had resided in this island for several years, and who solemnly assured me that every circumstance was true. But indeed our own observation left us without the least room for doubt, and the singular appearance of the ladies fully evinced the truth of our friend's relation. In walking through the town it is easy to perceive, from the whimsical manners of the female passengers, that the women, according to the vulgar phrase, *wear the breeches*. They frequently stopped us in the streets, examined our dress, interrogated us with a bold manly air, laughed at our foreign garb and appearance, and showed so little attention to that decent modesty , which is, or ought to be, the true characteristic of the sex, that there is every reason to suppose that they could, in spite of their haughtiness, be the kindest ladies upon earth, if they were not strictly watched by the Turks, who are here very numerous, and would be ready to punish any transgression of their ungallant laws with arbitrary fines.

In all their customs they seem to have changed sexes with the men. The lady rides astride. The man sits sideways upon the horse. Nay, I have been assured that the husband's distinguishing name is his wife's patronymic. The women have town and country- houses, in the property and management of which the husband never dares interfere. Their gardens, their servants, are all their own, and the husband from every circumstance of his behaviour, plainly appears to be no other than his wife's first domestic, perpetually bound to her service and slave to her caprice. Hence it is that a tradition obtains in the country that this island was formerly inhabited by Amazons, a tradition however founded upon no ancient history that I know of. Sappho indeed, the most renowned female which this island has ever produced, is said to have had manly inclinations, in which, as Lucian informs us, she did but conform with the whimsical manners of her countrywomen, but I do not find that the mode in which she chose to show these inclinations is imitated by the present female inhabitants, who seem perfectly content with the dear prerogative of absolute sway, without endeavouring any other particular to change the course of nature. Yet will this circumstance serve to show that the women of Lesbos had always something peculiar, and even peculiarly manly, in their manners and propensities. But be this as it may, it is certain that no country whatsoever can afford a more perfect idea of an Amazonian commonwealth than this island of Metelin.

These lordly ladies are for the most part very handsome in spite of their dress, which is singular and disadvantageous. Down almost to the waist they wear nothing but a shift of thin and transparent gauze, red, green, or brown, through which everything is visible, except their breasts which they cover with a sort of handkerchief; and this, as we are informed, the Turks have obliged them to wear, while they look upon it as an incumbrance, and as no inconsiderable portion of Turkish tyranny. Their principal ornaments are chains of pearl, to which they hang small pieces of gold coin. Their complexions are naturally fine, but they spoil them by paint, of which they make great use; and they disfigure their pretty faces by shaving the arched part of the eyebrow and replacing it with a straight line of hair, neatly applied with some sort of gum, the brow being thus continued in a straight and narrow line till it joins the hair on each side of their face. They are well made, of the middle size, and for the most part plump, but they are distinguished by nothing so much as by a haughty, disdainful, and supercilious air, with which they seem to look down upon all mankind, as creatures of an inferior nature, born for their service, and doomed to be their slaves. Neither does this peculiarity take away from their natural beauty, but rather adds to it that sort of bewitching attraction which the French call piquant...

Since my writing the text I have found this singular custom respecting the women of Metelin, mentioned, but by no means detailed in its circumstances or consequences, in the letters concerning Greece, written from Constantinople by Monsieur de Guys. 'He had,' as he tells us, 'been informed that, according to an ancient institution at Metelin, all estates, both real and personal, descend to the eldest daughter, whereby the males, and the younger children of the female sex, are disinherited. I was assured,' continues he, 'by one of the inhabitants of that part where I landed, that my information was literally true, that the custom was of very ancient date, and that the males had consented to it, out of love to their sisters, and to procure better establishments for them. The men, said my informer, would have no difficulty in getting their right of inheritance, if they chose to claim the benefit of the Turkish law, which admits the children of both sexes to an equal share in the parents' fortune; but the man, who should attempt to promote his interest by an appeal to a foreign power, would appear infamous in the eyes of his countrymen' (*Sentimental Journey Through Greece*, vol. 2 p. 205).

We may perceive, from the manner in which this institution is mentioned, that Monsieur de Guys' information was partial, and by no means sufficiently circumstantial, a defect which was occasioned, as I suppose, from his having as he himself tells us, made no stay in the island. I cannot however avoid feeling much pleasure to have found some authority for the existence of an usage of a nature so very extraordinary as not to be easily believed upon the credit of a single testimony, Neither can I help expressing my surprise that a matter so singular in the history of mankind should have been deficient in point of evidence, and should have escaped the notice of such travellers as have spent much time in these islands.

Monsieur de Guys next proceeds to account for the rise of this custom, which he supposes to have been very ancient in the island. And this he does, in a manner that appears to me rather unsatisfactory by a detail extracted for the most part from Diodorus Siculus, [12. 55], of the bloody quarrels between the Lesbians and the Athenians, and of the many revolutions to which the island had been subject, during the course of which, as there must have been a great slaughter of the men, he supposes that the women would naturally have made their own terms with the few who remained alive in the island, and with those who returned from exile; and this usage, he concludes, was probably the result of such negotiation.

I cannot entirely agree with Monsieur de Guys that a scarcity of men affords to the women the best opportunity of making their own terms – *tout au contraire*. I fear however that I have misunderstood my author, who, upon a second perusal, appears to suppose that the Lesbian ladies, having lost the greater part of their own men, and consequently of the heirs male in the island, made these extraordinary terms with the conquering Athenians. But this seems still more improbable, as terms are seldom made by the women with successful invaders, who are but too apt to take their wicked will.

But unfortunately there are few countries in Greece, or indeed I fear in the world, where the women might not have had, at some time or other, the same opportunity. for encroachment. Neither can we allow the probability of their hazarding so strange a proposition, unless indeed we should suppose some pre-existing peculiarity in their manners, and in the ancient customs of their country, which might induce them to propose such extraordinary terms, and encourage them with some hope of their being accepted. And this supposition will bring us back to the early establishment of the Lycian usage, as mentioned in the text, which, having possibly grown into disuse in a long course of ages, may have been renewed upon this occasion when the ladies found themselves strong enough to reassume that ancient superiority which, though for a time they might have been compelled to yield, it is highly probable they never would forget.

The Forced Marriage of Strangers

Monsieur de Guys, upon the faith of a travelled friend, in the same letter tells us another story of the Metelinean ladies. "About three days' journey from the capital," says he, "is a small town, where every stranger upon his arrival is compelled to marry, and, after cohabiting with his wife, leaves her as soon as he pleases, she, and her parents being thoroughly contented if the obstacle, which is, it seems, in that country, not only ignominious but disgusting, be completely removed. This requisite being performed, which must be done by a stranger, the people of the province thinking, as it should seem, the operation troublesome and undignified, the lady is at liberty, after a year has passed, to marry with whoever offers, and seldom fails of a good husband.

c.1790-1801 James Dalloway

Arbitrary Authority

Passages such as the following reveal how venal and capricious Turkish rule was, and how not even important Turks themselves were safe from arbitrary persecution.

[W]e dined most comfortably with Hadji Bekir Effendi. In the early part of his life, having great property in olives, he conducted the commerce himself; and had made many voyages into the Mediterranean and Atlantic. His conversation therefore was much more rational than that of many of his countrymen. About two years since he was appointed Agha of Cyprus, where, growing suddenly rich, he was threatened with decapitation, which he escaped by the mediation of Kara Osman Oglu, and the payment of many purses of piastres. He is now retired to his patrimony, to end his days by the course of nature, and in secret.

1831-2 Dr. J. E. Dekaye

Throwing Fish

At nine o'clock we returned to our little craft, and while our crew were making preparations for departure, my attention was called to a scene which, I am told, is not unusual in Greece. A fishing boat had just arrived, and was lying about ten feet from the wharf, which was crowded with people. Handkerchiefs, baskets, and other missiles were flying to and fro between the wharf and the boat; and upon enquiry, I was informed that this was the usual manner in which fish or other commodities are vended among the Greeks. The money was tied up in a handkerchief and thrown on board; the value in fish was returned in the same way; and the cautious distance between the boat and the wharf was preserved in order to prevent them from coming on board to steal...

Psara

c.1680 Bernard Randolph

A Remarkable Deliverance and a Remarkable Souvenir

Ipsara is a small island which lies to the west of Scio, very poorly inhabited. It hath a safe port. Its west side is secured with a small island lying before it. At the entrance from the north, there runs a ridge of rocks from the great island almost half a mile into the sea, being about sixteen foot under water. Upon these rocks the ship *Plymouth* stuck fast, having aboard her the Right Honourable the Earl of Winchelsea, a true relation of which follows:

In the year 1660 his lordship embarked on the *Plymouth*, on an embassy from His Majesty of Great Britain to the Grand Signior, and about the end of December arrived at Smyrna, where his lordship tarried till January the 6th, when he embarked again for his voyage to Constantinople. So soon as his lordship was aboard, they set sail, with the wind at east, sailing towards the castle, which is about three leagues from Smyrna. It fell calm; then they came to anchor and tarried all night, having in their company the Smyrna-factor and a ketch; the latter waited upon the man-of-war. Next morning being the seventh the wind at south-east was a fine gale, they weighed anchor, the weather promising them a speedy passage. But the wind veering to the north-east with a strong gale, they weathered Caraborun standing for the island of Metelino; intending to spend the night under the lee of that island in smooth water, bringing their ship under a Maine-course. All that night the wind increased every hour more and more, so that in the morning it was a most violent storm: the sea in a breach, the sky very black and thick, and the sun lowering and red, which were the undoubted indications of its continuance. The spray of the sea was so forcibly carried by the wind over the ship, that the masts, yards and decks were querned with the white salt.

This extremity of weather made them think of some port to secure themselves. The island of Ipsara lying about eight leagues distant south by west from Metelino, it was supposed by the master a safe place with this wind to spend the fury of the storm in. So they put her before it with foresail down, and mainsail in the brailes; but the wind soon blew away their foresail like paper, and in bringing another to the yard, it had the misfortune to become foul of the flook of the anchor, and soon became as unserviceable as the other. Being thus deprived of their commanding sails, they loosed their spritsail and set their maine-course. Steering in between the greater and lesser islands, the ship had swift way, being shot within the northernmost point, luffing to near the great island, on a sudden, stuck fast on the rock, which astonished them with a strange amazement. The poor ship knocked five several times to clear herself from a total wrack and ruin.

They all began to despair of her, and with cast up eyes and stretched out arms, thought now of no other but their last and final Port. But in the midst of this horrid consternation and distress, it pleased God, who is their best pilot, to bring the ship off, and to all their appearances without the least damage: an escape so wonderful and miraculous (on the eighth day of January) as it ought to be ever recorded to admiration by all who were partakers in the danger, and an anniversary of thanksgiving be made to God for his Providence over and protection of them.

When they were in this distress, they fired a gun to give warning to the Smyrna-factor and ketch, who thereupon stood away for Milo.

The storm continued all that day, so that with two anchors down, (the sheet-anchor being one) they had much ado to secure the ship fast, the storm continuing so very violent. The tenth, the wind abated; and the fourteenth, it veered about to the south-west, so they sailed toward the Dardenelle. The fifteenth, they got to Tenedos about eight in the morning, and about three in the afternoon entered the Old Castles. From the New Castles a boat came off, in which was a messenger to acquaint his lordship that the Vizier had sent orders that a free passage should be granted his lordship and his attendance with the ship, without any hindrance or molestation... On the seventeenth, (it being three months since his lordship embarked in England) they came to anchor near the Seven Towers, till such time as Sir Thomas Bendish had notice; then weighed anchor and stood for port... With a fresh gale of wind they had all their colours abroad with their guns and wastecloths out. Being almost opposite to the Seraglio point the ... Bustangee went aboard ..., telling them that it was the Grand Signior's pleasure that they should rejoice with guns (which was his expression) upon which they fired six guns and came to an anchor at Toppanna, when Sir Thomas Bendish came aboard to congratulate his lordship's arrival. His lordship, the next day, being the eighteenth, was received ashore, and indeed with that great state and handsome equipage that no ambassador from England, France or Germany ever passed with more honour or wonder of the multitude.

Where we will leave his lordship and come back with the ship, which tarried some time at Constantinople, and in her return called in at Messina, Legone and several ports in Spain, having undergone many storms at sea, and at last arrived in safety in the River Thames. At Woolwich she was hauled into the dry-dock, being searched, there was found a great piece of rock in the bottom of her, so fast that it could not but with much difficulty be got out. It passed the keel of the ship, and was so close fixed in that it stopped the water from coming in. This piece of rock was carried to His Majesty's closet at Whitehall, where it is carefully preserved.

1829-32 E.C.Wines

An Abandoned Island

The following melancholy passage refers to the state of the island following its devastation by the Turks during the War of Independence, when they sought to depopulate the island entirely.

We left Ipsara on our left early in the day. The late revolution has given a melancholy celebrity and interest to this rocky little island. Only a few years ago it was inhabited by one of the most enterprising, intelligent and thrifty communities to be met with in the East. Its women were distinguished for their beauty, sprightliness and modesty. It was the birthplace of the ... generous and heroic Canaris. The canvas of its little navy of merchantmen whitened every port of the Black Sea, the Archipelago and the Mediterranean; and the shops and warehouses of its merchants were enriched by the commerce which it carried on with the countries bordering on those seas. It was, in short, one of the few places in the Turkish dominions inhabited exclusively by Greeks, where prosperity and contentment made the descendents of Leonidas forget that they were slaves. But one night was sufficient for Turkish ferocity to destroy the result of so many years of commercial enterprise. The city was reduced to a heap of ruins, its inhabitants were either massacred or driven into the sea, and the island abandoned to solitude and sterility.

Chios

1599 Thomas Dallam

An Expedition Ashore

The 12th day we discried Scio. The 13th we sailed by the shore of that island. The 14th we came to an anchor in a road, two leagues short of the great town or city of Scio, so called by the name of the island.

The 15th day, in the morning, our long boat being ready to go ashore for fresh water, which we stood great need of, for in 3 days before we had nothing to eat but rice boiled in stinking water, and our beverage did also stink. The boat being launched, three of our gentlemen passengers came unto me and asked me if I would go ashore to see if we could buy some fresh victuals, and I said: "Yea, with all my heart." As soon as we were in the boat, the Master was told of it, and he looked over the ship side, and spoke unto me.. for the other might have gone with his good will, and never come again, neither would he have stayed half an hour for them; but they did know that he would not leave me behind. So the Master asked me whether I would go, and I told him but to set foot on shore, drink some fresh water, and come aboard with the boat. Then he bid me come aboard again presently, but the gentleman had me betwixt them, and held me fast; nether did I mean to do as he bid me. "Well," said the Master, "I see ye will go ashore, and the company that is with you will draw you up to yonder town which you see, and I will tell you before you go that which you shall find true. In no part of the world doth grow any mastic but in this island, and now is the time for it. The commodities here are nothing but mastic, cotten wool, and wines. You cannot go to yonder town but you must needs go through the gardens where these things grow; and if you be seen to take one sprig of mastic, or one pod of cotton wool, or one bunch of grapes, it is a whole year's imprisonment, and there will be no redemption for you. Therefore do not say but that I gave you sufficient warning, etc."

This island of Scio is rising from the seaside some three or four miles, and this town which we meant to go unto is two mile from the sea, and it seemed, afar off, to be a pretty town, with a castle in the midst of it. When the Master had told us his mind, for the dangers we might fall into unawares, then he said to me that if I came not back again with the boat when she had taken in water, he would set sail and be gone; but we feared not that, for as soon as we came to land, we went directly to the town. It was upon the Sunday, and the people seeing our ship come to an anchor, and seldom had seen the like in that country, and likewise saw us come ashore, many women and children came to meet us, who wondered as much at us as we did at them. We went on right forwards, giving no body one word till we came into the middle of the town under the castle wall, and there standing still looking about us, there came a Greek unto us, and demanded whom we sought for, or whither we would go. Two of our company could speak Italian well, who answered that our coming was to buy some victuals. This man said there was a consul in the town, and we must repair unto him before we could have anything, so he went with us unto the Consul's house. The streets were full of people, which flocked together to look upon us.

When we came to the consul's house, we were to go up a pair of stairs, made like a ladder at one end of the house without. This ladder went up to a stage or scaffold which was on the backside of his house, that looked right towards the sea where our ship lay at an anchor. The consul was upon this stage, sitting at a table, and with him there were six very gallant gentle-women, and very beautiful. As soon as we came up, these brave women arose and went away, and the consul came unto us, embracing us one after another, and bid us very welcome. He caused the table to be furnished with a very fine banquet of sweetmeats, and but two little cakes of bread; our drink was very good raspberry. Whilst we sat there talking, the common sort of the people in that town came to the garden walls, for on that side of the house was the consul's garden, and the walls were of stone without mortar, and the people did so much desire to see us, that they did climb upon the walls. The consul many times stood up chiding them, and shaking his hand at them, threatening punishment; but the more he chid, the more the people did climb upon the wall, and the wall being overladen, down came the wall, making a great noise, the length of a pair of boats, and almost so much in another place; the which made the consul very angry, and he might very well have wished that we had not come there.

Where we sat we might see our ship right before us, and we see the boat go aboard with water. In this meantime, the consul had sent two women about the town, to see what victuals they could get for us; at the end of two hours they came again, and told us that they could find nothing that was to be sold at that time, being Sunday, but about a bushel of garlic, the which we were contented to take, because we would have something; and we saw that we were trouble-some to the consul. So, having taken our leaves of the consul, he appointed one to carry our garlic to the town's end before us. Going down the ladder from the scaffold, upon both sides of the ladder did stand the cheifest women in the town, in degrees one above another, to see us at our going away. They stood in such order as we might see their faces and breasts naked, yet were they very richly apparelled, with chains about their necks, and jewels in them and in their ears, their heads very comely dressed with ribboning of diverse colours; but that which made us most admire them was their beauty and clear complexion. I think that no part of the world can compare with the women in that country for beauty. But afterwards we understood that if we had gone to the city, which was but six miles further, we should have been much better entertained, for in that city was an English consul, whose name was Mr. Willyam Aldridge, a fine gentleman, but our master would not put in there, for fear of being put to some charge; for he was a very miserable and sparing man, all for his own profit, and not regarding to satisfy other men's desires, or to give his passengers any content.

Being come aboard our ship with our bag of garlic, it was not so slenderly regarded but that we might have had chapmen [*buyers*] for it, and our money again with profit.

1609-10 William Lithgow

Shipwrecked

As we left the isle Venico on our left hand, and entered in the gulf between Sio, and Eolida, the firm land is called Aeolida, there fell down a deadly storm, at the Grecoe Levante, or at the north-east, which split our mast, carrying sails and all overboard, whereupon every man looked (as it were) with the stamp of death in his pale visage. The tempest continuing (our boat not being able to keep the seas) we were constrained to seek into a creek, betwixt two rocks, for safety of our lives; where, when we entered, there was no likelihood of relief: for we had a shelfie shore, and giving ground to the anchors, they came both home.

The sorrowful master seeing nothing but shipwreck, took the helm in hand, directing his course to rush upon the face of a low rock, whereupon the sea most fearfully broke. As we touched, the mariners contending who should first leap out, some fell overboard, and those that got land, were pulled back by the reciprocating waves. Neither in all this time durst I once move; for they had formerly sworn, if I pressed to escape before the rest were first forth, they would throw me headlong into the sea. So being two ways in danger of death, I patiently offered up my prayers to God.

At our first encounter with the rocks, (our foredecks, and boats gallery being broke, and a great lake made) the recoiling waves brought us back from the shelves a great way; which the poor master perceiving, and that there were seven men drowned, and eleven persons alive, cried with a loud voice: "Be of good courage, take up oars, and row hastily; it may be, before the barque sink we shall attain to yonder cave, which then appeared to our sight. Every man working for his own deliverance (as it pleased God) we got the same with good fortune: for no sooner were we disbarked, and I also left the last man, but the boat immediately sunk. There was nothing saved but my coffino, which I kept always in my arms: partly, that it might have brought my dead body to some creek, where being found, might have been by the creeks buried; and partly I held it fast also, that saving my life, I might save it too; it was made of reeds and would not easily sink, notwithstanding of my papers and linen I carried into it: for the which safety of my things, the Greeks were in admiration. In this cave, which was thirty paces long, within the mountain, we abode three days without either meat or drink: upon the fourth day at morn, the tempest ceasing, there came fisher-boats to relieve us, who found the ten Greeks almost famished for lack of food; but I in that hunger-starving fear, fed upon the expectation of my doubtful relief.

True it is, a miserable thing it is for man, to grow an example to others in matters of affliction, yet it is necessary that some men should be so; for it pleased God, having shown a sensible disposition of favour upon me, in humbling me to the very pit of extremities, taught me also by such an unexpected deliverance, both to put my confidence in his eternal goodness, and to know the frailty of my own self, and my ambition, which drove me often to such disasters.

The dead men being found on shore, we buried them; and I learned at that instant time, there were seventeen boats cast away on the coast of this land, and never a man saved. In this place the Greeks set up a stone cross in the memorial of such a woeful mischance, and mourned heavily, fasting and praying. I rejoicing and thanking God for my safety (leaving them sorrowing for their friends and goods) took journey through the land to Sio, for so is the city called, being thirty miles distant: In my way I past by an old castle standing on a little hill, named Garbos, now Helias; where (as I was informed by two Greeks in my company) the sepulchre of Homer was yet extant: for this Sio is one of the seven nes and towns, that contended for his birth...

The which I willing to see, I entreated my associates to accompany me thither; where, when we came, we descended by sixteen degrees into a dark cell; and passing that, we entered in another four squared room, in which I saw an ancient tomb, whereon were engraven Greek letters, which we could not understand for their antiquity; but whether it was this tomb or not, I do not know, but this they related, and yet very likely to have been his sepulchre.

This isle of Sio is divided into two parts, to wit, Appanomera, signifying the higher, or upper parts of it: the other Catomerea, that is, the level, or lower parts of the isle. It was first called Ethalia. It aboundeth so in oranges and lemons, that they fill barrels and pipes with the juice thereof, and carry them to Constantinople, which the Turks use at their meat, as we do the verges. .. It is of circuit an hundreth miles, and famous for the medicinable mastic that groweth there on trees. I saw many pleasant gardens in it, which yield in great plenty, oranges, lemons, apples, pears, prunes, figs, olives, apricots, dates, adams apples, excellent herbs, fair flowers, sweet honey, with store of cypress and mulbery-trees, and excceding good silk is made here.

At last I arrived at the city of Sio, where I was lodged, and kindly used with an old man, of the Genovesen race, for the space of eight days: I found here three monasteries of the order of Rome, one of the Jesuits, another of Saint Francis, and the third of the Dominican Friers, being all come from Genoa ; and because the greatest part of the city is of that stock, and of the Papal See, these cloisters have a braver life for good cheer, fat wines, and delicate lechery, than any sort of friars can elsewhere find in the world.

The women of the city Sio, are the most beautiful dames, (or rather angelical creatures) of all the Greeks, upon the face of the earth, and greatly given to venery... They are for the most part exceeding proud, and sumptuous in apparel, and commonly go (even artificers' wives) in gowns of satin and taffety; yea, in cloth of silver and gold, and are adorned with precious stones, and gems, and towels about their necks, and hands, with rings, chains, and bracelets. Their husbands are their panders, and when they see any stranger arrive, they will presently demand of him; if he would have a mistress: and so they make whores of their own wives, and are contented for a little gain, to wear horns: such are the base minds of ignominious cuckolds. If a stranger be desirous to stay all night with any of them, their price is a chicken of gold, nine shillings English, out of which this companion receiveth his supper, and for his pains, a bellyful of sinful content.

This city of Sio hath a large and strong fortress, which was built by the Genovese, and now detained by a garrison of Turks, containing a thousand fine houses within it, some whereof are Greeks, some Genovese, some Turks, and Moors. The city itself is unwalled, yet a populous and spacious place, spread along by the seaside, having a goodly harbour for galleys and ships, the chief inhabitants there, are descended of the Genovese, and profess the superstition of Rome. The people whereof were once lords of the Aegean Sea, maintaining a navy of eighty ships. In the end they became successively subject to the Roman and Greek princes; till Andronico Paleologus, gave them and their isle to the Justinianes, a noble family of the Genovese: from whom it was taken by Solyman the Magnificent on Easter day 1566.

1610 Sir George Sandys

The Economy of the Island

Three days after our imbarkment (as quick a passage as ever was heard of) we arrived at Sio, famous island called formerly Chios, which signifieth white, of Chione a nymph ... others say of the snow, that sometimes covers those mountains. Six score and five miles it containeth in circuit, extending from south unto north: the north and west quarters extraordinarily hilly. In the midst of the island is the mountain Arvis [now Amista] producing the best Greek wines... But the lentisk tree, which is well-nigh only proper to Sio, doth give it the greatest renown and endowment. These grow at the south end of the island, and on the leisurely ascending hills that neighbour the shore. In height not much exceeding a man, leafed like a service, and bearing a red berry , but changing into black as it ripeneth... which yearly yields to the inhabitants eighteen thousand sultanies. In the beginning of August lanch they the rine, from whence the mastic distilleth until the end of September, at which time they gather it. None is suffered to come amongst them during the interim, it being death but to have a pound of new mastic found in their houses. The wood thereof is excellent for toothpicks.

By reason of these trees they have the best honey of the world, which intermingled with water, is not much inferior in relish to the costly sherbets of Constantinople: the island produceth corn and oil in indifferent plenty. Some silk they make, and some cottons here grow, but short in worth to those of Smyrna. It hath also quarries of excellent marble: and a certain green earth, like the rust of brass, which the Turks call Terra Chia: but not that so reputed of by the ancient physicians. The coast, especially towards the south, is set with small watch-towers, which with smoke by day and fire by night, do give knowledge unto one another (and so to the upland) of suspected enemies. The environing sea being free from concealed rocks, and consequently from peril ...

Their orchards are here enriched with excellent fruits: amongst the rest, with oranges, lemons, citrons, pomegranates, and figs, so much esteemed by the Romans for their tartness... Upon the fig-trees they hang a kind of unsavoury fig, out of whose corruption certain small worms are engendered, which by biting the other (as they say) procure them to ripen. Partridges are here an ordinary food: whereof they have an incredible number, greater than ours, and differing in view: the beak and feet red, the plume ash-colour. Many of them are kept tame: these feeding abroad all day, at night upon a call return unto their several owners.

1674 Father Jacques-Paul Babin, S.J.

A Privileged Town

At each side of the city are abundance of pleasant gardens, abounding with all sorts of fruit. Coming in from sea there gardens and summer-houses do give a most delightsome prospect; the houses being for the most part very well built, with their windows red and green. The inhabitants are most Greeks, of which many are of the Church of Rome. Here are several good churches which remain since the time the Genovese had possession of the island; as that of the Jesuits, the Dominicans, and the Capuchins; the two former are in the city, the latter is at the north west end, where they have a large convent, with pleasant gardens. In the time of holy days they carry their processions in the streets without any molestation, but it must be after sunset. The same have I seen in Smyrna on Good Friday by the Greeks, and also at Galatta of Constantinople. The Vizier Cupri Ogle at his return from Candy, tarried here several days, and lodged in the house of one Signior Dominico Mascardi, which joins to the Capuchin's Convent; one day asking what bell it was that he heard, one told him it was some bells of mules; says the Vizier to him that made that answer, and you are an ass for endeavouring to make me believe so. This is some bell to call you to prayers and be not ashamed to enjoy the freedom which is given you. He was several times in the garden, and commended their way of living. Before the Vizier came, order was given by the elders to forbid the women's walking the streets as their custom was, fearing least some soldiers should abuse them, and so occasion a disorder. The Vizier having been two or three days in town, and not finding the divertissement he expected from what he had been told, he asked what was the reason, it was told him that fearing some disturbance might be, orders were given to forbid the women to walk the streets. The Vizier made answer; That seeing they had such privileges, they should enjoy them while he was there, otherwise he would recall the liberty they had. Next morning the streets were full with all sorts, and in the evening by the seaside singing and dancing most part of the nights. The Turks hold the Sciotes for a soft sort of people calling them, *prassinos* which signifies green: a Basha saying, it was impossible to see a wise Sciote, as to see a green horse. All the time that the Vizier was here, there was not the least disorder amongst the officers, but all were in clover; and notwithstanding there were upwards of fifty thousand strangers in town and in the fleet, the price of provision was not advanced.

The town lies about twelve miles from the Asian shore almost opposite to a very strong castle called Chisme; from whence they are supplied with most of their provision; Scio not affording sufficient for the inhabitants, and those passengers which are continually here. All vessels from

Constantinople bound for the south usually call in here, both going and coming. There are above thirty villages upon the island, which are well inhabited most by Greeks; those who belong to the mastic villages, to the south-ward, have their hair long. The time for gathering the mastic, is in August and September. The customer goes out to the villages, where they receive him with music, and feasting. What mastic is gathered, it is all delivered to the customer, for the Grand Signior's store, and he soon dispatches it up to Constantinople to serve in the Serraglio for several uses. What remains of the Grand Signior's store, the customer sells to merchants. It is very dangerous for the inhabitants, to keep any mastic by them. In Turkey they use it to chew and some mix it in their bread. The Turks call it sacks, and the island has the same name. The Italians call it mastice, and masticare is to chew. When any company of women meet in Turkey, some mastic is brought them on a server, and each taking a little, they are chewing, and spitting most of the time. It is comical to see the old women roll it about their gums; the effects which they find by it are, that it carries away the phlegm, cleanses and prevents the aching of the teeth; and causes a sweet breath. Here is a continual watch kept round the island; when they see any ships or other vessels in the day time they make a smoke, and in the night show lights; the light tower lends a man to acquaint the customer, what vessels are on the coast. If any passengers land in any part of the island, the sentinels accompany them to the customer, who inquires whence they came, and what business they have there; this to prevent spies. Betwixt this island and the main are several small islands called Spallnadori, which are much frequented with privateers as those before Metelino; they lie about twelve miles to the north from the city. In the year 1666 a Malta ship Commanded by the Chevalier Tincourt was at anchor between those islands a fisher man passing by see the ship; and coming to Scio finds the Captain Basha with about forty galleys. And going immediately to him asked for a *mustalook* (a gift upon good tidings) for he had news to tell him. The Basha hearing the news ordered the boatman to have ten dollars, and put to sea, it being very calm. The sentinels from the hills came down, and acquainted Monsieur Tincourt, that the Turkish fleet was rowing toward the islands, so he with his boats towed the ship out to the eastward, before the galleys came up to him, and had time to provide himself to receive them. A desperate fight was maintained for several hours, and not a breath of wind stirring; so as the ship lay to their mercy, and was boarded by them several times, but were torched often again, leaving many men dead behind them. In the afternoon a fresh gale of wind began, at which those in the ship took courage, and forced the Basha to retire under the guns of the castles of Scio, firing several broadsides into the town. The Captain Basha sent to the Capuchins to have them to go off in a boat, and persuade the captain to forbear firing into the town. The Capuchins went aboard, carrying some fresh provision as a present, desiring Monsieur Tincourt to forbear, for that most darnage was to the poor Christians. So he retired, and went to Micone to repair his ship. He was a French man born, - not above 24 years of age; he built and fitted out the ship at his own charge, styling himself the Champion of Christ. His father or uncle died in fight against the Turks, while he was but a child. To revenge whose blood, he took this resolution; not above two months after, his ship was carried away on the island of Scyros, where he perished; and of two hundred and fifty men not above five escaped, which caused a great grief to all who had heard of his valour. He had not been in the Archipeligo above two months, before he fought with the Turkish fleet; and intended to have past the Dardanells (as a merchant ship) to do what mischief he could, to the city of Constantinople, by firing against it and then to make his escape out of the castles or perish in the action. I lived in Smyrna when this fight was, and had the particular relation from one of the Capuchins.

The profit which the Turks receive from Scio, is double what any other island in the Archipelago pays. Nor are there any subjects in the Turk's dominions, of Greeks, that are richer. Their habit is different from all other islanders. The women have their coats to their ankles, their bodies short and thick waisted, their head dress with linen close to their ears, raised up behind, (not unlike the Doge of Venice his cornet) in which their hair is laid. They esteem great legs, and little feet. Some, to be in the fashion, will have four or more pair of stirrup stockings. Before their breasts hangs a bib which reaches a little below their waist, under it they have their hands covered when they are abroad; when they dance a round dance they hold a pocket handkerchief in their hands, that they may not have their hands touched. They have earrings, necklaces, and bracelets of gold. The men wear strait bodied jackets, with four broad skirts below the waist, strait kneed breeches, to button, or tie at the knees, ilioes and stockings moil: according to the Genovese, they have a broad lappet of linen fastened to the neck-band of their shirts, which hangs down behind over their backs. Their hair is cut short to their ears, and generally they wear little red caps or broad brimmed hats, But their Vecchiardi do wear long loose garments over their jackets and breeches.

1745 Pockocke, Richard

The Garden-Suburbs of Scio

The Campo or plain of Scio to the north [*south*, ed.] of this town is a very beautiful country, about two leagues long, and a league broad, but it consists entirely of country houses and gardens walled round, great part of them are groves of orange and lemon trees, - and the houses are so near to one another that it appears like the suburb of a town; and from sea it looks almost like one continual city. The plain country to the north and south is about four leagues long, and a league broad, in most parts, and in some more. There are also in it several gardens of mulberry trees for silkworms; those that are most beautiful have a walk in the middle, and to the right and left from the house, with square pillars on each side, and seats built between them of hewn stone; the pillars support a trellis-work which is covered with vines, and on the spaces on each side there are groves of orange and lemon trees. Some have chapels in their gardens, with a family vault under them. Here almost all the people of the city retire in the summer, and as instantly return to the town in winter; they go also out of the town to their country-houses when there is any plague; and the spring before I was there, when there were such terrible earthquakes, many went out of the town; but found that it was more secure to stay in the city, where the houses being contiguous, support one another better against the shock. To the south and south-west part of this country are the villages of the Campo; but these, as well as most of the others in the island, which are sixty in all, are really like towns; the houses are built together, and consist of several narrow streets, having gates at the entrance, and many of them a castle in the middle, especially the villages of mastic; which manner of building in the country seems to have been introduced as a defence against the incursions from the continent, which were often made when this island was not under the same government.

Pet Ewes

The want of herbage makes all sorts of meat very dear except goat's flesh, which they have in the mountains, but sheep are so scarce, that in the villages of mastic every family has a domestic ewe for breeding, which follows them about like a dog.

1764-6 Richard Chandler

At the Baths

The next morning we were set on shore again, and I went with Captain Jolly to the principal bagnio or public bathing-place, which is a very noble edifice, with ample domes, all of marble. I shall attempt to give an account of the mode of bathing. We undressed in a large square room, where linen is hung to dry, and the keeper attends with his servants. We had each a long towel given us to wrap round our middle, and a pair of tall wooden pattens to walk in. We were led through a warm narrow passage into the inner room, which is yet more spacious, and made very hot by stoves, which are concealed. In this was a water-bath, and recesses, with partitions, on the sides. The pavement in the centre under the dome was raised, and covered with linen cloths, on which we were instructed to lie down. We were soon covered with big drops of sweat, and two men naked, except the waist, then entered, and began kneading our flesh, tracing all the muscles and cleansing the pores. By the time they had finished, our joints were sufficiently suppled, and they commenced the formidable operation of snapping all of them, not only the toes, ankles, knees, fingers and the like, but the vertebrae of the back, and the breast; one while wrenching our necks; then turning us on our bellies, crossing our arms behind us, and placing their right knee between our shoulders. The feats they perform cannot easily be described, and are hardly credible. When this was over, we were rubbed with a mohair-bag fitted to the hand, which, like the ancient strigil, brings away the gross matter perspired. We were then led each to a recess, supplied by pipes with hot and cold water, which we tempered to our liking. The men returned with soap-lather and tow in a wooden bowl, with which they cleaned the skin, and then poured a large quantity of warm water on our heads. Our spirits were quite exhausted when they covered us with dry cloths and led us back to the first room, where beds were ready for us. On waking, after a gentle slumber, we were presented each with a lighted pipe and a dish of coffee. We rose much refreshed, and as the ladies of the Aga or Turkish governor were expected there, hastened away. The common Turks and Greeks pay a very small gratuity for the use of the bath, which they frequent once a week or oftener. I have sometimes been regaled, while in the inner room, with ripe fruits and sherbet, and with incense burning to scent the air. One of my companions repeatedly partook with me in this innocent and wholesome luxury at Smyrna and at Athens.

1811-12 C. R. Cockerell

Dispersing a Waterspout

We were carried gently along between Scio and the mainland till we reached the north end of the passage. There we fell in with a storm. The wind rose very strong; all around us grew fearfully black, and close to us fell a waterspout. Hereupon the man at the helm sunk terrified on his knees and made a large cross in the air with his hand. But our old pilot ordered him to look to the helm, for that he would save us from the danger. Drawing out a knife with a black handle (a very important point, I understand), he with it made also a cross in the air, and then stuck it into the deck and pronounced the words: "In the beginning was the Word." Whereupon, or very shortly after, the waterspout did disperse and our pious Greek took to himself all the credit for having saved us from a considerable danger.

Samos

1599 Thomas Dallam

Bluff

When we saw that we could not prevail against the wind, we came round to that place where we did first anchor, thinking there to get some better store of victuals and fresh water; but being very dark before we could get into the harbour, by the negligence of him that sounded, our ship was aground, the which turned us to great fear and much trouble a great part of that night; yet in the end all was well. But in the morning, when we did think to have gone ashore, we espied four galleys and a frigate, which came stealing by the shore. The galleys stayed a league off, under the shore of Asia the lesser, but the frigate came into the road to see what we were, and there came to an anchor; the which when our Master persevered, not knowing what their intent was, he caused anchor to be weighed with all speed, and being under sail, the frigate went before us, and also the galleys; for than our Master purposed to go that way which before he durst not adventure; for whereas we should have left this island on our right hand, now we left it on our left hand, and ventured to go betwixt Samos and the mainland of Asia the less, the which is a marvellous strait passage for such a ship as ours was. Even in the straitest place these four galleys stayed for us, but when they see our strength and boldness, they were afraid of us. They had placed their galleys close by the shore, so that either the beak head did touche the shore or else there ours might, and yet had we hardly room enough to pass betwixt their oars and the mainland. Our Master caused all our company to stand up and make as great a show as we could, and when we were right over against them, our five trumpets sounded suddenly, which made them wonder, looking earnestly upon us, but gave us not a word; so we dashed them out of countenance who meant to have feared us, and we left them by the shore of Samos, being the eleventh day of July.

1616 Sir Henry Blount

Sponge Fishing

Some early travellers were apparently rather credulous, although no doubt the genuine achievements of the islanders were cause enough for admiration.

Samos is the only place in the world, under whose rocks grow sponges: the people from their infancy, are bred up with dry biscuit, and other extenuating diet, to make them extreme lean; then taking a sponge wet in oil they hold it, part in their mouths and part without, so they go under water, where at first they cannot stay long; but after practice, some of the leanest stay above an hour and a half, even till all the oil of the sponge be corrupted; and by the law of the island, none of that trade is suffered to marry, until he have stayed half an hour under water. Thus they gather sponges from the bottom of the rocks, more than an hundred fathom deep; which with many stories of these islands was told me by certain Greeks in our galleon.

c.1692 "Mr. Roberts"

Freedom Regained on Samos

Now I come to relate the manner of my escape from the corsairs. You must note, I would have put it in practice sooner than I did, but I had all the while a little Dutch boy in my company, that came out of England with me in the *Arcana* Galley, and my resolution was to have lived and died there, had I not got the boy away as well as myself: which at last I did effect at noonday. For lying at Antiparos with a Prize, I got ashore, and lighting on a small Greek boat, I made him carry me to Melo, where I could be safe; but there not being able to subsist without money, I set on a new project, and having got another small boat for our selves I was resolved to sail for Smirna: but herein I was frustrated again, for under Cherso, meeting with five half galleys belonging to Stancu, it appeared worse and worse for us: For now we thought we should be sold to Matsa Mama at Rhodes; yet it fell out better than we expected, the Turks proving to be very kind, and never fettered us. So we went for Samos, from whence having been now five days in their custody, I, with the boy on my back, committed my self to the mercy of the sea in the night and got ashore. But there being many of the Turks, I was afraid to stir and so lay in the crevices of a rock six days and nights together, not daring to move, for fear of being retaken; and all the sustenance we had there, was three dew snails, and some roots of wild weeds. But at length we saw the half galleys go away, though by this time the youngster was almost dead, and my self little better: However, I could stand and go a little, but the boy was not able to budge. We were remote from any village, yet I would fain have carried the lad to that which was next, but we fell sometimes both together; then I dragged him a little way, but was so faint that I was quickly forced to rest my self. Yet at length meeting with a poor Greek, with one ass laden with wood, and another unladen; after having some discourse with him, (telling him who we were, and how we came thither) he took pity on us, and put the boy upon one ass, and me on the other, leaving his wood behind him, and brought us to the monastery at Samos. There for twelve days the friars took great care of us, and saw us safely sent for Smyrna, by a French ship: where, God be thanked, I thought my self in paradise to be at liberty; which I pray God to preserve to every man, and more particularly a deliverance out of a crusal.

Being safely arrived at Smirna, I could get never a voyage, save with the French, with whom I refused to embark, but waited with patience, till at last I obtained the favour of a passage with a Venetian…

1801 Edward Daniel Clarke

Infestation with Monks and Tigers

This island, the most conspicuous object, not only of the Ionian Sea, but of all the Aegean, is less visited, and of course less known, than any other: it is one of the largest and most considerable of them all; and so near to the mainland that it has been affirmed persons upon the opposite coasts may hear each other speak….

One of the monasteries is called Our Lady of Thunder. There are four nunneries upon the island, and above three hundred private chapels; yet the population does not exceed 12,000 men; which is explained by Tournefort, who says, that the island is entirely in the hands of churchmen, possessing seven monasteries. The swarm of caloyers and Greek Papas have made a desert of this fine island; where all the qualification necessary to become a priest, and live by the industry of others, is the talent of being able to repeat the mass from memory. The bishop of

Samos, who is also bishop of Nicaria, enjoys an annual income of two thousand crowns; and derives, besides a considerable revenue from the important services he renders to the islanders, in blessing for them their water and their cattle in the beginning of May. All the produce of the dairies on that day belongs to him: he has also two beasts out of every herd. In such state of affairs, we cannot wonder at the change that has taken place between the ancient and the modern population of Samos: its fertility in former ages made it the subject of proverbial admiration and praise. It is related in Athenaeus, that the fruit and rose trees off the island bore twice a year. Tournefort says, that Samos is infested with wolves; and that tigers sometimes arrive from the mainland, after crossing the little Boccaze; thereby confirming all observation made by the author in the former section, with regard to the existence of tigers in Asia Minor.

Some Travel Clichés Discovered

It is difficult to believe that the most banal clichés of tourist literature were once seen as original observations.

Passing across the great Boccaze, between Samos and Icaria, we were much struck by the extraordinary intensity of the deep blue colour of the sea; and this, which is as much a distinguishing characteristic of the Archipelago as the brightness of its sky, has been noticed by no writer, excepting our enchanting bard, whose poems arc now so deservedly the theme of general praise.

> "He that has sailed on the dark blue sea,
> Has viewed at times, I ween, a fair sight."

> Byron's *Childe Harold* p.68 (London, 1812)

1811-12 C. R. Cockerell

Columns as Targets

I made the acquaintance of a pleasant Russian, Monsieur Marschall, and with him crossed the island to see the antiquities - first of the ancient city and then of the Temple of Juno, lying three-quarters of an hour to the eastward of it. There is only one column of it remaining, but that one very finely cut and of beautiful marble. A few years ago, I understand, there were still many standing; but some were blown up for the sake of the metal rivets, and others knocked over by the Turkish men of war, who, as they were very white, used them as a target for gunnery practice.

1812-15 William Turner

Bad Character of the Wealthy Samiotes

The higher order of Samiotes are the most unprincipled miscreants in existence. They are always intriguing one against the other, and no ties of nature can restrain their hatred or their violence. Five years ago a young man of the island, by false accusation and bribery, caused his uncle to be hung. They tyrannize over their inferiors in the island, who are so oppressed and fleeced, that they would willingly receive new masters. They detest all Franks because they are independent of their jurisdiction; and the firmans of the Sultan or buyourdis of the Captain Pasha have no effect on them, as they secure friends in the Government of Constantinople by giving in presents large sums, for the levying of which they grind the people. The lower orders, if left to themselves, would not be of bad dispositions, but being constantly urged by their superiors, to support one cause or another, they lose all idea of order, learn to think violence the only mode of government; and the struggles that ensue amongst them at the frequent revolutions and changes of their governors seldom end without bloodshed. But, I am told, that the common people of Vathi, being the most conversant with commerce, which among Levantines is almost always a synonym for fraud, are much more unprincipled than their compeers throughout the rest of the island.

1890 The Rev. Henry Fanshawe Tozer
The Tunnel-Aqueduct of Eupalinus

The next morning (April 8) was devoted to exploring the aqueduct and tunnel of Eupalinus, the discovery of which has been one of the greatest archaeological triumphs of our generation. But before proceeding thither, it may be well for me to quote the passage of Herodotus in which the historian has described it together with the other wonders of Samos. It runs thus in Canon Rawlinson's translation:-

"I have dwelt the longer on the affairs of the Samians, because three of the greatest works in all Greece were made by them. One is a tunnel, under a hill 150 fathoms high, carried entirely through the base of the hill, with a mouth at either end. The length of the cutting is seven furlongs, the height and width are each eight feet. Along the whole course there is a second cutting twenty cubits deep and three feet broad, whereby water is brought, through pipes, from an abundant source into the city. The architect of this tunnel was Eupalinus, son of Naustrophus, a Megarian. Such is the first of their great works; the second is a mole in the sea, which goes all round the harbour, near twenty fathoms deep, and in length above two furlongs. The third is a temple; the largest of all the temples known to us, whereof Rhoecus, son of Phileus, a Samian, was first architect." (Herodotus 3. 60).

About the position of two of these works, the mole and the temple, there never has been any doubt, but this remarkable tunnel is not mentioned by any other ancient author, and all trace of it seemed to have disappeared. The first person who attempted a systematic exploration was M. Guerin, the author of a book on Patmos and Samos, who visited this island about 1853. He rightly judged that the source of water should be made the starting-point in the investigation, and discovered that there was a copious spring about half a mile from the northern foot of the lofty hill on which the city was built - that is, towards the interior and away from the sea. By digging in the neighbourhood of this he found an underground passage, leading in the direction of the hillside, in which were earthen pipes intended for the passage of water; and though it was much blocked up from the soil having fallen in, he traced it nearly to the foot of the hill. He was forced, however, to discontinue the work before arriving at that point, and consequently did not reach the tunnel which Herodotus describes. After all, the real discovery was made by accident, and on the opposite side of the mountain.

Seven years ago a priest from the neighbouring monastery of Hagia Triada, called Cyril, who possessed a piece of ground not very far from the ancient theatre which I have described, chanced to find an opening, which led into the tunnel near the point where it issued from the mountain-side; and so great was the enthusiasm aroused in Samos by this discovery that a large sum of money was soon forthcoming with the object of clearing it out and restoring it. As yet, owing to the magnitude of the task, this has not been fully accomplished, but enough has been done to give an accurate idea of the work, and to confirm the statements of Herodotus. We now know that the water was carried underground the whole way from the spring to the heart of the city; first by the passage which M. Guérin explored, then by the tunnel through the bowels of the mountain which Herodotus describes, and finally by another passage in the direction of the port. There were also independent entrances at either end of the tunnel. The first intelligence of this discovery was sent to the ACADEMY by Mr. Dennis from Smyrna shortly after it was made; and the place has since been described by Mr. Bent both in the ACADEMY and the ATHENAEUM … The following account is that of a passing traveller, and for more exact information I may refer the reader to the authorities above mentioned.

We started for the tunnel in the company of a *Chorophylax* or gendarme, who proved to be a most painstaking guide. Before reaching it we found sitting under some trees two monks, one of whom was Cyril, the discoverer of the entrance; they volunteered to join us, and with this admirable escort we arrived at the opening, which I have mentioned. Candles were now lighted, and when we had descended a little way into the ground, we entered a narrow passage constructed with large hewn stones, the upper of which were cut angularly so as to form an arch; after passing through this, in a short time we found ourselves in the tunnel. This was an excavation seven or eight feet wide, the sides of which curved somewhat outwards; and about two-thirds of its width was occupied by a footway, which ran along by the wall on our left-hand as we proceeded north-westwards in the direction of the source, while the rest of the space was taken up with the channel for the water, the sides of which descended perpendicularly to a depth of thirty feet. This was not open throughout, for spaces remained at intervals where the rubbish which had choked it had not been removed. In the process of clearing it the pipes which served to convey the water were found at the bottom. The height of the roof of the tunnel varied in different parts, for in some places it was eight feet high, or even more; while in others we had for some distance to stoop in walking. The roof was not arched but flattened, though rounded at the angles; and its surface, though, like that of the rest of the tunnel, it had been cut to a fairly smooth face, was often ridged owing to the character of the rock, as we discovered when our heads came into contact with it in places where our attention was diverted by the risk of slipping into the watercourse.

The *Chorophylax* and the second monk did not accompany us for any great distance, but Cyril conducted us as far as a point where a considerable quantity of water had collected on the path, and about which were the remains of stalactites. When the place was first explored a great quantity of these had to be broken away before the passage could he cleared. Here, also, strange to say, a large piece of a fluted column was lying half-immersed in the water, showing apparently that at one time a small *sacrarium* must have existed on the spot. We now proceeded alone, until we reached a place where the height of the tunnel was greater than before, and both tunnel and watercourse made a bend; on the further side of this the passage was obstructed, the clearing not having been continued further in this direction. As our progress thus far had occupied twenty minutes, we could not have been far from the middle of the tunnel, for its length is probably less, certainly not more, than the seven furlongs at which Herodotus estimates it. The change in the elevation which has just been mentioned, coinciding as it does with an alteration in the course of the tunnel, renders it almost certain that this was the meeting-point of two working parties, and that the excavation was carried on simultaneously from the two ends...

We now retraced our steps, but before we reached the entrance we noticed a number of cuttings or niches in the side of the rock, which probably were resting-places for lamps, since earthenware lamps were found in them; and in one place a deeper hollow had been made, concerning which it has been conjectured that it was intended to receive the tools of the work-men. Near the point where the transverse passage by which we entered meets the tunnel, a section of the rock was left, so as to form a wall across the passage; here no doubt there was originally a gate, for at the side it was pierced by a hole, through which a person desiring admission might call. During the forty minutes that we remained underground we found the air warm, but nowhere close or foul. The tunnel is continued by a subterranean passage, which runs parallel to the mountain-side in the direction of the port; this has been excavated as far as the theatre, but its exit into the city has not yet been found. Its course may be traced above ground by the stone-cased openings, resembling large vents, that form the heads of the shafts, through which both in ancient and modern times, the earth and rubbish were removed from below.

The point that we next made for was the northern entrance of the tunnel; and in order to reach this we crossed the mountain under the guidance of the *Chorophylax*, and descended to a point beneath the north-west angle of the city walls, where another opening had been made. By this the roof of the underground passage leading from the spring has been broken through from above, just where it makes a sharp turn at its junction with the tunnel; the tunnel itself is blocked with *débris* a little way beyond its mouth. In the steep hillside close above, an arched entrance, flanked with stone walls, has been discovered, corresponding to that through which we had first passed on the southern side, only here the gallery is longer, and runs at first above the tunnel, instead of striking it transversely. We penetrated into it for a quarter of an hour, until the passage became extremely narrow, and the water that had collected in it reached nearly to our knees; here it appeared useless to proceed further, and turning round with some difficulty, we returned to our starting-point. In one place a hole in the floor, which in the dim light of our candles required to be passed with great care, seemed to communicate, through a shaft or otherwise, with the tunnel below; but we had no means of discovering where is the ultimate point of junction of the two. The underground passage which brought the water from the spring has been completely cleared out, so that it is possible to pass from one end to the other. Owing to the nature of the ground its course was very irregular, for it was carried round the heads of two small valleys, where we traced it from outside by the openings of the shafts, which were constructed in the same way as those which I have already described. The fountain, which is close to the commencement of the passage, but has now no communication with it, lies beneath a small chapel of St. John the Baptist; the reservoir which contains it, is of ancient construction. In the middle of the floor of the chapel there is a square wooden cover, and when this is removed the water can be seen welling out in a large volume.

Two questions naturally suggest themselves in connection with this interesting work. First; what was the object of boring such a tunnel, with enormous expenditure of labour, through the rock, when, so far as the position of the ground is concerned, the water might have been carried in an open channel round the flank of the mountain into the city? We naturally conjecture that it was to secure the water supply in case of war; but then we are met by the difficulty that the spring was situated some way outside the walls, and consequently was in the power of an attacking force. I can only suggest that the source may have been completely concealed from view, and at that time or M. Guérin's visit it was so, for in order to discover it one of the flags or the pavement had to be removed. This idea is rendered probable by the fact that the water was carried underground to the foot of the mountain. If this was the case, the existence of the source, and probably that of the tunnel also, must have been a state secret, confined to a few persons; otherwise the city would have been at the mercy of every traitor. Secondly; what explanation is to be given of the extraordinary depth of the waterway, which so far exceeds all the requirements of the supply 'To this question the only satisfactory answer is to be found in the suggestion of M. Fabricius, that as the depth is more remarkable in the southern part of the channel, which is furthest from the source, it may have been deepened as the work proceeded in consequence of insufficient allowance having been originally made for the fall of the water.

Ikarios

c.1609 William Lithgow

Escape!

As we fetched up the sight of Nicaria, we espied two Turkish galleots who gave us the chase, and pursued us straight into a bay betwixt two mountains, where we left the laden boat and fled to the rocks, from whence we mightily annoyed with huge tumbling stones the pursuing Turks. But in our flying, the Master was taken, and two other old men, whom they made captives and slaves; and also seized upon the boat, and all their goods. The number of us that escaped were nine persons.

1674 Father Jacques-Paul Babin, S.J.

Fishing in the Nude

Nicaria formerly called Icaria lies to the north of Scio about 25 miles distant. It is in compass about 70 miles, having no harbour for great shipping, and therefore incapable of any trade. The land is also very barren being most mountainous, and rocky, so that they of Samos have a saying that when God made those islands he ordered all the rubbish should be cast upon Icaria, which they have no great reason to say, for they have their share also of mountains.

The inhabitants are generally very poor, as the privateers cannot get any thing out of them; nor can the Turks bring them to pay any considerable tribute. They have some wine, but none of the best; it being hard. But here are the best winter grapes which I did ever see, they being round and red, growing between the rocks and in such dangerous places to come at as that with much hazard they are gathered. Sheep they have none, but goats are the chief of their food.

I have seen several of the Nicariotes in their boats that row all naked, for which they give two reasons: one that with their coats they cannot be so active at the oar, the other that they wear out their clothes much; for every time that they tug the oar they rise with their bodies, and fall back on the banks as is usual in the galleys.

The Temple of Hera, Samos

(Contemporary print)

The Dodecanese

These islands, lying close to the coast of Anatolia, enjoyed special privileges under Turkish rule, which were only cancelled in 1908. They were seized by Italy during the Italo-Turkish War of 1911-12. Arrangements were made by the Great powers for these islands to pass to Greece following the First World War, but Italy repudiated this settlement. During 1944-45 they were occupied by British forces, and in 1947, finally united to Greece.

Street of the Knights, Rhodes
(Contemporary print)

Patmos

c.1680 Bernard Randolph
The Sights of Patmos

Upon this island did St. John the Divine write the *Revelations* (a manuscript of which they have) and here, if we may believe the inhabitants, is to be seen the pulpit in which he preached, and the font where he used to baptise.

Also here is a mountain where is a deep cave in which they say Cynops the magician lived in the time of Saint John; this cave they believe to be haunted; and to try it, a man was let down by a cord to see what was in the cave, but he was pulled up almost dead.

c. 1692 "Mr. Roberts
The Miraculously Preserved Body of Saint John

On this island stands a famous monastery on a high hill over the town, which is dedicated by the Greeks to St. John the Divine. In this monastery is a stone tomb, cased within with wainscot, and lined with black cloth, wherein lies the body of a man very fair and sound, affirmed by the inhabitants to be the very body of St. John the Divine; and it is certain it has lain there many hundred years. This I can assure, that the body is as firm as any living man's, and not the least sign of putrefaction upon it; and that at the same time, it is no ways embalmed. Several English men have told me, that they had seen it ten years before my arrival there; and therefore there is something of truth in it.

1801 Edward Daniel Clarke
Helping Some Stranded French Soldiers

This incident, taking place as it did during the extended period of the Revolutionary and Napoleonic Wars, is an indication of the limited and comparatively "civilised" character of warfare at that period. Not only did English and Frenchmen meeting in the Levant, outside the immediate theatre of war, fail to engage in hostilities, but one party found it quite the natural thing to do to offer their assistance to those from "the other side" who were in difficulties in a very practical way.

At half-past eight am we made the island of Patmos; and afterwards passing between Leria and Lepsia, Samos appeared most beautifully in view, covered by a silvery mist, softening every object, but concealing none, Lepsia is now called Lipso. At eleven o'clock am. we entered the port of La Scala, in Patmos. We were surprised by meeting several boats filled with French soldiers, fishing. In order to prevent our caique from being fired at, as a pirate vessel (which she much resembled, and probably had been), we had hoisted an English flag given to us by Captain Clarke, and recommended for our use in the Archipelago. The Frenchmen, seeing this proud distinction upon our humble skiff, called out, by way or taunt, "Voilà un beau venez-y voir! Le Pavillon Anglois! Tremblez, Messieurs." They were much too numerous to venture a reply, if we had been so disposed; and as soon as we landed, we found the quay covered with French privates, among whom were some of the inferior officers of the French army. These men were part of the army which had surrendered to our troops in Egypt, on their passage to France. The transport hired for their conveyance was commanded by an Algerine: this man had put into Patmos, under the pretence of careening his vessel, saying that it was unsafe to continue the voyage until this had been done; but it was feared that he intended to seize an opportunity, after landing these Frenchmen, to escape with the ship and all the booty on board. We had been but a short time on shore, when a petition was brought to us signed by the French officers, stating their fears, and begging that we would represent their case to our Minister at Constantinople. They said that they had already removed their trunks, and were resolved to return no more on board the Algerine; the rascally captain having twice attempted to poison their food. All this was uttered in a very different sort of tone from that in which we had been hailed upon our coming into the harbour, and we entered warmly into their cause. The situation was, to be sure, critical. They had property belonging to some of the French generals, besides their own effects; and all the cases containing those things were lying upon the open quay. They were forced to appoint a regular guard, day and night; hourly dreading, as they told us, a visit from some of the numerous pirates which swarm around Patmos: besides all this, the mutinous behaviour of their own men made it impossible for them to rely even upon the sentinels set over the baggage, for they were constantly in a state of intoxication with the wine of the island. As Mr. Riley was going to Constantinople, we wrote to the British Ambassador, briefly explaining the event that had taken place: and our letter, as we were afterwards told, procured them another ship. In the meantime, it was necessary to take some immediate step for the security of their baggage. For this purpose we proposed making an application to the monks of the Monastery of the Apocalypse, which is situate two miles and a half from the quay, upon the top of a mountain in the highest part of all the island, close to the town of Patmos. Here it might be secure from pirates; for the building is strongly fortified, and is proof against any attack of that nature. A Commissary of the French army proposed to accompany us upon this expedition; and, as the plan was highly approved, we set off without further delay for the Convent.

The ascent is steep and rugged, but practicable for ass's and mules; and upon the backs of these animals we proposed to convey the trunks. When we arrived at the Monastery, we were quite struck by its size and substantial appearance. It is a very powerful fortress, built upon a sheer rock, with several towers and lofty thick walls; and if duly mounted with guns, might be made impregnable. According to Tournefort, it is said to have been founded by Alexius Comnenus, in consequence of the persuasion of St. Christodulus; but Dapper relates, that the saint himself founded the Monastery, having obtained permission to this effect from Alexius, towards the end of the tenth century, when he retired to Patmos to avoid the persecution of the Turks. St. Christodulus had been Abbot of Latros, a day and a half's journey from Ephesus, where he presided over twenty convents. We were received by the Superior and by the Bursar of the Monastery, in the Refectory. Having made known the cause of our coming, we presented to them our circular letter from the Capudan Pasha: this, being written in Turkish, was interpreted by Mr. Riley. After a short consultation, they acquiesced in the proposal made for the French officers; and agreed to receive the whole of the luggage at the quay, within their walls; also a single officer to superintend the care of it, until a vessel should arrive from Constantinople, or from Smyrna, for its removal. This business being settled, we asked permission to see the library, which was readily granted; and while the French commissioner went into the town to hire some mules, the two caloyers, by whom we had been received, conducted us thither.

An Unappreciated Treasury

We entered a small, oblong chamber, having a vaulted stone roof; and found it to be nearly filled with books, of all sizes, in a most neglected state; some lying upon the floor, a prey to the damp and to worms; others standing upon shelves, but without any kind of order. The books upon the shelves were all printed volumes; for these, being more modern, were regarded as the more valuable, and had a better station assigned them than the rest, many of which were considered only as so much rubbish.

Some of the printed books were tolerably well bound, and in good condition. The Superior said, these were his favourites; but when we took down one or two of them to examine their contents, we discovered that neither the Superior nor his colleague were able to read. They had a confused traditionary recollection of the names of some of them, but knew no more of their contents than the Grand Signior. We saw here the first edition of the *Anthologia*, in quarto, printed at Florence, in capital letters. A.D. MCCCCXCIV - a beautiful copy. At the extremity of this chamber, which is opposite to the window, a considerable number of old volumes of parchment, some with covers and some without, were heaped upon the floor, in the utmost disorder; and there were evident proofs that these had been cast aside, and condemned to answer any purpose for which the parchment might be required. When we asked the superior what they were, he replied, turning up his nose with an expression of indifference and contempt, cheirographa [manuscripts]! It was, indeed, a moment in which a literary traveller might be supposed to doubt the evidence of his senses; for the whole of this condemned heap consisted entirely of Greek manuscripts, and some of them were of the highest antiquity. We sought in vain for the manuscript of Homer, said to have been copied by a student from Cos... We even ventured to ask the ignorant monks if they had ever heard of the existence of such a relic in their library. The bursar maintained that he had, and that he should know the manuscript if he saw it. Presently he produced from the heap the volume he pretended to recognise: it was a copy of the *Poems* of Gregory of Nazianzus, written upon vellum, evidently as old as the ninth century. The cover and some of the outer leaves had been torn off; but the rest was perfect. The ink had become red; a circumstance alluded to by Montfaucon, in ascertaining the age of Greek manuscripts; and the writing throughout manifested an equal degree of antiquity. What was to be done? To betray any extraordinary desire to get possession of these treasures, would inevitably prevent all possibility of obtaining any of them. We referred the matter to Mr. Riley, as to a person habituated in dealing with knavish Greeks; and presently such a jabbering took place, accompanied with so many significant shrugs, winks, nods, and grimaces, that it was plain something like a negotiation was going on. The author, meanwhile, continued to inspect the heap; and had soon selected the fairest specimen of Grecian calligraphy which has descended to modern times. It was a copy of the twenty-four first Dialogues of Plato, written throughout upon vellum, in the same exquisite character; concluding with a date, and the name of the calligraphist. The whole of this could not be ascertained at the instant. It was a single volume in folio, bound in wood. The cover was full of worms, and falling to pieces: a paper label appeared at the back, inscribed, in a modern hand, *Dialogues of Socrates*: but the letters of Plato's name, separated by stars, appeared very distinctly as a head-piece to the first page of the Manuscript ... A postscript at the end of the volume stated that the Manuscript had been "written by John the calligraphist, for Arethas, Dean of Patras, in the month of November 896, the 14th year of the Indiction, and 6404 year of the world, in the reign of Leo son of Basilius, for the sum of thirteen Byzantine nomismata," about eight guineas of our money...

The author afterwards discovered a lexicon of St. Cyril of Alexandria, written upon paper, without any date, and contained in a volume of *Miscellanies*. He also found two small volumes of the *Psalms* and of *Greek Hymns*, accompanied by unknown characters, serving as ancient Greek musical notes. They are the same which the Abbé Barthelemy and other writers have noticed; but their history has never been illustrated. Besides these, he observed, in a manuscript of very diminutive size, the curious work of Phile upon animals, containing an account of the ibis, bound up with twenty-three other tracts upon a great variety of subjects. After removing these volumes from a quantity of theological writings, detached fragments, worm-eaten wooden covers (that had belonged to books once literally bound in boards), scraps of parchment lives of hermits, and other litter, all further inquiry was stopped by the promptitude and caution of Mr. Riley, who told us the Superior had agreed to sell the few articles we had selected, but that it would be impossible to purchase more; and that even these would be lost, if we ventured to expose them to the observation of any of the inhabitants of the town. Then telling us what sum he had agreed to give for them, he concealed two of the smaller volumes in the folds of his Turkish habit, entrusting to the humour of the two calloyers the task of conveying the others on board our vessel in the harbour. Upon this honour, it must be confessed, we did not rely with so much confidence as we ought to have done; but as there was no other method which promised any chance of success, we were forced to comply; and we left, as we believed, the most valuable part of our acquisition in very doubtful hands. Just as we had concluded this bargain, the French Commissary returned; and finding us busied in the library, afforded an amusing specimen of the sort of system pursued by his countrymen, upon such occasions. "Do you find," said he, "any thing worth your notice, among all this rubbish?" We answered, that there were many things we would gladly purchase, "Purchase! he added, "I should never think of purchasing from such a herd of swine. If I saw any thing I might require, I should, without ceremony, put it in my pocket, and say, Bonjour!"

After this, some keys were produced, belonging to an old chest that stood opposite to the door of the library; and we were shown a few antiquities which the monks had been taught to consider as valuable. Among these, the first thing they showed to us was an original letter from the emperor Alexius Comnenus, concerning the establishment of their monastery, inscribed upon a large roll, and precisely corresponding, in the style of the manuscript, with the fragment preserved by Montfaucon, in his *Palaeographia*. Besides this, were other rolls of record, the deeds of succeeding emperors, with their seals affixed, relating to the affairs of the convent. We calculated the number of volumes in the library to be about a thousand; and of this number, above two hundred were in manuscript. After we had left the library, we saw, upon a shelf in the refectory, the most splendid manuscript of the whole collection, in two folio volumes, richly adorned: it was called the *Theology* of Gregory Nazianzus, and purported to be throughout in the handwriting of the emperor Alexius. Nothing could be more beautiful. As a singular circumstance, it may also be mentioned, that we saw upon the same shelf, and by the side of this, a manuscript of the writings of Gregory's greatest admirer, Erasmus.

The Cave of the Apocalypse

As we descended from the great Monastery of St. John, we turned off, upon our right, to visit a smaller edifice of the same nature, erected over a cave or grot, where the *Apocalypse*, attributed to that evangelist, is said to have been written. It can hardly be considered as any other than a hermitage, and it is entirely dependent upon the principal monastery. As to the cave itself, whence this building derives its origin, and to which it owes all its pretended sanctity, it may be supposed that any other cave would have answered the purpose fully as well: it is not spacious enough to have afforded a habitation even for a hermit; and there is not the slightest probability that any thing related concerning it, by the monks, is founded in truth…

It affords another striking proof: in addition to many already enumerated, that there is no degree of absurdity too gross for the purposes of *altarage* and superstition. There seemed to be something like a school held in the building erected about this cave; but the only monk who showed the place to us, and who appeared to superintend the seminary, was not much better informed than his godly brethren in the parent monastery.

A Discontented Ally

Descending from this place towards the Port of La Scalla, we were met by several of the Frenchmen, coming with the commissary to invite us to dinner: so grateful were they for the attention paid to their request, and the consequent safety of their baggage, that each seemed to strive with the other who could render us the greater civility. We accepted their invitation; and were conducted into a warehouse near the quay, where a large table was prepared, with fish, wine, and biscuit. Here we found several French women, conversing with their usual gaiety; and we all sat down together. During dinner, the conversation turned upon the events that had happened in Egypt: and, as each began to boast of his personal prowess in the late campaign, some contradictions took place, and a most turbulent scene of dispute ensued. In the midst of this, a figure entered the warehouse, whose appearance silenced the whole party, and was particularly gratifying to our curiosity. It was Barthelemy, the famous Greek pirate, who engaged in the French service under Buonaparte, and was chief of a regiment of Mamelukes in Egypt. His figure was uncommonly martial and dignified: he wore the Mameluke dress, and carried a large knotted club as a walking-staff. Placing himself at the table, he began to complain, in a very hoarse voice, of the treatment he had experienced, which he stated to be contrary to the most solemn stipulations; contrary to his deserts; and highly dishonourable to the French army, for whom he had fought so many battles, and made such important sacrifices. They made free, it seemed, with his women; of whom, he had many, that he was conveying, as his property, to France. One or two of the principal persons present tried to pacify him, by the assurance that he should not be molested in future; and filling a large goblet of wine, proposed to him to drink "Success to the Republic, and the liberation of Greece." The wary old corsair did not appear to relish the toast; and had probably, by this time, both heard and seen quite enough of Gallic emancipation.

A Stupid Impatience Subsequently Regretted

This being the evening of the sixth day since our first arrival in Patmos, and perhaps being as well acquainted with it as if we had spent a year in its examination, we became impatient to leave it; and began to fancy that as our caïque was hired by the month, its owners would create as much delay as possible, and loiter in port when they might safely venture out. Accordingly, after midnight, having roused the captain, we told him that it was a fine night, and that we wished he would put to sea. This man was one of the most experienced pilots of the Archipelago, and as worthy a Greek as ever navigated these seas; but we had not at that time learned to place the confidence in him which he so highly deserved. He was very poor; and having become a widower in an early period of his life, had suffered his beard to grow, according to the manner of mourning in his native island of Casos, wearing, at the same time a black turban. Without making any answer to our proposal, he continued for the space of a minute, looking up attentively, with his eyes fixed towards the zenith. Presently he shook his head; and pointing upwards, with his arms extended, asked us, how we liked the sky? As it seemed to be very clear, and there were many stars visible, we replied that there was every sign of fair weather. Do you not see," said he, "some small clouds; which now and then make their appearance, and instantly afterwards vanish?" We confessed that we did; but rather hastily insisted that instead of peering after signs in the sky, he should get the vessel out of harbour as speedily as possible. His only comment upon this order, so inconsiderately given, was a summons to his companions to heave the anchor, and hoist the sails.

We had barely light enough to steer through the narrow channel at the entrance, without running against the rocks; and we had no sooner cleared the port, than there fell a dead calm. A prodigious sea, tossing our vessel in all directions, soon convinced us of the nature of the situation for which we had exchanged our snug berth but a few minutes before. Surrounded as we had been by the lofty cliffs of the island, we had not the most distant conception of the turbulent sea we should encounter. Our steady helmsman endeavoured in vain to keep the prow of his vessel to any particular point; and calling to our interpreter, bade him notice what he termed, in Greek, "the belching of the deep." This happens during the roll of a calm, when a wave, lifted to a great height, suddenly subsides, with a deep and hollow sound, like air bursting through a narrow channel. Our apprehensions had already got the better of our indifference to such observations; and in a very different tone of voice from that in which we had ordered him out of port, we asked the Captain, what that noise denoted? He calmly replied, that it was generally considered as a bad omen; but that he more disliked the appearance which he had desired us to notice before we left the harbour. Being by this time heartily sick of our usurped authority, we begged that he would be guided in future by the dictates of his own experience; and, further, requested that he would put back into port. This he affirmed to be impossible; that he would not venture towards a lee-shore during the night for any consideration. We prepared therefore to suffer, as we had deserved, for our extreme folly and rashness, and, strange as it may seem, not without many an anxious thought for the ancient manuscripts we had on board. The crew lighted a wax taper before a small picture of some saint in the foreship; all the after-part of the hold being occupied by our cots and baggage. Here, when we endeavoured to lie down for rest, we were overrun by swarms or stinking cockroaches; we remained therefore sitting upon some planks that we had placed to serve as a floor, with our heads touching the roof which the deck afforded, sustaining the violent motion of the vessel, and anxiously expecting the coming of the morning.

1870s-80s The Rev. Henry Fanshawe Tozer
A Haphazard Collection of Buildings

Tozer points here to the surprising (to someone from Western Europe) lack of any monumental quality in the vast majority of the monastery buildingsof Greece

With the exception of one or two Greek monasteries which are built in the interior of caverns - such as those of Megaspelaeon in the Morea and Sumelas at the back of Trebizond - none that I can remember is so closely and strangely packed together as that of St. John on Patmos; its staircases are quite a puzzle, and passages occur in the most unexpected places, and diverge in a variety of directions. The court round which it is built is very irregular in shape, and several pointed arches are thrown across it to strengthen the buildings on either side: within it are numerous cisterns for storing water and troughs for washing. The upper part is a wilderness of chimneys, bells, domes, and battlements. A pavement of tiles or flags covers the flat roof, or rather roofs, for different parts have different levels, and the communication between these is made by steps constructed at various angles.

Kalymnos

Mid-1850s Charles T. Newton

Wretched Isolation

You cannot imagine any isolation more complete than that of an European compelled to sojourn in such an island in winter time. It is something like living at the bottom of a well and seeing the same bit of sky every day. The winter has been an unusually severe one.

The house I lived in, though once the residence of a Greek archbishop, was a wretched squalid barrack with no glass in the windows. The roof being flat and covered with earth, the rain in wet weather dripped through on to my pillow. There being no fireplace, I could only keep myself warm by cowering over an earthen pan just 8 inches in diameter filled with charcoal.

After standing all day watching my workmen in the field, I was generally obliged to take an active part in the cooking of my own supper, in which I had the assistance of my trusty Albanian cavasso To obtain every day wholesome food and fuel was a business requiring much forethought and trouble; and the absolute necessity of exerting myself in order to exist kept my mind from the utter stagnation into which it would otherwise have fallen, from the extreme monotony and eventless character of the life I led. My communications with the outer world of civilization were carried on by stray caiques which sometimes wandered about the Archipelago for many days unable to pass Cape Crio, but which ultimately succeeded in conveying to me huge packets of letters and newspapers from Rhodes...

The Sponge Divers

The first sheet of this letter has been at the bottom of the sea in several fathoms water. The caique in which it was despatched to Rhodes was capsized by the carelessness of the captain, and sank. The Calymniote divers, notwithstanding the coldness of the weather, contrived to descend several fathoms, fasten ropes to the caique, and drag it into shallow water. The inhabitants of Calymnos, like those of Syme, Chalce, and other small islands near Rhodes, are celebrated as divers, and spend the whole summer in fishing up sponges on the coasts of Asia Minor and Syria. In the month of May a little fleet of caiques sets sail from Calymnos, manned by the greater part of the able-bodied male population. The profits of the sponge-fishery are very considerable. The divers in each caique enter into partnership. They are generally poor men, and the money for rigging out the caiques and for the, maintenance of the crew during their voyage is lent to them by the richer Calymniotes, who stay at home and trade in sponges. On the return of the caiques in the autumn, the merchants who made the advances to the divers reimburse themselves by purchasing the produce of the season at a price very much below the real value of each cargo. The sponge-merchant then sends his sponges direct to Smyrna, Syra, or Trieste, where they are repurchased by the great traders who supply the European market; and thus, when the sponge arrives in England, the price, after passing through so many hands, is very much raised. But the cause of the dearness of sponges is the great risk of life and capital incurred in the first instance. The diver descends, holding a flat stone in both hands, to assist him in sinking, on which stone a cord is fastened. When he gets to the bottom, he puts this flat stone under his arm, and walks about in search of sponges, putting them in a net hung round his neck, as fast as he uproots them; he then pulls the cord as a signal, and is drawn up again. It is said that the best divers they can remain under water for as long a period as three minutes. From inquiries which I have made, it does not appear that they are often cut off by sharks, though these monsters are not infrequent in the southern part of the .Archipelago. It is possible that the rapid descent of the diver may scare away this fish, who generally seizes his prey on the surface. A Calymniote told me that the most terrible sensation he had, ever experienced was finding himself close to an immense fish at the bottom of the sea. Under the root of the sponge is a parasitical substance of a caustic nature. This often bursts when the sponge is suspended round the diver's neck, and the liquid it contains causes deep ulcers in his flesh.

Before the sponges are exported, they are cleaned and spread out in fields to dry. In fine weather, many acres of sponges may be seen at Calymnos thus exposed. Part of the process of preparing them for the European market is the filling them with sand. The reason assigned for this singular practice is that, the sponges being always sold by weight, it was the practice fraudulently to increase the weight of the fine sponges by surreptitiously introducing a little sand. To meet this fraud, the sponge-merchants require all sponges to be filled with as much sand as they can hold; and as the quantity which each sponge can contain may be calculated, this amount is always deducted from the weight. The sand thus serves as a common measure...

The roving and varied life of the sponge-divers, and the address and courage required in their calling, render them very much more intelligent than the ordinary peasantry of the Sporades.

On the other hand, the large profits of the sponge fishery in good years rather lead them to despise agricultural pursuits, and they leave much of the operations of husbandry to be performed by women, passing their time in winter in the cafes, where they sit smoking over a pan of charcoal, and recounting the singular adventures which they have met with in the course of their rambles, and which give an Odyssean character to the lives of some of them. Most of the seafaring men bring back a pocketful of Greek coins after the summer cruise, and, from the variety of remote and unfrequented places which they visit, they often pick up very rare and curious specimens. There is no better place in the Archipelago to buy coins than this island immediately after the return of the sponge-divers in the autumn. I bought an interesting coin of Cilicia which was found in a cargo of wheat from Tarsus.

The New Town

In the old times, when the Archipelago swarmed with pirates, the Calymniotes dwelt in a fortified city perched on the top of a steep rock, as the inhabitants of Astypalaea do to this day. Sentinels were perpetually stationed on the hills to give a signal in case of the approach of pirates. This custom is curiously commemorated in the names of two of the highest mountains in the island, one of which is called *Vigli*, "the watch," the other *Mero Vigli*, "the day-watch."

Since the Greek War of Independence, the greater security of the Archipelago has led the Calymniotes to desert their old fortified city, and to build a new one a little lower down the mountain-side. This town is situated on the neck of land halfway between Linaria and the harbour of Pothia. At this latter place a second town is growing up, which will probably some day be the capital. The houses are very studiously whitewashed outside, and from their extreme regularity and uniformity of size, look, at a distance, like those cubes of chalk which are given to beginners to draw from. Inside, I missed the neatness and comparative cleanliness of the Rhodian peasant's house. Generally the house in Calymnos has two stories, in order to have more room for the stowage of sponges.

The Hard Life of Women and Children

There are hardly any shops. Each man lays up his own stock of provisions for the winter, so that a stranger has difficulty in existing at all, unless he has some friend to purvey for him. As from the scarcity of fodder there are very few beasts of burden, most of the necessaries of life imported into the island, such as corn, fuel, wine, and even timber and stone for building, have to be carried on the backs of men, and oftener of women and children, from the port to the higher town, a distance of about two miles. There are no fountains in the town of Calymnos; the wells are very deep, and at some distance from the town. When the supply of water gets low, the women descend to the bottom of the wells, inserting their hands and feet in the crevices between the stones on each side with great dexterity.

Nothing would be easier than to make a road for wheeled vehicles; but the Calymniotes are still very far from this stage of civilization. The constant labour of transport presses very heavily on the women, who are puny and undersized. They are usually married at the age of fourteen, and sometimes as early as twelve. It is a common sight to see a young girl, herself a mere child, tottering under the weight of a sack of flour or load of wood, under which, slung in a kind of scarf, is a bambino so tightly swathed as to be no more than a flexible cylinder. Many of these children die off when they are very young, from imperfect nourishment, dirt, and general neglect. Those who are strong enough to pass the ordeal of so rough a nurture are left to shift for themselves at a very early age, and very soon take to the water like young spaniels.

The women of Calymnos, from always remaining in the island, are very much less civilized than the men. Their dialect is very barbarous and difficult to understand; but since the establishment of schools is gradually disappearing.

The Rigorous Fast

Fasts are kept in Calymnos with extraordinary rigour. When the caique was shipwrecked in which my former letter was sent, two of the passengers were drowned; the rest, who happened to be Franks, were fished out of the water and brought more dead than alive on shore into the house of a rich Greek merchant. It was bitterly cold December weather, and the Italian doctor, on being called in to restore the half-drowned survivors, immediately ordered some substantial food to be prepared for them. Their host then observed that, as it was one of the most strict fasts in the whole year, he had the greatest scruple in allowing animal food to be cooked in his house; but that, as a great favour, he would allow them a broth made of *butter stirred round in hot water*.

The Italian doctor here during the last great fast ventured to eat meat every day. This was an offence not to be forgiven. Stones and pieces of iron were thrown over the wall of his courtyard, with the remark that he might as well eat them as meat in Lent. One of these pieces of iron struck, his wife on the breast; and the family were kept in such constant fear that the doctor, being the possessor of a British passport, appealed to me for protection. I had no jurisdiction whatever in the island; but I did not hesitate to summon the Demarchia to my own house; and, rather to my surprise, they came. I remonstrated with them in very decided language, and told them that, after so much had been done by the Western powers for the protection of the Christians in the East, no one sect of Christians would be permitted to annoy or persecute another, and that religious toleration was the principle which we were resolved to maintain in the Turkish empire. The sleek primates listened with an air of extreme contrition, and apologized for the insult offered to the Italian doctor, which, they said, had been the work of some boys. I remember, when the Turks at Rhodes last year took to menacing the Christians, the same excuse was offered. It is always the children who are put forward on these occasions in the Levant to commence a war of petty insults and annoyances.

Kos

1609-10 William Lithgow
The Watchful Islanders

South-east from this lieth the isle of Coos now Lango: by the Turks called Stanccow, the capital town is Arango, where Hypocrates and Apelles the Painter were born. In this isle, there is a wine named by the Greeks, Hyppocon, that excelleth in sweetness all other wines except the Malvasie, and it aboundeth in cypress and turpentine trees. There is here a part of the isle uninhabited, in regard of a contagious lake, that infecteth the air, both Summer, and Winter. There is abundance of alloes found here, so much esteemed by our pothecaries; the rest of this isle shall be touched in the own place.

And near to Lango, lieth the isle Giara, now Stopodia, it is begirded with rocks and deserted, unto which the Romans were wont to send in banishment such as deserved death. In general of these isles Cyclads, because they are so near one to another, and each one in sight of another, there are many corsairs and Turkish galleots, that still afflict these islanders: Insomuch that the inhabitants are constrained to keep watch day and night, upon the tops of the most commodious mountains, to discover these pirates; which they easily discern from other vessels, both because of their sails and oars. And whensoever discovered, according to the number of cursary boats, they make as many fires, which giveth warning to all the ports to be on guard. And if the sea voyagers in passing see no sign on these isles, of fire or smoke, then they perfectly know, these labyrinthine seas, are free from pestilent raveners.

1674 Father Jacques-Paul Babbin, S.J.
"A Most Delicate Shade"

The great plane tree described by Babbin still exists. Naturally, it is now called the plane tree of Hippocrates. Although this is extremely unlikely, it may be the oldest tree in Europe, and it is customary to touch it for good luck on the first day of September every year.

Stanco formerly called Coos, is a very large island near eighty miles about, lying to the west of the Bay of Halicarnassos. Though Rhodes exceeds it in bigness, this doth that as much in beauty; most part of it being low land, in comparison to the other islands about it. Here are woods of cypress trees, of a great many years standing, and the Turks are so pleased with them that they will not suffer them to be cut down. The inhabitants are Turks, Greeks, and some Jews. There are several villages inhabited by the Greeks, and one large town, with a strong castle, near the haven which hath the name of the island. A little above the castle is a very large, and rich Seraglio for the Governor; close to which runs a small rivulet, which is very clear, and not deep. Here are twenty very large plane trees, that make a most delicate shade, and being on a rising ground may be seen at a great distance. Here is one very large tree which the Turks call *Kavak agatz*, the body is above thirty foot about, spreading its boughs to a great distance, under the boughs are twelve very stately marble pillars to support them; but it appears they were for a temple, for part of a wall is yet remaining. The Turks make this their place for recreation in hot weather, there being several shops for barbers, and where coffee and sherbet is sold, The river head is within musket shot of these trees. At each side are many pleasant gardens full of all sorts of delicious fruits. Oranges and lemons are in great abundance; lemons are sold for half a dollar the thousand. All ships that go from Constantinople and those parts, bound to Egypt, or that come from Egypt and bound upwards, usually call in here, it being almost the midway between Rhodes and Scio. The Port is secured with a good moat, which (to wonder) is kept in repair. No Christian is suffered to go into the castle, so the Cadde hath his house without. Every night here is very good watch kept, and the privateers dare not venture to come near, for here are galleys, or ships of Barbary almost continually. In some maps I find this island called Lango; from whence they derive the word I know not; for as the Turks call it Stancoi the Greeks do Stincos.

1801 Edward Daniel Clarke

A "Guilty Island"

A remarkable case was tried while we were in Cos; and a statement of the circumstance on which it was founded will serve to exhibit a very singular part of the Mohammedan law; namely, that which relates to "Homicide by implication."

An instance of a similar nature was before noticed, when it was related that the Capudan Pasha reasoned with the people of Samos upon the propriety of their paying for a Turkish frigate which was wrecked upon their territory; "because the accident would not have happened unless their island had been in the way." This was mentioned as a characteristic feature of Turkish justice, and so it really was; that is to say, it was a sophistical application of a principle rigidly founded upon the fifth species of homicide, according to the Mohammedan law; or "Homicide by an intermediate Cause," which is strictly the name it bears. The case which occurred at Cos fell more immediately under the cognisance of this law. It was as follows.

A young man desperately in love with a girl of Stanchio, earnestly sought to marry her; but his proposals were rejected. In consequence of his disappointment, he bought some poison and destroyed himself. The Turkish police instantly arrested the father of the young woman, as the cause, by implication, of the man's death: under the fifth species of homicide, he became therefore amenable for this act of suicide. When the cause came before the Magistrate, it was urged literally by the accusers, that "If he, the accused, had not had a daughter, the deceased would not have fallen in love; consequently, he would not have been disappointed; consequently, he would not have swallowed poison; consequently, he would not have died :- but he, the accused, had a daughter; and the deceased had fallen in love ; and had been disappointed; and had swallowed poison; and had died... Upon all these counts, he was called upon to pay the price of the young man's life; and this being fixed at the sum of eighty piastres, was accordingly exacted.

Depopulation

The population of Cos had much diminished of late years. There were formerly 20,000 inhabitants; and of this number only eight or ten thousand now remained. Three thousand had been carried off by a severe plague the year before; and great numbers had been drafted, to serve as soldiers in the war.

Syme

c.1680 Bernard Randolph

The Skill of the Sponge-Divers

Their chief livelihood is by diving for sponges, of which they make great merchandise, supplying all parts in the Levant, from whence they are brought to most places in Europe. They will dive fifteen fathom under water, being brought up to this profession from their childhood. They reckon those the best of men who can keep longest under water.

I was a passenger in the *Zante* frigate with Captain Robert Wilkinson from Venice to Constantinople. Through bad weather we sprang a leak, which we could not stop unless we landed most of our goods. Being at anchor in the port of Milo, and continually pumping, an old Greek priest told the captain that he would undertake to get a man that should stop the leak, though it were at the keel of the ship. The Captain offered him fifty pieces of eight to get it done out of hand. Next morning the priest brings one of the islanders. He took a good swig at the bottle, and by our directions he soon found out the hole. He ordered a piece of lead to be cut square, and daubed with oakham and tar, which he nailed over the leak, so as our ship was again very sound. He first put the nails into the lead, then diving, by degrees drove them into the ship's side. He was sometimes a minute under water.

When they hear of any vessels being cast away, the first fair weather, they go to the place and agree with the inhabitants to whom they give the tenths of what they shall get and keep the rest. The Bassha of Candia gave them two hundred dollars for diving to get the guns of the *Thersia*, a French ship blown up at Standia.

1812-15 William Turner

Island Peculiarities

It is perhaps on the smaller islands that the divergence of customs occasioned when small communities live in some degree of isolation from each other becomes most evident.

I went in the morning to the principal coffee-house, a large naked chamber, with broad high-raised platform on each side, on which were sitting crowds of Greeks playing at drafts, backgammon, and a game called magala. Here I found a Greek doctor dressed as an European, who had studied medicine in Pisa, (whence he had a regular diploma,) and was a sensible well-informed man. I was glad to contract his acquaintance, to ask him a few questions, especially as our illustrious consul was by no means of brilliant abilities, and had a systematic habit of not answering to a question till it had been asked him three times. I walked a good deal about the town in the day-time, and in the evening went with the old gentleman and two of his grand-children ... to church, where I was witness to a custom which I never saw before. The men alone entered the church; the women remained praying outside; (they are never admitted inside till the men have left it.) The pavement of the churchyard consisted of tombstones and each woman brought to the grave of him in whom she was interested, a lantern, and a small pot of incense, which she waved over it, and then setting them down on it remained praying and crossing herself over the tomb as long as the church-service lasted, when she went away with the rest, taking the lantern and incense with her. There were above twenty women thus employed. The Greeks assured me that this was a general custom, but could not be everywhere followed, as the Turks would not allow them to have their churchyards by the side of their churches...

From questions and observation, I have obtained the following information respecting Symi. The island is only nominally governed by the Aga deputed from Rhodes: The real power is in the hands of about twenty chief Greek families, (distinguished by riches,) of whom an unfixed number govern by rotation under the title of *proxenoi* and without the consent of these the Aga can do nothing. These families are all at daggers drawn with each other, but a majority always decides on the just rotation of the candidates. The *Proesti* dictate to the Aga, (in whose name every thing is done,) all the affairs of the people, what duties are to be paid, whether a Greek ought to be punished, etc., and the Aga always finds it his interest to be well with the Greeks. In consequence the islanders enjoy entire liberty, and are subject to no vexations; the Aga being the only Mussulman resident in the island. The only inhabitants of the island, (except the priests of three Greek convents,) live in the town, (there being no villages) which is built near the top of a high rocky mountain, and contains from 1,800 to 2,000 houses.

The island, consisting almost exclusively of mountains of rock, produces nothing except a little fruit in a few gardens of the richer inhabitants: every necessary of life is imported, and the sea being their only resource, all the men of the placc are naturally seamen. There are belonging to the island fifty large saccolevas and as many small fishing boats; and it would seem that their gains abroad are great, for though this is the Greek Christmas fast, (of forty days,) and the stationary inhabitants would pay any sum in reason for fish, the sailors will not go out to bring them a supply, and on an average not above fifty okes of fish a day are brought into the town. They might gain greatly by going to fish at Rhodes. where there are great quantities of fish, but no fishers; but they fear, least the Turks of Rhodes should compel them to work gratis, and detain them there. While the men are thus abroad, gaining by a carrying trade between Smyma, Constantinople, Salonica, etc., all the domestic affairs of the island are carried on by women, who are the porters, bakers, butchers, shopkeepers, etc., of the place. I never was more astonished than when on telling George to find a porter to bring up my trunk (weighing about forty pounds) from the scala to the town, I saw him enter followed by an old woman of sixty carrying it on her back, and for having brought it up that steep rocky hill of a mile's length - which I would not have done myself for fifty pounds - I was told I was to pay her three paras, and when I offered her twenty, I could hardly persuade the old lady to take them, for she said it was a shame.

c. 1820 William Rae Wilson

An Unusual Fashion in Hats

Many of the women emigrate to Rhodes, and are employed there as servants. They are remarkable for their very singular head dress consisting of a great quantity of small handkerchiefs tied one over the other. They begin with one or two, and as their wealth accumulates increase their number till the head is at least swelled out to an enormous size and most uncouth shape.

Rhodes

1599 Thomas Dallam

Hostages to a Disappointed Turk

This town is double-walled, betwixt the walls the distance of a pair of short boats, and the ditch is very deep, but dry. To be short, having past around about the town without any contradiction or stare, only the time that we drank a pitcher of wine which cost us but one penny, we made haste unto the seaside, and so to go aboard. When we were without the gate, looking for our boat, we see it coming of from our ship. When it came to the shore, there was in it Mr. Maye, our preacher, and one that was appointed to be our ambassador's under butler. Quoth Mr. Maye to me: "Are you ready to go aboard?" "Yea, truly!" said I; "for I am very hungry and weary with travel." "I pray you," said he, "go back again with me to the gate, that I may but see the superscription over it, and set one foot within the gate, and then I will go back again with you." So we went all back with Mr. Maye to the gate. When we were there, he saw afar off a fountain of water, made like one of our conduits, with a fair, bright dish of steel hanging on a chain, for the Turks drink nothing but water. "I pray you," quoth he Mr. Maye, go with me to yonder fountain, that I may drink some of that water, for it seemeth to be very good, and I have a great desire to drink some of it. So we went all with him to the fountain, and every one of us did drink a dish of water. As we were a drinking, there came unto us two stout Turks, and said: "Parlye Francko, sinyore?" which is: "Can ye speak Italian, sinyor?" So quoth Mr. Maye. So, as there were a talking, I looked about me, and a Turk, sitting upon his stall, who did know me - for he had heard me play on my virginals and kissed me aboard our ship - he beckoned me to come unto him; and when I came somewhat near him, in kindness and some love he bore unto me, made me a sign to be gone; and pointed to the gate, and bid me make haste. So to the gate went I as fast as I could trudge, and my mate Harvie and the rest of my company followed after as fast as they could; leaving Mr. Maye and the under butler talking with the Turks, for they too could speak Italian a little, and so could none of us. When we were gotten without the gate we looked back towards the fountain, but we see nobody there; for the Turks had carried Mr. Maye and the other man to prison. By chance we found our boat and sailors there ready, and aboard our ship we went. When we came aboard, I went presently to our master, and told him all that had happened. When I told him how I had been about the town, he imagined that we by that means had given some offence; because it is dangerous for a stranger, being a Christian, to take a view of that town, and so thought that for our fault these men were taken prisoners. What words did pass betwixt our master and me I will omit till God send us into Inglande. No man durst be so bold as to go ashore all that day, neither did any come aboard us.

The next morning a little Greek boat came from the town aboard our ship with a letter from Mr. Maye, directed not only to our master and merchants, but also to the rest of their company. This letter was written so pitifully, as if there had been prisoners there seven years: showing how they were taken from the fountain and coupled together, like as they had been two dogs, with a chain of cold rusty iron, and led into a dark dungeon, their chain fastened with a staple unto a post where they must continually stand, and nether sit nor kneel, and every two hours were shaken over them whips made of wire, threatening most cruel punishment; and therefore desired that by all means they would seek some means for their speedy release, or else that they might be presently put to death, for they were not able to endure that miserable life and sharp punishment, which was likely to be inflicted upon them if the ship did once depart. Our master and merchants were so wounded with reading this letter, and pitying the prisoners' case, and banishing all fear, they resolved to go ashore. Our master and five merchants having made themselves as brave as they could, they went ashore very stoutly to the Captain's house, desiring to speak with the Chial, the Captain bassha his deputy, who after he had made them to stay while he came unto them to know the cause of their coming, one of our men that could best speak Italian told him that they found themselves very much aggrieved that their men should be stayed as prisoners, and not to be informed of the cause; and likewise wondered how they durst be so bold as to make stay of any one of our men, we being going with so rich a present to the Grand Seigneur, and those two men which they had stayed were two special men, one of them our divine and preacher, the other the chief and principal man for the present. This, with other words, they said to fear them; also they said that if he would not presently deliver those men, they would hire a galley and send to the Grand Seigneur, that he might understand how they were wronged and hindered in their voyage without any occasion given to our knowledge.

The Answer of the Chial was this: "Yesterday I was aboard your ship presenting my Captain's person in his absence; you gave me not such entertainment as my place did require; you made me no good cheer, nether did you give me a present for my captain."

Our men answered: "The best entertainment that we could give unto you for the time you had; good cheer we could make you none, for we had nothing for ourselves. Our coming to this place was to have some relief here, and to furnish our selves with such victuals as this country yieldeth for our money. Whereas you say that you had no present for your Captain, you say not truly, for you had so much abroad cloth as would make your captain a vest. But than said the chial: I had none for myself, and one will I have before you have your men." Then said they: "Is that all the occasion that moved you to imprison our men? And will the gift of such a present give you content that we may have our men?"

"Yea, surely," said the chiao. And so this quarrel was ended. Here you are see the base and covetous condition of these rude and barbarous dogged Turks, and how little they do regard Christians.

This city wall which is next unto the sea is marvellous strong, and so fortified with great ordinance, not upon the wall, but their noses do look through the wall, so placed that no ship can pass on that side of the land without leave. Within the town, in most streets, a man cannot trot a horse, the streets lie so full of bullets, made of marble; and of all sizes, from 16 inches to 3 inches. Many other things concerning this city and land I do omit till my return into Inglande; but of all the towns or cities that in my life I have seen, for strength I never saw the like.

Now, having redeemed our men out of prison, the next day being the 30th, or last day of June, we weighed anchor, hoisted sail, and so to sea.

1609-10 William Lithgow

A Murderous Rainstorm

This Isle of Rhodes within the space of twenty-five years was three times mightily endangered by violent and extreme impetuosities of rain: in such sort that the last flood did drown the greatest part of the inhabitants: which beginning in the springtime, did continue to summer, and in all this time, it broke violently down their houses, and in the night killed the people lying in their beds; and in the day time such as were sheltered under safeguard of their dwellings: which was a miserable destruction, and the like of it scarcely heard of since the universal deluge.

But true it is, as these ominous judgements falling upon particular parts and parcels of people, are justly executed; yet they serve for caveats for all others in general, (sin being the original of all) to take heed of offending the Creator, in abusing the best use of the creature.

1755 C-É. Savary

The Play of Light

The isle of Rhodes is now in full view, and presents a range of hills resembling an amphitheatre, and terminated by a lofty mountain. We are going as near the wind as possible, and with a crowd of sail, to gain the harbour .But we shall not reach it before night. Already the sun is setting behind the mountains, which hide him from us, while his radiant beams still streak the clouds with gold and purple! How vivid are their colours! Some of them concentring thousands of his rays, again reflect them, and resemble globes of fire floating through the air. Others, the lower parts of which are entirely dark, assume the appearance of dusky mountains of various forms, and emit, from their luminous points, the flash of the ruby, or the fire of the topaz, some opening in the centre, and edged with the brightest and liveliest colours, exhibit the azure of the sky set in gold. Others diversified with satiny stripes, are slightly bounded with a yellowish border. How admirable, how magnificent, is this scene! What a sublime idea does it give of Him who said, Let there be light, and there was light! Night has thrown her dark veil over this glorious picture, yet the eye remains still fixed on the heavens, and the soul still feels deeply penetrated with sentiments of admiration and gratitude. How great are the works of the Creator! and how feeble the conceptions of man!

c.1830 Alphonse de Lamartine

An Indolent Air

The impression surpasses that from the horizons of Greece; - one feels a milder atmosphere; the sea and the sky are tinged with a calmer and paler blue; nature defines herself in more majestic masses! I breathe, and feel my entrance into a wider and loftier region! Greece is small - it is tormented and despoiled - it is the skeleton of a dwarf! - here is that of a giant! Dark forests stain the sides of the mountains of Marmoriza, and one sees from afar white torrents of foam falling into the profound ravines of Caramania.

Rhodes springs up like a verdant nosegay from the bosom of the waves; the light and graceful minarets of its white mosques rear themselves above its forests of palms, carobs, sycamores, planes, and fig-trees; they attract from a distance the mariner's eye to those delicious retreats or the Turkish cemeteries; where are to be seen, every evening, Mussulmans stretched out on the turf that covers the tomb of their friends, and quietly smoking and chatting, like sentries waiting till they are relieved, like indolent men that love to lie down in bed, and make an essay of sleep before the hour of their last repose. At ten o'clock in the morning, our brig was suddenly surrounded by five or six Turkish frigates, under full sail, that were cruising off Rhodes. One of them approached within hail, and interrogated us in French; they saluted us politely, and we soon came to an anchor in the roadstead of Rhodes, in the midst of thirty-six men-of-war of the Capitan-Pacha, Halil Pacha. Two French vessels of war, one a steamer, *Le Sphinz*, commanded by Captain Sarlat, the other a corvette, *L' Actéon*, commanded by Captain Vaillant, were lying at anchor not far from us.

The officers came on board to ask us the news from Europe. In the evening we delivered our thanks to M. d'Ornano, the commander of the brig *Le Génie* - he proceeded on his return with the *Actéon*. We were now to continue our voyage alone to Cyprus and Syria.

I passed two days at Rhodes in examining this first specimen we had of a Turkish town - the oriental character of the bazaars, or Moorish shops, of carved wood - the street of the Knights, where every house still preserves uninjured, over the door, the escutcheons of the ancient families of France, Spain, Italy, and Germany. Rhodes presents some fine remains of its antique fortifications; the rich Asiatic vegetation with which they are crowned and enveloped, imparts to them more grace and beauty than those of Malta can lay claim to - an Order that could allow itself to be expelled from such a magnificent possession, received its death-blow! Heaven seems to have formed this island as an advanced post on Asia - a European power that should be mistress of it, would hold at the same time the key of the Archipelago, of Greece, Smyrna, the Dardanelles, and of the Egyptian and Syrian seas. I know not in the world either a finer military maritime position, or a lovelier sky, or a more smiling and fertile land. The Turks have impressed upon them that character of inaction and indolence which they carry everywhere! Every thing here is in a state of inertia, and in what may be called misery; but this people, who create nothing, who renew nothing, never break nor destroy any thing either - they at least allow nature to act freely around them - they respect trees even in the very middle of the streets, and of the houses which they inhabit; water and shade, the lulling murmur and voluptuous coolness, are their first, their only wants. Thus, as soon as you approach a land possessed by Mahomedans, whether in Europe or in Asia, you recognise from afar the rich and sombre verdure which covers it, the trees for shade, the spouting fountains for lulling to repose, the silence, and the mosques with their light minarets rising at every step from the bosom of a religious soil - it is all that is necessary to this people. They leave this soft and philosophic apathy only to mount their desert coursers, the first servants of man, and fearlessly to rush upon death for their prophet and their God. The dogma of fatalism has made them the bravest people on the earth, and although existence may be to them both light and pleasant, that promised by the Koran as the reward of a life given up for its sake is the more prized, from their requiring but one weak effort to throw themselves from this to the celestial world, which they see before them redolent in beauty, repose, and love! It is the religion of heroes - but this religion grows faint in the faith of the Mussulman, and heroism is extinguished with the faith which is its principle, so that as the people shall believe , less either in a dogma or an idea, they will die less willingly and less nobly. It is as in Europe; why die if life avails more than death, if there is no immortal gain from the sacrifice to duty? Thus war will diminish and be abolished in Europe, until some faith shall reanimate and move the heart of man more highly than the base instinct of life.

The Women of Rhodes

The forms of women seated on the terraces by the light of the moon, are ravishing to behold. There is the eye of the Italian women, but softer, more timid, expressing more of tenderness and love; there is the figure of the Grecian women, but more rounded, more supple, with more gracious and winning motions. Their forehead is large, white, and polished, like that of the most beautiful women of England or of Switzerland, but the regular, straight, and high profile of the nose, gives to the countenance more majesty and nobleness. The Greek sculptors would have been yet more perfect, if they had taken their models or female figures from Asia! How sweet is it for a European, accustomed to the hard features, the studied and contracted expression of the women of Europe, especially of drawing-room women, to behold countenances as simple, pure, and smooth, as the marble broken from the quarry - countenances which have but one expression, the repose of tenderness, and which the eye can scan as quickly, and as easily, as the large type of some magnificent publication.

Society and civilisation are evidently enemies of physical beauty. They multiply impressions and sentiments too much; and as the features receive and involuntarily preserve their marks, they become complicated, and, as it were, adulterated; they acquire a certain confusion and uncertainty, which destroy their simplicity and their charm; they are like a tongue too, full of words, which is inarticulate because it is too rich.

Lady Hester Stanhope

A Traveller Marooned but Surviving

The contrast of this passage with the previous one in tone serves to remind us that what is perceived as the characteristic atmosphere of a place is to some extent generated from within the traveller.

I write one line by a ship which came in here for a few days, just to tell you we are all safe and well. Starving thirty hours on a bare rock, even without fresh water, being half-naked and drenched with wet, having traversed an almost trackless country, over dreadful rocks and mountains; partly on foot and partly on a mule for eight hours, laid me up at a village for a few days: but I have since crossed the island on an ass, going for six hours a day, which proves I am pretty well now at least.

The Consul here is a dear old fellow of seventy five, who thinks he cannot do too much for us; but the bey pretends to be so poor, that he cannot give us more than £30, which will neither clothe nor feed eleven people for long; so we must send an express to Smyrna to get what we want. My locket, and the valuable snuff box Lord Sligo gave me, are all I have saved; -all the travelling equipage for Syria, etc., all gone; -the servants naked and unarmed: but the great loss of all is the medicine chest, which saved the lives of so many travellers in Greece. How to repair it, I know not. I expected more medicine out by Mr. Liston; but whether he has forwarded it, or kept it, I know not: if you could assist me in this once more, I should thank you much. I may be able to get a little at Smyrna, but I am told all the medicine shops were burnt by the late fire ...

Remember me most kindly to Mr. Taylor: tell him I make conquests of Turks everywhere. Here they are ten times more strict than in Constantinople; yet a Turk has lent me a house and bath in the middle of an orange-grove, where I go tomorrow. The houses on the outsides of the walls where Franks live are only fit for poultry.

1845 William Makepiece Thakeray

The Jewish Quarter

The sailing of a vessel direct for Jaffa brought a great number of passengers together, and our decks were covered with Christian, Jew, and Heathen. In the cabin we were Poles and Russians, Frenchmen, Germans, Spaniards, and Greeks; on the deck were squatted several little colonies of people of different race and persuasion. There was a Greek Papa, a noble figure with a flowing and venerable white beard, who had been living on bread-and-water for I don't know how many years, in order to save a little money to make the pilgrimage to Jerusalem. There were several families of Jewish Rabbis, who celebrated their "feast of tabernacles" on board; their chief men performing worship twice or thrice a day, dressed in their pontifical habits, and bound with phylacteries: and there were Turks, who had their own ceremonies and usages, and wisely kept aloof from their neighbours of Israel.

The dirt of these children of captivity exceeds all possibility of description; the profusion of stinks which they raised, the grease of their venerable garments and faces, the horrible messes cooked in the filthy pots, and devoured with the nasty fingers, the squalor of mats, pots, old bedding, and foul carpets of our Hebrew friends, could hardly be painted by Swift in his dirtiest mood, and cannot be, of course, attempted by my timid and genteel pen. What would they say in Baker Street to some sights with which our new friends favoured us? What would your ladyship have said if you had seen the interesting Greek nun combing her hair over the cabin — combing it with the natural fingers, and, averse to slaughter, flinging the delicate little intruders, which she found in the course of her investigation, gently into the great cabin? Our attention was a good deal occupied in watching the strange ways and customs of the various comrades of ours.

The Jews were refugees from Poland, going to lay their bones to rest in the valley of Jehoshaphat, and performing with exceeding rigour the offices of their religion. At morning and evening you were sure to see the chiefs of the families, arrayed in white robes, bowing over their books, at prayer. Once a week, on the eve before the Sabbath, there was a general washing in Jewry, which sufficed until the ensuing Friday. The men wore long gowns and caps of fur, or else broad-brimmed hats, or, in service time, bound on their heads little iron boxes, with the sacred name engraved on them. Among the lads there were some beautiful faces; and among the women your humble servant discovered one who was a perfect rosebud of beauty when first emerging from her Friday's toilet, and for a day or two afterwards, until each succeeding day's smut darkened those fresh and delicate cheeks of hers. We had some very rough weather in the course of the passage from Constantinople to Jaffa, and the sea washed over and over our Israelitish friends and their baggages and bundles; but though they were said to be rich, they would not afford to pay for cabin shelter. One father of a family, finding his progeny half drowned in a squall, vowed he WOULD pay for a cabin; but the weather was somewhat finer the next day, and he could not squeeze out his dollars, and the ship's authorities would not admit him except upon payment.

This unwillingness to part with money is not only found amongst the followers of Moses, but in those of Mahomet, and Christians too. When we went to purchase in the bazaars, after offering money for change, the honest fellows would frequently keep back several piastres, and when urged to refund, would give most dismally: and begin doling out penny by penny, and utter pathetic prayers to their customer not to take any more. I bought five or six pounds' worth of Broussa silks for the womankind, in the bazaar at Constantinople, and the rich Armenian who sold them begged for three-halfpence to pay his boat to Galata. There is something naif and amusing in this exhibition of cheatery — this simple cringing and wheedling, and passion for twopence-halfpenny. It was pleasant to give a millionaire beggar an alms, and laugh in his face and say, "There, Dives, there's a penny for you: be happy, you poor old swindling scoundrel, as far as a penny goes." I used to watch these Jews on shore, and making bargains with one another as soon as they came on board; the battle between vendor and purchaser was an agony — they shrieked, clasped hands, appealed to one another passionately; their handsome noble faces assumed a look of woe - quite an heroic eagerness and sadness about a farthing.

Ambassadors from our Hebrews descended at Rhodes to buy provisions, and it was curious to see their dealings: there was our venerable Rabbi, who, robed in white and silver, and bending over his book at the morning service, looked like a patriarch, and whom I saw chaffering about a fowl with a brother Rhodian Israelite. How they fought over the body of that lean animal! The street swarmed with Jews: goggling eyes looked out from the old carved casements - hooked noses issued from the low antique doors - Jew boys driving donkeys, Hebrew mothers nursing children, dusky, tawdry, ragged young beauties and most venerable grey-bearded fathers were all gathered round about the affair of the hen! And at the same time that our Rabbi was arranging the price of it, his children were instructed to procure bundles of green branches to decorate the ship during their feast. Think of the centuries during which these wonderful people have remained unchanged; and how, from the days of Jacob downwards, they have believed and swindled!

The Rhodian Jews, with their genius for filth, have made their quarter of the noble desolate old town the most ruinous and wretched of all. The escutcheons of the proud old knights are still carved over the doors, whence issue these miserable greasy hucksters and pedlars. The Turks respected these emblems of the brave enemies whom they had overcome, and left them untouched. When the French seized Malta they were by no means so delicate: they effaced armorial bearings with their usual hot-headed eagerness; and a few years after they had torn down the coats-of-arms of the gentry, the heroes of Malta and Egypt were busy devising heraldry for themselves, and were wild to be barons and counts of the Empire.

Remnants of Chivalry

The chivalrous relics at Rhodes are very superb. I know of no buildings whose stately and picturesque aspect seems to correspond better with one's notions of their proud founders. The towers and gates are warlike and strong, but beautiful and aristocratic: you see that they must have been high-bred gentlemen who built them.

The edifices appear in almost as perfect a condition as when they were in the occupation of the noble Knights of St. John; and they have this advantage over modern fortifications, that they are a thousand times more picturesque. Ancient war condescended to ornament itself, and built fine carved castles and vaulted gates: whereas, to judge from Gibraltar and Malta, nothing can be less romantic than the modern military architecture; which sternly regards the fighting, without in the least heeding the war-paint.

Some of the huge artillery with which the place was defended still lies in the bastions; and the touch-holes of the guns are preserved by being covered with rusty old corselets, worn by defenders of the fort three hundred years ago. The Turks, who battered down chivalry, seem to be waiting their turn of destruction now. In walking through Rhodes one is strangely affected by witnessing the signs of this double decay. For instance, in the streets of the knights, you see noble houses, surmounted by noble escutcheons of superb knights, who lived there, and prayed, and quarrelled, and murdered the Turks; and were the most gallant pirates of the inland seas; and made vows of chastity, and robbed and ravished; and, professing humility, would admit none but nobility into their order; and died recommending themselves to sweet St. John, and calmly hoping for heaven in consideration of all the heathen they had slain. When this superb fraternity was obliged to yield to courage as great as theirs, faith as sincere, and to robbers even more dexterous and audacious than the noblest knight who ever sang a canticle to the Virgin, these halls were filled by magnificent Pashas and Agas, who lived here in the intervals of war, and having conquered its best champions, despised Christendom and chivalry pretty much as

587

an Englishman despises a Frenchman. Now the famous house is let to a shabby merchant, who has his little beggarly shop in the bazaar; to a small officer, who ekes out his wretched pension by swindling, and who gets his pay in bad coin.

A Walk through the Town

All the town of Rhodes has this appearance of decay and ruin, except a few consuls' houses planted on the seaside, here and there, with bright flags flaunting in the sun; fresh paint; English crockery; shining mahogany, etc., - so many emblems of the new prosperity of their trade, while the old inhabitants were going to rack - the fine Church of St. John, converted into a mosque, is a ruined church, with a ruined mosque inside; the fortifications are mouldering away, as much as time will let them. There was considerable bustle and stir about the little port; but it was the bustle of people who looked for the most part to be beggars; and I saw no shop in the bazaar that seemed to have the value of a pedlar's pack.

I took, by way of guide, a young fellow from Berlin, a journeyman shoemaker, who had just been making a tour in Syria, and who professed to speak both Arabic and Turkish quite fluently - which I thought he might have learned when he was a student at college, before he began his profession of shoemaking; but I found he only knew about three words of Turkish, which were produced on every occasion, as I walked under his guidance through the desolate streets of the noble old town. We went out upon the lines of fortification, through an ancient gate and guard-house, where once a chapel probably stood, and of which the roofs were richly carved and gilded. A ragged squad of Turkish soldiers lolled about the gate now; a couple of boys on a donkey; a grinning slave on a mule; a pair of women flapping along in yellow papooshes; a basket-maker sitting under an antique carved portal, and chanting or howling as he plaited his osiers: a peaceful well of water, at which knights' chargers had drunk, and at which the double-boyed donkey was now refreshing himself—would have made a pretty picture for a sentimental artist. As he sits, and endeavours to make a sketch of this plaintive little comedy, a shabby dignitary of the island comes clattering by on a thirty-shilling horse, and two or three of the ragged soldiers leave their pipes to salute him as he passes under the Gothic archway.

The astonishing brightness and clearness of the sky under which the island seemed to bask, struck me as surpassing anything I had seen - not even at Cadiz, or the Piraeus, had I seen sands so yellow, or water so magnificently blue. The houses of the people along the shore were but poor tenements, with humble courtyards and gardens; but every fig-tree was gilded and bright, as if it were in an Hesperian orchard; the palms, planted here and there, rose with a sort of halo of light round about them; the creepers on the walls quite dazzled with the brilliancy of their flowers and leaves; The people lay in the cool shadows, happy and idle, with handsome solemn faces; nobody seemed to be at work; they only talked a very little, as if idleness and silence were a condition of the delightful shining atmosphere in which they lived.

We went down to an old mosque by the seashores, with a cluster of ancient domes hard by it, blazing in the sunshine, and carved all over with names of Allah, and titles of old pirates and generals who reposed there. The guardian of the mosque sat in the garden-court, upon a high wooden pulpit, lazily wagging his body to and fro, and singing the praises of the Prophet gently through his nose, as the breeze stirred through the trees overhead, and cast chequered and changing shadows over the paved court, and the little fountains, and the nasal psalmist on his perch. On one side was the mosque, into which you could see, with its white walls and cool-matted floor, and quaint carved pulpit and ornaments, and nobody at prayers. In the middle distance rose up the noble towers and battlements of the knightly town, with the deep sea-line behind them.

A Lotus Land

It really seemed as if everybody was to have a sort of sober cheerfulness, and must yield to indolence under this charming atmosphere. I went into the courtyard by the seashores (where a few lazy ships were lying, with no one on board), and found it was the prison of the place. The door was as wide open as Westminster Hall. Some prisoners, one or two soldiers and functionaries, and some prisoners' wives, were lolling under an arcade by a fountain; other criminals were strolling about here and there, their chains clinking quite cheerfully; and they and the guards and officials came up chatting quite friendly together, and gazed languidly over the portfolio, as I was endeavouring to get the likeness of one or two of these comfortable malefactors. One old and wrinkled she-criminal, whom I had selected on account of the peculiar hideousness of her countenance, covered it up with a dirty cloth, at which there was a general roar of laughter among this good-humoured auditory of cut-throats, pickpockets, and police-men. The only symptom of a prison about the place was a door, across which a couple of sentinels were stretched, yawning; while within lay three freshly-caught pirates - chained by the leg. They had committed some murders of a very late date, and were awaiting sentence; but their wives were allowed to communicate freely with them: and it seemed to me that if half-a-dozen friends would set them free, and they themselves had energy enough to move, the sentinels would be a great deal too lazy to walk after them.

The combined influence of Rhodes and Ramazan, I suppose, had taken possession of my friend the Schustergesell from Berlin. As soon as he received his fee, he cut me at once, and went and lay down by a fountain near the port, and ate grapes out of a dirty pocket-handkerchief. Other Christian idlers lay near him, dozing, or sprawling, in the boats, or listlessly munching watermelons. Along the coffee-houses of the quay sat hundreds more, with no better employment; and the captain of the *Iberia* and his officers, and several of the passengers in that famous steamship, were in this company, being idle with all their might. Two or three adventurous young men went off to see the valley where the dragon was killed; but others, more susceptible of the real influence of the island, I am sure would not have moved though we had been told that the Colossus himself was taking a walk half a mile off.

1850s Charles T. Newton

Inside a Rhodian House

On our way back we slept at a village near Rhodes called Koskino, one of the cleanest and most flourishing in the island. Here most of the inhabitants are muleteers, and own a little land besides. They are a thriving, active, fine-grown set of men, good specimens of the peasant proprietor.

Externally the house of the Rhodian peasant much resembles those in the villages of Malta. It is built of squared blocks of freestone, the door on one side, and very high up under the roof, two small windows. The roof is, flat, and supported inside by one large arch traversing the whole width of the house. The ceiling is made of reeds, over which outside is a thick bed of earth, which intercepts the fiercer rays of the sun, and, if duly rolled, keeps out the winter rain.

Internally, the house forms one large room very destitute of furniture. In one corner is the nuptial bed, raised high above the floor on a kind of platform; in another corner the fireplace. The wall opposite the door is ornamented with an imposing array of plates of the old Lindos ware, each hung by a string. They are for ornament, not for use, and form part of the dower which every bride brings with her. The designs of these plates are generally floral patterns; the fabric seems similar to that of the Italian Majolica, though coarser in material and execution. The designs are so Persian in character, that it has been thought by some archaeologists that these plates were all imported from the East to Rhodes. There is, however, reason to believe that the greater part of those still existing in the island are of native manufacture, for on some of them are escutcheons with heraldic bearings. Below these plates a string stretches right across the wall; from it hang embroidered napkins wrought with very good taste by the women of the place; below these ornamental hangings is a row of .large cupboards, containing various household implements. In another corner hangs the breadbasket, which is a large tray made of reeds, suspended from the ceiling, so as to be quite out of the way of all animals. Arriving just after Easter-day, we saw the Easter bread which had just been made, and which lasts as a stock for many weeks: it is in form like a ring. On another wall was a horizontal string, from which depended the Sunday clothes of both men and women, all beautifully embroidered and scrupulously clean. On one side of the fireplace I noticed a round earthen pot shaped like a bushel in which the forks and spoons are kept...

1890 The Rev. Henry Fanshawe Tozer

The Disappearance of Two Landmarks

Of the magnificence of that time little remains beyond the Hellenic foundations of the moles, and the numerous sepulchral monuments of grey marble-resembling small round altars or pedestals of statues - which are met with in the city and the suburbs. But as a specimen of a mediaeval fortress the existing city is almost unrivalled; and the objects that remain there, notwithstanding the ravages of time, illustrate in an impressive manner the organisation of the Order of the Knights of St, John. The enormous moat, wide and deep, and faced on both sides with stone; the solid walls, with towers at intervals, forming sometimes a double, and at the highest point, where the palace of the Grand Master stood, a triple line of defence, and drawn in a horseshoe form over the sloping heights from either side of the central harbour, and along the line of the harbour itself; and the fortifications by which the moles themselves were protected - all remain unchanged, to attest the strength of this bulwark, on which for centuries the attacks of its powerful foes broke in vain. And in like manner the names of saints attached to the various gates, and their figures sculptured in relief above them; the Priories, which formed the headquarters of each nationality or Tongue, as they were called, while the affairs of the Order at large were discussed in their common place of meeting; the bastions, or portions of the wall which were permanently assigned to each nationality to defend; and the escutcheons over the dwellings or the gateways, denoting either the possessor or the person by whom they were erected, but all of them containing the cross of the Order; all these bear witness to the religious character of the institution, and to the principle according to which the independent position of each people was recognised.

Within the memory of the present generation, however, two objects, which were among the greatest glories of the place, have been destroyed. One of these was the Tour de Naillac, which bore the name of the Grand Master by whom it was constructed, and formed a conspicuous object in views of the place as seen from the sea, rising, as it did, on the northern side of the central harbour; this was ruined by an earthquake in 1863. The other was the church of St. John, the Sanctuary of the Order, of which no trace now remains; it was destroyed in 1856 by an explosion of gunpowder, which was set on fire by a flash of lightning that struck an adjoining minaret. The neighbouring palace of the Grand Master, which was already in a ruinous condition, was still further damaged by the same catastrophe, so that now only the lower storey remains.

It is an interesting question at what period, and by whom, the powder was stored in this neighbourhood, for the Turkish authorities at the time of the explosion were ignorant of its existence. At first it was suggested that it was deposited there when Rhodes was besieged by the Ottomans in 1522; and that this was the act of Amaral, the chancellor of the Order, who turned traitor through jealousy in consequence of L 'Isle Adam being preferred to him as Grand Master, and might have concealed a quantity of the gunpowder belonging to the besieged, in order to hasten the fall of the place. To this view, however, there are two objections, which appear to be fatal. In the first place, there is no historical evidence of the concealment of the powder, and without that we are in the region of conjecture. Secondly, the doubt not unreasonably suggests itself, whether it is possible for gunpowder to retain its explosive power for more than three centuries. This question has been submitted to Sir F. Abel, the highest authority on explosives in this country; and his opinion is that, though gunpowder may retain its explosive properties for an indefinite period, provided that it is so packed and enclosed that moisture cannot have access to it, yet it is scarcely probable that packages such as were available at that period, even if they were in the first instance fairly impervious to moisture, could have preserved this essential feature for so long a time. It follows that the attractive view which would invest this gunpowder with a historical interest must be set aside; and we must content ourselves with the more prosaic supposition, that it was deposited in the vaults underneath the church at some comparatively recent period, and was subsequently forgotten.

1926 Paul Wilsach
In a Mosque during a Festival

Although a visit to a mosque is part of the ordinary experience of the traveller to a Muslim country today, this was rarely possible under Ottoman rule. Wilsach must have been one of the first to take advantage of the more relaxed attitude which followed the imposition of Italian rule over the Dodecanese.

There are few experiences so difficult of attainment for the so-called infidel in the Levant as admission to a mosque while the Moslems are at prayer. The pressure of a certain expediency has made it possible for tourists to visit a few particular mosques in such centres as Algiers, Constantinople and Cairo at particular hours, but not at a time of general prayers. In a place so remote from tourist paths as Rhodes, therefore, where the Moslems are under no pressure to allow the infidel to violate their houses of prayer, it was especially surprising to be invited to visit the principal mosque during the celebration of Mevlùd, or the Birthday of the Prophet.

In the first hour after sundown we climbed the hill to the Amboise Gate. Above the walls rose the double galleried minaret of the Mosque of Soliman. It was no mere cold gray monolith against the sky. Its balustrades were twinkling with bands of lamps which shone like brilliants about a white neck. No other minaret was illuminated, for under that one was to be held the single service for the entire city .The lights disappeared as we passed into the gateway, and we picked our way through the dim passages of the medieval city until we turned through an arch into the even more shadowy courtyard of the mosque itself.

One scarcely saw the fountain which invariably stands before a mosque, but one knew it was there by the music of the dripping waters and the soft splash of the faithful, as they laved hands and feet and the organs of the head, before entering for prayer. The wide open portal framed a segment of the Moslem gathering, squat on the scarlet rugs, fezzes and turbans outlined against the whitewashed walls. We, however, were led by a *hoja* up a dozen winding stone steps in the minaret and on to an inner balcony which commanded a view of the entire interior.

The mosque was already crowded. The lights of pendent crystal chandeliers were given added luster by the white walls and ceiling. The floor presented a hit-and-miss pattern of white and black and blue and brown figures. There were only men in sight The women were concealed behind an arras. Some of the men sat cross-legged, others knelt and rested on their heels. The Mussulman in his mosque reverses the practise of the Christian in his church, for while the latter retains his shoes and uncovers his head, the former covers his head and removes his shoes.

At an angle in the wall, in a position where he could best be seen and heard, a *hoja* sat cross-legged on a cushioned box behind a desk, explaining the significance of the occasion. On the floor about him squatted other *hojas*, priests of Islam, who may be recognized by the white turban wrapped about their fez. The mufti, or chief hoja, portly and venerable, squatted in the folds of his gabardine on the rug before the prayer niche which is on the side toward Mecca. Behind the flight of steps which in every mosque leads up to a platform against the eastern wall, where on Friday the hojas reads [*sic*] the prayers, we saw a green turban and knew by it that the wearer thus distinguished was believed to be a descendant of the Prophet.

The service consisted of the chanting of an ancient version of the story of the Prophet's birth. It is divided into four parts, each one of which was sung by a different cantor. The music was weirdly of the East, nasal and shrill, incoherent to a Western ear, with casual arpeggios and unexpected emphasis, and the recital was made impressive by silences between the verses longer than the verses themselves. The singer generally held the palm of his hand to his cheek and ear, and swayed gently forward and back. This motion was caught by many of the faithful and it gave a peculiar eye-rhythm to the assembly.

When the narrative approached the account of the birth of the Prophet a strange exotic aroma seemed to suffuse the whole place, and it was no imaginary aroma, for an attendant presently came into sight, threading his way through the huddled figures on the rugs, sprinkling rose-water into the outspread palms of the faithful, and they rubbed it over their faces and heads.

At the moment of the recital of the birth, the entire assembly rose and stood facing Mecca-ward, and joined in a treble canticle which raised the moment to a kind of ecstasy.

When every one was seated again the concluding strophes were chanted by a young *hoja* whom we not before observed in the balcony beside us. His voice had a sweetness that made the chant more lyric than the others had been and it lost nothing of the serene ardour reflected in his olive Oriental features. He was the muezzin of this mosque who ascended at prayer-time to the balcony of the minaret to call the faithful to prayer.

While he chanted the occasion was given the further character of a festival by the reappearance of the sprinkler .This time he had the ends of a blue tablecloth tied about his waist and the fold made by gathering the other ends overflowed with brown paper cones of sweet-meats which he distributed. It gave the feast of Mevlùd another kinship with our Christian Christmas.

A final detail of the service, particular to this night, were the prayers for the souls of those who in life had been noted for their charity. They were mentioned by name, and it was hinted that the distinction thus given beneficence was designed to encourage others to give. During the recital every one spread his hands palms upward before him, the Moslem attitude of prayer. Each prayer was punctuated by an echo from the congregation. With rigid attention I thought the sound "Aameen," resembling our Amen, and such exactly it was in the Arabic of their ritual.

On the final Aameen the assembly rose and drifted out into the night. W e wound our way down to the portico, bearing the cones of confections, followed by the fragrance of the scented waters and the echo of the plaintive chant. The mufti and other *hojas* were there, and we were presented and they gave us good night.

The shadowy courtyard was crowded with the silent but active figures, scurrying for foot-gear and shuffling into them. Dimly the women came out of the obscurity of which their nun-like figures seemed a part, mantled in brown and black from head to foot. They must have searched out their men, for certainly there was neither line nor feature by which the men could identify them.

We strolled with the Mussulmans out through the arch and along the winding streets. As they disappeared at other doors and arches along the way, and we came alone to the moonlit battlements, it seemed as if we were emerging from Asia and coming back again to Christendom. But not to a Rhodes of later than the fifteenth century, the latest days of the knights, the suggestion of whom rose in dark massive walls, tunnelled towers, and the broad moat which showed no bottom in the darkness.

Church of Saint John, Rhodes (Contemporary print)

Eighteenth Century Lindos (Contemporary print)

Select Biographical Notes

About, Edmund: A controversial French writer, who visited Greece in 1852, his novel, based on the *kleftes* and their relations with the state and law-enforcement agencies *The King of the Mountain*, became a well-known comic-opera.

Anderson, The Rev. Rufus: A clergyman selected by the American Board as its agent in Greece; sailed with the Rev. Eli Smith on the to make a survey of the situation in Greece in 1828.

Babin, Jacques-Paul, SJ: a Jesuit missionary based in Smyrna. After visiting Greece he returned by way of Constantinople, where, in 1672, the abbé Pecoil, in the service of the French ambassador to the Port, asked him to write down his impressions of the region, which is the earliest description of the state of the parts of the country he visited.

Baird, Henry M.: A US citizen, he spent one year in Athens during the 1850s for study, staying with the Rev. Jonas King. He died in 1906.

Barrows, Samuel J: accompanied the archaeologist Dörpfeld in his excavations of Troy in 1893.

Bent, James Theodore: travelled around the Aegean during the winter of 1883-4, and managed to visit all the inhabited islands of the Cyclades. He was chiefly interested in contemporary Greeks, and the connections between their customs and those of the ancients. An indefatigable traveller and observer, who wrote with wit and charm, he also excavated the ruins of Great Zimbabwe, but could not bring himself to believe that native Africans could have been responsible for so impressive a civilisation.

Blount, Sir Henry: arrived in the East in 1634. He later became a member of the notorious Green Ribbon Club, a Whig faction hostile to the Court which met at the King's Head tavern at Chancery Lane End, sometimes known as the" King's Head Club, which organized sedition, and was probably the first genuinely modern political organization in England.

Bodenham, Roger: His groundbreaking voyages to the Levant in the *Aucher* are mentioned in Charles Kingley's *Westward Ho!*

Brassey, "Mrs. Annie":   It has been said that "The Victorian public welcomed Annie Brassey's books with an enthusiasm reserved nowadays for episodes of a soap opera."

Bulwer-Lytton, Edward George Earle Lytton, first Baron Lytton: son of General Bulwer, who added his mother's surname to his own when he inherited Knebworth in 1843. Educated at Trinity Hall, Cambridge, he embarked on a career in politics as MP for St Ives and a was keen Reform member in 1831; he was subsequently MP for Lincoln and in 1858-9 secretary for the colonies. He financed an extravagant life-style as a man of fashion by his prolific writing as a novelist, poet, dramatist and magazine editor, publishing anonymously or under the name "Bulwer Lytton". He was a friend, among others, of Disraeli and Dickens.

Chandler, Richard: a fellow of Magdalen College, Oxford, and a literary figure of some eminence, he was selected by the Dilettanti Society to lead their first sponsored expedition, in 1764-6, to record Greek antiquities, chiefly those of Ionia. In addition to his historical concerns, he showed some interest in the contemporary inhabitants of the region. Chandler's account of Athens was the most detailed that had appeared at the time. It was he who announced the discovery of the temple of Apollo at Bassae.

Charlemont, James Caulfield, Earl of: the young fourth Viscount, and later the first Earl, of Charlemont, worried his recently widowed mother by his association with dissolute aristocrats, and was sent on a Grand Tour in 1746. He was away for many years travelling throughout southern Europe and the Near East. The company he kept on his journey seems to have been little better than that his travels were designed to remove him from, and his chief interest seems to have centred upon observation of the women of the countries through which he passed. He later became chairman of the Dilettanti Club and a prominent statesman, devoted to the social and cultural development of the Irish. He became commander in chief of the Irish Volunteers in 1780, and in 1785 he was elected the first president of the Royal Irish Academy.

Chateaubriand, François-René: a Breton army officer and writer who fled France at the outbreak of the Revolution, but returned to fight under Condé in 1792, escaping to England. He held various ministerial posts until the revolution of 1830. He is chiefly known as a superb stylist.

Chishull, Edmund: became chaplain to the factory of the Worshipful Turkey Company in Smyrna in 1698. A fellow of Corpus Christi, Oxford, he was given a grant by the college to travel. His son, Edmund, later collected and published his papers.

Clarke, Edward Daniel: An indefatigable traveller, he arrived in Greece from the Holy Land in 1801 and stayed with Tarsia Makris. A friend of Lusieri, he was, in spite of that, horrified at the destruction of the Parthenon. Yet this failed to deter him from amassing his own collection of at least one thousand coins and many vases and "marbles". The most bulky memento of his travels was a two-ton statue he thought to be a representation of Ceres, from Eleusis. He later became Professor of Mineralogy at Cambridge.

Cochrane, George: nephew of Admiral Lord Cochrane, a Philhellene leaders in the War of Independence, he became his private secretary in 1826.

Cockerell, Charles Robert: A descendent of the diarist Samuel Pepys, he initially went out to the Mediterranean as a King's Messenger with dispatches for the fleet. He arrived in Greece in 1810 in a small party which included the artist Stackelberg. During a four year stay he excavated and uncovered marbles from the temple of Aphaia in Aigina and the temple of Apollo at Bassae, got them out of the country, and auctioned them to the highest bidder. Later in life he became an eminent architect, designed the Ashmolean Museum, and member of the Royal Academy. His journals were published after his death by his son, famous landscape architect Samuel Pepys Cockerell.

Corrigan, Dr.: physician to the Queen in Ireland and President of the Irish College of Physicians, Dr. Corrigan travelled to Greece during the summer of 1861.

Cotton, The Rev. Walter: a chaplain in the US Navy. While at Mahon he defended a sailor who was court-martialled, and during the trial, took time off to make a sightseeing tour of the monastery of Mount Tauro. The accused was found guilty.

Covel, Dr. John: Chaplain to the Levant trading company during 1670-77, during which period he resided in Constantinople. He was subsequently appointed chaplain to the Princess of Orange and resided at the Hague, but was sent home in disgrace in 1865 for getting involved in court and family intrigue. He later became Master of Christ's College, Cambridge, and Vice-Chancellor of the University; and wrote an account of the Greek Church which became the authoritative view of Orthodoxy in England for many years.

Craven, Lady Elizabeth: Although she had six children by him, Lady Craven (Pouqueville) left her husband after thirteen years of marriage. Still only thirty years of age herself, and attractive, she met the Margrave of Brandenburg and Anspach while living in Paris, and lived with him "in chaste sisterly intercourse". In 1785, she set out to tour to the East with Fauvel. Crossing the Black Sea from Crimea. As her ship approached Constantinople it was discovered that the Greek pilot, the only man who had ever taken that route before, was hopelessly drunk. From a map she spotted that there were several dangerous obstacles to be cleared in order to arrive safely in harbour. She took command of the situation, gave orders to the captain, and so steered the ship safely into port. A guest of the French Consul, the Comte de Choiseul Gouffier, he loaned her his small frigate to sail to Greece. A young and pretty woman who demonstrated initiative and independence, she was assumed in social circles to be a chronic nymphomaniac. Later she married her "sisterly friend", became the Margravine of Hansbach, settled in England, and wrote English and French comedies, in some of which she also acted.

Curzon, The Hon. Robert (Junior): Between 1834 and 1837, Robert Curzon visited Egypt, Syria, Albania and Mount Athos, in order to collect ancient manuscripts. A dozen years later, he wrote an account of some of the MSS, the places in which they were found, and some of the adventures he encountered in the pursuit of them. Afterwards he became the fourteenth baron Zouche.

Dallam, Thomas: An organ-maker from Lancashire, he was sent by Queen Elizabeth I to deliver an organ to the Porte as a present in 1599.

Dallaway, James: became chaplain and physician to the British ambassador to the Porte. An active traveller and antiquarian, in 1795 he made a study of the walls of Constantinople, and in 1801 travelled to the Troad in the company of Gell and Morritt. He later became a member of the Dilettanti Society.

Dekaye, Dr. J. E.: A New York physician and naturalist who visited Greece during 1831-2, he admired the Turks and exhibits a strong antipathy to the Greeks.

De Pouqueville, François-Charles: a French doctor, diplomat and historian, captured by Algerian pirates on his return from a scientific mission in Egypt. He was taken to Tripolis and held there for ten months, before being transferred to Constantinople. He spent two years in prison there, before being appointed French representative at the court of Ali Pasha. He returned to Paris after 1815, and became a prolific writer.

De Vere, Aubrey Thomas Hunt: was a romantic essayist and poet who fell under the influence of William Wordsworth, never omitting to make an annual pilgrimage to his grave.

Digby, Sir Kenelm: In 1627 he launched a naval expedition to harass the Turks in the Aegean.

Dodwell, Edward: travelled to the Ionian Isles in 1801 in the company of Sir William Gell. Taken prisoner by the French on the way back in Italy, he was freed at the intercession of the archaeologist Lechevalier. Apparently undaunted by this experience, he returned to Greece in 1805-6, and travelled extensively in the company of the painter Simone Pomardi.

Emerson, James: An English Philhellene who had enlisted in the War under Lord Byron, after the poet's death he returned home for a while, and then returned to travel through southern Greece in 1825.

Finlay, George: A Scottish Philhellene who took part in the War of Independence and afterwards settled in Greece to become the leading historian of modern Greece, and an opponent of the Bavarian monarchy.

Fuller, John: a painter, he arrived in Athens in 1818, travelled on to Asia and returned to Greece two years later, leaving after the outbreak of the War of Independence. He grew a substantial beard and wore Turkish clothes, something which got him into danger after the outbreak of the War of Independence.

Galt, John: a prolific Scottish writer who toured the Eastern Mediterranean during 1809-10. He exhibits an antipathy to modern Greeks.

Gell, Sir William: a topographical archaeologist nicknamed "Classic Gell" by Byron, , he first visited Greece in 1801 with Dodwell, touring Attica, the Peloponnese and the Troad. In 1805 he visited the Ionian Islands, again with Dodwell. In 1811 he headed an archaeological mission for the Dilettanti Society. During the course of these visits, he changed from being a strong supporter of Greek rights to an opponent.

Giffard, Edward: Suffering from the "disagreeable symptoms" of some undisclosed complaint, he travelled to Greece in January 1836 on medical advice, in company with a fellow-sufferer. Apparently, the trip worked, for the symptoms, whatever they were, disappeared.

Hobhouse, John C.: travelled in company with his friend, Lord Byron, and visited Greece in 1809-10. He was very interested in the modern Greeks but sometimes he was inaccurate in his observations, or in the subsequent writing up of them. Leake later detailed many of his errors. Later he became Lord Broughton, a friend of Koraïs, and a member of the Greek Committee of 1823.

Holland, Dr. Henry: a physician, he travelled out to Portugal to view military hospitals during the Peninsula War, and then went on to the Balkans during 1812 and 1813. He was professionally consulted by Ali Pasha of Ioannina and Velli Pasha during his journey.

Hughes, Reverend Thomas Smart: arrived in Greece in 1813 with R. Townley Parker and made friends with Lusieri.

La Guillatière, M. de: spent four years enslaved by corsairs, leaving Tunis in 1669.

Lamartine, Alphonse Marie Louis de: an aristocratic poet from Mâcon, France, he lost his only daughter on his luxury trip to the Levant, and after publishing an account of it in 1835, he thereafter limited himself to prose writing. He was an eloquent opponent of King Louis Philippe in the National Assembly, but was swept from politics by the revolution of 1848.

Leake, Colonel William Martin: an army officer, the son of a herald who lived in Mayfair, he is undoubtedly the most important of the travellers to Greece, judged by the results of his work. He arrived in Constantinople in 1799 at the age of twenty-two to instruct the Turkish army in artillery practice. He visited Greece three times. In 1802, after a survey of Egypt, he sailed home from Athens on the ship which carried the Parthenon (Elgin) Marbles. When the ship sank off Kythera he drew his pistol and prevented a general panic. Then he organised divers to recover the Marbles. In 1805 was sent to take orders Nelson to the British fleet in the Aegean, and thereafter to investigate and report on the military preparedness of Turkish governors for an invasion of the

Balkans by the French under Napoleon, siezing the opportunity to travel throughout southern Greece. He was taken prisoner when war broke out between England and the Porte. After his release, he met Ali Pasha and persuaded him to bring about the reconciliation which ended hostilities. He again went to Greece in 1808 to supply Ali with arms, including cannon, to be used against the French, and became resident at Ioannina and Preveza, travelling throughout northern Greece. In 1809 he met Byron and returned with him to the United Kingdom. A reliable and disciplined observer, topographer archaeologist, numismatologist, antiquary, historian and student of contemporary life, Leake was a founder of what is today called landscape archaeology, and personally established the locations of most of the then unidentified ancient sites of Greece.

Lear, Edward: Employed as a draughtsman by the London Zoological society, he produced some of the first colour plates of animals ever made in Britain. A humorist, he is most famous for his nonsense verse. Lear visited Corfu in 1848 then travelled to Constantinople with Sir Stafford and Lady Canning, and on his return overland from Salonica he visited Macedonia and Albania. A second journey saw Lear return to Albania, as well as taking in Epirus and Thessaly.

Lithgow, William: A tailor from Lanark, Scotland, William Lithgow suffered injury at the hands of the outraged relatives of a lady, and in consequence was afterwards known as "Cut-lugged Willie". As a result of this incident, he found it advisable to leave his home town and seek his fortune in the Levant in or near 1609. Although full of incident, Lithgow's understanding of geography seems to have been "approximate": for example, he thought that Athens was in the Peloponnese. He had little time for niceties, dogged as the unfortunate man seems to have been by a succession of mishaps and disasters, ending with what Eisner describes as "an unpleasant encounter with the Spanish Inquisition."

Melville, Herman: Born in New York City into an established merchant family, his father went bankrupt and lost his sanity, dying when Melville was twelve. He soon left Albany Classical School in New York State, and from the age of twelve he worked as a clerk, teacher, and farmhand. In search of adventure, he shipped out in 1839 as a cabin boy on a whaler, and later joined the US Navy, voyaging in the Atlantic and the South Seas. He spent some time as a clerk and bookkeeper in general store in Honolulu and lived briefly among the Typee cannibals in the Marquesas Islands. His account of this, and a sequel based on his experiences in Polynesian Islands, were huge successes, although he was more highly estimated in Britain than in America. In 1847 he bought a farm near Nathaniel Hawthorne's home at Pittsfield, Massachusetts, and the two authors became friends. Hawthorne encouraged him in the composition of what was to be his most famous work, *Moby-Dick*.

Meryon, Charles: had graduated as a medical stident when, in 1810, he set out for the East in the company of the indefatigable Lady Hester Stanhope.

Morritt, John Bacon Sawry: Inheriting the estate of Rokeby, in Yorkshire, at the age of nineteen, having graduated at Cambridge, he set off on the Grand Tour in 1794 with the Reverend James Galloway. They crossed Europe by land, skirting the fighting in the Revolutionary War, and stayed in the house of Procopius Makris. Morritt tried to detach and take home several slabs from the Pathenon frieze to adorn the sculpture gallery at Rokesby, but was prevented by the authorities. He later became a Tory MP and a friend of Sir Walter Scott.

Moryson, Fynes: The son of the MP for Grimsby during the 1570-80s, he set out for Germany in 1591, and spent most of the next decade travelling about Europe. On his return, he became secretary to Charles Blount, Lord Mountjoy, retiring from his service in 1606 to write up his travels.

Newton, Charles T.:   appointed vice-consul of Mytilene in 1852 by Lord Granville, spent seven years in the Aegean, during which he conducted extensive excavations in Anatolia.

Pashley, Robert: left England at the end of 1832 on a one and a half year journey throughout the Eastern Mediterranean. He arrived in Khania in February 1834 and explored Crete by land accompanied by a draughtsman and a Turkish guide.

Pockoke, Richard: Born in Southampton, the son of a headmaster of a public school, he attended Corpus Christi College, Oxford and then went on his travels, touring Egypt during 1837-8. Despite being described as "the dullest man who ever travelled," his account, published in 1743-5, was celebrated at the time and translated into French, German and Dutch, Although interested in geography, archaeology, history, and mythology, there is little of a personal nature in his account. He subsequently became domestic chaplain to Lord Chesterfield, and died very unexpectedly in September of 1765, shortly after being made Bishop of Ossary and Meath.

Post, Henry Albertson VanZo: A Professor of Columbia College, he sailed on the relief ship *Jane* from New York in May 1827 and spent four months in Greece, travelling with General George Jarvis. He was a "sharpshooter" in the army of the Potomac.

Randolph, Bernard: was unusual for his age in that he was chiefly interested in contemporary affairs rather than antiquities.

Robson, Rev. Charles: A chaplain at Aleppo, Robson travelled through the Greek islands during 1628, returning to England with some ancient manuscripts in 1630.

Sandwich, John Montague, fourth Earl of: Twenty years old in 1738, he set out on a tour in a galley with a group of friends and sixteen cannon. He later became famous for his collection of Egyptian mummies, and as a member of the notorious Medmenham Brotherhood. he served as First Lord of the Admiralty, and has been described as "possibly the most hated politician of the eighteenth century."

Sandys, Sir George: Son of the archbishop of York, he travelled to the East in 1610, passing through France when King Henry IV was assassinated. Subsequently he helped establish the new colony of Virginia in North America, where he passed his time translating Ovid into English.

Sandys, John Edwin: A fellow of St John's College and Public Orator of Cambridge University, he visited Greece with his wife during Spring 1886.

Senior, Nassau W.:   A British economist and social scientist, who taught at Oxford. He held that capital accumulation is a cost of production, distinguished wealth and welfare, and originated "Abstinence theory": that interest is a reward for saving money rather than spending it. He advised the Whig party and he wrote the revised Poor Law of 1834.

Skinner, J.E.Hillary: A strong Philhellene, he sailed on the *Arcady*, which was running guns to Christian rebels in Crete during the revolt of 1867.

Snider, Denton J.:   A schoolmaster from Saint Louis Missouri, he stayed for three months in Athens in 1879.

Spratt, Captain Thomas A.B: became director of the Mediterranean Survey in 1851. He took command of the *Spitfire*, a paddle steamer, and went to Crete. Two years later, his work was interrupted by the outbreak of the Crimean War and not finished until 1860. The results of the survey were published in 1861, but Spratt's archaeological, ethnological and linguistic interests prompted him to publish a fuller account of the island. He later became an admiral.

Stanhope, Lady Hester: the eldest daughter of Charles Viscount Mahon, an eccentric who inherited the Chevening estate, in Kent, in 1786. An inventor, he developed a new design of printing press and a screw-propelled steamship, and worked on a mechanical calculating machine. After her mother died and her father remarried, the young Lady Hester went to live with her uncle, prime minister William Pitt. Following his death in 1810, she set out for the Levant with Charles Meryon. She sometimes dressed as a Turkish man, and made several expeditions into the desert, where she became known to the Bedouin as "Queen of the Desert". She finally settled in a former monastery at Djoun in the Lebanon mountains where, abandoned by friends and family, she died alone, an impoverished recluse, in 1839.

Stephens, John Lloyd: His travel writing was universally admired and widely imitated by others during the mid-nineteenth century.

Taylor, Bayard: recorded his sojourn in Athens during the unusually harsh winter of 1857-8.

Thackeray, William Makepeace: was born in 1811 in India, where his father worked for the East India Company. Sent to school in England in 1817, he was unhappy because he was not good at sports. He went to Cambridge University, where he lost in a poetry contest to Alfred Tennyson. He studied law, supporting himself by selling sketches and working for a financial house. He got into bad company and built up large gambling debts. After trying to launch his own newspaper, he was briefly an art student before falling in love. Since he needed money to marry, William's mother and stepfather scraped together all they could find and started a newspaper called the *Constitution, and* William was appointed the paper's Paris correspondent. He began writing as many articles as possible, and sending them to any newspaper that would print them. Over the next few years, he wrote several novels, made two lecture tours of America, and stood as an independent candidate in an Oxford by-election. Through all this, he was continually ill with recurrent kidney infections caused by syphillis contracted in his youth. In 1859, he and a friend named George Smith started the *Cornhill Magazine.* William, besides editing, contributed a great series of essays called the *Roundabout Papers.* In 1863, he sensed that his health was deteriorating and travelled around his old haunts and friends to say goodbye. On Christmas Eve, he died of a burst blood vessel. Among the mourners at his funeral was Charles Dickens.

Tournefort, Joseph Pitton de: was selected by the French Government to travel throughout the East to collect information about the state of the Ottoman Empire. He set out in 1700 with a remit to concern himself with geography, natural history, antiquities, commerce, and the religion and customs of the people. With his companions, he travelled as far as Georgia and Armenia, returning to France in 1702.

Tozer, The Reverend Henry Fanshaw: A fellow of Exeter College, he made three journeys to Greece during the 1870s and 1880s

Trelawny, E. J.:   He deserted from the Royal Navy, and went to Italy, where he later falsely claimed to have become a corsair. He met Lord Byron and the ageing Shelley, whose cremation he conducted in 1822. He went to Greece in 1823 with Byron to join in the War of Independence. When Byron died, he joined the band of the *kleft* Odysseus, in his mountain stronghold. He later returned to England and took upon himself "the role of guardian of Shelley's romantic ideals." In 1833 he travelled to the US, and almost drowned trying to swim across the Niagara Falls. At the age of eighty-two he threatened to fight a duel with Millais over a portrait the artist had made of him. After his death in 1881, his ashes were buried next to the monument to Shelley in the Protestant cemetery in Rome.

Tuckerman, Charles K.:   of New York State, was the first US Minister Resident in Athens, serving from 1868 to 1871. The Senate refused to confirm his re-nomination to this post in 1867.

Turner, William: Serving under the Marquis of Wellesley in the Peninsula War, Turner was assigned to the staff of Mr. Liston on his embassy of to the Sublime Porte in 1812. He spent three years in Constantinople, but also managed to travel throughout the Near East.

Twain, Mark (Samuel Langhorne Clemens):   lived as a child in Hannibal, on the Mississippi River. He had little formal education, but he worked in print shops and newspaper offices as a youth. In 1853 he left Hannibal to travel. After an unsuccessful attempt at gold and silver mining he joined the staff of a newspaper in Virginia City, Nevada, where he first wrote under the pen name, "Mark Twain" in 1863. He sailed from New York on the Quaker City in summer 1867 on a voyage to the Holy Land, and in 1869 his travel letters were collected into the popular *The Innocents Abroad*. Afterwards, Twain married and settled down in Hartford, Connecticut to write, including seven novels, and became perhaps the greatest influence on American literature.

Urquhart, David: of Speke Hall, visited European Turkey before spending ten years on the Bosporous, returning to Britain in 1830. He prided himself in discounting all his Western preconceptions and appreciating Eastern cultures in their own terms. However, A sceptical Eisner points out that "A number of his descriptions seem taken from a painting by Claude or Delacroix than from life… Urquhart's scenes ... arrange themselves too easily into compositions lacking just those details that could mar the cliché or reflect the author as a chump." It does seem likely that some of his work lies at the "creative" end of the spectrum of travel writing, and consists more of "what I would have said or done, had I thought of it at the time," than an accurate narrative of experiences that had actually happened.

Walsh, The Rev. R.:   In 1821 he was appointed chaplain to Lord Strangford, the British Ambassador in Constantinople. During 1824-5 he made a tour of Greece.

Wheler, George: He was born in 1650, in Holland, where his parents were royalist exiles from Cromwell's England. Later a graduate of Lincoln College, Oxford and a botanist, he met Jacob Spon in Venice in 1675. In 1677 he took holy orders. Richard Stoneman argues that the era of accurate description in travel narrative began with the visit to Greece of this duo. Among their accomplishments was the first correct identification of the shrine at Delphi, and the first detailed modern eyewitness account of the monuments of Athens.

Williams, Hugh William: made a painting tour that earned him the nickname "Grecian Williams".

Willis, N. Parker: A US poet, who travelled to Greece on the *Constitution* in 1833. He seems to have been intensely anti-British, despite constantly seeking out, and enjoying, the hospitality of British residents.

Woodruff, Judge Samuel: A philhellene from Granby, Con., USA. He was a member of the New York Greek Committee, selected to sail in the brig *Herald* to bring provisions, such as food and clothes to refugees from the war in the liberated areas of Greece in 1828.

Wordsworth, Christopher: A nephew of the poet William Wordsworth, he toured Greece during 1832-3, when he was stabbed in the neck by brigands and nearly died. This seemed only to whet his appetite, and he returned to Greece in 1836 and 1840. Later he became headmaster of Harrow School and bishop of Lincoln.

Bibliography

Sources

About, Edmund, *Greece and the Greeks of the Present Day* (Edinburgh, 1855)

Anderson, Rufus, *Observations upon the Peloponnese and Greek Islands made in 1829* (Boston, 1830)

A Picturesque Tour through Part of Europe, Asia and Africa, by "An Italian Gentleman" (London, 1793)
    "Athens," *Harper's Monthly Magazine* (May 1881)

Babin, Father Jacques-Paul, S.J., *Relation de l'état présent de la ville d'Athenes*, (Lyons, 1674)

Baird, Henry M., *Modern Greece: A Narrative of a Residence and Travels in that Country...* (New York, 1856)

Barrows, Samuel J., *The Isles and Shrines of Greece*, (Boston, 1898)

Bent, James Theodore, *The Cyclades or Life among the Insular Greeks*, (London, 1885)

Blount, H., *Á Voyage into the Levant* (London, 1616)

Bosanquet, Mrs. R.C., *Days in Attica* (London, 1914)

Bracebridge, Charles, appended to C. Wordsworth, *Athens and Attica* (London, 1837)

Brassey, Mrs. Annie, *Sunshine and Storm in the East*, (London, 1874)

Bulwer, Lytton, *An Autumn in Greece*, (London, 1827)

[Byron, Dr] V*oyages and Travels of Princess Caroline* (London, 1821)

Byron, Robert, *The Station, Athos: Treasures and Men* (London, 1949)

Carnarvon, Earl of, *Reminiscences of Athens and the Morea* (London, 1869)

Chandler, Richard, *Travels in Asia Minor and Greece, 3rd ed.* (London, 1817)

Charlemont, *The Travels of Lord Charlemont in Greece and Turkey* (London, 1749)

Chateaubriand, F. de, *Travels in Greece, Palestine, Egypt and Barbary,* tr. F. Shobel (1811)

Clark, William George, *Peloponnesus: Notes of Study and Travel* (London, 1858)

Clarke, Edward Daniel, *Travels in Various Countries of Europe, 8v* (London, 1825)

Cochrane, George, *Wanderings in Greece* (London, 1837)

Corrigan, Dr., *Ten Days in Athens, with Notes by the Way* (London, 1862)

Cotton, The Rev. Walter, *Land and Lee in the Bosphorus and the Aegean*, ed. The Rev. Henry T. Cheever (New York, 1851)

Covel, Dr John, *Diary* (1669-77)

Cox, S.S., *A Buckeye Abroad* (New York, 1852)

Craven, Lady Elizabeth, *A Journey Through the Crimea to Constantinople* (London, 1789)

Curzon, The Hon. Robert (Junior), *Visits to Monasteries in the Levant* (New York, 1849)

Dallam, Thomas, *Diary*, 1599-1600, ed. J. T. Bent, *Hakluyt Society 87* (London, 1893)

[Dekaye, Dr. J. E.,] *Sketches of Turkey in 1831 and 1832 by an American* (New York, 1833).

De Vere, Aubrey, *Picturesque Sketches of Greece and Turkey* (London, 1850)

Diehl, Charles, *Excavations in Greece*, Tr. Emma R. Perkins (London, 1893)

Dodwell, Edward, *A Classical and Topographical Tour through Greece in the years 1801, 1805 and 1806* (London, 1819)

Dodwell, *Views in Greece* (London, 1821)

Douglas, Frederick Sylvester North, *An Essay on Certain Points of Resemblance between the Ancient and Modern Greeks*, 2nd corrected ed. (London, 1813)

Edwards, Charles, *Letters from Crete: Letters written during the Spring of 1886,* (London, 1887)

Emerson, James, "Journal of a Residence in Greece in 1825," in *Emerson, James, etc. A Picture of Greece...*

Emerson, Richard, Count Pecchio & Humphreys, W. H., *A Picture of Greece...* 2v (London, 1826)

Finlay, George, *The Hellenic Kingdom and the Greek Nation* (London, 1846)

Galt, John, *Letters from the Levant* (London, 1813)

Galt, John, *Voyages and Travels in the Years 1809, 1810 and 1811* (London, 1812)

Garston, Edgar, *Greece Revisited* (London, 1842)

Gell, W., *Narrative of a Journey in the Morea* (London, 1823)

Giffard, E., *A Short Visit to the Ionian Islands, Athens and the Morea* (London, 1837)

Goodell, Thomas Dwight, "A Journey in Thessaly," *Century Illustrated Monthly Magazine 54 (4)* (Aug. 1897)

Harrison, James Albert, *Greek Vignettes: A Sail in the Greek Seas, Summer of 1877* (Boston, 1878)

Hervé, Francis, *A Residence in Greece and Turkey...* 2v (London, 1826)

Hobhouse, John, *A Journey through Albania and Other Provinces of Turkey*, 2nd ed. (London, 1913)

Holland, Henry, *Travels in the Ionian Islands, Albania, Thessaly, Macedonia, etc. during the years 1812 and 1813* (London, 1815)

Hughes Thomas Smart, *Travels in Sicily, Greece and Albania* (London, 1820)

La Guillatière, M. de, *Voyage to Athens*, (London, 1676)

Lamartine, Alphonse de, *Travels in the East, including a journey in the Holy Land*, Tr. the author (Edinburgh, 1839)

Laurent, Peter Edmund, *Recollections of a Classical Tour through Various Parts of Greece, Turkey and Italy, Made in the years 1818 and 1819*, 2v (London, 1822)

Leake, William, *The Topography of Athens* (London, 1821)

Leake, William, *Travels in the Morea*, 3v (London, 1830)

Leake, William, *Travels in Northern Greece* (London, 1835)

Lear, Edward, *Journals of a Landscape Painter in Greece and Albania* (London, 1851)

Lithgow, William, *Totall Discourse of the Rare and Painefull Peregrinations* (London, 1632)

Mahaffy, John Pentland, *Rambles and Studies in Greece,* 4th ed. (London, 1892)

Memoirs relating to European and Asiatic Turkey, ed. Rev. Robert Walpole (London, 1917)

Meryon, Charles, *The Travels of Lady Hester Stanhope, forming the Completion of her Memoirs, Narrated by her Physician* (London, 1846)

Miller, William, *Greece* (London, 1828)

Miller, William, *Greek Life in Town and Country* (London, 1905)

Morritt, John Bacon Sawry, *The Letters of John B.S. Morritt of Rokeby, Descriptive of Journeys in Europe and Asia Minor in the Years 1794–1796,* ed. G.E. Marindin (London, 1914)

Moryson, Fynes, *An Itinerary*, 4v (Glasgow, 1907)

"Mr. Robert's his Voyage to the Levant, with an account of his sufferings among the Corsairs, their Villainous way of Living, and his description of the Archipelago…" in *A Collection of Original Voyages*, ed. Capt. William Hacks (London, 1699)

Mure, William, *Journal of a Tour in Greece*, 2v (London, 1842)

Newton, Charles T., *Travels and Discoveries in the Levant* (London, 1865)

Pashley, Robert, *Travels in Crete* 2v (Cambridge/London, 1837)

Pecchio, Count, *Journal, in Emerson, James, eyc., A Picture of Greece...*

Pitton de Tournefort, Joseph, *A Voyage Into the Levant... 3v,* tr. J. Ozell, (London, 1741)

Pococke, Richard, *A Description of the East and Some Other Countries* 3v (London, 1743)

Pouqueville, F.C.H.L., *Travels through the Morea, Albania and Other Parts of the Ottoman Empire to Constantinople during the Years 1798, 1799, 1800*, 1806, *3 v,*, trans. anon. (London, 1805)

Porter, Sir Robert Ker, *Travels in Georgia, Persia, Armenia...* (London, 1822)

Post, Henry A. V., *A Visit to Greece and Constantinople in the year 1827-8* (New York, 1830)

Postlethwaite, Edward, *A Tour in Crete* (London, 1868)

Pouqueville, François-Charles, *Travels in the Morea, Albania and other Parts of the Ottoman Empire*, Tr. A. Plumptre (London, 1813).

Raikes, Mr., *Journal* in *Travels in Various Countries of the East*, ed. Robert Walpole (London, 1820)

Randolph, Bernard, *The Present State of the Morea* (London, 1686)

Randolph, Bernard, *Present State of the Islands in the Archipelago* (Oxford, 1687)

Robson, Rev. Charles, *News from Aleppo* (London, 1628)

Ross, H.J., *Letters from the East, 1837-57* (London, 1902)

Sandwich, John Montague, Earl of, *A Voyage Performed by the late Earl of Sandwich* (London, 1799)

Sandys, Sir George, *A Relation of a Journey begun 1610* (London, 1615)

Sandys, John Edwin, *An Easter Vacation in Greece* (London, 1887)

Savary, C-É., *Letters on Greece* (Dublin, 1755)

Seymour, Thomas D., "Life and Travel in Modern Greece", *Scribner's Magazine* (New York, July 1888)

Ship and Shore, by an Officer of the United States' Navy (New York, 1835)

Skene, Felicia Mary, *Wayfaring Sketches among the Greeks and Turks by a Seven Years' Resident in Greece* (London, 1847)

Skinner, J. E. Hillery, *Roughing it in Crete in 1867* (London, 1868)

Slade, Capt. Adolphus, R.N., *Records of Travels in Turkey, Greece, etc., and of a Cruise in the Black Sea with the Capitan Pacha, New ed.* (London, 1854)

Snider, Denton Jacques, *A Walk in Hellas 2v* (St. Louis, 1881)

Spratt, Captain T. A. B., *Travels and Researches in Crete 2v* (London, 1865)

Stephens, J.L., *Incidents of Travel in Greece, Turkey, Russia and Poland* (Edinburgh, 1839)

Swan, Charles, *Voyage to the Eastern Mediterranean* (London, 1826)

Taylor, Bayard, *Travels in Greece and Russia with an Excursion to Crete* (London, 1859)

Thackeray, William Makepeace, *Notes on a Journey from Cornhill to Grand Cairo* (London, 1845)

Tozer, The Rev. Henry Fanshawe, *Islands of the Aegean* (Oxford, 1890)

Travels in Southern Europe and the Levant, 1810-17: the Journal of C.R. Cockerell RA, ed. Samuel Pepys Cockerell (London, 1903)

Travels in various Countries of the East, ed. Rev. Robert Walpole (London, 1820)

Trelawny, E. J., *Records of Shelley, Byron and the Author* (London, 1878)

Tuckerman, Charles Keating, *Personal Recollections* (London, 1895)

Turner, William, *Journal of a Tour in the Levant*, 3v (London, 1820)

Twain, Mark, *Innocents Abroad* (Hartford, Con., 1839)

Urquhart, David, *The Spirit of the East* (London, 1839)

Walsh, R., *Narrative of a Journey from Constantinople to England*, 3rd ed. (London, 1829)

Wheler, George, *A Journey into Greece* (London, 1682)

Williams, Hugh William, *Travels in Italy, Greece and the Ionian Isles*, 2v (Edinburgh, 1820)

Willis, N. Parker, *Summer Cruise in the Mediterranean* (London, 1853)

Wilsach, Paul, *Islands of the Mediterranean: A Holiday* (Indianapolis, 1926)

Wines, E.C., *Two Years and a Half in the American Navy ... during 1829-1831* (London, 1833)

Woodruff, Samuel, *Journal of a Tour to Malta, Asia Minor, Carthage, Algiers, Port Mahon and Spain* (Hartford, 1831)

Wordsworth, Christopher, *Athens and Attica* (London, 1837)

General Bibliography

British Travellers in Greece 1750-1820, ed. G. Tolias, (Athens, 1995)

Eisner, Robert, *Travelers to an Antique Land: The History of Travel to Greece*, (Ann Arbor, 1991)

Tregaskis, Hugh, *Beyond the Grand Tour*, (London, 1980)

Tsigakou, Fani-Maria, *The Rediscovery of Greece*, (London, 1982)

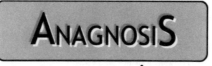

www.anagnosis.gr

GREECE BEYOND THE GUIDEBOOKS

The Stories BEHIND the Sites

with

Stories the Guidebooks Do Not Tell

and

Sites the Guidebooks Overlook

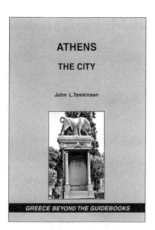

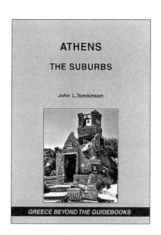

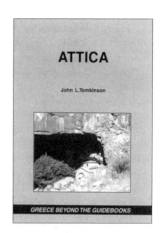

1. Athens: The City

• A Plot to Kill Winston Churchill • The "Hard Men" of Old Athens
• The Amazons in Athens: Legend or History? • A Roman Meterological Station
• The Secrets of the Parthenon The Column which Imprisons the Plague
• The First Modern Olympic Games • A Greek Dimension to Watergate
• When the Three Fates Visited Every Child • An Armoury Under a Church
• Male Chauvinism in Ancient Athens • The Swastika Over the Acropolis
• The Plaka Orphan who Murdered her Son, and became an Empress and Saint
• The "Christmas Spirits" of Old Athens • An Island Village in Central Athens
• Did Byron Really Love the Maid of Athens? • Subterranean Museums
• Ancient Athenian Democracy: How Democratic Was It?

... and much, much more...

2. Athens: The Suburbs

• A Monastery Born of a Romance • The "Bastille" of Greece
• Self-Castration and the Bloody Rites of the Great Goddess
• An Unspoken "No!" which Altered the Course of a World War
• The Iron Bedstead of Death • When Greeks were Hunted for Sport
• A Girl who Went to Join the Neraïdes • A School for a Prince
• The Oldest Family Name in the World • A City Built Over a Lake
• The Royal Air Force Besieged • The "Beast" of Kifissia
• The First Ever "Marathon Man" • A Vision over Mount Hymettos
• When the Allies Helped Cause a Famine • A Quarrelsome Saint
• When Politicians were Really Held Accountable for their Actions
• The Billionaire who Created a Philosophers' Paradise
• A Cannibal Island off the Coast of Attica

... and much, much more.

3. Attica

• The SS and a Hill of Horrors in Pallene • Nymph-Descended Families
• A Fatal Monkey-Bite that Led to Disaster • The Devil's Cave
• A Wagnerian Death • Rough Justice Peasant-Style • Jesus Christ in Attica?
• The Best Kept Secret of the Ancient World • A Fatal Hair Shampoo
• Strangled Monks • A Tailor, His Wife and Two Lightouses • A Dream Oracle
• A Road which Seems to Defy Gravity • The Virgin's Pulley
• A Close Encounter of the Third Kind that Predates the UFO Mania
• A Graveyard Wager that Went Wrong • A Haunted Mansion
• The Vanished Villagers • A Secret Concentration Camp in the "Free" West
• The Dark Foundations of Athenian Greatness • The Laws of the Brigands

... and much, much more.

All the above are by John L. Tomkinson

Now in Preparation…

4. The Saronic Gulf

Including the islands of **Salamis (Salamina), Aigina, Angistri, Hydra, Poros and Spetses,**
together with the area of Attica on the coast of the Saronic Gulf in the Peloponnese, including
Troizen (Damala) and **Methana.**

5. The Isthmus

Korinthia and **the Megarid**: including: **Megara, Loutraki, Isthmia, Corinth, Acrocorinth,
Nemea, Stymphalos, Sikyon, Phlious, Dervenakia, Kleonai, Sofikon,** etc.

6. The Northern Cyclades

Including the islands of **Andros, Tinos, Mykonos** and **Delos.**

ANAGNOSIS

For up-to-date information on all Anagnosis books, visit our website:
www.anagnosis.gr

or write to us at

Harilaou Trikoupi 130, Kifissia, 14563 Athens, Greece
or
anagnosis@anagnosis.gr